Signal Processing

Signal Processing

Edited by
Sebastian Miron

Signal Processing
Edited by Sebastian Miron

CBS, Edition 2016

Published by InTech
Janeza Trdine 9, 51000 Rijeka, Croatia

Technical Editor Teodora Smiljanic

Cover Designer Dino Smrekar

Additional hard copies can be obtained from orders@intechopen.com

Signal Processing, Edited by Sebastian Miron
p. cm.
ISBN 978-953-7619-91-6

Preface

The exponential development of sensor technology and computer power over the last few decades, transformed signal processing in an essential tool for a wide range of domains such as telecommunications, medicine or chemistry. Signal processing plays nowadays a key role in the progress of knowledge, from the discoveries on the universe underlying structure, to the recent breakthroughs in the understanding of the sub-atom structure of the matter. Internet, GSM, GPS, HDTV technologies are also indebted to the accelerated evolution of signal processing methods. Today, a major challenge in this domain is the development of fast and efficient algorithms capable of dealing with the huge amount of data provided by the modern sensor technology.

This book intends to provide highlights of the current research in signal processing area, to offer a snapshot of the recent advances in this field. This work is mainly destined to researchers in the signal processing related areas but it is also accessible to anyone with a scientific background desiring to have an up-to-date overview of this domain. The twenty-five chapters present methodological advances and recent applications of signal processing algorithms in various domains as telecommunications, array processing, biology, cryptography, image and speech processing. The methodologies illustrated in this book, such as sparse signal recovery, are hot topics in the signal processing community at this moment.

The editor would like to thank all the authors for their excellent contributions in the different areas of signal processing and hopes that this book will be of valuable help to the readers.

January 2010

Editor

Sebastian MIRON

Centre de Recherche en Automatique de Nancy

Nancy-Université, CNRS

Contents

1

New Adaptive Algorithms for the Rapid Identification of Sparse Impulse Responses

Mariane R. Petraglia
Federal University of Rio de Janeiro
Brazil

1. Introduction

It is well known that the convergence of the adaptive filtering algorithms becomes slow when the number of coefficients is very large. However, in many applications, such as digital network and acoustical echo cancelers, the system being modeled presents sparse impulse response, that is, most of its coefficients have small magnitudes. The classical adaptation approaches, such as the least-mean square (LMS) and recursive least squares (RLS) algorithms, do not take into account the sparseness characteristics of such systems.

In order to improve the convergence for these applications, several algorithms have been proposed recently, which employ individual step-sizes for the updating of the different coefficients. The adaptation step-sizes are made larger for the coefficients with larger magnitudes, resulting in a faster convergence for the most significant coefficients. Such idea was first introduced in (Duttweiler, 2000) resulting in the so-called proportionate normalized least mean square (PNLMS) algorithm. However, the performance of the PNLMS algorithm for the identification of non-sparse impulse response can be very poor, even slower than that of the conventional LMS algorithm. An improved version of such algorithm, which employs an extra parameter to control the amount of proportionality in the step-size normalization, was proposed in (Benesty & Gay, 2002).

An observed characteristic of the PNLMS algorithm is a rapid initial convergence, due to the fast adaptation speed of the large value coefficients, followed by an expressive performance degradation, owing to the small adaptation speed of the small value coefficients. Such behavior is more significant in the modeling of not very sparse impulse responses. In order to reduce this problem, the application of a non-linear function to the coefficients in the step-size normalization was proposed in (Deng & Doroslovacki, 2006).

The well-known slow convergence of the gradient algorithms for colored input signals is also observed in the proportionate-type NLMS algorithms. Implementations that combine the ideas of the PNLMS and transform-domain adaptive algorithms were proposed in (Deng & Doroslovacki, 2007) and (Petraglia & Barboza, 2008) for accelerating the convergence for colored input signals.

In this chapter, we give an overview of the most important adaptive algorithms developed for the fast identification of systems with sparse impulse responses. The convergence of the proposed algorithms are compared through computer simulations for the identification of the channel impulse responses in a digital network echo cancellation application.

2. Sparse Impulse Response Systems

Sparse impulse responses are encountered in several applications, such as in acoustic and digital network echo cancelers. The adaptive filters employed in the modeling of the unknown system in such applications present a small number of coefficients with significant magnitude. Figure 1 illustrates the modeling of an unknown system $\mathbf{w}^o$, which is assumed to be linear, time-invariant and of finite impulse response length (N), by an adaptive filter. The vector containing the adaptive filter coefficients is denoted as $\mathbf{w}(n) = [w_0(n)\ w_1(n) \cdots w_{N-1}(n)]^T$ and its input vector as $\mathbf{x}(n) = [x(n)\ x(n-1) \cdots x(n-N+1)]^T$. The adaptive filter output is denoted as $y(n)$, the desired response as $d(n)$ and the estimation error as $e(n)$. One of the most used adaptation techniques is the normalized least mean-square (NLMS) algorithm, shown in Table 1, where β is a fixed step-size factor and δ is a small constant needed in order to avoid division by zero.
As shown in Table 1 for the NLMS algorithm, typical initialization parameters are given for all algorithms studied in this chapter.

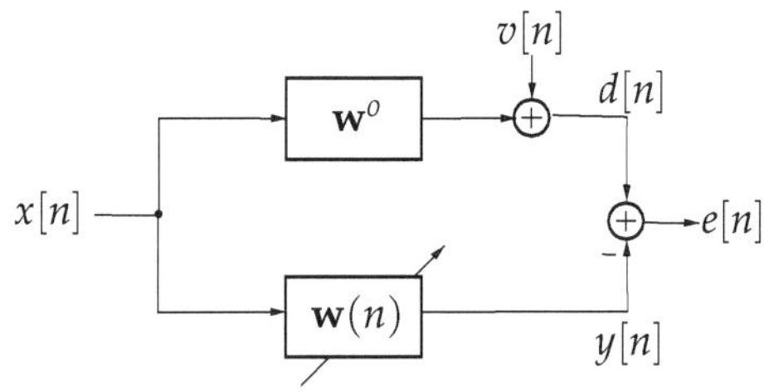

Fig. 1. System identification through adaptive filtering.

Initialization (typical values)

$\delta = 0.01,\ \beta = 0.25$

$\mathbf{w}(0) = [\ w_0(0)\quad w_1(0)\quad \cdots\quad w_{N-1}(0)\ ]^T = \mathbf{0}$

Processing and Adaptation

For $n = 0, 1, 2, \cdots$

$$\mathbf{x}(n) = [\ x(n)\quad x(n-1)\quad \cdots\quad x(n-N+1)\ ]^T$$
$$y(n) = \mathbf{x}^T(n)\mathbf{w}(n)$$
$$e(n) = d(n) - y(n)$$
$$\mathbf{w}(n+1) = \mathbf{w}(n) + \beta \frac{\mathbf{x}(n)e(n)}{\mathbf{x}^T(n)\mathbf{x}(n) + \delta}$$

End

Table 1. NLMS Algorithm

Described in the next sections, adaptive algorithms that take into account the sparseness of the unknown system impulse response have been recently developed. The convergence behavior of such algorithms depends on how sparse the modeled impulse response is. A sparseness measure of an N-length impulse response $\mathbf{w}$ was proposed in (Hoyer, 2004) as

$$\xi_{\mathbf{w}} = \frac{N}{N - \sqrt{N}} \left(1 - \frac{||\mathbf{w}||_1}{\sqrt{N}||\mathbf{w}||_2}\right) \quad (1)$$

where $||\mathbf{w}||_l$ is the l-norm of the vector $\mathbf{w}$. It should be observed that $0 \leq \xi_{\mathbf{w}} \leq 1$, and that $\xi_{\mathbf{w}} = 0$ when all elements of $\mathbf{w}$ are equal in magnitude (non-sparse impulse response) and $\xi_{\mathbf{w}} = 1$ when only one element of $\mathbf{w}$ is non-zero (the sparsest impulse response).
In the simulations presented throughout this chapter, the identification of the digital network channels of ITU-T Recommendation G.168 (G.168, 2004), by an adaptive filter with $N = 512$ coefficients, will be considered. Figures 2(a) and 2(b) show the impulse responses of the most and least sparse digital network channel models (gm1 and gm4, respectively) described in (G.168, 2004). Figure 2(c) presents the gm4 channel impulse response with a white noise (uniformly distributed in [-0.05,0.05]) added to it, such as to simulate a non-sparse system. The corresponding sparseness measures are $\xi_{\mathbf{w}} = 0.8970$ for the gm1 channel, $\xi_{\mathbf{w}} = 0.7253$ for the gm4 channel and $\xi_{\mathbf{w}} = 0.2153$ for the gm4 plus noise channel.

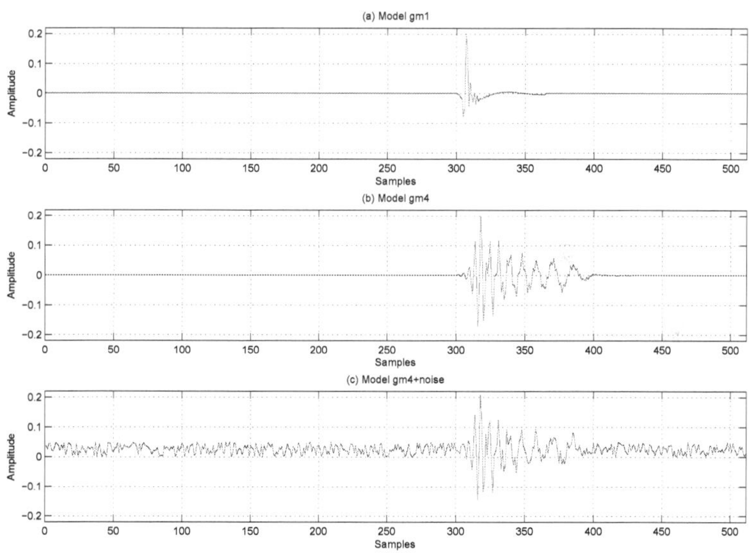

Fig. 2. Channel impulse responses: (a) gm1, (b) gm4 and (c) gm4+noise.

3. Proportionate-type NLMS Algorithms

The proportionate-type NLMS algorithms employ a different step-size for each coefficient, such that larger adjustments are applied to the larger coefficients (or active coefficients), resulting in faster convergence rate when modeling systems with sparse impulse responses. The main algorithms of such family are described next.

3.1 PNLMS Algorithm

For an adaptive filter with coefficients $w_i(n)$, for $1 \leq i \leq N-1$, the proportionate normalized least mean-square (PNLMS) algorithm is presented in Table 2. In this algorithm, a time-varying step-size control matrix $\mathbf{\Gamma}(n)$, whose elements are roughly proportional to the absolute values of the corresponding coefficients, is included in the update equation (Duttweiler, 2000). As a result, the large coefficients at a given iteration get significantly more update energy than the small ones. The parameter β is a fixed step-size factor, δ is a small constant needed in order to avoid division by zero, and δ_p and ρ are small positive constants which are important when all the coefficients are zero (such as in the beginning of the adaptation process) or when a coefficient is much smaller than the largest one.

Initialization (typical values)

$\delta_p = \delta = 0.01,\ \beta = 0.25, \rho = 0.01$

$\mathbf{w}(0) = \begin{bmatrix} w_0(0) & w_1(0) & \cdots & w_{N-1}(0) \end{bmatrix}^T = \mathbf{0}$

Processing and Adaptation

For $n = 0, 1, 2, \cdots$

$\quad \mathbf{x}(n) = \begin{bmatrix} x(n) & x(n-1) & \cdots & x(n-N+1) \end{bmatrix}^T$

$\quad y(n) = \mathbf{x}^T(n)\mathbf{w}(n)$

$\quad e(n) = d(n) - y(n)$

$\quad \gamma_{min}(n) = \rho\max\{\delta_p, |w_0(n)|, \cdots, |w_{N-1}(n)|\}$

$\quad$ For $i = 0, 1, \cdots, N-1$

$\quad\quad \gamma_i(n) = \max\{\gamma_{min}(n), |w_i(n)|\}$

$\quad$ End

$\quad$ For $i = 0, 1, \cdots, N-1$

$$g_i(n) = \frac{\gamma_i(n)}{\frac{1}{N}\sum_{j=0}^{N-1}\gamma_j(n)}$$

$\quad$ End

$\quad \mathbf{\Gamma}(n) = \mathrm{diag}\{g_0(n), \cdots, g_{N-1}(n)\}$

$$\mathbf{w}(n+1) = \mathbf{w}(n) + \beta\frac{\mathbf{\Gamma}(n)\mathbf{x}(n)e(n)}{\mathbf{x}^T(n)\mathbf{\Gamma}(n)\mathbf{x}(n) + \delta}$$

End

Table 2. PNLMS Algorithm

Figure 3 displays the experimental MSE evolutions of the PNLMS and NLMS algorithms for the three channels of Fig. 2 with white Gaussian noise input. In all experiments a white Gaussian measurement noise of variance $\sigma_v^2 = 10^{-6}$ was added to the desired signal. It can

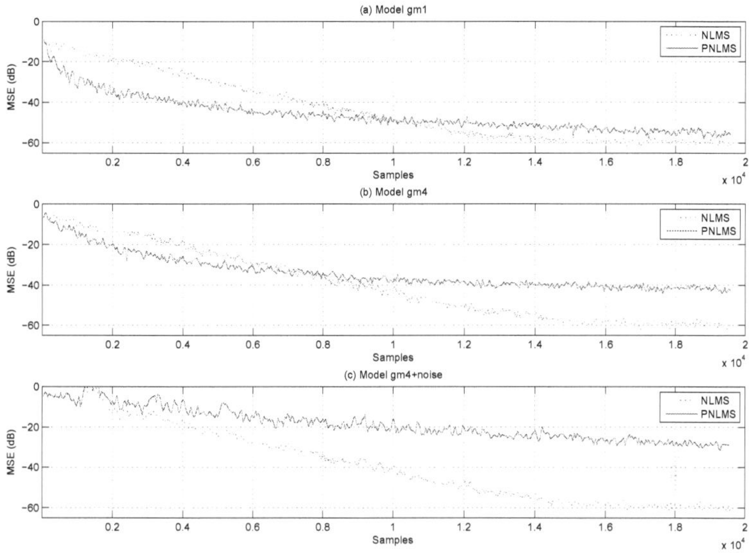

Fig. 3. MSE evolution for the PNLMS and NLMS algorithms for white noise input and channels (a) gm1, (b) gm4 and (c) gm4+noise.

be observed in Fig. 3 that the PNLMS algorithm converges much faster than the NLMS algorithm for the sparse channel gm1. However, for the dispersive channel gm4+noise the PNLMS behaves much worse than the NLMS. For channel gm4 the PNLMS algorithm presents a fast initial convergence, which is significantly reduced after 2000 iterations, becoming slower than that of the NLMS algorithm.

3.2 IPNLMS Algorithm

In the improved proportionate normalized least mean-square (IPNLMS) algorithm, the individual step-sizes are a compromise between the NLMS and the PNLMS step-sizes, resulting in a better convergence for different degrees of sparseness of the impulse response (Benesty & Gay, 2002). The IPNLMS algorithm is listed in Table 3. It can be observed that for $\alpha = -1$ the step-size control matrix $\mathbf{\Gamma}(n)$ reduces to $\frac{1}{N}\mathbf{I}$ and hence the IPNLMS and NLMS algorithms turn identical. For $\alpha = 1$, the elements of $\mathbf{\Gamma}(n)$ become proportional to the absolute values of the coefficients, in which case the IPNLMS and PNLMS algorithms show practically the same behavior. A typical value for this parameter is $\alpha = -0.5$.

Figure 4 presents the experimental MSE evolutions of the IPNLMS and NLMS algorithms for the three channels of Fig. 2 with white Gaussian noise input. From this figure, it can be observed that for the sparse channel gm1, the IPNLMS algorithm produces similar performance as the PNLMS algorithm, that is, significantly better than the NLMS algorithm. For the dispersive channel gm4+noise, the IPNLMS performance is similar to that of the NLMS algorithm, not presenting the severe convergence degradation of the PNLMS algorithm. For channel

Initialization (typical values)

$\delta = 0.01,\ \epsilon = 0.001,\ \beta = 0.25, \alpha = -0.5$

$\mathbf{w}(0) = \begin{bmatrix} w_0(0) & w_1(0) & \cdots & w_{N-1}(0) \end{bmatrix}^T = \mathbf{0}$

Processing and Adaptation

For $n = 0, 1, 2, \cdots$

$\quad \mathbf{x}(n) = \begin{bmatrix} x(n) & x(n-1) & \cdots & x(n-N+1) \end{bmatrix}^T$

$\quad y(n) = \mathbf{x}^T(n)\mathbf{w}(n)$

$\quad e(n) = d(n) - y(n)$

$\quad$ For $i = 0, 1, \cdots, N-1$

$$g_i(n) = \frac{1-\alpha}{2N} + \frac{(1+\alpha)|w_i(n)|}{2\sum_{j=0}^{N-1}|w_j(n)| + \epsilon}$$

$\quad$ End

$\quad \mathbf{\Gamma}(n) = \mathrm{diag}\{g_0(n), \cdots, g_{N-1}(n)\}$

$$\mathbf{w}(n+1) = \mathbf{w}(n) + \beta\frac{\mathbf{\Gamma}(n)\mathbf{x}(n)e(n)}{\mathbf{x}^T(n)\mathbf{\Gamma}(n)\mathbf{x}(n) + \delta}$$

End

Table 3. IPNLMS Algorithm

gm4, the IPNLMS algorithm does not present the performance degradation (after the initial convergence period) observed in the PNLMS algorithm; however, there is almost no gain in the initial convergence speed when compared to the NLMS algorithm.

3.3 MPNLMS and SPNLMS Algorithms

In the μ-law improved proportionate normalized least mean-square (MPNLMS) algorithm, the step-sizes are optimal in the sense of minimizing the convergence rate (considering white noise input signal) (Deng & Doroslovacki, 2006). The resulting algorithm employs a non-linear (logarithm) function of the coefficients in the step-size control. A simplified version of the MPNLMS, referred to as the segmented PNLMS (SPNLMS) algorithm, also proposed in (Deng & Doroslovacki, 2006), employs a segmented linear function in order to reduce its computational complexity. These two algorithms are presented in Table 4, where the function $\mathrm{F}(\cdot)$ is defined as

$$\mathrm{F}(x) = \ln(1 + \mu x) \tag{2}$$

for the MPNLMS algorithm and

$$\mathrm{F}(x) = \begin{cases} 600x, & x < 0.005 \\ 3, & x \geq 0.005 \end{cases} \tag{3}$$

for the SPNLMS algorithm (Deng & Doroslovacki, 2006).

Figure 5 shows the experimental MSE evolutions of the MPNLMS and NLMS algorithms for the three channels of Fig. 2 with white Gaussian noise input. From this figure, it can be noticed

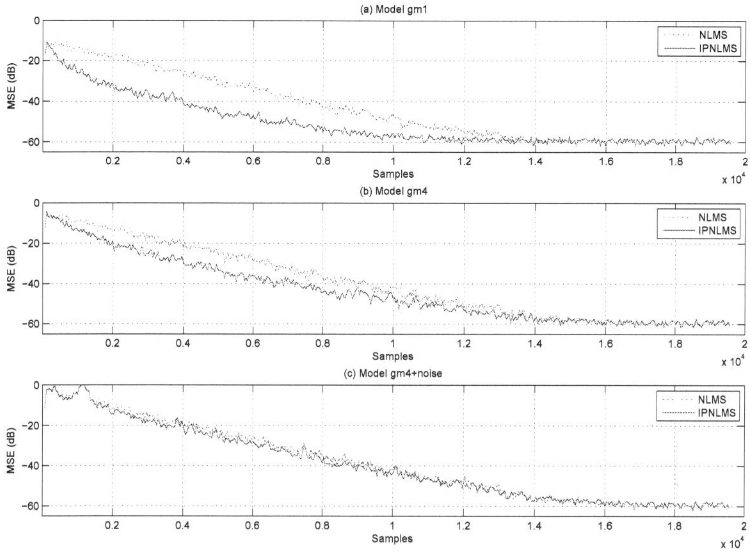

Fig. 4. MSE evolution for the IPNLMS and NLMS algorithms for white noise input and channels (a) gm1, (b) gm4 and (c) gm4+noise.

that the MPNLMS algorithm presents significantly faster convergence, when compared to the NLMS, PNLMS and IPNLMS algorithms, mainly for the sparse channels gm1 and gm4. However, for the dispersive channel gm4+noise, its convergence is severely degraded, being much slower than that of the NLMS algorithm.

Figure 6 presents the experimental MSE evolutions of the SPNLMS and NLMS algorithms for the three channels of Fig. 2 with white Gaussian noise input. Comparing Figs. 5 and 6, it can be verified that the use of the simplified non-linear function does not deteriorate meaningfully the performance of the MPNLMS algorithm.

3.4 Variable-Parameter IMPNLMS Algorithm

The variable-parameter improved μ-law PNLMS (IMPNLMS) algorithm was proposed in (L. Liu & Saiki, 2008). In this algorithm, the channel sparseness measure of Eq. (1) was incorporated into the μ-law PNLMS algorithm in order to improve the adaptation convergence for dispersive channels. Since the real channel coefficients are not available, the corresponding sparseness measure is estimated recursively using the current adaptive filter coefficients. The resulting algorithm is summarized in Table 5, where the parameter $\alpha(n)$, which in the improved PNLMS algorithm of Table 4 was a predetermined fixed factor, is made variable and related to the estimated impulse response sparseness measure $\xi_{\mathbf{w}}(n)$. In addition, also proposed in (L. Liu & Saiki, 2008), was the use of the line segment function

$$\mathrm{F}(x) = \begin{cases} 400x, & x < 0.005 \\ 8.51|x| + 1.96, & x \geq 0.005 \end{cases} \tag{4}$$

Initialization (typical values)

$\delta_p = \delta = 0.01,\ \beta = 0.25, \rho = 1/N$

$\mathbf{w}(0) = [\ w_0(0) \quad w_1(0) \quad \cdots \quad w_{N-1}(0)\ ]^T = \mathbf{0}$

Processing and Adaptation

For $n = 0, 1, 2, \cdots$

$\mathbf{x}(n) = [\ x(n) \quad x(n-1) \quad \cdots \quad x(n-N+1)\ ]^T$

$y(n) = \mathbf{x}^T(n)\mathbf{w}(n)$

$e(n) = d(n) - y(n)$

$\gamma_{min}(n) = \rho \max\{\delta_p, \mathrm{F}(|w_0(n)|), \cdots, \mathrm{F}(|w_{N-1}(n)|)\}$

For $i = 0, 1, \cdots, N-1$

$\gamma_i(n) = \max\{\gamma_{min}(n), \mathrm{F}(|w_i(n)|)\}$

End

For $i = 0, 1, \cdots, N-1$

$$g_i(n) = \frac{\gamma_i(n)}{\frac{1}{N}\sum_{j=0}^{N-1}|\gamma_j(n)|}$$

End

$\mathbf{\Gamma}(n) = \mathrm{diag}\{g_0(n), \cdots, g_{N-1}(n)\}$

$$\mathbf{w}(n+1) = \mathbf{w}(n) + \beta\frac{\mathbf{\Gamma}(n)\mathbf{x}(n)e(n)}{\mathbf{x}^T(n)\mathbf{\Gamma}(n)\mathbf{x}(n) + \delta}$$

End

Table 4. MPNLMS and SPNLMS Algorithms

with which the steady-state misalignment is decreased in comparison to those of the MPNLMS and SPNLMS algorithms (Eqs. (2) and (3)), which place too much emphasis on small coefficients.

Figure 7 presents the experimental MSE evolutions of the IMPNLMS and NLMS algorithms for the three channels of Fig. 2 with white Gaussian noise input. The good convergence behavior of the IMPNLMS algorithm for the sparse and dispersive channels can be observed in this figure.

4. Wavelet-based proportionate-type NLMS Algorithms

Although the proportionate-type NLMS algorithms produce better convergence than the NLMS algorithm when modeling sparse impulse responses with white noise inputs, they suffer from the same performance degradation as the NLMS when the excitation signal is colored. Figure 8 illustrates the performance of the NLMS, MPNLMS and IMPNLMS algorithms for a colored input signal, generated by passing a white Gaussian noise with zero-mean and unit variance through the filter with transfer function

$$H(z) = \frac{0.25\sqrt{3}}{1 - 1.5z^{-1} - 0.25z^{-2}}. \tag{5}$$

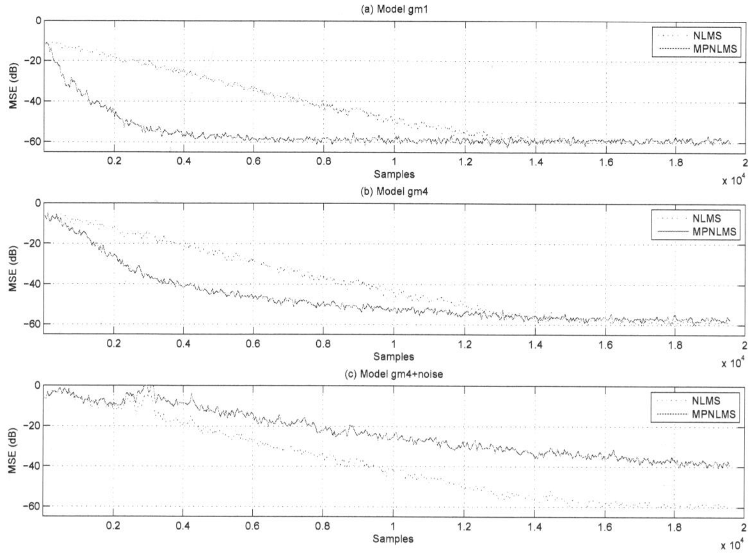

Fig. 5. MSE evolution for the MPNLMS and NLMS algorithms for white noise input and channels (a) gm1, (b) gm4 and (c) gm4+noise.

Such input signal has power spectrum similar to speech signal (Ikeda & Sugiyama, 1994). In order to improve the adaptation speed of these algorithms in dispersive channels with colored input signals, the use of wavelet transform was proposed independently in (Deng & Doroslovacki, 2007) and (Petraglia & Barboza, 2008). The resulting algorithms are described next.

4.1 Wavelet-based MPNLMS algorithm (Transform-Domain)

The transform-domain proportionate technique presented in (Deng & Doroslovacki, 2007) employs the μ-law PNLMS algorithm in the wavelet-domain. Besides improving the convergence of the conventional algorithms owing to power normalization of the step-sizes, the wavelet-domain approach may be advantageous in the modeling of non-sparse impulse responses, since they usually become more sparse in the transformed domain. The resulting algorithm, termed as wavelet-based MPNLMS in the transform-domain (WMPNLMS-TD), is described in Table 6. The transformation matrix $\mathbf{T}$ is formed by the coefficients of the wavelet filters, as defined in (Attallah, 2000), the vector $\mathbf{z}(n) = [z_0(n) \cdots z_{N-1}(n)]^T = \mathbf{T}\mathbf{x}(n)$ is the transformed input vector and $p_i(n)$ is the power estimate of $z_i(n)$. The matrix $\mathbf{D}(n)$ introduced in the update equation assigns a different step-size normalization to each coefficient.

Figure 9 presents the experimental MSE evolutions of the WMPNLMS-TD algorithm for the three channels of Fig. 2 and colored noise input with the following wavelet functions: Haar, Daubechies 2 (Db2) and Daubechies 4 (Db4). Comparing the simulation results of the

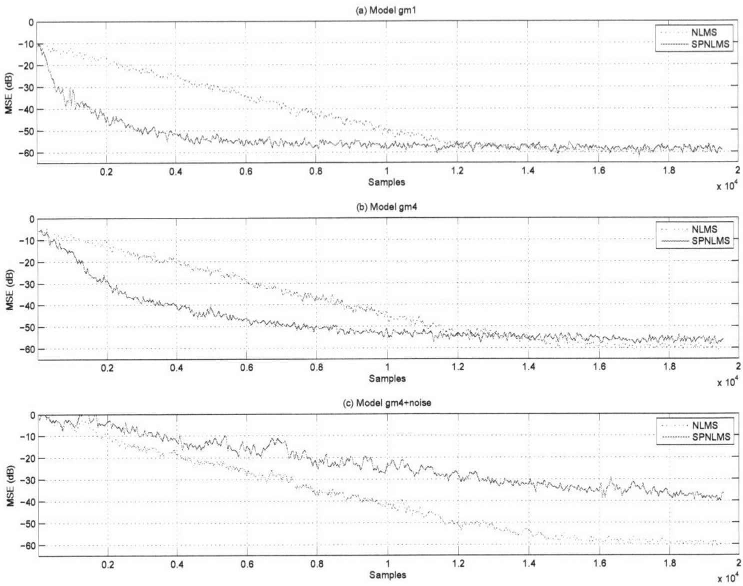

Fig. 6. MSE evolution for the SPNLMS and NLMS algorithms for white noise input and channels (a) gm1, (b) gm4 and (c) gm4+noise.

WMPNLMS-TD algorithm with those of Fig. 8, it can be observed that, for colored input, there is a significant improvement in the performance of the MPNLMS algorithm when it is applied in the wavelet-domain. The more selective wavelet (Daubechies 4) produced the fastest convergence, as expected.

4.2 Wavelet-based MPNLMS Algorithm (Sparse Filters)

The wavelet-based proportionate NLMS algorithm proposed in (Petraglia & Barboza, 2008) employs a wavelet transform and sparse adaptive filters. Illustrated in Fig. 10, the wavelet transform is represented by a non-uniform filter bank with analysis filters $H_k(z)$, and sparse adaptive subfilters $G_k(z^{L_k})$ (Petraglia & Torres, 2002). For an octave-band wavelet, the equivalent analysis filters of the M-channel filter bank are (Vaidyanathan, 1993)

$$
\begin{aligned}
H_0(z) &= \prod_{j=0}^{M-2} H^0(z^{2^j}), \\
H_k(z) &= H^1(z^{2^{M-1-k}}) \prod_{j=0}^{M-k-2} H^0(z^{2^j}),\; k = 1, \cdots, M-1,
\end{aligned} \tag{6}
$$

Initialization (typical values)

$\delta = 0.01,\ \epsilon = 0.001,\ \beta = 0.25, \lambda = 0.1, \xi(-1) = 0.96$

$\mathbf{w}(0) = [\ w_0(0) \quad w_1(0) \quad \cdots \quad w_{N-1}(0)\ ]^T = \mathbf{0}$

Processing and Adaptation

For $n = 0, 1, 2, \cdots$

$\mathbf{x}(n) = [\ x(n) \quad x(n-1) \quad \cdots \quad x(n-N+1)\ ]^T$

$y(n) = \mathbf{x}^T(n)\mathbf{w}(n)$

$e(n) = d(n) - y(n)$

$$\xi_{\mathbf{w}}(n) = \frac{N}{N-\sqrt{N}}\left(1 - \frac{\sum_{j=0}^{N-1}|w_j(n)|}{\sqrt{N\sum_{j=0}^{N-1}|w_j(n)|^2}}\right)$$

$\xi(n) = (1-\lambda)\xi(n-1) + \lambda\xi_{\mathbf{w}}(n)$

$\alpha(n) = 2\xi(n) - 1$

For $i = 0, 1, \cdots, N-1$

$$g_i(n) = \frac{1-\alpha(n)}{2N} + \frac{(1+\alpha(n))F(|w_i(n)|)}{2\sum_{j=0}^{N-1}F(|w_j(n)|) + \epsilon}$$

End

$\boldsymbol{\Gamma}(n) = \mathrm{diag}\{g_0(n), \cdots, g_{N-1}(n)\}$

$$\mathbf{w}(n+1) = \mathbf{w}(n) + \beta\frac{\boldsymbol{\Gamma}(n)\mathbf{x}(n)e(n)}{\mathbf{x}^T(n)\boldsymbol{\Gamma}(n)\mathbf{x}(n) + \delta}$$

End

Table 5. Variable-Parameter IMPNLMS Algorithms

where $H^0(z)$ and $H^1(z)$ are, respectively, the lowpass and high-pass filters associated with the wavelet functions (Vaidyanathan, 1993). The sparsity factors are

$$L_0 = 2^{M-1}, \quad L_k = 2^{M-k}, \quad k = 1, \cdots, M-1, \tag{7}$$

and the delays Δ_k in Fig. 10, introduced for the purpose of matching the delays of the different length analysis filters, are given by $\Delta_k = N_{H_0} - N_{H_k}$, where N_{H_k} is the length of the kth analysis filter. This structure yields an additional system delay (compared to a direct-form FIR structure) equal to $\Delta_D = N_{H_0}$. For the modeling of a length N FIR system, the number of adaptive coefficients of the subfilters $G_k(z)$ (non-zero coefficients of $G_k(z^{L_k})$) should be at least

$$N_k = \left\lfloor \frac{N + N_{F_k}}{L_k} \right\rfloor \tag{8}$$

where N_{F_k} are the lengths of the corresponding synthesis filters which, when associated to the analysis filters $H_k(z)$, lead to perfect reconstruction.

The resulting proportionate-type NLMS algorithm, referred here as wavelet-based MPNLMS with sparse filters (WMPNLMS-SF), is presented in Table 7, where $x_k(n)$ is the input signal of

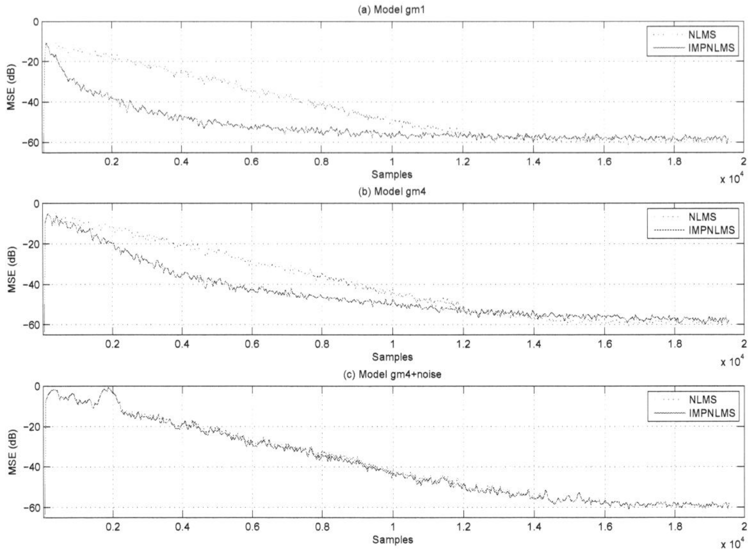

Fig. 7. MSE evolution for the IMPNLMS and NLMS algorithms for white noise input and channels (a) gm1, (b) gm4 and (c) gm4+noise.

the k-th subband ($x(n)$ filtered by $H_k(z)$) and $w_{k,i}$ is the i-th coefficient of $G_k(z)$. For colored input signals, the WMPNLMS-SF algorithm presents faster convergence than the time-domain MPNLMS algorithm, since its step-size normalization strategy uses the input power at the different frequency bands. It should be observed that the step-size normalization takes into account the absolute value of each coefficient in comparison to the values of the corresponding subfilter coefficients (and not to all coefficients, as is done in the WMPNLMS-TD algorithm (Deng & Doroslovacki, 2007)). As a result, the large coefficients of a given subfilter get significantly more of the update energy assigned to the corresponding subband than the small ones.

Figure 11 shows the experimental MSE evolution of the WMPNLMS-SF algorithm for a two-level decomposition ($M = 3$ subbands) using the following wavelet functions: Haar, Daubechies 2, Daubechies 4 and Biorthogonal 4.4 (Bior4.4). With such wavelets, the increase in the complexity (compared to the MPNLMS algorithm) and the delay introduced by the decomposition are not very large, owing to the reduced orders of the corresponding prototype filters.

From Figs. 8 and 11 we conclude that, for the colored input signal employed in the simulations, the use of the very simple Haar wavelet transform improves significantly the convergence rate of the MPNLMS algorithm. The fastest convergence of the WMPNLMS-SF algorithm was obtained with the more selective Daubechies 4 and Biorthogonal 4.4 wavelets.

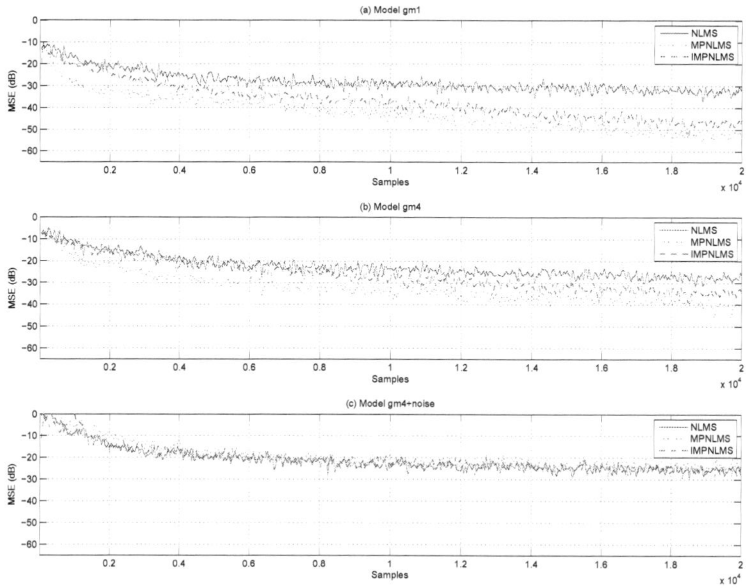

Fig. 8. MSE evolution for the NLMS, MPNLMS and IMPNLMS algorithms for colored noise input and channels (a) gm1, (b) gm4 and (c) gm4+noise.

Comparisons with Figs. 9 and 11 indicate that the step-size normalization strategy adopted by the WMPNLMS-SF method is advantageous when compared to that of the WMPNLMS-TD method.

The convergence performance of the WMPNLMS-SF algorithm for non-sparse channels can be improved by using the IMPNLMS algorithm independently for each adaptive subfiter. Figure 12 shows the MSE evolution of the resulting algorithm, referred therein as WIMPNLMS-SF, for different wavelets with colored input signal. The improvement in the convergence rate for the dispersive channel gm4+noise can be observed by comparing Figs. 11(c) and 12(c).

5. Conclusions

In this chapter we presented a family of algorithms developed in the last years for improving the convergence of adaptive filters when modeling sparse impulse responses. The performances of the described techniques, known as proportionate-type LMS algorithms, were illustrated through computer simulations in the identification of the digital network channels of ITU-T recommendation G.168. The first proposed approach, the PNLMS algorithm, was shown to produce fast initial convergence for sparse impulse responses, followed by a significant reduction after the fast initial period. Also, its performance was poor for non-sparse impulse responses. Improved versions of the PNLMS algorithm were then described and

Initialization (typical values)

T: wavelet transform matrix

$\delta_p = \delta = 0.01,\ \beta = 0.25/N,\ \rho = 0.01, \alpha = 0.9$

$\mathbf{w}(0) = [\ w_0(0) \quad w_1(0) \quad \cdots \quad w_{N-1}(0)\ ]^T = \mathbf{0}$

Processing and Adaptation

For $n = 0, 1, 2, \cdots$

$\mathbf{x}(n) = [\ x(n) \quad x(n-1) \quad \cdots \quad x(n-N+1)\ ]^T$

$\mathbf{z}(n) = \mathbf{T}\mathbf{x}(n)$

$y(n) = \mathbf{z}^T(n)\mathbf{w}(n)$

$e(n) = d(n) - y(n)$

$\gamma_{min}(n) = \rho\max\{\delta_p, \mathrm{F}(|w_0(n)|), \cdots, \mathrm{F}(|w_{N-1}(n)|)\}$

For $i = 0, 1, \cdots, N-1$

$\gamma_i(n) = \max\{\gamma_{min}(n), \mathrm{F}(|w_i(n)|)\}$

End

For $i = 0, 1, \cdots, N-1$

$$g_i(n) = \frac{\gamma_i(n)}{\frac{1}{N}\sum_{j=0}^{N-1}|\gamma_j(n)|}$$

$p_i(n) = \alpha p_i(n-1) + (1-\alpha) * z_i^2(n)$

End

$\mathbf{D}(n) = \mathrm{diag}\{1/p_0(n), \cdots, 1/p_{N-1}(n)\}$

$\mathbf{\Gamma}(n) = \mathrm{diag}\{g_0(n), \cdots, g_{N-1}(n)\}$

$\mathbf{w}(n+1) = \mathbf{w}(n) + \beta\mathbf{D}(n)\mathbf{\Gamma}(n)\mathbf{z}(n)e(n)$

End

Table 6. WMPNLMS-TD Algorithm

their advantages were verified in the simulation results. Whereas the IPNLMS algorithm produced enhanced convergence performance when modeling dispersive impulse responses, the MPNLMS employed a non-linear function of the coefficients in the step-size normalization in order to obtain optimal convergence rate. The combination of these two techniques and the use of a sparseness measure of the impulse response resulted in the variable-parameter IMPNLMS algorithm. The fast convergence rate of the proportionate-type algorithms was limited to white input signals. In order to extend their performance advantages to colored input signals, wavelet-domain algorithms, whose step-size normalization takes into account the value of each coefficient as well as the input signal power in the corresponding frequency band, were described. Simulations showed that the wavelet-domain PNLMS methods present significantly faster convergence rate than do the time-domain PNLMS ones for applications in which the system has sparse impulse responses and is excited with colored input signal.

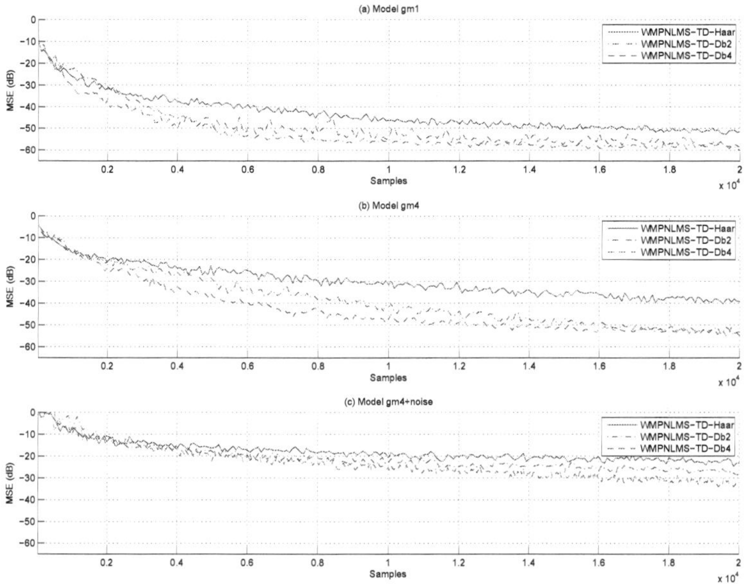

Fig. 9. MSE evolution for the WMPNLMS-TD with Haar, Db2 and Db4 wavelets for colored noise input and channels (a) gm1, (b) gm4 and (c) gm4+noise.

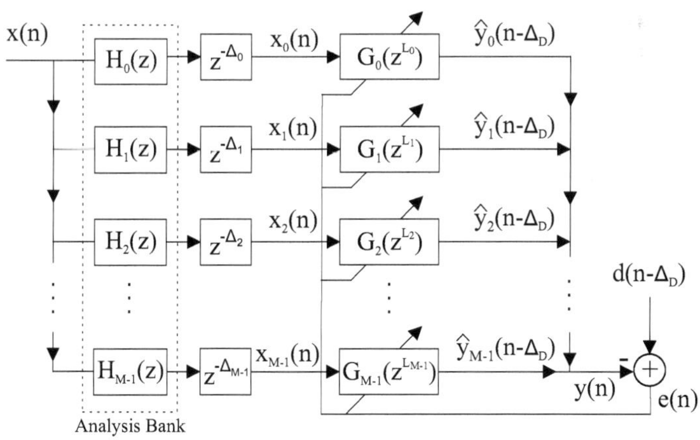

Fig. 10. Adaptive subband structure composed of a wavelet transform and sparse subfilters.

Initialization $\delta_p = \delta = 0.01,\ \beta = 0.25, \rho = 0.01$ For $k = 0, 1, \cdots, M-1$ $\quad \mathbf{w}_k(0) = [\ w_{k,0}(0) \quad w_{k,1}(0) \quad \cdots \quad w_{k,N_k-1}(0)\ ]^T = \mathbf{0}$ End Processing and Adaptation For $n = 0, 1, 2, \cdots$ $\quad$ For $k = 0, 1, \cdots, M-1$ $\quad\quad x_k(n) = \sum_{i=0}^{N_{H_k}-1} h_k(i)x(n-i)$ $\quad\quad \mathbf{x}_k(n) = [\ x_k(n) \quad x_k(n-L_k) \quad \cdots \quad x_k(n-(N_k-1)L_k)\ ]^T$ $\quad\quad \hat{y}_k(n-\Delta_D) = \mathbf{x}_k^T(n)\mathbf{w}_k(n)$ $\quad$ End $\quad y(n) = \sum_{k=0}^{M-1} \hat{y}_k(n-\Delta_D)$ $\quad e(n) = d(n-\Delta_D) - y(n)$ $\quad$ For $k = 0, 1, \cdots, M-1$ $\quad\quad \gamma_{min,k}(n) = \rho\max\{\delta_p, \mathrm{F}(\lvert w_{k,0}(n)\rvert), \cdots, \mathrm{F}(\lvert w_{k,N_k}(n)\rvert)\}$ $\quad\quad$ For $i = 0, 1, \cdots, N_{k-1}$ $\quad\quad\quad \gamma_{k,i}(n) = \max\{\gamma_{min,k}(n), \mathrm{F}(\lvert w_{k,i}(n)\rvert)\}$ $\quad\quad$ End $\quad\quad$ For $i = 0, 1, \cdots, N_{k-1}$ $\quad\quad\quad g_{k,i}(n) = \frac{\gamma_{k,i}(n)}{\frac{1}{N_k}\sum_{j=0}^{N_{k-1}} \gamma_{k,j}(n)}$ $\quad\quad$ End $\quad\quad \mathbf{\Gamma}_k(n) = \mathrm{diag}\{g_{k,0}(n), \cdots, g_{k,N}(n)\}$ $\quad\quad \mathbf{w}_k(n+1) = \mathbf{w}_k(n) + \beta\frac{\mathbf{\Gamma}_k(n)\mathbf{x}_k(n)e(n)}{\mathbf{x}_k^T(n)\mathbf{\Gamma}_k(n)\mathbf{x}_k(n) + \delta}$ $\quad$ End End

Table 7. WMPNLMS-SF Algorithm

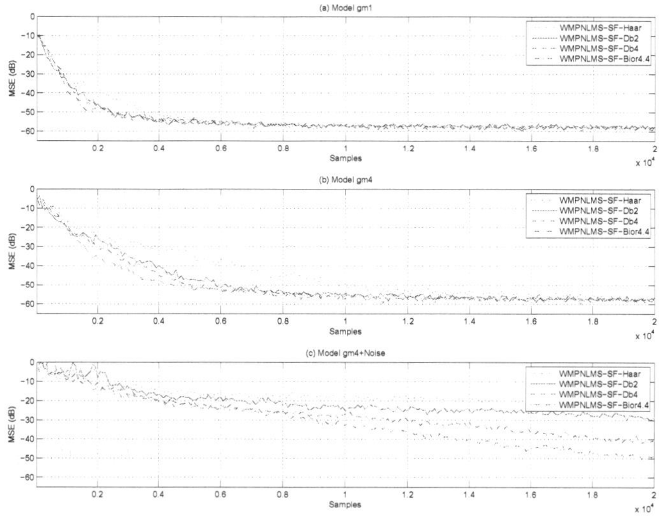

Fig. 11. MSE evolution for the WMPNLMS-SF algorithm with Haar, Db2, Db4 and Bior4.4 wavelets and $M = 3$, for colored noise input and channels (a) gm1, (b) gm4 and (c) gm4+noise.

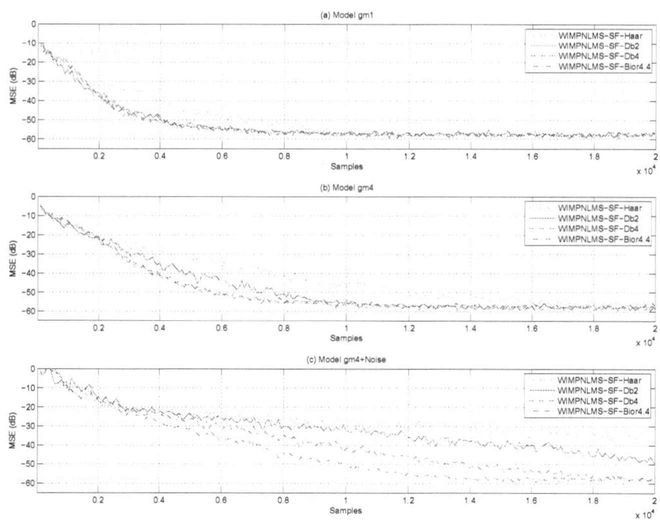

Fig. 12. MSE evolution for the WIMPNLMS-SF algorithm with Haar, Db2, Db4 and Bior4.4 wavelets and $M = 3$, for colored noise input and channels (a) gm1, (b) gm4 and (c) gm4+noise.

6. References

Attallah, S. (2000). The wavelet transform-domain lms algorithm: a more practical approach, *IEEE Trans. Circ. and Syst. II: Analog and Digital Sig. Proc.*. **47**(3): 209–213.

Benesty, J. & Gay, S. L. (2002). An improved PNLMS algorithm, *Proc. IEEE Int. Conf. Acoust., Speech, Signal Process.*, pp. 1881–1884.

Deng, H. & Doroslovacki, M. (2006). Proportionate adaptive algorithms for network echo cancellation, *IEEE Trans. Signal Process.* **54**(5): 1794–1803.

Deng, H. & Doroslovacki, M. (2007). Wavelet-based MPNLMS adaptive algorithm for network echo cancellation, *EURASIP Journal on Audio, Speech, and Music Processing* .

Duttweiler, D. L. (2000). Proportionate normalized least mean square adaptation in echo cancelers, *IEEE Trans. Speech Audio Process.* **8**(5): 508–518.

G.168, D. N. E. C. I.-T. R. (2004).

Hoyer, P. O. (2004). Non-negative matrix factorization with sparseness constraints, *Journal of Machine Learning Res.* (5): 1457–1469.

Ikeda, S. & Sugiyama, A. (1994). A fast convergence algorithm for sparse-tap adaptive fir filters for an unknown number of multiple echos, *Proc. IEEE Int. Conf. Acoust., Speech, Signal Process.*, pp. 41–44.

L. Liu, M. F. & Saiki, S. (2008). An improved mu-law proportionate nlms algorithm, *Proc. IEEE Int. Conf. Acoust., Speech, Signal Process.*, pp. 3793–3800.

Petraglia, M. & Barboza, G. (2008). Improved pnlms algorithm employing wavelet transform and sparse filters, *Proc. 16th European Signal Process. Conf.*

Petraglia, M. R. & Torres, J. C. B. (2002). Performance analysis of adaptive filter structure employing wavelet and sparse subfilters, *IEE Proc. - Vis. Image Signal Process.* **149**(2): 115–119.

Vaidyanathan, P. P. (1993). *Multirate Systems and Filter Banks*, Prentice-Hall, Englewood Cliffs, NJ.

2

Vector sensor array processing for polarized sources using a quadrilinear representation of the data covariance

Sebastian Miron*, Xijing Guo*,† and David Brie*
*Centre de Recherche en Automatique de Nancy, Nancy-Université, CNRS
France
† Department of Information and Communication Engineering, Xi'an Jiaotong University
China

1. Introduction

Array processing techniques aim principally at estimating source Directions Of Arrivals (DOA's) based on the observations recorded on a sensor array. The *vector-sensor* technology allows the use of polarization as an additional parameter, leading to *vector sensor array processing*. In electromagnetics, a vector sensor is composed of six spatially collocated but orthogonally polarized antennas, measuring all six components (three for the electric and three for the magnetic fields) of the incident wave. The benefits of considering source polarization in signal estimation were illustrated in Burgess and Van Veen (1994); Le Bihan et al. (2007); Li (1993); Miron et al. (2006); Nehorai and Paldi (1994); Rahamim et al. (2003); Weiss and Friedlander (1993a); Wong and Zoltowski (1997) for diverse signal processing problems. Most of these algorithms are based on *bilinear* polarized source mixture models which suffers from identifiability problems. This means that, without any additional constraint, the steering vectors of the sources (and implicitly their DOA's) cannot be uniquely determined by matrix factorization. The identifiability issues involved in vector sensor applications are investigated in Ho et al. (1995); Hochwald and Nehorai (1996); Tan et al. (1996a;b).

The use of polarization as a third diversity, in addition to the temporal and spatial diversities, in vector sensor array processing, leading to a trilinear mixture model, was proposed for the first time in Miron et al. (2005). Based on this model, a PARAFAC-based algorithm for signal detection, was later introduced in Zhang and Xu (2007). Multilinear models gave rise to a great interest in the signal processing community as they exhibit interesting identifiability properties; their factorization is unique under mild conditions. Several multilinear algorithms were proposed, mainly in telecommunication domain, using different diversity schemes such as code diversity Sidiropoulos et al. (2000a), multi-array diversity Sidiropoulos et al. (2000b) or time-block diversity Rong et al. (2005). For the trilinear mixture model with polarization diversity, we derived in Guo et al. (2008) the identifiability conditions and showed that in terms of source separation, the performance of the proposed algorithm is similar to the classical non-blind techniques.

Nevertheless, the joint estimation of all the three parameters of the sources (DOA, polarization, and temporal sequence) is time-consuming, and it does not always have a practical interest, especially in array processing applications. A novel stochastic algorithm for DOA estimation of polarized sources is introduced in this chapter, allowing the estimation of only two source parameters (DOA and polarization), and thus presenting a smaller computational complexity than its trilinear version Guo et al. (2008). It is based on a quadrilinear (fourth-order tensor) representation of the polarized data covariance. The parameters are then obtained by CANDECOMP/PARAFAC (CP) decomposition the covariance tensor of the polarized data, using a quadrilinear alternating least squares (QALS) approach. A significant advantage of the proposed algorithm lies in the fact that the methods based on statistical properties of the signals proved to outperform deterministic techniques Swindlehurst et al. (1997), provided that the number of samples is sufficiently high. The performance of the proposed algorithm is compared in simulations to the trilinear deterministic method, MUSIC and ESPRIT for polarized sources and to the Cramér-Rao Bound.

This chapter is organized as follows. Section 2 provides some multilinear algebra notions, necessary for the presentation of the multilinear models. In Section 3 we introduce the quadrilinear model for the covariance of the polarized data and the identifiability conditions for this model are discussed in Section 4. Section 5 presents the QALS algorithm for parameter estimation; performance and computational complexity issues are also addressed. Section 6 compares in simulations the quadrilinear algorithm to its trilinear version Guo et al. (2008), to polarized versions of MUSIC Miron et al. (2005) and ESPRIT Zoltowski and Wong (2000b) and to the CRB for vector sensor array Nehorai and Paldi (1994). We summarize our findings in Section 7.

2. Multilinear algebra preliminaries

In multilinear algebra a *tensor* is a multidimensional array. More formally, an N-way or Nth-order tensor is an element of the tensor product of N vector spaces, each of which has its own coordinate system. A first-order tensor is a vector, a second-order tensor is matrix and tensors of order three or higher are called higher-order tensors. Extending matrix notations to multilinear algebra we denote by

$$\boldsymbol{\mathcal{X}} \in \mathbb{C}^{I_1 \times I_2 \times \cdots \times I_N} \tag{1}$$

a Nth-*order* tensor with complex entries. In (1), $I_1, I_2, \ldots, I_N$ are the dimensions of the N *modes* of $\boldsymbol{\mathcal{X}}$. The entry $(i_1, i_2, \ldots, i_N)$ of $\boldsymbol{\mathcal{X}}$ is denoted by $x_{i_1 i_2 \ldots i_N}$ or by $(\boldsymbol{\mathcal{X}})_{i_1 i_2 \ldots i_N}$. For an overview of higher-order tensor their applications, the reader is referred to De Lathauwer (1997); Kolda and Bader (2007). In this section we restrain ourselves to some basic definitions and elementary operations on tensors, necessary for the understanding of the multilinear models and algorithms presented in the paper.

Definition 1 (Norm of a tensor). *The norm of a tensor* $\boldsymbol{\mathcal{X}} \in \mathbb{C}^{I_1 \times I_2 \times \cdots \times I_N}$ *is the square root of the sum of the squares of all its elements,* i.e.,

$$\|\boldsymbol{\mathcal{X}}\| \triangleq \sqrt{\sum_{i_1}^{I_1} \sum_{i_2}^{I_2} \cdots \sum_{i_N}^{I_N} |x_{i_1 i_2 \ldots i_N}|^2}. \tag{2}$$

This is analogous to the matrix Frobenius norm.

Definition 2 (Outer product). *The outer product of two tensors* $\mathcal{X} \in \mathbb{C}^{I_1 \times I_2 \times \cdots \times I_N}$ *and* $\mathcal{Y} \in \mathbb{C}^{J_1 \times J_2 \times \cdots \times J_P}$ *is a tensor* $\mathcal{X} \circ \mathcal{Y} \in \mathbb{C}^{I_1 \times \cdots \times I_N \times J_1 \times \cdots \times J_P}$ *defined by* $(\mathcal{X} \circ \mathcal{Y})_{i_1 \dots i_N j_1 \dots j_p} \triangleq x_{i_1 \dots i_N} y_{j_1 \dots j_P}$.

The outer product allows to extend the rank-one matrix definition to tensors.

Definition 3 (Rank-one tensor). *An N-way tensor* $\mathcal{X} \in \mathbb{C}^{I_1 \times I_2 \times \cdots \times I_N}$ *is rank-one if it can be written as the outer product of N vectors, i.e.,*

$$\mathcal{X} = \mathbf{a}_1 \circ \mathbf{a}_2 \circ \cdots \circ \mathbf{a}_N \tag{3}$$

with $\mathbf{a}_n \in \mathbb{C}^{I_n}$.

Tensors can be multiplied together though the notation is much more complex than for matrices. Here we consider only the multiplication of a tensor by a matrix (or a vector) in mode n.

Definition 4 (n-mode product). *The n-mode product of a tensor* $\mathcal{X} \in \mathbb{C}^{I_1 \times \cdots \times I_n \times \cdots \times I_N}$ *with a matrix* $\mathbf{U} \in \mathbb{C}^{J \times I_n}$ *is denoted by* $\mathcal{X} \times_n \mathbf{U}$ *and is of size* $I_1 \times \cdots \times I_{n-1} \times J \times I_{n+1} \times \cdots \times I_N$. *It is defined as :*

$$(\mathcal{X} \times_n \mathbf{U})_{i_1 \dots i_{n-1} j i_{n+1} \dots i_N} = \sum_{i_n=1}^{I_n} x_{i_1 i_2 \dots i_N} u_{j i_n}. \tag{4}$$

Several matrix products are important in multilinear algebra formalism, two of which being recalled here.

Definition 5 (Kronecker product). *The Kronecker product of matrices* $\mathbf{A} \in \mathbb{C}^{I \times J}$ *and* $\mathbf{B} \in \mathbb{C}^{K \times L}$, *denoted by* $\mathbf{A} \otimes \mathbf{B}$, *is a matrix of size* $IK \times JL$ *defined by*

$$\mathbf{A} \otimes \mathbf{B} = \begin{bmatrix} a_{11}\mathbf{B} & \dots & a_{1J}\mathbf{B} \\ \vdots & \ddots & \vdots \\ a_{I1}\mathbf{B} & \dots & a_{IJ}\mathbf{B} \end{bmatrix} \tag{5}$$

Definition 6 (Khatri-Rao product). *Given matrices* $\mathbf{A} \in \mathbb{C}^{I \times K}$ *and* $\mathbf{B} \in \mathbb{C}^{J \times K}$, *their Khatri-Rao product is a* $IJ \times K$ *matrix defined by*

$$\mathbf{A} \odot \mathbf{B} = [\mathbf{a}_1 \otimes \mathbf{b}_1 \quad \mathbf{a}_2 \otimes \mathbf{b}_2 \quad \dots \quad \mathbf{a}_K \otimes \mathbf{b}_K], \tag{6}$$

where $\mathbf{a}_k$ *and* $\mathbf{b}_k$ *are the the columns of* $\mathbf{A}$ *and* $\mathbf{B}$, *respectively.*

A tensor can be also represented into a matrix form, process known as *matricization* or *unfolding*.

Definition 7 (Matricization). *The n-mode matricization of a tensor* $\mathcal{X} \in \mathbb{C}^{I_1 \times \cdots \times I_n \times \cdots \times I_N}$ *is a* $I_n \times I_1 \dots I_{n-1} I_{n+1} \dots I_N$ *size matrix denoted by* $\mathbf{X}_{(n)}$. *The tensor element* $(i_1, i_2, \dots, i_N)$ *maps to matrix element* (i_n, j) *where*

$$j = 1 + \sum_{k=1, k \neq n}^{N} (i_k - 1) J_k \quad \text{with} \quad J_k = \prod_{m=1, m \neq n}^{k-1} I_m \tag{7}$$

This operation is generally used in the alternating least squares algorithms for fitting the CP models, as illustrated in section 5.1.

3. The quadrilinear model of the data covariance

We introduce in this section a quadrilinear model for electromagnetic source covariance, recorded on a six-component vector sensor array. Suppose the sources are completely polarized and the propagation takes place in an isotropic, homogeneous medium. We start by modeling the data measurements under the narrowband assumptions.
Consider an uniform array of M identical sensors spaced by Δx along the x-axis, collecting narrowband signals emitted from K (known *a priori*) spatially distinct far-field sources. For the kth incoming wave, its DOA can be totally determined by the azimuth angle $\phi_k \in [0, \pi)$ (measured from $+x$-axis) and the elevation angle $\psi_k \in [-\pi/2, \pi/2]$ (measured from the ground)[1], as shown in Fig. 1.

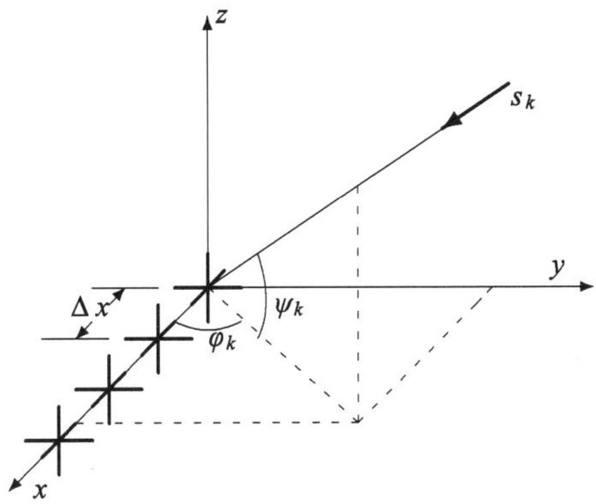

Fig. 1. 2D-DOA on a vector-sensor array

On an electromagnetic vector sensor, if the incoming wave has unit power, the electric- and magnetic-field measurements in Cartesian coordinates, $\mathbf{e}(\phi_k, \psi_k, \alpha_k, \beta_k) \triangleq [e_x^{(k)}, e_y^{(k)}, e_z^{(k)}]^T$ and $\mathbf{h}(\phi_k, \psi_k, \alpha_k, \beta_k) \triangleq [h_x^{(k)}, h_y^{(k)}, h_z^{(k)}]^T$, can be stacked up in a 6×1 vector $\mathbf{b}_k$ Nehorai and Paldi (1994)

$$\mathbf{b}_k \triangleq \begin{bmatrix} \mathbf{e}(\phi_k, \psi_k, \alpha_k, \beta_k) \\ \mathbf{h}(\phi_k, \psi_k, \alpha_k, \beta_k) \end{bmatrix} = \underbrace{\begin{bmatrix} -\sin\phi_k & -\cos\phi_k \sin\psi_k \\ \cos\phi_k & -\sin\phi_k \sin\psi_k \\ 0 & \cos\psi_k \\ -\cos\phi_k \sin\psi_k & \sin\phi_k \\ -\sin\phi_k \sin\psi_k & -\cos\phi_k \\ \cos\psi_k & 0 \end{bmatrix}}_{\mathbf{F}(\phi_k, \psi_k)} \mathbf{g}_k. \tag{8}$$

The 6×2 matrix $\mathbf{F}_k \triangleq \mathbf{F}(\phi_k, \psi_k)$ is referred to as the steering matrix Nehorai et al. (1999) and characterizes the capacity of a vector sensor to convert the information carried on an impinging polarized plane wave defined in polar coordinates, into the six electromagnetic-field-associated electric signals in the corresponding Cartesian coordinates. A 2×1 complex

[1] We assume the sources are all coming from the $+y$ side of the $x - z$ plane.

vector

$$\mathbf{g}_k \triangleq \mathbf{g}(\alpha_k, \beta_k) = \begin{bmatrix} g_\phi(\alpha_k, \beta_k) \\ g_\psi(\alpha_k, \beta_k) \end{bmatrix} = \begin{bmatrix} \cos\alpha_k & \sin\alpha_k \\ -\sin\alpha_k & \cos\alpha_k \end{bmatrix} \begin{bmatrix} \cos\beta_k \\ j\sin\beta_k \end{bmatrix} \quad (9)$$

is used to depict the polarization state of the kth signal in terms of the orientation angle $\alpha_k \in (-\pi/2, \pi/2]$ and the ellipticity angle $\beta_k \in [-\pi/4, \pi/4]$ Deschamps (1951). Now we have a compact expression $\mathbf{b}_k = \mathbf{F}(\phi_k, \psi_k)\mathbf{g}(\alpha_k, \beta_k)$ modeling the vector sensor response to the kth polarized source.

Under the far-field assumption, the spatial response of a M-sensor uniform linear array to the kth impinging wave, *i.e.* the steering vector, presents a Vandermonde structure that can be expressed as

$$\mathbf{a}_k \triangleq \mathbf{a}(\phi_k, \psi_k) = [1,\ a_k,\ \cdots,\ a_k^{M-1}]^T, \quad (10)$$

where $a_k = \exp(jk_0\Delta x \cos\phi_k \cos\psi_k)$ is the inter-sensor phase shift and k_0 is the wave number of the electromagnetic wave.

Let p ($p = 1, 2, \cdots, 6$) index the six field components of the vector $\boldsymbol{b}_k$ respectively. Define

$$\mathbf{A} \triangleq [\mathbf{a}_1, \ldots, \mathbf{a}_K] = \begin{bmatrix} 1 & \cdots & 1 \\ a_1 & \cdots & a_k \\ \vdots & & \vdots \\ a_1^{M-1} & \cdots & a_K^{M-1} \end{bmatrix} \quad (11)$$

a $M \times K$ matrix containing the spatial responses of the array to the N sources,

$$\mathbf{B} \triangleq [\mathbf{b}_1, \ldots, \mathbf{b}_K] = [\mathbf{F}_1\mathbf{g}_1, \ldots, \mathbf{F}_K\mathbf{g}_K] \quad (12)$$

a $6 \times K$ matrix containing the polarization responses and

$$\mathbf{S} \triangleq \begin{bmatrix} s_1 & \cdots & 0 \\ \vdots & \ddots & \vdots \\ 0 & \cdots & s_K \end{bmatrix} \quad (13)$$

a $K \times K$ diagonal matrix containing the K source signals at some fixed instant. With these notations, a snapshot of the output of the array can be organized as a $M \times 6$ matrix

$$\mathbf{X} = \mathbf{ASB}^T + \mathbf{N} \quad (14)$$

with $\mathbf{N}$ a $M \times 6$ matrix expressing the noise contribution on the antenna.

The following assumptions are made

(A1) Sources are zero-mean, stationary, mutually uncorrelated, ergodic processes

(A2) The noise is i.i.d. centered, complex Gaussian process of variance σ^2, non-polarized and spatially white

(A3) The sources have distinct DOAs

We define the 4-way covariance of the received data as the $M \times 6 \times M \times 6$ array

$$\mathcal{C}_{XX} \triangleq \mathrm{E}\{\mathbf{X} \circ \mathbf{X}^*\} \quad (15)$$

where $\mathrm{E}\{.\}$ denotes the mathematical expectation operation. We define also the source covariance as the $K \times K \times K \times K$ fourth-order tensor

$$\mathcal{C}_{SS} \stackrel{\triangle}{=} \mathrm{E}\{\mathbf{S} \circ \mathbf{S}^*\} \tag{16}$$

From (14) and (16) and using assumptions (A1) and (A2) the covariance tensor of the received data takes the following form

$$\mathcal{C}_{XX} = \mathcal{C}_{SS} \times_1 \mathbf{A} \times_2 \mathbf{B} \times_3 \mathbf{A}^* \times_4 \mathbf{B}^* + \mathcal{N} \tag{17}$$

where $\mathcal{N}$ is a $M \times 6 \times M \times 6$ tensor containing the noise power on the sensors. Assumption (A1) implies that $\mathcal{C}_{SS}$ is a hyperdiagonal tensor (the only non-null entries are those having all four indices identical), meaning that $\mathcal{C}_{XX}$ presents a *quadrilinear* CP structure Harshman (1970). The inverse problem for the direct model expressed by (17) is the estimation of matrices **A** and **B** starting from the 4-way covariance tensor $\mathcal{C}_{XX}$.

4. Identifiability of the quadrilinear model

Before addressing the problem of estimating **A** and **B**, the identifiability of the quadrilinear model (17) must be studied first. The polarized mixture model (17) is said to be *identifiable* if **A** and **B** can be uniquely determined (up to permutation and scaling indeterminacies) from $\mathcal{C}_{XX}$. In multilinear framework Kruskal's condition is a sufficient condition for unique CP decomposition, relying on the concept of Kruskal-rank or (k-rank) Kruskal (1977).

Definition 8 (k-rank). *Given a matrix* $\mathbf{A} \in \mathbb{C}^{I \times J}$*, if every linear combination of* l *columns has full column rank, but this condition does not hold for* $l+1$*, then the k-rank of* **A** *is* l*, written as* $k_{\mathbf{A}} = l$.

Note that $k_{\mathbf{A}} \leq \mathrm{rank}(\mathbf{A}) \leq \min(I, J)$, and both equalities hold when $\mathrm{rank}(\mathbf{A}) = J$.
Kruskal's condition was first introduced in Kruskal (1977) for the three-way arrays and generalized later on to multi-way arrays in Sidiropoulos and Bro (2000). We formulate next Kruskal's condition for the quadrilinear mixture model expressed by (17), considering the noiseless case ($\mathcal{N}$ in (17) has only zero entries).

Theorem 1 (Kruskal's condition). *Consider the four-way CP model (17). The loading matrices* **A** *and* **B** *can be uniquely estimated (up to column permutation and scaling ambiguities), if but not necessarily*

$$k_{\mathbf{A}} + k_{\mathbf{B}} + k_{\mathbf{A}^*} + k_{\mathbf{B}^*} \geq 2K + 3 \tag{18}$$

This implies

$$k_{\mathbf{A}} + k_{\mathbf{B}} \geq K + 2 \tag{19}$$

It was proved Tan et al. (1996a) that in the case of vector sensor arrays, the responses of a vector sensor to every three sources of distinct DOA's are linearly independent regardless of their polarization states. This means, under the assumption (A3) that $k_{\mathbf{B}} \geq 3$. Furthermore, as **A** is a Vandermonde matrix, (A3) also guarantees that $k_{\mathbf{A}} = \min(M, K)$. All these results sum up into the following corollary:

Corollary 1. *Under the assumptions (A1)-(A3), the DOA's of K uncorrelated sources can be uniquely determined using an M-element vector sensor array if* $M \geq K - 1$*, regardless of the polarization states of the incident signals.*

This sufficient condition also sets an upper bound on the minimum number of sensors needed to ensure the identifiability of the polarized mixture model. However, the condition $M \geq K - 1$ is not necessary when considering the polarization states, that is, a lower number of sensors can be used to identify the mixture model, provided that the polarizations of the sources are different. Also the symmetry properties of $\mathcal{C}_{XX}$ are not considered and we believe that they can be used to obtain milder sufficient conditions for ensuring the identifiability.

5. Source parameters estimation

We present next the algorithm used for estimating sources DOA's starting from the observations on the array and address some issues regarding the accuracy and the complexity of the proposed method.

5.1 Algorithm

Supposing that L snapshots of the array are recorded and using (A1) an estimate of the polarized data covariance (15) can be obtained as the temporal sample mean

$$\hat{\mathcal{C}}_{XX} = \frac{1}{L}\sum_{l=1}^{L} \mathbf{X}(l) \circ \mathbf{X}^*(l). \tag{20}$$

For obvious matrix conditioning reasons, the number of snapshots should be greater or equal to the number of sensors, *i.e.* $L \geq K$.

The algorithm proposed in this section includes three sequential steps, during which the DOA information is extracted and then refined to yield the final DOA's estimates. These three steps are presented next.

5.1.1 Step 1

This first step of the algorithm is the estimation of the loading matrices $\mathbf{A}$ and $\mathbf{B}$ from $\hat{\mathcal{C}}_{XX}$. This estimation procedure can be accomplished via the *Quadrilinear Alternative Least Squares (QALS)* algorithm Bro (1998), as shown next.
Denote by $\hat{\mathbf{C}}_{pq} = \hat{\mathcal{C}}_{XX}(:,p,:,q)$ the (p,q)th matrix slice $(M \times M)$ of the covariance tensor $\hat{\mathcal{C}}_{XX}$. Also note $\mathrm{D}_p(\cdot)$ the operator that builds a diagonal matrix from the pth row of another and $\mathbf{\Delta} = \mathrm{diag}\left(E\|s_1\|^2, \ldots, E\|s_K\|^2\right)$, the diagonal matrix containing the powers of the sources. The matrices $\mathbf{A}$ and $\mathbf{B}$ can then be determined by minimizing the Least Squares (LS) criterion

$$\phi(\sigma, \mathbf{\Delta}, \mathbf{A}, \mathbf{B}) = \sum_{p,q=1}^{6} \left\| \hat{\mathbf{C}}_{pq} - \mathbf{A}\mathbf{\Delta}\mathrm{D}_p(\mathbf{B})\mathrm{D}_q(\mathbf{B}^*)\mathbf{A}^H - \sigma^2\delta_{pq}\mathbf{I}_M \right\|_F^2 \tag{21}$$

that equals

$$\begin{aligned}\phi(\sigma, \mathbf{\Delta}, \mathbf{A}, \mathbf{B}) = &\sum_{p,q} \left\| \hat{\mathbf{C}}_{pq} - \mathbf{A}\mathbf{\Delta}\mathrm{D}_p(\mathbf{B})\mathrm{D}_q(\mathbf{B}^*)\mathbf{A}^H \right\|_F^2 \\ &- 2\sigma^2 \sum_{p} \Re\left\{\mathrm{tr}\left(\hat{\mathbf{C}}_{pp} - \mathbf{A}\mathbf{\Delta}\mathrm{D}_p(\mathbf{B})\mathrm{D}_p(\mathbf{B}^*)\mathbf{A}^H\right)\right\} + 6M\sigma^4\end{aligned} \tag{22}$$

where $\mathrm{tr}(\cdot)$ computes the trace of a matrix and $\Re(\cdot)$ denotes the real part of a quantity.

$$\phi(\sigma, \Delta, \mathbf{A}, \mathbf{B}) = \sum_{p,q} \left\| \hat{\mathbf{C}}_{pq} - \mathbf{A}\Delta \mathrm{D}_p(\mathbf{B})\mathrm{D}_q(\mathbf{B}^*)\mathbf{A}^H \right\|_F^2 - 2\sigma^2 \sum_p \Re\left\{ \mathrm{tr}\left(\hat{\mathbf{C}}_{pp} - 2M\Delta \right) \right\} + 6M\sigma^4 \tag{23}$$

Thus, finding **A** and **B** is equivalent to the minimization of (23) with respect to **A** and **B**, i.e.

$$\{\hat{\mathbf{A}}, \hat{\mathbf{B}}\} = \min_{\mathbf{A},\mathbf{B}} \omega(\Delta, \mathbf{A}, \mathbf{B}) \tag{24}$$

subject to $\|\boldsymbol{a}_k\|^2 = M$ and $\|\boldsymbol{b}_k\|^2 = 2$, where

$$\omega(\Delta, \mathbf{A}, \mathbf{B}) = \sum_{p,q} \left\| \hat{\mathbf{C}}_{pq} - \mathbf{A}\Delta \mathrm{D}_p(\mathbf{B})\mathrm{D}_q(\mathbf{B}^*)\mathbf{A}^H \right\|_F^2 \tag{25}$$

The optimization process in (24) can be implemented using QALS algorithm, briefly summarized as follows.

Algorithm 1 QALS algorithm for four-way symmetric tensors

1: INPUT: the estimated data covariance $\hat{\mathcal{C}}_{XX}$ and the number of the sources K
2: Initialize the loading matrices **A**, **B** randomly, or using ESPRIT Zoltowski and Wong (2000a) for a faster convergence
3: Set $\mathbf{C} = \mathbf{A}^*$ and $\mathbf{D} = \mathbf{B}^*$.
4: **repeat**
5: $\quad \mathbf{A} = \mathbf{X}_{(1)}[(\mathbf{B} \odot \mathbf{C} \odot \mathbf{D})^{\dagger}]^T$
6: $\quad \mathbf{B} = \mathbf{X}_{(2)}[(\mathbf{C} \odot \mathbf{D} \odot \mathbf{A})^{\dagger}]^T$
7: $\quad \mathbf{C} = \mathbf{X}_{(3)}[(\mathbf{D} \odot \mathbf{A} \odot \mathbf{B})^{\dagger}]^T$
8: $\quad \mathbf{D} = \mathbf{X}_{(4)}[(\mathbf{A} \odot \mathbf{B} \odot \mathbf{C})^{\dagger}]^T$,
where $(\cdot)^{\dagger}$ denotes Moore-Penrose pseudoinverse of a matrix
9: Update **C**, **D** by $\mathbf{C} := (\mathbf{A}^* + \mathbf{C})/2$ and $\mathbf{D} := (\mathbf{B}^* + \mathbf{D})/2$
10: **until** convergence
11: OUTPUT: estimates of **A** and **B**.

Once the $\hat{\mathbf{A}}$, $\hat{\mathbf{B}}$ are estimated, the following post-processing is needed for the refined DOA estimation.

5.1.2 Step 2

The second step of our approach extracts separately the DOA information contained by the columns of $\hat{\mathbf{A}}$ (see eq. (10)) and $\hat{\mathbf{B}}$ (see eq. (8)).

First the estimated matrix $\hat{\mathbf{B}}$ is exploited via the physical relationships between the electric and magnetic field given by the Poynting theorem. Recall the Poynting theorem, which reveals the mutual orthogonality nature among the three physical quantities related to the kth source: the electric field $\mathbf{e}_k$, the magnetic field $\mathbf{h}_k$, and the kth source's direction of propagation, *i.e.*, the normalized Poynting vector $\mathbf{u}_k$.

$$\mathbf{u}_k = \begin{bmatrix} \cos\phi_k \cos\psi_k \\ \sin\phi_k \cos\psi_k \\ \sin\psi_k \end{bmatrix} = \Re\left(\frac{\mathbf{e}_k \times \mathbf{h}_k^*}{\|\mathbf{e}_k\| \cdot \|\mathbf{h}_k\|}\right). \tag{26}$$

Equation (26) gives the cross-product DOA estimator, as suggested in Nehorai and Paldi (1994). An estimate of the Poynting vector for the kth source $\hat{\mathbf{u}}_k$ is thus obtained, using the previously estimated $\hat{\mathbf{e}}_k$ and $\hat{\mathbf{b}}_k$.

Secondly, matrix $\hat{\mathbf{A}}$ is used to extract the DOA information embedded in the Vandermonde structure of its columns $\hat{\mathbf{a}}_k$.
Given the noisy steering vector $\hat{\mathbf{a}} = [\hat{a}_0\, \hat{a}_1\, \cdots\, \hat{a}_{M-1}]^T$, its Fourier spectrum is given by

$$A(\omega) = \frac{1}{M}\sum_{m=0}^{M-1} \hat{a}_m \exp(-jm\omega) \tag{27}$$

as a function of ω.
Given the Vandermonde structure of the steering vectors, the spectrum magnitude $|A(\omega)|$ in the absence of noise is maximum for $\omega = \omega_0$. In the presence of Gaussian noise, $\max_\omega |A(\omega)|$ provides an maximum likelihood (ML) estimator for $\omega_0 \triangleq k_0 \Delta x \cos\phi \cos\psi$ as shown in Rife and Boorstyn (1974).
In order to get a more accurate estimator of $\omega_0 \triangleq k_0 \Delta x \cos\phi \cos\psi$, we use the following processing steps.

1) We take uniformly Q ($Q \geq M$) samples from the spectrum $A(\omega)$, say $\{A(2\pi q/Q)\}_{q=0}^{Q-1}$, and find the *coarse* estimate $\hat{\omega} = 2\pi\check{q}/Q$ so that $A(2\pi\check{q}/Q)$ has the maximum magnitude. These spectrum samples are identified via the fast Fourier transform (FFT) over the zero-padded Q-element sequence $\{\hat{a}_0, \ldots, \hat{a}_{M-1}, 0, \ldots, 0\}$.
2) Initialized with this coarse estimate, the *fine* estimate of ω_0 can be sought by maximizing $|A(\omega)|$. For example, the *quasi-Newton* method (see, *e.g.*, Nocedal and Wright (2006)) can be used to find the maximizer $\hat{\omega}_0$ over the local range $\left(\frac{2\pi(\check{q}-1)}{Q}, \frac{2\pi(\check{q}+1)}{Q}\right)$.

The normalized phase-shift can then be obtained as $\varrho = (k_0\Delta x)^{-1} \arg(\hat{\omega}_0)$.

5.1.3 Step 3

In the third step, the two DOA information, obtained at **Step 2**, are combined in order to get a refined estimation of the DOA parameters ϕ and ψ. This step can be formulated as the following non-linear optimization problem

$$\min_{\psi,\phi} \left\| \begin{bmatrix} \cos\phi \cos\psi \\ \sin\phi \cos\psi \\ \sin\psi \end{bmatrix} - \hat{\mathbf{u}} \right\| \quad \text{subject to } \cos\phi\cos\psi = \varrho. \tag{28}$$

A closed form solution to (28) can be found by transforming it into an alternate problem of 3-D geometry, *i.e.* finding the point on the vertically posed circle $\cos\phi\cos\psi = \varrho$ which minimizes its Euclidean distance to the point $\hat{\mathbf{u}}$, as shown in Fig. 2.
To solve this problem, we do the orthogonal projection of $\hat{\mathbf{u}}$ onto the plane $x = \varrho$ in the 3-D space, then join the perpendicular foot with the center of the circle by a piece of line segment.

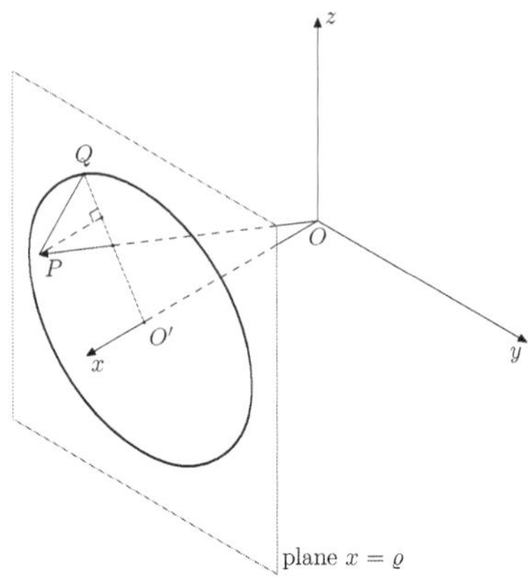

Fig. 2. Illustration of the geometrical solution to the optimization problem (28). The vector $\vec{OP}$ represents the coarse estimate of Poynting vector $\hat{\mathbf{u}}$. It is projected orthogonally onto the $x = \varrho$ plane, forming a shadow cast $\overline{O'Q}$, where O' is the center of the circle of center O on the plane given in the polar coordinates as $\cos\phi\cos\psi = \varrho$. The refined estimate, obtained this way, lies on $\overline{O'Q}$. As it is also constrained on the circle, it can be sought as their intersection point Q.

This line segment collides with the circumference of the circle, yielding an intersection point, that is the minimizer of the problem.
Let $\hat{\mathbf{u}} \triangleq [\hat{u}_1\ \hat{u}_2\ \hat{u}_3]^T$ and define $\kappa \triangleq \hat{u}_3/\hat{u}_2$, then the intersection point is given by

$$\begin{bmatrix} \varrho & \pm\sqrt{\frac{1-\varrho^2}{1+\kappa^2}} & \pm|\kappa|\sqrt{\frac{1-\varrho^2}{1+\kappa^2}} \end{bmatrix}^T \tag{29}$$

where the signs are taken the same as their corresponding entries of vector $\hat{\mathbf{u}}$. Thus, the azimuth and elevation angles estimates are given by

$$\hat{\phi} = \begin{cases} \arctan\frac{1}{|\varrho|}\sqrt{\frac{1-\varrho^2}{1+\kappa^2}}, & \text{if } \varrho \geq 0 \\ \pi - \arctan\frac{1}{|\varrho|}\sqrt{\frac{1-\varrho^2}{1+\kappa^2}}, & \text{if } \varrho < 0 \end{cases} \tag{30a}$$

$$\hat{\psi} = \arcsin\sqrt{\varrho^2 + \frac{1-\varrho^2}{1+\kappa^2}}, \tag{30b}$$

which completes the DOA estimation procedure. The polarization parameters can be obtained in a similar way from $\hat{\mathbf{B}}$.
It is noteworthy that this algorithm is not necessarily limited to uniform linear arrays. It can be applied to arrays of arbitrary configuration, with minimal modifications.

5.2 Estimator accuracy and algorithm complexity issues

This subsection aims at giving some analysis elements on the accuracy and complexity of the proposed algorithm (QALS) used for the DOA estimation.

An exhaustive and rigorous performance analysis of the proposed algorithm is far from being obvious. However, using some simple arguments, we provide elements giving some insights into the understanding of the performance of the QALS and allowing to interpret the simulation results presented in section 6.

Cramér-Rao bounds were derived in Liu and Sidiropoulos (2001) for the decomposition of multi-ways arrays and in Nehorai and Paldi (1994) for vector sensor arrays. It was shown Liu and Sidiropoulos (2001) that higher dimensionality benefits in terms of CRB for a given data set. To be specific, consider a data set represented by a four-way CP model. It is obvious that, unfolding it along one dimension, it can also be represented by a three-way model. The result of Liu and Sidiropoulos (2001) states that than a quadrilinear estimator normally yields better performance than a trilinear one. In other word, the use of a four-way ALS on the covariance tensor is better sounded that performing a three-way ALS on the unfolded covariance tensor. A comparaison can be conducted with respect to the three-way CP estimator used in Guo et al. (2008), that will be denoted TALS. The addressed question is the following : is it better to perform the trilinear decomposition of the 3-way raw data tensor or the quadriliear decomposition of the 4-way convariance tensor ?
To compare the accuracy of the two algorithms we remind that the variance of an unbiased linear estimator of a set of independant parameters is of the order of $\mathcal{O}\left(\frac{\mathrm{P}}{\mathrm{N}}\sigma^2\right)$, where P is the number of parameters to estimate and N is the number of samples.
Coming back to the QALS and TALS methods, the main difference between them is that the trilinear approach estimates (in addition to $\mathbf{A}$ and $\mathbf{B}$), the K temporal sequences of size L. More precisely, the number of parameters to estimate equals $(6 + M + L)K$ for the three-way approach and $(6 + M)K$ for the quadrilinear method. Nevertheless, TALS is directly applied on the three-way raw data, meaning that the number of available observations (samples) is $6ML$ while QALS is based on the covariance of the data which, because of the symmetry of the covariance tensor, reduces the samples number to half of the entries of $\hat{\mathcal{C}}_{XX}$, that is $18M^2$. The point is that the noise power for the covariance of the data is reduced by the averaging in (20) to σ^2/L. If we resume, the estimation variance for TALS is of the order of $\mathcal{O}\left(\frac{(6+M+L)K}{6ML}\sigma^2\right)$ and of $\mathcal{O}\left(\frac{(6+M)K}{18M^2}\frac{\sigma^2}{L}\right)$ for QALS. Let us now analyse the typical situation consisting in having a large number of time samples. For large values of L, $(L \gg (M+6))$, the variance of TALS tends to a constant value $\mathcal{O}\left(\frac{K}{6M}\sigma^2\right)$ while for QALS it tends to 0. This means that QALS improves continuously with the sample size while this is not the case for TALS. This analysis also applies to the case of MUSIC and ESPRIT since both also work on time averaged data.

We address next some computational complexity aspects for the two previously discussed algorithms. Generally, for an N-way array of size $I_1 \times I_2 \times \cdots \times I_N$, the complexity of its CP decomposition in a sum of K rank-one tensors, using ALS algorithm is $\mathcal{O}(K\prod_{n=1}^{N} I_n)$ Rajih and Comon (2005), for each iteration. Thus, for one iteration, the number of elementary operations involved is QALS is of order $\mathcal{O}(6^2KM^2)$ and of the order of $\mathcal{O}(6KML)$ for TALS. Normally $6M \ll L$, meaning that for large data sets QALS should be much faster than its trilinear counterpart. In general, the number of iterations required for the decomposition convergence, is not determined by the data size only, but is also influenced by the initialisation and the

parameter to estimate. This makes an exact theoretical analysis of the algorithms complexity rather difficult. Moreover, trilinear factorization algorithms have been extensively studied over the last two decades, resulting in improved, fast versions of ALS such as COMFAC[2], while the algorithms for quadrilinear factorizations remained basic. This makes an objective comparison of the complexity of the two algorithms even more difficult.
Compared to MUSIC-like algorithms, which are also based on the estimation of the data covariance, the main advantage of QALS is the identifiability of the model. While MUSIC generally needs an exhaustive grid search for the estimation of the source parameters, the quadrilinear method yields directly the steering and the polarization vectors for each source.

6. Simulations and results

In this section, some typical examples are considered to illustrate the performance of the proposed algorithm with respect to different aspects. In all the simulations, we assume the inter-element spacing between two adjacent vector sensors is half-wavelength, *i.e.*, $\Delta x = \lambda/2$ and each point on the figures is obtained through $R = 500$ independent Monte Carlo runs. We divided this section into two parts. The first aims at illustrating the efficiency of the novel method for the estimation of both DOA parameters (azimuth and elevation angles) and the second shows the effects of different parameters on the method. Comparisons are conducted to recent high-resolution eigenstructure-based algorithms for polarized sources and to the CRB Nehorai and Paldi (1994).

Example 1: This example is designed to show the efficiency of the proposed algorithm using a uniform linear array of vector sensors for the 2D DOA estimation problem. It is compared to MUSIC algorithm for polarized sources, presented under different versions in Ferrara and Parks (1983); Gong et al. (2009); Miron et al. (2005); Weiss and Friedlander (1993b), to TALS Guo et al. (2008) and the Cramér-Rao bound for vector sensor arrays proposed by Nehorai Nehorai and Paldi (1994). A number of $K = 2$ equal power, uncorrelated sources are considered. The DOA's are set to be $\phi_1 = 20°$, $\psi_1 = 5°$ for the first source and $\phi_2 = 30°$, $\psi_2 = 10°$ for the other; the polarization states are $\alpha_1 = \alpha_2 = 45°$, $\beta_1 = -\beta_2 = 15°$. In the simulations, $M = 7$ sensors are used and in total $L = 100$ temporal snapshots are available. The performance is evaluated in terms of root-mean-square error (RMSE). In the following simulations we convert the angular RMSE from radians to degrees to make the comparisons more intuitive. The performances of these algorithms are shown in Fig. 3(a) and (b) versus the increasing signal-to-noise ratio (SNR). The SNR is defined per source and per field component ($6M$ field components in all). One can observe that all the algorithms present similar performance and eventually achieve the CRB for high SNR's (above 0 dB in this scenario). At low SNR's, nonetheless, our algorithm outperforms MUSIC, presenting a lower SNR threshold (about 8 dB) for a meaningful estimate. CP methods (TALS and QALS), which are based on the LS criterion, are demonstrated to be less sensitive to the noise than MUSIC. This confirms the results presented in Liu and Sidiropoulos (2001) that higher dimension (an increased structure of the data) benefits in terms of estimation accuracy.
Example 2: We examine next the performance of QALS in the presence of four uncorrelated sources. For simplicity, we assume all the elevation angles are zero, $\psi_k = 0°$ for $k = 1, \ldots, 4$, and some typical values are chosen for the azimuth angles, respectively: $\phi_1 = 10°$, $\phi_2 = 20°$,

[2] COMFAC is a fast implementation of trilinear ALS working with a compressed version of the data Sidiropoulos et al. (2000a)

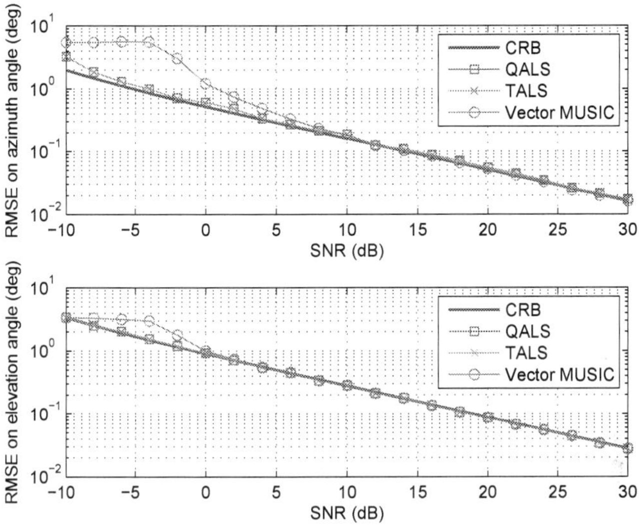

(a) RMSE of the DOA estimation for the first source

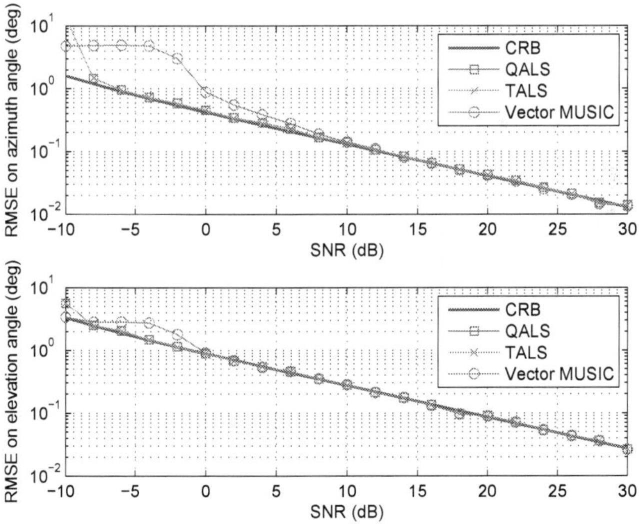

(b) RMSE of the DOA estimation for the second source

Fig. 3. RMSE of the DOA estimation versus SNR in the presence of two uncorrelated sources

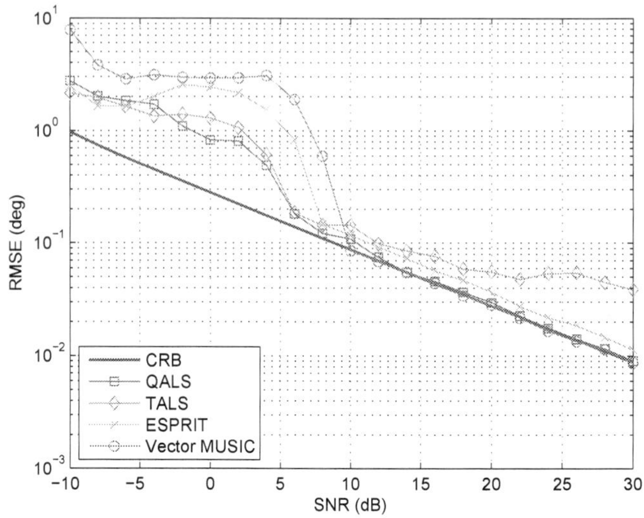

Fig. 4. RMSE of azimuth angle estimation versus SNR for the second source in the presence of four uncorrelated sources

$\phi_1 = 30^\circ$, $\phi_1 = 40^\circ$. The polarizations parameters are $\alpha_2 = -45^\circ$, $\beta_2 = -15^\circ$ for the second source and for the others, the sources have equal orientation and ellipticity angles, 45° and 15° respectively. We keep the same configuration of the vector sensor array as in example 1. For this example we compare our algorithm to polarized ESPRIT Zoltowski and Wong (2000a;b) as well. The following three sets of simulations are designed with respect to the increasing value of SNR, number of vector sensors and snapshots.

Fig. 4 shows the comparison between the four algorithms as the SNR increases. Once again, the advantage of the multilinear approaches in tackling DOA problem at low SNR's can be observed. The quadrilinear approach seems to perform better than TALS as the SNR increases. The MUSIC algorithm is more sensitive to the noise than all the others, yet it reaches the CRB as the SNR is high enough. The estimate obtained by ESPRIT is mildly biased.

Next, we show the effect of the number of vector sensors on the estimators. The SNR is fixed to 20 dB and all the other simulation settings are preserved. The results are illustrated on Fig. 5. One can see that the DOA's of the four sources can be uniquely identified with only two vector sensors (RMSE around 1°), which substantiates our statement on the identifiablity of the model in Section 4. As expected, the estimation accuracy is reduced by decreasing the number of vector sensors, and the loss becomes important when only few sensors are present (four sensors in this case). Again ESPRIT yieds biased estimates. For the trilinear method, it is shown that its performance limitation, observed on Fig. 4, can be tackled by using more sensors, meaning that the array aperture is a key parameter for TALS. The MUSIC method shows mild advantages over the quadrilinear one in the case of few sensors (less than four sensors), yet the two yield comparable performance as the number of vector sensors increases (superior to the other two methods).

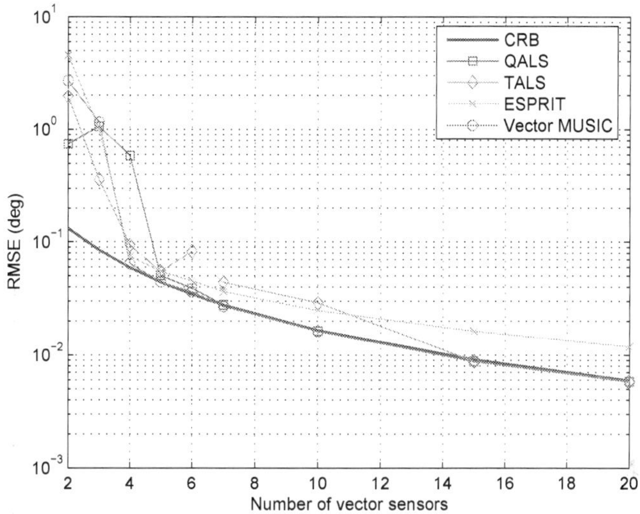

Fig. 5. RMSE of azimuth angle estimation versus the number of vector sensors for the second source in the presence of four uncorrelated sources

Finally, we fix the SNR at 20 dB, while keeping the other experimental settings the same as in Fig. 4, except for an increasing number of snapshots L which varies from 10 to 1000. Fig. 6 shows the varying RMSE with respect to the number of snapshots in estimating azimuth angle of the second source. Once again, the proposed algorithm performs better than TALS. Moreover as L becomes important, one can see that TALS tends to a constant value while the RMSE for QALS continues to decrease, which confirms the theoretical deductions presented in subsection 5.2.

7. Conclusions

In this paper we introduced a novel algorithm for DOA estimation for polarized sources, based on a four-way PARAFAC representation of the data covariance. A quadrilinear alternated least squares procedure is used to estimate the steering vectors and the polarization vectors of the sources. Compared to MUSIC for polarized sources, the proposed algorithm ensures the mixture model identifiability; thus it avoids the exhaustive grid search over the parameters space, typical to eigestructure algorithms. An upper bound on the minimum number of sensors needed to ensure the identifiability of the mixture model is derived. Given the symmetric structure of the data covariance, our algorithm presents a smaller complexity per iteration compared to three-way PARAFAC applied directly on the raw data. In terms of estimation, the proposed algorithm presents slightly better performance than MUSIC and ESPRIT, thanks to its higher dimensionality and it clearly outperforms the three-way algorithm when the number of temporal samples becomes important. The variance of our algorithm decreases with an increase in the sample size while for the three-way method it tends asymptotically to a constant value.

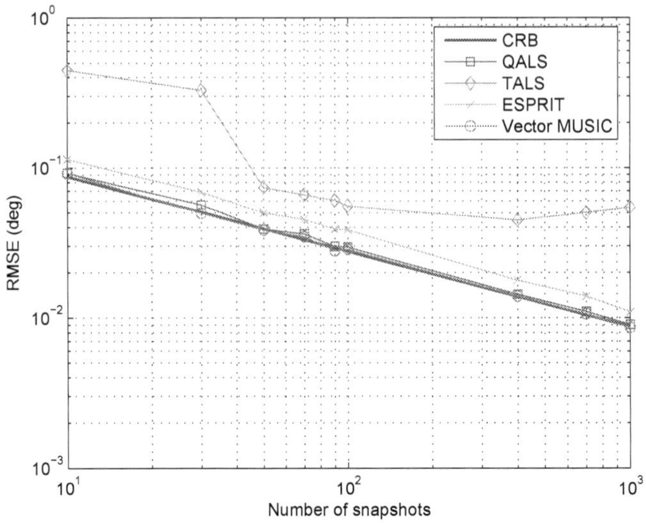

Fig. 6. RMSE of azimuth angle estimation versus the number of snapshots for the second source in the presence of four uncorrelated sources

Future works should focus on developing faster algorithms for four-way PARAFAC factorization in order to take full advantage of the lower complexity of the algorithm. Also, the symmetry of the covariance tensor must be taken into account to derive lower bounds on the minimum number of sensors needed to ensure the source mixture identifiability.

8. References

Bro, R. (1998). Multi-way Analysis in the Food Industry - Models, Algorithms, and Applications. Ph.D. dissertation. Royal Veterinary and Agricultural University. Denmark.

Burgess, K. A. and B. D. Van Veen (1994). A subspace GLRT for vector-sensor array detection. In: *Proc. IEEE Int. Conf. Acoust., Speech, Signal Process. (ICASSP)*. Vol. 4. Adelaide, SA, Australia. pp. 253–256.

De Lathauwer, L. (1997). Signal Processing based on Multilinear Algebra. PhD thesis. Katholieke Universiteit Leuven.

Deschamps, G. A. (1951). Geometrical representation of the polarization of a plane electromagnetic wave. *Proc. IRE* **39**, 540–544.

Ferrara, E. R., Jr. and T. M. Parks (1983). Direction finding with an array of antennas having diverse polarizations. *IEEE Trans. Antennas Propagat.* **AP-31**(2), 231–236.

Gong, X., Z. Liu, Y. Xu and M. I. Ahmad (2009). Direction-of-arrival estimation via twofold mode-projection. *Signal Processing* **89**(5), 831–842.

Guo, X., S. Miron and D. Brie (2008). Identifiability of the PARAFAC model for polarized source mixture on a vector sensor array. In: *Proc. IEEE ICASSP 2008*. Las Vegas, USA.

Harshman, R. A. (1970). Foundations of the PARAFAC procedure: Model and conditions for an explanatory multi-mode factor analysis. *UCLA Working Papers Phonetics,* **16**, 1–84.

Ho, K.-C., K.-C. Tan and W. Ser (1995). An investigation on number of signals whose directions-of-arrival are uniquely determinable with an electromagnetic vector sensor. *Signal Process.* **47**(1), 41–54.

Hochwald, B. and A. Nehorai (1996). Identifiability in array processing models with vector-sensor applications. *IEEE Trans. Signal Process.* **44**(1), 83–95.

Kolda, T. G. and B. W. Bader (2007). Tensor decompositions and applications. Technical Report SAND2007-6702. Sandia National Laboratories. Albuquerque, N. M. and Livermore.

Kruskal, J. B. (1977). Three-way arrays: Rank and uniqueness of trilinear decompositions, with application to arithmetic complexity and statistics. *Linear Algebra Applicat.* **18**, 95–138.

Le Bihan, N., S. Miron and J. I. Mars (2007). MUSIC algorithm for vector-sensors array using biquaternions. *IEEE Trans. Signal Process.* **55**(9), 4523–4533.

Li, J. (1993). Direction and polarization estimation using arrays with small loops and short dipoles. *IEEE Trans. Antennas Propagat.* **41**, 379–387.

Liu, X. and N. D. Sidiropoulos (2001). Camér-Rao lower bounds for low-rank decomposition of multidimensional arrays. *IEEE Trans. Signal Processing* **49**, 2074–2086.

Miron, S., N. Le Bihan and J. I. Mars (2005). Vector-sensor MUSIC for polarized seismic sources localisation. *EURASIP Journal on Applied Signal Processing* **2005**(1), 74–84.

Miron, S., N. Le Bihan and J. I. Mars (2006). Quaternion MUSIC for vector-sensor array processing. *IEEE Trans. Signal Process.* **54**(4), 1218–1229.

Nehorai, A. and E. Paldi (1994). Vector-sensor array processing for electromagnetic source localisation. *IEEE Trans. Signal Processing* **42**(2), 376–398.

Nehorai, A., K. C. Ho and B. T. G. Tan (1999). Minimum-noise-variance beamformer with an electromagnetic vector sensor. *IEEE Trans. Signal Processing* **47**(3), 601–618.

Nocedal, J. and S. J. Wright (2006). *Numerical Optimization.* Springer-Verlag. New York.

Rahamim, D., R. Shavit and J. Tabrikian (2003). Coherent source localisation using vector sensor arrays. *IEEE Int. Conf. Acoust., Speech, Signal Processing* pp. 141–144.

Rajih, M. and P. Comon (2005). Enhanced line search: A novel method to accelerate PARAFAC. In: *Proc. EUSIPCO 2005.* Antalya, Turkey.

Rife, D. C. and R. R. Boorstyn (1974). Single-tone parameter estimation from discrete-time observation. *IEEE Trans. Inform. Theory* **IT-20**(5), 591–598.

Rong, Y., S. A. Vorobyov, A. B. Gershman and N. D. Sidiropoulos (2005). Blind spatial signature estimation via time-varying user power loading and parallel factor analysis. *IEEE Trans. Signal Processing* **53**(5), 1697–1710.

Sidiropoulos, N. D. and R. Bro (2000). On the uniqueness of multilinear decomposition of N-way arrays. *Journal of chemometrics* (14), 229–239.

Sidiropoulos, N. D., G. B. Giannakis and R. Bro (2000*a*). Blind PARAFAC receivers for DS-CDMA systems. *IEEE Trans. Signal Processing* **48**(3), 810–823.

Sidiropoulos, N. D., R. Bro and G. B. Giannakis (2000*b*). Parallel factor analysis in sensor array processing. *IEEE Trans. Signal Processing* **48**(8), 2377–2388.

Swindlehurst, A., M. Goris and B. Ottersten (1997). Some experiments with array data collected in actual urban and suburban environments. In: *IEEE Workshop on Signal Proc. Adv. in Wireless Comm.*. Paris, France. pp. 301–304.

Tan, K.-C., K.-C. Ho and A. Nehorai (1996*a*). Linear independence of steering vectors of an electromagnetic vector sensor. *IEEE Trans. Signal Process.* **44**(12), 3099–3107.

Tan, K.-C., K.-C. Ho and A. Nehorai (1996*b*). Uniqueness study of measurements obtainable with arrays of electromagnetic vector sensors. *IEEE Trans. Signal Process.* **44**(4), 1036–1039.

Weiss, A. J. and B. Friedlander (1993*a*). Analysis of a signal estimation algorithm for diversely polarized arrays. *IEEE Trans. Signal Process.* **41**(8), 2628–2638.

Weiss, A. J and B. Friedlander (1993*b*). Direction finding for diversely polarized signals using polynomial rooting. *IEEE Trans. Signal Processing* **41**(5), 1893–1905.

Wong, K. T. and M. D. Zoltowski (1997). Uni-vector-sensor ESPRIT for multisource azimuth, elevation, and polarization estimation. *IEEE Trans. Antennas Propagat.* **45**(10), 1467–1474.

Zhang, X. and D. Xu (2007). Blind PARAFAC signal detection for polarization sensitive array. *EURASIP Journal on Advances in Signal Processing* **2007**, Article ID 12025, 7 pages.

Zoltowski, M. D. and K. T. Wong (2000*a*). Closed-form eigenstructure-based direction finding using arbitrary but identical subarrays on a sparse uniform cartesian array grid. *IEEE Trans. Signal Process.* **48**(8), 2205–2210.

Zoltowski, M. D. and K. T. Wong (2000*b*). ESPRIT-based 2-D direction finding with a sparse uniform array of electromagnetic vector sensors. *IEEE Trans. Signal Process.* **48**(8), 2195–2204.

3

New Trends in Biologically-Inspired Audio Coding

Ramin Pichevar, Hossein Najaf-Zadeh, Louis Thibault and Hassan Lahdili
Advanced Audio Systems, Communications Research Centre
Ottawa, Canada

1. Abstract

This book chapter deals with the generation of auditory-inspired spectro-temporal features aimed at audio coding. To do so, we first generate sparse audio representations we call spikegrams, using projections on gammatone or gammachirp kernels that generate neural spikes. Unlike Fourier-based representations, these representations are powerful at identifying auditory events, such as onsets, offsets, transients and harmonic structures. We show that the introduction of adaptiveness in the selection of gammachirp kernels enhances the compression rate compared to the case where the kernels are non-adaptive. We also integrate a masking model that helps reduce bitrate without loss of perceptible audio quality. We then quantize coding values using the genetic algorithm that is more optimal than uniform quantization for this framework. We finally propose a method to extract frequent auditory objects (patterns) in the aforementioned sparse representations. The extracted frequency-domain patterns (auditory objects) help us address spikes (auditory events) collectively rather than individually. When audio compression is needed, the different patterns are stored in a small codebook that can be used to efficiently encode audio materials in a lossless way. The approach is applied to different audio signals and results are discussed and compared. This work is a first step towards the design of a high-quality auditory-inspired "object-based" audio coder.

2. Introduction

Non-stationary and time-relative structures such as transients, timing relations among acoustic events, and harmonic periodicities provide important cues for different types of audio processing techniques including audio coding, speech recognition, audio localization, and auditory scene analysis. Obtaining these cues is a difficult task. The most important reason why it is so difficult is that most approaches to signal representation/analysis are block-based, i.e. the signal is processed piecewise in a series of discrete blocks. Therefore, transients and non-stationary periodicities in the signal can be temporally smeared across blocks. Moreover, large changes in the representation of an acoustic event can occur depending on the arbitrary alignment of the processing blocks with events in the signal. Signal analysis techniques such as windowing or the choice of the transform can reduce these effects, but it would be preferable if the representation was insensitive to signal shifts. Shift-invariance alone, however, is not a sufficient constraint on designing a general sound processing algorithm. A desirable representation should capture the underlying 2D-time-frequency structures, so that they are more directly observable and well represented at low bit rates (Smith & Lewicki, 2005). These structures must be easily extractable as auditory objects for further processing in coding, recognition, etc.

The aim of this chapter is to first introduce sparse biologically-inspired coding and then propose an auditory-inspired coding scheme, which includes many characteristics of the auditory pathway such as sparse coding, masking, auditory object extraction, and recognition (see Fig. 6). In the next section we will see how sparse codes are generated and why they are efficient.

3. Sparse Coding

Research on sparse coding is generally conducted almost independently by two group of researchers: signal processing engineers and biophysicists. In this chapter, we will try to make a link between these two realms. In a mathematical sense, sparse coding generally refers to a representation where a small number of components are active. In the biological realm, a sparse code generally refers to a representation where a small number of neurons are active with the majority of neurons being inactive or showing low activity (Graham & Field, 2006). Over the last decade, mathematical explorations into the statistics of natural auditory and visual scenes have led to the observation that these scenes, as complex and varied as they appear, have an underlying structure that is sparse. Therefore, one can learn a possibly overcomplete basis[1] set such that only a small fraction of the basis functions is necessary to describe a given audio or video signal. In section 5.1, we will see how these codes can be generated by projecting a given signal onto a set of overcomplete kernels. When the cell's amplitude is different from zero, we say that the neuron or cell is active and has emitted a spike. To show the analogy between sparse 2-D representations and the underlying neural activity in the auditory or visual pathway, we call the 2-D sparse representation spikegram (in contrast with spectrograms) and the components of a sparse representation cells or neurons throughout this chapter.

In a sparse code, the dimensionality of the analyzed signal is maintained (or even increased). However, the number of cells responding to any particular instance of the input signal is minimized. Over the population of likely inputs, every cell has the same probability of producing a response but the probability is low for any given cell (Field, 1994). In other words, we have a high probability of no response and a high probability of high response, but a reduction in the probability of a mid-level response for a given cell. We can thus increase the peakiness (kurtosis) of the histogram of cell activity and be able to reduce the total number of bits (entropy) required to code a given signal in sparse codes by using any known arithmetic coding approach. The sparse coding paradigm is in contrast with approaches based on Principal Component Analysis (PCA) (or Karhunen-Loeve transform), where the aim is to reduce the number of signifcant signal components. Fig. 1 shows the conceptual differences between the two approaches as described above.

Normally, sparseness occurs in space (population sparseness) or in time (lifetime sparseness). Population sparseness means that our 2-D sparse representation (spikegram) has very few active cells at each instance of time, while lifetime sparseness means that each cell in the representation is acitve only for a small fraction of the time span of the audio/video signal.

3.1 *Sparse Coding and ICA*

Sparse coding as described in this chapter can also be related to Independent Component Analysis (ICA) (Hyvarinen et al., 2009). In fact for some signals (i.e., an ensemble of natural images), the maximization of sparseness for a linear sparse code is basically the same as

[1] A set of bases in which the number of kernels/atoms is higher than the dimension of the audio/video signal

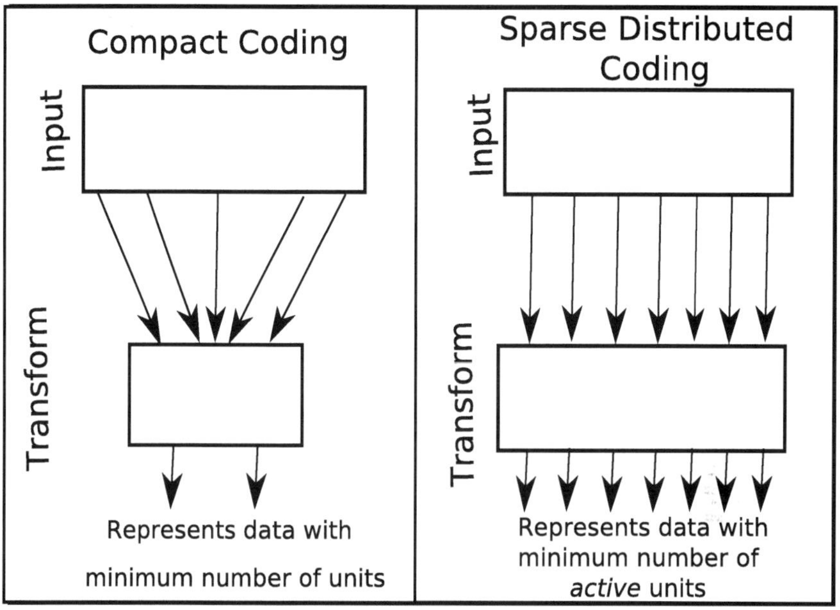

Fig. 1. Conceptual differences between sparse representations and PCA/Karhunen-Loeve transform (reproduced from (Field, 1994)). Note that in some cases the dimensionality of the sparse code is even higher than the input signal.

the maximization of non-gaussianity in the context of overcomplete ICA (Hyvarinen et al., 2009). Karklin and Lewicki also discussed the limits of applicability of the aforementioned equivalence in (Karklin & Lewicki, 2005) (Karklin & Lewicki, 2009). However, in the general case where components (cell activities) are not statistically independent (i.e., small patches of natural images) and noise is present in the system, maximizing sparseness is not equivalent to maximizing non-gaussianity and as a consequence ICA is not equivalent to sparse coding anymore.

4. Advantages of Sparse Coding

In this section we give some reasons (among others) on why sparse coding is such a powerful tool in the processing of audio and video materials.

Signal-to-Noise Ratio

A sparse coding scheme can increase the signal-to-noise ratio (Field, 1994). In a sparse code, a small subset of cells represents all the variance present in the signal (remember that most of the cells are inactive in a sparse code). Therefore, that small active subset must have a high response relative to the cells that are inactive (or have outputs equal to zero). Hencce, the probability of detecting the correct signal in the presence of noise is increased in the sparse coding paradigm compared to the case of a transform (e.g., Fourier Transform) where the variance of the signal is spread more uniformly over all coefficients. It can also be shown that sparse/overcomplete coding is optimal when a transmission channel is affected by quantization noise and is of limited capacity (see (Doi et al., 2007) and (Doi & Lewicki, 2005)).

Correspondence and Feature Detection

In an ideal sparse code, the activity of any particular basis function has a low probability. Since the response of each cell is relatively rare, tasks that require matching of features should be more successful, since the search space is only limited to those active cells (Field, 1994).
It has also be shown that the inclusion of a non-negativeness constraint into the extraction of sparse codes can generate representations that are part-based (Pichevar & Rouat, 2008) (Lee & Seung, 1999) (Hoyer, 2004). It is presumably easier to find simple parts (primitives) in an object than identifying complex shapes. In addition, complex shapes can be charachterized by the relationship between parts. Therefore, it seems that non-negative sparse coding can be potentially considered as a powerful tool in pattern recognition.

Storage and Retrieval with Associative Memory

It has been shown in the literature that when the inputs to an associative memory[2] network are sparse, the network can store more patterns and provide more effective retrieval with partial information (Field, 1994) (Furber et al., 2007).
As a simple argument of why sparse codes are efficient for storage and retrieval, Graham and Field (Graham & Field, 2006) gave the follwoing example. Consider a collection of 5x5 pixel images that each contain one block letter of the alphabet. If we looked at the histogram of any given pixel, we might discover that the pixel was on roughly half the time. However, if we were to represent these letters with templates that respond uniquely to each letter, each template would respond just 1/26th of the time. This letter code is more sparse-and more efficient-relative to a pixel code. Although no information is lost, the letter code would produce the lowest information rate. Moreover, a representation that was letter-based (and sparse) would provide a more efficient means of learning about the association between letters. If the associations were between individiual pixels, a relatively complex set of statistical relationships would be required to describe the co-occurences of letters (e.g., between the Q and U). Sparseness can assit in learning since each unit is providing a relatively complete representation of the local structure.

Shift Invariance

In transform-based (block-based) coding (e.g., Fourier Transforms), representations are sensitive to the arbitrary alignment of the blocks (analysis window) (see Fig. 2). Even wavelets are shift variant with respect to dilations of the input signal, and in two dimensons, rotations of the input signal (Simoncelli et al., 1992). However, with sparse coding techniques as defined in this manuscript this sensitivity problem is completely solved, since the kernels are positioned arbitrarily and independently (Smith & Lewicki, 2005).

4.1 Physiological evidence for sparse coding

Much of the discussion in recent years regarding sparse coding has come from the the theoretical and computational communities but there is substantial physiological evidence for sparse

[2] An associative memory is a dynamical system that saves memory attributes in its state space via attactors. The idea of associative memory is that when a memory clue is presented, the actual memory that is most like the clue will be recapitulated (see (Haykin, 2008) for details).

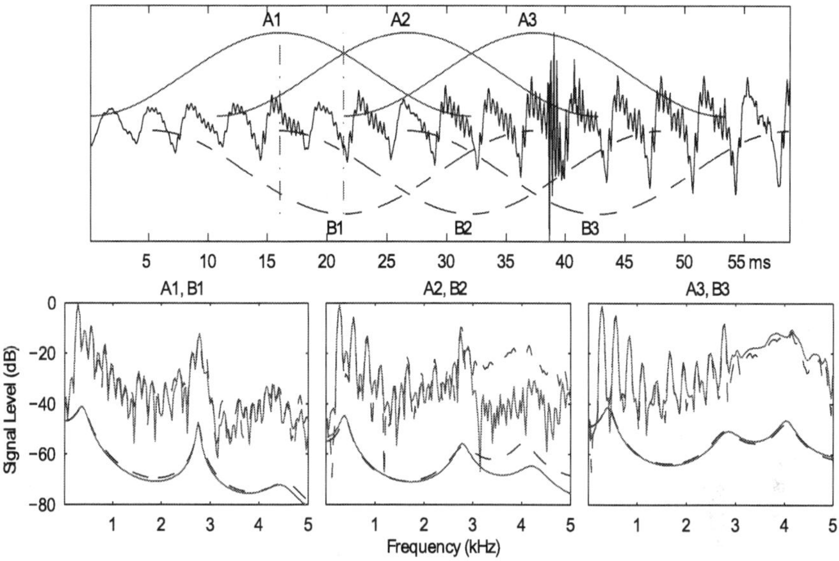

Fig. 2. Block-based representations are sensitive to temporal shifts. The top panel shows a speech waveform with two sets of overlaid Hamming windows, A1-3 (continuous lines above waveform) and B1-3(dashed lines below waveform). In the three lower panels, the power spectrum (jagged) and Linear Prediction Coding (LPC) spectrum of hamming windows offset by <5ms are overlaid (A, continuous; B, dahsed). In either of these, small shifts (e.g., from A2 to B2) can lead to large changes in the representation (reproduced from (Smith & Lewicki, 2005)).

coding in most biological systems. One neurophysiological theory that predicts the presence of sparse codes in the neural system is the efficient coding theory (Barlow, 1961) (Simoncelli & Olshausen, 2001). Efficient coding theory states that a sensory system should preserve information about its input while reducing the redundancy of the employed code (Karklin, 2007). As stated earlier, an efficient way of reducing redundancy is to make cell activity as sparse as possible (both in time and space). On the experimental side, Lennie (Lennie, 2003) estimated that given the limited resources of a neuron (i.e., limited energy consumption), the maximum number of active neurons is only 1/50th of any population of cortical neurons at any given time (see also (Baddeley, 1996) for a discussion on the energy efficiency of sparse codes). DeWeese and colleagues (DeWeese et al., 2003), recording from auditory neurons in the rat, have demonstrated that neurons in A1 (a specific cortical area) can reliably produce a signle spike in response to a sound. Also, evidence from olfactory systems in insects, somatosensory neurons in rat, and recording from rat hippocampus all demonstrate highly sparse responses (Graham & Field, 2006).

Sparse coding in its extreme forms a representation called "grandmother cell" code. In such a code, each object in the world (e.g., a grandmother) is represented by a single cell. Some evidence from neurophysiology may be linked to the presence of this very hierarchical repre-

sentation of information (Afraz et al., 2006). However, this coding scheme does not seem to be the prevelant mode of coding in sensory systems.
Sparse coding prevents accidental conjunction of attributes, which is related to the so-called binding problem (Barlow, 1961) (von der Malsburg, 1999) (Wang, 2005) (Pichevar et al., 2006). Accidental conjunction is the process in which different features from different stimuli are associated together, giving birth to illusions or even hallucinations. Although, sparsely coded features are not mutually exclusive, they nonetheless occur infrequently. Therefore, the accidental conjunction occurs rarely and not more frequently than in real life where "illusory conjunction" (the illusion to associate two different features from different stimuli together) occurs rarely.

5. The Mathematics of Sparse Coding

In most cases, in order to generate a sparse representation we need to extract an overcomplete representation. In an overcomplete representation, the number of basis vectors (kernels) is greater than the real dimensionality (number of non-zero eigenvalues in the covariance matrix of the signal) of the input. In order to generate such overcomplete representations, the common approach consists of matching the best kernels to different acoustic cues using different convergence criteria such as the residual energy. However, the minimization of the energy of the residual (error) signal is not sufficient to get an overcomplete representation of an input signal. Other constraints such as sparseness must be considered in order to have a unique solution. Thus, sparse codes are generated using matching pursuit by matching the most optimal kernels to the signal.

5.1 Generating Overcomplete Representations with Matching Pursuit (MP)

Matching Pursuit (MP) is a greedy search algorithm (Tropp, 2004) that can be used to extract sparse representations over an overcomplete set of kernels. Here is a simple analogy showing how MP works. Imagine you want to buy a coffee that costs X units with a limited number of coins of higher and lower values. You first pick higher valued coins until you cannot use them anymore to cover the differnce between the sum of your picked up coins and X. You then switch to lower-valued coins to reach the amount X and continue with smaller and smaller coins till either there is no smaller coin left or you reach X units. MP is doing the exact same thing in the signal domain. It tries to reconstruct a given signal $x(t)$ by decreasing the energy of the atom used to shape the signal at each iteration. In mathematical notations, the signal $x(t)$ can be decomposed into the overcomplete kernels as follow

$$x(t) = \sum_{m=1}^{M} \sum_{i=1}^{n_m} a_i^m g_m(t - \tau_i^m) + r_x(t), \tag{1}$$

where τ_i^m and a_i^m are the temporal position and amplitude of the i-*th* instance of the kernel g_m, respectively. The notation n_m indicates the number of instances of g_m, which need not be the same across kernels. In addition, the kernels are not restricted in form or length.
In order to find adequate τ_i^m, a_i^m, and g_m matching pursuit can be used. In this technique the signal $x(t)$ is decomposed over a set of kernels so as to capture the structure of the signal. The approach consists of iteratively approximating the input signal with successive orthogonal projections onto some basis. The signal can be decomposed into

$$x(t) = < x(t), g_m > g_m + r_x(t), \tag{2}$$

where $< x(t), g_m >$ is the inner product between the signal and the kernel and is equivalent to a^m in Eq. 1. $r_x(t)$ is the residual signal.
It can be shown (Goodwin & Vetterli, 1999) that the computational load of the matching pursuit can be reduced, if one saves values of all correlations in memory or finds an analytical formulation for the correlation given specific kernels.

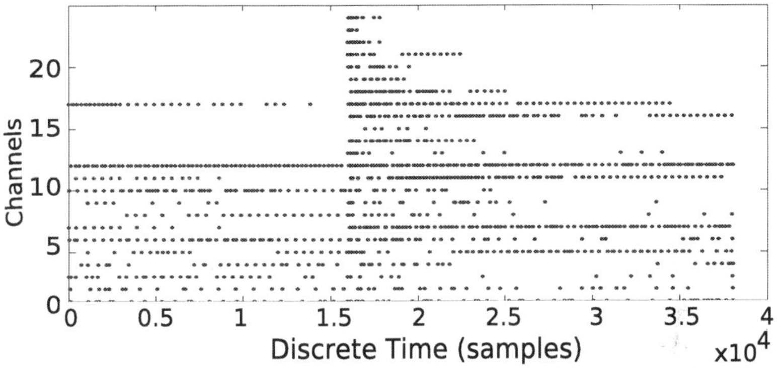

Fig. 3. Spikegram of the harpsichord using the gammatone matching pursuit algorithm (spike amplitudes are not represented). Each dot represents the time and the channel where a spike is fired.

5.2 Shape of Kernels

In the previous section we showed how a signal $x(t)$ can be projected onto a basis of kernels g_m. The question we address in this section is to find optimal bases for different types of signals (e.g., image, audio). As mentioned before, the efficient coding theory states that sensory systems might have evolved to highly efficient coding strategies to maximize the information conveyed to the brain while minimizing the required energy and neural ressources. This fact can be the starting point to finding "optimal waveforms "g_m for different sensory signals.

5.2.1 *Best Kernels for Audio*

Smith and Lewicki (Smith & Lewicki, 2006) found the optimal basis $g_m \in G$ for environmental sounds by maximizing the Maximum Likelihood (ML) $p(x|G)$ given that the prior probability of a spike, $p(s)$, is sparse. Note that the ML part of the optimization deals with the maximization of the information transfer to the brain and the sparseness prior minimizes the energy consumption. Therefore, the optimization here is totally inspired by the efficient coding theory. In mathematical notation, the kernel functions, g_m, are optimized by performing gradient ascent on the log data probability (including ML and sparseness terms),

$$E = \frac{\partial}{\partial g_m} \log p(x|G) = \frac{\partial}{\partial g_m} [\log p(x|G, \hat{s}) + \log(p(\hat{s}))] \tag{3}$$

If we assume that the noise present in the system is gaussian, Eq. 3 can be rewritten as:

$$E = \frac{1}{\sigma_e} \sum_i a_i^m [x - \hat{x}]_{\tau_i^m} \tag{4}$$

where $[x - \hat{x}]_{\tau_i^m}$ indicates the residual error over the extent of kernel g_m at position τ_i^m and $\hat{s}$ is the estimated s. At the start of the training, Smith and Lewicki initialized g_m as Gaussian noise and trained (found optimal g_m) by running the optimization on a database of natural sounds. The natural sounds ensemble used in training combined a collection of mammalian vocalizations with two classes of environmental sounds: ambient sounds (rustling brush, wind, flowing water) and transients (snapping twigs, crunching leaves, impacts of stone or woood). Results from optimization show only slight differences between the optimal kernels obtained by Eq. 3 and the gammatone/gammachirp (Irino & Patterson, 2006) family of filters that approximate cochlea in the inner ear (see Fig. 4). However, as pointed out by Smith and Lewicki, totally different kernels will be obtained, if we restrain our training set to only a subclass of environmental sound or if we change the type of signal used as the training set. In the remaining of this chapter, we use the safe assumption that the physiologically optimal kernels for audio are the gammatone/gammachirp filters.

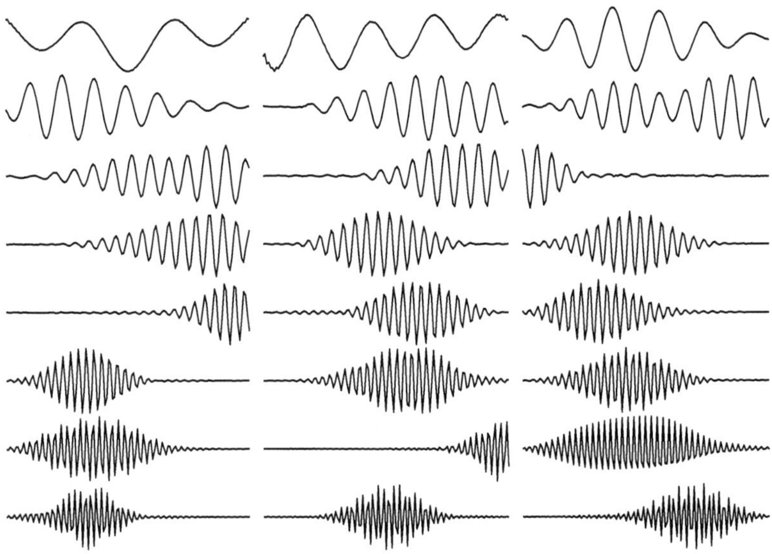

Fig. 4. Efficient coding of a combined sound ensemble consisting of environmental sounds and vocalization yields filters similar to the gammatone/gammachirp family. The impulse response of some of the optimal filters are shown here (reporduced from (Lewicki, 2002)).

5.2.2 *Best kernels for Image*

By using the same efficient coding theory, and by following the same steps as for extracting the optimal basis g_m for audio (i.e., optimizing an ML with sparseness prior and Eq. 3), Olshausen and Field found that the physiologically optimal kernels for image are Gabor wavelets (Olshausen & Field, 1996) (see Fig. 5). Since our focus in this chapter is on audio coding, we refer the reader to (Olshausen & Field, 1996) (among others) for furhter discussion on the extraction of optimal kernels for images.

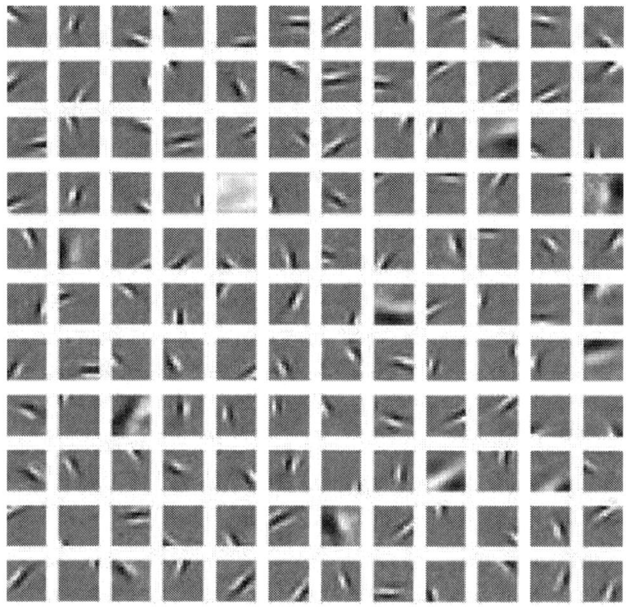

Fig. 5. Results of the search for optimal kernels using maximum likelihood with sparseness prior on 12x12 pixel images drawn from natural scenes. The kernels are Gabor-like. Reproduced from (Olshausen & Field, 1996).

6. A New Paradigm for Audio Coding

In the second half of this chapter, we will briefly describe the biologically-inspired audio coder we have developped based on the concepts already presented in the first half of this chapter (i.e., sparse coding).

6.1 The Bio-Inspired Audio Coder

The analysis/synthesis part of our universal audio codec is based on the generation of auditory-inspired sparse 2-D representations of audio signals, dubbed as spikegrams. The spikegrams are generated by projecting the signal onto a set of overcomplete adaptive gammachirp (gammatones with additional tuning parameters) kernels (see section 6.2.2). The adaptiveness is a key feature we introduced in Matching Pursuit (MP) to increase the efficiency of the proposed method (see section 6.2.2). An auditory masking model has been developed and integrated into the MP algorithm to extract audible spikes (see section 7). In addition a differential encoder of spike parameters based on graph theory is proposed in (Pichevar, Najaf-Zadeh, Lahdili & Thibault, 2008). The quantization of the spikes is given in section 8. We finally propose a frequent pattern discovery block in section 10. The block diagram of all the building blocks of the receiver and transmitter of our proposed universal audio coder is depicted in Fig. 6 of which the graph-based optimization of the differential encoder is explained in (Pichevar, Najaf-Zadeh, Lahdili & Thibault, 2008).

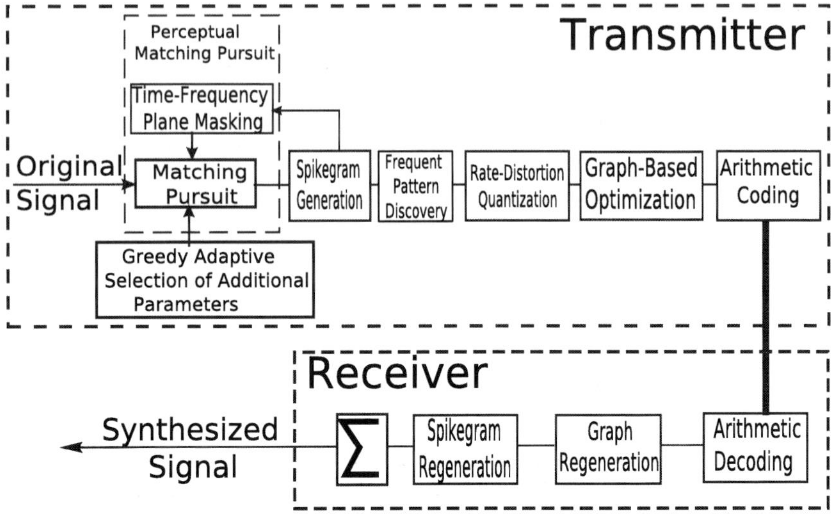

Fig. 6. Block diagram of our proposed Universal Bio-Inspired Audio Coder.

6.2 Generation of the spike-based representation

We use here the concept of generating sparse overcomplete representations as described in section 5 to design a biologically-inspired sparse audio coder. In section 5.2, we saw that the gammatone family of kernels is the optimal class of kernels according to the efficient coding theory. Therefore, they are used in our approach. In addition, using asymmetric kernels such as gammatone/gammachirp atoms is that they do not create pre-echos at onsets (Goodwin & Vetterli, 1999). However, very asymmetric kernels such as damped sinusoids (Goodwin & Vetterli, 1999) are not able to model harmonic signals suitably. On the other hand, gammatone/gammachirp kernels have additional parameters that control their attack and decay parts (degree of symmetry), which are modified suitably according to the nature of the signal in our proposed technique. As described in section 5, the approach used to find the projections is an iterative one. In this section, we will compare two variants of the projection technique. The first variant, which is non-adaptive, is roughly similar to the general approach used in (Smith & Lewicki, 2006), which we applied to the specific task of audio coding. However, we proposed the second adaptive variant in (Pichevar et al., 2007), which takes advantage of the additional parameters of the gammachirp kernels and the inherent nonlinearity of the auditory pathway (Irino & Patterson, 2001)(Irino & Patterson, 2006). Some details on each variant are given below.

6.2.1 Non-Adaptive Paradigm

In the non-adaptive paradigm, only gammatone filters are used. The impulse response of a gammatone filter is given by

$$g(f_c, t) = t^3 e^{-2\pi b t} \cos(2\pi f_c t) \quad t > 0, \tag{5}$$

where f_c is the center frequency of the filter, distributed on Equal Rectangular Bandwith (ERB) scales. At each step (iteration), the signal is projected onto the gammatone kernels (with different center frequencies and different time delays). The center frequency and time delay that give the maximum projection are chosen and a spike with the value of the projection is added to the "auditory representation" at the corresponding center frequency and time delay (see Fig. 3). The signal is decomposed into the projections on gammatone kernels plus a residual signal $r_x(t)$ (see Eqs. 1 and 2).

6.2.2 Adaptive Paradigm

In the adaptive paradigm, gammachirp filters are used. The impulse response of a gammachirp filter with the corresponding tuning parameters (*b*,*l*,*c*) is given below

$$g(f_c, t, b, l, c) = t^{l-1} e^{-2\pi b t} \cos(2\pi f_c t + c \quad \ln t) \quad t > 0. \tag{6}$$

It has been shown that the gammachirp filters minimize the scale/time uncertainty (Irino & Patterson, 2001). In this approach the chirp factor c, l, and b are found adaptively at each step. The chirp factor c allows us to slightly modify the instantaneous frequency of the kernels, l and b control the attack and decay of the kernels. However, searching the three parameters in the parameter space is a very computationally intensive task. Therefore, we use a suboptimal search (Gribonval, 2001) in which, we use the same gammatone filters as the ones used in the non-adaptive paradigm with values of l and b given in (Irino & Patterson, 2001). This step gives us the center frequency and start time (t_0) of the best gammatone matching filter. We also keep the second best frequency (gammatone kernel) and start time.

$$G_{max1} = \underset{f,t_0}{\operatorname{argmax}} \{|< r, g(f, t_0, b, l, c) >|\}, \quad g \in G \tag{7}$$

$$G_{max2} = \underset{f,t_0}{\operatorname{argmax}} \{|< r, g(f, t_0, b, l, c) >|\}, \quad g \in G - G_{max1} \tag{8}$$

For the sake of simplicity, we use f instead of f_c in Eqs. 8 to 11. We then use the information found in the first step to find c. In other words, we keep only the set of the best two kernels in step one, and try to find the best chirp factor given $g \in G_{max1} \cup G_{max2}$.

$$G_{maxc} = \underset{c}{\operatorname{argmax}} \{|< r, g(f, t_0, b, l, c) >|\}. \tag{9}$$

We then use the information found in the second step to find the best b for $g \in G_{maxc}$ in Eq. 10, and finally find the best l among $g \in G_{maxb}$ in Eq. 11.

$$G_{maxb} = \underset{b}{\operatorname{argmax}} \{|< r, g(f, t_0, b, l, c) >|\} \tag{10}$$

$$G_{maxl} = \underset{l}{\operatorname{argmax}} \{|< r, g(f, t_0, b, l, c) >|\}. \tag{11}$$

Therefore, six parameters are extracted in the adaptive technique for the "auditory representation": center frequencies, chirp factors (c), time delays, spike amplitudes, b, and l. The last two parameters control the attack and the decay slopes of the kernels. Although, there are additional parameters in this second variant, as shown later, the adaptive technique contributes to better coding gains. The reason for this is that we need a much smaller number of filters (in the filterbank) and a smaller number of iterations to achieve the same SNR, which roughly reflects the audio quality.

	Speech		Castanet		Percussion	
	Adapt.	Non-Adapt.	Adapt.	Non-Adapt.	Adapt.	Non-Adapt.
Number of spikes	10492	35208	6510	24580	9430	29370
Spike gain	0.13N	0.44N	0.08N	0.30N	0.12N	0.37N
Bitrate (bit/sample)	1.98	3.07	1.54	3.03	1.93	2.90

Table 1. Comparison of the adaptive and non-adaptive schemes for spike generation for three different audio signals. The average saving in bitrate over all materials is around 45%. N is the signal length (number of samples in the signal).

6.3 Comparison of Adaptive and Non-Adaptive Paradigms

In this section we compare the performance of the adaptive and non-adaptive schemes. Results and a comparison of the two different schemes in terms of bitrate and number of spikes extracted for high quality (scale 4 on ITU-R impairment scale) are given in Table 1. With the adaptive scheme, we observe an average drop of 45% in the bitrate compared to the non-adaptive approach. The spike gain (decrease in spikes for a given signal of N samples) decreases drastically when the adaptive paradigm is used as well. Fig. 7 compares the adaptive to the non-adaptive approach for different numbers of cochlear channels (the number of center frequencies used in the gammatone kernels).

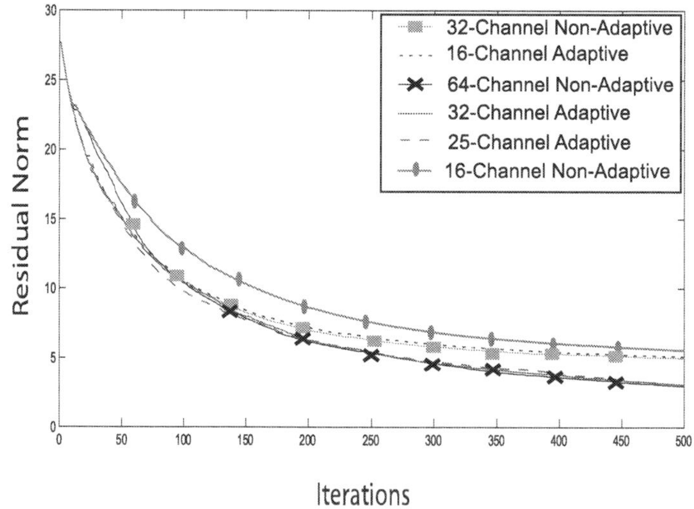

Fig. 7. Comparison of the adaptive and non-adaptive spike coding schemes of speech for different number of channels. In this figure, only the chirp factor is adapted. For the case where all three parameters are adapted see Fig. 3 in (Pichevar et al., 2007).

7. Masking of Spikes

In previous sections, we showed how sparse representations based on spikes can be generated using our proposed alogrithm based on MP. We also showed how we can increase the performance of our system by shaping adaptively the kernels used in MP to our signal. However, in the previous section we generated a sparse signal that is close to the original signal in the mean-squared error sense and we ignored the effects of perceptual masking on the generation of the signal. In fact, we will see later in this section that some of the spikes generated in section 6 are not perceptible by the human ear. To this end, we will first review the basics of masking in the auditory system.

7.1 Fundamentals of Masking

Auditory masking occurs when the perception of one sound (the maskee) is affected by the presence of another sound (the masker). This happens because the original neural activity caused by the first signal is reduced by the neural activity of the other sound in the brain. Masking can be classified in two distinct categories. In temporal (non-simultaneous masking) the masker and the maskee are not present at the same time. In the case of a spikegram, the temporal masking is present when two spikes are fired in the same channel (two dots in the same horizontal line on the spikegram) and are relatively close in time. On the other hand, simultaneous masking happens when two spikes fire at the same time in different channels. Fig. 8 outlines the mechanism of different types of masking. The masker (a spike on the spikegram) is presented. This masker can potentially mask another spike (or make the presence of another spike inaudible) if the latter falls within the pre- or post-synaptic curves with an amplitude below the curve or if it is applied simultaneously with a frequency close enough to the masker and with the appropriate amplitude.

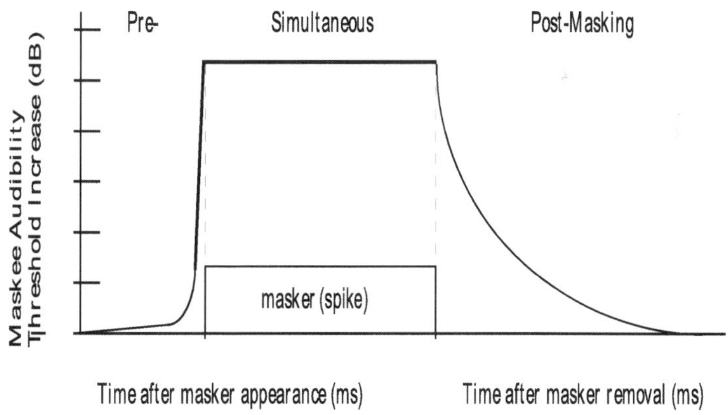

Fig. 8. Temporal masking of the human ear. Pre-masking occurs prior to masker onset and lasts only a few milliseconds; Post-masking may persist for more than 100 milliseconds after masker removal (after (Painter & Spanias, 2000))

Audio Material	Mean Subj. Score for MP	Mean Sub. Score for PMP	PEAQ Obj. Score for MP	PEAQ Obj. Score for PMP
Susan Vega	-0.7500	-0.9667	-0.593	-0.330
Trumpet	-0.9667	-0.4333	-1.809	-0.791
Orchestra	-0.7667	-0.4000	-1.239	-0.915
Harpsichord	-0.5000	-0.3667	-1.699	-0.867
Bagpipe	-0.4000	-0.2000	-0.765	-0.502
Glockenspiel	-0.2000	-0.333	-0.925	-1.266
Plucked Strings	-0.4667	-0.2667	-1.050	-1.050

Table 2. Mean subjective and objective scores for a few audio files processed with MP and PMP. Objective Difference Grade (ODG) are shown in the table for subjective tests.

7.2 Perceptual Matching Pursuit

Based on the masking mechanism explained above, we proposed in (Najaf-Zadeh et al., 2008) the Perceptual Matching Pursuit, which basically extend MP to the perceptual domain. By doing so, only an audible kernel is extracted at each iteration. Moreover, contrary to the matching pursuit algorithm, PMP will stop decomposing an audio signal once there is no audible part left in the residual. Details of how the pre- and post-masking curves as in Fig. 8 are extracted for spikegrams as well as the simultaneous masking are given in (Najaf-Zadeh et al., 2008). Here, in table 2 we give results on how PMP retains the same audio quality as MP. In order to verify the objective scores, we conducted a semi-formal listening test, based on the ITU.R BS. 1116 method, to evaluate the quality of the test signals. Six subjects took part in a Ştriple stimulus hidden referenceŤ test and listened to the audio materials (presented in Table 2) over the headphone in a quiet room. The CRC SEAQ software was used in the test which allowed the listener to seamlessly switch among the three stimuli. In each trial, the stimuli ŞAŤ was always the reference stimulus known by the subject. Two other stimuli, ŞBŤ or ŞCŤ, were either a hidden reference, identical to ŞAŤ, or a synthesized version of the same audio material. None of ŞBŤ or ŞCŤ was known to the subject. The listener had to identify the synthesized version (either ŞBŤ or ŞCŤ) and to grade its quality relative to that of the reference on ŞAŤ. The grading scale was continuous from 1 (very annoying) to 5 (no difference between the reference and the synthesized file). The average subjective scores for MP and PMP were 4.4214 and 4.5762, and the standard deviations of the scores were 0.2522 and 0.2612 respectively. Values in Table 2 are the mapping of the subjective test scores (between 1 and 5) to the Objective Difference Grade (ODG) that varies between -4 to +4, according to the ITU.R BS 1116 standard. Positive values in the ODG represents evaluation errors by subjects (basically errors in identifying the hidden reference), while negative values are the subjective scores, with 0 being the case where no difference between the reference and the coded material is detected by the subject[3] and -4 representing the biggest difference between the reference and the coded signal. Although the confidence intervals for the subjective scores are overlapping, the majority of the test materials received higher subjective scores for PMP, which is consistent with the objective evaluation. The reader may notice that PMP reduces the total number of spikes to be extracted for the same audio quality, thus requires lower bitrate for the same audio quality.

[3] http://www.itu.int/rec/R-REC-BS.1116-1-199710-I/e

8. Quantization of Spikes

The amplitude of spikes generated in spikegrams should be quantized before transmission. The cost function we use to find the optimal levels of quantization is a trade-off between the quality of reconstruction and the number of bits required to code each modulus. More precisely, given the vector of quantization levels (codebook) $\mathbf{q}$, the cost function to optimize is given by (R is the bitrate and D is the distortion):

$$\widehat{E}(\mathbf{q}) = D + \lambda R = \frac{\|\sum_i \hat{\alpha}_i g_i - \sum_i \alpha_i g_i\|^2}{\|\sum_i \alpha_i g_i + \eta\|^\gamma} + \lambda H(\hat{\mathbf{ff}}), \tag{12}$$

where $\eta = 10^{-5}$, $\gamma = 0.001$ are set empirically using informal listening tests. The entropy, $\widehat{E}(\mathbf{q})$, is computed using the absolute value of spike amplitudes. $\hat{\mathbf{ff}}$ is the vector of quantized amplitudes and is computed as follows:

$$\hat{\alpha}_i = q_i \quad \text{if} \quad q_{i-1} < \alpha_i < q_i \tag{13}$$

$H(\hat{\mathbf{ff}})$ is the per spike entropy in bits needed to encode the information content of each element of $\hat{\mathbf{ff}}$ defined as:

$$H(\hat{\mathbf{ff}}) = -\sum_i p_i(\hat{\alpha}_i)\log_2 p_i(\hat{\alpha}_i), \tag{14}$$

where $p_i(\hat{\alpha}_i)$ is the probability density function of $\hat{\alpha}_i$. The way the quantizer is defined in Eq. 13 reduces the dead zone problem (defined in (Neff & Zakhor, 2000)). To proceed with the optimization at a given number of quantization levels, we randomly set the initial values (initial population) for the q_i and perform Genetic Algorithm to find optimal solutions. The goal of the weighting in the denominator of D (Eq. 12) is to give a better reconstruction of low-energy parts of the signal.

Note that in Eq. 12 many different $\hat{\alpha}_i$ can contribute to the reconstruction of the original signal at a given instance of time t, which is not the case when quantization is applied on time samples (Lloyd algorithm). Therefore, the optimal $\hat{\alpha}_k$ are not statistically independent. In addition, in contrast with transform-based coder quantizations (done for instance with Lloyd algorithm), g_k are a few atoms selected from a large set of different atoms (tens of thousand) in the dictionary and there is an entropy maximization term in our cost function. It is therefore impossible to derive a closed-form theoretical solution for the optimal $\hat{\alpha}_i$ in the case of sparse representations. Hence, we should use adaptive optimization techniques. In order to avoid local minima, in (Pichevar, Najaf-Zadeh, Thibault & Lahdili, 2008) we derived optimal quantization levels using Genetic Algorithm (GA) (Mitchell, 1998). Results obtained in (Pichevar, Najaf-Zadeh, Thibault & Lahdili, 2008) showed that the optimal quantizer is not linear in the case of spikegrams.

9. Piecewise Uniform Quantization

Running GA for each signal is a time consuming task. In addition, sending a new codebook for each signal type and/or frame is an overhead we may want to avoid. In this section we propose faster ways to find a suboptimal solution to the quantization results that keeps transparency in quality. The goal is achieved by performing a piecewise uniform approximation of the codebook by using the histogram of the moduli.

Fig. 9 shows the optimal quantization levels (q_i) for four different types of signals. The optimal signal is obtained using the GA algorithm explained in the previous section.

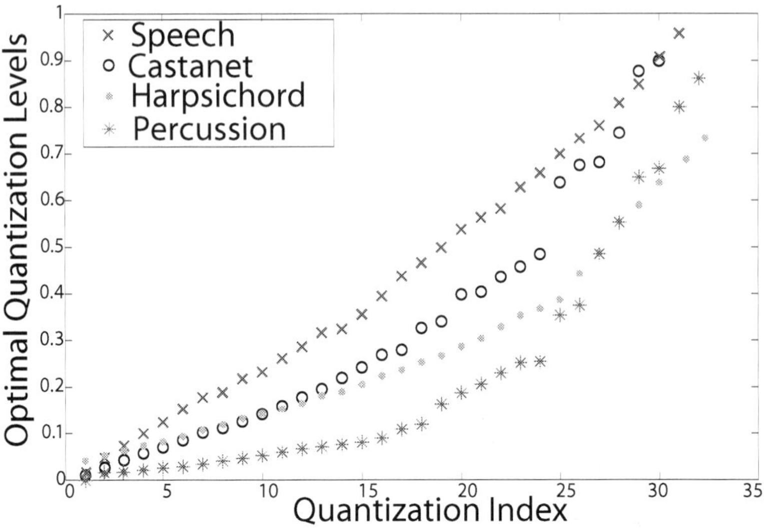

Fig. 9. Optimal quantization levels for different sound categories. Spike amplitudes are normalized to one.

As we can see, the optimal levels can be approximated as piecewise linear segments (meaning that the quantizer is "piecewise" linear). The optimal levels are updated by the following method for each one-second-long frame:

- Find the 40-bin histogram h of the spike amplitudes.
- Threshold the histogram by the sign function so that $h_t = \text{sign}(h)$ to find spike amplitude clusters (concentrations). Smooth out the curves by applying a moving average filter with the following impulse response: $m(n) = \sum_k 0.125\delta(n-k)$ for $k = 1, 2, ...8$.
- Set a crossing threshold of 0.4 on the smoothed curve. Each time the curve crosses the threshold, define a new uniform quantizer between the two last threshold crossings.

9.1 Results from Piecewise Uniform Quantization

For the different signal types we used in section 2.3, we proceeded with the fast piecewise uniform quantization described in the previous subsection. We noticed that the 32-level quantizer gives only near-transparent coding results with CRC-SEAQ (see Table 3) for the piecewise uniform quantizer. However, the quality is transparent when 64 levels are used. These observations have been confirmed with informal listening tests. This behavior is due to the fact that the 64-level quantizer has more uniform quantization levels than the 32-level quantizer. Therefore, we recommend the 64-level quantizer when the piecewise uniform approximation is used.

The overall codec bitrate can be computed by combining the bitrate in Tables 1-3 of (Pichevar et al., 2007) for the unquantized case and values for amplitude quantization in Table 3 of this article.

	CRC-SEAQ	
	32-Levels	64 Levels
Percussion	-1.30	-0.25
Castanet	-0.50	-0.10
Harpsichord	-1.10	-0.15
Speech	-0.95	-0.44

Table 3. Comparison of 32-level and 64-level piecewise uniform quantizers for different audio signals. A CRC-SEAQ score between 0 and -1 is associated with transparent quality. No codebook side information is sent to the receiver in this case.

10. Extraction of Patterns in Spikegrams

As mentioned in previous sections, the spike activity of each channel can be associated to the activity of a neuron tuned to the center frequency of that channel. The ultimate goal in the pattern recognition paradigm is to find a generative neural architecture (such as a synfire chain (Abeles, 1991) or a polychronous network (Izhikevich, 2006)) that is able to generate a spikegram such as the one we extract by MP (see Fig. 3) for a given audio signal. However, for the time being we proposed a solution to a simplified version of the aforementioned problem in (Pichevar & Najaf-Zadeh, 2009). In fact, we propose to extract "channel-based or frequency-domain patterns" in our generated spikegrams using temporal data mining (Mannila et al., 1997) (Patnaik et al., 2008). Since these patterns are repeated frequently in the signal and are the building blocks of the audio signal, we may call them auditory objects (Bregman, 1994). In contrast with other approaches (i.e., Harmonic Matching Pursuit and Meta-Molecular Matching Pursuit) that are able to extract some predefined sound structures such as harmonics (Krstulovic et al., 2005) very precisely, our proposed approach is able to extract patterns without any a priori knowledge of the type of structure present in the sound. The reader may also refer to (Karklin, 2007) and (Karklin & Lewicki, 2009) for another approach to extract statistical dependencies in a sparse representation that uses latent (hidden) variables to exploit higher order statistics.

10.1 Frequent Episode Discovery

The frequent episode discovery framework was proposed by Mannila and colleagues (Mannila et al., 1997) and enhanced in (Laxman et al., 2007). Patnaik *et al.* (Patnaik et al., 2008) extended previous results to the processing of neurophysiological data. The frequent episode discovery fits in the general paradigm of temporal data mining. The method can be applied to either serial episodes (ordered set of events) or to parallel episodes (unordered set of events). A frequent episode is one whose frequency exceeds a user specified threshold. Given an episode occurrence, we call the largest time difference between any two events constituting the occurrence as the span of the occurrence and we use this span as a temporal constraint in the algorithm. The details of the algorithm can be found in (Pichevar & Najaf-Zadeh, 2009).

In (Pichevar & Najaf-Zadeh, 2009), we showed that the extraction of patterns in the spikegram is biased towards denser regions. Therefore we proposed a 3-pass extraction algorithm in which extracted patterns are subtracted from the original signal at each pass and explore sparser regions as well.

Fig. 10 shows the extracted patterns for each of the three distinct passes for percussion. Since unordered episodes are discovered, the order of appearance of spikes in different channels

Percussion	Pass 1	Pass 2	Pass 3	Overall
No. extracted spikes	1682	771	335	2788
No. codebook elements	47	36	11	94
Codebook size in bits	2200	1976	320	4496
Raw bit saving	9968	4403	1820	16191
Effective bit saving	7768	2427	1500	11695
Castanet	**Pass 1**	**Pass 2**	**Pass 3**	**Overall**
No. extracted Spikes	596	684	580	1860
No. codebook elements	8	20	37	65
Codebook size in bits	440	1436	2340	4216
Raw bit saving	2660	4095	3253	10008
Effective bit saving	2220	2659	913	5792
Speech	**Pass 1**	**Pass 2**	**Pass 3**	**Overall**
No. extracted Spikes	1262	689	395	2346
No. codebook elements	8	21	11	40
Codebook size in bits	338	1053	288	1679
Raw bit saving	3238	3859	2250	11026
Effective bit saving	2899	2806	1962	7667

Table 4. Results for a 3-Pass pattern extraction on 1-second frames. **Percussion:** The total number of bits to address channels when no pattern recognition is used equals 23704 and the saving in addressing channels due to our algorithm is 49%. **Castanet:** The total number of bits to address channels when no pattern recognition is used is 21982 and there is a saving of 26% with our proposed algorithm. **Speech:** The total number of bits to address channels when no pattern recognition is used is 19118 and there is a saving of 40%.

can change for a given pattern. However, the channels in which spike activity occurs are the same for all similar patterns. In other words the patterns are similar up to a permutation in the order of appearance of each spike. Fig. 10 also shows that our 3-pass algorithm is able to extract patterns in the high, low and mid-frequency ranges, while a 1-pass algorithm would have penalized some sparser spikegram regions.

In Table 4, the number of extracted spikes is shown for each pass and the raw bit saving and effective bit saving in addressing channels as described above are given for percussion, castanet, and speech. Our algorithm was able to extract between 1860 and 2788 spikes in different episodes out of the total 4000 spikes. The longest pattern found in percussion is 13-spike long and is repeated on average 17 times in the signal frame, while the longest pattern for castanet is 14-spike long and is repeated 33 times on average in frames. In the meantime, the longest pattern for speech is 100-spike element and is repeated 8 times on average in the frames. Results show that the bitrate coding gain obtained in addressing frequency channels ranges from 26 % to 49% depending on signal type. Note that since the pattern extraction coding is lossless, the informal subjective quality evaluations in (Pichevar et al., 2007) for the audio materials still hold when our new audio extraction paradigm is applied.

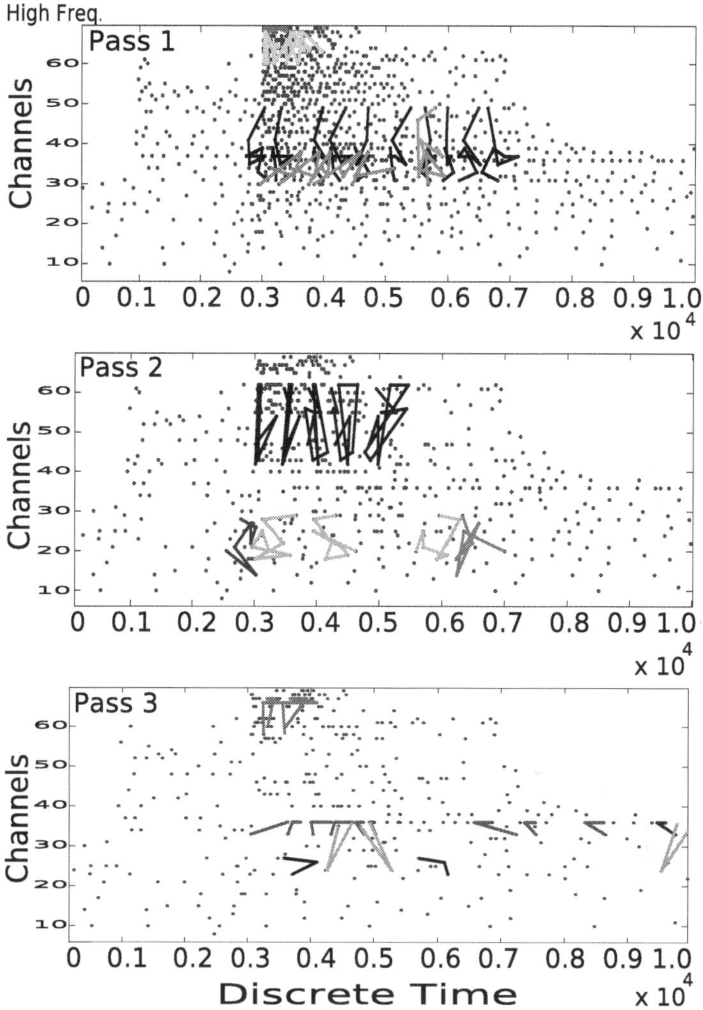

Fig. 10. Spikegrams (dots) and the most *relevant* extracted patterns (lines) at each of the 3 passes for percussion for a 250 ms frame. Different colors/grayscales represent different episodes. Only spikes not discovered during the previous pass are depicted at each pass. Note that since unordered episodes are discovered, patterns are similar up to a permutation in the temporal order.

11. Conclusion

We outlined in this chapter, a new type of emergent signal coding called sparse representation, which is able to preserve the exact timing of acoustical events and edges of images.

Sparse codes have also other interesting properties such as shift invariance. Furthermore, we discussed the biological plausibiltiy of sparse representations in the brain when it comes to the processing of audio and video. We then described our proposed audio coder, which is a merger of sparse coding with biologically-inspired coding. We showed how sparse code generation (spikegrams), masking, quantization and pattern extraction can be done in our proposed framework. Our proposed approach is a first step towards the development of an object-based universal audio coder. Object-based coders belong to a totally new generation of coders that can potentially reduce current achievable bitrates by an order of magnitude; as an analogy, consider the amount of information we can save by transmitting only the color, radius, and position of a given circle in a visual scene instead of sending all pixels of that circle one by one!

In a future work, we will extract the structural dependencies of spike amplitudes and/or other parameters in the spikegram such as the chirp factor, etc. We will also investigate the design of a generative neural model based on spikegrams. Formal subjective listening tests for the overall system will be conducted in the future. In order to speed up the spikegram extraction of audio signals, we have conducted preliminary tests on replacing the MP stage (see Fig. 6) by neural circuitry that can be implemented on embedded and parallel hardware. We will further explore this avenue in a future work. The application of different ideas outlined in this chapter (i.e., pattern recognition and masking model) are not limited to spikegrams and can be applied to other sparse representations found in the literature. In addition, the frequency episode discovery algorithm discussed in this article can be used in other applications such as speech recognition, sound source separation, and audio classification.

12. References

Abeles, M. (1991). *Corticonics: Neural circuits of the cerebral cortex*, Cambridge University Press.

Afraz, S., Kiani, R. & Esteky, H. (2006). Microstimulation of inferotemporal cortex influences face categorization, *Nature* **442**: 692–695.

Baddeley, R. (1996). An efficient code in V1?, *Nature* **381**: 560–561.

Barlow, H. (1961). Possible principles underlying the transformation of sensory messages, *Sensory Communication* pp. 217–234.

Bregman, A. (1994). *Auditory Scene Analysis: The Perceptual Organization of Sound*, MIT Press.

DeWeese, M., Wehr, M. & Zador, A. (2003). Binary spiking in auditory cortex, *J. Neuroscience* **23**: 7940–7949.

Doi, E., Balcan, D. & Lewicki, M. (2007). Robust coding over noisy overcomplete channels, *IEEE Transactions on Image Processing* **16**(2): 442–452.

Doi, E. & Lewicki, M. (2005). Sparse coding of natural images using an overcomplete set of limited capacity units, *Advances in Neural Information Processing Systems*, pp. 442–452.

Field, D. (1994). What is the goal of sensory coding?, *Neural Computation* **6**: 559–601.

Furber, S., Brown, G., Bose, J., Cumpstey, J., Marshall, P. & Shapiro, J. (2007). Sparse distributed memory using rank-order neural codes, *IEEE Transactions on Neural Networks* **18**(3): 648–659.

Goodwin, M. & Vetterli, M. (1999). Matching pursuit and atomic signal models based on recursive filter banks, *IEEE Transaction on signal processing* **47**(7): 1890–1902.

Graham, D. & Field, D. (2006). Sparse coding in the neocortex, *Evolution of Nervous Sys. ed. J. H. Kaas and L. A. Krubitzer* .

Gribonval, R. (2001). Fast matching pursuit with a multiscale dictionary of gaussian chirps, *IEEE Transaction on signal processing* **49**(5): 994–1001.

Haykin, S. (2008). *Neural networks: a comprehensive foundation*, Prentice Hall.

Hoyer, P. (2004). Non-negative matrix factorization with sparseness constraints, *Journal of Machine Learning Research* **5**: 1457–1469.

Hyvarinen, A., Hurri, J. & Hoyer, P. (2009). *Natural Image Statistics- A probalistic approach to early computational vision*, Springer-Verlag, Berlin.

Irino, T. & Patterson, R. (2001). A compressive gammachirp auditory filter for both physiological and psychophysical data, *JASA* **109**(5): 2008–2022.

Irino, T. & Patterson, R. (2006). A dynamic compressive gammachirp auditory filterbank, *IEEE Trans. on Audio and Speech Processing* **14**(6): 2008–2022.

Izhikevich, E. (2006). Polychronization: Computation with spikes, *Neural Computation* **18**: 245–282.

Karklin, Y. (2007). *Hierarchical statistical models of computation in the visual cortex*, PhD thesis, Carnegie Mellon University.

Karklin, Y. & Lewicki, M. (2005). A hierarchical bayesian model for learning non-linear statistical regularities in non-stationary natural signals, *Neural Computation* **17**(2): 397–423.

Karklin, Y. & Lewicki, M. (2009). Emergence of complex cell properties by learning to generalize in natural scenes, *Nature* **457**: 83–86.

Krstulovic, S., Gribonval, R., Leveau, P. & Daudet, L. (2005). A comparison of two extensions of the matching pursuit algorithm for the harmonic decomposition of sounds, *Workshop on the Applications of Signal Processing to Audio and Acoustics, New Platz, New York*.

Laxman, S., Sastry, P. & Unnikrishnan, K. (2007). Discovery of frequent generalized episodes when events persist for different durations, *IEEE Trans. on Knowledge and Data Eng.* **19**: 1188–1201.

Lee, D. & Seung, S. (1999). Learning the parts of objects by non-negative matrix factorization, *Nature* **401**: 788Ű791.

Lennie, P. (2003). The cost of cortical computation, *Curr. Biol.* **13**: 493–497.

Lewicki, M. (2002). Efficient coding of natural sounds, *Nature Neuroscience* **5**: 356–363.

Mannila, H., Toivonen, H. & Verkamo, A. (1997). Discovery of frequent episodes in event sequences, *Data Mining and Knowledge Discovery* **1**: 259–289.

Mitchell, M. (1998). *An Introduction to Genetic Algorithms (Complex Adaptive Systems)*, MIT Press.

Najaf-Zadeh, H., Pichevar, R., Thibault, L. & Lahdili, H. (2008). Perceptual matching pursuit for audio coding, *Audio Engineering Society Convetion, Amsterdam, The Netherlands*.

Neff, R. & Zakhor, A. (2000). Modulus quantization for matching pursuit video coding, *IEEE Trans. on Circuits and Systems for Video Technology* **10**(6): 895–912.

Olshausen, B. & Field, D. (1996). Emergence of simple-cell receptive field properties by learning a sparse code for natural images, *Nature* **381**: 607–609.

Painter, T. & Spanias, A. (2000). Perceptual coding of digital audio, *Proceedings of the IEEE* **88**: 451–515.

Patnaik, D., Sastry, P. & Unnikrishnan, K. (2008). Inferring neural network connectivity from spike data: A temporal mining approach, *Scientific Programming* **16**: 49–77.

Pichevar, R. & Najaf-Zadeh, H. (2009). Pattern extraction in sparse representations with application to audio coding, *European Signal Processing Conf., Glasgow, UK*.

Pichevar, R., Najaf-Zadeh, H., Lahdili, H. & Thibault, L. (2008). Differential graph-based coding of spikes in a biologically-inspired universal audio coder, *Audio Engineering Society Convetion, Amsterdam, The Netherlands*.

Pichevar, R., Najaf-Zadeh, H. & Thibault, L. (2007). A biologically-inspired low-bit-rate universal audio coder, *Proceedings of Audio Engineering Society Convention*.

Pichevar, R., Najaf-Zadeh, H., Thibault, L. & Lahdili, H. (2008). Entropy-constrained spike modulus quantization in a bio-inspired universal audio coder, *European Signal Processing Conf., Switzerland*.

Pichevar, R. & Rouat, J. (2008). An improved sparse non-negative part-based image coder via simulated annealing and matrix pseudo-inverse, *IEEE Conf. on Audio, Speech, and Signal Proc., Las Vegas, USA*.

Pichevar, R., Rouat, J. & Tai, L. (2006). The oscillatory dynamic link matcher for spiking-neuron-based pattern recognition, *Neurocomputing* **69**: 1837–1849.

Simoncelli, E., Freeman, W., Adelson, E. & Heeger, D. (1992). Shiftable multi-scale transforms, *IEEE Transactions on Information Theory* **38**(2): 587–607.

Simoncelli, E. & Olshausen, B. (2001). Natural image statistics and neural representation, *Annual Review of Neuroscience* **24**: 1193–1216.

Smith, E. & Lewicki, M. (2005). Efficient coding of time-relative structure using spikes, *Neural Computation* **17**: 19–45.

Smith, E. & Lewicki, M. (2006). Efficient auditory coding, *Nature* **7079**: 978–982.

Tropp, J. (2004). Greed is good: Algorithmic results for sparse approximation, *IEEE Trans. on information theory* **50**(10): 2231–2242.

von der Malsburg, C. (1999). The what and why of binding: the modelers perspective, *Neuron* **24**: 692–695.

Wang, D. (2005). The time dimension for scene analysis, *IEEE Trans. On Neural Networks* **16**: 1401–1426.

4

Constructing wavelet frames and orthogonal wavelet bases on the sphere

Daniela Roşca[a] and Jean-Pierre Antoine[b]
[a]*Department of Mathematics, Technical University of Cluj-Napoca*
RO-400020 Cluj-Napoca, Romania
Daniela.Rosca@math.utcluj.ro
[b]*Institut de Physique Théorique, Université catholique de Louvain*
B-1348 Louvain-la-Neuve, Belgium
Jean-Pierre.Antoine@uclouvain.be

1. Introduction

A classical problem is to analyse a signal (function) by decomposing it into suitable building blocks, then approximate it by truncating the expansion. Well-known examples are Fourier transform and its localized version, the Short Time Fourier transform (sometimes called the Gabor transform), and the wavelet transform. In the best case, the elementary blocks form a basis in the space of signals, with the pleasant consequence that the expansion coefficients are uniquely defined. Unfortunately, this is not always possible and often one has to resort to frames. In image processing, in particular, two-dimensional wavelets are by now a standard tool in image processing, under the two concurrent approaches, the Discrete Wavelet Transform (DWT), based on the concept of multiresolution analysis, and the Continuous Wavelet Transform (CWT). While the former usually leads to wavelet bases, the CWT has to be discretized for numerical implementation and produces in general only frames.

Nowadays, many situations yield data on *spherical* surfaces. For instance, in Earth and Space sciences (geography, geodesy, meteorology, astronomy, cosmology, etc), in crystallography (texture analysis of crystals), in medicine (some organs are regarded as sphere-like surfaces), or in computer graphics (modelling of closed surfaces as the graph of a function defined on the sphere). So one needs a suitable analysis tool for such data. In the spherical case, the Fourier transform amounts to an expansion in spherical harmonics, whose support is the whole sphere. Fourier analysis on the sphere is thus global and cumbersome. Therefore many different methods have been proposed to replace it with some sort of wavelet analysis.

In addition, some data may live on more complicated manifolds, such as a *two-sheeted hyperboloid*, in cosmology for instance (an open expanding model of the universe). In optics also, in the catadioptric image processing, where a sensor overlooks a mirror with the shape of a hyperboloid or a *paraboloid*. Another example is a closed *sphere-like surface*, that is, a surface obtained from a sphere by a smooth deformation. Thus it would be useful to have a wavelet transform available on such manifolds as well.

In this chapter, we will review the various aspects of the wavelet transform on the two-sphere, both continuous and discrete, with some emphasis on the construction of bases and frames.

We will also quickly indicate generalizations to other curved manifolds. Besides the original papers, partial reviews of some of this material may be found in (Antoine & Vandergheynst, 2007; Antoine & Roşca, 2008). The present chapter is an elaboration of the paper (Roşca & Antoine, 2008).

2. The CWT on the two-sphere

2.1 Heuristics

We consider first the extension of the CWT to the two sphere $\mathbb{S}^2 = \{\mathbf{x} \in \mathbb{R}^3, \ \|\mathbf{x}\| = 1\}$. A complete solution was obtained in (Antoine & Vandergheynst, 1999; Antoine et al., 2002) by a group-theoretical method (which actually works in any dimension (Antoine & Vandergheynst, 1998)). As it is well-known in the planar case, the design of a CWT on a given manifold X starts by identifying the operations one wants to perform on the finite energy signals living on X, that is, functions in $L^2(X, d\nu)$, where ν is a suitable measure on X. Next one realizes these operations by unitary operators on $L^2(X, d\nu)$ and one looks for a possible group-theoretical derivation.

In the case of the two-sphere $\mathbb{S}^2$, the required transformations are of two types: (i) *motions*, which are realized by rotations $\varrho \in SO(3)$, and (ii) *dilations* of some sort by a scale factor $a \in \mathbb{R}^*_+$. The problem is how to define properly the dilation *on* the sphere $\mathbb{S}^2$. The solution proposed in (Antoine & Vandergheynst, 1999; Antoine et al., 2002) consists in lifting onto the sphere, by inverse *stereographic projection*, the usual radial dilation in the tangent plane at the South Pole. More precisely, one proceeds in three steps: Project a point $A \in \mathbb{S}^2$ onto the point B in the tangent plane, perform the usual 2-D dilation $B \mapsto B_a$ by a factor a, and project back to $A_a \in \mathbb{S}^2$. The map $A \mapsto A_a$ is the *stereographic dilation*.

Now, the Hilbert space of spherical signals is $L^2(\mathbb{S}^2, d\mu)$, where $d\mu = \sin\theta \, d\theta \, d\varphi$, $\theta \in [0, \pi]$ is the colatitude angle, $\varphi \in [0, 2\pi)$ the longitude angle, $\omega = (\theta, \varphi) \in \mathbb{S}^2$. In that space, the desired operations are realized by the following unitary operators:

$$. \text{ rotation } R_\varrho \ : \ (R_\varrho f)(\omega) = f(\varrho^{-1}\omega), \ \varrho \in SO(3), \tag{1}$$

$$. \text{ dilation } D_a \ : \ (D_a f)(\omega) = \lambda(a, \theta)^{1/2} f(\omega_{1/a}), \ a \in \mathbb{R}^*_+. \tag{2}$$

In relation (2), $\omega_a := (\theta_a, \varphi)$, θ_a is defined by $\cot\frac{\theta_a}{2} = a \cot\frac{\theta}{2}$ for $a > 0$ and the normalization factor (Radon-Nikodym derivative, cocycle) , given as

$$\lambda(a, \theta)^{1/2} := 2a \left[(a^2 - 1)\cos\theta + (a^2 + 1)\right]^{-1}, \tag{3}$$

is needed for compensating the noninvariance under dilation of the natural measure $d\mu(\omega)$ on $\mathbb{S}^2$. Thus, starting from a function $\psi \in L^2(\mathbb{S}^2)$, we consider the whole family it generates, namely, $\{\psi_{\varrho,a} := R_\varrho D_a \psi, \ \varrho \in SO(3), \ a > 0\}$.

By analogy with the plane case, the spherical wavelet transform of a function $f \in L^2(\mathbb{S}^2)$, with respect to the wavelet ψ, will be defined as

$$W_\psi f(\varrho, a) := \langle \psi_{\varrho,a} | f \rangle. \tag{4}$$

The question, of course, is to determine which functions ψ can qualify as wavelets, that is, to determine the wavelet admissibility condition. Apart from an educated guess, the natural way to find the answer is through a group-theoretical analysis, mimicking the familiar one of planar 2-D wavelets.

2.2 The group-theoretical or coherent state approach

As a matter of fact, this spherical CWT was obtained in (Antoine & Vandergheynst, 1999) by the group-theoretical approach familiar in the planar 2-D case. The point is to embed the rotations from SO(3) and the dilations into the Lorentz group $SO_o(3,1)$, the argument being that this group is the *conformal* group both of the sphere $\mathbb{S}^2$ and of the tangent plane $\mathbb{R}^2$. The embedding results from the so-called *Iwasawa decomposition*:

$$SO_o(3,1) = SO(3) \cdot A \cdot N,$$

where $A \sim SO_o(1,1) \sim \mathbb{R} \sim \mathbb{R}_*^+$ (boosts in the z-direction) and $N \sim \mathbb{C}$.
Then it turns out that the Lorentz group $SO_o(3,1)$ has a transitive action on the sphere $\mathbb{S}^2$. In particular, a boost from A corresponds to a stereographic dilation. Now $SO_o(3,1)$ has a natural unitary representation U in $L^2(\mathbb{S}^2, d\mu)$, namely,

$$[U(g)f](\omega) = \lambda(g,\omega)^{1/2} f\left(g^{-1}\omega\right), \text{ for } g \in SO_o(3,1),\ f \in L^2(\mathbb{S}^2, d\mu), \tag{5}$$

where $\lambda(g,\omega) \equiv \lambda(a,\theta)$ is the Radon-Nikodym derivative (3).
Thus the parameter space of the spherical CWT is the quotient

$$X = SO_o(3,1)/N \sim SO(3) \cdot A,$$

which is *not* a group. Therefore, in order to apply the general formalism, we must introduce a *section* $\sigma : X \to SO_o(3,1)$ and consider the reduced representation $U(\sigma(\varrho,a))$. Choosing the natural (Iwasawa) section $\sigma(\varrho,a) = \varrho\, a$, $\varrho \in SO(3)$, $a \in A$, we obtain

$$U(\sigma(\varrho,a)) = U(\varrho\, a) = U(\varrho)U(a) = R_\varrho\, D_a, \tag{6}$$

exactly as before, in (1)-(2).
The following three propositions show that the representation (5) has all the properties that are required to generate a useful CWT. First of all, it is square integrable on the quotient manifold $X = SO_o(3,1)/N \simeq SO(3) \cdot \mathbb{R}_*^+$. For simplicity, we shall identify these two isomorphic manifolds.

Proposition 2.1. *The UIR (5) is square integrable on X modulo the section σ, that is, there exist nonzero (admissible) vectors $\psi \in L^2(\mathbb{S}^2, d\mu)$ such that*

$$\int_0^\infty \frac{da}{a^3} \int_{SO(3)} d\varrho\, |\langle U(\sigma(\varrho,a))\psi|\phi\rangle|^2 := \langle \phi | A_\psi \phi \rangle < \infty, \textit{ for all } \phi \in L^2(\mathbb{S}^2, d\mu). \tag{7}$$

Here $d\varrho$ is the left invariant (Haar) measure on SO(3).
The resolution operator *(also called* frame operator*) A_ψ is diagonal in Fourier space (i.e., it is a Fourier multiplier):*

$$\widehat{A_\psi f}(l,m) = G_\psi(l)\widehat{f}(l,m), \tag{8}$$

where

$$G_\psi(l) = \frac{8\pi^2}{2l+1} \sum_{|m| \leqslant l} \int_0^\infty \frac{da}{a^3} |\widehat{\psi}_a(l,m)|^2, \quad \textit{for all } l \in \mathbb{N}, \tag{9}$$

and $\widehat{\psi}_a(l,m) = \langle Y_l^m | \psi_a \rangle$, where Y_l^m is a spherical harmonic and $\psi_a := D_a \psi$.

Next, we have an exact admissibility condition on the wavelets (this condition was also derived by Holschneider (1996)).

Proposition 2.2. *An admissible wavelet is a function $\psi \in L^2(S^2, d\mu)$ for which there exists a positive constant $c < \infty$ such that $G_\psi(l) \leqslant c$, for all $l \in \mathbb{N}$. Equivalently, the function $\psi \in L^2(S^2, d\mu)$ is an admissible wavelet if and only if the resolution operator A_ψ is bounded and invertible.*

As in the plane case (Antoine et al., 2004), there is also a weaker admissibility condition on ψ:

$$\int_{S^2} \frac{\psi(\theta, \varphi)}{1 - \cos\theta} \, d\mu(\omega) = 0. \tag{10}$$

Here too, this condition is only necessary in general, but it becomes sufficient under mild regularity conditions on ψ. This is clearly similar to the "zero mean" condition of wavelets on the line or the plane. As in the flat case, it implies that the spherical CWT acts as a *local filter*, in the sense that it selects the components of a signal that are similar to ψ, which is assumed to be well localized.
Finally, our spherical wavelets generate continuous frames. Indeed:

Proposition 2.3. *For any admissible wavelet ψ such that $\int_0^{2\pi} d\varphi \; \psi(\theta, \varphi) \neq 0$, the family $\{\psi_{a,\varrho} := R_\varrho D_a \psi : a > 0, \varrho \in SO(3)\}$ is a continuous frame, that is, there exist two constants $\mathsf{m} > 0$ and $\mathsf{M} < \infty$ such that*

$$\mathsf{m} \, \|\phi\|^2 \leqslant \int_0^\infty \frac{da}{a^3} \int_{SO(3)} d\varrho \, |\langle \psi_{a,\varrho} | \phi \rangle|^2 \leqslant \mathsf{M} \, \|\phi\|^2, \; \textit{for all} \; \phi \in L^2(S^2, d\mu), \tag{11}$$

or, equivalently, there exist two positive constants $d > 0$ and $c < \infty$ such that

$$d \leqslant G_\psi(l) \leqslant c, \; \textit{for all} \; l \in \mathbb{N}$$

(in other words, the operators A_ψ and A_ψ^{-1} are both bounded).

Note that the condition $\int_0^{2\pi} d\varphi \; \psi(\theta, \varphi) \not\equiv 0$ is automatically satisfied for any nonzero axisymmetric (zonal) wavelet. The frame so obtained is not tight, unless $G_\psi(l) = \text{const}$. For an axisymmetric wavelet, $\widehat{\psi}_a(l, m) \equiv \widehat{\psi}_a(l)$ is independent of m, hence tightness would require that $G_\psi(l) = 8\pi^2 \int_0^\infty a^{-3} da \, |\widehat{\psi}_a(l)|^2 = \text{const}$, which seems difficult to obtain.
With all the ingredients thus available, we may now define the spherical CWT as in (4), namely,

Definition 2.4. *Given the admissible wavelet ψ, the* spherical CWT *of a function $f \in L^2(S^2, d\mu)$ with respect to ψ is defined as*

$$W_\psi f(\varrho, a) := \langle \psi_{\varrho,a} | f \rangle = \int_{S^2} \overline{[R_\varrho D_a \psi](\omega)} \, f(\omega) \, d\mu(\omega). \tag{12}$$

As in the planar case, this spherical CWT may be inverted and one gets the following *reconstruction formula*. For $f \in L^2(S^2)$ and ψ an admissible wavelet such that $\int_0^{2\pi} \psi(\theta, \varphi) \, d\varphi \neq 0$, one has

$$f(\omega) = \int_{\mathbb{R}_+^*} \int_{SO(3)} W_\psi f(\varrho, a) [A_\psi^{-1} R_\varrho D_a \psi](\omega) \, a^{-3} \, da \, d\varrho.$$

In addition, the spherical CWT has two important properties:
(1) It has a correct *Euclidean limit*. By this we mean that, if we construct the transform on a sphere of radius R and then let $R \to \infty$, the spherical CWT tends to the usual planar 2-D

CWT on the tangent plane at the South Pole. We refer to (Antoine & Vandergheynst, 1999) for mathematical details.
(2) Unlike the usual 2-D CWT, which is fully covariant with respect to translations, rotations and dilations, the spherical CWT is only partially covariant. It is covariant under motions on $\mathbb{S}^2$: for any $\varrho_o \in SO(3)$, the transform of the rotated signal $f(\varrho_o^{-1}\omega)$ is the function $W_\psi f(\varrho_o^{-1}\varrho, a)$. But it is *not* covariant under dilations. Indeed the wavelet transform of the dilated signal $(D_{a_o}f)(\omega) = \lambda(a_o,\theta)^{1/2} f(\omega_{1/a_o})$ is $\langle U(g)\psi|f\rangle$, with $g = a_o^{-1}\varrho a$, and the latter, while a well-defined element of $SO_o(3,1)$, is *not* of the form $\sigma(\varrho', a')$. This reflects the fact that the parameter space X of the spherical CWT is not a group, but only a homogeneous space.
A byproduct of this analysis is a complete equivalence between the spherical CWT and the usual planar CWT in the tangent plane, in the sense that the stereographic projection induces a unitary map $\pi : L^2(\mathbb{S}^2) \to L^2(\mathbb{R}^2)$. This fact allows one to lift any plane wavelet, including directional ones, onto the sphere by inverse stereographic projection. The same technique will be used in Section 3.3 below for lifting the discrete WT onto the sphere and thus generating orthogonal wavelet bases on it.
The advantages of this method are that it is easy to implement (the wavelet ψ is given explicitly), it leaves a large freedom in choosing the mother wavelet ψ, it allows the use of directional wavelets, it preserves smoothness and it gives no distortion around poles, since all points of $\mathbb{S}^2$ are equivalent under the action of the operator R_ϱ. However, it is computationally intensive. As for the disadvantages, the method yields only frames, not bases, as we will see in the next section.
Although this spherical CWT was originally obtained by a group-theoretical method, this mathematically sophisticated approach may be short-circuited if one remarks that it is uniquely determined by the geometry, in the sense that it suffices to impose *conformal* behavior of the relevant maps. More precisely, the stereographic projection is the unique conformal diffeomorphism from the sphere to its tangent plane at the South Pole. Similarly, the stereographic dilation (2) is the unique longitude-preserving dilation on the sphere that is conformal (Wiaux et al., 2005). Thus one gets the formula (12) directly, without the group-theoretical calculation.
There is an alternative that also leads to a half-continuous wavelet representation on $\mathbb{S}^2$. It consists in using the so-called *harmonic* dilation instead of the stereographic one. This dilation acts on the Fourier coefficients of a function f, that is, the numbers $\widehat{f}_{\ell,m} := \langle Y_\ell^m | f\rangle_{\mathbb{S}^2}$, where $\{Y_\ell^m, \ell \in \mathbb{N}, m = -\ell,\dots,\ell\}$ is the orthonormal basis of spherical harmonics in $L^2(\mathbb{S}^2)$. The dilation d_a is defined by the relation

$$\widehat{(d_a f)}_{\ell,m} := f_{a\ell,m}, \quad a > 0.$$

This technique, originally due to Holschneider (1996) and Freeden & Windheuser (1997), has recently been revived in the applications to astrophysics (Wiaux et al., 2008). However, although this definition leads to a well-defined, uniquely invertible wavelet representation, with steerable wavelets and full rotation invariance, there is no proof so far that it yields a frame. Hence one may question the stability of the reconstruction process, since it is the lower frame bound that guarantees it.

2.3 Spherical frames

The spherical CWT (12) may be discretized and one obtains frames, either half-continuous (only the scale variable a is discretized) or fully discrete (Antoine et al., 2002; Bogdanova et al.,

2005). To be more precise, one gets generalized frames, called *weighted frames* and *controlled frames*, respectively. They are defined as follows (Jacques, 2004; Bogdanova et al., 2005; Balazs et al., 2009).

Let $\{\phi_n : n \in \mathcal{I}\}$ be a countable family of vectors in a (separable) Hilbert space $\mathfrak{H}$ (the index set $\mathcal{I}$ may be finite or infinite). Then, the family $\{\phi_n\}$ is a *weighted frame* in $\mathfrak{H}$ if there are positive weights w_n and two constants $\mathsf{m} > 0$ and $\mathsf{M} < \infty$ such that

$$\mathsf{m}\,\|f\|^2 \leqslant \sum_{n\in\mathcal{I}} w_n\,|\langle\phi_n|f\rangle|^2 \leqslant \mathsf{M}\,\|f\|^2, \text{ for all } f \in \mathfrak{H}. \tag{13}$$

The family $\{\phi_n\}$ is a *controlled frame* in $\mathfrak{H}$ if there is a positive bounded operator C, with bounded inverse, such that

$$\mathsf{m}\,\|f\|^2 \leqslant \sum_{n\in\mathcal{I}} \langle\phi_n|f\rangle\,\langle f|C\phi_n\rangle \leqslant \mathsf{M}\,\|f\|^2, \text{ for all } f \in \mathfrak{H}. \tag{14}$$

Clearly this reduces to standard frames for $w_n = $ const and $C = I$, respectively.

These two notions are in fact mathematically equivalent to the classical notion of frame, namely, a family of vectors $\{\phi_n\}$ is a weighted frame, resp. a controlled frame, if and only if it is a frame in the standard sense (with different frame bounds, of course) (Balazs et al., 2009). However, this is not true numerically, the convergence properties of the respective frame expansions may be quite different (Antoine et al., 2004; Bogdanova et al., 2005). And, indeed, the new notions were introduced precisely for improving the convergence of the reconstruction process.

Following Bogdanova et al. (2005), we first build a half-continuous spherical frame, by discretizing the scale variable only, while keeping continuous the position variable on the sphere. We choose the half-continuous grid $\Lambda = \{(\omega, a_j) : \omega \in \mathbb{S}^2, j \in \mathbb{Z}, a_j > a_{j+1}\}$, where $\mathcal{A} = \{a_j : j \in \mathbb{Z}\}$ is an arbitrary decreasing sequence of scales, and $\nu_j := (a_j - a_{j+1})/a_j^3$ are weights that mimic the natural (Haar) measure da/a^3. Then a tight frame might be obtained, as shown in following proposition.

Proposition 2.5. *Let $\mathcal{A} = \{a_j : j \in \mathbb{Z}\}$ be a decreasing sequence of scales. If ψ is an axisymmetric wavelet for which there exist two constants $\mathsf{m}, \mathsf{M} \in \mathbb{R}_+^*$ such that*

$$\mathsf{m} \leqslant g_\psi(l) \leqslant \mathsf{M}, \text{ for all } l \in \mathbb{N}, \tag{15}$$

where

$$g_\psi(l) = \frac{4\pi}{2l+1} \sum_{j\in\mathbb{Z}} \nu_j\,|\widehat{\psi}_{a_j}(l,0)|^2,$$

then any function $f \in L^2(\mathbb{S}^2, d\mu)$ may be reconstructed from the corresponding family of spherical wavelets, as

$$f(\omega) = \sum_{j\in\mathbb{Z}} \nu_j \int_{\mathbb{S}^2} d\mu(\omega')\, W_\psi f(\omega', a_j) \left[\ell_\psi^{-1} R_{[\omega']} D_{a_j} \psi\right](\omega'), \tag{16}$$

where ℓ_ψ is the (discretized) resolution operator defined by $\widehat{\ell_\psi^{-1} h}(l,m) = g_\psi(l)^{-1}\, h(l,m)$.

Note that the resolution operator ℓ_ψ is simply the discretized version of the continuous resolution operator A_ψ. Clearly (16) may be interpreted as a (weighted) tight frame controlled by the operator ℓ_ψ^{-1}.

Next, still following Bogdanova et al. (2005), one designs a fully discrete spherical frame by discretizing all the variables. The scale variable is discretized as before. As for the positions, we choose an equiangular grid $\mathcal{G}_j$ indexed by the scale level:

$$\mathcal{G}_j = \{\omega_{jpq} = (\theta_{jp}, \varphi_{jq}) \in \mathbb{S}^2 : \theta_{jp} = \tfrac{(2p+1)\pi}{4B_j}, \varphi_{jq} = \tfrac{q\pi}{B_j}\}, \tag{17}$$

for $p, q \in \mathcal{N}_j := \{n \in \mathbb{N} : n < 2B_j\}$ and some range of bandwidths $\mathcal{B} = \{B_j \in 2\mathbb{N} : j \in \mathbb{Z}\}$. Note that, in (17), the values $\{\theta_{jp}\}$ constitute a pseudo-spectral grid, with nodes on the zeros of a Chebyshev polynomial of degree $2B_j$. Their virtue is the existence of an *exact* quadrature rule (Driscoll & Healy, 1994), namely,

$$\int_{\mathbb{S}^2} d\mu(\omega) f(\omega) = \sum_{p,q \in \mathcal{N}_j} w_{jp}\, f(\omega_{jpq}), \tag{18}$$

with certain (explicit) weights $w_{jp} > 0$ and for every band-limited function $f \in L^2(\mathbb{S}^2, d\mu)$ of bandwidth B_j (i.e., $\widehat{f}(l,m) = 0$ for all $l \geqslant B_j$). Thus the complete discretization grid is $\Lambda(\mathcal{A}, \mathcal{B}) = \{(a_j, \omega_{jpq}) : j \in \mathbb{Z},\ p, q \in \mathcal{N}_j\}$.

For this choice of discretization grid, one obtains a discrete *weighted, nontight frame, controlled by the operator* A_ψ^{-1}, namely, $\{\psi_{jpq} = R_{[\omega_{jpq}]} D_{a_j} \psi : j \in \mathbb{Z},\ p, q \in \mathcal{N}_j\}$ (Bogdanova et al., 2005):

$$\mathsf{m}\, \|f\|^2 \leqslant \sum_{j \in \mathbb{Z}} \sum_{p,q \in \mathcal{N}_j} \nu_j w_{jp}\, W_\psi f(\omega_{jpq}, a_j)\, \overline{\widetilde{W}_\psi f(\omega_{jpq}, a_j)} \leqslant \mathsf{M}\, \|f\|^2, \tag{19}$$

where $\nu_j = (a_j - a_{j+1})/a_j^3$ are the same positive weights as in Proposition 2.5 and

$$\widetilde{W}_\psi f(\varrho, a) := \langle \widetilde{\psi}_{a,\varrho} | f \rangle = \langle A_\psi^{-1} R_\varrho D_a \psi | f \rangle. \tag{20}$$

A sufficient condition for (19) to hold may be given, but it is very complicated, involving the determinant of an ∞-dimensional matrix, unless f is band-limited. As usual, when the frame bounds are close enough, approximate reconstruction formulas may be used. The convergence of the process may still be improved by combining the reconstruction with a conjugate gradient algorithm.

As a matter of fact, no discretization scheme leading to a wavelet *basis* is known and, in practice, the method applies to band-limited functions only. This entails high *redundancy* and thus a higher computing cost, which is not suitable for large data sets. There is also the problem of finding an appropriate discretization grid which leads to good frames. Some of them, e.g. the equi-angular grid $\Lambda(\mathcal{A}, \mathcal{B})$ described above, yield exact quadrature rules for the integration of band-limited signals on $\mathbb{S}^2$, but other ones (typically, the familiar HEALPix) are only approximate. This is actually a general feature: when discretizing a CWT, it is not easy to prove that a given discretization leads to a frame, even less to a good frame or a tight frame.

For all those reasons, one would prefer to try and build directly a DWT on the sphere.

3. The DWT on the sphere

3.1 General requirements

Many authors have designed methods for constructing discrete spherical wavelets. All of them have advantages and drawbacks. These may be characterized in terms of several properties which are desirable for *any* efficient wavelet analysis, planar or spherical (a thorough discussion of this topic may be found in Antoine & Roşca (2008)).

· *Basis:* The redundancy of frames leads to nonunique expansions. Moreover, the existing constructions of spherical frames are sometimes computationally heavy and often applicable only to band-limited functions. Thus, in some applications, genuine bases are preferable.
· *Orthogonality:* This method leads to orthogonal reconstruction matrices, whose inversion is trivial. Thus, orthogonal bases are good for compression, but this is not always sufficient: sparsity of reconstruction matrices is still needed in the case of large data sets.
· *Local support:* This is crucial when working with large data sets, since it yields sparse matrices in the implementation of the algorithms. Also, it prevents spreading of "tails" during approximation.[1]
· *Continuity, smoothness:* These properties are always desirable in approximation, but not easily achieved.

3.2 Some known methods

Let us quote a few of those methods, with focus on the properties just mentioned, without being exhaustive. A more comprehensive review, with all references to original papers, may be found in (Antoine & Roşca, 2008).

(1) The spherical DWT using spherical harmonics

Various constructions of discrete spherical wavelets using spherical harmonics may be found in the literature, leading to frames or bases. The advantages of this method is that it produces no distortion (since no pole has a privileged role) and that it preserves smoothness of the wavelets. However, the wavelets so obtained have in general a localized support, but not a local one, i.e., it covers the whole sphere. Since this implies full reconstruction matrices, the result is not suitable for large amount of data. Examples are the works of Potts et al. (1996) or Freeden & Schreiner (1997).

(2) The spherical DWT via polar coordinates

The polar coordinate map $\rho : I = [0, \pi] \times [0, 2\pi) \to S^2$ has the familiar form

$$\rho : (\theta, \varphi) \mapsto (\cos\varphi \sin\theta, \sin\varphi \sin\theta, \cos\theta)\,.$$

A problem here is *continuity*. Indeed a continuous function f defined on I remains continuous after mapping it onto S^2 if and only if $f(\theta, 0) = f(\theta, 2\pi)$, for all $\theta \in [0, \pi]$, and there exists two constants P_N, P_S such that $f(0, \varphi) = P_N$ and $f(\pi, \varphi) = P_S$, for all $\varphi \in [0, 2\pi)$. Unfortunately, these continuity conditions are not easily satisfied by wavelets on intervals.
The obvious advantage of this approach is that many data sets are given in polar coordinates and thus one does not need to perform additional interpolation when implementing. However, there are disadvantages. First, no known construction gives both continuity and local support. Next, there are distortions around the poles: ρ maps the whole segment $\{(0, \varphi),\ \varphi \in [0, 2\pi)\}$ onto the North Pole, and the whole segment $\{(\pi, \varphi),\ \varphi \in [0, 2\pi)\}$ onto the South Pole. Representative examples are papers by Dahlke et al. (1995) or Weinreich (2001).

(3) The spherical DWT via radial projection from a convex polyhedron

Let S^2 be the unit sphere centered in 0 and let Γ be a convex polyhedron, containing 0 in its interior and with triangular faces (if some faces are non-triangular, one simply triangularizes

[1] A wavelet has *local support* if it vanishes identically outside a small region. It is *localized* if it is negligible outside a small region, so that it may have (small, but nonzero) "tails" there. Since these tails may spread in the process of approximation of data and spoil their good localization properties, local support is definitely preferred (see the example in (Roşca & Antoine, 2009)).

them). The idea of the method, due to one of us (Roşca, 2005; 2007a;b), is to obtain wavelets on $\mathbb{S}^2$ first by moving planar wavelets to wavelets defined on the faces of Γ and then projecting these radially onto $\mathbb{S}^2$. This proceeds as follows. Let $\Omega = \partial\Gamma$ denote the boundary of Γ and let $p : \Omega \to \mathbb{S}^2$ denote the radial projection from the origin:

$$p(x,y,z) = \rho \cdot (x,y,z), \quad \text{where } \rho := \rho(x,y,z) = 1/\sqrt{x^2+y^2+z^2}.$$

Let $\mathcal{T}$ denote the set of triangular faces of Γ and consider the following weighted scalar product on $L^2(\mathbb{S}^2)$:

$$\langle F|G\rangle_\Gamma = \sum_{T\in\mathcal{T}} \int_{p(T)} F(\zeta)\, G(\zeta)\, w_T(\zeta)\, d\mu(\zeta), \quad \zeta = (\zeta_1,\zeta_2,\zeta_3) \in \mathbb{S}^2,\ F,G \in L^2(\mathbb{S}^2). \tag{21}$$

Here $w_T(\zeta_1,\zeta_2,\zeta_3) = 2d_T^2 \left|a_T\zeta_1 + b_T\zeta_2 + c_T\zeta_3\right|^{-3}$, with a_T, b_T, c_T, d_T the coefficients of $x, y, z, 1$, respectively, in the determinant

$$\begin{vmatrix} x & y & z & 1 \\ x_1 & y_1 & z_1 & 1 \\ x_2 & y_2 & z_2 & 1 \\ x_3 & y_3 & z_3 & 1 \end{vmatrix} = a_T x + b_T y + c_T z + d_T 1,$$

where (x_i, y_i, z_i), $i = 1,2,3$, are the vertices of the planar triangle $T \in \mathcal{T}$. Then one proves that the norm $\|\cdot\|_\Gamma := \langle\cdot|\cdot\rangle_\Gamma^{1/2}$ is equivalent to the usual norm in $L^2(\mathbb{S}^2)$, i.e., there exist constants $\mathsf{m}_\Gamma > 0$, $\mathsf{M}_\Gamma < \infty$ such that

$$\mathsf{m}_\Gamma \|f\|_\Gamma \leqslant \|f\|_2 \leqslant \mathsf{M}_\Gamma \|f\|_\Gamma,\ \forall f \in L^2(\mathbb{S}^2).$$

Explicit expressions for optimal bounds m_Γ and M_Γ are given in (Roşca, 2009).
The resulting wavelets are orthogonal with respect to the weighted scalar product (21) on $L^2(\mathbb{S}^2)$. This method offers many advantages: no distortion around the poles, possible construction of continuous and locally supported stable wavelet bases, local support of the wavelets (leading to sparse matrices), easy implementation, possible extension to sphere-like surfaces (Roşca, 2006). As a disadvantage, we may note the lack of smoothness of the wavelets.

(4) Needlets

A new class of discrete spherical wavelets, called *needlets*, has been introduced recently (Narcowich et al., 2006a;b; Baldi et al., 2009). These functions, which are actually special spherical harmonics kernels, are derived by combining three ideas, namely, a Littlewood-Paley decomposition, a suitable distribution of (finitely many) points on the sphere, called *centers*, and an exact quadrature rule. The dilation takes place in the space of spherical harmonics, effectively in Fourier space, i.e., it is a harmonic dilation as described at the end of Section 2.2. The upshot is a new class of tight frames on the sphere. The frame functions are both compactly supported in the frequency domain (i.e., band-limited in l) and almost exponentially localized around each center. When combined with a new statistical method, they offer a powerful tool for analysing CMB (WMAP) data, e.g. for analysing the cross-correlation between the latter and galaxy counts from sky surveys (Pietrobon et al., 2006; Marinucci et al., 2008). They have also found nice applications in statistics (Baldi et al., 2008; 2009).
As a matter of fact, no construction so far has led to wavelet bases on the sphere which are *simultaneously* continuous (or smoother), orthogonal and locally supported, although any two of these three conditions may be met at the same time. This suggests to try another approach.

3.3 Lifting the DWT from the plane to the sphere

The method we propose consists in lifting wavelets from the tangent plane to the sphere by inverse stereographic projection (Roşca & Antoine, 2009). It yields simultaneously smoothness, orthogonality, local support, vanishing moments. The disadvantage is that it gives distortions around a pole. In addition, it is not suitable for the whole sphere $\mathbb{S}^2$, but only for data "away" from that pole. However, the latter can be taken anywhere on the sphere, for instance, in a region where no data is given. To give an example, European climatologists routinely put the North Pole of their spherical grid in the middle of the Pacific Ocean. Therefore, this is in fact a minor inconvenient in practice.

Our sphere is

$$\mathbb{S}^2 = \{\zeta = (\zeta_1, \zeta_2, \zeta_3) \in \mathbb{R}^3,\ \zeta_1^2 + \zeta_2^2 + (\zeta_3 - 1)^2 = 1\},$$

where we have used the parametrization $\zeta_1 = \cos\varphi \sin\theta, \zeta_2 = \sin\varphi\sin\theta, \zeta_3 = 1 + \cos\theta$, for $\theta \in (0, \pi], \varphi \in [0, 2\pi)$. The pointed sphere is $\dot{\mathbb{S}}^2 = \mathbb{S}^2 \setminus \{(0,0,2)\}$.

Let now $\mathsf{p} : \dot{\mathbb{S}}^2 \to \mathbb{R}^2$ be the stereographic projection from the North Pole $N(0,0,2)$ onto the tangent plane $\zeta_3 = 0$ at the South Pole. The area elements $d\mathbf{x}$ of $\mathbb{R}^2$ and $\mu(\zeta)$ of $\dot{\mathbb{S}}^2$ are related by $d\mathbf{x} = \nu(\zeta)^2\, d\mu(\zeta)$, where the weight factor $\nu : \dot{\mathbb{S}}^2 \to \mathbb{R}$ is defined as

$$\nu(\zeta) = \frac{2}{2 - \zeta_3} = \frac{2}{1 - \cos\theta},\ \zeta = (\zeta_1, \zeta_2, \zeta_3) \equiv (\theta, \varphi) \in \dot{\mathbb{S}}^2.$$

Notice that $L^2(\dot{\mathbb{S}}^2) := L^2(\dot{\mathbb{S}}^2, d\mu(\zeta)) = L^2(\mathbb{S}^2)$, since the set $\{N\}$ is of measure zero. As mentioned in Section 2, the stereographic projection p induces a unitary map $\pi : L^2(\dot{\mathbb{S}}^2) \to L^2(\mathbb{R}^2)$, with inverse $\pi^{-1} : L^2(\mathbb{R}^2) \to L^2(\dot{\mathbb{S}}^2)$ given by $\pi^{-1}(F) = \nu \cdot (F \circ \mathsf{p}),\ \forall F \in L^2(\mathbb{R}^2)$. As a consequence, we have

$$\langle F|G\rangle_{L^2(\mathbb{R}^2)} = \langle \nu \cdot (F \circ \mathsf{p}) | \nu \cdot (G \circ \mathsf{p})\rangle_{L^2(\dot{\mathbb{S}}^2)},\ \forall F, G \in L^2(\mathbb{R}^2). \tag{22}$$

This equality allows us to construct orthogonal bases on $L^2(\dot{\mathbb{S}}^2)$ starting from orthogonal bases in $L^2(\mathbb{R}^2)$. More precisely, we will use the fact that, if the functions $F, G \in L^2(\mathbb{R}^2)$ are orthogonal, then the functions $F^s = \nu \cdot (F \circ \mathsf{p})$ and $G^s = \nu \cdot (G \circ \mathsf{p})$ will be orthogonal in $L^2(\dot{\mathbb{S}}^2)$. Thus, the construction of multiresolution analysis (MRA) and wavelet bases in $L^2(\dot{\mathbb{S}}^2)$ is based on the equality (22).

The starting point is a MRA in $L^2(\mathbb{R}^2)$ (for a thorough analysis of MRAs in 1-D and in 2-D, we refer to the monograph (Daubechies, 1992)). For simplicity, we consider 2-D tensor wavelets, that is, we take the tensor product of two 1-D MRAs, with scaling function ϕ, mother wavelet ψ, and diagonal dilation matrix $D = \mathrm{diag}(2,2)$. Thus we get a 2-D MRA of $L^2(\mathbb{R}^2)$, i.e., an increasing sequence of closed subspaces $\mathbf{V}_j \subset L^2(\mathbb{R}^2)$ with $\bigcap_{j\in\mathbb{Z}} \mathbf{V}_j = \{0\}$ and $\overline{\bigcup_{j\in\mathbb{Z}} \mathbf{V}_j} = L^2(\mathbb{R}^2)$, satisfying the following conditions:

(1) $f(\cdot) \in \mathbf{V}_j \iff f(D\,\cdot) \in \mathbf{V}_{j+1}$,

(2) There exists a function $\Phi \in L^2(\mathbb{R}^2)$ such that the set $\{\Phi(\cdot - \mathbf{k}),\ \mathbf{k} \in \mathbb{Z}^2\}$ is an orthonormal basis (o.n.b.) of $\mathbf{V}_0$.

In terms of the original 1-D MRA, the 2-D scaling function is $\Phi(\mathbf{x}) = \phi(x)\phi(y)$ and for the 2-D MRA it generates, one has

$$\begin{aligned}\mathbf{V}_{j+1} &= V_{j+1} \otimes V_{j+1} = (V_j \oplus W_j) \otimes (V_j \oplus W_j)\\ &= (V_j \otimes V_j) \oplus [(W_j \otimes V_j) \oplus (V_j \otimes W_j) \oplus (W_j \otimes W_j)]\\ &= \mathbf{V}_j \oplus \mathbf{W}_j.\end{aligned}$$

Thus $\mathbf{W}_j$ consists of three pieces, with the following orthonormal bases:

$$\{\psi_{j,k_1}(x)\phi_{j,k_2}(y),\ (k_1,k_2) \in \mathbb{Z}^2\} \text{ o.n.b. in } W_j \otimes V_j,$$
$$\{\phi_{j,k_1}(x)\psi_{j,k_2}(y),\ (k_1,k_2) \in \mathbb{Z}^2\} \text{ o.n.b. in } V_j \otimes W_j,$$
$$\{\psi_{j,k_1}(x)\psi_{j,k_2}(y),\ (k_1,k_2) \in \mathbb{Z}^2\} \text{ o.n.b. in } W_j \otimes W_j.$$

This leads us to define three wavelets

$$^{h}\Psi(x,y) = \phi(x)\psi(y),$$
$$^{v}\Psi(x,y) = \psi(x)\phi(y),$$
$$^{d}\Psi(x,y) = \psi(x)\psi(y).$$

Then, $\{^{\lambda}\Psi_{j,\mathbf{k}},\ \mathbf{k} = (k_1,k_2) \in \mathbb{Z}^2,\ \lambda = h,v,d\}$ is an orthonormal basis for $\mathbf{W}_j$ and $\{^{\lambda}\Psi_{j,\mathbf{k}},\ j \in \mathbb{Z},\ \mathbf{k} \in \mathbb{Z}^2,\ \lambda = h,v,d\}$ is an orthonormal basis for $\overline{\bigoplus_{j\in\mathbb{Z}} \mathbf{W}_j} = L^2(\mathbb{R}^2)$. Here, for $j \in \mathbb{Z}$, $\mathbf{k} = (k_1,k_2) \in \mathbb{Z}^2$ and for $F \in L^2(\mathbb{R}^2)$, the function $F_{j,\mathbf{k}}$ is defined as

$$F_{j,\mathbf{k}}(x,y) = 2^j F(2^j x - k_1, 2^j y - k_2).$$

Now we can proceed and lift the MRA to the sphere. To every function $F \in L^2(\mathbb{R}^2)$, one may associate the function $F^s \in L^2(\dot{\mathbb{S}}^2)$ as $F^s = \nu \cdot (F \circ \mathsf{p})$. In particular,

$$F^s_{j,\mathbf{k}} = \nu \cdot (F_{j,\mathbf{k}} \circ \mathsf{p}) \text{ for } j \in \mathbb{Z},\ \mathbf{k} \in \mathbb{Z}^2, \tag{23}$$

and similarly for the spherical functions $\Phi^s_{j,\mathbf{k}}$ and $^{\lambda}\Psi^s_{j,\mathbf{k}}$, where $\Phi_{j,\mathbf{k}}, ^{\lambda}\Psi_{j,\mathbf{k}}, \lambda = h,v,d$, are the planar 2-D scaling functions and wavelets, respectively. For $j \in \mathbb{Z}$, we define $\mathcal{V}_j$ as $\mathcal{V}_j := \{\nu \cdot (F \circ \mathsf{p}),\ F \in \mathbf{V}_j\}$. Then we have:

(1) $\mathcal{V}_j \subset \mathcal{V}_{j+1}$ for $j \in \mathbb{Z}$, and each $\mathcal{V}_j$ is a closed subspace of $L^2(\dot{\mathbb{S}}^2)$;

(2) $\bigcap_{j\in\mathbb{Z}} \mathcal{V}_j = \{0\}$ and $\bigcup_{j\in\mathbb{Z}} \mathcal{V}_j$ is dense in $L^2(\dot{\mathbb{S}}^2)$;

(3) $\{\Phi^s_{0,\mathbf{k}},\ \mathbf{k} \in \mathbb{Z}^2\}$ is an orthonormal basis for $\mathcal{V}_0$.

A sequence $(\mathcal{V}_j)_{j\in\mathbb{Z}}$ of subspaces of $L^2(\dot{\mathbb{S}}^2)$ satisfying (1), (2), (3) constitutes a MRA of $L^2(\dot{\mathbb{S}}^2)$. Define now the wavelet spaces $\mathcal{W}_j$ by $\mathcal{V}_{j+1} = \mathcal{V}_j \oplus \mathcal{W}_j$. Then $\{^{\lambda}\Psi^s_{j,\mathbf{k}},\ \mathbf{k} \in \mathbb{Z}^2,\ \lambda = h,v,d\}$ is an orthonormal basis for $\mathcal{W}_j$ and $\{^{\lambda}\Psi^s_{j,\mathbf{k}},\ j \in \mathbb{Z},\ \mathbf{k} \in \mathbb{Z}^2,\ \lambda = h,v,d\}$ is an orthonormal basis for $\overline{\left(\bigoplus_{j\in\mathbb{Z}} \mathcal{W}_j\right)} = L^2(\dot{\mathbb{S}}^2)$. This the orthonormal wavelet basis on $\mathbb{S}^2$.

Thus, an orthonormal 2-D wavelet basis yields an orthonormal spherical wavelet basis. In addition, if Φ has compact support in $\mathbb{R}^2$, then $\Phi^s_{j,\mathbf{k}}$ has local support on $\mathbb{S}^2$ (and $\operatorname{diam}\operatorname{supp}\Phi^s_{j,\mathbf{k}} \to 0$ as $j \to \infty$), and similarly for the respective wavelets. Smooth 2-D wavelets yield smooth spherical wavelets. In particular, Daubechies wavelets yield locally supported and orthonormal wavelets on $\dot{\mathbb{S}}^2$. Thus the same tools as in the planar 2-D case can be used for the decomposition and reconstruction matrices (so that existing toolboxes may be used).

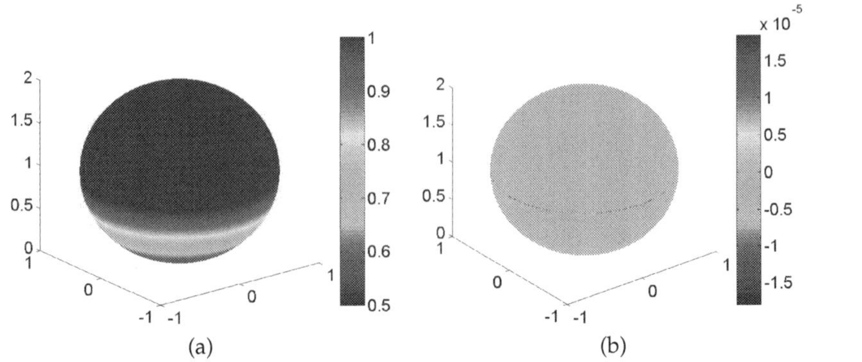

Fig. 1. (a) The graph of the function $f(\theta,\varphi)$ defined in (24); (b) Its analysis with the spherical wavelet associated to the Daubechies wavelet db3, the familiar 6-coefficient filter.

3.4 An example: Singularity detection

As an application of our construction, we analyse the following zonal function on S^2:

$$f(\theta,\varphi) = \begin{cases} 1, & \theta \leqslant \frac{\pi}{2}, \\ (1+3\cos^2\theta)^{-1/2}, & \theta \geqslant \frac{\pi}{2}. \end{cases} \tag{24}$$

The function f and its gradient are continuous, but the second partial derivative with respect to θ has a discontinuity on the equator $\theta = \frac{\pi}{2}$. The function f is shown in Figure 1 (a). Detecting properly such a discontinuity requires a wavelet with three vanishing moments at least, so that, as far as we know, none of the existing constructions of discrete spherical wavelets could detect this discontinuity.

Instead, we consider the discretized spherical CWT with the spherical wavelet $\Psi^s_{H_2}$ associated to the planar wavelet

$$\begin{aligned} \Psi_{H_2}(x,y) &= \Delta^2[e^{-\frac{1}{2}(x^2+y^2)}] \\ &= (x^4+y^4+2x^2y^2-8(x^2+y^2)+8)e^{-\frac{1}{2}(x^2+y^2)}. \end{aligned} \tag{25}$$

This wavelet has four vanishing moments (again a planar wavelet with less than three vanishing moments could not detect this discontinuity). The analysis is presented in Figure 2. Panels (a), (b), (c) and (d) present the spherical CWT at smaller and smaller scales, $a = 0.08, 0.04, 0.02$ and 0.0165, respectively. From Panels (a)-(c), it appears that the discontinuity along the equator is detected properly, and the precision increases as the scale decreases. However, there is a limit: when the scale a is taken below $a = 0.018$, the singularity is no more detected properly, and the transform is nonzero on the upper hemisphere, whereas the signal is constant there. This is visible on Panel (d), which shows the transform at scale $a = 0.01655$. In fact, the wavelet becomes too narrow and "falls in between" the discretization points, ripples appear in the Southern hemisphere. This effect is described in detail in (Antoine et al., 2002).

On the contrary, the well-known Daubechies wavelet db3 lifted on the sphere by (23) does the job better than the wavelet $\Psi^s_{H_2}$ mentioned above, as one can see in Figure 1, Panel (b). The computational load is smaller and the precision is much better, in the sense that the width of the detected singular curve is narrower.

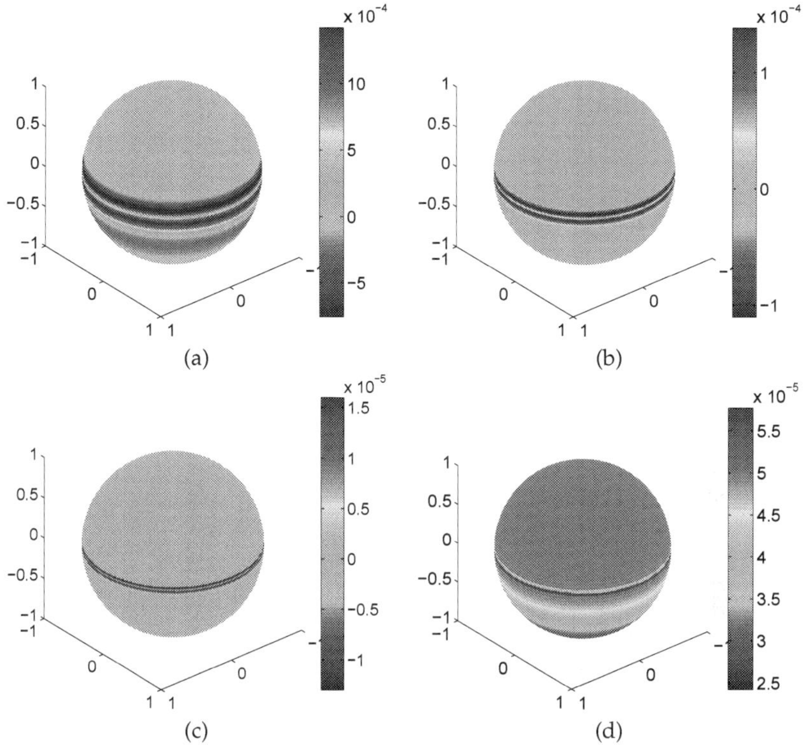

Fig. 2. Analysis of the function $f(\theta, \varphi)$ by the discretized CWT method with the wavelet $\psi^s_{H_2}$, at scales: (a) $a = 0.08$ (b) $a = 0.04$ (c) $a = 0.02$ (d) $a = 0.0165$. The sampling grid is 256×256.

The same tests were performed for the function $f_{\pi/7}$, obtained from f by performing a rotation around the axis Ox with an angle of $\pi/7$. The results are presented in Figure 3. Panel (a) shows the analysis of the function $f_{\pi/7}$ with the discretized CWT method, using the wavelet $\psi^s_{H_2}$, at scale $a = 0.0165$. Panel (b) gives the analysis with the Daubechies wavelet db3 lifted onto the sphere. No appreciable distortion is seen, the detection is good all along the discontinuity circle, and again the precision is better with the lifted Daubechies wavelet. Notice that the computation leading to the figure of Panel (a) was made with a grid finer than that used in Figure 2, so that the detection breaks down at a smaller scale (here below $a = 0.01$).
Of course, this example is still academic, but it is significant. More work is needed, in particular, for estimating the degree of distortion around the pole and applying the method to real life signals.

4. Generalizations

As we have seen up to now in the case of the two-sphere, the main ingredients needed for construction of a wavelet transform on a manifold are harmonic analysis and a proper notion

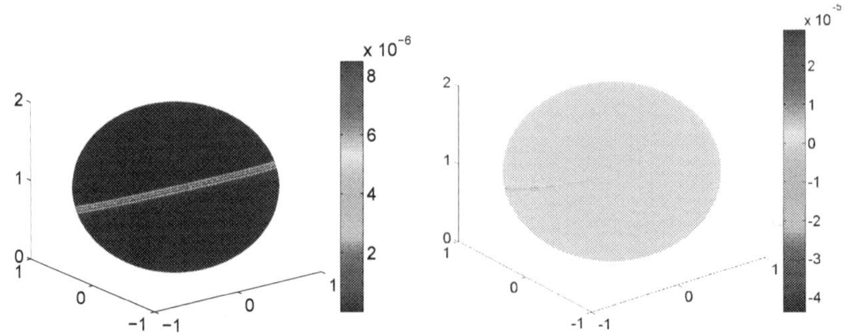

(a) (b)

Fig. 3. (a) Analysis of the function $f_{\pi/7}(\theta,\varphi)$ by the discretized CWT method with the wavelet $\psi^{s}_{H_2}$, at scale $a = 0.0165$ (the sampling grid here is 512×512); (b) Analysis of the function $f_{\pi/7}(\theta,\varphi)$, with the spherical wavelet associated to db3.

of dilation *on* the manifold. Suitable notions of dilation may be obtained by a group-theoretical approach or by lifting from a fixed plane by some inverse projection.

These generalizations do not have a purely academic interest. Indeed, some data live on manifolds more complicated than the sphere, such as a *two-sheeted hyperboloid* or a *paraboloid*. In optics also, data on such manifolds are essential for the treatment of omnidirectional images, which have numerous applications in navigation, surveillance, visualization, or robotic vision, for instance. In the catadioptric image processing, a sensor overlooks a mirror, whose shape may be spherical, hyperbolic or parabolic. However, instead of projecting the data from that mirror onto a plane, one can process them directly on the mirror, which then suggests to use wavelets on such manifolds (Bogdanova, Bresson, Thiran & Vandergheynst, 2007).

4.1 The two-sheeted hyperboloid $\mathbb{H}^2$

The upper sheet $\mathbb{H}^2_+ = \{\zeta = (\zeta_1,\zeta_2,\zeta_3) \in \mathbb{R}^3,\ \zeta_1^2+\zeta_2^2-\zeta_3^2 = -1,\ \zeta_3 > 0\}$ of the two-sheeted hyperboloid may be treated exactly as the sphere, replacing SO(3) by the isometry group $SO_o(2,1)$. For dilations, however, a choice has to be made, since there are many possibilities, each type being defined by some projection. Details may be found in (Bogdanova, 2005; Bogdanova, Vandergheynst & Gazeau, 2007). Given an (admissible) hyperbolic wavelet ψ, the hyperbolic CWT of $f \in L^2(\mathbb{H}^2_+)$ with respect to ψ is

$$W_\psi f(g,a) := \langle \psi_{g,a} | f\rangle = \int_{\mathbb{H}^2_+} \overline{\psi_a(g^{-1}\zeta)}\, f(\zeta)\, d\mu(\zeta),\ g \in SO_o(2,1), a > 0, \tag{26}$$

a formula manifestly analogous to its spherical counterpart (12). As in the spherical case, $\psi_a(\zeta) = \lambda(a,\zeta)\psi(d_{1/a}\zeta)$, with d_a an appropriate dilation, $\lambda(a,\zeta)$ is the corresponding Radon-Nikodym derivative, and μ is the $SO_o(2,1)$-invariant measure on $\mathbb{H}^2$.

The key for developing the CWT is the possibility of performing harmonic analysis on $\mathbb{H}^2_+$, including a convolution theorem, thanks to the so-called Fourier-Helgason transform. As a consequence, the usual properties hold true, for instance, an exact reconstruction formula. However, no result is known concerning frames that would be obtained by discretization.

On the other hand, it is possible to construct wavelet orthonormal bases on $\mathbb{H}^2_+$ by lifting them from the equatorial plane $\zeta_3 = 0$ by inverse orthographic (i.e., vertical) projection. In this case, no point has to be avoided, since only one pole is present, but distortions will occur again if one goes sufficiently far away from the tip (pole).

4.2 The paraboloid and other manifolds

Among the three shapes for a catadioptric mirror, the parabolic one is the most common (think of the headlights of a car). And this case brings us back to the topic of Sections 2.2 and 3.3. Indeed it has been shown by Geyer & Daniilidis (2001) that the reconstruction of the orthographic projection from a parabolic mirror can be computed as the inverse stereographic projection from the image plane onto the unit sphere. Thus wavelet frames and wavelet orthogonal bases may be obtained from the corresponding spherical constructions. Alternatively, one may lift planar orthogonal wavelet bases onto the paraboloid directly by inverse orthographic projection, as for the hyperboloid, with the same danger of distortions far away.
For a more general manifold, a local CWT may be designed, using a covering of the manifold by local patches (charts, in the language of differential geometry) and the projection along the normal at the center of each patch (Antoine et al., 2009) (this is also the idea behind needlets (Narcowich et al., 2006b)). One would then get orthogonal wavelet bases in each patch, but there remains the problem of connection of one patch with the next one, using transition functions (the concatenation of all the local bases may also be considered as a dictionary). Notice the same problem of combining local orthogonal wavelet bases has been encountered, and solved, in the wavelet construction based on radial projection from a convex polyhedron (Roşca, 2005), described briefly in Section 3.2(3).
A final example of orthogonal wavelet basis is that of the wavelet transform on graphs (Antoine et al., 2009). A graph is a good model for pairwise relations between objects of a certain collection, such as the nodes of a sensor network or points sampled out of a surface or manifold. Thus a wavelet transform on a graph could be a welcome addition.
A graph is defined as a collection V of vertices or nodes and a collection of edges that connect pairs of vertices. In the present context, one considers finite graphs only, with d nodes. Thus the signals of interest are functions $f : V \to \mathbb{R}$, which can be identified with d-dimensional real vectors $f \in \mathbb{R}^d$. In order to design a wavelet transform on such a graph, one considers the so-called Laplacian matrix, a positive semi-definite $d \times d$ matrix. Its eigenvectors form an orthonormal system that can be used to decompose any signal. Next one defines a dilation by dilating the "Fourier" coefficients — once again the needlet idea. The resulting functions are the wavelets on the graph and they form an orthogonal basis (everything is finite-dimensional). We refer to (Antoine et al., 2009) for further details of the construction.

5. Outcome

We have surveyed a number of techniques for generating orthogonal wavelet bases or wavelet frames on the two-sphere S^2, plus some generalizations. Two approaches have been privileged, both of them based on some notion of inverse projection, namely, (1) the construction of a CWT on S^2 by inverse stereographic projection from a tangent plane, which leads to nontight frames upon discretization; and (2) the construction of orthogonal wavelet bases by lifting in the same way a planar orthogonal basis. Of course, many other methods are available in the literature, especially in the discrete case, and we have mentioned some of them. Clearly many open questions remain, but we want to emphasize that progress in this field is likely to be motivated by physical applications, in particular, astrophysics and optics.

6. References

Antoine, J.-P., Demanet, L., Jacques, L. & Vandergheynst, P. (2002). "Wavelets on the sphere: Implementation and approximations", *Applied Comput. Harmon. Anal.* **13**: 177–200.

Antoine, J.-P., Murenzi, R., Vandergheynst, P. & Ali, S. T. (2004). *Two-dimensional Wavelets and Their Relatives*, Cambridge University Press, Cambridge (UK).

Antoine, J.-P. & Roşca, D. (2008). "The wavelet transform on the two-sphere and related manifolds — A review", *Optical and Digital Image Processing, Proc. SPIE* **7000**: 70000B–1–15.

Antoine, J.-P., Roşca, D. & Vandergheynst, P. (2009). "Wavelet transform on manifolds: Old and new approaches". Preprint.

Antoine, J.-P. & Vandergheynst, P. (1998). "Wavelets on the n-sphere and other manifolds", *J. Math. Phys.* **39**: 3987–4008.

Antoine, J.-P. & Vandergheynst, P. (1999). "Wavelets on the 2-sphere: A group-theoretical approach", *Applied Comput. Harmon. Anal.* **7**: 262–291.

Antoine, J.-P. & Vandergheynst, P. (2007). "Wavelets on the two-sphere and other conic sections", *J. Fourier Anal. Appl.* **13**: 369–386.

Balazs, P., Antoine, J.-P. & Gryboś, A. (2009). "Weighted and controlled frames: Mutual relationship and first numerical properties", *Int. J. Wavelets, Multires. and Inform. Proc.* p. (to appear).

Baldi, P., Kerkyacharian, G., Marinucci, D. & Picard, D. (2008). "high frequency asymptotics for wavelet-based tests for Gaussianity and isotropy on the torus", *J. Multivariate Anal.* **99**(4): 606–636.

Baldi, P., Kerkyacharian, G., Marinucci, D. & Picard, D. (2009). Asymptotics for spherical needlets, *Ann. of Stat.* **37**(3): 1150–1171.

Bogdanova, I. (2005). *Wavelets on non-Euclidean manifolds*, PhD thesis, EPFL, Lausanne, Switzerland.

Bogdanova, I., Bresson, X., Thiran, J.-P. & Vandergheynst, P. (2007). "Scale space analysis and active contours for omnidirectional images", *IEEE Trans. Image Process.* **16**(7): 1888–1901.

Bogdanova, I., Vandergheynst, P., Antoine, J.-P., Jacques, L. & Morvidone, M. (2005). "Stereographic wavelet frames on the sphere", *Appl. Comput. Harmon. Anal.* **26**: 223–252.

Bogdanova, I., Vandergheynst, P. & Gazeau, J.-P. (2007). "Continuous wavelet transform on the hyperboloid", *Applied Comput. Harmon. Anal.* **23**(7): 286–306.

Dahlke, S., Dahmen, W., Schmidt, E. & Weinreich, I. (1995). "Multiresolution analysis and wavelets on S^2 and S^3", *Numer. Funct. Anal. Optim.* **16**: 19–41.

Daubechies, I. (1992). *Ten Lectures on Wavelets*, SIAM, Philadelphia.

Driscoll, J. R. & Healy, D. M. (1994). "Computing Fourier transforms and convolutions on the 2-sphere", *Adv. Appl. Math.* **15**: 202–250.

Freeden, W. & Schreiner, M. (1997). "Orthogonal and non-orthogonal multiresolution analysis, scale discrete and exact fully discrete wavelet transform on the sphere", *Constr. Approx.* **14**: 493–515.

Freeden, W. & Windheuser, U. (1997). "Combined spherical harmonic and wavelet expansion — A future concept in Earth's gravitational determination", *Appl. Comput. Harmon. Anal.* **4**: 1–37.

Geyer, C. & Daniilidis, K. (2001). "Catadioptric projective geometry", *Int. J. Computer Vision* **45**(3): 223–243.

Holschneider, M. (1996). "Continuous wavelet transforms on the sphere", *J. Math. Phys.* **37**: 4156–4165.

Jacques, L. (2004). *"Ondelettes, repères et couronne solaire"*, PhD thesis, Université catholique de Louvain, Louvain-la-Neuve, Belgium.

Marinucci, D., Pietrobon, D., Baldi, A., Baldi, P., Cabella, P., Kerkyacharian, G., Natoli, P., Picard, D. & Vittorio, N. (2008). "spherical needlets for CMB data analysis", *Mon. Not. R. Astron. Soc.* **383**: 539–545.

Narcowich, F. J., Petrushev, P. & Ward, J. D. (2006a). "Decomposition of Besov and Triebel-Lizorkin spaces on the sphere", *J. Funct Anal.* **238**: 530–564.

Narcowich, F. J., Petrushev, P. & Ward, J. D. (2006b). "Localized tight frames on spheres", *SIAM J. Math. Anal.* **38**: 574–594.

Pietrobon, D., Baldi, P. & Marinucci, D. (2006). "Integrated Sachs-Wolfe effect from the cross correlation of WMAP3 year and the NRAO VLA sky survey data: New results and constraints on dark energy", *Phys. Rev. D* **74**: 043524.

Potts, D., Steidl, G. & Tasche, M. (1996). "Kernels of spherical harmonics and spherical frames", *in* F. Fontanella, K. Jetter & P. Laurent (eds), *Advanced Topics in Multivariate Approximation*, World Scientific, Singapore, pp. 287–301.

Roşca, D. (2005). "Locally supported rational spline wavelets on the sphere", *Math. Comput.* **74**(252): 1803–1829.

Roşca, D. (2006). "Piecewise constant wavelets defined on closed surfaces", *J. Comput. Anal. Appl.* **8**(2): 121–132.

Roşca, D. (2007a). "Wavelet bases on the sphere obtained by radial projection", *J. Fourier Anal. Appl.* **13**(4): 421–434.

Roşca, D. (2007b). Weighted Haar wavelets on the sphere, *Int. J. Wavelets, Multires. and Inform. Proc.* **5**(3): 501–511.

Roşca, D. (2009). "On a norm equivalence on $L^2(S^2)$", *Results Math.* . (53(3-4):399-405).

Roşca, D. & Antoine, J.-P. (2008). "Constructing orthogonal wavelet bases on the sphere", *in* J.-P. Thiran (ed.), *Proc. 16th European Signal Processing Conference (EUSIPCO2008)*, EPFL, Lausanne, Switzerland. Paper # 1569102372.

Roşca, D. & Antoine, J.-P. (2009). "Locally supported orthogonal wavelet bases on the sphere via stereographic projection". Math. Probl. Eng vol. 2009, art ID 124904 (14 pages).

Weinreich, I. (2001). "A construction of C^1-wavelets on the two-dimensional sphere", *Applied Comput. Harmon. Anal.* **10**: 1–26.

Wiaux, Y., Jacques, L. & Vandergheynst, P. (2005). "Correspondence principle between spherical and Euclidean wavelets", *Astrophys. J.* **632**: 15–28.

Wiaux, Y., McEwen, J. D., Vandergheynst, P. & Blanc, O. (2008). "Exact reconstruction with directional wavelets on the sphere", *Mon. Not. R. Astron. Soc.* **388**: 770.

5

MIMO Channel Modelling

Faisal Darbari, Robert W. Stewart and Ian A. Glover
University of Strathclyde, Glasgow
United Kingdom

1. Introduction

Multiple antenna communications technologies offer significant advantages over single antenna systems. These advantages include extended range, improved reliability in fading environments and higher data throughputs. If multiple antennas are provided only at the transmitting end of a link then the system is referred to as multiple input single output (MISO). If multiple antennas are provided only at the receiving end of a link then the system is referred to as single input multiple output (SIMO). If multiple antennas are provided at both ends of a link then the system is referred to as multiple input multiple output (MIMO).

Multiple antenna systems can be divided into two classes depending on the signal processing employed. These are: (i) smart antennas and (ii) spatial multiplexors.

Smart antennas provide increased signal-to-noise-and-interference ratio (SNIR) via diversity gain, array gain and/or interference suppression. Each transmit antenna radiates, to within a simple gain and delay difference, the same signal. Similarly, each receive antenna contributes its signal to a gain and delay weighted sum. By setting transmit and receive gains and delays appropriately, improved SNIR is achieved which may be used to realise greater spectral efficiency (and, therefore, greater channel capacity), greater range and/or decreased latency (due to a reduced requirement for channel coding).

Spatial multiplexors can provide increased channel capacity directly. Each transmit antenna radiates an independent signal sub-stream. With N transmit and N receive antennas, for example, an N-fold increase in data-rate is possible (in principle) over that achievable with a single input single output (SISO) antenna system (without any increase in total transmitted power).

In this chapter a theoretical framework for describing MIMO channels is presented followed by a brief outline of MIMO channel modelling principles [P. Almer et. al., 2007]. The rest of the chapter describes a selection of widely adopted MIMO channel models, their capabilities and limitations, in the context of specific standards.

2. MIMO channel framework

Wireless channels are linear. They may, therefore, be represented by a linear filter and described by their impulse response. If the transmit and receive antennas, and the scattering objects in the environment, are static then the channel will be time-invariant and the impulse response, $h(\tau)$, will be a function of delay, τ, only. If the transmit antenna, receive antenna or scattering objects move then the channel will be time-variant and the impulse response, $h(t, \tau)$, will be a function of time, t.

From a communication systems point of view $h(t, \tau)$ is an entirely adequate channel description, i.e. it represents sufficient information to predict the (noiseless) received signal from the transmitted signal. It has the limitation, however, of obscuring the underlying propagation physics. If $h(t, \tau)$ is to be predicted from full or partial knowledge of the physical environment, then models linking it to the most important aspect of the environment, i.e. the spatial distribution of scattering objects, is required. The double-directional impulse response is a channel description that makes explicit this connection between the systems-level impulse response and propagation physics.

2.1 Double-directional impulse response

The impulse response of the wireless transmission channel describes the cascaded effect of transmit antenna, propagation channel and receive antenna. Changing an antenna, therefore, may change the impulse response, even though the propagation channel (i.e. the physical arrangement of scatterers) may remain the same. The effects on $h(t, \tau)$ of the antennas and propagation environment can be decoupled using a description of the channel called the double-directional impulse response [M. Steinbauer et. al., 2001], i.e.:

$$h(t,\tau) = \int_{4\pi}\int_{4\pi} g_T(\boldsymbol{\varphi}_T)p(t,\tau,\boldsymbol{\varphi}_R,\boldsymbol{\varphi}_T)g_R(\boldsymbol{\varphi}_R)d\boldsymbol{\varphi}_T d\boldsymbol{\varphi}_R \tag{1}$$

where the integrand is the component of impulse response represented by power leaving the transmit antenna with (vector) direction $\boldsymbol{\varphi}_T$ (or, more strictly speaking, within the element of solid angle, $d\boldsymbol{\varphi}_T$, centred on $\boldsymbol{\varphi}_T$) and arriving at the receive antenna with (vector) direction $\boldsymbol{\varphi}_R$. $g_R(\boldsymbol{\varphi}_R)$ and $g_T(\boldsymbol{\varphi}_T)$ are the complex (field-strength or voltage) gains of the receive and transmit antennas, respectively, in the directions $\boldsymbol{\varphi}_R$ and $\boldsymbol{\varphi}_T$. (The magnitude of the voltage gain is the square root of the conventional antenna (power) gain and is proportional to an antenna's effective length - the square root of its effective area - via the antenna reciprocity formula.) For isotropic antennas $g_R(\boldsymbol{\varphi}_R) = g_T(\boldsymbol{\varphi}_T) = 1$. $p(t, \tau, \boldsymbol{\varphi}_R, \boldsymbol{\varphi}_T)$ is the component of impulse response assuming isotropic antennas. It incorporates all propagation related losses including free-space path loss, absorption and scattering loss. The integral in Eq. (1) sums over all possible directions-of-departure (DODs) at the transmitter and all possible directions-of-arrival (DOAs) at the receiver.

If propagation is via K discrete paths then Eq. (1) can be written as a summation over K multipath components (MPCs), i.e.:

$$h(t,\tau) = \sum_{i=1}^{K} g_T(\varphi_{T_i}) p(t,\tau,\varphi_{R_i},\varphi_{T_i}) g_T(\varphi_{T_i}) \tag{2}$$

Recognising that the channel characteristics are a function of transmit and receive antenna locations, denoted by the position vectors $\mathbf{r}_T$ and $\mathbf{r}_R$, respectively then the double-directional impulse response may be more fully expressed using $p(\mathbf{r}_T, \mathbf{r}_R, t, \tau, \varphi_R, \varphi_T)$, i.e.:

$$h(\mathbf{r}_T,\mathbf{r}_R,t,\tau) = \sum_{i=1}^{K} g_T(\varphi_{T_i}) p(\mathbf{r}_T,\mathbf{r}_R,t,\tau,\varphi_{R_i},\varphi_{T_i}) g_T(\varphi_{T_i}) \tag{3}$$

The description above relates to singly-polarised antennas. A more complete channel description can be devised by introducing a matrix of impulse responses defining the coupling between, for example, the vertically- and horizontally-polarised ports of a dual-polarised transmit antenna and the vertically- and horizontally-polarised ports of a dual-polarised receive antenna, i.e.:

$$\mathbf{h}(t,\tau) = \begin{bmatrix} h_{vv}(t,\tau) & h_{vh}(t,\tau) \\ h_{hv}(t,\tau) & h_{hh}(t,\tau) \end{bmatrix} \tag{4}$$

The leading diagonal (co-polar) elements of Eq. (4) describe coupling between the vertically polarised port of the transmit antenna and the vertically polarised port of the receive antenna (h_{vv}), and the horizontally polarised port of the transmit antenna and the horizontally polarised port of the receive antenna (h_{hh}). The off diagonal (cross-polar) elements describe coupling between the horizontally polarised port of the transmit antenna and the vertically polarised port of the receive antenna (h_{vh}), and the vertically polarised port of the transmit antenna and the horizontally polarised port of the receive antenna (h_{hv}). In principle, the ports could have any pair of orthogonal polarisations. In practice, however, they are almost always perpendicular linear polarisations (typically vertical and horizontal for terrestrial links) or counter-rotating (right-handed and left-handed) circular polarisations.

Eq. (4) is a systems description. To express the cross-polarising effects of the antenna and propagation medium separately a cascade of three polarisation matrices (one each for transmit antenna, medium and receive antenna) is required for each propagation path. The system matrix for a discrete set of propagation paths is then given by:

$$\begin{bmatrix} h_{vv}(t,\tau) & h_{vh}(t,\tau) \\ h_{hv}(t,\tau) & h_{hh}(t,\tau) \end{bmatrix} = \sum_{i=1}^{K} \left\{ \begin{array}{l} \begin{bmatrix} g_{R,vv_i}(\varphi_R) & g_{R,vh_i}(\varphi_R) \\ g_{R,hv_i}(\varphi_R) & g_{R,hh_i}(\varphi_R) \end{bmatrix} \\ \times \begin{bmatrix} p_{vv_i}(t,\tau,\varphi_R,\varphi_T) & p_{vh_i}(t,\tau,\varphi_R,\varphi_T) \\ p_{hv_i}(t,\tau,\varphi_R,\varphi_T) & p_{hh_i}(t,\tau,\varphi_R,\varphi_T) \end{bmatrix} \\ \times \begin{bmatrix} g_{T,vv_i}(\varphi_T) & g_{T,vh_i}(\varphi_T) \\ g_{T,hv_i}(\varphi_T) & g_{T,hh_i}(\varphi_T) \end{bmatrix} \end{array} \right\} \qquad (5)$$

The use of vertical and horizontal basis polarisations (or, more generally, any pair of perpendicular linear polarisations) in Eq. (5) is problematic. A simple cartesian definition of a pair of basis polarisations (definition 1, Fig. 1) is adequate only for the single propagation path described by $\varphi_R = \varphi_T = 0$. For propagation paths with non-zero DODs and DOAs some other pair of basis polarisations must be adopted [A. C. Ludwig., 1973]. The polarisations of a pair of dipoles (one electric, one magnetic) can be used - definition 2, Fig. 1 - as can the polarisations of a pair of perpendicular Huygens' sources - definition 3, Fig. 1. (A Huygens' source is the elementary radiating source of an electromagnetic wave referred to in Huygens ' Principle which states that each point on a propagating wave-front acts as a secondary source of radiation.)

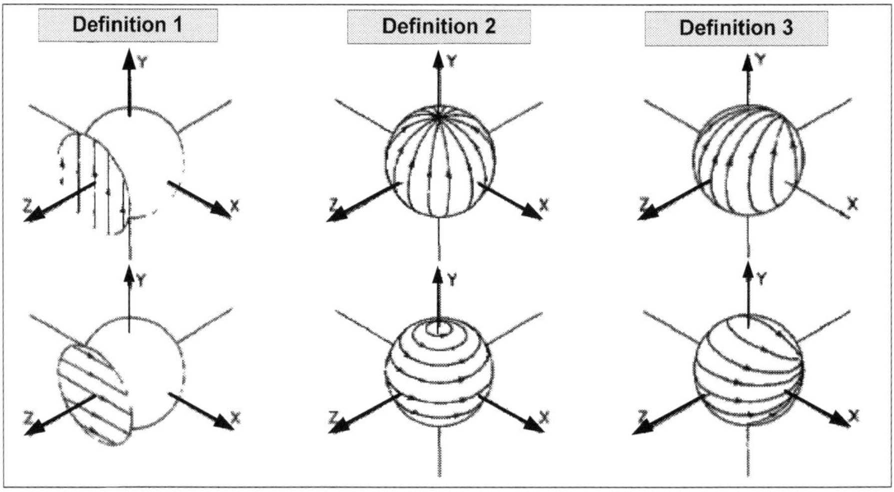

Fig. 1. Ludwig's three definitions of orthogonal basis polarisations (After [A. C. Ludwig, 1973]. (© 1973 IEEE))

Definitions 2 and 3 allow a pair of perpendicular polarisations to be defined for directions other than $\varphi_R = \varphi_T = 0$ whilst preserving the requirement for transverse electromagnetic fields. They still suffer from limitations, however, since definition 2 does not define polarisation in the ±Y direction and definition 3 does not define polarisation in the –Z direction. (This is reflected physically by the fact that a dipole does not radiate along its axis - it has a toroidal radiation pattern - and a Huygens source does not radiate in the backward propagating direction - its radiation pattern is a cardioid of revolution.)

For radio links with columnated-beam antennas, and DODs and DOAs closely clustered about transmit and receive antenna boresights, the most appropriate choice of basis polarisations is probably definition 3. (As the spread DODs and DOAs about boresight tends to zero then all three definitions converge.) For links with omnidirectional antennas, and DODs and/or DOAs widely spread in azimuth (but not too widely spread in elevation), then definition 2 is probably more appropriate.

2.2 The MIMO channel impulse response

Fig. 2 shows a schematic diagram of a MIMO channel.

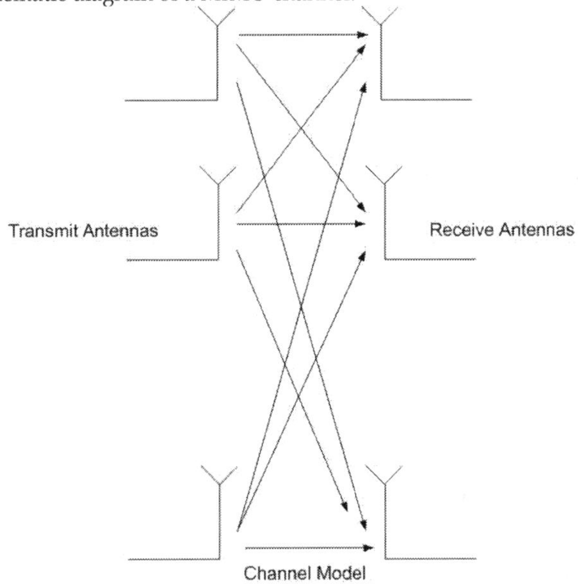

Fig. 2. MIMO channel

The MIMO channel must be described for all transmit and receive antenna pairs. For M transmit antennas and N receive antennas the MIMO transmission channel can be represented by an $N \times M$ channel matrix, i.e.:

$$\mathbf{h}(t,\tau) = \begin{bmatrix} h_{11}(t,\tau) & h_{12}(t,\tau) & . \; . \; . & h_{1M}(t,\tau) \\ h_{21}(t,\tau) & h_{22}(t,\tau) & . \; . \; . & h_{2M}(t,\tau) \\ . & . & . \; . \; . & . \quad .. \\ . & . & . \; . \; . & . \\ . & . & . \; . \; . & . \\ h_{N1}(t,\tau) & h_{N2}(t,\tau) & . \; . \; . & h_{NM}(t,\tau) \end{bmatrix} \tag{6}$$

where $h_{nm}(t, \tau)$ represents the time-variant impulse response between the input of the mth transmit antenna and the output of the nth receive antenna. Each impulse response is the cascaded effect of transmit antenna, the propagation medium and a receive antenna. This is therefore a system-level representation. If polarisation diversity is employed then each element of the matrix must be replaced by the polarisation matrix of Eq. (4). This is equivalent to doubling the number of antennas at each end of the link; a dual-polarised antenna being treated, effectively, as two singly-polarised antennas. Any time variation, due to shadowing and/or multipath fading, arises from antenna motion or the motion of environmental scatterers. The spatial, polarisation and temporal correlations between the signals at the terminals of different receiving antennas are reflected in the correlation properties of the matrix elements.

MIMO channel models may be physical or analytical. Physical models are based either on a physical theory (often geometrical optics) or on physical measurements. They are site-specific or specific to an environment type (e.g. urban suburban, rural) and are particularly useful in network planning. Analytical models are based on mathematical assumptions about channel behaviour. They are generally site-independent and are mostly used for system design, comparison and testing.

Physical models can be subdivided into deterministic and stochastic variants. Deterministic models are environment specific and are derived from the underlying physical radio propagation processes, e.g. reflection, diffraction, shadowing and wave-guiding. The most important example is ray tracing. Stochastic (physical) models are more generic than deterministic models. They are based on the fact that whilst, in the absence of a detailed environment database, the precise physical propagation parameters (e.g. DOD, DOA, number of paths, path delay, path power) are unpredictable, they nevertheless have well-defined statistical behaviours. Probability models can therefore be constructed for these propagation parameters. They are generally more computationally efficient than deterministic models. The Spatial Channel Model (SCM) and the Spatial Channel Model - Extended (SCME) described in sections 4.1.1 and 4.1.2 are stochastic physical models.

Analytical channel models derive the MIMO channel matrix without any consideration of propagation parameters. Examples include Independent Identically Distributed (i.i.d.), Weichselberger and Kronecker models. The WiMAX and IEEE 802.11n channel models described in sections 4.2 and 4.3 are Kronecker models. Since MIMO channel matrices are easily generated using analytical models, and since the statistics of these matrices are both unvarying (repeatable) and environment independent, they are popular for the development, verification and optimisation of system hardware and software (especially signal processing algorithms).

3. Link-level and system-level simulations

Most standardised MIMO channel models provide link-level and system-level simulation. The former refers to a single point-to-point link (but including, of course, multiple transmit and receive antennas). The latter refers to multiple communication links, potentially including multiple base-stations (BSs). In the case of an SCM channel, for example, a calibration process is undertaken at the link-level prior to a system-level simulation.

The SCM and SCME system-level model defines a 'drop' concept where a mobile is placed (dropped) in a sequence of different network locations. The locations may be random or pre-defined by the user. Each drop represents a snapshot of the fading channel. The statistics of the channel parameters within a single drop are assumed to be stationary and, for the duration of the drop all large scale parameters (DOA, DOD, mobile station velocity etc.) are assumed to be constant. The drop concept is illustrated in Fig. 3.

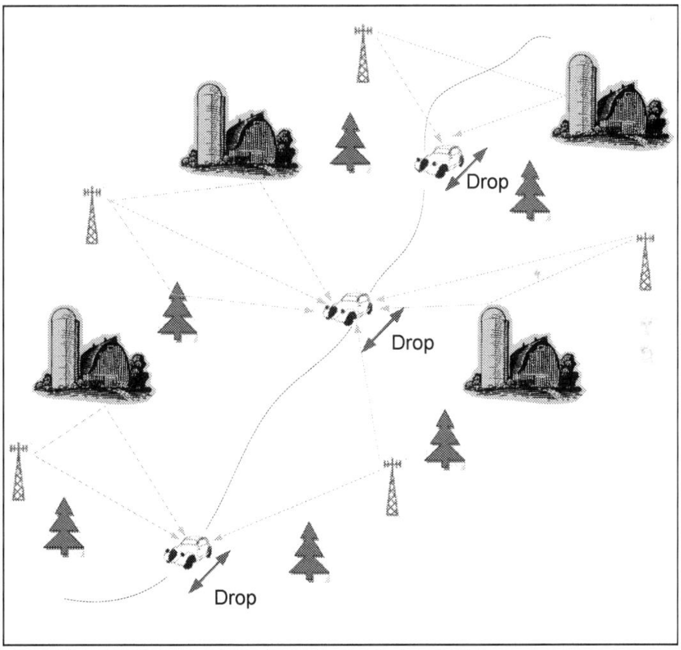

Fig. 3. Quasi-stationary drop periods in a channel simulation

A variation of the drop-based simulation allows the large-scale channel parameters to evolve (change gradually and continuously) at each simulation step inside a drop. This approach is more realistic than the stationary assumption but represents an increase in complexity and results in increased simulation time.

If motion of the mobile station (MS) and scatterers is assumed to be negligible during the course of a packet transmission the channel is said to be quasi-static. Such a channel has a decorrelation time, T_c, which is greater than the packet duration. If T_c is defined as the time shift resulting in a correlation coefficient of 0.5 then it may be related (approximately) to the maximum Doppler shift, f_m (speed/wavelength) [T. S. Rappaport., 2002], by:

$$T_c \approx \frac{9}{16\pi f_m} \tag{7}$$

For a carrier frequency of 2 GHz and a terminal speed of 3 km/h the maximum Doppler shift would be 5.6 Hz and the channel decorrelation time would be 32 ms. The assumption that the channel is quasi-static could then be justified providing the transmitted packet duration is less than this.

4. Channel model standards

Specific standardised channel models have been developed for the testing and optimisation of particular wireless standards in a manner that is repeatable and widely agreed. These wireless channel models are important for the development of new wireless devices. Examples of standardised channel models include COST 207, SCM and SCME. These are wideband power delay profile (PDP) models used in the development of GSM, WCDMA and LTE systems, respectively. Standardised channel models provide a framework to test algorithms and investigate design trade-offs thereby informing key design decisions relating to modulation, coding and multiple-accessing etc.

A selection of standardised channel models for mobile, broadband wireless access (BWA) and wireless local area network (WLAN) applications is given below:

Channel Model	Origin	Application
SCM	3GPP/3GPP2	3G Outdoor
SCME	WINNER	3G Outdoor
WIN II	WINNER II	3G Outdoor
SUI	Stanford University	Fixed BWA
WiMAX- ITU-TDL	WiMAX form	Fixed/Mobile BWA
IEEE 802.11n	IEEE 802.11n TGn (High throughput task group)	Indoor Channel

4.1 WINNER

The European WINNER (wireless world initiative new radio) project began in 2004 with the aim to develop a new radio concept for beyond third generation (B3G) wireless systems. Work Package 5 (WP5) of the WINNER projects focused on multi-dimensional channel modelling for carrier frequencies between 2 and 6 GHz and bandwidths up to 100 MHz. In total six organisations were formally involved in WP5 (Elektrobit, Helsinki University of Technology, Nokia, Royal Institute of Technology (KTH), the Swiss Federal Institute of Technology (ETH) and the Technical University of Ilmenau.

At the start of the project there was no widely accepted channel model suitable for WINNER system modelling. Two existing channel models, 3GPP/3GPP2 Spatial Channel Model (SCM), were selected as starting points for outdoor simulation and one existing channel model (IEEE 802.11 TGn Model [3GPP TR25.996 V6.1.0, 2003-09]) was selected as a starting point for indoor simulation. The SCM had insufficient bandwidth and too few scenarios. In 2005 the first extension of SCM, SCM Extended (SCME), was therefore proposed. Despite the modifications to SCM, SCME was deemed inadequate for the simulation of B3G systems.

At the end of 2005 the WINNER channel model - Phase 1 (WIM1) was described in the deliverable D5.4 [WINNER, 2005]. WIM1 has a unified structure for indoor and outdoor environments and is based on double-directional measurement campaigns carried out in the 5 GHz ISM2 band with bandwidths of up to 120 MHz. It covers six different propagation scenarios, i.e.(i) indoor small office, (ii) indoor hall, (iii) urban microcell, (iv) urban macrocell, (v) suburban macrocell, and (vi) rural . Both line-of-sight (LOS) and non-line-of-sight (NLOS) propagation conditions are catered for [H. El-Sallabi et. al., 2006].

In September 2007, the WINNER channel model - Phase II (WIM2) was described [WINNER II interim, 2006]. This model, which evolved from WIM1 and the WINNER II interim channel models, extended the propagation scenarios to: (i) indoor office, (ii) large indoor hall, (iii) indoor-to-outdoor, (iv) urban microcell, (v) bad urban microcell, (vi) outdoor-to-indoor, (vii) stationary feeder, (viii) suburban macrocell, (ix) urban macrocell, (x) rural macrocell, and (xi) rural moving networks. In the course of the WINNER project channel models were implemented in MATLAB and made available through the official web site [WINNER II, 2007].

4.1.1 Spatial Channel Model (SCM)

SCM was developed by 3GPP/3GPP2 (third generation partnership project) for outdoor environments at a carrier frequency of 2 GHz. It was designed to test 5 MHz CDMA channels [P.Almer et. al., 2007] and consists of two parts: (i) a link level simulation model and (ii) a system-level simulation model. The SCM system level model is currently used as a de-facto standard for LTE, WCDMA, UMTS and WiMAX system level evaluation and performance verification.

4.1.1.1 Link-level model

The link-level model which might also be referred to as a reference model is a single link channel model. It provides a well-defined, convenient, interface for different equipment manufacturers to compare their proprietary implementations of the same signal processing algorithms. Link-level simulations alone are not recommended for performance testing of different algorithm because they reflect only a single snapshot of the (dynamic) channel. Link-level simulations do not, therefore, allow conclusions to be made about the general behaviour of a system and if such conclusions are required system-level simulations must be performed.

The link-level SCM can be implemented as either a stochastic physical or analytical model. In the former the wideband characteristics of the channel are modelled as a tapped delay line (TDL). Each tap is independently faded and is characterised by an azimuth DOD/DOA angular spectrum described by a uniform distribution (for MSs) or a Laplacian distribution (for BSs). The mean direction and angular spread at BS and MS are fixed (and thus represent stationary channel conditions). The Doppler spectrum is calculated based on the MS velocity (speed and direction relative to the line connecting MS and BS). The model also defines the number and configuration of antennas at MS and BS. Given all these parameters the physical model can be transformed to an analytical model [P.Almer et. al., 2007].

4.1.1.2 System-level model

The system-level model is a multi-link physical model intended for performance evaluation in which each link represents a cell or a sector within a cell. Fig. 4 illustrates a system-level simulation in which an MS receives interference from adjacent sectors of adjacent cells.

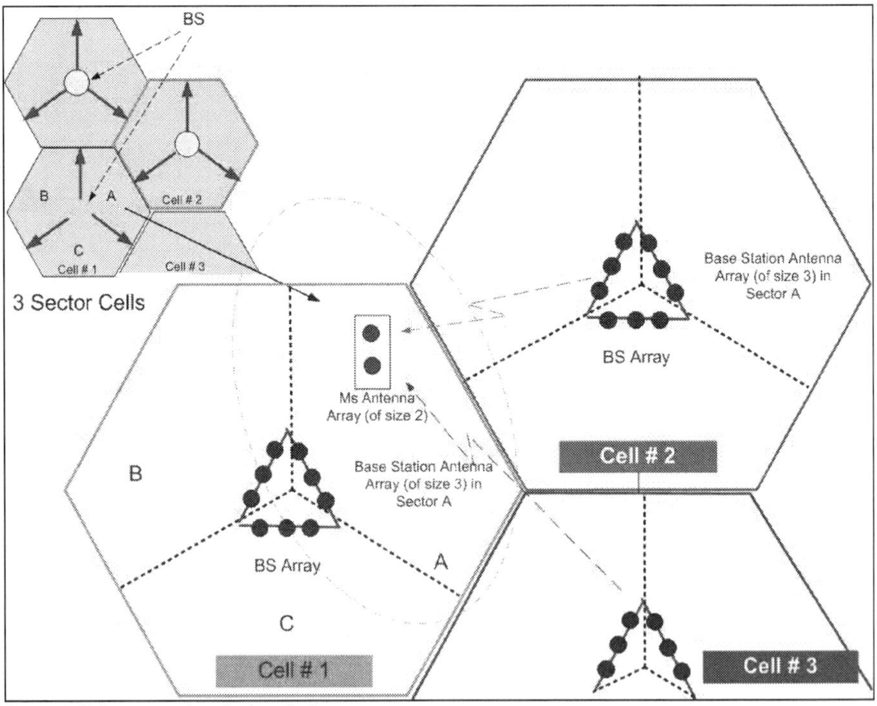

Fig. 4. SCM system level simulation.

Each link comprises an MS and BS MIMO antenna array. Propagation is via multipaths and sub-paths. The excess delays of sub-paths are closely clustered around the delay of their (parent) multipath. This is assumed to originate from an environment with closely spaced clusters of scatterers. Fig. 5 illustrates the clustered scatterers and resulting multipaths and sub-paths.

The SCM distinguishes between three different environments, i.e. (i) urban macrocell, (ii) suburban macrocell and (iii) urban microcell. The modelling and simulation methodology are identical for all three environments but the parameters (e.g. azimuth spread, delay-spread, shadow fading and path loss) are different [P. Almer et. al., 2007].

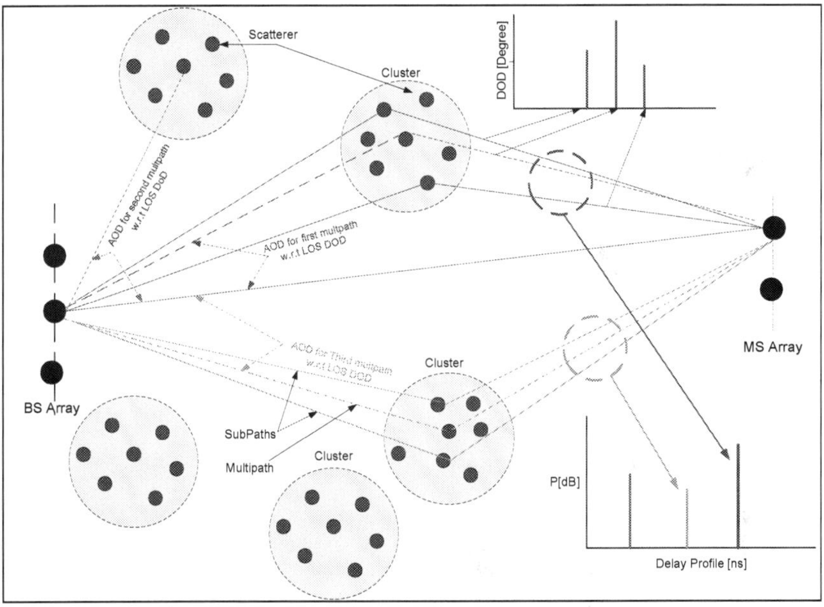

Fig. 5. Clustered scatterers, multipaths and sub-paths in an SCM simulation.

4.1.1.3 Software implementation of SCM

The modelling approach can be divided in to three parts: (i) antenna correlation (ii) spatial correlation and (iii) polarisation correlation. This is illustrated schematically in Fig. 6 which represents the impulse response of the nth multipath component.

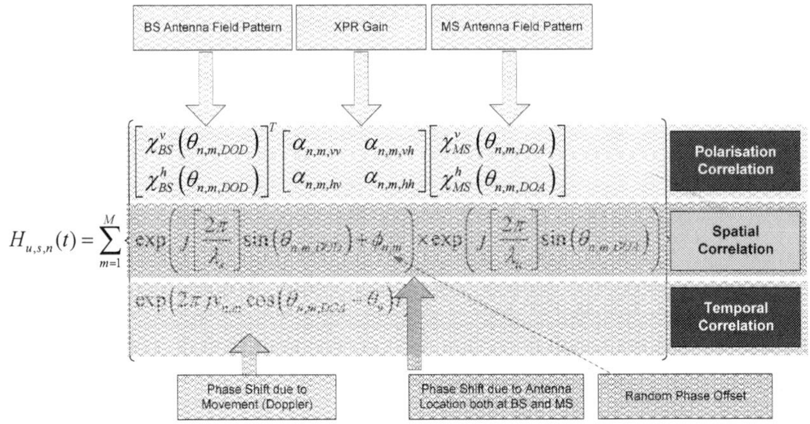

Fig. 6. Tap n complex gain for SCM

Where $H_{u,s,n}(t)$ is the complex gain of the nth tap (corresponding to the nth MPC) between the sth element of a linear BS array and the uth element a linear MS array. $x^{v}{}_{BS}(\theta_{n,m,DOD})$ and $x^{h}{}_{BS}(\theta_{n,m,DOD})$ are, respectively, the BS antenna complex field patters for vertically and horizontally polarised fields. Matrix $\alpha_{n,m}$ represents cross-polarised coupling between vertically and horizontally polarised components. $x^{v}{}_{MS}(\theta_{n,m,DOA})$ and $x^{h}{}_{MS}(\theta_{n,m,DOA})$ are, respectively, the MS antenna complex field patterns for vertically and horizontally polarised fields. (Note that the DOD and DOA are each defined by a single angle. This reflects the assumption that there is spreading in azimuth only. Whilst energy is unlikely to be completely constrained to a single azimuthal (horizontal) plane in reality the spread of energy in elevation (out of the horizontal plane) is likely to be relatively modest. The spatial correlation is a function of separation between BS and MS antenna array elements and their respective DODs and DOAs. A random phase offset $\varphi_{n,m}$ (uniformly distributed between 0 and 360°) is added to ensure a random starting point for fast fading. Temporal correlation is a function of the magnitude and direction of MS motion. Fig. 7 shows a pseudo-code flow diagram for the model. The simulation steps implied by Fig. 7 are:

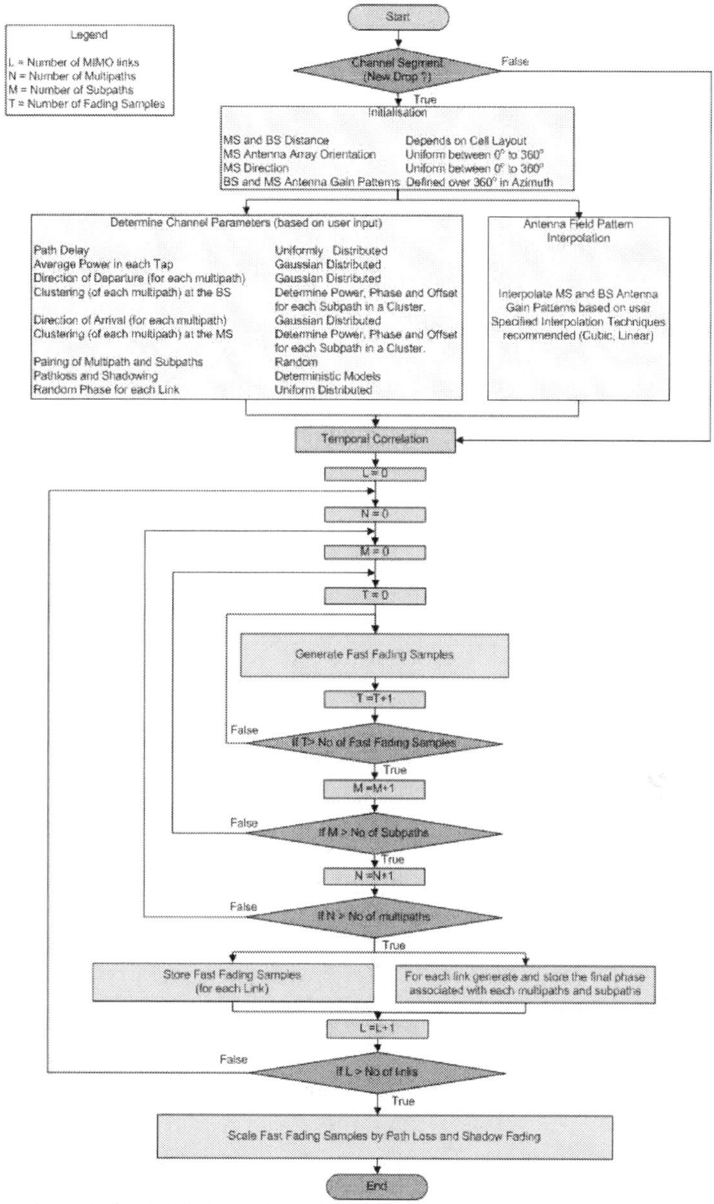

Fig. 7. Pseudo-code for SCM channel model

1. For a given drop the multiple MSs are placed at random locations within a sector/cell. The MS (linear array) antenna orientation and the MS direction of motion are selected at random.
2. Path-loss is calculated based on the separation between MS and BS. The path-loss model used is the COST 231 (Hata) model for macrocells and the COST 231 (Walfish-Ikegami) model for microcells. The number of multipath components is fixed in all three cases at six and their delay and average power are chosen randomly using appropriate probability distributions.
3. Angular dispersion at the MS and BS is incorporated by assuming each multipath component comprises a cluster of 20 sub-paths having the same delay but (randomly modelled) different DOD and DOA [3GPP TR.996 V6.1.0 (2003 09)]. The overall mean DOD and DOA is determined by the relative locations of BS and MS and the orientation of their antenna arrays. The mean DOD or DOA for each tap is chosen at random from a Gaussian distribution that is centred on the overall mean. (DOA and DOD variances are model parameters.) . The sub-paths have deterministic amplitude and random phase. Their sum is therefore subject to Rayleigh or Ricean fading.
4. Temporal fading may be generated either by using a sum of sinusoids or by applying white Gaussian noise to a Doppler filter.
5. Temporal variation of the impulse response is determined by the speed and direction of the MS. The different Doppler shift for each sub-path leads to a different phase for each sub-path. The phase for each sub-path at the end of each call within a single simulation drop is stored in order to ensure continuity, Fig. 8.

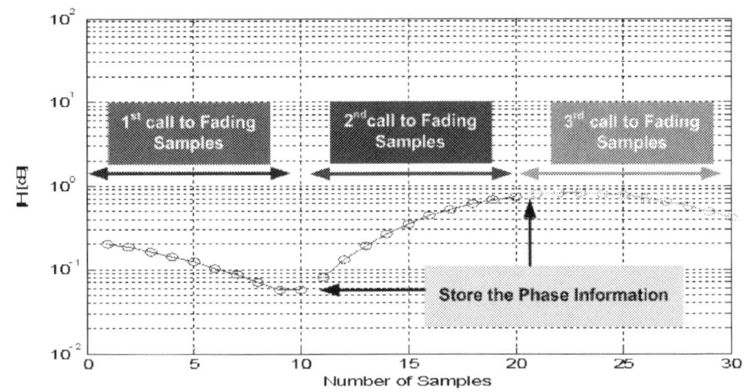

Fig. 8. Fast fading samples for one tap corresponding to successive calls of the same channel drop.

5. For system level simulations (which consider multiple MSs and BSs in different cells/sectors) a sequence of drops is executed. All parameters are independent of those in prior or succeeding drops. The drop period is assumed to be sufficiently short for large-scale channel parameters (e.g. angle spread, mean DOD/DOA, delay-spread and shadowing) to be constant during the drop. The MS position is determined at random during the start of each drop.

4.1.1.4 Model features

1. Each drop reflects a snapshot of the fading channel.
2. The COST 231 Urban Hata (macrocell) and COST 231 Walfish-Ikegami (microcell) path-loss models are adjusted for a frequency of 1.9 GHz. The applicability to a frequency other than 1.9 GHz is not analysed [M. Narandzic., 2007].
3. The model provides a bandwidth of 5 MHz which is not adequate for the most recent wireless standards (e.g. LTE which requires bandwidth of 20 MHz).
4. During a drop the channel undergoes fast fading due to MS movement. Delays, DOD and DOA, however, are kept constant. Any two consecutive drops are independent and are based on randomly located clusters. This makes the channel model discontinuous across drops.
5. Six clusters of scatterers are considered. Each cluster corresponds to a resolvable MPC (referred to as a multipath). Within a resolvable path (cluster), there are 20 irresolvable sub-paths. Each of the multipaths is modelled as a Dirac (delta) function of delay. Each multipath is subject to angular dispersion across its 20 sub-paths. The summing of the sub-path carriers results in Rayleigh fading of each multipath [D.S. Baum., 2005].
6. The correlation of the standard deviation (in dB) of lognormal fading due to shadowing (between the links from a single MS to multiple BSs) is 0.5. The correlation is independent of the range of BSs or their relative angular locations as seen from the MS. Shadowing and its correlation between multiple MS-BS paths are therefore assumed independent of network topology and topography [3GPP TR25.996 V6.1.0, 2003-09].
7. Elevation spread is not considered.
8. Antenna radiation pattern, array geometry and array orientation are arbitrary. When all propagation and antenna parameters are defined an analytic formulation can be extracted from the physical model. Each drop results in a different instance of the correlation matrix.
9. Most model parameters are described by their PDFs. While this provides a rich source of variability, it has the disadvantage that simulation time grows exponentially with the number of random parameters.
10. As a consequence of the assumption that each multipath is flat-faded, the model's utility for bandwidths above 5 MHz is questionable. (This motivates the extended, SCME, version of SCM.)
11. Uplink and downlink reciprocity is assumed, i.e. DOD and DOA values are identical for both uplink and downlink simulation of the channel.
12. The uplink and downlink sub-path (random) phases are uncorrelated for frequency division duplex (FDD) systems but correlated for TDD systems. .

4.1.2 Extended Spatial Channel Model (SCME)

SCME is an extension of SCM. The extension is not associated with the 3GPP working group but was developed in WP5 of the WINNER project. SCME extends the channel bandwidth of SCM from 5 MHz to 20 MHz. It was adopted as the channel standard for the development and testing of the 3GPP Long Term Evolution (LTE) standard. The channel bandwidth was subsequently further extended to 100 MHz. (The required bandwidth of B3G systems is up to 100 MHz in both 2 GHz and 5 GHz bands.) A limitation of SCM is the drop-based approach with the consequence that there is no short-term variability in the channel transfer function. This corresponds to fixed DOAs as seen by a moving MS. SCM also has a limited range of scenarios (it does not include, for example, outdoor-to-indoor paths) and, in some scenarios, does not incorporate *K*-factor to support LOS paths.

SCME uses the intra-cluster delay-spread to effect bandwidth extension. Since backward compatibility with SCM was required the number of clusters (i.e. multipaths) is not increased from six. Each cluster of 20 sub-paths (which in SCM have identical delay) is subdivided into 3 or 4 sub-clusters (for macrocell and microcell scenarios respectively) called mid-paths with different delays, Fig. 9.

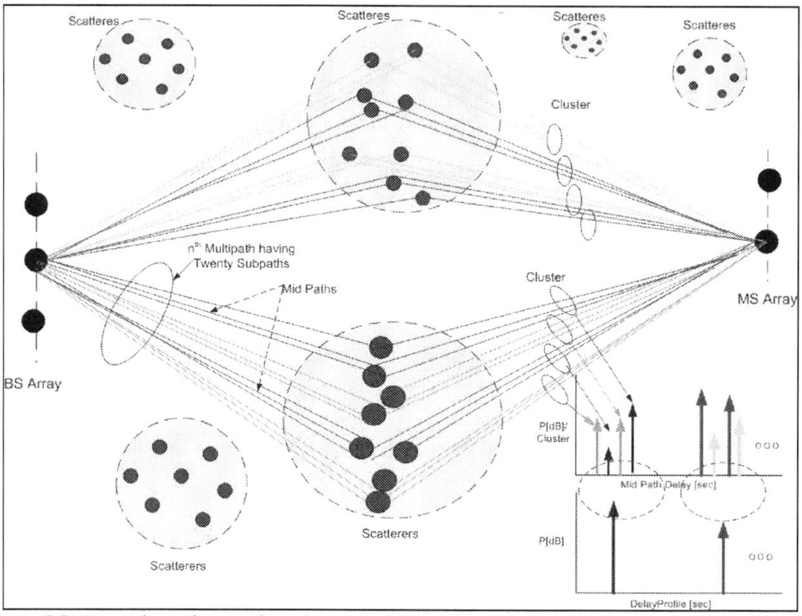

Fig. 9. SCME multipaths, mid-paths and clusters

(The total number of sub-paths for SCME, however, remains the same as for SCM, i.e. 20.) Bandwidth extension is realised by introducing delay (and power) difference between the mid-paths The number of delay taps is therefore increased from 6 in SCM to 18 or 24 in SCME (depending on the scenario [Spirent Communications, 2008]). The 20 sub-paths are split into groups of 10, 6, and 4 (for scenarios with three mid-paths) or groups of 6, 6, 4 and 4 (for scenarios with four mid-paths). The relative power of each mid-path is scaled by this ratio as shown in Fig. 10.

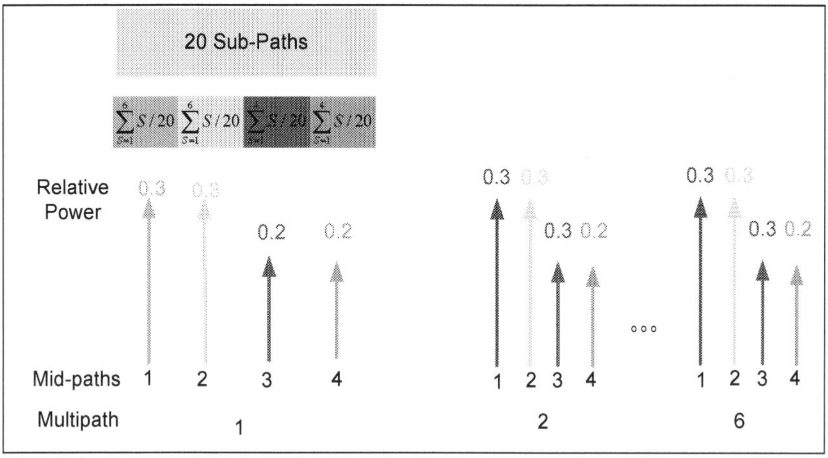

Fig. 10. Multipaths, mid-paths and sub-path in SCME.

Sub-paths within a mid-path have identical delay. Each mid-path has the same azimuth spread as in SCM. SCME is a continuous evolution model since it allows drifting of DODs, DOAs and delays for every multipath at each simulation step within a drop.

4.1.2.1 Additional features of SCME

SCME contains the following additional features when compared to SCM [D.S Baum et. al., 2005; M. Narandzic., 2007; SCME Project., 2005]:

1. Addition of intra-cluster delay-spread within a multipath

The introduction of intra-cluster delay-spread to increase bandwidth. The 20 subpaths of SCM are grouped into three (in case of macrocells) or four (in case of microcells) mid-paths with different delays. This results in about 10 ns of intra-cluster RMS delay spread. The delays, which are fixed, are given in [D.S Baum et al., 2005]. A mid-path, which represents a single resolvable delay (or tap), comprises a collection of sub-paths and therefore has a fading distribution close to Rayleigh.

2. Frequency

Carrier frequency is extended to 5 GHz.

3. Path-loss models

Two path-loss models are used. The long-range model (identical to that defined in the SCM 2 GHz model) and an alternative, short-range, model. The extension of frequency to 5 GHz is applied to both. SCME selects the path-loss model (long-range/short-range/2 GHz/5 GHz) depending on the user input. The 5 GHz path-loss model offsets loss by +8 dB with respect to the existing 2 GHz model.

4. LOS model for all scenarios

The LOS option affects path-loss and shadow-fading variance. The choice between LOS and NLOS within a drop is based on the probability of LOS versus BS-MS distance. The LOS model in SCM defines a path-loss and Ricean *K*-factor which is applicable to urban microcell scenario only. With the alternative path-loss model in SCME, the LOS option (with appropriate *K*-factor model) is defined for all scenarios and is thus available whenever the current drop is LOS.

5. Time-variant shadowing
Each drop consists of time samples within a channel snapshot. In SCM the fading due to shadowing is constant for the duration of a drop. In SCME shadow induced fading (in dB) changes within a drop thus modelling time-varying shadowing. The decorrelation distance of shadowing is predefined (i.e. 5 m, 50 m and 250 m in urban microcells, urban macrocells, and suburban macrocells, respectively). The standard deviation of shadow induced fading for all scenarios is 4 dB for LOS and 10 dB for NLOS.

6. Time-variant DODs, DOAs and delays
For all sub-paths, DODs and distances are calculated once for every channel snapshot. It is assumed, therefore, that the locations of scatterers relative to the BS are fixed for the duration of a drop. This results in fixed DODs as seen by the BS (with the exception of any LOS DOD which does change). The DOAs as seen from the MS and the sub-path delays change during a drop due to the MS movement.

4.1.2.2 Model features

1. SCME is a stochastically controlled spatial channel model. The model is based on the same design philosophy as SCM i.e. the summation of specular components to define the changing impulse response. The model is backward compatible with the existing SCM model.
2. SCME provides a channel bandwidth of up to 100 MHz which is sufficient to characterise B3G wireless technologies and networks.
3. In addition to fast fading (due to multipath propagation), SCME can model the evolution of slow fading (due to shadowing), sub-path delay and DOA during each drop. This results in, time-varying, spatial correlations between transmit and receive antenna elements as shown in Fig. 11.

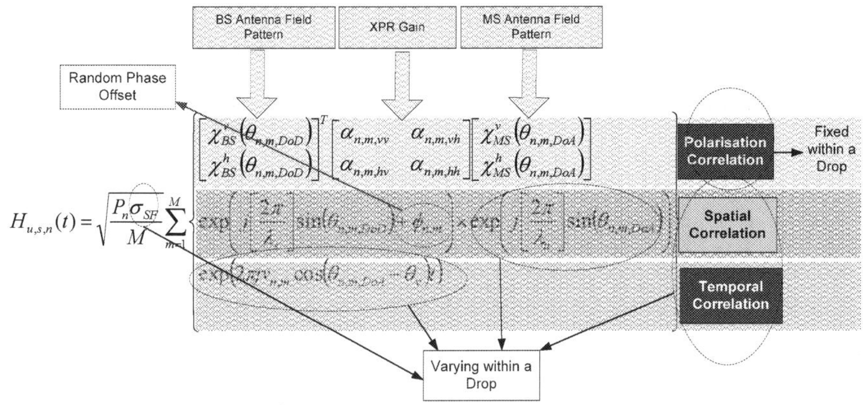

Fig. 11. Tap n complex gain for SCME

4. SCME considers six clusters of scatterers. Each cluster corresponds to a resolvable path. Within a resolvable path (cluster), there are 20 sub-paths. The 20 sub-paths are divided into mid-paths which are then assigned different delays relative to the original path. The mid-paths are delay resolvable but sub-paths within a mid-path are irresolvable. The mid-path (which is a collection of subpaths) corresponds to a single tap.
5. SCME includes a LOS K-factor option which is switch selectable for all urban and suburban macrocell scenarios. (SCM includes a LOS model for the urban microcell scenario only.)
6. A simplified tap delay line model referred to as the cluster delay line (CDL) model is used for calibration and comparison purposes. In this model, the DODs and DOAs are fixed for each path. Also, fixed delays are defined resulting in a fixed power delay profile (PDP) [Spirent Communications, 2008].

4.1.2.3 Software implementation of SCME

1. The drop concept in SCM corresponds to a relatively short channel-observation period that is significantly separated from adjacent drops in both time and space. The channel parameters are therefore constant within the drop and independent between drops. Short-term variability of channel parameters within a drop is incorporated by introducing drifting of (i) path delays (ii) DOAs and (iii) shadow induced fading.
2. The position of scatters is fixed within a drop. As a consequence the scattering angles as seen from the BS (DOD) do not change (with the exception of the LOS DOD in LOS scenarios). This assumption is common to SCM. The initial values of random parameters such as DODs, DOAs, K-factor, path phases etc. are generated in the same way as in SCM.
3. The scatter angles as seen from the MS (DOAs) and sub-path delays change (in contrast to SCM) during a drop reflecting MS movement. Similarly the LOS direction from the BS to MS varies in time. This results in time-varying spatial correlation between MS and BS antenna array elements.

4. An initial value of distance ($d_{j,i}$) between the MS and the last bounce scatter (LBS) of the ith sub-path of the jth multipath is required in order to calculate DOA drifts as the MS moves. This distance is unknown but can be inferred from a stochastic model as proposed in [D. S. Baum et. al., 2005].
5. Time evolution, or drifting, of slow fading (shadowing) is determined by the spatial auto-correlation function.

Fig. 12 shows the pseudo-code flow diagram for an implementation of SCME.

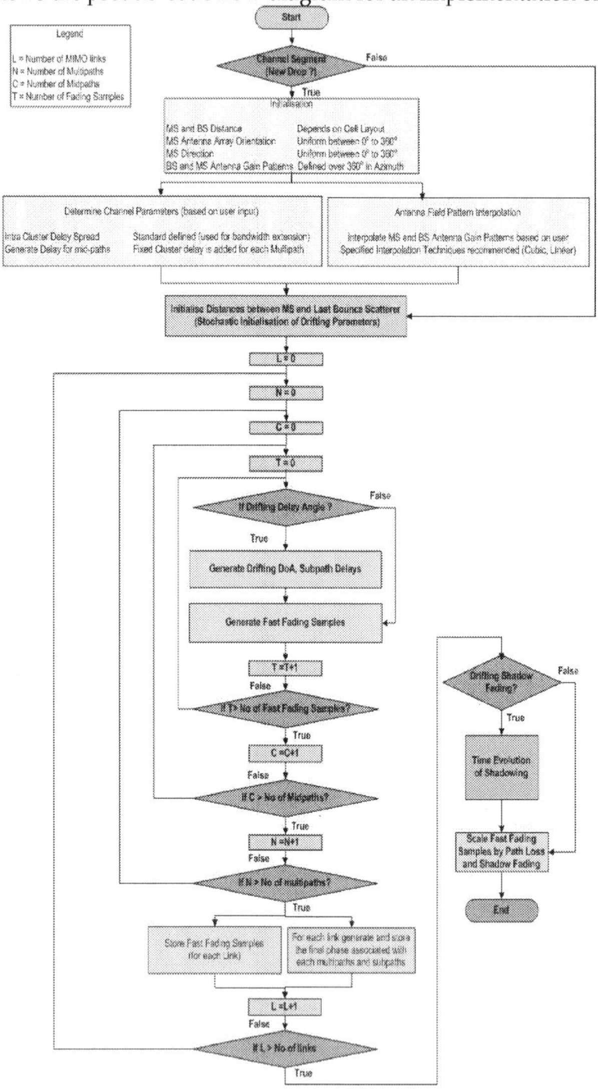

Fig. 12. Pseudo-code flow diagram of SCME channel model.

4.1.3 WIM2

The WIM2 channel model (also referred to as WINNER II [WINNER II Channel Models, 2006]) is defined for both link-level and system-level simulations. It encompasses a wide range of scenarios relevant to local, metropolitan and wide-area systems. WIM2 evolved from the WINNER I and WINNER II (interim) channel models.

WIM2 is a double-directional geometry-based stochastic channel model. It incorporates generic multilink models for system-level simulations and clustered delay line (CDL) models, with fixed large-scale channel parameters, for calibration and comparison purposes.

Initially, the WINNER group selected SCM for immediate simulation but later extended this to SCME. In spite of the greater bandwidth and higher frequency capability of SCME it was still deemed inadequate for advanced WINNER II simulations. The novel features of WIM2 are its parameterisation, the addition of further outdoor and indoor scenarios and the consideration of both azimuth and elevation spreading for indoor environments. (This is in contrast to SCM and SCME which restrict spreading to the azimuthal plane only.) WIM2 also includes correlation modelling of large-scale parameters and scenario-dependent polarisation modelling [WINNER II Channel Models, 2007].

4.1.3.1 Model features

1. It is a geometry-based stochastic channel model, which allows the creation of an arbitrary double-directional model. The channel impulse response is the sum of specular components. This is the same principle as used in the SCM and SCME channel model. The channel parameters are determined randomly, based on probability distributions extracted from channel measurement.
2. It covers 12 scenarios which is a larger number than SCM or SCME. These include indoor environments. (SCM and SCME include only outdoor environment.) Each scenario allows LOS or NLOS conditions. The model supports mobile, nomadic and fixed systems.
3. It allows transitions between different propagation conditions, the most important of which are transitions between LOS and NLOS within the same scenario. In the A1 (indoor) or B1 (urban microcell) scenarios, for example, transitions from LOS to NLOS can occur as a result of the MS turning a corner to leave a corridor or street in which the BS is located.
4. It can be used to characterise systems operating in the 2 - 6 GHz frequency range with a bandwidth up to 100 MHz. Like SCME, intra-cluster delay spread is used to support this bandwidth.
5. It specifies DOA and DOD as two-dimensional variables (whereas only a single (azimuthal) angle is considered in SCM and SCME).
6. It employs a sophisticated correlation model to the multiple links in system level simulations [M. Narandzic et. al., 2007]. (This contrasts with SCM which adopts a fixed correlation (0.5) for slow fading to model multiple links between a MS and different BSs.)
7. A drop, or channel segment, represents a quasi-stationary period during which the probability distributions of most channel parameters do not change. The advantage of this approach is simplicity. The disadvantage is that it is not

possible to adequately simulate cases where variable channel conditions are needed. Drop-based simulation is the principal approach used by both WINNER I (SCM and SCME) and WIM2 models. WIM2, however, also allows simulation with time evolution in which the drops are correlated and a smooth transition between consecutive drops is engineered. (The drops in WIM2 are usually referred to as channel segments since they are no longer 'dropped in' at random.) This smooth transition between channel segments is realised by spacing the segments in time by the quasi-stationary duration and dividing the transition region into a number of sub-intervals. The number of sub-intervals is chosen to be the same as the higher of the number of clusters in either channel segment. In each sub-interval the strength (amplitude) of a cluster from the earlier segment is ramped linearly down and the strength of the cluster from the later segment is ramped up. The pair of clusters is chosen to be, as far as possible, 'matched' in strength. Where the number of clusters in earlier and later segments are not equal then the weakest paths in the segment with more clusters are left unpaired and are ramped up or down alone. This process is illustrated schematically in Fig. 13.

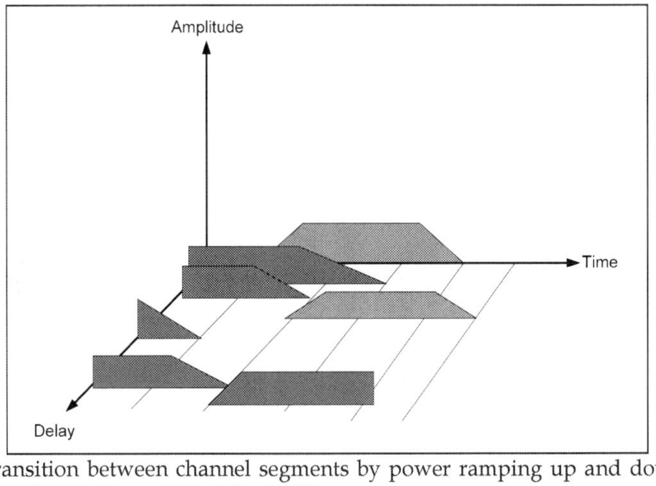

Fig. 13. Transition between channel segments by power ramping up and down of clusters (After [WINNER II Channel Models, 2007]).

8. For time division duplex (TDD) systems WIM2 (like SCM and SCME) uses the same parameters for both uplink and downlink. For frequency division duplex (FDD) systems a different path-loss is used on uplink and downlink and the random phases of sub-paths on uplink and downlink are modelled independently [M. Narandzic et. al., 2007].

4.1.3.1 Channel modelling approach

The modelling process can be divided into three phases. These are illustrated in Fig. 14.

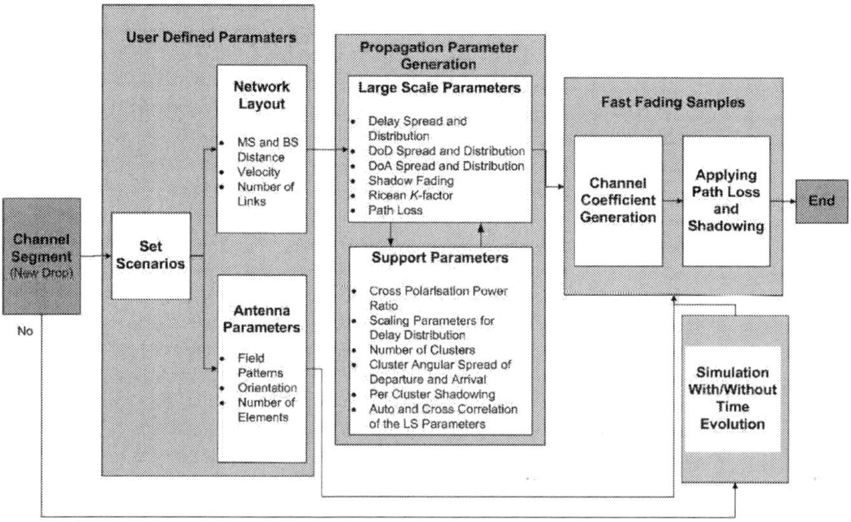

Fig. 14. WIM2 channel modelling process.

1. The environment, network layout and antenna array parameters are defined.
2. The large-scale parameters such as slow fading (shadowing), power, DODs, DOAs and delay-spread are drawn randomly from tabulated distribution functions. At this stage the geometry (i.e. network layout) is fixed and the only free variables are the random initial phases of the sub-paths. By picking different initial phases (randomly), an unlimited number of different realisations of the model can be generated. When the initial phases are fixed, the model is deterministic.
3. Fast fading samples are generated using the sum of sinusoids technique. (This is the same as in SCM and SCME.) The model implements time evolution (depending on user input) in order to generate correlated channel samples if the required channel simulation period is longer than the quasi-stationery period of the channel.

4.2 WiMAX

IEEE working group 802.16 has been central to the development of technical standards for fixed wireless access networks. Broadband wireless access (BWA) technology provides last mile access for high-speed residential and commercial Internet services. It is a promising alternative to digital subscriber line (DSL), cable and fibre technologies which are struggling to meet world-wide demand, especially outside metropolitan centres, for Internet services at reasonable cost. The IEEE 802.16 standard for BWA and its associated industry consortium, the WiMAX forum, has the potential to offer broadband access to virtually all users irrespective of location. WiMAX (the Worldwide Interoperability for Microwave Access) is a consortium of telecommunication equipment manufacturers, vendors and service providers, formed to promote the compatibility and interoperability of BWA devices incorporating the IEEE 802.16 and ETSI HiperMAN wireless standards.

IEEE 802.16 was designed for LOS links operating at carrier frequencies between 10 and 66 GHz. The first release of the standard (IEEE 802.16-2001) specifies a set of medium access control (MAC) and physical-layer standards intended to provide fixed broadband access using a point-to-point (PP) or point-to-multipoint (PMP) topology. The standard was revised in January 2003 to included NLOS links operating at frequencies in both licensed and unlicensed bands between 2 and 11 GHz. A consolidated standard, IEEE 802.16-2004, was issued in 2004.

IEEE 802.16e-2005, was issued in December 2005 which includes enhancements for physical and MAC layers that support nomadic and mobile operation in 2 to 11 GHz range.

The WiMAX forum has adopted the IEEE 802.16-2004 and ETSI HyperMAN standards for fixed and nomadic access and the IEEE 802.16e standard for portable access.

Two channel models are used for fixed and portable systems complying with the IEEE 802.16 standard. The Stanford University Interim (SUI) channel model is used for fixed broadband access and the ITU Tapped-Delay-Line channel model is used for portable broadband access.

4.2.1 SUI

The Stanford University Interim (SUI) suite of channel models was designed for fixed macrocell networks operating at 2.5 GHz. It contains the definition of six specific channel implementations which were initially developed for Multipoint Microwave Distribution Systems (MMDSs) in the USA operating in the 2.5 - 2.7 GHz frequency band. Their applicability to the 3.5 GHz frequency band that is in use in the UK has so far not been conclusively established.

The model generates both SISO and MIMO channel parameters. The six specific channel implementations represent different terrain types. The targeted scenarios are based on the following assumptions:

1. Cell radius less than 10 km.
2. Cell coverage (80 - 90%).
3. Fixed directional receiving antenna installed at a height of 2 - 10 m (below rooftop height since LOS is not required).
5. Base-station antenna installed at a height of 15 - 40 m (above rooftop height).
6. Flexible channel bandwidth between 2 and 20 MHz.

Three terrain types are defined: A for hilly terrain with moderate to heavy tree density (representing the highest path-loss terrain type), B for either flat terrain with moderate to heavy tree density or hilly terrain with light tree density and C for flat terrain with moderate to light tree density (representing the lowest path-loss terrain).

The SUI models corresponding to these terrain types are:

1. A: SUI-5 and SUI-6
2. B: SUI-3 and SUI-4
3. C: SUI-1 and SUI-2

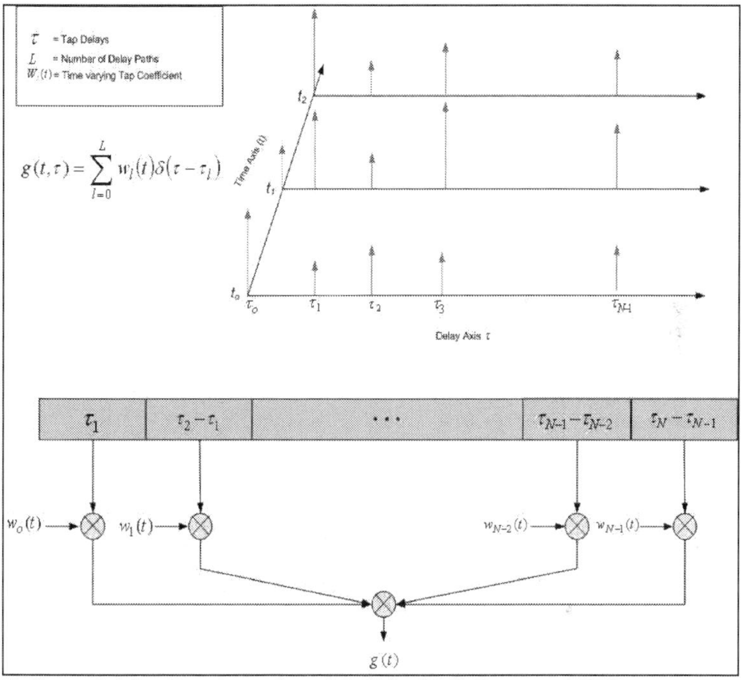

Fig. 15. Tapped delay line channel model. (After[T. S. Rapport, 2002])

4.2.1.1 Model features

1. Claimed to be valid between 2 and 4 GHz (although no tests of its performance in the European 3.5 GHz band are known) and for up to 7 km separation between transmitter and receiver.
2. Fading modelled as tapped delay line, Fig. 15, with three taps having non-uniform delays. The delays are specified in the standard document [IEEE 802.16 (BWA), 2003].
3. Omni-directional antennas are assumed at both transmitter and the receiver in the original SUI models. A modified version of the model assumes directional antennas with 30° beamwidths.
4. A lognormal model [L.J. Greenstein et. Al., 1999] for the distribution of *K*-factor is adopted. The *K*-factor for each tap is specified by exceedance values corresponding to cell coverage areas of 90% and 75% (SUI-1 to SUI-4) and 90%,

75% and 50% (SUI-5 to SUI-6). Taps 2 and 3 are always, effectively, Rayleigh faded. Tap 1 may be Ricean or Rayleigh faded.

5. Correlation between multipath components (tap weights) for the same taps of different receiving antennas at the MS is fixed irrespective of MS array configuration. The correlation between multipath components for the same taps of different receiving antennas at the BS is zero (corresponding to an assumption of large antenna spacing.
6. Channel coefficients with the probability distribution and power spectral density specified in the standard document [IEEE 802.16 (BWA), 2003] are generated by filtering noise. In a fixed wireless system the Doppler power spectral density is concentrated around $f = 0$ Hz. The shape of the spectrum, which different from the classical Jakes spectrum (that is more relevant to urban mobile scenarios), is given by:

$$S(f_D) = \begin{Bmatrix} 1.72(f_D / f_m)^2 + 0.785(f_D / f_m)^4 & f_D \le f_m \\ 0 & f_D > f_m \end{Bmatrix} \tag{8}$$

where f_m is the maximum Doppler frequency. This is usually referred to as the 'rounded' Doppler spectrum [IEEE 802.16 (BWA), 2003].
7. Validity restricted to distances less than 7 km (which is less than the targeted maximum range of 10 km). A modified version of SUI channel model has been proposed in order to scale transmit-receive distances to ranges greater than 7 km.
8. Propagation environments characterised in terms of power delay profiles.
9. Actual antenna array configurations not considered.
10. Simple and suited for rapid proto-typing or equipment/algorithm development. Unsuited to comprehensive, location-specific, network/system planning.

5.2.1.2 Generic structure

The generic structure of the SUI channel model is shown in Fig. 16 [IEEE 802.16 (BWA), 2003].

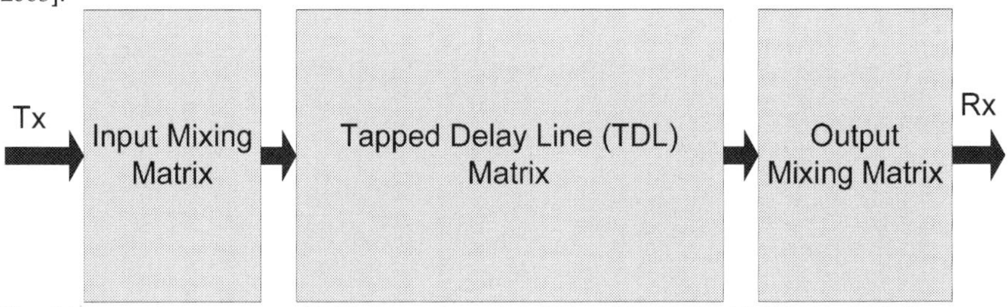

Fig. 16. Generic structure of SUI channel model. (After [IEEE 802.16 (BWA), 2003].)

The input mixing matrix models the spatial correlation between inputs if multiple antennas are used at the transmitter. The tapped delay line matrix models multipath fading. Each filter tap is characterised by a Ricean or Raleigh fading process. The output mixing matrix models the spatial correlation between output signals if multiple antennas are used at the receiver.

5.2.1.3 Channel modelling approach

1. RMS delay-spread is calculated based on user specified parameters.
2. A set of complex zero-mean Gaussian random numbers are generated for each tap leading to a Rayleigh distributed tap magnitude. If a Ricean distribution ($K > 0$) is required a constant path component is added to the Rayleigh set of coefficients.
3. The random numbers generated are independent (and therefore uncorrelated) and thus have a white spectrum. The SUI channel model specifies a 'rounded' power spectrum. The uncorrelated samples are filtered to generate channel coefficients with the required correlation properties.
4. An antenna envelope correlation value (i.e. the correlation between the amplitude of signals received at corresponding taps of two antenna elements) is defined for multiple transmit or receive elements.

The simulation steps are summarised in Fig. 17.

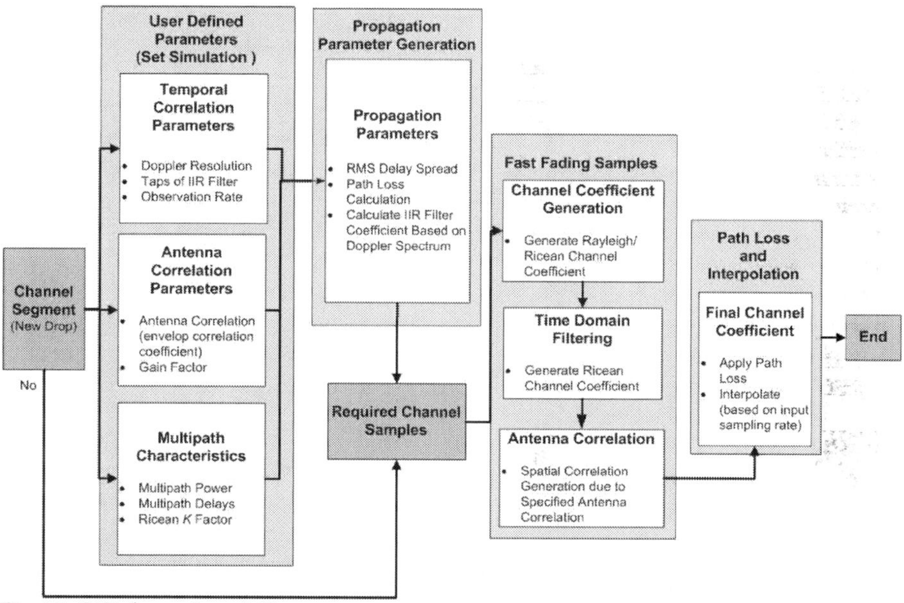

Fig. 17. SUI channel modelling process

4.2.2 WiMAX- ITU-TDL

The WiMAX forum approved the mobile WiMAX system profile in 2006. Mobile WiMAX, based on 802.16e-2005, enables WiMAX systems to address portable and mobile devices in addition to fixed and nomadic applications. The WiMAX forum Mobile release 1.0 channel model [WiMAX forum, 2008] defines the SISO and MIMO channel model requirements for mobile applications governed by the IEEE 802.11e standard. The purpose of the model is to provide a realistic and repeatable channel context for the testing and comparison of portable and mobile WiMAX-enabled devices.

4.2.2.1 Model features

Mobile WiMAX specifies SISO/MIMO channel models for radio conformance testing (RCT) of WiMAX products. The WiMAX forum has selected the ITU Pedestrian-B and Vehicular-A 6-tap TDL models for test and verification of SISO devices. The WiMAX-ITU-TDL channel model extends the ITU-TDL model to the MIMO systems encompassing spatial correlation for each multipath component. One of the novel features of the model is the definition of three levels of channel correlation (low, medium and high) between antenna elements. The following are the main features of the model:

1. It is a physical model, using a stochastic modelling approach similar to SCM.
2. ITU propagation scenarios are extended by defining the azimuth angle spread and shape (Laplacian) of the azimuth spectrum for each tap. Tap-wise MIMO correlation matrices are determined based on the spatial information (i.e. high, medium and low antenna correlation) of multipath components combined with specific antenna configurations.

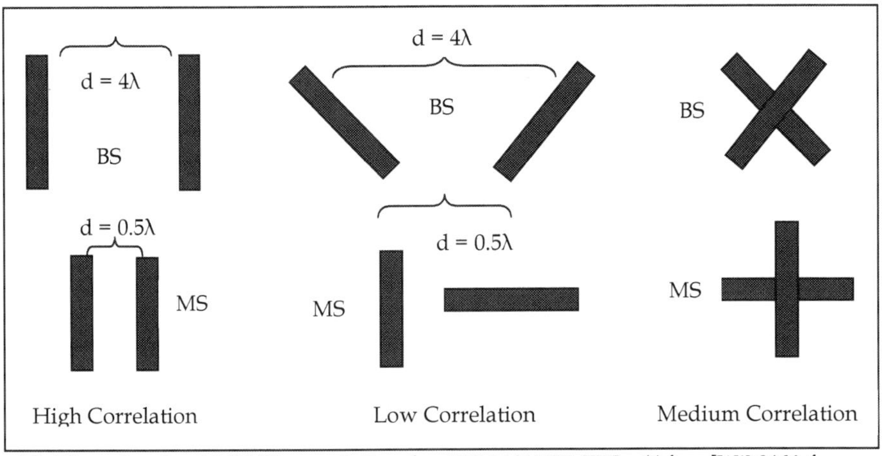

Fig. 18. Three levels of MIMO correlation for WiMAX-ITU-TDL. (After [WiMAX forum, 2008].)

3. Three pairs of reference antenna configurations are defined that typify low, medium and high correlation. The reference configurations specify the spacing of elements and their relative polarisations at MS and BS. This is illustrated schematically in Fig. 18.
4. The azimuth spread in all WiMAX-ITU-TDL scenarios for all taps is 2° at the BS and 35° at the MS.
5. The Doppler spectrum has the classical Jakes U-shape [Jakes model].
6. The strength of each tap is Raleigh distributed.
7. To model long channel impulse response (>10 μs) and for high-speed MSs (>120 km/h), the ITU Vehicular A channel is used but modified such that the last tap is

moved from 2510 ns to 10,000 ns. (The strength of the last tap remains unchanged at -20dB.)

8. Each cluster corresponds to a resolvable multipath. Within each of the six multipaths there are 20 irresolvable sub-paths. Each of the six multipaths is modelled as Dirac (delta) function of delay. The 20, spatially separated, sub-paths have equal delay.

4.2.2.2 WiMAX-ITU-TDL model design

1. The model can be separated into three components addressing (i) spatial correlation, (ii) polarisation correlation and (iii) temporal correlation. The spatial and polarisation correlation are modelled using square matrices of dimensions $(K\times M\times N)\times(K\times M\times N)$ where K is the number of multipaths, and M and N are the number of elements in the transmit and receive antenna arrays respectively. The temporal correlation matrix has same number of rows as the spatial or polarisation matrices and the same number of columns as the number of required channel samples.
2. Spatial correlation is calculated independently at transmit and receive antenna and is based on antenna geometry. A 2×2 MIMO system results in the following spatial correlation matrices at transmit and receive antenna elements:

$$R_{BS} = \begin{bmatrix} 1 & \alpha \\ \alpha^{*} & 1 \end{bmatrix} \qquad 9(a)$$

$$R_{MS} = \begin{bmatrix} 1 & \beta \\ \beta^{*} & 1 \end{bmatrix} \qquad 9(b)$$

where α and β are the spatial correlations between antenna elements at BS and MS respectively. The MIMO correlation matrix is given by the Kronecker product of independent spatial correlation matrices, i.e.:

$$\mathbf{R_{S\text{-}MIMO}} = \mathbf{R_{BS}} \otimes \mathbf{R_{MS}} = \begin{bmatrix} R_{MS} & \alpha R_{MS} \\ \alpha^{*} R_{MS} & R_{MS} \end{bmatrix} = \begin{bmatrix} 1 & \beta & \alpha & \alpha\beta \\ \beta^{*} & 1 & \alpha\beta^{*} & \alpha \\ \alpha^{*} & \alpha^{*}\beta & 1 & \beta \\ \alpha^{*}\beta^{*} & \alpha^{*} & \beta^{*} & 1 \end{bmatrix} \qquad 10$$

3. The use of the Kronecker product corresponds to an assumption that the correlation between elements in the received antenna array is not affected by changes in the spatial configuration of elements in the transmit antenna array.

4. The polarisation model (which originated in the ITU) assumes a cross-polar ratio (XPR = cross-polar power/co-polar power) of -8 dB for each tap [WiMAX forum, 2008]. The polarisation matrix is denoted by:

$$\mathbf{S} = \begin{bmatrix} S_{vv} & S_{vh} \\ S_{hv} & S_{hh} \end{bmatrix} \quad 11$$

where v and h denote vertical and horizontal polarisation respectively. (The first subscript refers to the BS and the second subscript refers to the MS.) The downlink polarisation correlation matrix for a 2×2 MIMO system [WiMAX forum, 2008] is given by:

$$\mathbf{R}_{\mathbf{P,MIMO}} = \begin{bmatrix} 1 & \gamma & 0 & 0 \\ \gamma & 1 & 0 & 0 \\ 0 & 0 & 1 & -\gamma \\ 0 & 0 & -\gamma & 1 \end{bmatrix} \quad 12$$

where γ depends on XPR (expressed as a power ratio). The structure of $\mathbf{R}_{\mathbf{P,MIMO}}$ depends on the MS and BS antenna polarisations and orientations. Further detail can be found in [WiMAX forum, 2008].

5. Temporal correlation refers to the auto-correlation of the signal received at a single antenna element. There are two ways of generating temporal (fast fading) tap coefficients. Since the Doppler spectrum is classical and the amplitude is Rayleigh distributed the temporal fading samples can be generated using either the sum of sinusoids technique (Jakes' method) or by filtering white Gaussian noise. Fig. 19 summarises the process of generation of channel weights.

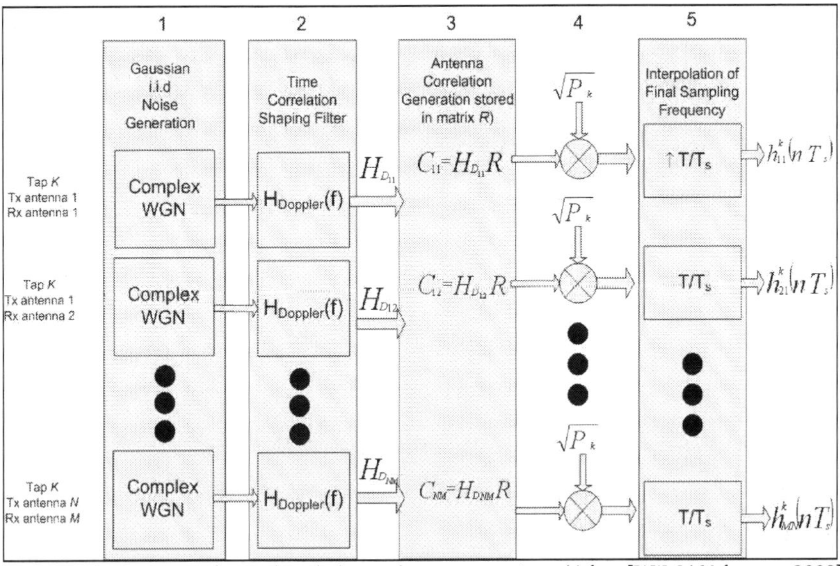

Fig. 19. Block diagram of correlated channel tap generation. (After [WiMAX forum, 2008].)

4.2.2.3 Software implementation of WiMAX-ITU-TDL

Fig. 20 shows pseudo-code for a WiMAX-ITU-TDL channel model. The modelling process is divided into the following principal components:

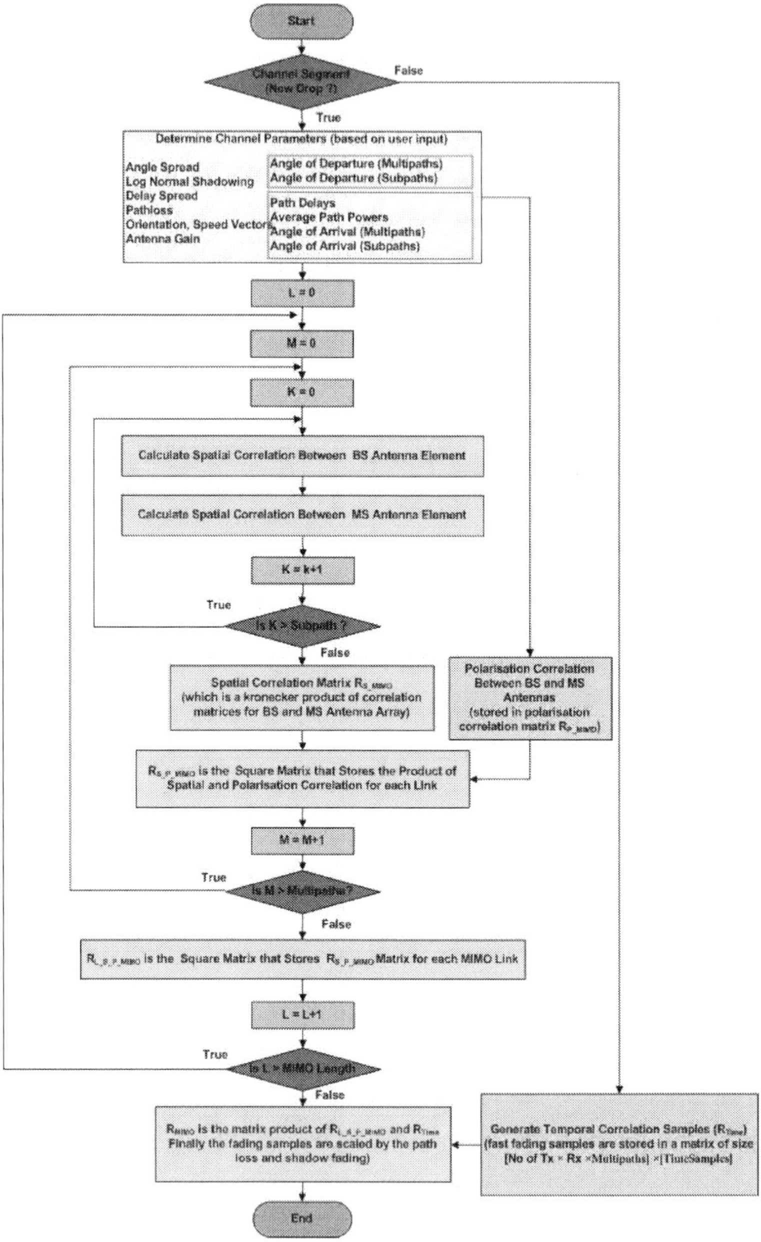

Fig. 20. Pseudo-code flow diagram for WiMAX-ITU-TDL channel model.

The generation of secondary channel statistics (e.g azimuth spread, offset DOA and offset DOD) is based on the user specified scenario. The channel segment (drop) represents a quasi-stationary period in which the probability distributions of parameters are unchanged. Unlike SCME the underlying large-scale parameters such as DOD and DOA remain constant within a single a channel segment.

The spatial correlation matrices for the BS and MS antenna elements are generated for all multipaths of each link. The BS and MS antenna spatial correlation matrices are Kronecker multiplied. The spatial correlation matrix remains unchanged between multiple drops of the same simulation.

Like spatial correlation the polarisation matrix remains unchanged between multiple drops of the same simulation.

Temporal correlation refers to the autocorrelation of the signal received at a single antenna element. During each drop of the simulation fast fading samples of the tap weights are generated either by the summing sinusoids or filtering a white Gaussian random process.

4.3 IEEE 802.11n

IEEE 802.11n is an amendment to the IEEE 802.11-2007 wireless local area network (WLAN) standard [IEEE 802.11, 2009]. It gives higher network throughput compared with earlier variants of the standard, e.g. 802.11b and 802.11g. The maximum raw (physical-layer) data rate is 600 Mbit/s. The IEEE 802.11n channel model [V. Erceg et. al., 2004] was developed for systems using the 2 GHz and 5 GHz bands operating in indoor environments and employing MIMO technology. Measurement results from these two frequencies bands were combined to develop the model. Only the path-loss element of the model depends on frequency. The channel model is based on the clustering approach developed by Saleh and Valenzula [A. A. M. Saleh et. al., 1987] and illustrated in Fig. 21.

4.3.1 Model features

The principal features of the model [P. Almer et. al., 2007] are:

1. It is a physical model based on stochastic modelling approach.
2. It can be applied to both 2 GHz and 5 GHz frequency bands.
3. A dual-slope, frequency dependent, model for path-loss is adopted.
4. The channel impulse response is a sum of clusters where each cluster consists of up to 18 multipaths. (The precise number depends on the scenario.) These multipaths are modelled as filter taps which are separated in delay by at least 10 ns.
5. Five scenarios are defined [P. Almer et. al., 2007]: A, B, C, D, E and F. Scenarios A-C represent small environments (RMS delay-spread <30 ns), such as residential homes and small offices. (Scenario A is optional and not recommended for system performance comparison.) Scenarios D-F represent large open spaces with maximum RMS delay-spread <150 ns.

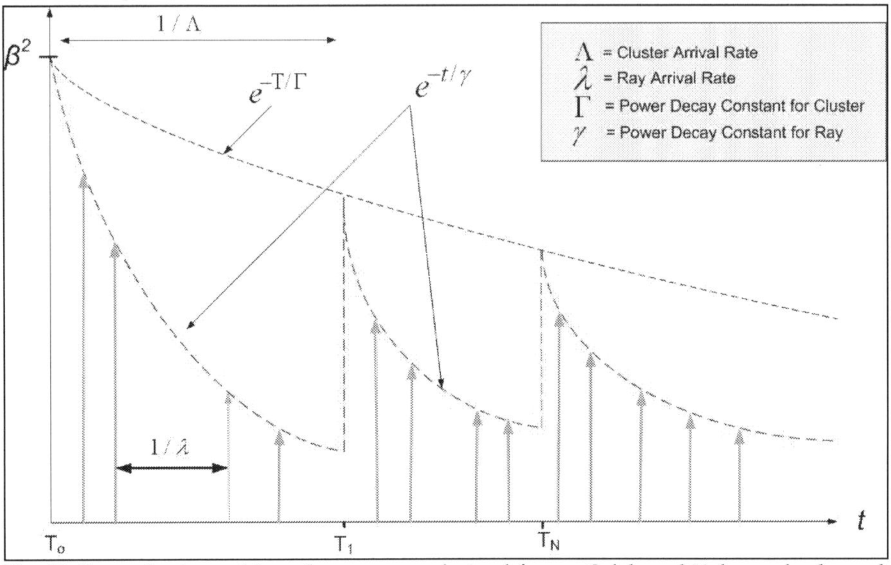

Fig. 21. Example channel impulse response derived from a Saleh and Valenzuela channel model. (After [A. A. M. Saleh et. al.].)

6. The MIMO channel matrix **H** for each filter tap at each instant of time is separated into a fixed (constant) LOS matrix, $\mathbf{H_F}$, and a time-varying (Rayleigh distributed) NLOS matrix, $\mathbf{H_V}$ [V. Erceg et. al., 2004], i.e.:

$$\mathrm{H} = \left(\sqrt{\frac{K}{K+1}} \mathrm{H_F} + \sqrt{\frac{1}{K+1}} \mathrm{H_V} \right) \qquad 13$$

where K is the Ricean K-factor.

7. Each tap consists of a number of sub-paths having truncated Laplacian azimuth spectrum with an angular spread that varies between from 20° to 40° [V. Erceg et. al., 2004].
8. Elevation spread is not incorporated (since most building dimensions in azimuth are much larger than their dimensions in elevation) [V Erceg et. al., 2004]).
9. The mean DOA and DOD for each cluster is random with a uniform distribution over all azimuth angles. (For indoor WLANs the scattering environment is similar for both the access point and the user equipment. This is in contrast to outdoor scenarios where the BS is typically mounted sufficiently high to be relatively free of local scatter while the MS is often immersed in a rich scattering environment.)
10. Several channel taps in scenarios D and E are amplitude modulated to account for the effects of fluorescent lights [V. Erceg et. al., 2004] which represent time-

periodic scatterers; alternately present and absent at twice the frequency of the mains supply (2×50 Hz in Europe).

11. The model differentiates between uplink and downlink (unlike SCM and SCME).
12. Isotropic antenna elements are assumed.

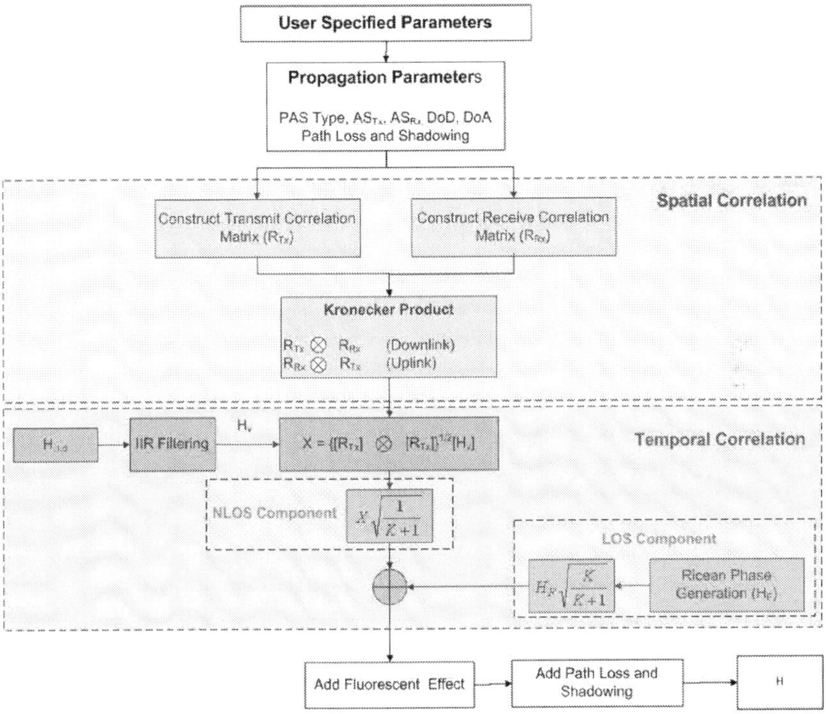

Fig. 22. IEEE 802.11n channel model

4.3.2 Model features

The various steps in the IEEE 802.11n channel model are illustrated in Fig. 22 and described below:

1. At each drop, during the initialisation phase, the model determines the delay profile and identifies clusters in the user-specified scenario.
2. The model assigns azimuth spread, mean DOD and DOA to each cluster and the corresponding taps. Spatial correlation is calculated independently at transmit and receive antennas and is based on antenna geometry.
3. The spatial correlation matrix is the Kronecker product of the individual spatial correlation matrices of transmit and receives antenna arrays, Fig. 22. The spatial correlation is a square matrix and is different for uplink and downlink.

4. Fast fading samples are generated by filtering uncorrelated (white) Gaussian noise. The filter final states are retained after a dummy run in order to avoid transient states. (Fading samples generated during the transient phase are not used because their variance is artificially low.)
5. In order to maintain continuity between successive channel calls (for the same drop) the filter states are stored.
6. The product of spatial and temporal correlation matrices results in the **H** matrix which is then scaled to account for path-loss and shadowing.

5. Summary and comparison of channel models

Table 1 summarises the principal features of those channel models that have been described and Table 2 compares some of their most important parameters.

	SCM	SCME	WINNER II	SUI	WiMAX	IEEE 802.11n
Bandwidth > 100 MHz	No	Yes *	Yes	No	No	Yes
Indoor scenarios	No	No	Yes	No	No	Yes **
Outdoor-to-indoor and indoor-to-outdoor scenarios	No	No	Yes	No	No	No
DoD/DoA elevation	No	No	Yes	No	No	No
Random selection of MPC from the appropriate probability distribution	Yes	Yes	Yes	No	No	No
Time evolution of large scale model parameters with in a drops	No	Yes	Yes	No	No	No
Time evolution of large scale model parameters between successive drops	No	No	Yes	No	No	No
Use of Intra-Cluster delay spread concept (based on Saleh and Valenzuela model	No	Yes	Yes	No	No	Yes
Cross correlation between large scale parameters	No	No	Yes	No	No	No

* SCME support both 20 MHz and 100 MHz bandwidth
** IEEE802.11n is an indoor channel model with only one case that typical open space (both indoor and outdoor)

Table 1. Principal features of standard channel models. (Extended from [M. Narandzic et. al., 2007].)

	Unit	SCM	SCME	WINNER II	SUI	WiMAX	IEEE 802.11n
Max bandwidth	MHz	5	100*	100**	2-20	2	100
Frequency range	GHz	2	2-6	2-6	1-4	2-11	2-5
No. of scenarios		3	3	12	6	3	6
No. of clusters		6	6	4-20	0	6	2-6
No. of taps		6	18-24	4-24	3-4	6	1-18
Doppler Spectrum		Classical	Classical	Classical	Standard Specific	Classical	Standard Specific
Normalised Delay spread	μs	1.2	1.2	1.2	0.9-20	2.51-10	0-1.05
Path azimuth spread at BS and MS	Degrees	2,5,35	2,5,35	5-50***	NA	2,35	20-40
Shadow fading (standard deviation)	dB	4-10	4-10	3-8	8.5-10.5****	8-12	3-6

* Artificial extension from 5 MHz bandwidth

** Based on 100 MHz measurements

*** Per tap azimuth spread in WINNER varies between 5°-50° depending on the scenario

**** The combined shadow fading/GRF standard deviation σ_c can be calculated using standard defined formula. The value represents a special case of 20° antenna beam width

Table 2. Comparison of standard channel model parameters. (Extended from [M. Narandzic et. al., 2007].)

6. Summary

Next generation wireless systems will offer wide bandwidth, high data-rates and greater mobility. MIMO technology will certainly play an important role in future wireless application. This chapter has presented a brief review of the theoretical framework used to describe MIMO channels and has described a selection of standard MIMO channel models. The characteristics of standard channel models have been summarised and compared.

7. Reference

A.A.M. Saleh. & R.A. Valenzuela (1987). "A statistical model for indoor multipath propagation," IEEE Journal on Selected Areas in Communications, vol. 5, 1987, pp. 128-137.

A.M. Sayeed, "Deconstructing multiantenna fading channels," IEEE Transactions on Signal Processing, vol. 50, no. 10, pp. 2563 - 2579, October 2002.

A. Burr, "Capacity bounds and estimates for the finite scatterers MIMO wireless channel," IEEE Journal on Selected Areas in Communications, vol. 21, no. 5, pp. 812–818, 2003.

A. C. Ludwig, "The definition of cross polarization, IEEE Transactions on Antennas and Propagation. AP-21(1) pp. 116-119, January 1973.

P. Almers.; F. Tufvesson.; A.F. Molisch., "Keyhold Effect in MIMO Wireless Channels: Measurements and Theory", IEEE Transactions on Wireless Communications, ISSN: 1536-1276, Vol. 5, Issue 12, pp. 3596-3604, December 2006.

D.S. Baum.; j. Hansen.; j. Salo., "An interim channel model for beyond-3G systems: extending the 3GPP spatial channel model (SCM)," Vehicular Technology Conference, 2005. VTC 2005-Spring. 2005 IEEE 61st , vol.5, no., pp. 3132-3136 Vol. 5, 30 May-1 June 2005.

N. Czink.; A. Richter.; E. Bonek.; J.-P. Nuutinen.; j. Ylitalo., "Including Diffuse Multipath Parameters in MIMO Channel Models," Vehicular Technology Conference, 2007. VTC-2007 Fall. 2007 IEEE 66th , vol., no., pp.874-878, Sept. 30 2007-Oct. 3 2007.

D.-S. Shiu.; G. J. Foschini.; M. J. Gans.; and J. M. Kahn, "Fading correlation and its effect on the capacity of multielement antenna systems," IEEE Transactions on Communications, vol. 48, no. 3, pp. 502–513, 2000.

H. El-Sallabi.; D.S Baum.; P. ZetterbergP.; P. Kyosti.; T. Rautiainen.; C. Schneider., "Wideband Spatial Channel Model for MIMO Systems at 5 GHz in Indoor and Outdoor Environments," Vehicular Technology Conference, 2006. VTC 2006-Spring. IEEE 63rd , vol.6, no., pp.2916-2921, 7-10 May 2006.

E. Telatar, "Capacity of multi-antenna Gaussian channels," European Transactions on Telecommunications, vol. 10, no. 6, pp. 585–595, 1999.

E.T. Jaynes, "Information theory and statistical mechanics," APS Physical Review, vol. 106, no. 4, pp. 620–630, 1957.

3GPP TR25.996 V6.1.0 (2003-09) "Spatial channel model for multiple input multiple output (MIMO) simulations" Release 6. (3GPP TR 25.996)

IEEE 802.16 (BWA) Broadband wireless access working group, Channel model for fixed wireless applications, 2003. http://ieee802.org/16

IEEE 802.11, WiFi. http://en.wikipedia.org/wiki/IEEE_802.11-2007. Last assessed on 01-May 2009.

International Telecommunications Union, "Guidelines for evaluation of radio transmission technologies for imt-2000," Tech. Rep. ITU-R M.1225, The International Telecommunications Union, Geneva, Switzerland, 1997

Jakes model; http://en.wikipedia.org/wiki/Rayleigh_fading

J. P. Kermoal.; L. Schumacher.; K. I. Pedersen.; P. E. Mogensen'; and F. Frederiksen, "A stochastic MIMO radio channel model with experimental validation," IEEE Journal on Selected Areas in Communications, vol. 20, no. 6, pp. 1211–1226, 2002.

J. W. Wallace and M. A. Jensen, "Modeling the indoor MIMO wireless channel," IEEE Transactions on Antennas and Propagation, vol. 50, no. 5, pp. 591–599, 2002.

L.J. Greenstein, S. Ghassemzadeh, V.Erceg, and D.G. Michelson, "Ricean K-factors in narrowband fixed wireless channels: Theory, experiments, and statistical models," WPMC'99 Conference Proceedings, Amsterdam, September 1999.

Merouane Debbah and Ralf R. M¨uller, "MIMO channel modelling and the principle of maximum entropy," IEEE Transactions on Information Theory, vol. 51, no. 5, pp. 1667–1690, May 2005.

M. Steinbauer, "A Comprehensive Transmission and Channel Model for Directional Radio Channels," COST 259, No. TD(98)027. Bern, Switzerland, February 1998. 13. M. Steinbauer, "A Comprehensive Transmission and Channel Model for Directional Radio Channels," COST259, No. TD(98)027. Bern, Switzerland, February 1998.

M. Steinbauer.; A. F. Molisch, and E. Bonek, "The doubledirectional radio channel," IEEE Antennas and Propagation Magazine, vol. 43, no. 4, pp. 51–63, 2001.

M. Narandzic.; C. Schneider .; R. Thoma.; T. Jamsa.; P. Kyosti.; Z. Xiongwen, "Comparison of SCM, SCME, and WINNER Channel Models," Vehicular Technology Conference, 2007. VTC2007-Spring. IEEE 65th , vol., no., pp.413-417, 22-25 April 2007.

M. Ozcelik.;N. Czink.; E. Bonek ., "What makes a good MIMO channel model?," Vehicular Technology Conference, 2005. VTC 2005-Spring. 2005 IEEE 61st , vol.1, no., pp. 156-160 Vol. 1, 30 May-1 June 2005.

P.Almer.; E.Bonek.; A.Burr.; N.Czink.; M.Deddah.; V.Degli-Esposti.; H.Hofstetter.; P.Kyosti.; D.Laurenson.; G.Matz.; A.F.Molisch.; C.Oestges and H.Ozcelik."Survey of Channel and Radio Propagation Models for Wireless MIMO Systems". EURASIP Journal on Wireless Communications and Networking, Volume 2007 (2007), Article ID 19070, 19 pages doi:10.1155/2007/19070.

Paul BS.; Bhattacharjee R. MIMO Channel Modeling: A Review. IETE Tech Rev 2008;25:315-9

Spirent Communications.; Path-Based Spatial Channel Modelling SCM/SCME white paper 102. 2008.

SCME Project; 3GPP Spatial Channel Model Extended (SCME); http://www.ist winner.org/3gpp_scme.html.

T. S. Rapport (2002). Wireless Communications Principles and Practice, ISBN 81-7808-648-4, Singapore.

T. Zwick.; C. Fischer, and W. Wiesbeck, "A stochastic multipath channelmodel including path directions for indoor environments,"IEEE Journal on Selected Areas in Communications, vol. 20, no. 6, pp. 1178–1192, 2002.

V Erceg.; L Schumacher.; P Kyristi.; A Molisch.; D S. Baum.; A Y Gorokhov.; C Oestges.; Q Li, K Yu.; N Tal, B Dijkstra.; A Jagannatham.; C Lanzl.; V J. Rhodes.; J Medos.; D Michelson.; M Webster.; E Jacobsen.; D Cheung.; C Prettie.; M Ho.; S Howard.; B Bjerke.; L Jengx.; H Sampath.; S Catreux.; S Valle.; A Poloni.; A Forenza.; R W Heath. "TGn Channel Model". IEEE P802.11 Wireless LANs. May 10, 2004. doc IEEE 802.11-03/940r4.

R. Verma.; S. Mahajan.; V. Rohila., "Classification of MIMO channel models," Networks, 2008. ICON 2008. 16th IEEE International Conference on , vol., no., pp.1-4, 12-14 Dec. 2008.

WINNER.; Final Report on Link Level and System Level Channel Models. IST-2003-507581 WINNER. D5.4 v. 1.4, 2005.

WINNER II Channel Models. IST-4-027756 WINNER II D1.1.2 V1.1, 2007.

WINNER II interim channel models. IST-4-027756 WINNER II D1.1.1 V1.1, 2006.

S. Wyne.; A.F. Molisch.; P. Almers.; G. Eriksson.; J. Karedal.; F. Tufvesson., "Statistical evaluation of outdoor-to-indoor office MIMO measurements at 5.2 GHz," Vehicular Technology Conference, 2005. VTC 2005-Spring. 2005 IEEE 61st , vol.1, no., pp. 146-150 Vol. 1, 30 May-1 June 2005

WiMAX forum®. Mobile Release 1.0 Channel Model. 2008.

wikipedia.org. http://en.wikipedia.org/wiki/IEEE_802.11n. Last assessed on May 2009.

6

Finite-context models for DNA coding*

Armando J. Pinho, António J. R. Neves, Daniel A. Martins,
Carlos A. C. Bastos and Paulo J. S. G. Ferreira
Signal Processing Lab, DETI/IEETA, University of Aveiro
Portugal

1. Introduction

Usually, the purpose of studying data compression algorithms is twofold. The need for efficient storage and transmission is often the main motivation, but underlying every compression technique there is a model that tries to reproduce as closely as possible the information source to be compressed. This model may be interesting on its own, as it can shed light on the statistical properties of the source. DNA data are no exception. We urge to find out efficient methods able to reduce the storage space taken by the impressive amount of genomic data that are continuously being generated. Nevertheless, we also desire to know how the code of life works and what is its structure. Creating good (compression) models for DNA is one of the ways to achieve these goals.

Recently, and with the completion of the human genome sequencing, the development of efficient lossless compression methods for DNA sequences gained considerable interest (Behzadi and Le Fessant, 2005; Cao et al., 2007; Chen et al., 2001; Grumbach and Tahi, 1993; Korodi and Tabus, 2005; 2007; Manzini and Rastero, 2004; Matsumoto et al., 2000; Pinho et al., 2006; 2009; 2008; Rivals et al., 1996). For example, the human genome is determined by approximately 3 000 million base pairs (Rowen et al., 1997), whereas the genome of wheat has about 16 000 million (Dennis and Surridge, 2000). Since DNA is based on an alphabet of four different symbols (usually known as nucleotides or bases), namely, Adenine (A), Cytosine (C), Guanine (G), and Thymine (T), without compression it takes approximately 750 MBytes to store the human genome (using $\log_2 4 = 2$ bits per symbol) and 4 GBytes to store the genome of wheat.

In this chapter, we address the problem of DNA data modeling and coding. We review the main approaches proposed in the literature over the last fifteen years and we present some recent advances attained with finite-context models (Pinho et al., 2006; 2009; 2008). Low-order finite-context models have been used for DNA compression as a secondary, fall back method. However, we have shown that models of orders higher than four are indeed able to attain significant compression performance.

Initially, we proposed a three-state finite-context model for DNA protein-coding regions, i.e., for the parts of the DNA that carry information regarding how proteins are synthesized (Ferreira et al., 2006; Pinho et al., 2006). This three-state model proved to be better than a single-state model, giving additional evidence of a phenomenon that is common in these protein-coding regions, the periodicity of period three.

*This work was supported in part by the FCT (Fundação para a Ciência e Tecnologia) grant PTDC/EIA/72569/2006.

More recently (Pinho et al., 2008), we investigated the performance of finite-context models for unrestricted DNA, i.e., DNA including coding and non-coding parts. In that work, we have shown that a characteristic usually found in DNA sequences, the occurrence of inverted repeats, which is used by most of the DNA coding methods (see, for example, Korodi and Tabus (2005); Manzini and Rastero (2004); Matsumoto et al. (2000)), could also be successfully integrated in finite-context models. Inverted repeats are copies of DNA sub-sequences that appear reversed and complemented ($A \leftrightarrow T$, $C \leftrightarrow G$) in some parts of the DNA.
Further studies have shown that multiple competing finite-context models, working on a block basis, could be more effective in capturing the statistical information along the sequence (Pinho et al., 2009). For each block, the best of the models is chosen, i.e., the one that requires less bits for representing the block. In fact, DNA is non-stationary, with regions of low information content (low entropy) alternating with regions with average entropy close to two bits per base. This alternation is modeled by most DNA compression algorithms by using a low-order finite-context model for the high entropy regions and a Lempel-Ziv dictionary based approach for the repetitive, low entropy regions. In this work, we rely only on finite-context models for representing both regions.
Modeling DNA data using only finite-context models has advantages over the typical DNA compression approaches that mix purely statistical (for example, finite-context models) with substitutional models (such as Lempel-Ziv based algorithms): (1) finite-context models lead to much faster performance, a characteristic of paramount importance for long sequences (for example, some human chromosomes have more than 200 million bases); (2) the overall model might be easier to interpret, because it is made of sub-models of the same type.
This chapter is organized as follows. In Section 2 we provide an overview of the DNA compression methods that have been proposed. Section 3 describes the finite-context models used in this work. These models collect the statistical information needed by the arithmetic coding. In Section 4 we provide some experimental results. Finally, in Section 5 we draw some conclusions.

2. DNA compression methods

The interest in DNA coding has been growing with the increasing availability of extensive genomic databases. Although only two bits are sufficient to encode the four DNA bases, efficient lossless compression methods are still needed due to the large size of DNA sequences and because standard compression algorithms do not perform well on DNA sequences. As a result, several specific coding methods have been proposed. Most of these methods are based on searching procedures for finding exact or approximate repeats.
The first method designed specifically for compressing DNA sequences was proposed by Grumbach and Tahi (1993) and was named *Biocompress*. This technique is based on the sliding window algorithm proposed by Ziv and Lempel, also known as LZ77 (Ziv and Lempel, 1977). According to this universal data compression technique, a sub-sequence is encoded using a reference to an identical sub-sequence that occurred in the past. *Biocompress* uses a characteristic usually found in DNA sequences which is the occurrence of inverted repeats. These are sub-sequences that are both reversed and complemented ($A \leftrightarrow T$, $C \leftrightarrow G$). The second version of *Biocompress*, *Biocompress-2*, introduced an additional mode of operation, based on an order-2 finite-context arithmetic encoder (Grumbach and Tahi, 1994).
Rivals et al. (1995; 1996) proposed another compression technique based on exact repetitions, *Cfact*, which relies on a two-pass strategy. In the first pass, the complete sequence is parsed using a suffix tree, producing a list of the longest repeating sub-sequences that have a potential

coding gain. In the second pass, those sub-sequences are encoded using references to the past, whereas the rest of the symbols are left uncompressed.

The idea of using repeating sub-sequences was also exploited by Chen et al. (1999; 2001). The authors proposed a generalization of this strategy such that approximate repeats of sub-sequences and of inverted repeats could also be handled. In order to reproduce the original sequence, the algorithm, named *GenCompress*, uses operations such as replacements, insertions and deletions. As in *Biocompress*, *GenCompress* includes a mechanism for deciding if it is worthwhile to encode the sub-sequence under evaluation using the substitution-based model. If not, it falls back to a mode of operation based on an order-2 finite-context arithmetic encoder. A further modification of *GenCompress* led to a two-pass algorithm, *DNACompress*, relying on a separated tool for approximate repeat searching, *PatternHunter*, (Chen et al., 2002). Besides providing additional compression gains, *DNACompress* is considerably faster than *GenCompress*.

Before the publication of *DNACompress*, a technique based on context tree weighting (CTW) and LZ-based compression, *CTW+LZ*, was proposed by Matsumoto et al. (2000). Basically, long repeating sub-sequences or inverted repeats, exact or approximate, are encoded by a LZ-type algorithm, whereas short sub-sequences are compressed using CTW.

One of the main problems of techniques based on sub-sequence matching is the time taken by the search operation. Manzini and Rastero (2004) addressed this problem and proposed a fast, although competitive, DNA encoder, based on fingerprints. Basically, in this approach small sub-sequences are not considered for matching. Instead, the algorithm focus on finding long matching sub-sequences (or inverted repeats). Like most of the other methods, this technique also uses fall back mechanisms for the regions where matching fails, in this case, finite-context arithmetic coding of order-2 (*DNA2*) or order-3 (*DNA3*).

Tabus et al. (2003) proposed a sophisticated DNA sequence compression method based on normalized maximum likelihood discrete regression for approximate block matching. This work, later improved for compression performance and speed (Korodi and Tabus (2005), *GeNML*), encodes fixed-size blocks by referencing a previously encoded sub-sequence with minimum Hamming distance. Only replacement operations are allowed for editing the reference sub-sequence which, therefore, always have the same size as the block, although may be located in an arbitrary position inside the already encoded sequence. Fall back modes of operation are also considered, namely, a finite-context arithmetic encoder of order-1 and a transparent mode in which the block passes uncompressed.

Behzadi and Le Fessant (2005) proposed the *DNAPack* algorithm, which uses the Hamming distance (i.e., it relies only on substitutions) for the repeats and inverted repeats, and either CTW or order-2 arithmetic coding for non-repeating regions. Moreover, *DNAPack* uses dynamic programming techniques for choosing the repeats, instead of greedy approaches as others do.

More recently, two other methods have been proposed (Cao et al., 2007; Korodi and Tabus, 2007). One of them (Korodi and Tabus, 2007), is an evolution of the normalized maximum likelihood model introduced by Tabus et al. (2003) and improved by Korodi and Tabus (2005). This new version, *NML-1*, is built on the *GeNML* framework and aims at finding the best regressor block using first-order dependencies (these dependencies were not considered in the previous approach).

The other method, proposed by Cao et al. (2007) and called *XM*, relies on a mixture of experts for providing symbol by symbol probability estimates which are then used for driving an arithmetic encoder. The algorithm comprises three types of experts: (1) order-2

Markov models; (2) order-1 context Markov models, i.e., Markov models that use statistical information only of a recent past (typically, the 512 previous symbols); (3) the copy expert, that considers the next symbol as part of a copied region from a particular offset. The probability estimates provided by the set of experts are them combined using Bayesian averaging and sent to the arithmetic encoder. Currently, this seems to be the method that provides the highest compression on the April 14, 2003 release of the human genome (see results in `ftp://ftp.infotech.monash.edu.au/software/DNAcompress-XM/XMCompress/humanGenome.html`). However, both *NML-1* and *XM* are computationally intensive techniques.

3. Finite-context models

Consider an information source that generates symbols, s, from an alphabet $\mathcal{A}$. At time t, the sequence of outcomes generated by the source is $x^t = x_1 x_2 \ldots x_t$. A finite-context model of an information source (see Fig. 1) assigns probability estimates to the symbols of the alphabet, according to a conditioning context computed over a finite and fixed number, M, of past outcomes (order-M finite-context model) (Bell et al., 1990; Salomon, 2007; Sayood, 2006). At time t, we represent these conditioning outcomes by $c^t = x_{t-M+1}, \ldots, x_{t-1}, x_t$. The number of conditioning states of the model is $|\mathcal{A}|^M$, dictating the model complexity or cost. In the case of DNA, since $|\mathcal{A}| = 4$, an order-M model implies 4^M conditioning states.

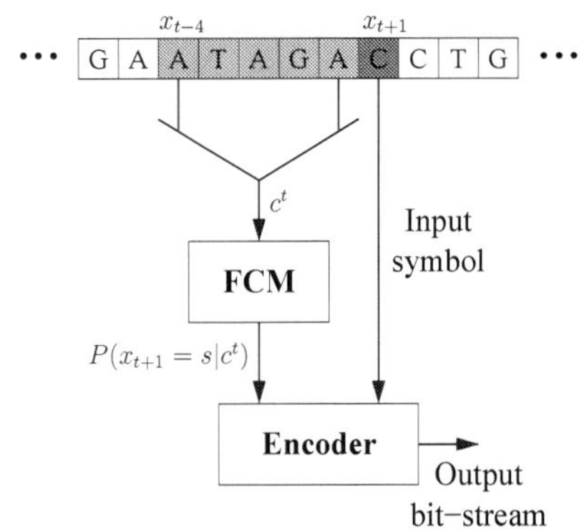

Fig. 1. Finite-context model: the probability of the next outcome, x_{t+1}, is conditioned by the M last outcomes. In this example, $M = 5$.

In practice, the probability that the next outcome, x_{t+1}, is s, where $s \in \mathcal{A} = \{A, C, G, T\}$, is obtained using the Lidstone estimator (Lidstone, 1920)

$$P(x_{t+1} = s|c^t) = \frac{n_s^t + \delta}{\sum\limits_{a \in \mathcal{A}} n_a^t + 4\delta}, \tag{1}$$

where n_s^t represents the number of times that, in the past, the information source generated symbol s having c^t as the conditioning context. The parameter δ controls how much probability is assigned to unseen (but possible) events, and plays a key role in the case of high-order

Context, c^t	n_A^t	n_C^t	n_G^t	n_T^t	$\sum_{a\in\mathcal{A}} n_a^t$
$AAAAA$	23	41	3	12	79
$\vdots$	$\vdots$	$\vdots$	$\vdots$	$\vdots$	$\vdots$
$ATAGA$	16	6	21	15	58
$\vdots$	$\vdots$	$\vdots$	$\vdots$	$\vdots$	$\vdots$
$GTCTA$	19	30	10	4	63
$\vdots$	$\vdots$	$\vdots$	$\vdots$	$\vdots$	$\vdots$
$TTTTT$	8	2	18	11	39

Table 1. Simple example illustrating how finite-context models are implemented. The rows of the table represent probability models at a given instant t. In this example, the particular model that is chosen for encoding a symbol depends on the last five encoded symbols (order-5 context).

models.[1] Note that Lidstone's estimator reduces to Laplace's estimator for $\delta = 1$ (Laplace, 1814) and to the frequently used Jeffreys (1946) / Krichevsky and Trofimov (1981) estimator when $\delta = 1/2$. In our work, we found out experimentally that the probability estimates calculated for the higher-order models lead to better compression results when smaller values of δ are used.

Note that, initially, when all counters are zero, the symbols have probability $1/4$, i.e., they are assumed equally probable. The counters are updated each time a symbol is encoded. Since the context template is causal, the decoder is able to reproduce the same probability estimates without needing additional information.

Table 1 shows an example of how a finite-context model is typically implemented. In this example, an order-5 finite-context model is presented (as that of Fig. 1). Each row represents a probability model that is used to encode a given symbol according to the last encoded symbols (five in this example). Therefore, if the last symbols were "$ATAGA$", i.e., $c^t = ATAGA$, then the model communicates the following probability estimates to the arithmetic encoder:

$$P(A|ATAGA) = (16+\delta)/(58+4\delta),$$

$$P(C|ATAGA) = (6+\delta)/(58+4\delta),$$

$$P(G|ATAGA) = (21+\delta)/(58+4\delta)$$

and

$$P(T|ATAGA) = (15+\delta)/(58+4\delta).$$

The block denoted "Encoder" in Fig. 1 is an arithmetic encoder. It is well known that practical arithmetic coding generates output bit-streams with average bitrates almost identical to the entropy of the model (Bell et al., 1990; Salomon, 2007; Sayood, 2006). The theoretical bitrate average (entropy) of the finite-context model after encoding N symbols is given by

$$H_N = -\frac{1}{N}\sum_{t=0}^{N-1} \log_2 P(x_{t+1} = s|c^t) \quad \text{bps,} \tag{2}$$

[1] When M is large, the number of conditioning states, 4^M, is high, which implies that statistics have to be estimated using only a few observations.

Context, c^t	n_A^t	n_C^t	n_G^t	n_T^t	$\sum_{a \in \mathcal{A}} n_a^t$
$AAAAA$	23	41	3	12	79
$\vdots$	$\vdots$	$\vdots$	$\vdots$	$\vdots$	$\vdots$
$ATAGA$	16	$\boxed{7}$	21	15	59
$\vdots$	$\vdots$	$\vdots$	$\vdots$	$\vdots$	$\vdots$
$GTCTA$	19	30	10	4	63
$\vdots$	$\vdots$	$\vdots$	$\vdots$	$\vdots$	$\vdots$
$TTTTT$	8	2	18	11	39

Table 2. Table 1 updated after encoding symbol "C", according to context "$ATAGA$".

where "bps" stands for "bits per symbol". When dealing with DNA bases, the generic acronym "bps" is sometimes replaced with "bpb", which stands for "bits per base". Recall that the entropy of any sequence of four symbols is, at most, two bps, a value that is achieved when the symbols are independent and equally likely.

Referring to the example of Table 1, and supposing that the next symbol to encode is "C", it would require, theoretically, $-\log_2((6+\delta)/(58+4\delta))$ bits to encode it. For $\delta = 1$, this is approximately 3.15 bits. Note that this is more than two bits because, in this example, "C" is the least probable symbol and, therefore, needs more bits to be encoded than the more probable ones. After encoding this symbol, the counters will be updated according to Table 2.

3.1 Inverted repeats

As previously mentioned, DNA sequences frequently contain sub-sequences that are reversed and complemented copies of some other sub-sequences. These sub-sequences are named "inverted repeats". As described in Section 2, this characteristic of DNA is used by most of the DNA compression methods that rely on the sliding window searching paradigm.

For exploring the inverted repeats of a DNA sequence, besides updating the corresponding counter after encoding a symbol, we also update another counter that we determine in the following way. Consider the example given in Fig. 1, where the context is the string "$ATAGA$" and the symbol to encode is "C". Reversing the string obtained by concatenating the context string and the symbol, i.e., "$ATAGAC$", we obtain the string "$CAGATA$". Complementing this string ($A \leftrightarrow T, C \leftrightarrow G$), we get "$GTCTAT$". Now we consider the prefix "$GTCTA$" as the context and the suffix "T" as the symbol that determines which counter should be updated. Therefore, according to this procedure, for taking into consideration the inverted repeats, after encoding symbol "C" of the example in Fig. 1, the counters should be updated according to Table 3.

3.2 Competing finite-context models

Because DNA data are non-stationary, alternating between regions of low and high entropy, using two models with different orders allows a better handling both of DNA regions that are best represented by low-order models and regions where higher-order models are advantageous. Although both models are continuously been updated, only the best one is used for

Context, c^t	n_A^t	n_C^t	n_G^t	n_T^t	$\sum_{a\in\mathcal{A}} n_a^t$
$AAAAA$	23	41	3	12	79
⋮	⋮	⋮	⋮	⋮	⋮
$ATAGA$	16	7	21	15	59
⋮	⋮	⋮	⋮	⋮	⋮
$GTCTA$	19	30	10	5	64
⋮	⋮	⋮	⋮	⋮	⋮
$TTTTT$	8	2	18	11	39

Table 3. Table 1 updated after encoding symbol "C" according to context "$ATAGA$" (see example of Fig. 1) and taking the inverted repeats property into account.

encoding a given region. To cope with this characteristic, we proposed a DNA lossless compression method that is based on two finite-context models of different orders that compete for encoding the data (see Fig. 2).

For convenience, the DNA sequence is partitioned into non-overlapping blocks of fixed size (we have used one hundred DNA bases), which are then encoded by one (the best one) of the two competing finite-context models. This requires only the addition of a single bit per data block to the bit-stream in order to inform the decoder of which of the two finite-context models was used. Each model collects statistical information from a context of depth $M_i, i = 1, 2, M_1 \neq M_2$. At time t, we represent the two conditioning outcomes by $c_1^t = x_{t-M_1+1}, \ldots, x_{t-1}, x_t$ and by $c_2^t = x_{t-M_2+1}, \ldots, x_{t-1}, x_t$.

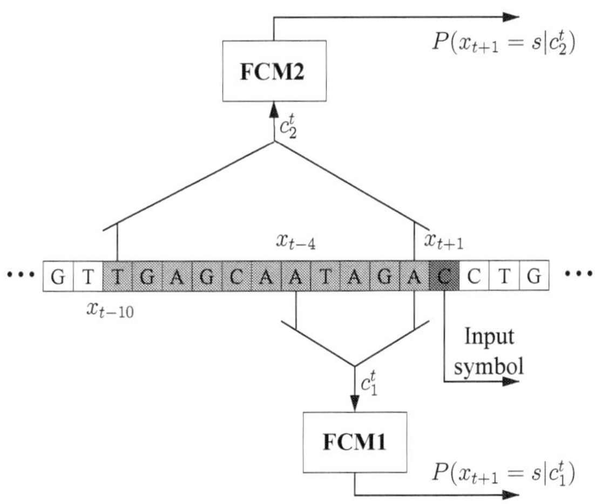

Fig. 2. Proposed model for estimating the probabilities: the probability of the next outcome, x_{t+1}, is conditioned by the M_1 or M_2 last outcomes, depending on the finite-context model chosen for encoding that particular DNA block. In this example, $M_1 = 5$ and $M_2 = 11$.

Using higher-order context models leads to a practical problem: the memory needed to represent all of the possible combinations of the symbols related to the context might be too large. In fact, as we mentioned, each DNA model of order-M implies 4^M different states of the Markov chain. Because each of these states needs to collect statistical data that is necessary to the encoding process, a large amount of memory might be required as the model order grows. For example, an order-16 model might imply a total of 4 294 967 296 different states.

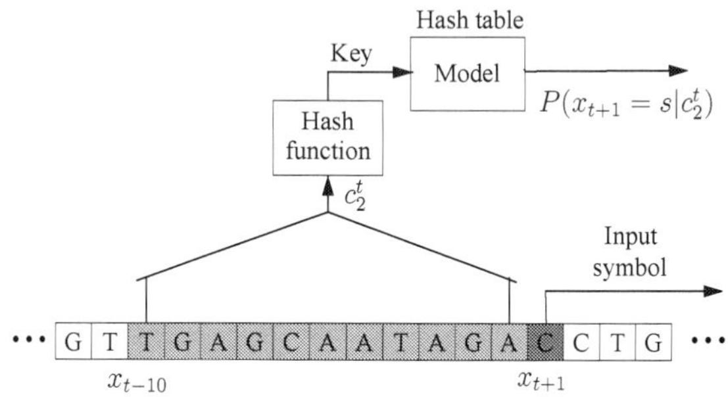

Fig. 3. The context model using hash tables. The hash table representation is shown in Fig. 4.

In order to overcome this problem, we implemented the higher-order context models using hash tables. With this solution, we only need to create counters if the context formed by the M last symbols appears at least once. In practice, for very high-order contexts, we are limited by the length of the sequence. In the current implementation we are able to use models of orders up to 32. However, as we will present later, the best value of M for the higher-order models is 16. This can be explained by the well known problem of context dilution. Moreover, for higher-order models, a large number of contexts occur only once and, therefore, the model cannot take advantage of them.

For each symbol, a key is generated according to the context formed by the previous symbols (see Fig. 3). For that key, the related linked-list if traversed and, if the node containing the context exists, its statistical information is used to encode the current symbol. If the context never appeared before, a new node is created and the symbol is encoded using an uniform probability distribution. A graphical representation of the hash table is presented in Fig. 4.

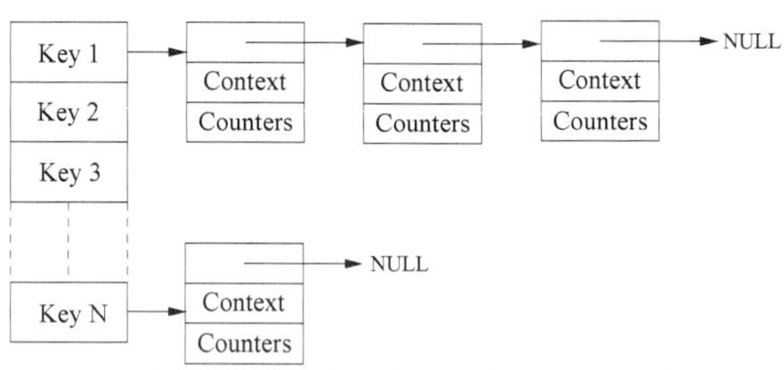

Fig. 4. Graphical representation of the hash table used to represent higher-order models. Each node stores the information of the context found (`Context`) and the counters associated to that context (`Counters`), four in the case of DNA sequences.

4. Experimental results

For the evaluation of the methods described in the previous section, we used the same DNA sequences used by Manzini and Rastero (2004), which are available from `www.mfn.unipmn.it/~manzini/dnacorpus`. This corpus contains sequences from four organisms: yeast (*Saccharomyces cerevisiae*, chromosomes 1, 4, 14 and the mitochondrial DNA), mouse (*Mus musculus*, chromosomes 7, 11, 19, x and y), arabidopsis (*Arabidopsis thaliana*, chromosomes 1, 3 and 4) and human (*Homo sapiens*, chromosomes 2, 13, 22, x and y).

First, we present results that show the effectiveness of the proposed inverted repeats updating mechanism for finite-context modeling. Next, we show the advantages of using multiple (in this case, two) competing finite-context models for compression.

4.1 Inverted repeats

Regarding the inverted repeats updating mechanism, each of the sequences was encoded using finite-context models with orders ranging from four to thirteen, with and without the inverted repeats updating mechanism. As in most of the other DNA encoding techniques, we also provided a fall back method that is used if the main method produces worse results. This is checked on a block by block basis, where each block is composed of one hundred DNA bases. As in the *DNA3* version of Manzini's encoder, we used an order-3 finite-context model as fall back method (Manzini and Rastero, 2004). Note that, in our case, both the main and fall back methods rely on finite-context models.

Table 4 presents the results of compressing the DNA sequences with the "normal" finite-context model (FCM) and with the model that takes into account the inverted repeats (FCM-IR). The bitrate and the order of the model that provided the best results are indicated. For comparison, we also included the results of the *DNA3* compressor of Manzini and Rastero (2004).

As can be seen from the results presented in Table 4, the bitrates obtained with the finite-context models using the updating mechanism for inverted repeats (FCM-IR) are always better than those obtained with the "normal" finite-context models (FCM). This confirms that the finite-context models can be modified according to the proposed scheme to exploit inverted repeats. Figure 5 shows how the finite-context models perform for various model orders, from order-4 to order-13, for the case of the "y-1" and "h-y" sequences.

4.2 Competing finite-context models

Each of the DNA sequences used by Manzini was encoded using two competing finite-context models with orders M_1, M_2, $3 \leq M_1 \leq 8$ and $9 \leq M_2 \leq 18$. For each DNA sequence, the pair M_1, M_2 leading to the lowest bitrate was chosen. The inverted repeats updating mechanism was used, as well as $\delta = 1$ for the lower-order model and $\delta = 1/30$ for the higher-order model. All information needed for correct decoding is included in the bit-stream and, therefore, the compression results presented in Table 5 take into account that information. The columns of Table 5 labeled "M_1" and "M_2" represent the orders of the used models and the columns labeled with the percent sign show the percentage of use of each finite-context model.

As can be seen from the results presented in Table 5, the method using two competing finite-context models always provides better results than the *DNA3* compressor. This confirms that the finite-context models may be successfully used as the only coding method for DNA sequences. Although we do not include here a comprehensive study of the impact of the δ parameter in the performance of the method, nevertheless we show an example to illustrate its influence on the compression results of the finite-context models. For example, using $\delta = 1$

Name	Size	DNA3	FCM		FCM-IR	
		bpb	Order	bpb	Order	bpb
y-1	230 203	1.871	10	1.935	11	1.909
y-4	1 531 929	1.881	12	1.920	12	1.910
y-14	784 328	1.926	9	1.945	12	1.938
y-mit	85 779	1.523	6	1.494	7	1.479
Average	–	1.882	–	1.915	–	1.904
m-7	5 114 647	1.835	11	1.849	12	1.835
m-11	49 909 125	1.790	13	1.794	13	1.778
m-19	703 729	1.888	10	1.883	10	1.873
m-x	17 430 763	1.703	12	1.715	13	1.692
m-y	711 108	1.707	10	1.794	11	1.741
Average	–	1.772	–	1.780	–	1.762
at-1	29 830 437	1.844	13	1.887	13	1.878
at-3	23 465 336	1.843	13	1.884	13	1.873
at-4	17 550 033	1.851	13	1.887	13	1.878
Average	–	1.845	–	1.886	–	1.876
h-2	236 268 154	1.790	13	1.748	13	1.734
h-13	95 206 001	1.818	13	1.773	13	1.759
h-22	33 821 688	1.767	12	1.728	12	1.710
h-x	144 793 946	1.732	13	1.689	13	1.666
h-y	22 668 225	1.411	13	1.676	13	1.579
Average	–	1.762	–	1.732	–	1.712

Table 4. Compression values, in bits per base (bpb), for several DNA sequences. The "DNA3" column shows the results obtained by Manzini and Rastero (2004). Columns "FCM" and "FCM-IR" contain the results, respectively, of the "normal" finite-context models and of the finite-context models equipped with the inverted repeats updating mechanism. The order of the model that provided the best result is indicated under the columns labeled "Order".

for both models would lead to bitrates of 1.869, 1.865 and 1.872, respectively for the "at-1", "at-3" and "at-4" sequences, i.e., approximately 2% worse than when using $\delta = 1/30$ for the higher-order model.

Finally, it is interesting to note that the lower-order model is generally the one that is most frequently used along the sequence and also the one associated with the highest bitrates. In fact, the bitrates provided by the higher-order finite-context models suggest that these are chosen in regions where the entropy is low, whereas the lower-order models operate in the higher entropy regions.

5. Conclusion

Finite-context models have been used by most DNA compression algorithms as a secondary, fall back method. In this work, we have studied the potential of this statistical modeling paradigm as the main and only approach for DNA compression. Several aspects have been addressed, such as the inclusion of mechanisms for handling inverted repeats and the use

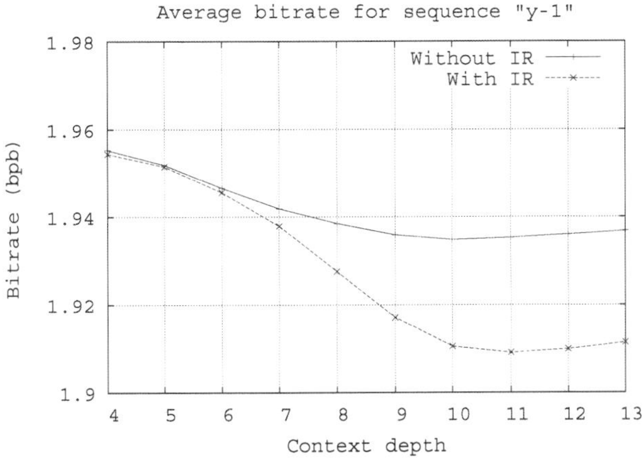

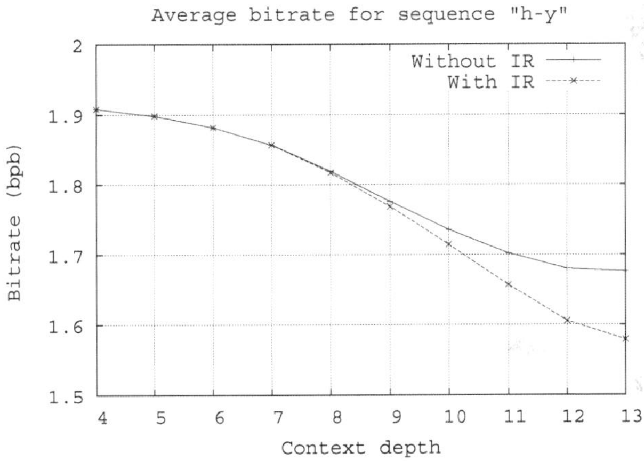

Fig. 5. Performance of the finite-context model as a function of the order of the model, with and without the updating mechanism for inverted repeats (IR), for sequences "y-1" and "h-y".

of multiple finite-context models that compete for encoding the data. This study allowed us to conclude that DNA models relying only on Markovian principles can provide significant results, although not as expressive as those provided by methods such as *MNL-1* or *XM*. Nevertheless, the experimental results show that the proposed approach can outperform methods of similar computational complexity, such as the *DNA3* coding method (Manzini and Rastero, 2004).

One of the key advantages of DNA compression based on finite-context models is that the encoders are fast and have $\mathcal{O}(n)$ time complexity. In fact, most of the computing time needed by previous DNA compressors is spent on the task of finding exact or approximate repeats of sub-sequences or of their inverted complements. No doubt, this approach has proved to give good returns in terms of compression gains, but normally at the cost of long compression

Name	Size	DNA3	FCM1			FCM2			FCM
		bps	M_1	%	bps	M_2	%	bps	bps
y-1	230 203	1.871	3	82	1.939	12	18	1.462	1.860
y-4	1 531 929	1.881	4	88	1.930	14	12	1.470	1.879
y-14	784 328	1.926	3	90	1.938	13	10	1.716	1.923
y-mit	85 779	1.523	5	83	1.533	9	17	1.178	1.484
Average	–	1.882	–	–	1.920	–	–	1.533	1.877
m-7	5 114 647	1.835	6	81	1.907	14	19	1.353	1.811
m-11	49 909 125	1.790	4	76	1.917	16	24	1.230	1.758
m-19	703 729	1.888	4	83	1.920	13	17	1.582	1.870
m-x	17 430 763	1.703	6	70	1.896	15	30	1.081	1.656
m-y	711 108	1.707	3	66	1.896	13	34	1.199	1.670
Average	–	1.772	–	–	1.911	–	–	1.206	1.738
at-1	29 830 437	1.844	6	82	1.898	16	18	1.475	1.831
at-3	23 465 336	1.843	6	80	1.901	16	20	1.495	1.826
at-4	17 550 033	1.851	6	80	1.897	15	20	1.560	1.838
Average	–	1.845	–	–	1.899	–	–	1.503	1.831
h-2	236 268 154	1.790	4	76	1.905	16	24	1.212	1.755
h-13	95 206 001	1.818	5	80	1.895	15	20	1.279	1.723
h-22	33 821 688	1.767	3	68	1.925	15	32	1.180	1.696
h-x	144 793 946	1.732	5	66	1.901	16	34	1.217	1.686
h-y	22 668 225	1.411	4	47	1.901	16	53	0.941	1.397
Average	–	1.762	–	–	1.903	–	–	1.212	1.711

Table 5. Compression values, in bits per symbol (bps), for several of DNA sequences. The "DNA3" column shows the results obtained by Manzini and Rastero (2004). Column "FCM" contains the results of the two combined finite-context models. The orders of the two models that provided the best result for each sequence are indicated under the columns labeled "M_1" and "M_2".

times. Although slow encoders could be tolerated for storage purposes (compression could be ran in batch mode), for interactive applications such as those involving the computation of complexity profiles (Dix et al., 2007) they are certainly not the most appropriate; faster methods, such as those examined in this chapter, could be particularly useful in those cases.

6. References

Behzadi, B. and F. Le Fessant (2005, June). DNA compression challenge revisited. In *Combinatorial Pattern Matching: Proc. of CPM-2005*, LNCS, Jeju Island, Korea. Springer-Verlag.

Bell, T. C., J. G. Cleary, and I. H. Witten (1990). *Text compression*. Prentice Hall.

Cao, M. D., T. I. Dix, L. Allison, and C. Mears (2007). A simple statistical algorithm for biological sequence compression. In *Proc. of the Data Compression Conf., DCC-2007*, Snowbird, Utah.

Chen, X., S. Kwong, and M. Li (1999). A compression algorithm for DNA sequences and its applications in genome comparison. In K. Asai, S. Miyano, and T. Takagi (Eds.), *Genome Informatics 1999: Proc. of the 10th Workshop*, Tokyo, Japan, pp. 51–61.

Chen, X., S. Kwong, and M. Li (2001). A compression algorithm for DNA sequences. *IEEE Engineering in Medicine and Biology Magazine 20*, 61–66.

Chen, X., M. Li, B. Ma, and J. Tromp (2002). DNACompress: fast and effective DNA sequence compression. *Bioinformatics 18*(12), 1696–1698.

Dennis, C. and C. Surridge (2000, December). *A. thaliana* genome. *Nature 408*, 791.

Dix, T. I., D. R. Powell, L. Allison, J. Bernal, S. Jaeger, and L. Stern (2007). Comparative analysis of long DNA sequences by per element information content using different contexts. *BMC Bioinformatics 8*(1471-2105-8-S2-S10).

Ferreira, P. J. S. G., A. J. R. Neves, V. Afreixo, and A. J. Pinho (2006, May). Exploring three-base periodicity for DNA compression and modeling. In *Proc. of the IEEE Int. Conf. on Acoustics, Speech, and Signal Processing, ICASSP-2006*, Volume 5, Toulouse, France, pp. 877–880.

Grumbach, S. and F. Tahi (1993). Compression of DNA sequences. In *Proc. of the Data Compression Conf., DCC-93*, Snowbird, Utah, pp. 340–350.

Grumbach, S. and F. Tahi (1994). A new challenge for compression algorithms: genetic sequences. *Information Processing & Management 30*(6), 875–886.

Jeffreys, H. (1946). An invariant form for the prior probability in estimation problems. *Proc. of the Royal Society (London) A 186*, 453–461.

Korodi, G. and I. Tabus (2005, January). An efficient normalized maximum likelihood algorithm for DNA sequence compression. *ACM Trans. on Information Systems 23*(1), 3–34.

Korodi, G. and I. Tabus (2007). Normalized maximum likelihood model of order-1 for the compression of DNA sequences. In *Proc. of the Data Compression Conf., DCC-2007*, Snowbird, Utah.

Krichevsky, R. E. and V. K. Trofimov (1981, March). The performance of universal encoding. *IEEE Trans. on Information Theory 27*(2), 199–207.

Laplace, P. S. (1814). *Essai philosophique sur les probabilités (A philosophical essay on probabilities)*. New York: John Wiley & Sons. Translated from the sixth French edition by F. W. Truscott and F. L. Emory, 1902.

Lidstone, G. (1920). Note on the general case of the Bayes-Laplace formula for inductive or a posteriori probabilities. *Trans. of the Faculty of Actuaries 8*, 182–192.

Manzini, G. and M. Rastero (2004). A simple and fast DNA compressor. *Software—Practice and Experience 34*, 1397–1411.

Matsumoto, T., K. Sadakane, and H. Imai (2000). Biological sequence compression algorithms. In A. K. Dunker, A. Konagaya, S. Miyano, and T. Takagi (Eds.), *Genome Informatics 2000: Proc. of the 11th Workshop*, Tokyo, Japan, pp. 43–52.

Pinho, A. J., A. J. R. Neves, V. Afreixo, C. A. C. Bastos, and P. J. S. G. Ferreira (2006, November). A three-state model for DNA protein-coding regions. *IEEE Trans. on Biomedical Engineering 53*(11), 2148–2155.

Pinho, A. J., A. J. R. Neves, C. A. C. Bastos, and P. J. S. G. Ferreira (2009, April). DNA coding using finite-context models and arithmetic coding. In *Proc. of the IEEE Int. Conf. on Acoustics, Speech, and Signal Processing, ICASSP-2009*, Taipei, Taiwan.

Pinho, A. J., A. J. R. Neves, and P. J. S. G. Ferreira (2008, August). Inverted-repeats-aware finite-context models for DNA coding. In *Proc. of the 16th European Signal Processing Conf., EUSIPCO-2008*, Lausanne, Switzerland.

Rivals, E., J.-P. Delahaye, M. Dauchet, and O. Delgrange (1995, November). A guaranteed compression scheme for repetitive DNA sequences. Technical Report IT–95–285, LIFL, Université des Sciences et Technologies de Lille.

Rivals, E., J.-P. Delahaye, M. Dauchet, and O. Delgrange (1996). A guaranteed compression scheme for repetitive DNA sequences. In *Proc. of the Data Compression Conf., DCC-96*, Snowbird, Utah, pp. 453.

Rowen, L., G. Mahairas, and L. Hood (1997, October). Sequencing the human genome. *Science 278*, 605–607.

Salomon, D. (2007). *Data compression - The complete reference* (4th ed.). Springer.

Sayood, K. (2006). *Introduction to data compression* (3rd ed.). Morgan Kaufmann.

Tabus, I., G. Korodi, and J. Rissanen (2003). DNA sequence compression using the normalized maximum likelihood model for discrete regression. In *Proc. of the Data Compression Conf., DCC-2003*, Snowbird, Utah, pp. 253–262.

Ziv, J. and A. Lempel (1977). A universal algorithm for sequential data compression. *IEEE Trans. on Information Theory 23*, 337–343.

7

Space-filling Curves in Generating Equidistrubuted Sequences and Their Properties in Sampling of Images

Ewa Skubalska-Rafajłowicz and Ewaryst Rafajłowicz
Institute of Computer Eng., Control and Robotics,
Wrocław University of Technology Wybrzeże Wyspiańskiego 27, 50 370, Wrocław
Poland

1. Introduction

Intensive streams of video sequences arise more and more frequently in monitoring the quality of production processes. Such streams not only have to be processed on-line, but also stored in order to document production quality and to investigate possible causes of insufficient quality. Direct storage of a video stream, coming with the intensity 10-30 frames per second with a resolution of 1-8 megapixels, from one production month would require 100-500 terra bytes of a disk (or tape) space. A common remedy is to apply compression algorithms (like MPEG or H264), but compression algorithms usually introduce changes in gray-levels or colors, which is undesirable from the point of view of identifying defects and their causes.

For these reasons we return to the traditional idea of sampling images, followed by loss-less compression. However, classical sampling on a rectangular grid is insufficient for our purposes, since it is still too demanding from the point of view of storage capacity. Our experience of using equidistributed (or quasirandom) sequences as experimental sites in nonparametric regression function estimation Rafajłowicz and Schwabe (2003); Rafajłowicz and Schwabe (2006); Rafajłowicz and Skubalska-Rafajłowicz (2003) suggests that such sequences can be good candidates for sampling sites. Roughly speaking, the reason is in that the projection of a 100×100 rectangular grid on the axes has 100 points, while a typical equidistributed sequence of the length 10^4 provides again 10^4 points when projected onto the same axes. The idea of using equidistributed (EQD) sequences in sampling images was firstly described in Thevenaz (2008), where it was used for image registration. Our goals are different and we need more specialized sampling schemes than a "general purpose" Halton's sequence, which was used in Thevenaz (2008).

Our aim is to propose a new method of generating equidistributed sequences, which is based on space-filling curves. Due to the remarkable properties of space-filling curves (SFC), which preserve volumes and (to some extent) neighborhoods, the proposed sequences are well-suited for sampling of images in such a way that samples can be processed similarly as an original image. We concentrate mainly on 2D images here, but 3D images are also covered by the theoretical properties. Simple reconstruction schemes, which are well-suited for industrial images, are also briefly discussed. We also indicate ways of generating sampling sequences

and reconstructing underlying images by neural networks, which are based on weighted averaging of gray-levels of nearest neighbors.
Let us note that space-filling curves have been used in image processing for image compression Kamata et all (1996); Lempel and Ziv (1986); Schuster and Katsaggelos (1997); Skubalska-Rafajłowicz (2001b), dithering Zhang (1998); Zhang (1997) halftoning Zhang and Webber (1993) and median filtering Regazzoni and Teschioni (1997); Krzyżak (2001). However, the measure and neighborhoods-preserving properties of these curves were not fully exploited.
The chapter is organized as follows.

1. In Section 2 we collect some known and certain not so well-known properties of space-filling curves, including the Hilbert, the Peano and the Sierpiński curves. In addition to measure-preserving properties, we provide an efficient algorithms for calculating approximations to selected space-filling curves. The definition and elementary properties of equidistributed sequences are recalled at the end of Section 2 with the emphasis on the Weyl sequences, which are used as the building block in the rest of the chapter.
2. The proposed way of generating equidistributed sequences is presented in Section 3. It is based on transforming the Weyl one-dimensional sequence $t_i = fractionalpart(i\,\theta)$, $i = 1, 2, \ldots, \theta$ – irrational, by a space-filling curve. We shall prove that sequences generated in this way are also equidistributed. The choice of θ is crucial for the practical behavior of the sampling scheme. Roughly speaking, θ should be an irrational number, which approximates badly by rational numbers.
3. In Section 4 we discuss some properties of our equidistributed sequences as a sampling scheme for 2D images.
   - We shall prove that the spectrum of a wide class of images can be reconstructed from samples when their number grows to infinity. By "wide class" we mean measurable functions, which allow for discontinuities.
   - We exploit the measure-preserving properties of space-filling curves in order to show that moments of images can easily be approximated from samples.
   - It will also be shown how simple image processing tasks can be performed, utilizing natural ordering of samples, which preserves neighbors in an image.
4. In section 5 we discuss two algorithms for the approximate reconstruction of the underlying image from samples. The first is based on the inversion of the spectrum estimate and it can be used for one image. The second one is based on the nearest neighbor (NN) technique, but it can be speeded up by preprocessing and storing (NN) addresses. This technique is useless for one image, but it is valuable when one needs to store a very long video sequence without degradation of pixel values, since NN addresses use only a very small portion of storage memory, while we gain on the reconstruction speed. The next reconstruction scheme, which is proposed here is based on neural networks of the radial-basis functions (RBF) type. We shall also provide the examples of sampling, processing and reconstructing industrial images.

2. Preliminaries

Our aim in this section is to collect known facts concerning space-filling curves and quasi-random sequences, which are useful for explaining the proposed way of sampling.

2.1 Space-filling curves – basic facts

In the 19th and at the beginning of the 20th century, space-filling curves were developed and investigated as mathematical "monsters", since they are continuous, but nowhere differentiable.

2.1.1 Definition

From those pioneering times researches more frequently treat space-filling curves as useful tools. The first applications were in approximate, multidimensional integration, see, e.g., Kuipers and Niederreiter (1974). The next area where they happened to be useful is scanning images Lamarque and Robert (1996); Cohen et all (2007) and the bibliography cited therein. Note that scanning images by a space-filling curve is the task, which is different from our goals, since the curve is expected to visit all the pixels in an image. Thus, scanning along a space-filling curve provides only linear ordering of pixels. Furthermore, in the above-mentioned papers additional features of space-filling curves, such as their ability to preserve closeness or area, were not used. Scanning images with utilization of some properties of space-filling curves for estimating the median was proposed in Krzyżak (2001). One more area of applications was proposed in Skubalska-Rafajłowicz (2001a), where space-filling curves were used as a tool in the Bayesian pattern recognition problems.

Definition 1. *A space-filling curve is a continuous mapping* $\Phi : I_1 \overset{onto}{\rightarrow} I_d$*, where* $I_d \overset{def}{=} [0, 1]^d$ *is d-dimensional unit cube (or interval* $I_1 = [0, 1]$*),* $d \geq 1$.

We cannot draw a space-filling curve, since it maps $[0, 1]$ onto I_2. Thus, the image of I_1 by Φ would be completely black in the unit square. However, we can draw an approximation to such a curve, as is illustrated in Fig. 1.
It is important to mention that these curves can be approximated to the desired accuracy by implementable algorithms (see below).
The well-known curves constructed by Hilbert, Peano and Sierpiński possess properties Sagan (1994); Milne (1980); Moore (1900); Sierpiński (1912); Platzman and Bartholdi (1989); Skubalska-Rafajłowicz (2001a), which are stated in the two next subsections. These properties are stated for $d = 2$, but they holds for $d > 2$ with obvious changes.

2.1.2 Most important properties

The formula for changing variables in integrals, which is stated below, was used for constructing multidimensional quadratures. Here, we shall need it for approximating the Fourier spectrum of images from samples.

Property 1 (F1 – Change of variables). *Let* $\Phi : I_1 \overset{onto}{\rightarrow} I_d$ *be a space-filling curve. Then, for every measurable function* $g : I_2 \rightarrow R$

$$\int_{I_2} g(x)\, dx = \int_0^1 g(\Phi(t))dt, \tag{1}$$

where $x = [x^{(1)}, x^{(2)}]^T$ *and T denotes the transposition and the integrals in (1) are understood in the Lebesgue sense.*

The Lipschitz continuity of the curves constructed by Hilbert, Sierpiński and Peano is somewhat more demanding property, than the continuity required in the above definition, but is less than necessary for the first order differentiability.

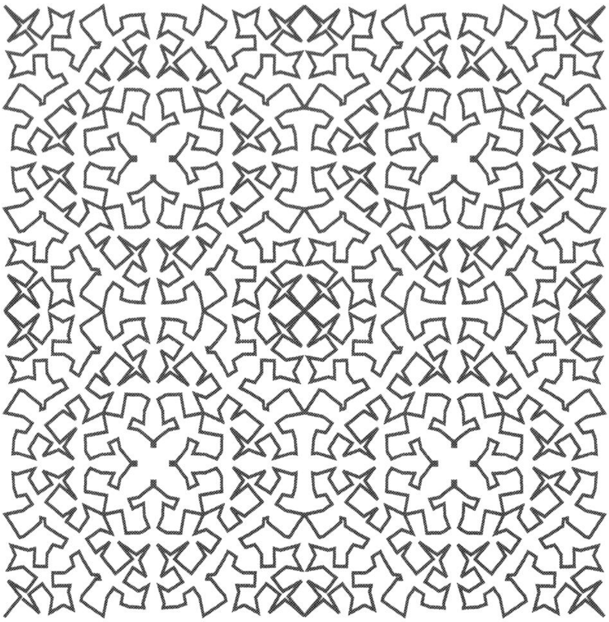

Fig. 1. An approximation to the Sierpiński SFC.

Property 2 (F2 – Lipschitz continuity). *There exists* $C_\Phi > 0$ *such that*

$$||\Phi(t) - \Phi(t')|| \leq C_\Phi |t - t'|^{1/2}, \tag{2}$$

where $||.||$ *is the Euclidean norm in* R^2.

The Lipschitz continuity (2) is stated above for a 2D case and it reads intuitively as a distance preserving property in the sense that points close to each other in the interval are transformed by Φ onto points close together in I_2, but the converse is not necessarily true, since curve $\Phi(t)$, $t \in I_1$ intersects itself many times.
The next property will be useful for evaluating areas from samples along a space-filling curve.

Property 3 (F3 – measure preservation). *Space-filling curve* Φ *is the Lebesgue measure preserving in the sense that for every Borel* $A \subset I_2$ *we have* $\mu_2(A) = \mu_1(\Phi^{-1}(A))$, *where* μ_1 *and* μ_2 *denote the Lebesgue measure in* R_1 *and* R_2, *respectively.*

At first glance, this property is strange. Note that it means that only values of lengths and areas before and after the transformation by Φ are equal. For example, an interval of the length $0.1\,cm$ is transformed into a set having the area $0.1\,cm^2$.

2.1.3 Quasi-inverses of space-filling curves

As mentioned above, points which are close in I_2 may have far, but not very far (see F2)) pre-images in I_1. The reason is that Φ does not have the inverse Sagan (1994) in the usual sense (intuitively, because a curve intersects itself). For our purposes it is of interest to find at least one $t \in I_1$ such that $\Phi(t) = x$ for given x. Consider a transformation $\Psi : I_2 \to I_1$, such that $\Psi(x) \in \Phi^{-1}(x)$, where $\Phi^{-1}(x)$ denotes the inverse image of x, i.e., the set $\{t \in I_1 : \Phi(t) = x\}$. Φ^{-1} allows to order linearly pixels in an image. We shall call Ψ a quasi-inverse of Φ.

Property 4 (F4 – Quasi-invers). *Let $\Phi : I_1 \overset{onto}{\to} I_d$ be a space-filling curve of the Hilbert, the Peano or the Sierpiński type. One can construct its quasi-inverse $\Psi : I_d \to I_1$ in such a way that it is also Lebesgue measure preserving.*

See Skubalska-Rafajłowicz (2004) for the constructive proof of this property.

2.1.4 Remarks on generating space-filling curves

It is important that there exist algorithms for calculating approximate value of the Peano, Hilbert and Sierpiński curves at a given point $t \in I_1$ with $O\left(\frac{d}{\varepsilon}\right)$ of arithmetic operations, where $\varepsilon > 0$ denotes the accuracy of approximation Butz (1971); Skubalska-Rafajłowicz (2003); Skubalska-Rafajłowicz (2001a)). Furthermore, quasi-inverses of these curves can also be calculated with the same computational complexity Skubalska-Rafajłowicz (2004); Skubalska-Rafajłowicz (2001b); Skubalska-Rafajłowicz (2001a)).

The specific self-similarities and the symmetries that space-filling curves usually possess, allow us to define a given space-filling curve. For example, consider Sierpiński's 2D curve. $\Phi(t) = (x(t), y(t))$ is uniquely defined by the following set of functional equations (see Sierpiński (1912) for the equivalent definition)

$$
\begin{cases} x(t) = 1/2 - x(4t + 1/2)/2, \\ y(t) = 1/2 - y(4t + 1/2)/2 \\ 0 \le t \le 1/8, \end{cases}
\begin{cases} x(t) = 1/2 + x(4(t - 7/8))/2, \\ y(t) = 1/2 - y(4(t - 7/8))/2 \\ 7/8 \le t \le 1, \end{cases}
\begin{cases} x(t) = 1/2 + x(1 - 4(t - 1/8))/2, \\ y(t) = 1/2 - y(1 - 4(t - 1/8))/2 \\ 1/8 \le t \le 3/8, \end{cases}
\begin{cases} x(t) = x(3/4 - t) \\ y(t) = 1 - y(3/4 - t) \\ 3/8 \le t \le 7/8. \end{cases}
\tag{3}
$$

It follows from (3) that $x(0) = y(0) = 0$ and $x(1/2) = y(1/2) = 1$. After above observation, one can convert (3) into recurrent algorithm of computing $\Phi(t),\ t \in I_1$. If t has a finite binary expansion, $\Phi(t)$ is obtained in a finite number of iterations. The code for generating the Sierpiński space-filling curve is provided in the Appendix.

2.2 Equidistributed sequences in general

Equidistributed sequences are deterministic sequences, which behave like random variables, which are drawn from a uniform distribution, but they are much more regular. They arise as a tool for numerical integration, which is applied like the well known Monte-Carlo method, but provides much more accurate results, at least for carefully selected sequences.

Definition 2. *A deterministic sequence* $(x_i)_{i=1}^n$ *is called equidistributed (EQD) (or uniformly distributed or quasi-random) sequence in* I_d *if*

$$\lim_{n\to\infty} n^{-1}\sum_{i=1}^{n} g(x_i) = \int_{I_d} g(x)dx \tag{4}$$

holds for every continuous function g *on* I_d.

We refer the reader to Kuipers and Niederreiter (1974) for account on properties of EQD sequences and on their discrepancies, which are measures of their "uniformity". We shall use this definition mainly for $d = 1$ and $d = 2$, but the properties, which are proved below hold also for $d > 2$.
The well-known way of generating EQD sequences in $[0, 1]$ is as follows

$$t_i = \text{frac}(i\,\theta), \qquad i = 1, 2, \ldots, \tag{5}$$

where the fractional part is denoted as frac(.), θ is an irrational number.
A large number of methods for generating multivariate EQD sequences have been proposed in the literature, including generalizations of (5), Van der Corput sequences, Halton sequences and many others Davis and Rabinowitz (1984); Kuipers and Niederreiter (1974). As far as we know, none of them have properties which are needed for our purposes.

3. Generating sequences equidistributed along a space-filling curve

We propose a new class of equidistributed multidimensional sequences, which is obtained from one-dimensional equidistributed sequences by transforming it by a space-filling curve. In fact, one can combine any reasonable way of generating a one-dimensional EQD sequence with one of the space-filling curves of the Hilbert, Peano or Sierpiński type.

3.1 A new scheme of generating EQD sequences

The proposed scheme of generating an equidistributed sequence along a space-filling curve is as follows.

Step 1) Calculate t_i's as in (5) (or as a one-dimensional Van der Corput sequence),

Step 2) Select one of the above space-filling curves as $\Phi : I_1 \to I_d$ and calculate x_i's as follows:

$$x_i = \Phi(t_i), i = 1, 2, \ldots, n. \tag{6}$$

For given n and θ it suffices to perform Steps 1) and 2) only once and store the resulting sequence x_i, $i = 1, 2, \ldots, n$. An example is shown in Fig. 2.

Proposition 1. *Sequence* $\{x_i\}_{i=1}^n$, $x_i \in R^d$, *which is generated according to the above method is the equidistributed sequence in* I_d.

Proof. For continuous $g : I_d \to R$,

$$n^{-1}\sum_{i=1}^{n} g(x_i) = n^{-1}\sum_{i=1}^{n} g(\Phi(t_i)) \to \int_0^1 g(\Phi(t))dt = \int_{I_2} g(x)\,dx, \tag{7}$$

since $\{t_i\}_{i=1}^n$ are EQD, Φ is continuous, while the last equality follows from F1).•

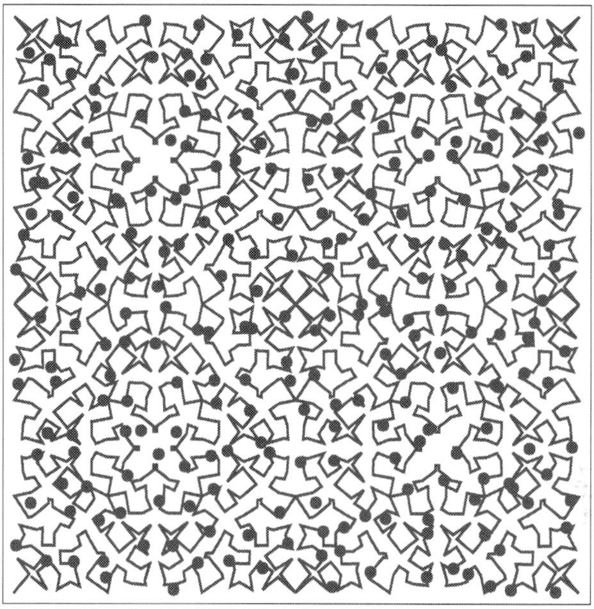

Fig. 2. The Sierpiński SFC and $n = 256$ EQD points.

3.2 Sampling of images

Application of the above sequence for sampling images is straightforward, but requires some preparation.

Preparation Perform Step 1 and Step 2, described in Section 3.1, for $d = 2$ in order to obtain EQD sequence $[x_i^{(1)}, x_i^{(1)}]$, $i = 1, 2, \ldots, n$.

Step 3 Scale and round sequence (6) as follows:

$$n_h(i) = round(N_h\, x_i^{(1)}), \quad n_v(i) = round(N_v\, x_i^{(1)}), \quad i = 1, 2, \ldots, n, \tag{8}$$

where $[n_h(i), n_v(i)]$ denote coordinates of pixels in a real image, which has N_h pixels width and N_v pixels height.

Step 4 Read out samples $f_i = f([n_h(i), n_v(i)]))$, $\quad i = 1, 2, \ldots, n$.

Remark 1. *In practice, samples are collected as in Step 4 above, but for theoretical discussions we shall consider "theoretical" sample values* $f_i = f(x_i)$, $i = 1, 2, \ldots, n$.

Remark 2. *Note that gray levels* f_i*'s are usually stored as integers from* 0 *to* 255, *instead of* $[0, 1]$, *as it is assumed about* f *and* f_i *later on in this chapter.*

4. Properties of the sampling scheme

This section is the central point of the chapter, since we collect here basic properties of the proposed sampling scheme. Some of them can be obtained by using known equdistributed sequences, but properties presented in Section 4.3 and the reconstruction methods discussed in Section 5 essentially use unique features of sequences, which are equidistributed along a space-filling curve.

4.1 Images as measurable functions

Function $f : R^d \to R$ is called measurable if for every $c \in R$ the following level sets $\{x : f(x) < c\}$ are measurable (see, e.g., Wheeden and Zygmund (1977) for the definition). In this chapter we treat images f as measurable functions. This is convenient from a mathematical point of view. On the other hand, the class of measurable functions is sufficiently wide to include real life gray level images. This class, in particular, contains discontinuous functions, which can be expressed as limits of sequences of continuous functions. Furthermore, limits of such limits are also measurable functions and this process can be iterated, leading again to measurable functions.
Color images in RGB format can be modelled as triples of measurable functions.

4.2 Spectrum approximation

Denote by $\mathcal{F}(\omega)$, $\omega = [\omega^{(1)}, \omega^{(2)}]^T$ the Fourier transform of image f, i.e.,

$$\mathcal{F}(\omega) = \int_{I_2} \exp(-\mathbf{j}\, \omega^T x)\, f(x)\, dx, \tag{9}$$

where $\mathbf{j}^2 = -1$. We approximate spectrum $\mathcal{F}$ by

$$\hat{\mathcal{F}}_n(\omega) = n^{-1} \sum_{i=1}^{n} \exp(-\mathbf{j}\, \omega^T x_i)\, f_i, \tag{10}$$

where x_i's are EQD along a space-filling curve.

Proposition 2. *If f is measurable in I_2 and sampled at EDQ points along a space-filling curve, then for every ω we have*

$$\lim_{n\to\infty} \left|\mathcal{F}(\omega) - \hat{\mathcal{F}}_n(\omega)\right| = 0. \tag{11}$$

The proof of this property is deferred to the Appendix. Note that this result was obtained without assuming that f is band-limited. For earlier results in this direction see Unser (1998). A detailed discussion of the convergence rate of $\hat{\mathcal{F}}_n(\omega)$ to $\mathcal{F}(\omega)$ is outside the scope of this chapter, since it requires some smoothness assumptions imposed on f. We only mention that if for f the Lipschitz condition with the exponent $0 < \alpha \leq 1$ holds, i.e.,

$$|f(x') - f(x'')| \leq C_f\, ||x' - x''||^{\alpha},$$

where $C_f > 0$ is a constant, then

$$\left|\mathcal{F}(\omega) - \hat{\mathcal{F}}_n(\omega)\right| \leq C\, (log(n)/n)^{\alpha/2},$$

where $C > 0$ is a constant, which may depend on f, the kind of a space-filling curve and ω, but not on n.

4.3 Fast approximate segmentation and blob analysis based on samples

The segmentation of images is a basic technique for marking objects, which are characterized by (approximately) the same gray level. In other words, our aim is to mark (approximately) regions such that

$$\{x \in I_2 : G_1 < f(x) < G_2\}, \tag{12}$$

where $0 \leq G_1 < G_2 \leq 1$ are specified thresholds. The next step is to find blobs, which are cluster of points, which are close to each other and far from points, which belong to another cluster. The segmentation and blob analysis task is time consuming, since it requires to not only visit each pixel and to mark it (as black, say), if $G_1 < f(x) < G_2$, but also to group marked into clusters, which usually requires to visit marked pixels several times (see, e.g., Davies (2005)).

We can reduce the computational burden by performing the segmentation and the blob analysis directly on samples. The blob analysis is also called silhouettes analysis, which are extracted by the segmentation.

Assume that sample points (t_i, f_i), $i = 1, 2, \ldots, n$ are reordered according to their first coordinates. Denote by $t_{(i)}$ i-th point of the equidistributed sequence in I_1. Thus, after sorting $t_{(i)} < t_{(i+1)}$, $i = 1, 2, \ldots, n$. Simultaneously – we keep the corresponding gray levels, which are denoted by $f_{(i)}$'s, i.e.,

$$f_{(i)} = f(\Phi(t_{(i)})), \quad i = 1, 2, \ldots, n \tag{13}$$

Thus, our samples have the form $(t_{(i)}, f_{(i)})$. Now the procedure for approximate segmentation and blob analysis runs as follows.

Segmentation For each sample point mark $t_{(i)}$ as "black", if

$$G_1 < f_{(i)} < G_2 \quad i = 1, 2, \ldots, n.$$

Blob analysis Starting from $t_{(1)}$, search for the first group of consecutive points

$$t_{(p)} < t_{(p+1)} < \ldots < t_{(q)}, \quad 1 \leq p < q,$$

which are marked as "black". Then, repeat this search starting from $t_{(q+2)}$ ($t_{(q+1)}$ cannot be a member of the first group) and find the second group etc. Attach a label, e.g., number or color, to each group and treat it as the approximation of a blob.

Measuring blobs For each blob calculate the difference between the last point and the first point, i.e., $t_{(q)} - t_{(p)}$ and treat it as the approximation of the area of the corresponding blob.

The segmentation step does not require explanation (see Fig. 3). In the second step we use F2) property of space-filling curves that is if points $t_{(j)}$ and $t_{(j+1)}$ are close, the also points $x_{(j)} = \Phi(t_{(j)})$ and $x_{(j+1)} = \Phi(t_{(j+1)})$ are close in the image. To justify the last step, let us note that, according to F3) and F4), the length $\left|t_{(q)} - t_{(p)}\right|$ can be used as the approximation of the area of the smallest polygon containing $x_{(j)}$, $j = p, p+1, \ldots, q$.

The idea of the approximate blob analysis is illustrated in Fig. 3. The white, gray and black squares (left panel) were sampled in 512 points, which are equidistributed along the Sierpiński space-filling curve. The resulting gray levels are shown in the right panel. Note that samples from the white square are almost perfectly grouped as samples, which are numbered as 320 to 440. Similarly, samples from the black and light gray squares are grouped in the right panel as samples from 60 to (almost) 200 and from 200 to 320, respectively. Samples from the dark gray square are split into two groups. The first one is numbered from 1 to 60. the second one, from 420 to 512. The consequence of this (unavoidable) split is not too severe, since we obtain two blobs of dark gray color (if $G_1 \approx 185$, $G_2 \approx 195$) instead of one, but when transformed to the image space, these two blobs will be close to each other. The only points, which would lead to false grouping are shown as separate points in the right panel of Fig. 3. This is the price paid for speeding up grouping. We can avoid even these false classifications by checking a proper classification of small clusters, but at the expense of an additional computational burden. The above approach can be applied to images in RGB format, just by applying it to each channel separately, but keeping the same sequence $t_{(i)}$'s.

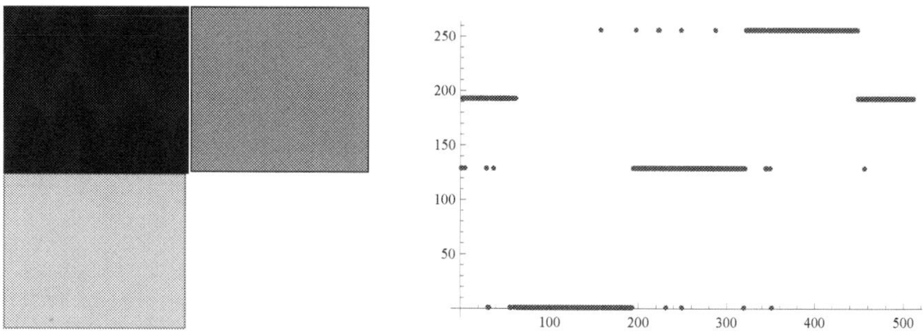

Fig. 3. Explanation why (approximate) segmentation and blob analysis work.

4.4 Approximating moments

Moments a_k of image f with respect to linearly independent functions $v_k(x)$ are defined as

$$a_k = \int_{I_2} f(x)\, v_k(x)\, dx, \quad k = 1, 2, \ldots. \tag{14}$$

a_k's are usually approximated by the sums of gray levels located at all the pixels. We can gain much on efficiency using $\hat{\alpha}_k^{(n)} = n^{-1} \sum_{i=1}^{n} f_i$ to evaluate theoretical moments from samples.

Proposition 3. *Let f and v_k, $k = 1, 2, \ldots$ be measurable functions in I_2. Then, for f_i sampled at points x_i, which are equidistributed along a space-filling curve, we have*

$$\lim_{n \to \infty} |\alpha_k - \hat{\alpha}_k^{(n)}| = 0, \tag{15}$$

i.e., approximate moments converge to the theoretical moments as the number of samples grows to infinity.

We omit the proof, since it is similar to the one for the spectrum approximation.
The role of moments in image analysis is well established (see, e.g., Davies (2005); Pawlak (2006). In particular, selecting $v_k(x)$'s as ordered monomials one can evaluate centroids of blobs, their area etc. Central moments, in turn, provides translation invariant information about shape parameters describing blobs.

4.5 Moving mean and median filtering

The moving mean and the moving median are the most popular filters applied in image processing. A rectangular window of size $(2P+1) \times (2Q+1)$, say, is scanning the image and the mean value (or the empirical median) of gray levels of the corresponding pixels replaces the central pixel value.

Assuming that samples are ordered as in Section 4.3, one can perform (approximately) the same kind of filtering directly on samples. The filtering process runs as follows.

Step 1 Sort samples according to their first coordinates in order to obtain $(t_{(i)}, f_{(i)})$.

Step 2 Select half of the size of a neighborhood, which is used for filtering. Denote it by S.

Step 3 Starting from $i = S+1$ to $i = n-(S+1)$, perform the following operations:

1. calculate

$$\hat{f}_i = (2S+1)^{-1} \sum_{m=-S}^{S} f_{(i-m)} \tag{16}$$

   or the empirical median of the following gray levels

$$\{f_{(i-m)} : m = -S, \ldots, 0, 1, \ldots, S\},$$

2. $\hat{f}_i$ (or by the empirical median) is attached to the point $t_{(i)}$ in the filtered sample.

As usual, we are faced with the boundary problem, since we cannot filter samples numbered by $i \leq S$ and $i \geq n-S$. The simplest remedy is to leave these samples unchanged.

Somewhat more sophisticated way of median filtering along a space-filling curve was proposed in Krzyżak (2001), but – in opposite to the present chapter – neighbors were not equidistributed.

As is known, sampling of images and sapce-filling curves have many other applications (see, e.g., Davies (2001); Lamarque and Robert (1996)), in which the sampling scheme proposed here can also be useful.

5. Approximate reconstruction by k-nearest neighbors RBF nets

Our aim is to demonstrate that images can be efficiently reconstructed from the samples, which are equidistributed along a space-filling curve. We shall concentrate on reconstruction schemes, which are based on nearest neighbors and artificial neural networks from the radial basis functions (RBF) class.

An alternative way would be to estimate the spectrum of an image according to (10) on a regular grid and to calculate the inverse discrete Fourier transform by the FFT algorithm.

5.1 Reconstruction using RBF nets and exact neighbors

Consider $N_h \times N_v$ image. The coordinates of its pixels are denoted as (h, v), while positions of sample points are denoted as $(n_h(i), n_v(i))$, $i = 1, 2, \ldots, n$. Abusing the notation, we shall write $f_{(k,m)}$, forgetting for a while that earlier f was defined in $[0, 1]^2$.

5.1.1 1-NN reconstruction scheme

A seemingly naive algorithm of reconstructing the underlying image is the following.

Preparations For all $N_h N_v$ positions (h, v) pixels find the nearest neighbor (1-NN) among positions of samples $(n_h(i), n_v(i))$, $i = 1, 2, \ldots, n$ and store these positions in $N_h \times N_v$ table C, say. Its elements $c(h, v)$, $h = 1, 2 \ldots, N_h$, $v = 1, 2 \ldots, N_v$ contain addresses to the closest sample point.

Step 1 Repeat Step 2 for $h = 1, 2 \ldots, N_h$, $v = 1, 2 \ldots, N_v$.

Step 3 Attach gray level of the nearest sample point $f_{(c(h,v))}$ to pixel (h, v).

The most time consuming Step 1 is performed only once. As a result we obtain table C, which is of the same size as an original image and – at a first glance – all the compression effect is distracted. Note however, that when frames from a long video sequence are sampled and later some of them have to be reconstructed, then it pays to store matrix C in order to have an almost immediate reconstruction of selected frames. This is exactly the case when a production quality is monitored by a camera and we have to store (and keep for a long time) very long sequences of images, which document the quality of products.

5.1.2 k-NN reconstruction using RBF net

We can generalize the above reconstruction scheme by taking into account gray levels of nearest neighbors starting from the first one, second nearest up to k-th nearest. It is convenient to express such a generalized reconstruction scheme as a neural network from the well known radial basis functions (RBF) class.

To this end, we select a nonnegative kernel $K : R_1 \to R_1$, which is a function such that

$$\int_{-\infty}^{\infty} t\,K(t)\,dt = 0, \quad \int_{-\infty}^{\infty} t^2\,K(t)\,dt < \infty, \tag{17}$$

which is normalized $K(0) = 1$. This kind of normalization is not typical, but convenient for our purposes. Typical examples include the uniform kernel ($K(t) = 1$, $|t| < 1$ and zero otherwise), the Epanechnikov kernel etc.

Denote by $\tilde{f}_{(h,v)}$ the reconstructed gray level at (h, v), which is calculated as follows

$$\tilde{f}_{(h,v)} = \sum_{j=1}^{k} w_j(h, v)\, f_{c(j,h,v)}, \tag{18}$$

where $c(j, h, v)$ is the address of j-th closest point among positions of samples $(n_h(i), n_v(i))$, $i = 1, 2, \ldots, n$, while weights $w_j(h, v)$ are defined as follows:

$$w_j(h, v) = \frac{K\left(||(h, v) - c(j, h, v)||^2 / H(k)\right)}{\sum_{j=1}^{k} K\left(||(h, v) - c(j, h, v)||^2 / H(k)\right)}, \tag{19}$$

where

$$H(k) \stackrel{def}{=} ||(h, v) - c(k, h, v)||^2. \tag{20}$$

Note that when $k = 1$ and kernel K is the uniform one, then (18) reduces to 1-NN reconstruction scheme.

We remark that (18) is the approximation scheme rather than interpolatory one, as it was used in Anton et all (2001).

5.2 Reconstruction using RBF nets and neighbors along SFC

We can reduce the computational burden on finding nearest neighbors by replacing the exact search by the approximate one, which is performed along a space-filling curve. The proposed method is as follows.

1-NN along SFC

Step 1 For all pixels (h, v) perform the following steps:

1. normalize current pixel (h, v) to I_2 as $x_{h,v} \stackrel{def}{=} (h/N_h, v/N_v)$.
2. calculate its quasi-inverse $t_{h\,v} \stackrel{def}{=} \Psi(x_{h,v})$
3. find its nearest neighbor among all $t_{(i)}$'s and denote its number by $\hat{c}(h, v)$.

and store the resulting $N_h \times N_v$ matrix as $\hat{C}$.

Step 2 As the approximate value of f at pixel (h, v) (or at $x_{h,v}$) take f at $\hat{c}(h, v)$.

Step 3 Repeat Step 2 for all (h, v).

The main advantage of this scheme is in that finding NN among ordered $t_{(i)}$'s has computational complexity $O(\log_2(n))$. The price for that is a possibility of missing the true NN in I_2, since in Step 1 we use the quasi-inverse of SFC. Nevertheless, a point found in this is close to NN in I_2 due to F2). Matrix $\hat{C}$ can be treated as approximation of matrix C in the sense that many of its entries are the same as the corresponding entries of matrix C. The differences arise due to self-crossing of SFC.
We do not provide details of reconstruction by RBF net, which is based on approximate nearest neighbors, since changes in (19) and (20) are obvious.

5.3 Reconstruction by local random spreading of grey levels

In opposite to the above-described reconstruction schemes, which are based on searching (approximate) neighbors to each pixel, the method considered here spreads gray levels of samples in their neighborhoods. Below, we describe the simplest way of such spreading, which is based on a random choice of neighbors.

Reconstruction by random spreading

Step 1 Prepare $N_h \times N_v$ matrix S, say, as follows. Fill its entries, denoted as $s(h, v)$ by sampled gray levels at appropriate positions. The remaining entries fill by "empty" symbol (coded as a number greater than 1 (or 255)).

Step 2 Check whether "empty" entries are present in S. If not, the stop and S contains the reconstructed image. Otherwise, go to Step 3.

3 Find the position of the next "empty" element of matrix S and denote it by (h, v).

Step 4 Select at random (with equal probabilities) one of the following directions "up", "down", "left", "right".

Step 5 Assign the contents of $s(h-1, v)$ to $s(h, v)$, if the direction is "left". Assign the contents of $s(h+1, v)$ to $s(h, v)$, if the direction is "right" etc. Go to Step 2.

In Step 5 it may happen that the contents assigned to $s(h, v)$ is still "empty", but after a short time gray levels of samples nicely "smear" over the image. The result of the reconstruction is random, but repeated reconstructions produce visually stable images in a relatively short time. In Steps 4 and 5 one can use the neighborhood containing eight or more pixels.

5.4 Examples

As explained in the Introduction, the proposed sampling and reconstruction schemes are dedicated mainly for industrial images. However, it is instructive to verify their performance using the well-known example, which is shown in Fig. 4. Analysis of the differences between the original and the reconstructed images indicate that 1-NN reconstruction scheme provides the most exact reconstruction, but the reconstruction by random spreading provides the nicest looking image.

The application to industrial images is illustrated in Fig. 5, in which a copper slab with defects is shown. Note that it suffices to store 4096 samples in order to reconstruct 1000×1000 image, without distorting gray levels of samples from the original image. This is equivalent to the compression ratio of about $1/250$. Such a compression rate plus loss-less compression allows us to store a video sequence (30 fps) from one month of a continuous production process on a disk or tape, having 1 TB (terra byte) capacity.

6. Appendix – proof of Proposition 3

Take arbitrary $\epsilon > 0$. By the Lusin theorem, there exists a set $E = E(\epsilon/4)$ such that $f|_E$ is continuous and $\mu_2(E - I_2) < \epsilon/4$. Denote by $\mathcal{F}_E(\omega)$ the Fourier transform of $f|_E$. Then, for $D \stackrel{def}{=} E - I_2$ we have

$$|\mathcal{F}(\omega) - \mathcal{F}_E(\omega)| = \left| \int_D e^{-\mathbf{j}\,\omega^T x} f(x)\, dx \right| < \mu_2(D) < \frac{\epsilon}{4}, \tag{21}$$

since both integrands do not exceed 1. Let

$$\hat{\mathcal{F}}_E(\omega) = n^{-1} \sum_{x_i \in E} \exp(-\mathbf{j}\,\omega^T x_i)\, f_i. \tag{22}$$

Define $\Delta_n = \left|\hat{\mathcal{F}}_n(\omega) - \hat{\mathcal{F}}_E(\omega)\right|$. Then

$$\Delta_n = \left| n^{-1} \sum_{x_i \notin E} \exp(-\mathbf{j}\,\omega^T x_i)\, f_i \right|. \tag{23}$$

Clearly, $\Delta_n \leq \mathcal{N}(I_2 - E)/n$, where

$$\mathcal{N}(I_2 - E) \stackrel{def}{=} \mathrm{card}\{i :\, x_i \in (I_2 - E)\}.$$

From Proposition 1 it follows that for $n \to \infty$

$$\Delta_n \leq \frac{\mathcal{N}(I_2 - E)}{n} \to \mu_2(I_2 - E) < \epsilon/4. \tag{24}$$

Thus, for n sufficiently large we have $\Delta_n < \epsilon/4$. Define

$$\delta_n = \left| \left(\frac{1}{n} - \frac{1}{\mathcal{N}(E)} \right) \sum_{x_i \in E} \exp(-\mathbf{j}\,\omega^T x_i)\, f_i \right|$$

where $\mathcal{N}(E) \stackrel{def}{=} \mathrm{card}\{i :\, x_i \in E\}$. Clearly,

$$\left| \sum_{x_i \in E} \exp(-\mathbf{j}\,\omega^T x_i)\, f_i \right| \leq \mathcal{N}(E).$$

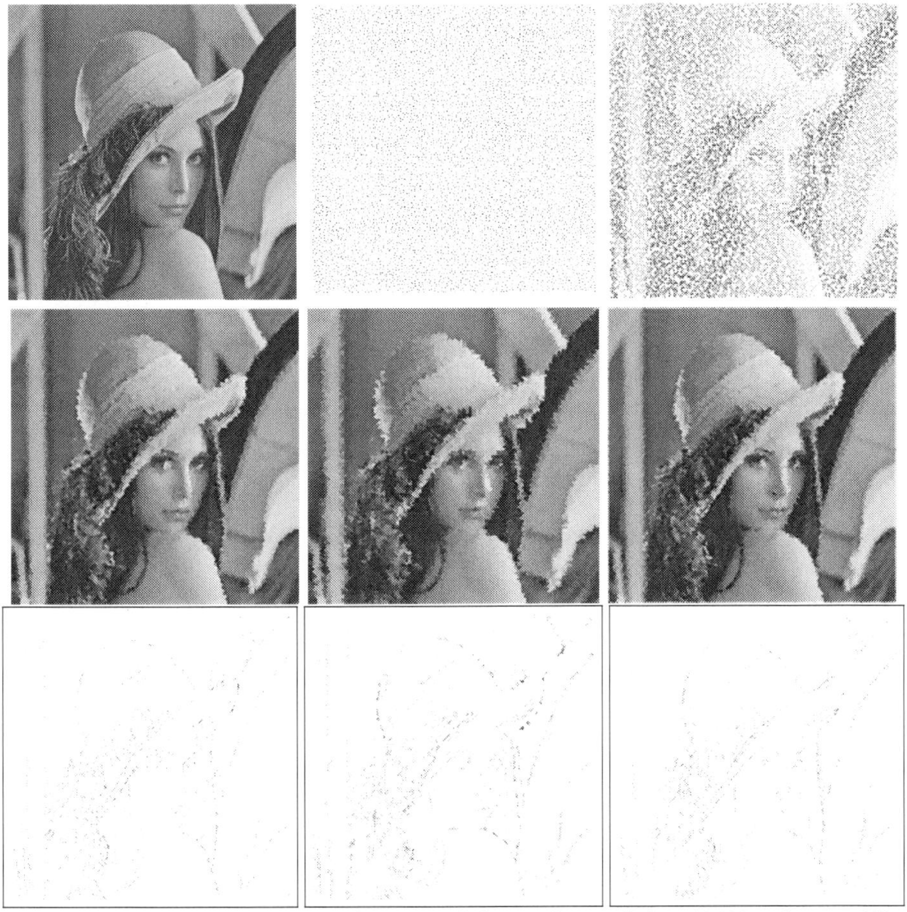

Fig. 4. Lena image, 512 × 512 pixels, (upper-left panel) sampled at 10 000 points equidistributed along the Sierpiński space-filling curve (upper-middle panel). Gray levels at sample points are shown in the upper-right panel. The results of reconstruction by 1-NN method (middle left panel), by 1-NN along the space-filling curve (central panel) and by spread to random-NN (middle right panel). The differences between the original image and the reconstructed one are shown in the last row of this figure.

Thus, for n large enough

$$\delta_n \leq |(\mathcal{N}(E)/n - 1|) < \epsilon/4, \tag{25}$$

since, by Proposition 1, $|(\mathcal{N}(E)/n - \mu_2(I_2)|) \to 0$ as $n \to \infty$. We omit argument ω in the formulas that follow. Summarizing, we obtain.

$$\left|\mathcal{F} - \hat{\mathcal{F}}_n\right| < \epsilon/4 + \left|F_E - \hat{\mathcal{F}}_n\right|, \tag{26}$$

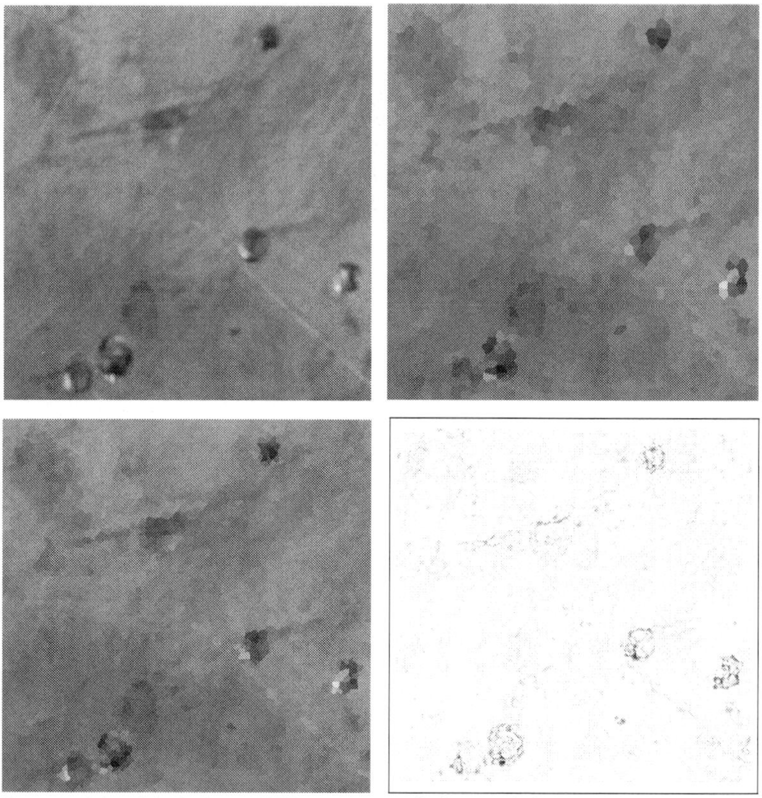

Fig. 5. Copper slab with defects, 1000×1000 pixels (upper left panel) and its reconstruction from $n = 2048$ samples by 1-NN method (upper right panel). The same slab reconstructed from $n = 4096$ samples (lower left panel) and the difference between the original image and the reconstructed one (lower right panel). Compression ratio 1/250.

since, by (21), $|\mathcal{F} - \mathcal{F}_E| < \epsilon/4$. Analogously,

$$\left|\mathcal{F}_E - \hat{\mathcal{F}}_n\right| < \epsilon/4 + \left|\hat{\mathcal{F}}_E - \hat{\mathcal{F}}_n\right|, \tag{27}$$

due to (24). Finally,

$$\left|\mathcal{F}_E - \hat{\mathcal{F}}_E\right| \leq \delta_n + \tag{28}$$

$$+ \left|\mathcal{F}_E - \frac{1}{\mathcal{N}(E)} \sum_{x_i \in E} \exp(-\mathbf{j}\,\omega^T x_i)\, f_i\right|.$$

The last term in (28) approaches zero, since f is continuous in E and Proposition 1 holds. Hence, $\left|\mathcal{F}_E - \hat{\mathcal{F}}_E\right| < \epsilon/2$ for n large enough, due to (25). Using this inequality in (27) and invoking (26) we obtain that for n large enough we have $\left|\mathcal{F} - \hat{\mathcal{F}}_n\right| < \epsilon$. •

7. Appendix – Generating the Sierpiński space-filling curve and equidistributed points along it.

In this Appendix we provide implementations of procedures for generating points from the Sierpiński space-filling curve and its quasi-inverse, which are written in Wolfram's Mathematica language. Special features of new versions of Mathematica are not implemented with the hope that the code should run and be useful for all versions, starting from version 3.
The following procedure `tranr` calculates one point of the Sierpiński curve, i.e., for given $t \in I_1$ an approximation to $\Phi(t) \in I_d$ is provided, but only for $d \geq 2$ and even. Parameter k of this procedure controls the accuracy to which the curve is approximated. It should be a positive integer. In the examples presented in this chapter $k = 32$ was used.

```
tranr[d_,k_,t_]:= Module[{bd,cd,ii,j,jj,tt,KM,km,be,kb},
bd=1; tt:=t;xx={1};
Do[bd=2^ii-bd+1; AppendTo[xx,1],{ii,d-1}];
cd=bd*2^(-d); km={};
Do[kb=Floor[(tt-cd/2^d)*2^d]+1;
   tt=2^d*(tt-cd/2^d-(kb-1)*2^(-d));
   If[kb==2^d, kb=0];
   If[ Floor[kb/2]<kb/2,tt=1-tt]; AppendTo[km,kb] ,{j,k}];
Do[ KM=km[[k-j+1]]; ww={};
  Do[ If[KM< 2^(d-jj),be=0,be=1]; AppendTo[ww,be];
      KM=KM-be*2^(d-jj);
      If[be==1,KM=2^(d-jj)-KM-1] ,{jj,d}];
Do[xx[[d-jj+1]]=1/2-(1/2-ww[[jj]])*xx[[d-jj+1]] ,{jj,d}] ,{j,k}];
  (*out*) xx]
```

The following lines of the Mathematica code generate the sequence of 2D points, which are equidistributed along the Siepinski space-filling curve.

```
dim = 2; deep = 32; n = 512;  th = (Sqrt[5.] - 1.)/2.;   {i, 1, n}]];
points = Map[tranr[dim, deep, #] &, Sort[Table[FractionalPart[i*th]];
```

8. References

Anton F.; Mioc D. & Fournier A. (2001) Reconstructing 2D images with natural neighbour interpolation. *The Visual Computer*, Vol. 17, No. 1, (2001) pp. 134-146, ISSN: 0178-2789

Butz A. (1971) Alternative Algorithm for Hilbert's Space-filling Curve. *IEEE Trans. on Computing*, Vol. C-20, No. 4, (1971) pp. 424-426, ISSN: 0018-9340

Cohen A.; Merhav N. & Weissman T. (2007) Scanning and sequential decision making for multidimensional data Part I: The noiseless case. *IEEE Trans. Information Theory*, Vol. 53, No. 9, (2007) pp. 3001-3020, ISSN: 0018-9448

Davies, E.R. (2001) A sampling approach to ultra-fast object location. *Real-Time Imaging*, Vol. 7, No. 4, pp. 339-355, ISSN: 1077-2014

Davies, E.R. (2005) *Machine Vision*, Morgan Kaufmann, ISBN: 0-12-206093-8, San Francisco

Davis P. & Rabinowitz P. (1984) *Methods of Numerical Integration*, Academic Press, ISBN: 0-12-206360-0, Orlando FL

Kamata S.; Niimi M. & Kawaguchi, E. (1996) A gray image compression using a Hilbert scan. *Proceedings of the 13th International Conference on Pattern Recognition*, Vienna, Austria, August, 1996, Vol. 3, pp. 905-909

Krzyżak A.; Rafajłowicz E. & Skubalska-Rafajłowicz E. (2001) Clipped median and space-filling curves in image filtering. *Nonlinear Analysis: Theory, Methods and Applications,* Vol. 47, No. 1, pp 303-314, ISSN: 0362-546X

Kuipers L. & Niederreiter H. (1974) *Uniform Distribution of Sequences.* Wiley, ISBN: 0471510459/9780471510451, New York

Lamarque C. -H. & Robert F. (1996) Image analysis using space-filling curves and 1D wavelet bases, *Pattern Recognition,* Vol. 29, No. 8, August 1996, pp 1309-1322, ISSN: 0031-3203

Lempel, A. & Ziv, J. (1986) Compression of two-dimensional data. *IEEE Transactions on Information Theory,* Vol. 32, No. 1, January 1986, pp. 2-8, ISSN: 0018-9448

Milne S. C. (1980) Peano curves and smoothness of functions. *Advances in Mathematics,* Vol. 35, No. 2, 1980, pp. 129-157, ISSN: 0001-8708

Moore E.H. (1900) On certain crinkly curves. *Trans. Amer. Math. Soc.,* Vol. 1, 1900, pp. 72–90

Pawlak M. (2006) *Image Analysis by Moments,* Wrocław University of Techmology Press, ISBN: 83-7085-966-6, Wrocław

Platzman L.K . & Bartholdi J.J. (1898) Spacefilling curves and the planar traveling salesman problem. *Journal of the ACM,* Vol. 36, No. 4, October 1989, pp. 719-737, ISSN: 0004-5411

Rafajłowicz E. & Schwabe R. (2003) Equidistributed designes in nonparametric regression. *Statistica Sinica,* Vol. 13, No 1, 2003, pp. 129-142, ISSN: 1017-0405

Rafajłowicz E. & Skubalska-Rafajłowicz E. (2003) RBF nets based on equidistributed points. *Proceedings of the 9th IEEE International Conference on Methods and Models in Automation and Robotics MMAR 2003,* Vol. 2, pp. 921-926, ISBN: 83-88764-82-9, Międzyzdroje, August 2003

Rafajłowicz E. & Schwabe R. (1997) Halton and Hammersley sequences in multivariate nonparametric regression. *Statistics and Probability Letters,* Vol. 76, No. 8, 2006, pp. 803-812, ISSN: 0167-71-52

Regazzoni, C.S. & Teschioni, A. (1997) A new approach to vector median filtering based on space filling curves. *IEEE Transactions on Image Processing,* Vol. 6, No, 7, 1997, pp. 1025-1037, ISSN: 1057-7149

Sagan H. (1994) *Space-filling Curves,* Springer ISBN: 0-387-94265-3, New York

Schuster, G.M. & Katsaggelos, A.K. (1997) A video compression scheme with optimal bit allocation among segmentation, motion, and residual error. *IEEE Transactions on Image Processing,* Vol. 6, No. 11, November 1997, pp. 1487-1502, ISSN: 1057-7149

Sierpiński W. (1912) Sur une nouvelle courbe continue qui remplit toute une aire plane. *Bull. de l'Acad. des Sci. de Cracovie A.,* 1912, pp. 463–478

Skubalska-Rafajłowicz E. (2001a) Pattern recognition algorithms based on space-filling curves and orthogonal expansions. *IEEE Trans. Information Theory,* Vol. 47, No. 5, 2001, pp. 1915-1927, ISSN: 0018-9448

Skubalska-Rafajłowicz E. (2001b) Data compression for pattern recognition based on space-filling curve pseudo-inverse mapping. *Nonlinear Analysis: Theory, Methods and Applications* Vol. 47, No. 1, (2001), pp. 315-326, ISSN: 0362-546X

Skubalska-Rafajłowicz Ewa. (2003) Neural networks with orthogonal activation function approximating space-filling curves. *Proc. 9th IEEE Int. Conf. Methods and Models in Automation and Robotics. MMAR 2003,* Vol. 2, pp. 927-934, ISBN: 83-88764-82-9, Międzyzdroje, August 2003,

Skubalska-Rafajłowicz E. (2004) Recurrent network structure for computing quasi-inverses of the Sierpiński space-filling curves. *Lect. Notes in Comp. Sci.*, Springer 2004, Vol. 3070, pp. 272–277, ISSN: 0302-9743

Thevenaz P.; Bierlaire M. & Unser M. (2008) Halton Sampling for Image Registration Based on Mutual Information, *Sampling Theory in Signal and Image Processing,* Vol. 7, No. 2, 2008, pp. 141-171, ISSN: 1530-6429

Unser M.& Zerubia J. (1998) A generalized sampling theory without band-limiting constraints, *IEEE Trans. Circ. Systems II,* Vol. 45, No. 8, 1998, pp. 959-969, ISSN: 1057-7130

Wheeden R. & Zygmund A. (1977) *Measure and Integral,* Marcell Dekker, ISBN: 0-8247-6499-4, New York

Zhang Y. (1997) Adaptive ordered dither. *Graphical Models and Image Processing,* Vol. 59, No. 1, January 1997, pp. 49-53, ISSN: 1077-3169

Zhang Y. (1998) Space-filling curve ordered dither. *Computers and Graphics,* Vol. 22, No 4, August 1998, pp 559-563, ISSN: 0097-84-93

Zhang Y. & Webber R. E. (1993) Space diffusion: an improved parallel halftoning technique using space-filling curves. *Proceedings of the 20th annual conference on Computer graphics and interactive techniques,* pp 305-312, ISBN: 0-89791-601-8, Anaheim, CA, August 1993

Acknowledgements This work was supported by a grant contract 2006-2009, funded by the Polish Ministry for Science and Higher Education.

8

Sparse signal decomposition for periodic signal mixtures

Makoto Nakashizuka
Graduate School of Engineering Science, Osaka University
Japan

1. Introduction

Periodicities are found in speech signals, musical rhythms, biomedical signals and machine vibrations. In many signal processing applications, signals are assumed to be periodic or quasi-periodic. Especially in acoustic signal processing, signal models based on periodicities have been studied for speech and audio processing.

The sinusoidal modelling has been proposed to transform an acoustic signal to a sum of sinusoids [1]. In this model, the frequencies of the sinusoids are often assumed to be harmonically related. The fundamental frequency of the set of sinusoids has to be specified for this model. In order to compose an accurate model of an acoustic signal, the noise-robust and accurate fundamental frequency estimation techniques are required. Many fundamental frequency estimation techniques are performed in the short-time Fourier transform (STFT) spectrum by peak-picking and clustering of harmonic components [2][3][4]. These approaches depend on the frequency spectrum of the signal.

The signal modeling in the time-domain has been also proposed to extract a waveform of an acoustic signal and its parameters of the amplitude and frequency variations [5]. This approach aims to represent an acoustic signal that has single fundamental frequency. For detection and estimation of more than one periodic signal hidden in a signal mixture, several signal decomposition that are capable of decomposing a signal into a set of periodic subsignals have been proposed.

In Ref. [7], an orthogonal decomposition method based on periodicity has been proposed. This technique achieves the decomposition of a signal into periodic subsignals that are orthogonal to each other. The periodicity transform [8] decomposes a signal by projecting it onto a set of periodic subspaces. In this method, seeking periodic subspaces and rejecting found periodic subsignals from the observed signal are performed iteratively. For reduction of the redundancy of the periodic representation, a penalty of sparsity has been introduced to the decomposition in Ref. [9].

In these periodic decomposition methods, the amplitude of each periodic signal in the mixture is assumed to be constant. Hence, it is difficult to obtain the significant decomposition results for the mixtures of quasi-periodic signals with time-varying amplitude. In this chapter, we introduce a model for periodic signals with time-varying amplitude into the periodic decomposition [10]. In order to reduce the number of resultant periodic subsignals obtained by the decomposition and represent the mixture with only significant periodic subsignals, we impose a sparsity penalty on the decomposition. This penalty is defined as the sum of l_2 norms of the resultant periodic subsignals to find the shortest path to the approximation of the mixture. The waveforms and amplitude of the hidden periodic signals are iteratively estimated with the penalty of sparsity. The proposed periodic decomposition can be interpreted as a sparse coding [15] [16] with non-negativity of the amplitude and the periodic structure of signals.

In our approach, the decomposition results are associated with the fundamental frequencies of the source signals in the mixture. So, the pitches of the source signals can be detected from the mixtures by the proposed decomposition.

First, we explain the definition of the model for the periodic signals. Then, the cost function that is a sum of the approximation error and the sparsity penalty is defined for the periodic decomposition. A relaxation algorithm [9] [10] [18] for the sparse periodic decomposition is also explained. The source estimation capability of our decomposition method is demonstrated by several examples of the decomposition of synthetic periodic signal mixtures. Next, we apply the proposed decomposition to speech mixtures and demonstrate the speech separation. In this experiment, the ideal separation performance of the proposed decomposition is compared with the separation method obtained by an ideal binary masking [10] of a STFT. Finally, we provide the results of the single-channel speech separation with simple assignment technique to demonstrate the possibility of the proposed decomposition.

2. Periodic decomposition of signals

For signal analysis, the periodic decomposition methods that decompose a signal into a sum of periodic signals have been proposed. Most fundamental periodic signal is a sinusoid. In speech processing area, the sinusoidal modeling [1] that represents the signal into the linear combination of sinusoids with various frequencies is utilized. The sinusoidal representation of the signal $f(n)$ with constant amplitude and constant frequencies is obtained as the form of

$$f(n)=\sum_{j=1}^{J} A_j \cos\left(\omega_j n+\phi_j\right). \tag{1}$$

This model relies on the estimation of the parameters of the model. Many estimation techniques have been proposed for the parameters. If the frequencies $\{\omega_j\}_{1\le j\le J}$ are harmonically related, all frequencies are assumed to be the multiples of the fundamental frequency. To detect the fundamental frequencies from mixtures of source signals that has periodical nature, multiple pitch detection algorithms have been proposed [2][3][4].

The signal modelling with (1) is a parametric modeling of the signal. On the contrast, the non-parametric modeling techniques that obtain a set of periodic signals that are specified in time-domain have been also proposed.

For time-domain approach of the periodic decomposition, the periodic signal is defined as a sum of time-translated waveforms. Let us suppose that a sequence $\{\mathbf{f}_p(n)\}_{0\le n<N}$ is a finite length periodic signal with a length N and an integer period $p\ge 2$. It satisfies the periodicity condition with an integer period p and is represented as

$$f_p(n)=a_p(n)\sum_{k=0}^{K} t_p(n-kp) \tag{1}$$

where $K = \lfloor (N\text{-}1)/p \rfloor$ that is the largest integer less than or equal to $(N\text{-}1)/p$. The sequence $\{t_p(n)\}_{0\le n<p}$ corresponds to a waveform of the signal within a period and is defined over the interval $[0, p\text{-}1]$. $t_p(n) = 0$ for $n \ge p$ and $n < 0$. This sequence is referred to as the p-periodic template. The sequence $\{a(n)\}_{0\le n<N}$ represents the envelope of the periodic signal. If the amplitude coefficient $a(n)$ is constant, the model is reduced to

$$f_p(n) = \sum_{k=0}^{K} t_p(n - kp). \tag{2}$$

Several periodic decomposition methods based on the periodic signal model (2) have been proposed [6] [7] [8] [9]. These methods decompose a signal f(n) into a set of the periodic signals as:

$$f(n) = \sum_{p\in \mathrm{P}} \sum_{k=0}^{K} t_p(n - kp) \tag{3}$$

where P is a set of periods for the decomposition. This signal decomposition can be represented in the matrix form as:

$$\mathbf{f} = \sum_{p\in \mathrm{P}} \mathbf{U}_p \mathbf{t}_p \tag{4}$$

where $\mathbf{t}_p$ is the vector which corresponds to the p-periodic template. The i-th column vector of $\mathbf{A}_p$ represent an impulse train with a period p. The elements of $\mathbf{U}_p$ are defined as

$$u_{n,i} = \begin{cases} 1 & \text{for } n = kp + i - 1 \text{ where } k = 0, 1, \cdots \\ 0 & \text{otherwise} \end{cases}. \tag{5}$$

The subspace that is spanned by the column vectors of $\mathbf{U}_p$ is referred to as the p-periodic subspace [8] [9].

If the estimations of the periods hidden in signal **f** are available, we can choose the periodic subspaces with the periods that are estimated before the decomposition. For MAS [6], the signal is decomposed into periodic subsignals as the least-squares solution along with an additional constrained matrix. In Ref. [8], the periodic bases are chosen to decompose a signal into orthogonal periodic subsignals. Therefore, these methods require that the number of the periodic signals and their periods have to be estimated before decomposition.

Periodic decomposition methods that do not require predetermined periods have also been proposed. In Ref. [7], the concept of periodicity transform is proposed. Periodicity transform decomposes a signal by projecting it onto a set of periodic subspaces. Each subspace consists of all possible periodic signals with a specific period. In this method, seeking periodic subspaces and rejecting found periodic subsignals from an input signal are performed iteratively. Since a set of the periodic subspaces lacks orthogonality and is redundant for signal representation, the decomposition result depends on the order of the subspaces onto which the signals are projected. In Ref. [7], four different signal decomposition methods - small to large, best correlation, M-best, and best frequency - have been proposed. In Ref. [9], the penalty of sparsity is imposed on the decomposition results in order to reduce the redundancy of the decomposition.

In this chapter, we discuss the decomposition of mixtures of the periodic signals with time-varying amplitude that can be represented in the form of (1). To simplify the periodic signal model, we assume that the amplitude of the periodic signal varies slowly and can be approximated to be constant within a period. By this simplification, we define an approximate model for the periodic signals with time-varying amplitude as

$$f_p(n) = \sum_{k=0}^{K} a_{p,k} t_p(n - kp) . \quad (6)$$

In order to represent a periodic component without a DC component, the average of $f_p(n)$ over the interval [0, p-1] is zero. The amplitude coefficients $a_{p,k}$ are restricted to non-negative values.

These p-periodic signals can also be represented in a matrix form as well as the previous periodic signal model. The matrix representation of (6) is defined as

$$\mathbf{f}_p = \mathbf{A}_p \mathbf{t}_p \quad (7)$$

In this form, the amplitude coefficients and the template are represented in an N by p matrix $\mathbf{A}_p$ and a p-dimensional template vector $\mathbf{t}_p$, which is associated with the sequence $t_p(n)$, respectively. $\mathbf{A}_p$ is a union of the matrices as

$$\mathbf{A}_p = \left(\mathbf{D}_{p,1}, \mathbf{D}_{p,2} \cdots \mathbf{D}_{p,K+1}\right)^{\mathrm{T}} \quad (8)$$

where superscript T denotes transposition.

$\{\mathbf{D}_{p,j}\}_{1 \le j \le K+1}$ are p by p diagonal matrices whose elements correspond to $a_{p,j-1}$. $D_{p,K+1}$ is the p by N-pK matrix whose non-zero coefficients that correspond to $a_{p,K}$ appear only in (i, i) elements. Since only one element is non-zero in any row of the $\mathbf{A}_p$, the column vectors of Ap are orthogonal to each other. The $l2$ norm of each column vector is supposed to be normalized to unity. In (6), the average of the waveform over the interval [0, p-1] must be zero. Hence, the condition

$$\mathbf{u}_p^{\mathrm{T}} \mathbf{t}_p = 0 \quad (9)$$

where $\mathbf{u}_p$ is a vector, of which elements correspond to the diagonal elements of $\mathbf{D}_{p,1}$.

Alternatively, the p-periodic signal in (2) can be represented as

$$\mathbf{f}_p = \mathbf{T}_p \mathbf{a}_p . \quad (10)$$

In this form, the amplitude coefficients and the template are represented in a N by K+1 matrix $\mathbf{T}_p$ and K+1-dimensional amplitude coefficients vector $\mathbf{a}_p$ whose elements are associated with the amplitude coefficients $a_{p,k}$, respectively. $\mathbf{T}_p$ consists of the column vectors that correspond to the shifted versions of the p-periodic template. As same as $\mathbf{A}_p$, only one element is non-zero in any row of $\mathbf{T}_p$. So, we defined Tp as the matrix which consists of the normalized vectors that are orthogonal to each other.

In this study, we propose an approximate decomposition method that obtains a representation of a given signal **f** as a form:

$$\mathbf{f} = \mathbf{e} + \sum_{p \in \mathrm{P}} \mathbf{f}_p \quad (11)$$

where **e** is an approximation error between the model and the signal **f**.

We suppose that the signal **f** is a mixture of some periodic signals that can be approximated by the form of (2), however, the periods of the source signals are unknown. So, we specify the set of periods P as a set of all possible periods of the source signals for the decomposition. If the number of the periods in P is large, the set of the periodic signals $\{\mathbf{f}_p\}_{p \in \mathrm{P}}$ that approximate the signal **f** with small error is not unique. To achieve the significant decomposition with the periodic signals that are represented in the form of (2), we introduce the penalty of the sparsity into the decomposition.

3. Sparse decomposition of signals

In Ref. [15] [16] [17], sparse decomposition methods that are capableof decomposing a signal into a small number of basis vectors that belong to an overcomplete dictionary have been proposed. Basis pursuit (BP) [17] is a well known sparse decomposition method and decomposes a signal into the vectors of a predetermined overcomplete dictionary. The signal $\mathbf{f}$ is represented as $\mathbf{\Phi c}$, where $\mathbf{\Phi}$ and $\mathbf{c}$ are the matrix that contains the normalized basis vectors and the coefficient vector, respectively.

In sparse decomposition, the number of basis vectors in $\mathbf{\Phi}$ is larger than the dimensionality of the signal vector $\mathbf{f}$. For this decomposition, the penalty of the sparsity is defined as l_1-norm of $\mathbf{c}$. The signal decomposition by BP is represented as a constrained minimization problem as follows:

$$\min \|\mathbf{c}\|_1 \text{ subject to } \mathbf{f} = \mathbf{\Phi c} \tag{12}$$

where $\|\cdot\|_1$ denotes the l_1 norm of a vector.

Since the l_1-norm is defined as the sum of the absolutes of the elements in the coefficient vector $\mathbf{c}$, BP determines the shortest path to the signal from the origin through the basis vectors. The number of the basis vectors with nonzero coefficients obtained by choosing the shortest path is much smaller than the least square solution obtained by minimizing the l_2-norm [17].

Usually, (12) is solved by linear programming [17]. However, it is difficult to apply linear programming to the large number of samples that appear in signal processing applications. So, an approximation of the solution of BP is obtained from the penalty problem of (12) as follows:

$$\hat{\mathbf{c}} = \arg\min_{\mathbf{c}} \frac{1}{2}\|\mathbf{f} - \mathbf{\Phi c}\|_2^2 + \lambda\|\mathbf{c}\|_1 \tag{13}$$

where λ denotes a Lagrange multiplier. $\|\cdot\|_2$ denotes the l_2 norm of the vector. This unconstrained minimization problem is referred to as a basis pursuit denoising (BPDN) [17] [18]. When $\mathbf{\Phi}$ is specified as a union of orthonormal bases, an efficient relaxation algorithm can be applied [18].

From Bayesian point of view, the minimization (13) is the equivalent of MAP estimation of the coefficient vector $\mathbf{c}$ under the assumption that the probability distribution of each element of the coefficient vector is an identical Laplace distribution [15].

The dictionary $\mathbf{\Phi}$ is fixed for signal representation in the BP and BPDN. In a sparse coding strategy [15] [16], the dictionary $\mathbf{\Phi}$ is adapted to the set of the signals. The dictionary is updated with the most probable one under the estimated sparse coefficients and the set of the signals [15].

For our periodic decomposition, we also impose the sparsity penalty on the decomposition under the assumption that the mixture contains a small number of periodic signals that can be approximated in the form of (6). Our objective is to achieve signal decomposition to obtain a small number of periodic subsignals rather than basis vectors. In order to achieve this, we define the sparsity measure as the sum of l_2 norms of the periodic subsignals to find the shortest path to the approximation of the signal as well as BPDN.

4. Sparse periodic decomposition

4. 1 Cost function for periodic decomposition

For our periodic decomposition, we also impose the sparsity penalty on the decomposition under the assumption that the mixture consists of a small number of periodic signals that can be approximated in the form of (2). Our objective is to achieve signal decomposition with a small number of periodic subsignals rather than the basis vectors. In order to achieve this, the probability distribution of the l_2 norm of each periodic signal is assumed to be a Laplace distribution, and then the probability distribution of the set of the periodic signals is

$$P\left(\{\mathbf{f}_p\}_{p\in \mathrm{P}}\right) \propto \prod_{p\in \mathrm{P}} \exp\left(-\alpha_p \|\mathbf{f}_p\|\right). \tag{14}$$

The noise is assumed to be Gaussian, and then the conditional probability distribution of **f** is

$$P\left(\mathbf{f}\,\middle|\,\{\mathbf{f}_p\}_{p\in P}\right) \propto \exp\left(-\frac{1}{2\lambda}\left\|\mathbf{f} - \sum_{p\in P}\mathbf{f}_p\right\|_2^2\right). \tag{15}$$

Along with Bayes' rule, the conditional probability distribution of the set of the periodic signals is

$$P\left(\{\mathbf{f}_p\}_{p\in P}\,\middle|\,\mathbf{f}\right) \propto P\left(\mathbf{f}\,\middle|\,\{\mathbf{f}_p\}_{p\in P}\right) P\left(\{\mathbf{f}_p\}_{p\in P}\right). \tag{16}$$

Substituting the prior distributions of the periodic signals and the noise into (16), we can derive the likelihood function of the set of periodic signals. From the likelihood function, we define the cost function E for the periodic decomposition as:

$$E \equiv \frac{1}{2}\left\|\mathbf{f} - \sum_{p\in P}\mathbf{f}_p\right\|_2^2 + \lambda \sum_{p\in P}\alpha_p \|\mathbf{f}_p\|_2 . \tag{17}$$

In our periodic decomposition, a signal **f** is decomposed into a set of periodic subsignals while reducing the cost E and maximizing the likelihood.

In the cost for BPDN (12), the sparsity penalty is defined as the l_1-norm of the coefficient vector that is identical the total length of the decomposed vector of the signal. In our periodic decomposition, the sparsity penalty is also defined as the sum of the decomposed vectors that are represented in the form of the periodic signal model shown in (6).

4. 2 Algorithm for sparse periodic decomposition

To find the set of the periodic subsignals $\{\mathbf{f}_p\}_{p\in \mathrm{P}}$, we employ a relaxation algorithm. This relaxation algorithm always updates one chosen periodic subsignal while decreasing the cost function (17). The template vector $\mathbf{t}_p$ and amplitude vector $\mathbf{a}_p$ of the chosen period p are alternatively updated in an iteration. In the algorithm, we suppose that the set of the periods P consists of M periods which are indexed as $\{p_1 \ldots p_M\}$.

The relaxation algorithm for the sparse periodic decomposition is as follows:

1) Set the initial amplitude coefficients for $\{\mathbf{A}_p\}$.
2) $i = 1$
3) Compute the residual

$$\mathbf{r} = \mathbf{f} - \sum_{j \neq i} \mathbf{f}_{p_j} \tag{18}$$

4) Represent $\mathbf{f}_{p_i}$ as $\mathbf{A}_{p_i}\mathbf{t}_{p_i}$. If $\left\|\mathbf{f}_{p_i}\right\| = 0$, then the amplitude coefficients in $\mathbf{A}_{p_i}$ are specified to be constant. Update the template $\mathbf{t}_{p_i}$ with the solution of a subproblem:

$$\min_{\mathbf{t}_{p_i}} \frac{1}{2}\left\|\mathbf{f} - \mathbf{A}_{p_i}\mathbf{t}_{p_i}\right\|_2^2 + \lambda\alpha_{p_i}\left\|\mathbf{t}_{p_i}\right\|_2 \text{ subject to } \mathbf{u}_{p_i}^{\mathrm{T}}\mathbf{t}_{p_i} = 0 \tag{19}$$

5) Represent $\mathbf{f}_{p_i}$ as $\mathbf{T}_{p_i}\mathbf{a}_{p_i}$. Update the amplitude coefficient vector $\mathbf{a}_{p_i}$ with the solution of a subproblem:

$$\min_{\mathbf{a}_{p_i}} \frac{1}{2}\left\|\mathbf{f} - \mathbf{T}_{p_i}\mathbf{a}_{p_i}\right\|_2^2 + \lambda\alpha_{p_i}\left\|\mathbf{a}_{p_i}\right\|_2 \text{ subject to } \mathbf{a}_{p_i} \geq 0 \tag{20}$$

where "$\mathbf{a} \geq 0$" denotes that the all elements of the vector $\mathbf{a}$ is positive.

6) If $i < M$, update $i \leftarrow i + 1$ and go to step 3). If $i = M$ and the stopping criterion is not satisfied, go to step 2).

For stable computation, the update stage of the amplitude coefficient in Step 5) is omitted when the l_2-norm of the template $\mathbf{t}_{p_i}$ becomes zero after Step 4).

The closed form solution of (19) is

$$\hat{\mathbf{t}}_{p_i} = \begin{cases} \dfrac{\|\mathbf{v}\|_2 - \lambda\alpha_{p_i}}{\|\mathbf{v}\|_2}\mathbf{v} & \textit{for } \|\mathbf{v}\|_2 > \lambda\alpha_{p_i} \\ 0 & \textit{for } \|\mathbf{v}\|_2 \leq \lambda\alpha_{p_i} \end{cases} \tag{21}$$

where

$$\mathbf{v} = \mathbf{A}_{p_i}^T\mathbf{r}_{p_i} - \frac{\mathbf{u}_{p_i}^T\left(\mathbf{A}_{p_i}^T\mathbf{r}_{p_i}\right)}{\left\|\mathbf{u}_{p_i}\right\|_2^2}\mathbf{u}_{p_i}. \tag{22}$$

The solution of (10) is

$$\hat{\mathbf{a}}_{p_i} = \begin{cases} \dfrac{\|\mathbf{w}\|_2 - \lambda\alpha_{p_i}}{\|\mathbf{w}\|_2} & \textit{for } \|\mathbf{w}\|_2 > \lambda\alpha_{p_i} \\ 0 & \textit{for } \|\mathbf{w}\|_2 \leq \lambda\alpha_{p_i} \end{cases} \tag{23}$$

where

$$\mathbf{w} = \left(\mathbf{T}_{p_i}^T\mathbf{r}_{p_i}\right)_+ \tag{24}$$

$(\cdot)_+$ denotes replacing the negative elements of a vector with zero. The both solutions of the subproblems guarantee the decrement of the cost E. Thus, the cost E decreases until convergence. However, the set of the resultant periodic subsignals after the convergence of the iteration does not always obtain a minimum of the cost function E exactly. If any periodic subsignal becomes zero in iteration, the amplitude coefficients are specified to be constant in step 4) of the next iteration. The proper search direction for $\mathbf{t}_{p_i}$ may not be obtained by these amplitude coefficients. However, the l_2 norms of the periodic signals that eliminated by the shrinkage in (21) and (23) is small enough to approximate the signal. Hence, we accept the periodic subsignals obtained by this algorithm as the result of the sparse decomposition instead of the proper minimiser of the cost E.

Tested set	*Ave.*	*Std. Dev*
28, 44, 52	14.6, 16.6, 12.6	2.4, 2.4, 2.2
30, 31, 32	16.9, 21.0, 20.7	3.1, 2.7, 2.7
50, 51, 52	10.8, 12.7, 10.8	1.7, 1.9, 1.7

Table 1. SNR improvements (dB) obtained by the sparse periodic decomposition for mixtures of three periodic signals.

5. Decomposition examples

In this section, we provide several examples of the sparse periodic decomposition. The examples demonstrate the decomposition of synthetic signals generated by adding three periodic signals. The length of the mixture and three source signals N is 256. Each source signal is generated with the model for the periodic signals shown in (1). Each waveform within a period is generated by Gaussian random variables. The average of the waveform of a period is normalized to zero. The amplitude envelope of one of the three source signals are specified as a constant. The envelopes of the other two source signals are specified as a decreasing Gaussian function

$$a(n) = \exp\left(-\left(\frac{2n}{N}\right)^2\right) \quad \text{for } n \geq 0$$

and an increasing Gaussian function

$$a(n) = \exp\left(-\left(\frac{2(n-N)}{N}\right)^2\right) \quad \text{for } n \geq 0,$$

respectively. The squared norms of the three source signals are normalized to unity. Since the three source periodic signals can be assumed to be independent to each other, the SNR of each source signal in the mixture is about -3.0 dB. The sets of three periods for mixtures are shown in the first column of Table. 1. The first set contains the periods have three divisors. The second and third consist of closely spaced periods. An example of the mixture is shown in Fig. 1(a). The three source periodic signals are shown in Fig. 1(b), (c) and (d), respectively.

For the sparse periodic decomposition, the sequence of the parameters $\{\alpha_p\}_{p \in \mathrm{P}}$ and the sparsity parameter λ have to be specified. The shrinkage of the l_2-norm of the periodic component in the decomposition algorithm is performed with the threshold $\lambda\alpha_p$ in (21) and (23). The periodic signal $\mathbf{f}_p$ with the l_2-norm that is less than the threshold is eliminated by the shrinkage. Obviously, if the residual $\mathbf{r}$ in (18) can be assumed to be a noise that is small enough to approximate the input signal, its periodic approximation has to be eliminated during the decomposition. We assume that the noise as a Gaussian noise with a variance σ^2. The product $\lambda\alpha_p$ is specified as proportional value to the expected l_2 norm of the approximated Gaussian noise with the periodic signal model. The expected l_2 norm of the periodic signal $\mathbf{f}_p$ that approximates a Gaussian noise, of which envelope is constant, is approximated as

$$E\left[\left\|\mathbf{f}_p\right\|_2\right] \approx \sigma\sqrt{p+1+\frac{N}{p}} \tag{25}$$

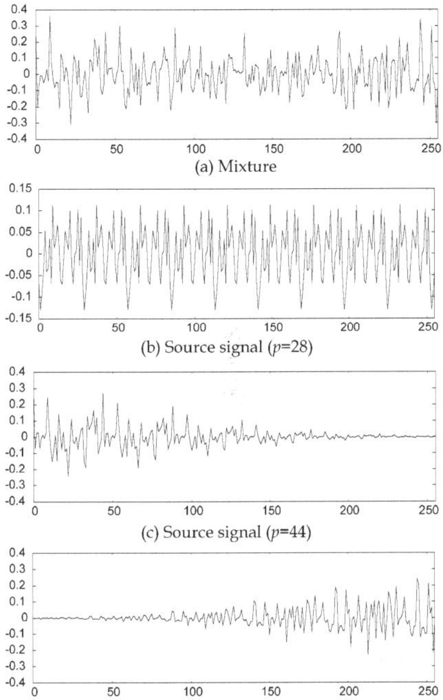

Fig. 1. (a) Example of mixture of three periodic signals, the source periodic signals, (a) p = 28, (c) p = 44 and (d) p =52.

The product $\lambda\alpha_p$ is hence specified to a value that is proportional to this expectation. In actual decomposition, σ is assumed to be 1% of the l_2-norm of the input signal. $\lambda\alpha_p$ is specified as the expectation shown in (25).

In the experiments, we supposed that the period of the source signals are integer in the range [10, 59]. The periods for the decomposition are also defined as integers in this range. So, the number of the periodic signals that are obtained by the decomposition is 60. The iteration of the decomposition algorithm explained in Sect. 4. 2 is stopped when l_∞-norm of the difference of the periodic signals before and after updating is lower than a threshold value. The threshold is specified as 0.01 $\times\lambda\alpha_p$ for all experiments.

In order to evaluate the decomposition, we compute the improvement in SNR. The improvement in SNR is computed as the difference of the SNRs of the mixture and decomposition results for each source period. We generate 1,000 mixtures to test the decomposition algorithm for each set of periods. Table 1 shows the averages and standard deviations of the SNR improvements of the decomposed periodic signals for 1,000 tests. The average SNR improvements of the decomposition results exceed 10 dB. By these results, we see that the proposed decomposition can obtain significant decomposition results and separate three sources into its periods. In Fig. 2 and 3, an example of the mixture and its decomposition result are shown. The discrete Fourier transform (DFT) spectrum of the mixture (Fig. 1(a)) is shown in Fig. 2(a).

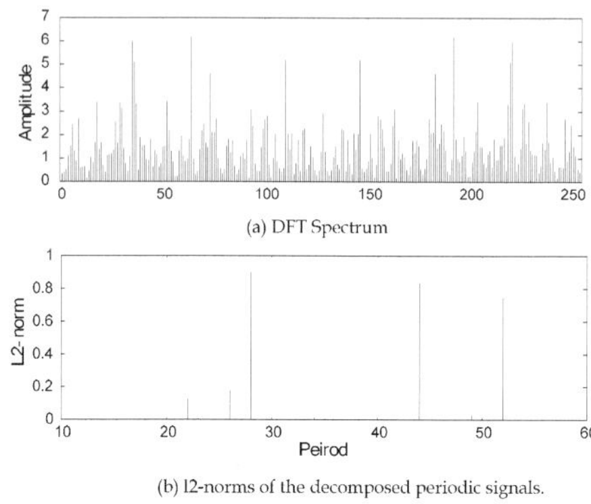

Fig. 2. (a) DFT spectrum of the mixture in Fig. 1(a) and (b) distribution of the l_2 norm of the decomposed periodic signals.

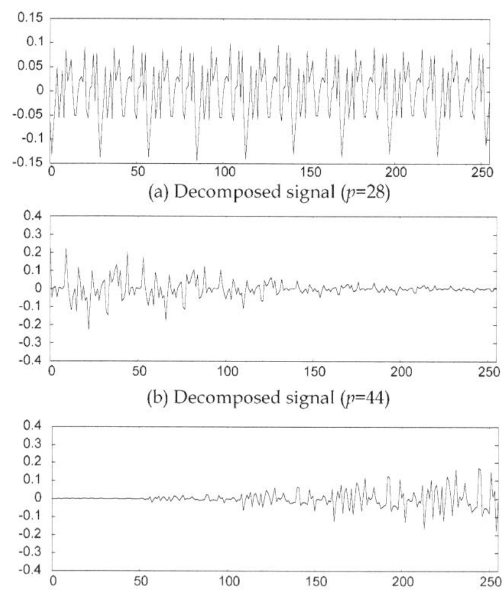

Fig. 3. Decomposed periodic signals, (a) p =28, (b) p = 44 and (c) p =52.

The distribution of l_2 norm of the resultant periodic signals of the mixture is shown in Fig. 2(b). As seen in Fig. 2(b), three periodic signals with large amplitude appear at the source periods. Small harmonics components are separated from the source periods due to the weighting of the sparsity penalty, however, the almost energy of the mixture is decomposed into the three source periods. In Fig. 3, the periodic signals that appear in the decomposition result are also shown. In this set of the periods, the harmonics with periods 1, 2, and 4 which are the common divisors of the source periods cannot be separated accurately. However, the other harmonics are well collected to three fundamental periods.

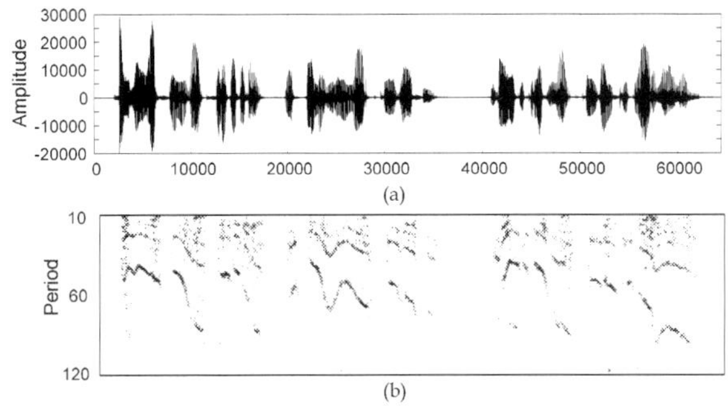

Fig. 4. (a) Speech signal (male, duration: 8.1 s, sampling freq. : 8 kHz) and (b) time-period energy distribution of (a).

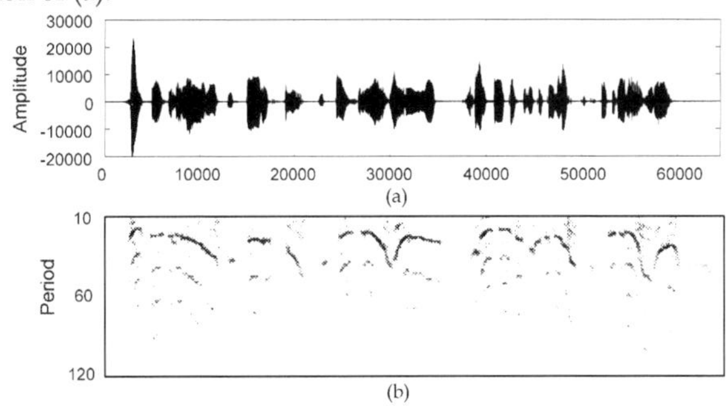

Fig. 5. (a) Speech signal (female, duration: 8.1 s, sampling freq. : 8 kHz) and (b) time-period energy distribution of (a).

6. Application to speech representation

In the synthetic signal examples, the signal mixtures consist of source periodic signals with integer periods. However, periods of many periodic signals that include speech and acoustic signals are not integer. In order to examine the sparse periodic decomposition for the signals with non-integer periods, we apply the proposed sparse decomposition to speech mixtures.

The speech signals for the experiments were selected 3 Japanese male and 3 female continuous speeches of about 8 s taken from ATR-SLDB (Spoken Language Database). The sampling rate of each speech signal is converted to 8 kHz. 15 speech mixtures that consist of two different speeches that are normalized to same power are generated.

For periodic decomposition, each mixture is divided into segments that contain 360 samples with 3/4 overlap. In each segment, the periods for decomposition are specified to be

integers in the range [10, 120] which corresponds to the range of the fundamental frequencies of most men and women. The stopping rule of the iteration of the relaxation method and the parameters are specified as the same rule that is mentioned in Sect. 5.
The examples of the male and female utterances and its time-period energy distributions are shown in Fig. 4 and Fig. 5, respectively. In Fig. 4(b) and 5(b), the brightness indicates the power of the resultant periodic signals for each segment and period. Darker pixels indicate higher powers of the resultant periodic subsignals.

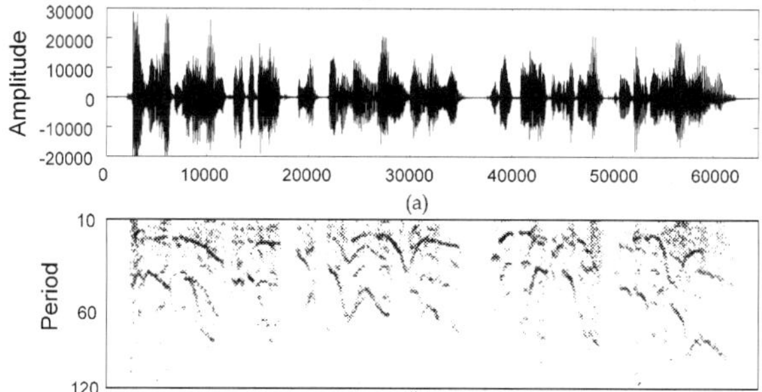

Fig. 6. (a) Mixture of female and male speeches and (b) time-period energy distribution of (a)

Speakers	*Ave. SNR*	*Min. SNR*	*Max. SNR*	*Ave. num. of periods*
(M, M)	20.1	10.4	28.9	16.1
(F, F)	20.2	10.3	27.6	11.2
(F, M)	20.2	10.2	28.9	14.0

Table. 2. Average, minimum and maximum SNRs (dB) of approximated speech segments and average numbers of periodic signals obtained by the sparse decomposition

Our method decomposes a signal into the periodic signals with only integer periods. Under this limitation, the speech components with non-integer periods and the frequency variations that occur in a segment are represented as the sum of some periodic signals. So, we see that the pitch contours are represented by some neighbouring periods in these time-period distribution. Moreover, small periodic components with periods that are multiples and divisors of the fundamental periods appear. These periodic components appear due to the non-integer periodic components of the speeches and the weighting of the sparsity measure in (17). However, the most of the signal energy is concentrated around the fundamental pitch periods of the speeches.
We also show the time-period energy distributions of the mixture of two speeches. Fig. 6(a) and (b) show the mixture of the source speech signals shown in Fig. 3(a) and Fig. 4(a) and its time-period energy distributions, respectively. We see that the time-period energy distribution of the mixture in Fig. 6 is almost equal to the sum of the two distributions of the source speeches shown in Fig. 4(b) and Fig. 5(b). The both of the pitch contours of the two source speeches are preserved in the distribution of the mixture. The proposed decomposition method can approximate the mixture while concentrating the energy of each speech to its pitch periods and provides sparse representation of the mixture. It is expected that the pitch periods of both the speech signals will be tracked in this time-period energy

distribution. Moreover, speech separation will be achieved by assigning the resultant periodic signals to the sources.
In order to evaluate the approximate decomposition, we compute the SNR and the number of the non-zero resultant periodic signals for each segment where the l_2 norm is greater than the noise level. The average, maximum and minimum SNRs over all voice active segments of mixtures are shown in Table 2. In this table, F an M denote female and male source speeches, respectively. The average numbers of periods for approximation of a segment are also shown. We see that the average approximation precision of the proposed decomposition is about 20 dB in the segmental SNR. The average number of the periods yield by the decomposition is about 14 for segments of speech mixtures consist of two speeches.

Speaker	*Proposed (with sources)*	*DFT (with sources)*	*Proposed (with ref. sig.)*
(M, M)	9.9±0.6	13.5±0.5	3.9±1.0
(F, F)	9.5±0.3	13.5±0.5	3.2±0.9
(F, M)	F: 10.1±1.5	F: 14.4±1.0	F: 6.5±2.5
	M: 9.8±1.0	M: 14.3±1.0	M: 6.7±2.7

Table 3. Average SNRs (dB) of separated speeches.

Next, we demonstrate the speech separation from a mixture with the sparse periodic decomposition. In this experiment, the speech separation is performed by assignment of the resultant periodic subsignals to the sources in each segment.
First, we use the clean source signals for assignment of the resultant periodic signals.
The separation is carried out by the following steps for each segment:

1. The segment of the mixture is decomposed into the set of the periodic signals $\{\mathbf{f}_p\}_{p\in P}$.
2. The normalized correlations between the resultant periodic signals and the clean source segments $\{\mathbf{s}_i\}_{i=1,2}$ are computed.
3. Each resultant periodic signal $\mathbf{f}_p$ are added to the separated output that is associated with the i-th source $\mathbf{s}_i$ that obtains larger correlation.

For recovering source signals, each resultant periodic signal is multiplied with a Hanning window in each segment. This assignment method does not obtain optimum separated results in terms of the SNR exactly. However, this experiment gives the rough ideal performance of the source separation by using the proposed sparse decomposition.
For comparison, the ideal separation results that are obtained by a STFT that is widely utilized for the sparse representation of speech signals are demonstrated. In the separation with the STFT, the ideal binary masks [20] are computed from the clean source speeches.
The mixture and the source signals are segmented by 512 points Hamming window with 3/4 overlap. In each segment, the DFT spectrum of the mixture and the source signals are computed. Each frequency bin of the DFT is assigned to the source whose amplitude of the frequency bin is larger than the other. The separation results obtained by the proposed decomposition and the DFT are shown in Table 3.
In this table, the SNRs of the separated speech signals are shown. We see that the SNRs of the separated speeches obtained by the proposed method are lower than the DFT by about

4dB. In the separation obtained by the proposed method, the approximation errors caused during the decomposition are involved in the separated output. Since the frequency resolution of the periodic decomposition is lower than the DFT at high frequency bands, the interferences between two speeches mainly occur at high-frequencies. However, the proposed representation is sparser than the DFT spectrum. In this experiment, the DFT yields 257 frequency bins for each segment. So, the DFT based separation is the problem of the assignment of the 257 frequency bins. In contrast, the average number of the periodic signals yield by the proposed method is about 14 for a segment. Comparing the proposed decomposition with the DFT, the separation problem can be reduced to relatively small size of a combinatorial optimization by the proposed decomposition.

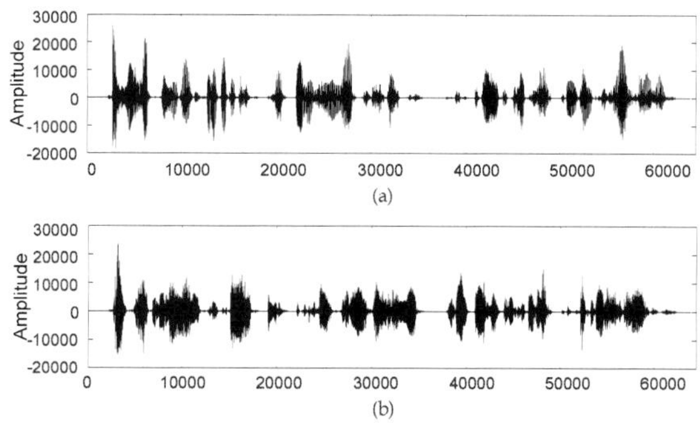

Fig. 7. Separated speech signals obtained by sparse periodic decomposition with reference speeches, (a) separated male speech (SNR: 7.2dB) and (b) female speech (SNR: 7.1dB) from the mixture shown in Fig. 5(a)

In above separation experiments, we assume that the source speeches are known. Next, we demonstrate the single-channel speech separation by referencing the clean speech segments. In this scenario of the separation, two speakers in a mixture are known and the clean speeches of the speakers are available, but the contents of the speeches in the mixture are unknown. In order to assign the periodic signals to the sources, a set of the clean speech segments of the i-th speaker is defined as $\{\mathbf{c}_{i,j}\}_{1\le j\le Nr}$ where Nr is the number of the reference segments.

The resultant periodic signal $\mathbf{f}_p$ is assigned to the i-th speaker that gives the maximum of the normalized correlation as:

$$\max_{i,j} \frac{\mathbf{f}_p^{\mathrm{T}} \mathbf{c}_{i,j}}{\left\|\mathbf{f}_p\right\|_2 \left\|\mathbf{c}_{i,j}\right\|_2}$$

For this experiment, segments that are generated from a clean speech of 20 s are used for the references of each speaker. The segments where the voice is not active are rejected from the references. The references do not include the source utterances in the mixtures. The SNRs obtained by the separation with the references are also shown in Table. 3. Obviously, such a simple separation method causes many false assignments. For separation of the mixture consists of the speakers of same gender, the averages of the improvements of SNR are lower than 4dB. However, the averages of SNR close to the ideal results and are about 6.5dB for

the speakers of opposite gender. The separated signals from the mixture in Fig. 6(a) are shown in Fig. 7(a) and (b).
The single channel speech separation methods based on frequency masking of spectrum have been proposed [12] [13] [14]. In these methods, statistical models for the frequency spectra of the speakers are preliminary learnt. The separation is performed on the frequency spectrum of the mixture by using the statistical models. In our approach, the proposed sparse decomposition yields the small number of the periodic signals which approximate the source signal due to the sparsity penalty. So, the separation of two speeches that have less similarity can be performed by such a lazy assignment method.

7. Conclusions

In this chapter, we present a sparse decomposition method for periodic signal mixtures. The proposed decomposition is based on the model for the periodic signals with time-varying amplitude and the sparsity of the periods that appear in the decomposition result. In decomposition experiments of the synthetic signal and the speech mixtures, we demonstrated that the proposed decomposition has the ability of source separation.
The assignment method that is employed for the single-channel speech separation demonstrated in this paper is too simple to obtain good separation results. In our decomposition results, as seen in the figures in Sect. 4, the speech pitch contours are involved. We can use the temporal continuity of the speech pitches and spectra over the consecutive segments for improvement of the accuracy of the assignment. The accurate and robust assignment of the decomposed periodic signals is a topic for future research.

8. References

McAulay, R.; and Quatieri, T. Speech analysis/synthesis based on a sinusoidal representation, *IEEE Trans. on Acoustics, Speech and Signal Processing*, Vol. 34, No. 8, pp. 744-754, Aug. 1986. [1]

Wu, M.; Wang, D.; & Brown, G. J. A multipitch tracking algorithm for noisy speech, *IEEE Trans. on Speech and Audio Processing*, Vol. 11, No. 3, pp. 229-241, May 2003. [2]

Goto, M. A real-time music scene description system: Predominant F0 estimation for detecting melody and bass lined in real-world audio signals, *Speech Commun.*, Vol. 43, No. 4, pp. 311-329, 2004. [3]

Le Roux, J.; Kameoka, H.; Ono, H.; Cheveigne, A. & Sagayama, S. Single and multiple F0 contour estimation through parametric sepectrogram modeling of speech in noisy enviroments, *IEEE Trans. on Audio, Speech and Language Processing*, Vol. 15, No. 4, pp. 1135-1145, May 2007. [4]

Triki, T. & Slock T. Periodic signal extraction with global amplitude and phase modulation for musical signal decomposition, *Proc. on ICASSP*, Vol. 3, pp. 233-236, 2005. [5]

Santhanam, B.; & Maragos, P. Harmonic analysis and restoration of separation methods for periodic signal mixtures: Algebraic separation versus comb filtering, *Signal Processing*, Vol. 69, No. 1, pp. 81-91, 1998. [6]

Muresan, D. D. & Parks, T. W. Orthogonal, exactly periodic subspace decomposition, *IEEE Trans. on Signal Processing*, vol. 51, no. 9, pp. 2270-2279, Nov. 2003. [7]

Sethares, W. A.; & Staley, T. W. Periodicity transform, *IEEE Trans. on Signal Processing*, vol. 47, no. 11, pp. 2953-2964, Nov. 1999. [8]

Nakashizuka, M. A sparse decomposition method for periodic signal mixtures, *IEICE Trans. on Fundamentals*, Vol.E91-A, No.3, pp. 791-800, March 2008. [9]

Nakashizuka, M. A sparse periodic decomposition and its application to speech representation, Proc. on EUSIPCO 2008, Aug. 2008. [10]

Yilmaz, O. & Rickard, S. Blind separation of speech mixtures via time-frequency masking, *IEEE Trans. on Signal Processing*, Vol. 52, No. 7, pp. 1830-1847, July 2004. [11]

Roweis, T. S. Factorial models and refiltering for speech separation and denoising, *Proc. on Eurospeech*, Vol. 7, No. 6, pp. 1009-1012, Geneva, 2003. [12]

Reddy, A. M. & Raj, B. Soft mask methods for single-channel speaker separation, *IEEE Trans. on Audio, Speech and Language Processing*, Vol. 15, No. 6, pp. 1766-1776, Aug. 2007. [13]

Radfar, M. H. & Dansereau, D. M. Single-channel speech separation using soft mask filtering, *IEEE Trans. on Audio, Speech and Language Processing*, Vol. 15, No. 8, pp. 2299-2310, Nov. 2007. [14]

Lewicki, M. S. & Olshausen, B. A. A probabilistic framework for the adaptation and comparison of image codes, *J. Opt. Soc. Amer. A, Opt. Image Sci.*, Vol. 16, No. 7, pp. 1587-1601, 1999. [15]

Plumbley, M. D.; Abdallah, S. A.; Blumensath, T. & Davies, M. E. Sparese representation of polyphonic music, *Signal Processing*, Vol. 86, No. 3, pp. 417-431, March 2006. [16]

Chen, S. S.; Donoho D. L. & Saunders, M. A. Atomic decomposition by basis pursuit, *SIAM Journal on Scientific Computing*, Vol. 20, No. 1, pp. 33-61, 1998. [17]

Sardy, S.; Bruce, A. G. & Tseng, P. Block coordinate relaxation methods for nonparametric wavelet denoising, *Journal of Computational and Graphical Statistics*, vol. 9, no. 2, pp. 361-379, 2000. [18]

9

Wavelet-based techniques in MRS

A. Suvichakorn[a] *, H. Ratiney[b], S. Cavassila[b,†] and J.-P Antoine[a,‡]
[a]Institut de physique théorique (FYMA),
Université catholique de Louvain, B-1348 Louvain-la-Neuve, Belgium
[b]CREATIS-LRMN, CNRS UMR 5220, Villeurbanne F-69621
Inserm, U630, Villeurbanne F-69621; INSA-Lyon, Villeurbanne F-69621
Université de Lyon, Lyon, F-69003; Université Lyon 1, Villeurbanne F-69622
France

1. Introduction: magnetic resonance spectroscopic (MRS) signals

A magnetic resonance spectroscopic (MRS) signal is made of several frequencies typical of the active nuclei and their chemical environments. The amplitude of these contributions in the time domain depends on the amount of those nuclei, which is then related to the concentration of the substance (Hornak, 1997).
This property is exploited in many applications of MRS, in particular in the clinical one. The MRS spectra contain a wealth of biochemical information characterizing the molecular content of living tissues (Govindaraju et al., 2000). Therefore, MRS is a unique non-invasive tool for monitoring human brain tumours, etc. (Devos et al., 2004), if it is well quantified.
When an MRS proton signal is acquired at short echo-time (TE), the distortion of spectral multiplets due to J-evolution can be minimized and the signals are minimally affected by transverse relaxation. Such signals exhibit many more metabolite contributions, such as glutamate and myo-inositol, compared to long TE spectra. Therefore, an MRS signal acquired at short TE presents rich *in vivo* metabolic information through complicated, overlapping spectral signatures. However, it is usually contaminated by water residue and a baseline which mainly originates from large molecules, known as macromolecules. As the shape and intensity of the baseline are not known *a priori*, this contribution becomes one of the major obstructions to accurately quantify the overlapping signals from the metabolites, especially by peak integration, which is commonly used in frequency-based quantification techniques. Also, by seeing only the frequency aspect, one loses all information about time localization.
A number of quantification techniques have been proposed, which work either in the time domain (see Vanhamme et al. (2001) for a review) or in the frequency domain (see Mierisová & Ala-Korpela (2001) for a review). The time-domain based methods are divided into two main classes: on one side, non-interactive methods such as SVD-based methods (Pijnappel et al., 1992) and, on the other side, methods based on iterative model function fitting using strong prior knowledge such as QUEST (Ratiney et al., 2004; 2005), LCModel (Provencher, 1993), AQSES (Poullet et al., 2007), or AMARES (Vanhamme et al., 1997).

*A. Suvichakorn is a Marie-Curie Research Fellow in the FAST (Advanced Signal Processing for Ultra-fast Magnetic Resonance) Marie-Curie Research Network (MRTN-CT-2006-035801, http://fast-mrs.eu)
†*E-mail address*: Sophie.Cavassila@univ-lyon1.fr
‡*E-mail address*: Jean-Pierre.Antoine@uclouvain.be

However, there also exist techniques that analyse a signal in the two domains simultaneously and are therefore more efficient than, say, the Fourier transform, which gives only spectral information. The result is a time-scale and or a time-frequency representation, such as provided by the wavelet transform (WT) and the Short-Time Fourier transform (STFT). In addition, both transforms are local, in the sense that a small perturbation of a signal which may occur during the data acquisition will result only in a small, local modification of the transform.
A number of wavelet-based techniques have been proposed for spectral line estimation in MRS, including the continuous wavelet transform (Delprat et al., 1992; Guillemain et al., 1992; Serrai et al., 1997) and the wavelet packet decomposition (Mainardi et al., 2002). Among the various possibilities, we will concentrate our discussion on the continuous wavelet transform (CWT) with the Morlet wavelet (MWT). All wavelet calculations have been performed by our own wavelet toolbox, called YAWTb (Jacques et al., 2007). Some of the experimental aspects have been reported in Suvichakorn et al. (2009). For the convenience of the reader we have collected in the Appendix the basic features and properties of the CWT.
In the following sections, we will study the performance of the Morlet WT to retrieve parameters of interest such as resonances frequencies, amplitude and damping factors, for nuisances or impairments generally encountered in *in vivo* MRS signals: noise, baseline, solvent, and non-Lorentzian lineshapes.

2. The Morlet wavelet transform

The wavelet transform (WT) of a signal $s(t)$ with respect to a basic wavelet $g(t)$ is

$$\begin{aligned} S(\tau,a) &= \frac{1}{\sqrt{a}} \int \overline{g\left(\frac{t-\tau}{a}\right)}\, s(t)\, dt \\ &= \frac{1}{2\pi}\sqrt{a} \int \overline{G(a\omega)}\, S(\omega)\, e^{i\omega\tau}\, d\omega, \end{aligned} \tag{1}$$

where $S(\omega)$ is the Fourier transform of the signal, $a > 0$ is a dilation parameter that characterizes the frequency of the signal (since $1/a$ is essentially a frequency), $\tau \in \mathbb{R}$ is a translation parameter that indicates the localization in time and $\overline{G(a\omega)}$ is the complex conjugate of the (scaled) Fourier transform of $g(t)$. We can think of the basic wavelet as a window which slides through the signal, giving the information at instantaneous time τ. The window is also dilated by a, so that a small a corresponds to a high frequency of the signal, and *vice versa*. As a result, the WT becomes a function of both time and frequency (scale). For more details, see the Appendix.
A technique based on the continuous wavelet transform (CWT) was proposed by Guillemain et al. (1992). By exploiting the ability of the CWT to see the information in the two domains simultaneously, it can extract the information from MRS signals directly without any decomposition or pre-processing, in order to quantify an MRS signal. The technique proceeds in two steps: (i) detection of the frequency of the peaks in MRS signals and (ii) characterization at each detected frequency. It can be described as follows.
At a particular value of a, the WT $S_a(\tau) \equiv S(\tau,a)$ can be represented in terms of its modulus $|S_a(\tau)|$ and phase $\Phi_a(\tau)$, namely,

$$S_a(\tau) = |S_a(\tau)| e^{i\Phi_a(\tau)}, \tag{2}$$

with an instantaneous frequency

$$\begin{aligned}\Omega_a(\tau) &= \frac{\partial}{\partial\tau}\Phi_a(\tau) \\ &= \frac{\partial}{\partial\tau}\mathrm{Im}[\ln S_a(\tau)] \\ &= \mathrm{Im}\left[\frac{1}{S_a(\tau)}\frac{d}{d\tau}S_a(\tau)\right],\end{aligned} \tag{3}$$

Next, let us consider an MRS signal with a Lorentzian damping function, namely,

$$s_L(t) = Ae^{-Dt}e^{i(\omega_s t+\varphi)} \Leftrightarrow S_L(\omega) = 2\pi Ae^{i\varphi}\delta(\omega - (\omega_s + iD)), \tag{4}$$

where D and φ denote the damping factor and the phase of the signal. Its WT is accordingly

$$\begin{aligned}S_L(\tau,a) &= \sqrt{a}Ae^{i\varphi}e^{-D\tau}e^{i\omega_s\tau}\overline{G(a(\omega_s+iD))} \\ &= \sqrt{a}s(\tau)\overline{G(a(\omega_s+iD))}.\end{aligned} \tag{5}$$

For a Morlet function scaled by a dilation parameter a (we omit the negligible correction term, see Eq.(A.9)), namely,

$$G_M(a\omega) = \exp\left(-\tfrac{1}{2}\sigma^2(a\omega-\omega_0)^2\right), \tag{6}$$

it can be seen that the modulus of $S(\tau,a)$ is maximum, i.e., $\frac{\partial}{\partial a}S(\tau,a) \to 0$, when $\frac{\partial}{\partial a}G \to 0$. Given that $a > 0$ and the assumption that $\omega_s \gg D$, the maximum can be found along the scale $a_r = \omega_0/\omega_s$ (this is called a *horizontal ridge*), which then gives

$$\overline{G_M(a_r(\omega_s+iD))} = \exp\left(\frac{\sigma a_r D}{\sqrt{2}}\right)^2, \tag{7}$$

and consequently

$$S_{a_r}(\tau) = \sqrt{a_r}\exp\left(\frac{\sigma a_r D}{\sqrt{2}}\right)^2 s(\tau), \tag{8}$$

which is identical to the signal $s(t)$ multiplied by a coefficient depending on the still unknown D. Consider the modulus of the Morlet wavelet transform (MWT) along a_r,

$$\begin{aligned}|S_{a_r}(\tau)| &= \sqrt{a_r}\exp\left(\frac{\sigma a_r D}{\sqrt{2}}\right)^2 |s(\tau)| \\ \ln|S_{a_r}(\tau)| &= \frac{1}{2}\ln a + \left(\frac{\sigma a_r D}{\sqrt{2}}\right)^2 + \ln A - D\tau.\end{aligned} \tag{9}$$

That is,

$$D = -\frac{\partial}{\partial\tau}\ln|S_{a_r}(\tau)|. \tag{10}$$

Knowing D can now lead to the estimation of the amplitude resonance A of the signal by

$$A = |s(t)|e^{Dt}. \tag{11}$$

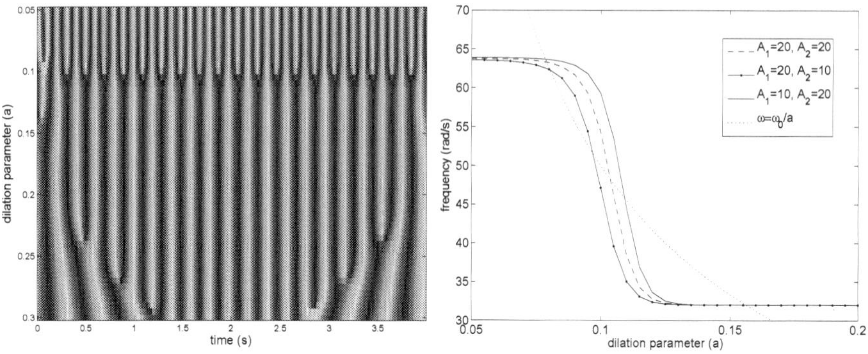

(a) (b)

Fig. 1. (a) Phase of the Morlet wavelet transform of a signal $s(t)$ containing two frequencies ω_s=32 and 64 rad/s and (b) its instantaneous frequency. Here $\sigma = 1, \omega_0 = 5$ rad/s, sampling frequency $F_s = 256\ \text{s}^{-1}$, data length $l = 1024$ points.

Since $S_{a_r}(\tau)$ is a function of time, the derived D is also a function of time. This is beneficial for analysing signals that do not have a steady damping function. In addition, considering the phase of the MWT along a_r, namely,

$$\arg S_{a_r}(\tau) = \omega_s \tau + \varphi,$$

we also have

$$\begin{aligned} \omega_s &= \frac{\partial}{\partial \tau} \arg S_{a_r}(\tau) \\ &= \Omega_{a_r}(\tau), \end{aligned} \tag{12}$$

as in Eq.(3). Strictly speaking, the instantaneous frequency at the scale a_r of the Morlet transform is ω_s. This can be observed in Figure 1, which shows that the instantaneous frequency intersects the line ω_0/a at $a = \omega_0/\omega_s$, where ω_s=32 and 64 rad/s are the frequencies of the signal. The phase of the signal $\varphi \in (-\pi, \pi)$ can also be derived from the phase of the WT, if needed. The property given in Eq.(12) is useful for analysing an n-frequency signal; it indicates the actual frequencies of the signal and the scale a that we should consider. In addition, if its frequencies are *sufficiently* far away from each other, so that $\overline{G(a\omega)}$ treats each spectral line independently (Barache et al., 1997), the amplitude at each frequency can thus be derived. When two frequencies are very close to each other (this also depends on the sampling frequency), increasing the frequency of the Morlet function ω_0 can better localize and distinguish the overlapping frequencies. On the other hand, ω_s can be obtained iteratively by

1. Initializing $a = a_i$ at some values.
2. Calculating the instantaneous frequency, namely Ω_{a_i}.
3. Assigning the new value to $a_{i+1} = \omega_0/\Omega_{a_i}$.
4. Repeating the process until a converges to ω_s.

Figure 2 illustrates an overlap of two frequencies and the derived instantaneous frequencies using the iteration method. The derived frequencies converge to the true frequencies within a few steps.

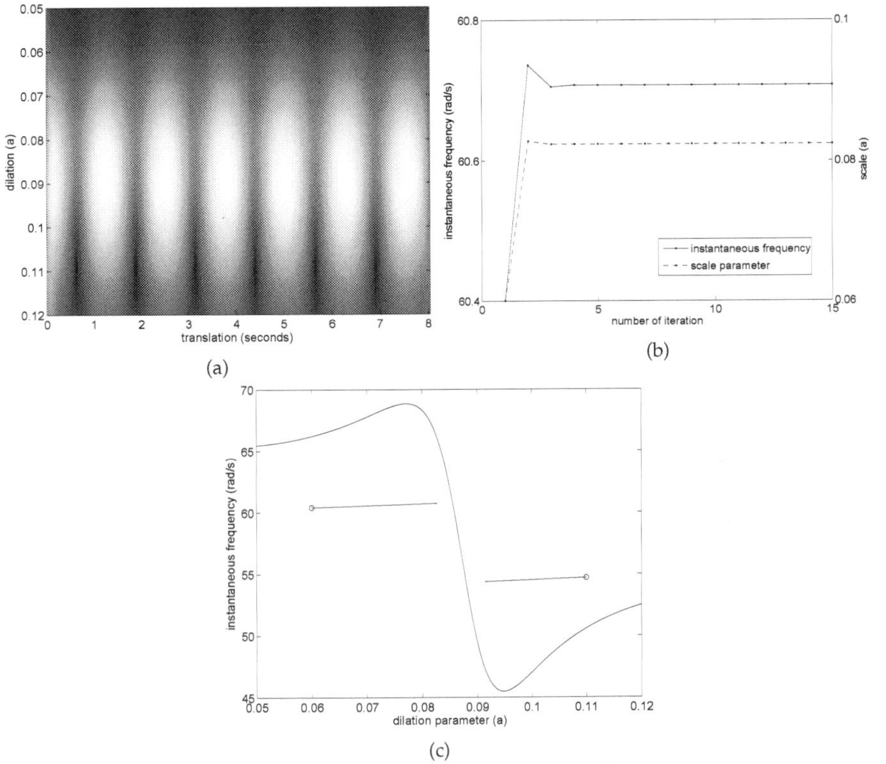

Fig. 2. (a) The MWT of $y(t) = \exp(i55t) + \exp(i60t)$ and (b) its instantaneous frequencies when using the iterative method. Here $\sigma = 1, \omega_0 = 5.5$ rad/s, $F_s = 800\ \mathrm{s}^{-1}, l = 1024$ points. (c) Comparison of the instantaneous frequencies by the non-iterative and the iterative method. The symbol $\circ$ indicates an initial value of a.

3. Continuous Wavelet Transform and the *in vivo* MRS challenges

3.1 Gaussian White Noise

An *in vivo* MRS signal is always impaired by additive noise, which is usually assumed to be white gaussian. This noise causes oscillations in the instantaneous frequency derived with the CWT representation, as illustrated in Figure 3 which shows the instantaneous frequency derived from a signal with a peak at a frequency of 32 rad/s with an additive Gaussian noise corresponding to a signal to noise ratio (SNR) of 10.[1] In order to reduce this effect, Guillemain

[1] The Signal to Noise ratio SNR is defined as the ratio of the time domain first point amplitude of the resonance to the time domain noise standard deviation

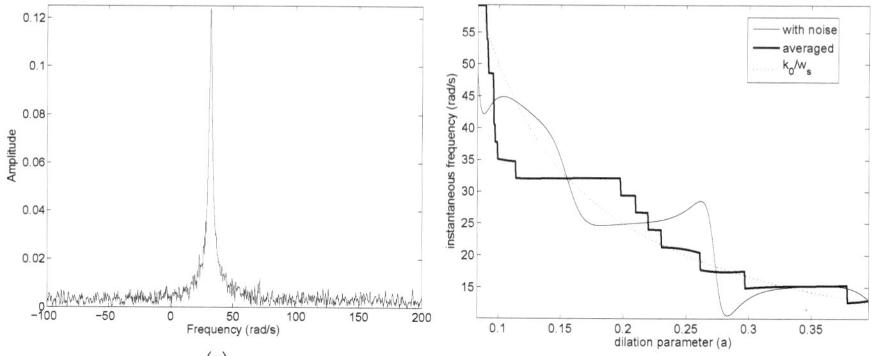

(a) (b)

Fig. 3. (a) A spectrum with one resonance at 32 rad/s with SNR=10 ($\sigma_n = 0.079$) and (b) its instantaneous frequency derived by the Morlet wavelet at $t = 4.7$ s ($\omega_0 = 5$ rad/s, σ=1, $Fs = 800\ \mathrm{s}^{-1}$).

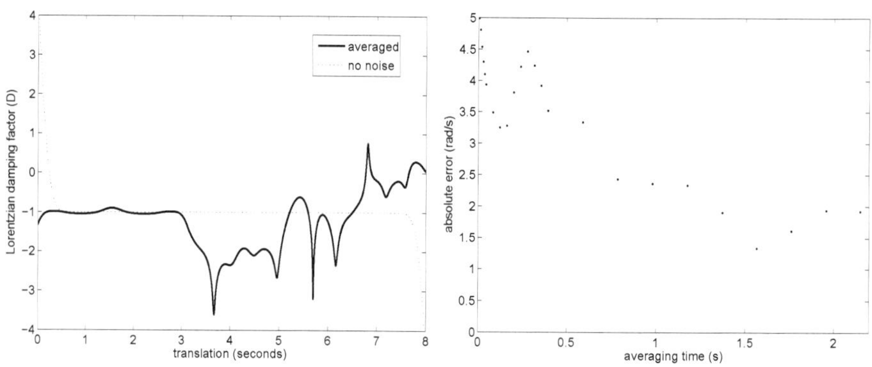

(a) (b)

Fig. 4. For the signal shown in Figure 3(a): Derived Lorentzian damping factor and (b) absolute frequency estimation error with respect to the averaging time, calculated at the scale $a = \omega_0/\omega_s$ of the Morlet wavelet transform (SNR = 10, ω_s = 32 rad/s,ω_0 = 5 rad/s, σ = 1, F_s = $800\ \mathrm{s}^{-1}$).

et al. (1992) suggested averaging in time the derived parameters, for instance $\Omega_a(\tau)$, i.e.,

$$\overline{\Omega_a} = \frac{1}{T}\int_{\tau_0}^{\tau_0+T} \Omega_a(\tau)d\tau. \tag{13}$$

As can be seen in Figure 3, averaging in time reduces the noise effect on the derivation of the instantaneous frequency.[2] One can see that averaging creates many steady points. At the scale $a = \omega_0/32$, the instantaneous frequency is about, but not exactly, 32 rad/s. Here, the

[2] This property might be used for denoising, but this has not been exploited.

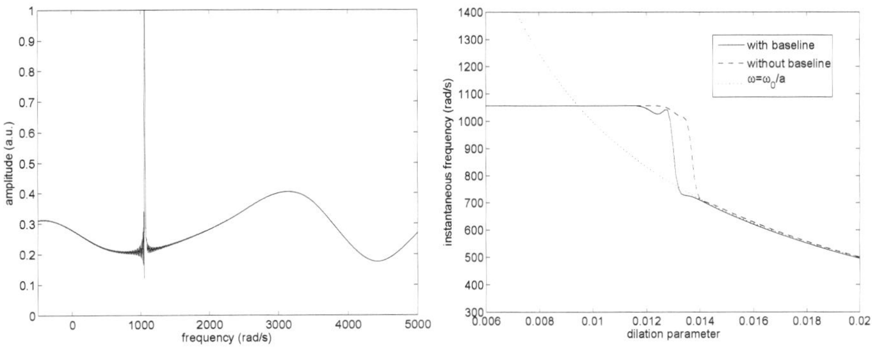

(a) (b)

Fig. 5. (a) The Fourier transform of a 1056-rad/s signal with baseline; b) Its instantaneous frequency ($\omega_0 = 10$ rad/s, $\sigma = 1$). The baseline is modelled by a cubic spline.

averaging time is 1.56 s. Figure 4(b) shows the evolution of the absolute frequency estimation with respect to the averaging time. Increasing the averaging time is likely to decrease the estimation error, as illustrated in Figure 4(b). The same approach can be used to derive the instantaneous damping factor. The estimated instantaneous damping factor is also smoother and closer to the actual damping factor when time averaging is employed. Although the method described above should work at any value of a, there is a particular range of a that is meaningful, and should be wisely selected. As a rule of thumb, this range should not be far from the scale that maximizes the modulus of the Morlet WT.

3.2 Baseline

The baseline corresponds to contributions from large molecules, with a broad frequency pattern in the MRS spectrum. Thus, it becomes a major obstruction in the quantification of metabolite contribution from the MRS signals. First, we simulate the baseline by cubic splines in order to study the performance of the MWT when a baseline is present. In the case of Figure 5, the simulated baseline has no effect on the instantaneous frequency derived from the WT. Then, we used a baseline modelled with 50 randomly distributed Lorentzian profiles with a large damping factor, compared to the signal-of-interest at 3447 rad/s, e.g. $s_L(t) = \exp(-10t)\exp(i3447t) + B(t)$ where $B(t) = \exp(-50t)[0.2\exp(i3447t) + 0.3\exp(i2000t) + \ldots]$ is the baseline (see Figure 6). The first component of $B(t)$ has the same frequency as the signal, in order to imitate the overlap between the baseline and the signal. It is found that the modelled baseline does not prevent an accurate estimation of both the damping factor and the amplitude derived from the Morlet WT, provided one waits until both the effect of the baseline and the edge effect (discussed in Section 4.1 below) have died out. In the example shown here, the waiting time is approximately 0.2 s.

The MWT in Figure 6(b) tells us that the baseline affects only the beginning of the transform in the time (τ) axis, comparing to the long, clear peak of our 3447-rad/s signal. This means that the baseline can be assumed to decay faster than the pure signal, and the method described should still be effective without removing the baseline beforehand. Such an assumption has been widely used in spectroscopic signal processing, where several authors have proposed truncation of the initial data points in the time domain, which are believed to contain a major

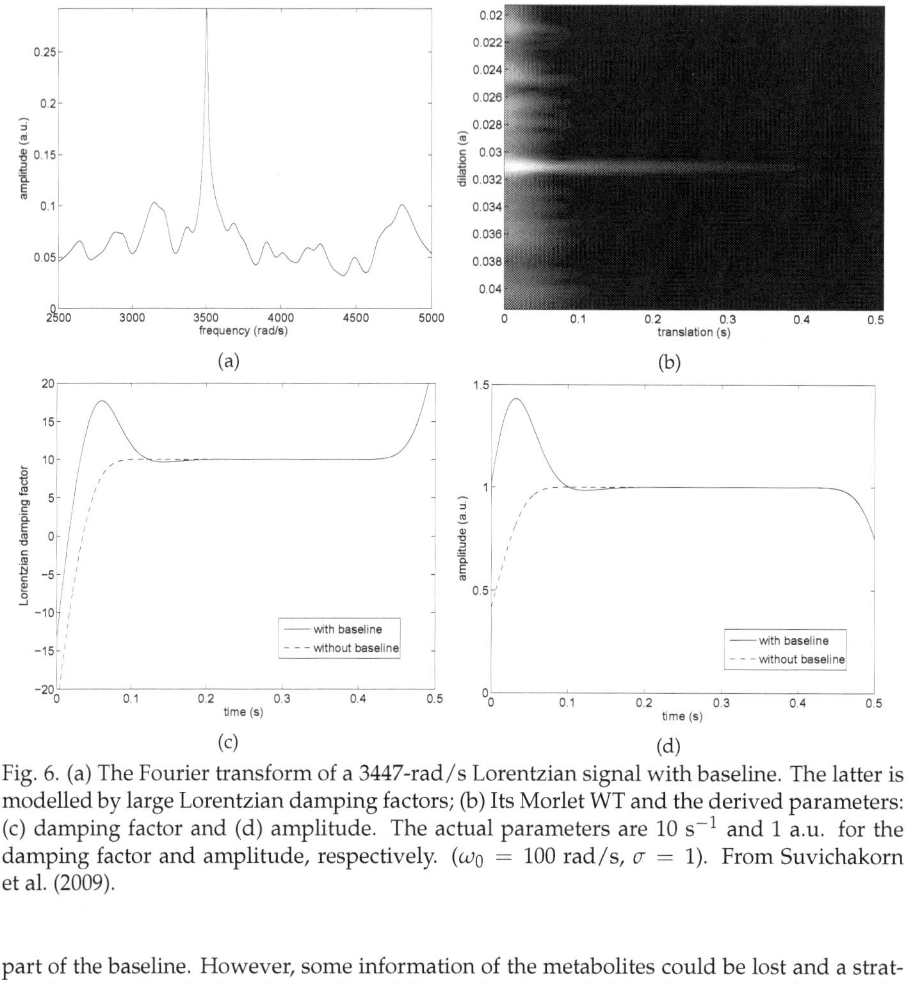

Fig. 6. (a) The Fourier transform of a 3447-rad/s Lorentzian signal with baseline. The latter is modelled by large Lorentzian damping factors; (b) Its Morlet WT and the derived parameters: (c) damping factor and (d) amplitude. The actual parameters are 10 s^{-1} and 1 a.u. for the damping factor and amplitude, respectively. (ω_0 = 100 rad/s, σ = 1). From Suvichakorn et al. (2009).

part of the baseline. However, some information of the metabolites could be lost and a strategy for properly selecting the number of data points is needed (see Rabeson et al. (2006) for examples and further references).

Next, in order to study the characteristics of the real baseline by the Morlet wavelet, an *in vivo* macromolecule MRS signal was acquired on a horizontal 4.7T Biospec system (BRUKER BioSpin MRI, Germany). The data acquisition was done using the differences in spin-lattice relaxation times (T1) between low molecular weight metabolites and macromolecules (Behar et al., 1994; Cudalbu et al., 2009; 2007).

As seen in Figure 7, the metabolite-nullified signal from a volume-of-interest (VOI) central-

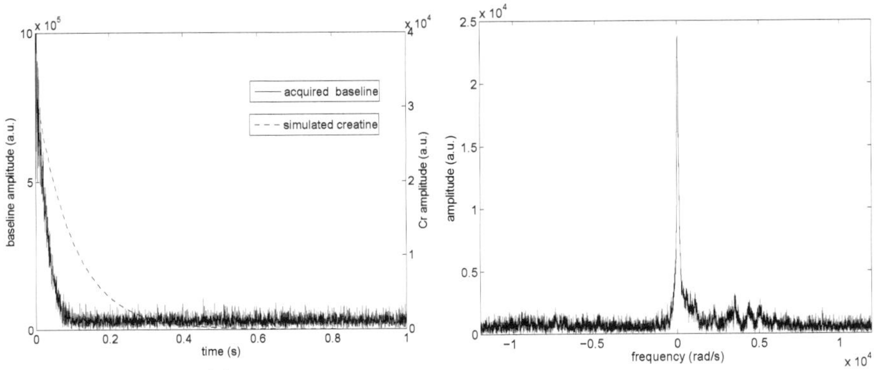

(a) (b)

Fig. 7. (a) The signal of baseline + residual water (a) in time domain; and (b) in frequency domain.

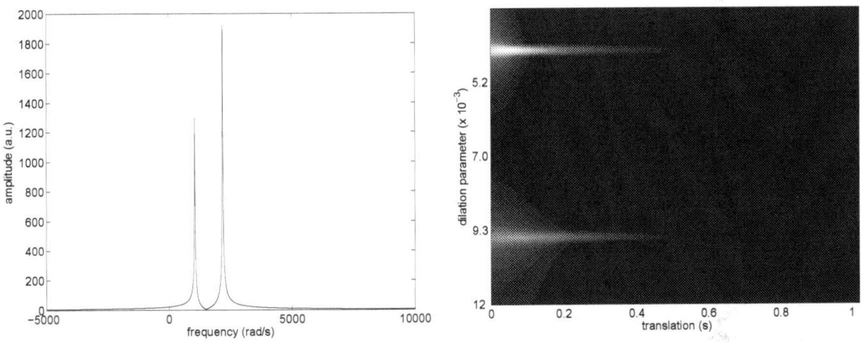

(a) (b)

Fig. 8. (a) Frequency response of creatine at 4.7 Tesla and (b) its Morlet WT ($\omega_0 = 10$ rad/s, $\sigma = 1$, $F_s = 4006.41\ \mathrm{s}^{-1}$). The parameters derived from the Morlet transform are $D = 10\ \mathrm{s}^{-1}$, $\omega_1 = 1056$ rad/s, $A_1 = 1330$ a.u. and $\omega_2 = 2168$ rad/s, $A_1 = 1965$ a.u.

ized in the hippocampus of a healthy mouse[3] resulted from a combination of residual water, baseline and noise. Compared to the simulated signal of creatine, whose frequency response and Morlet WT are shown in Figure 8, the signal decays much faster, making it suitable to use the Morlet wavelet to analyse the MRS signal as described earlier. For studying this, the two signals are normalised to the same amplitude and added together. Then the amplitude of the

[3] An Inversion-Recovery module was included prior to the PRESS sequence (echo-time = 20ms, repetition time = 3.5s, bandwidth of 4kHz, 4096 data-points) in order to measure the metabolite-nullified signal. The water signal was suppressed by variable power RF pulses with optimized relaxation delays (VAPOR). All first- and second-order shimming terms were adjusted using the Fast, Automatic Shimming technique by Mapping Along Projections (FASTMAP) for each VOI ($3 \times 3 \times 3\ \mathrm{mm}^3$). Inversion time = 700 ms.

creatine is derived with the Morlet WT. Next, we multiply the simulated, normalised creatine by 0.5, 1, 1.5,.... For each of these values, we derive the amplitude and plot the result in Figure 9. The recovery of the (simulated) creatine at different amplitudes, after adding it to the baseline signal, reveals that the amplitude of the metabolite can be correctly derived using $t = 0.4$ s, whereas at earlier time ($t < 0.2$ s) the derived amplitude still suffers from the boundary effect (we will discuss this effect in Section 4.1). However, the metabolite signal is covered later by noise ($t = 0.77$ s), giving an inaccurate amplitude estimate. Therefore, the time to monitor the amplitude of the metabolite should be properly selected. Another data set of the baseline[4] acquired at 9.4T, with a better signal to noise ratio and a better water suppression, shows similar characteristics (see Figure 10).

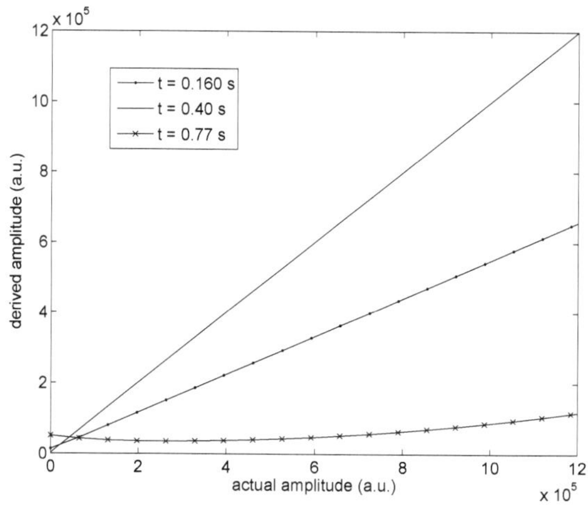

Fig. 9. Derived amplitude at $\omega = 1056$ rad/s, using $\omega_0 = 100$ rad/s and $\sigma = 1$ from a signal containing a simulated creatine signal and an *in vivo* acquired macromolecule signal.

3.3 Solvent

In MRS quantification, a large resonance from the solvent needs to be suppressed to unveil the metabolites without altering their magnitudes. The intensity of the solvent is usually several orders of magnitude larger than those of the metabolites.

[4] received from Cristina Cubaldu, Laboratory for Functional and Metabolic Imaging (LIFMET), Ecole Polytechnique Fédérale de Lausanne (EPFL).

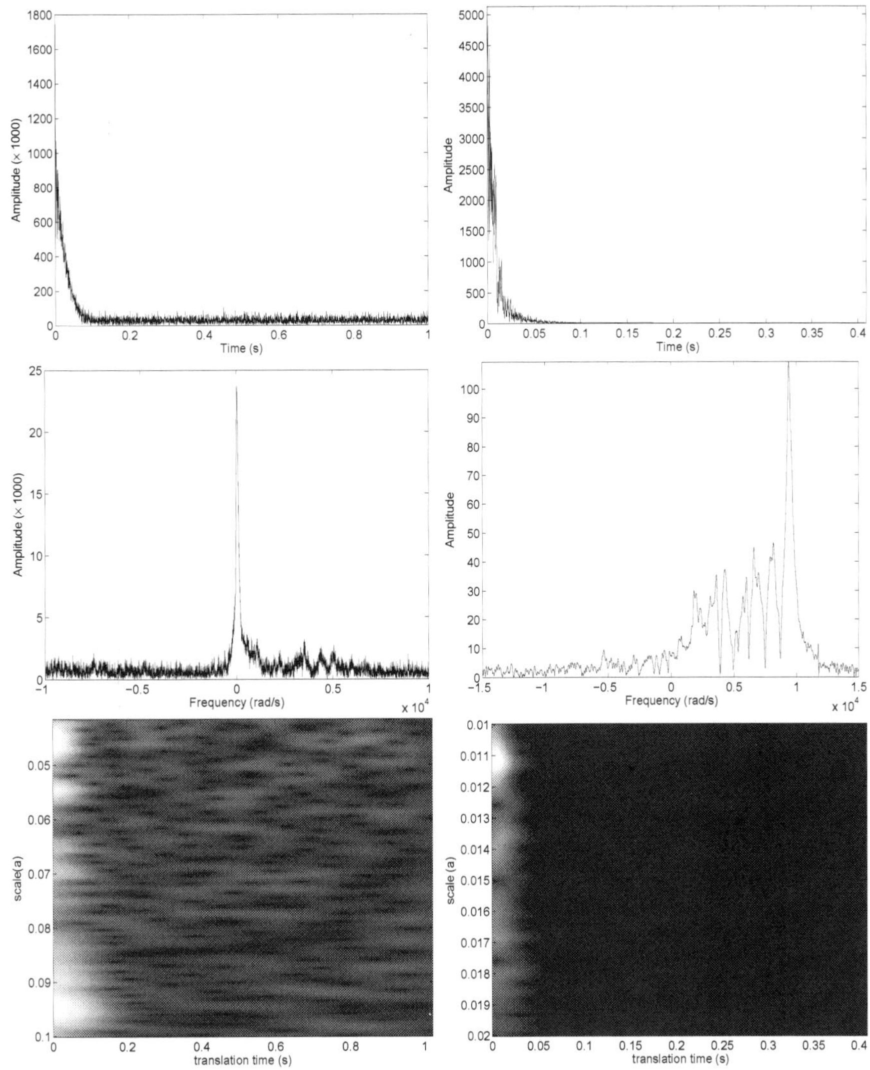

4.7 Teslas 9.4 Teslas

Fig. 10. Macromolecules MRS signals acquired at 4.7 Teslas and 9.4 Teslas, respectively, their Fourier transforms and their Morlet WT.

The Morlet WT sees the signal at each frequency individually, therefore it can work well even if the amplitudes at various frequencies are hugely different, which normally occurs when there is a solvent peak in the signal. In order to illustrate this, the Morlet WT has been applied to the following signal

$$s(t) = 100e^{-8.5t}e^{i32t} + e^{-1.5t}e^{i60t} + e^{-0.5t}e^{i90t} + e^{-t}e^{i120t} + e^{-2t}e^{i150t}, \tag{14}$$

as seen in Figure 11 (a). This signal has an amplitude of 100 at 32 rad/s and 1 elsewhere. The high amplitude can affect other frequencies if they are close to each other. This is illustrated in Figure 11 (b) when a Hann window is applied to the signal in order to separate each frequency. Using the aforementioned method, the amplitude of 1 is derived as 0.980, 0.911, 0.988 and 0.974 respectively. The error ranges within 1.2-8.9 %, without any preprocessing.

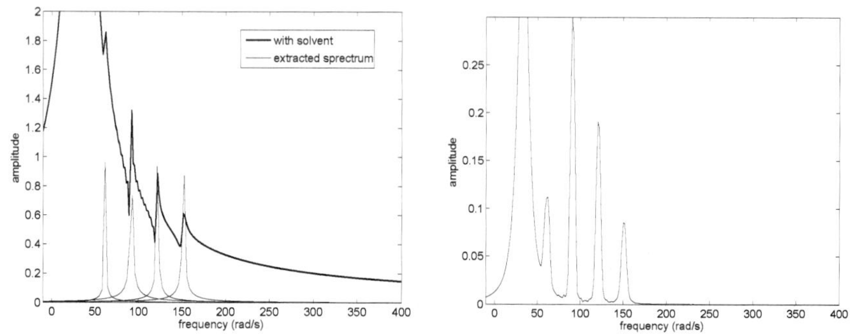

(a) (b)

Fig. 11. (a) The Fourier transform of a signal with different amplitudes and the spectrum extracted by the Morlet wavelet and (b) by a Hann window.

3.4 Non-Lorentzian lineshape

The ideal Lorentzian lineshape assumes that the homogeneous broadening is equally contributed from each individual molecule. However, imperfect shimming and susceptibility effects from internal heterogeneity within tissues lead to non-Lorentzian lineshapes in real experiments (Cudalbu et al., 2008). These effects are typically modelled by a Gaussian lineshape (Franzen, 2002; Hornak, 1997). Since the inhomogeneous broadening is often significantly larger than the lifetime broadening, the Gaussian lineshape is often dominant. If the lineshape is intermediate between a Gaussian and a Lorentzian form, the spectrum can be fitted to a convolution of the two functions (Marshall et al., 2000; Ratiney et al., 2008). Such lineshape is known as a *Voigt profile*.

Next we will explore how the Morlet WT can deal with the Gaussian and Voigt lineshapes. Consider a pure Gaussian function modulated at the frequency ω_s, namely,

$$s_G(t) = Ae^{-\gamma t^2}e^{i\omega_s t}. \tag{15}$$

Its Morlet WT is

$$\begin{aligned} S_G(\tau, a) &= \frac{1}{\sqrt{a}} \int \overline{g_M\left(\frac{t-\tau}{a}\right)} s_G(t)\, dt \\ &= \frac{A}{2\pi\sqrt{a\sigma}} \int e^{-\gamma t^2} e^{i\omega_s t} e^{-\left(\frac{t-\tau}{\sqrt{2}\sigma a}\right)^2} e^{-i\omega_0\left(\frac{t-\tau}{a}\right)} dt \\ &= \frac{A}{2\pi\sqrt{a\sigma}} \int e^{-(k_1 t^2 + k_2 t + k_3)} dt, \end{aligned} \tag{16}$$

where

$$k_1 = \gamma + \frac{1}{2\sigma^2 a^2}$$
$$k_2 = -i(\omega_s - \frac{\omega_0}{a}) - \frac{\tau}{\sigma^2 a^2}$$
$$k_3 = -i\frac{\omega_0 \tau}{a} + \frac{\tau^2}{2\sigma^2 a^2}.$$

Eq.(16) is known as a Gaussian integral and can be computed explicitly:

$$\int_{-\infty}^{\infty} e^{-(k_1 t^2 + k_2 t + k_3)} dt = \sqrt{\frac{\pi}{k_1}} e^{\frac{k_2^2}{4k_1} - k_3}. \tag{17}$$

As a result, the Morlet WT at the scale $a_r = \omega_0 / \omega_s$ is

$$S_{G,a_r}(\tau) = k_4 A e^{-k_5 \tau^2} e^{i\omega_s \tau}, \tag{18}$$

where

$$k_4 = \sqrt{\frac{a_r}{2\pi(2\gamma\sigma^2 a_r^2 + 1)}}$$
$$k_5 = \frac{\gamma}{2\gamma\sigma^2 a_r^2 + 1},$$

which is also a Gaussian function at the frequency ω_s. The width and amplitude of this new Gaussian function are functions of ω_s and of the width of the original Gaussian signal $s_G(t)$. Therefore, similarly to the process of the Lorentzian lineshape, the amplitude (A) and the width of the Gaussian function (inversely proportional to γ) can be obtained as follows:

1. Find $\omega_s = \frac{\partial}{\partial \tau} \arg S_{G,a_r}(\tau)$.
2. Find γ from the second derivative of $\ln |S_{G,a_r}(\tau)|$, which yields

$$\gamma = -\frac{0.5}{\left(\frac{\partial^2}{\partial \tau^2} \ln |S_{G,a_r}(\tau)|\right)^{-1} + \sigma^2 a_r^2}. \tag{19}$$

3. Find A from the calculated ω_s and γ.

On the other hand, the Morlet WT at the scale $a_r = \omega_0 / \omega_s$ of a Voigt lineshape,

$$s_V(t) = A e^{-\gamma t^2} e^{-Dt} e^{i\omega_s t}, \tag{20}$$

is given by

$$S_{V,a_r}(\tau) = k_6 A e^{-k_5(\tau - k_7)^2} e^{i\omega_s \tau}, \tag{21}$$

where

$$k_6 = k_4 e^{\frac{-D^2}{4\gamma}}$$
$$k_7 = \frac{D}{2\gamma}.$$

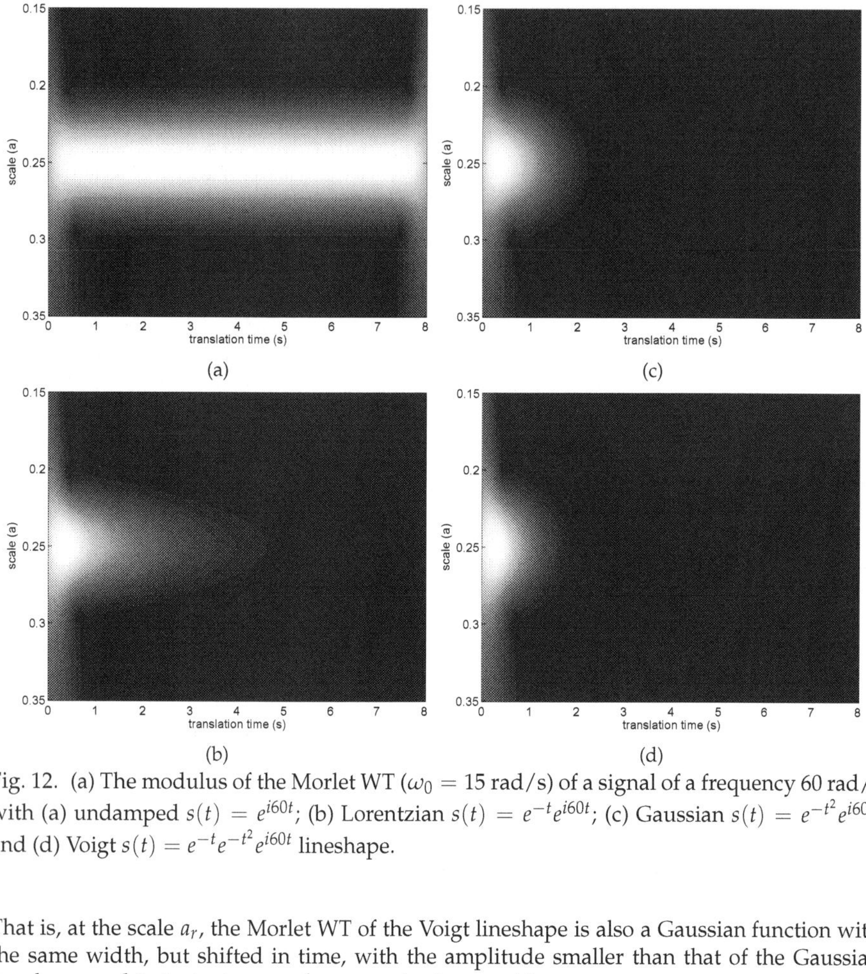

Fig. 12. (a) The modulus of the Morlet WT ($\omega_0 = 15$ rad/s) of a signal of a frequency 60 rad/s with (a) undamped $s(t) = e^{i60t}$; (b) Lorentzian $s(t) = e^{-t}e^{i60t}$; (c) Gaussian $s(t) = e^{-t^2}e^{i60t}$; and (d) Voigt $s(t) = e^{-t}e^{-t^2}e^{i60t}$ lineshape.

That is, at the scale a_r, the Morlet WT of the Voigt lineshape is also a Gaussian function with the same width, but shifted in time, with the amplitude smaller than that of the Gaussian lineshape, and its instantaneous frequency is also equal to ω_s.

Note that the scale $a_r = \omega_0/\omega_s$ does not give exactly the maximum modulus of the WT. However, as seen in Figure 12, the modulus of the Morlet WT of a signal with a Lorentzian lineshape or a Gaussian lineshape (and also a Voigt lineshape) are maximal at the same scale a_r, provided that $a \in \mathbb{R}$ and $\omega_s \gg D$.

Figure 13 shows that the second derivative of the modulus of the Morlet WT can be used to describe the second-order broadening of the lineshape, no matter whether it is Gaussian or Voigt. In the case of a Voigt lineshape, γ actually gives back a Lorentzian whose damping factor is obtained by Eq.(10).

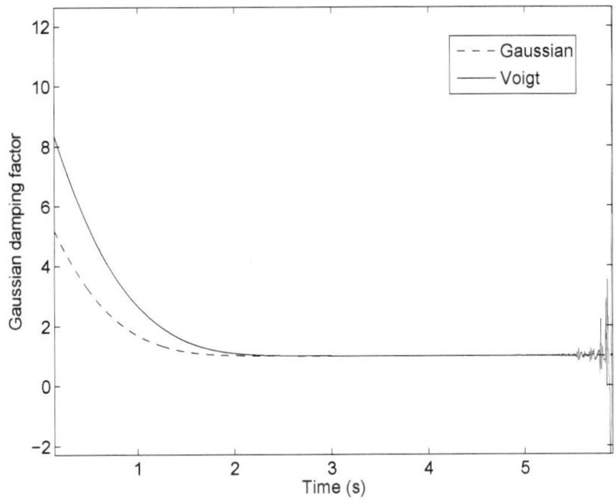

Fig. 13. The Gaussian damping factor derived from the pure Gaussian signal and the Voigt signal considered in Figure 12

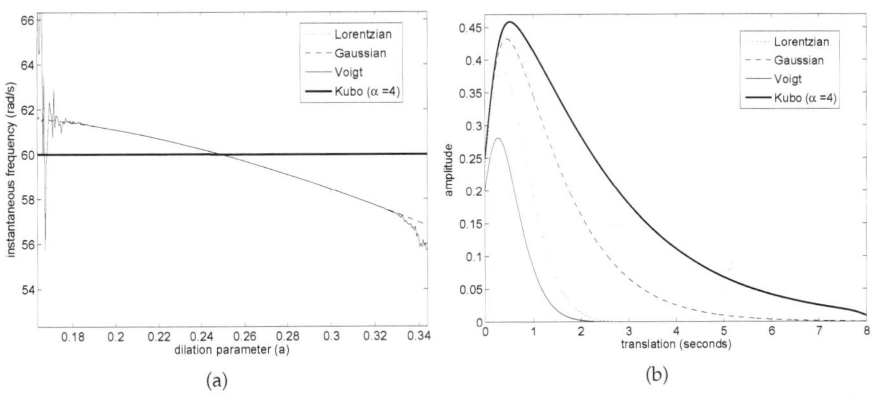

Fig. 14. (a) The comparison of the derived instantaneous frequency of the Morlet WT of a signal of a frequency 60 rad/s with different lineshapes, e.g. Lorentzian $s(t) = e^{-t}e^{i60t}$, Gaussian $s(t) = e^{-t^2}e^{i60t}$, Voigt $s(t) = e^{-t}e^{-t^2}e^{i60t}$ and Kubo $s(t) = e^{-0.25(e^{-t}-1+t)}e^{i60t}$ at t= 4.7 s. Panel (b) shows the modulus of the Morlet WT of each line at $a_r = \omega_0/60$. Note: σ =1, ω_0 =15 rad/s, F_s = 800 s^{-1}, l = 1024 points.

Kubo's lineshape

The interaction between the Lorentzian and Gaussian broadening of lineshape depends on the time scale. For example, if the relaxation time (T_2) is much longer than any effect modulating the energy of a molecule, the lineshape will approach the Lorentzian lineshape. On the contrary, if T_2 is short, the lineshape is likely to be Gaussian. In order to account for this time

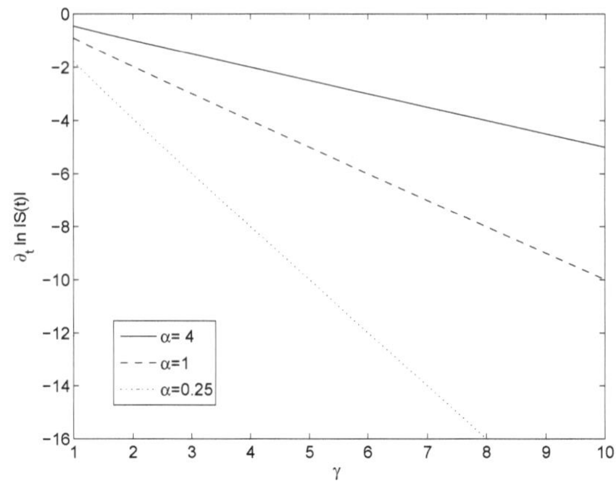

Fig. 15. $\frac{\partial}{\partial\tau}\ln|S_{G,a_r}(\tau)|$ with respect to Kubo's γ for the pure gaussian signal given in Eq.(15), at the scale $a_r = \omega_0/\omega_s$. We have put $\alpha = \gamma/\varsigma$, where γ and ς are the two parameters of the Kubo lineshape defined in Eq.(22).

scale, Kubo (1969) uses a so-called Gaussian-Markovian modulation, namely

$$s(t) = A\exp\Big(-\frac{\varsigma^2}{\gamma^2}\,(e^{-\gamma t} - 1 + \gamma t)\Big). \tag{22}$$

The parameter γ is inversely proportional to T_2 and ς is the amplitude of the solvent-induced fluctuations in the frequency. If $\alpha = \gamma/\varsigma \ll 1$, the lineshape becomes Gaussian, whereas $\alpha \gg 1$ leads to Lorentzian. The width of the lineshape is $\varsigma^2\gamma$.
Solving Eq.(22) seems to be complicated, though may be possible. However, it turns out that the maximum modulus of the Morlet WT of a Kubo lineshape at ω_s = 60 rad/s occurs also at the scale $a_r = \omega_0/\omega_s$, like those of the Gaussian and Lorentzian lineshapes. In addition, the instantaneous frequency is still able to derive the ω_s, even better than the Gaussian lineshape, as shown in Figure 14(a), although the amplitude is broader than those of the Lorentzian, Gaussian or Voigt profiles, as shown in Figure 14(b). The damping parameters can also be derived by the linear relation between $\frac{\partial}{\partial\tau}\ln|S_{G,a_r}(\tau)|$ and γ, as seen in Figure 15, whereas α is related directly to $\frac{\partial^2}{\partial\tau^2}\ln|S_{G,a_r}(\tau)|$.

4. Limitations of the Morlet wavelet transform

In the previous section, the Morlet WT shows its potential for analysing an MRS signal by means of its amplitude and phase, in addition to its time-frequency representation. However, these techniques can be applied to well-defined lineshapes only. Another limitation is the requirement of a proper ω_0 that should distinguish the signal from the solvent, but should not introduce noise in the result. In this section, we will look further on some more limitations that prevent the use of the Morlet WT to quantify MRS signals directly.

4.1 Edge effects

Errors in the wavelet analysis can occur at both ends of the spectrum due to the limited time series. The region of the wavelet spectrum in which effects become important[5] increases linearly with the scale a, thus it has a conic shape at both ends, as already seen in Figure 1(a) (see also the Appendix). The size of the forbidden region, which is affected by the boundary effect, varies with the frequency ω_0 of the Morlet wavelet function and the ratio between the frequency of the signal (ω_S) and the sampling frequency (F_S). Figure 16 shows that the size becomes larger for a large ω_0 and low ω_S/F_S. In practice, the working region is chosen so that the edge effects are negligible outside and the characterization of the MRS signals should be made inside this region, disregarding the presence of the macromolecular contamination.

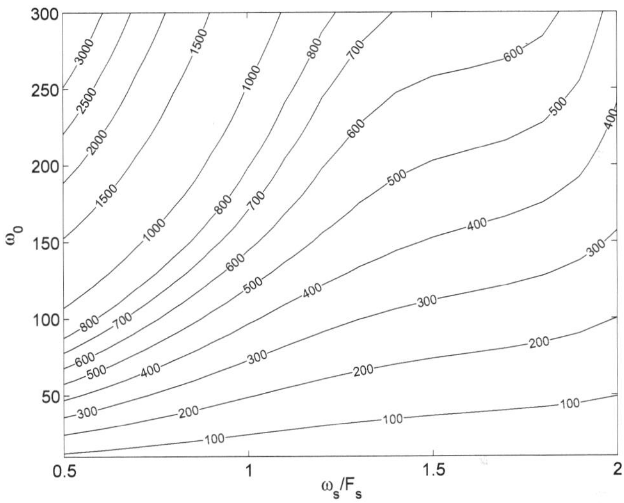

Fig. 16. Lines showing the width (in number of sample points) of the forbidden regions where the boundary effect becomes important, as a function of ω_0 (rad/s) and the ratio between the signal frequency (ω_S) and the sampling frequency (F_S). From (Suvichakorn et al., 2009).

4.2 Interacting/overlapping frequencies

If two frequencies of the signal are close to each other, the wavelet can interact with both of them at the same time. This was already observed in Figure 2(a). Barache et al. (1997) suggested the use of a linear equation system to solve the problem. In the sequel, the simulated N-Acetyl Aspartate (NAA) is used to illustrate how the problem could be solved. The spectrum of the NAA, shown in Figure 17(a), is composed of two different regions, the high, single peak (NAA–acetyl part) and a group of overlapping frequencies (NAA–aspartate part). By using a high ω_0 to separate the overlapping frequencies, the Morlet WT reveals that there are eight frequency peaks in the group as seen in Figure 17(b). The damping factors of the two parts of NAA are shown in Figure 18(a). Applying Eq.(10) directly to each peak causes an oscillation in the derived damping factor, compared to the smooth and stationary damping

[5] defined as the e-folding time for the autocorrelation of wavelet power at each scale.

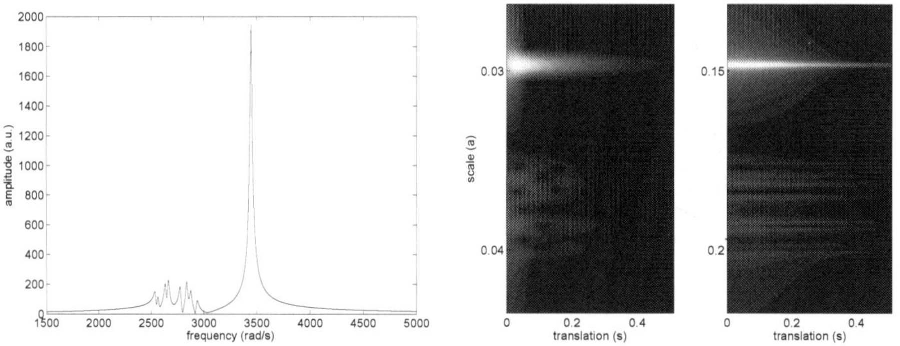

(a) (b)

Fig. 17. NAA : (a) Frequency response; (b) Its Morlet wavelet transform for $\omega_0 = 100$ rad/s (left) and $\omega_0 = 500$ rad/s (right). From (Suvichakorn et al., 2009).

factor of the single peak. The size and frequency of the oscillation depends on the numbers of neighbours of each peak and the spectral distance to these neighbours. A proper damping factor can be achieved by averaging these oscillations in time.

Next, we will try to derive the amplitude of each peak. Let us consider an MRS signal composed of n Lorentzian lines $s(t) = e^{-Dt} \sum_n s_n(t)$, where $s_n(t) = A_n e^{i\omega_n t + \varphi_n}$ and $n = 1, 2, \ldots$ is an indexing number. Its Morlet WT gives local maxima *close* to the scales $a_1 = \omega_0/\omega_1$, $a_2 = \omega_0/\omega_2$, and so on. Therefore, we can establish a systematic relation between S_{a_r} and $s_n(t)$ at each scale as follows:

$$\begin{bmatrix} \frac{S_{a_1}(\tau)}{\sqrt{a_1}} \\ \frac{S_{a_2}(\tau)}{\sqrt{a_2}} \\ \frac{S_{a_3}(\tau)}{\sqrt{a_3}} \\ \vdots \end{bmatrix} = \exp(-D\tau)\,\mathbf{C} \begin{bmatrix} s_1(\tau) \\ s_2(\tau) \\ s_3(\tau) \\ \vdots \end{bmatrix},$$

where $\mathbf{C} = [C_{mn}]$ is a matrix with

$$C_{nn} = \exp\left(\frac{\sigma^2 a_n^2 D^2}{2}\right)$$

$$C_{mn} = \exp\left[-\frac{\sigma^2 \omega_0^2}{2}\left(\frac{\omega_n - \omega_m - iD}{\omega_m}\right)^2\right], \qquad m \neq n.$$

The value of $|C_{mn}|$ decreases when the resonating peaks are well resolved (no overlapping frequencies), in fact, it goes to zero when $|\omega_m - \omega_n|$ increases, independently of D. Also, $|C_{mn}|$ decreases when ω_m is high. If C_{mn} is not negligible (overlapping frequencies), solving the linear equations gives the information for each $s_n(t)$.

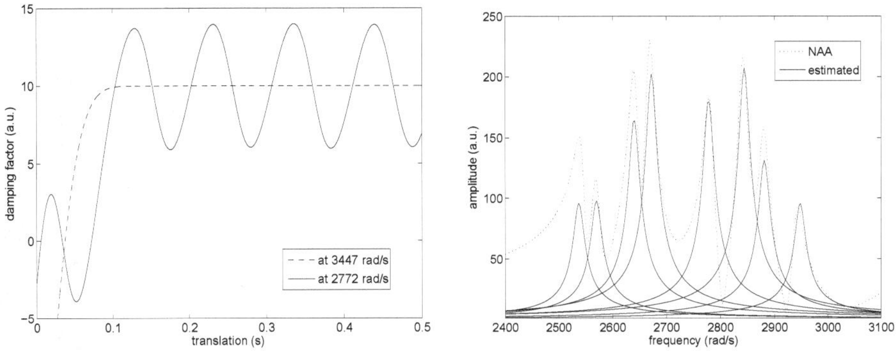

(a) (b)

Fig. 18. NAA: (a) Damping function derived by Eq.(10); (b) Amplitudes of NAA–aspartate part, derived by the linear equations (with zero phase). From (Suvichakorn et al., 2009).

The damping parameter D for the equations can be derived by Eq.(10), although the overlapping frequencies may cause oscillations in the solution, but these can be smoothened by averaging in time.
There can be a bias from the estimation, depending on the number and distribution of overlapping frequencies, e.g. the distance between neighbouring frequencies and ω_0. For the NAA ($\omega = 3447$ rad/s), the bias is approximately 1% of its amplitude (in time domain), when ω_0 = 200 rad/s is used. Note that Lorentzian lineshapes are assumed in these linear equations, and the result is presented in Figure 18(b). In case of non-Lorentzian lineshapes, the arbitrary damping function should be determined, and taken into account to solve the equation.

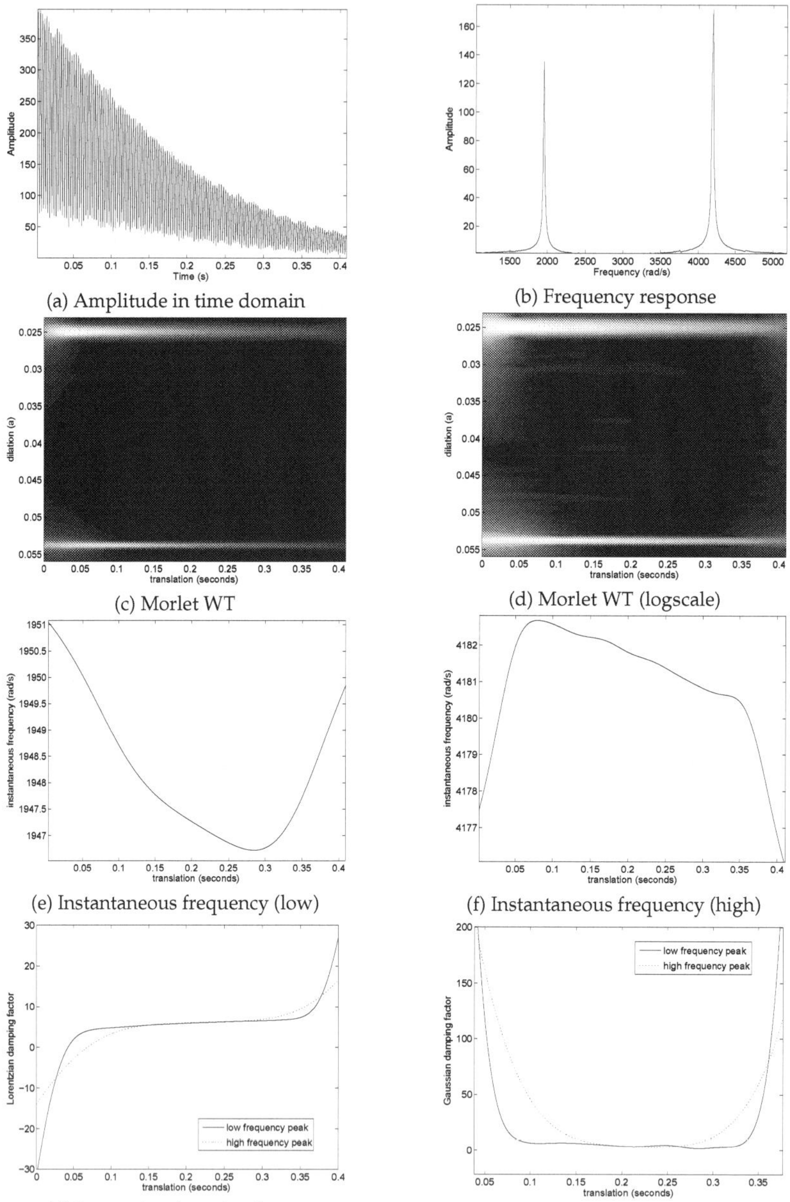

(a) Amplitude in time domain

(b) Frequency response

(c) Morlet WT

(d) Morlet WT (logscale)

(e) Instantaneous frequency (low)

(f) Instantaneous frequency (high)

(g) Lorentzian damping factor

(h) Gaussian damping factor

Fig. 19. *In vitro* measured Creatine at 9.4 T

4.3 Arbitrary lineshape

Let us consider a signal with an arbitrary damping function $D(t)$, namely,

$$s(t) = AD(t)e^{(i\omega_s t+\varphi)}. \quad (23)$$

Its Morlet WT is defined by

$$\begin{aligned}
S(\tau,a) &= \frac{Ae^{i\varphi}}{2\pi\sigma\sqrt{a}}\int D(t)e^{i\omega_s t}e^{-\frac{1}{2\sigma^2}\left(\frac{t-\tau}{a}\right)^2}e^{-i\omega_0\left(\frac{t-\tau}{a}\right)}dt \\
&= AC_1\int D(x+\tau)e^{i\omega_s x}e^{-\frac{1}{2\sigma^2}\left(\frac{x}{a}\right)^2}e^{-i\omega_0\left(\frac{x}{a}\right)}dx; \qquad x = t-\tau, \\
&= AC_1\int \mathcal{F}[D(x+\tau)]\overline{\mathcal{F}[e^{-\frac{x^2}{2\sigma^2a^2}}e^{\frac{-i(\omega_0-\omega_s)x}{a}}]}d\omega \text{ (Parseval's theorem)} \\
\frac{1}{\sqrt{a}}S(\tau,a) &= AC_2\int \mathcal{F}[D(x)]e^{i\tau\omega}e^{\frac{-\sigma^2}{2}(a\omega+\omega_s-\omega_0)^2}d\omega,
\end{aligned}$$

where $C_1 = \frac{e^{i(\omega_s\tau+\varphi)}}{2\pi\sigma\sqrt{a}}$ and $C_2 = (\sqrt{2\pi})^{-1}e^{i(\omega_s x+\varphi)}$. When implemented (thus discretized), the equation above can be seen as the product of two matrices, namely,

$$\mathbf{S} = C_2\mathbf{DG},$$

and the damping function could be solved from the following equations

$$\begin{aligned}
A\mathcal{F}[D(x)] &= C_2^{-1}\mathbf{S}\mathbf{G}^{-1}, \\
AD(x) &= C_2^{-1}\mathcal{F}^{-1}[\mathbf{S}\mathbf{G}^{-1}], \\
AD(t) &= C_2^{-1}\mathcal{F}^{-1}[\mathbf{S}\mathbf{G}^{-1}e^{i\tau\omega}],
\end{aligned}$$

where $\mathbf{S}$ is the matrix of the scaled wavelet coefficients, $\mathbf{G}$ is derived from the Morlet WT and the frequency-of-interest ω_s, and A is the unknown amplitude of the signal. For a combination of frequencies with the *same* damping function, dividing by $|D(t)|$ should give us a possibility for comparing the amplitude at each peak *relatively*.

5. Working in a real life environment

By real life environment, we mean genuine acquired data, either *in vitro* or *in vivo*, rather than simulated ones. In that case, the ideal Lorentzian lineshape of individual peaks gets distorted. To give an example, we show in Figure 19 the analysis of an *in vitro* creatine signal. We see that intermittent noise appears, in the form of many disrupted, horizontal bands in the WT. Thus the noise occurs for a while at some particular frequencies and then disappears.[6] Such characteristics differ from the Gaussian white noise that usually appears as vertical bands in the WT. It is also possible that the Gaussian white noise at that duration has the same intensity, however. The analysis of this *in vitro* creatine signal shows that the frequency distribution at each peak is broad and the *almost* stationary Gaussian damping factor indicates that the acquired signal has a lineshape close to that of the Gaussian function. Nevertheless, deriving the amplitude using the Gaussian assumption may lead to an inaccurate estimation.

[6] We don't know the origin of that noise, which in fact represents the part of the signal that we cannot identify in terms of specific, known contributions.

When the acquisition is made in an *in vivo* environment, the exponential decay of an MRS signal is severely distorted. This is due to the inhomogeneity of the static magnetic field and to eddy currents induced in the magnet walls by switching magnetic gradient fields on and off. Apart from the problem of overlapping frequencies in each metabolite, an *in vivo* MRS signal is composed of several metabolite signatures. Therefore, the challenge is to find a good combination of the amplitudes that the Morlet WT derives at each frequency. Determining complete spectra of each metabolite is preferred to individual resonance. This is yet to be solved.

Appendix:The mathematics of the CWT

A.1. General definitions and properties

The continuous WT is a mathematical tool which permits to decompose a signal in terms of elementary contributions called wavelets. A large body of literature exists for wavelet analysis. We might refer the interested reader to the textbooks of Daubechies (1992), Torrésani (1995), Ali et al. (2000), Antoine et al. (2004), or the elementary introductions (Antoine, 1994) and (Antoine, 2000). These wavelets are obtained from a single function g by translations and dilations,

$$g_{(\tau,a)}(t) = \frac{1}{\sqrt{a}}\, g\left(\frac{t-\tau}{a}\right), \tag{A.1}$$

where the parameters of translation, $\tau \in \mathbb{R}$, and dilation, $a > 0$, may be continuous or discrete. The CWT of a signal s with the analysing wavelet g is the convolution of s with a scaled and conjugated wavelet $g_a(t) = \overline{g(-t/a)}/a$, where the overbar denotes complex conjugation :

$$S(\tau,a) = g_a * s(\tau) = \frac{1}{\sqrt{a}} \int \overline{g\left(\frac{t-\tau}{a}\right)}\, s(t)\, dt. \tag{A.2}$$

It should be remarked that one uses often the so-called L^1-normalisation, with a factor $1/a$ in (A.1) and (A.2), instead of $1/\sqrt{a}$, in order to enhance small scales, where the finer details lie. In the Fourier domain, the expression (A.2) takes the following form:

$$S(\tau,a) = \frac{1}{2\pi} \int \overline{G(a\omega)}\, S(\omega)\, e^{i\omega\tau}\, d\omega, \tag{A.3}$$

where S and G are the Fourier transforms of the signal s and of the wavelet g, respectively. The equations (A.2) and (A.3) show clearly that the wavelet analysis is a time-frequency analysis, or, more properly, a time-scale analysis (the scale parameter a behaves as the inverse of a frequency). In particular, the relation (A.3) shows that the CWT of a signal s is a filter with a constant relative bandwidth $\Delta\omega/\omega = \text{const}$.

Then a straightforward calculation shows that this transform conserves energy (in the sense of signal processing), that is,

$$\iint |S(\tau,a)|^2 \frac{da\, d\tau}{a^2} = c_g \int_{-\infty}^{\infty} |s(t)|^2\, dt. \tag{A.4}$$

Clearly we must require the wavelet g to satisfy the so-called admissibility condition, namely,

$$c_g \equiv 2\pi \int |G(\omega)|^2 \frac{d\omega}{|\omega|} < \infty. \tag{A.5}$$

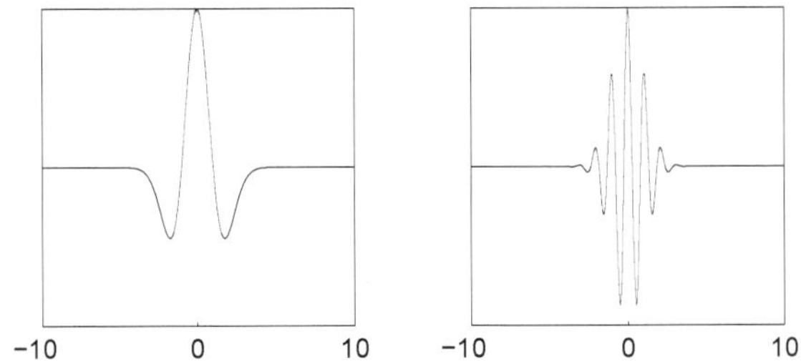

Fig. 20. Two usual one-dimensional wavelets: (left) The Mexican hat or Marr wavelet; (right) The real part of the 1-D Morlet wavelet, for $\omega_0 = 5.6$.

Eq.(A.4) means that the CWT is an isometry from the space of signals onto a closed subspace $\mathcal{H}_g$ of $L^2(\mathbb{R}^2_+, da\, d\tau/a^2)$, where $\mathbb{R}^2_+$ denotes the scale-position half-plane $\mathbb{R}^2_+ = \{(\tau, a), \tau \in \mathbb{R}, a > 0\}$. Therefore, the CWT may be inverted on its range $\mathcal{H}_g$ by the adjoint map, and this gives an *exact* reconstruction formula:

$$s(t) = c_g^{-1} \iint g_{(\tau,a)}(t)\, S(\tau, a)\, \frac{da\, d\tau}{a}. \tag{A.6}$$

This formula may also be interpreted as an expansion of the signal into the wavelets $g_{(\tau,a)}$, with (wavelet) coefficients $S(\tau, a)$.
A necessary (and almost sufficient) condition for admissibility is that the wavelet have no DC component:

$$G(0) = 0 \quad \Longleftrightarrow \quad \int g(t)\, dt = 0. \tag{A.7}$$

This is in fact the admissibility condition that is used in practice.
This transform is very general in the sense that there is one CWT for each choice of the analysing wavelet g. For each application, one should select an analysing wavelet adapted to the type of signal at hand. For instance, in order to detect and to characterize the singularities of a signal or a curve, it is advantageous to use as analysing wavelet a derivative of the Gaussian, for instance, the familiar *Mexican hat* (Figure 20, left),

$$g_H(x) = (1 - x^2)\, e^{-x^2/2} \quad \Leftrightarrow \quad G_H(\omega) = \omega^2\, e^{-\omega^2}. \tag{A.8}$$

In our case, MRS signals are relatively well defined in frequency, so it is more interesting to use analysing wavelets which are well localized in frequency space. This is the case of the Morlet wavelet, defined by

$$g_M(t) = e^{i\omega_0 t}\, e^{-t^2/(2\sigma_0^2)} + h(t) \quad \Leftrightarrow \quad G_M(\omega) = \sqrt{2\pi}\, \sigma_0\, e^{-(\omega-\omega_0)^2\sigma_0^2/2} + H(\omega), \tag{A.9}$$

where the correction term h is necessary to enforce the admissibility condition (in the sequel we shall use the value $\sigma_0 = 1$). If $\omega_0\sigma_0$ is sufficiently large (typically $\omega_0\sigma_0 > 5.5$), then h is numerically negligible, and will indeed be omitted. The Morlet wavelet can be interpreted as a bandpass linear filter centered around $\omega = \omega_0/a$ and of weight $1/(\sigma_0 a)$ (Figure 20, right).

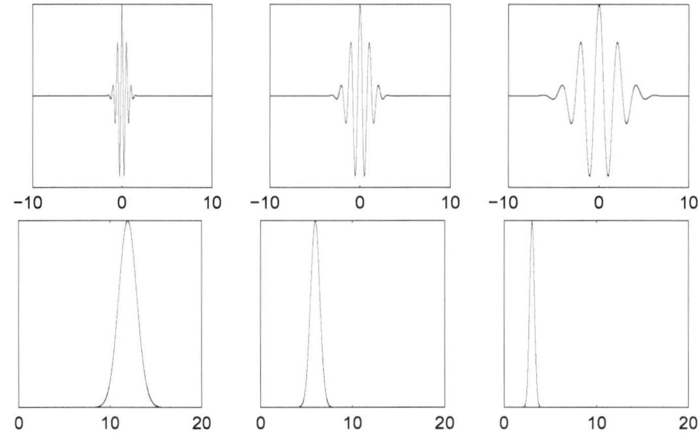

Fig. 21. Support properties of the Morlet wavelet g_M: for $a = 0.5, 1, 2$ (left to right), $g_{(\tau,a)}$ has width 3, 6, 12, respectively (top), while $G_{(\tau,a)}$ has width 3, 1.5, 0.75, and peaks at 12, 6, 3 (bottom).

All the results presented here have been obtained with the Morlet wavelet, but they can easily be generalized to any analysing wavelet whose Fourier transform has a single maximum at $\omega = \omega_0$, or even to the Short Time Fourier Transform (STFT)[7] (Delprat et al., 1992).

An important fact is the so-called reproduction property. Indeed it may be shown that the orthogonal projection P_g from $L^2(\mathbb{R}^2_+, da d\tau/a^2)$ onto the closed subspace $\mathcal{H}_g$ (the space of wavelet transforms) is an integral operator, with kernel

$$K(\tau', a'; \tau, a) = c_g^{-1} \langle g_{(\tau',a')} | g_{(\tau,a)} \rangle. \tag{A.10}$$

In other words, a function $f \in L^2(\mathbb{R}^2_+, da\, d\tau/a^2)$ is the WT of some signal if and only if it satisfies the reproduction identity

$$f(\tau', a') = \iint K(\tau', a'; \tau, a)\, f(\tau, a)\, \frac{da\, d\tau}{a^2}. \tag{A.11}$$

For this reason, K is called the *reproducing kernel* of g. It is also the autocorrelation function g and as such it plays an essential role in calibrating the CWT (Antoine, 1994).

Now the relation (A.11) shows that the CWT is enormously redundant (the signal has been unfolded from one variable t to two variables (τ, a)). Thus it is not surprising that the whole information is already contained in a small subset of the values of $S(\tau, a)$. An example of such a subset is the so-called *skeleton*, that is, the set of *ridges*, which are essentially the lines of maxima of the modulus of the WT (in the case of a monochromatic signal, the ridges become horizontal lines $a = a_r$, as we have seen in Section 2). Another example is obtained by taking an appropriate discrete subset $\Gamma = \{a_j, \tau_k\}$ of the half-plane $\mathbb{R}^2_+$, as it is necessary in any case

[7] The STFT is obtained by replacing scaling by modulation in the definition of the wavelets, that is, replacing Eq.(A.1) by $\widetilde{g}_{(\tau,a)}(t) = e^{it/a}\, g(t - \tau)$.

for numerical evaluation of the integrals. However, for most wavelets g, the resulting family $\{g_{(a_j,\tau_k)}\}$ is *never* an orthogonal basis (for the Morlet wavelet, for instance, the kernel K is a Gaussian, thus it never vanishes). At best, it is an overcomplete set of vectors, technically called a *frame*, provided Γ contains sufficiently many points (Daubechies, 1992).

A.2. Localization properties and interpretation

The main virtues of the CWT follow from the support properties of g. Assume g and G to be as well localized as possible (compatible with the Fourier uncertainty principle). More specifically, assume that g has an 'essential' support of width L, centered around 0, while G has an essential support of width Ω, centered around ω_0. Then the transformed wavelets $g_{(\tau,a)}$ and $G_{(\tau,a)}$ have, respectively, an essential support of width aL around τ and an essential support of width Ω/a around ω_0/a. This behavior is illustrated in Figure 21, which shows the Morlet wavelet in the time and frequency domains, for three successive scales $a = 0.5, 1$ and 2, from left to right. Notice that the product of the two widths is constant (we know it has to be bounded below by a fixed constant, by the (Fourier) uncertainty principle). Remember that $1/a$ behaves like a frequency. Therefore:

- if $a \gg 1, g_{(\tau,a)}$ is a wide window, whereas $G_{(\tau,a)}$ is very peaked around a small frequency ω_0/a: this transform is most sensitive to *low frequencies*.
- if $a \ll 1, g_{(\tau,a)}$ is a narrow window and $G_{(\tau,a)}$ is wide and centered around a high frequency ω_0/a: this wavelet has a good localization capability in the space domain and is mostly sensitive to *high frequencies*.

Combining now these localization properties with the zero mean condition and the fact that $g_{(\tau,a)}$ acts like a filter (convolution), we see that the CWT performs a *local filtering*, both in time and in scale. The WT $S(\tau,a)$ is nonnegligible only when the wavelet $g_{(\tau,a)}$ matches the signal $s(t)$, that is, it filters the part of the signal, if any, that lives around the time τ and the scale a. Taking all these properties together, one is naturally led to the interpretation of the CWT as a *mathematical microscope*, with optics g, position τ and global magnification $1/a$. In addition, the analysis works at constant relative bandwidth ($\Delta\omega/\omega$ = constant), so that it has a better resolution at high frequency, i.e., small scales. This property makes it an ideal tool for detecting *singularities* (for instance, discontinuities in the signal or one of its derivatives), and also scale dependent features, in particular, for analysing *fractals*.

A.3. Implementation questions

Faced with this new tool, one must begin by learning the rules of the trade, that is, one must learn how to read and understand a CWT (Grossmann et al., 1990). The simplest way is to get some practice on very simple academic signals, such as a simple discontinuity in time or a monochromatic signal (pure sinusoid). We note that it is natural to use a logarithmic scale for the scale parameter a. The visual effect is that the lines, τ/a = constant, are not straight lines, but hyperbolic curves; at the same time, the horizon $a = 0$ recedes to infinity (see Figure 22). The analysing wavelet g is supposed to be complex, so that we may treat separately the modulus and the phase of the transform. The scale axis, in units of $\ln a$, points downward, so that high frequencies (small a) correspond to the top of the plots, and low frequencies (large a) to the bottom. The results are presented by coding the height of the function by density of points (12 levels of gray, from white to black). The phase is 2π-periodic. When it reaches 2π, it is wrapped around to the value 0. Thus the lines of constant phase with value $2k\pi$ are lines of discontinuity, where the density of points drops abruptly from 1 (black) to 0 (white). In

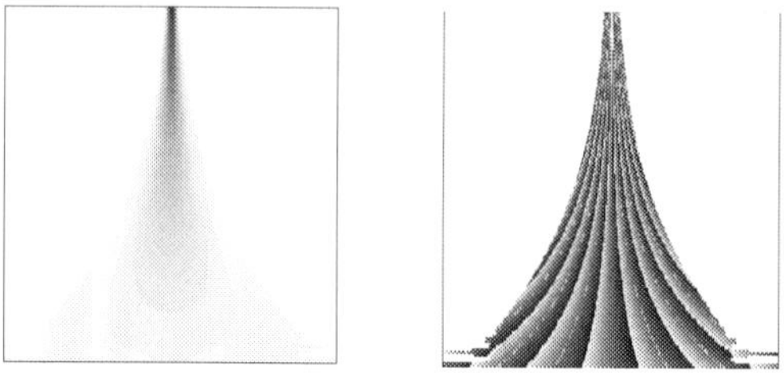

Fig. 22. Morlet WT of a δ function: (left) modulus; (right) phase.

addition, the functions plotted are thresholded at 1% of the maximum value of the modulus of $S(\tau, a)$. We will now analyse the two academic signals mentioned above.
(i) *A simple discontinuity*

The simplest signal is a simple discontinuity in time, at $t = t_0$, modelled by $s(t) = \delta(t - t_0)$. The WT is obtained immediately and reads

$$S(\tau, a) = a^{-1/2}\, \overline{g\left(a^{-1}(t_0 - \tau)\right)}. \tag{A.12}$$

The following features may be read off Eq.(A.12):

- The phase of $S(\tau, a)$ is constant on the lines $\tau / a =$ constant, originating from the point $\tau = t_0$ on the horizon. These lines point towards the position of the singularity, like a finger.
- On the same lines of constant phase, the modulus of $S(\tau, a)$ increases as $a^{-1/2}$ when $a \to 0$, so that the singularity is enhanced. The effect is even more pronounced if one uses the L^1 normalisation.

This is illustrated on Figure 22, which presents the modulus and phase of the WT of a δ function, using a standard Morlet wavelet (but the result is independent of the choice of g).
The interesting point is that this behavior is extremely robust. For instance, the 'finger' pointing to a δ-singularity remains clearly visible when the latter is superposed on a continuous signal (even if the amplitude of the δ function is too small to be invisible on the signal itself), or even in the presence of substantial background noise. Similarly, the discontinuity corresponding to the abrupt onset of a signal is readily identified with the CWT. We refer to (Grossmann et al., 1990) for several spectacular examples.
This is the origin of the *edge* or *boundary effects* that we have encountered in Section 4.1. The first notion is that of cone of confidence or *cone of influence*. Let the wavelet g vanish outside the interval $I_g = [t_{\min}, t_{\max}]$. Then, given a point t_0 in the support of the signal, the region in which it influences the WT is the cone $\tau \in aI_g + t_0 = [-at_{\min} + t_0, at_{\max} + t_0]$. Thus the region of influence increases linearly with a. The effect is clearly seen in Figure 1: the cones of influence of the two endpoints of the spectrum are the regions where the phase of the WT differs from that of a pure sinusoid (see (ii) below). This is the region to be avoided, as discussed in Section 4.1.
(ii) *A single monochromatic wave*

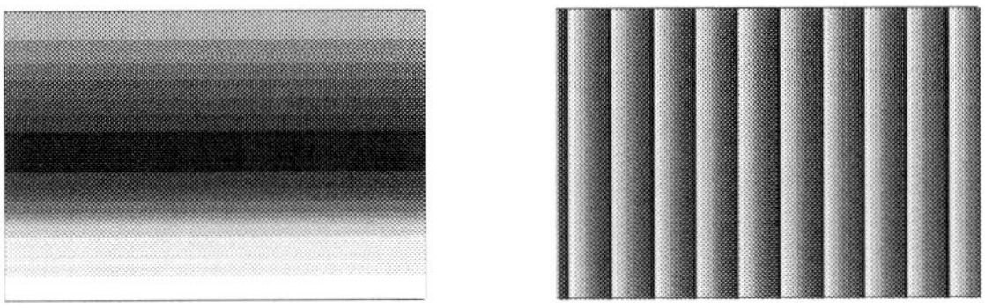

Fig. 23. Morlet WT of a single sinusoid: (left) modulus; (right) phase.

Equally simple is a single harmonic signal (monochromatic wave):

$$s(t) = e^{i\omega_s t} \Leftrightarrow S(\omega) = \frac{1}{\sqrt{2\pi}}\,\delta(\omega - \omega_s), \tag{A.13}$$

which gives

$$S(\tau, a) = \sqrt{\frac{a}{2\pi}}\,G(a\omega_s)\,e^{i\omega_s\tau} = S(a, 0)\,e^{i\omega_s\tau}. \tag{A.14}$$

The same relations remain true for a real monochromatic signal, $s(t) = \sin\omega_s t$ or $s(t) = \cos\omega_s t$, if the wavelet g is progressive (that is, $G(\omega) = 0$ for $\omega \leqslant 0$).
Again two important properties may be read off immediately from Eq.(A.14):

- The modulus of $S(\tau, a)$ is independent of τ. Hence, the graph of $|S(\tau, a)|$ consists of horizontal bands and the profile for a fixed time τ essentially reproduces the profile of G.
- The phase of $S(\tau, a)$ is linear in τ. Since the phase is 2π-periodic, the graph of $\Phi(\tau, a) := \arg S(\tau, a)$ is a linear sawtooth function:

$$\Phi(\tau, a) = \omega_s\tau \pmod{2\pi}. \tag{A.15}$$

These properties are illustrated on Figure 23 for a single sine function analysed with a Morlet wavelet. This pattern of equidistant vertical black-to-white bands is the signature of a pure frequency signal. This can be seen already in Figure 1.
Both the modulus and the phase allow to determine the frequency ω_s of the signal. If the modulus of the wavelet $G(\omega)$ has a single maximum for $\omega = \omega_0$, Eq.(A.14) gives immediately $\omega_s = \omega_0/a_r$, where a_r is the scale corresponding to the maximum in the profile of $|S(\tau, a)|$ for fixed τ. For instance, the (truncated) Morlet wavelet $g(t) = \exp(i\omega_0 t)\,\exp(-t^2/2)$ yields:

$$S(\tau, a) = \sqrt{a}\,e^{-\frac{1}{2}(a\omega_s - \omega_0)^2}\,e^{i\omega_s\tau}, \tag{A.16}$$

and the result is obvious. As for the phase, Eq.(A.15) gives, at least locally:

$$\frac{\partial\Phi(\tau, a)}{\partial\tau} = \omega_s = \frac{\omega_0}{a_r}. \tag{A.17}$$

A.4. The discrete wavelet transform

Notice that the discretized CWT which is used in practice, including in the present text, is totally different from the so-called *discrete WT* (DWT). Indeed, orthogonal bases of wavelets may be constructed, but from a completely different approach based on the notion of *multiresolution analysis*.

We emphasize that the DWT is totally different in spirit from the CWT, either truly continuous or discretized, and they have complementary ranges of applications:

- In the CWT, there is a lot of freedom in choosing the wavelet g, but one does not get an orthonormal basis, at best a frame. This is a tool for analysis and feature determination, as in MRS or other problems where the scaling properties of the signal are unknown *a priori*, for instance in fractal analysis.
- In the DWT, one insists on having an orthonormal basis, but the wavelet is *derived* from the multiresolution analysis. This is the preferred tool for data compression and signal synthesis, and the most popular in the signal processing community.

More radically, one may even say that the kind of problems treated here can be solved only with the CWT, the DWT is simply not adapted to the underlying physics, although it has been proposed for MRS (Neue, 1996). For instance, the algorithm for detecting spectral lines, as well as the ridge concept, rest upon a stationary phase argument. Similarly, the determination of fractal exponents exploits the scaling behaviour of homogeneous functions or distributions and the covariance properties of the CWT. All these notions are foreign to the DWT, which is more a signal processing tool.

6. References

Ali, S. T., Antoine, J.-P. & Gazeau, J.-P. (2000). *Coherent States, Wavelets and Their Generalizations*, Springer-Verlag, New York, Berlin, Heidelberg.

Antoine, J.-P. (1994). Wavelet analysis: A new tool in signal processing, *Physicalia Mag.* **16**: 17–42.

Antoine, J.-P. (2000). Wavelet analysis of signals and images, a grand tour, *Revista Ciencias Matematicas (La Habana)* **18**: 113–143.

Antoine, J.-P., Murenzi, R., Vandergheynst, P. & Ali, S. T. (2004). *Two-Dimensional Wavelets and their Relatives*, Cambridge University Press, Cambridge (UK).

Barache, D., Antoine, J.-P. & Dereppe, J.-M. (1997). The continuous wavelet transform, an analysis tool for NMR spectroscopy, *Journal of Magnetic Resonance* **128**: 1–11.

Behar, K. L., Rothman, D. L., Spencer, D. D. & Petroff, O. A. C. (1994). Analysis of macromolecule resonances in 1H NMR spectra of human brain, *Magnetic Resonance in Medicine* **32**(3): 294–302.

Cudalbu, C., Beuf, O. & Cavassila, S. (2009). *In vivo* short echo time localized 1H MRS of the rat brain at 7 T: influence of two strategies of background accommodation on the metabolite concentration estimation using QUEST, *J. Sign. Process. Syst.* **55**: 25–34.

Cudalbu, C., Bucur, A., Graveron-Demilly, D., Beuf, O. & Cavassila, S. (2007). Comparison of two strategies of background-accommodation: Influence on the metabolite concentration estimation from in vivo magnetic resonance spectroscopy data, *Proceedings of the 29th IEEE EMBC*, pp. 2077–2080.

Cudalbu, C., Cavassila, S., Rabeson, H., van Ormondt, D. & Graveron-Demilly, D. (2008). A comparison between the influence of in vitro and simulated basis-sets on estimated metabolite concentrations, *NMR in Biomedicine* **21**: 627–636.

Daubechies, I. (1992). *Ten Lectures on Wavelets*, SIAM, Philadelphia.

Delprat, N., Escudié, B., Guillemain, P., Kronland-Martinet, R., Tchamitchian, P. & Torrésani, B. (1992). Asymptotic wavelet and Gabor analysis extraction of instantaneous frequencies, *IEEE Transactions on Information Theory* **38**(2): 644–664.

Devos, A., Lukas, L., Suykens, J. A. K., Vanhamme, L., Tate, A. R., Howe, F. A., Majos, C., Moreno-Torres, A., Arus, C., der Graaf, M. V. & Huffel, S. V. (2004). Recent advances in magnetic resonance neurospectroscopy, *Journal of Magnetic Resonance* **170**: 164–175.

Franzen, S. (2002). *Lecture Notes on Molecular Spectroscopy*, Department of Chemistry, NC State University. http://chsfpc5.chem.ncsu.edu/ franzen/CH795Z/.

Govindaraju, V., Young, K. & Maudsley, A. A. (2000). Proton NMR chemical shifts and coupling constants for brain metabolites., *NMR in Biomedicine* **13**: 129–153.

Grossmann, A., Kronland-Martinet, R. & Morlet, J. (1990). Reading and understanding continuous wavelet transforms, *in* J.-M. Combes, A. Grossmann & P. Tchamitchian (eds), *Wavelets, Time-Frequency Methods and Phase Space (Proc. Marseille 1987), 2d ed.*, Springer-Verlag, Berlin, pp. 2–20.

Guillemain, P., Kronland-Martinet, R. & Martens, B. (1992). Estimation of spectral lines with the help of the wavelet transform, applications in NMR spectroscopy, *in* Y. Meyer (ed.), *Wavelets and applications— Proc. Int. Conf. Marseille, France, May 1989*, Masson, Paris, and Springer, Berlin, pp. 38–60.

Hornak, J. P. (1997). *The Basics of NMR*, Department of Chemistry, Rochester Institute of Technology, Rochester, NY. http://www.cis.rit.edu/htbooks/nmr/.

Jacques, L., Coron, A., Vandergheynst, P. & Rivoldini, A. (2007). The YAWTb toolbox : Yet Another Wavelet Toolbox. http://rhea.tele.ucl.ac.be/yawtb.

Kubo, R. (1969). A stochastic theory of line shape, *Advances in Chemical Physics: Stochastic Processes in Chemical Physics* **15**: 101–127.

Mainardi, L. T., Origgi, D., Lucia, P., Scotti, G. & Cerutti, S. (2002). A wavelet packets decomposition algorithm for quantification of in vivo 1H-MRS parameters, *Medical Engineering & Physics* **24**(3): 201–208.

Marshall, I., Bruce, S. D., Higinbotham, J., MacLullich, A., Wardlaw, J. M., Ferguson, K. J. & Seckl, J. (2000). Choice of spectroscopic lineshape model affects metabolite peak areas and area ratios, *Magnetic Resonance in Medicine* **44**: 646–649.

Mierisová, S. & Ala-Korpela, M. (2001). MR spectroscopy quantitation: a review of frequency domain methods, *NMR in Biomedicine* **14**(4): 247–259.

Neue, G. (1996). Simplification of dynamical NMR spectroscopy by wavelet transform, *Solid State Nuclear Magnetic Resonance* **5**: 305–314.

Pijnappel, W. W. F., van den Boogaart, A., de Beer, R. & van Ormondt, D. (1992). SVD-based quantification of magnetic resonance signals, *Journal of Magnetic Resonance* **97**(11): 122–134.

Poullet, J. B., Sima, D. M., Simonetti, A. W., Neuter, B. D., Vanhamme, L., Lemmerling, P. & Huffel, S. V. (2007). An automated quantitation of short echo time MRS spectra in an open source software environment: AQSES, *NMR in Biomedicine* **20**: 493–504.

Provencher, S. W. (1993). Estimation of metabolite concentrations from localized *in vivo* proton NMR spectra, *Magnetic Resonance in Medicine* **30**: 672–679.

Rabeson, H., Ratiney, H., Cudalbu, C., Cavassila, S., Capobianco, E., de Beer, R., van Ormondt, D. & Graveron-Demilly, D. (2006). Signal disentanglement in in vivo MR spectroscopy by semi-parametric processing or by measurement?, *Proceedings of the*

Annual Workshop on Circuits, Systems and Signal Processing (ProISC), IEEE Benelux, The Netherlands, pp. 176–183.

Ratiney, H., Bucur, A., Sdika, M., Beuf, O., Pilleul, F. & Cavassila, S. (2008). Effective Voigt model estimation using multiple random starting values and parameter bounds settings for *in vivo* hepatic 1H magnetic resonance spectroscopy data, *Proc. ISBI*, Paris, pp. 1529–1532.

Ratiney, H., Coenradie, Y., Cavassila, S., van Ormondt, D. & Graveron-Demilly, D. (2004). Time-domain quantitation of short echo-time signals: background accommodation, *Magn. Reson. Mater. Phy.* **16**: 284–296.

Ratiney, H., Sdika, M., Coenradie, Y., Cavassila, S., van Ormondt, D. & Graveron-Demilly, D. (2005). Time-domain semi-parametric estimation based on a metabolite basis set, *NMR in Biomedicine* **18**: 1–13.

Serrai, H., Senhadji, L., de Certaines, J. D. & Coatrieux, J. L. (1997). Time-domain quantification of amplitude, chemical shift, apparent relaxation time t_2^*, and phase by wavelet-transform analysis. application to biomedical magnetic resonance spectroscopy, *Journal of Magnetic Resonance* **24**: 20–34.

Suvichakorn, A., Ratiney, H., Bucur, A., Cavassila, S. & Antoine, J.-P. (2009). Toward a quantitative analysis of *in vivo* proton magnetic resonance spectroscopic signals using the continuous Morlet wavelet transform, *Meas. Sci. Technol.* p. Technol. 20: paper # 104029.

Torrésani, B. (1995). *Analyse continue par ondelettes*, InterEditions & CNRS Editions, Paris.

Vanhamme, L., Sundin, T., Hecke, P. V. & Huffel, S. V. (2001). MR spectroscopic quantitation: A review of time domain methods, *NMR in Biomedicine* **14**(4): 233–246.

Vanhamme, L., van den Boogaart, A. & Huffel, S. V. (1997). Improved method for accurate and efficient quantification of MRS data with use of prior knowledge, *Journal of Magnetic Resonance* **12**: 35–43.

10

Recent Fingerprinting Techniques with Cryptographic Protocol

Minoru Kuribayashi
Kobe University
Japan

1. Introduction

According to the development of the Internet, multi-media contents such as music, picture, movie, etc. are treated by digital format on the network. It enables us to purchase digital contents via a net easily. However, it causes several problems such as violation of ownership and illegal distribution of the copy. Digital fingerprinting is used to trace back the illegal users, where unique ID known as digital fingerprints is embedded into digital contents before distribution Wu et al. (2004). When a suspicious copy is found, the owner can identify illegal users by extracting the fingerprint. The fingerprinting techniques of multimedia contents involve the generation of a fingerprint, the embedding operation, and the realization of traceability from redistributed copies. The research on such fingerprinting techniques is classified into two studies; secure cryptographic protocol and design of collusion resistant fingerprint.

In a cryptographic protocol, the goal is to achieve the asymmetric property between a buyer and a seller such that only the former can obtain a uniquely fingerprinted copy because of the threat of dispute. If both of the parties know the fingerprinted copy, the buyer may redistribute a pirated copy but later repudiate it by insisting that it came from the seller. An asymmetric protocol Pfitzmann & Schunter (1996) is executed by exploiting the homomorphic property of the public key cryptosystem that enables a seller to produce the ciphertext of fingerprinted copy by operating an encrypted fingerprint with encrypted contents.

Since each user purchases multimedia contents involving his own fingerprint, each copy is slightly different. A coalition of users will therefore combine their different marked copies of a same content for the purpose of removing/changing the original fingerprint. A number of works on designing fingerprints that are resistant against the collusion attack have been proposed. Many of them can be categorized into two approaches. One is to exploit the Spread Spectrum (SS) technique Cox et al. (1997); Wang et al. (2004; 2005); Zhao et al. (2005), and the other approach is to devise an exclusive code, known as collusion-secure code Boneh & Shaw (1998); Staddon et al. (2001); Tardos (2003); Trappe et al. (2003); Yacobi (2001); Zhu et al. (2005), which has traceability of colluders. Although cryptographic protocols provide the asymmetric property, the production of embedding information is based on the design of collusion-resistant fingerprint.

In this chapter, we introduce the implementation method of watermarking technique in the encrypted domain during the fingerprinting protocol. As the robustness against attacks, a transformed domain like frequency domain is generally suitable to embed watermark information into an image. In such a case, the components of the transformed domain may be represented by real values. In order to apply a public-key cryptosystem, all frequency components of an image must be quantized to integer. In the operation, a fingerprinting information is embedded to the quantized value. From the perceptual property, the changes in low frequency components stand out compared with that of the other components and hence each component is quantized adaptively by a special quantization step size. In the conventional method Kuribayashi & Tanaka (2005), for the embedding of an information bit of which value is unknown, the frequency components in the embedding positions are quantized to a special number before embedding so that the value can be changed depending on the information bit, which embedding method is based on QIM watermarking Chen & Wornel (2001). We propose the method for implementing the spread spectrum watermarking technique by carefully designing parameters for rounding operation. As the precision of the representing watermark signal is sensitive for the implementation, the parameters are scaled by multiplying a constant factor. For the characteristic of the fingerprinting protocol, frequency components and the watermark signal must be separately encrypted after quantization. In such a case, the consistency of the precision is a sensitive issue. Then, the separate rounding operation causes interference term in a deciphered data at a buyer side. Without loss of secrecy of an original content, the interference term is removed after decryption in the post-processing. The proposed approach provides a guideline for the selection of watermarking technique suitable for a multimedia forensic system.

2. Fingerprinting Protocol

One of serious threats in the fingerprinting is dispute and repudiation of a purchase. The purpose of fingerprinting protocol is to solve such threats by achieving the asymmetric property, where only a buyer knows a fingerprinted copy. If both a buyer and a seller know a fingerprinted copy, the seller cannot prove to a third party whose copy it was even if the buyer's fingerprint can be extracted. This is because a malicious seller may distribute the copy in order to frame an innocent buyer. Hence, it is desirable that only a buyer is able to obtain his own fingerprinted copy in the protocol. Such a protocol is called the asymmetric fingerprinting protocol. As in real-life market places, it is desired that electronic market places offer privacy to the customers. It should be possible to buy different articles anonymously, since purchased items can reveal a lot of behavioristic information about a buyer. The solution is the anonymous fingerprinting protocol. Thus, the fingerprinting protocol is classified into the following three classes.

Symmetric: The operation to embed a fingerprint is performed only by a seller. Therefore, he cannot convince any third party of the traitor's treachery even if he has found out the identity of a traitor in an illegal copy.

Asymmetric: Fingerprinting is an interactive protocol between a buyer and a seller. After the sale, only the buyer obtains the copy with a fingerprint. If the seller finds the fingerprinted copy somewhere, he can identify the traitor and convince a third party that the the copy is illegally distributed by the traitor.

Anonymous: A buyer can purchase a fingerprinted copy without informing his identity to a seller, but he can identify the traitor later. It also retains the asymmetric property.

In asymmetric fingerprinting, the plain value of a fingerprint should not be revealed to a seller, otherwise he can produce a fingerprinted copy by himself. Therefore an interactive protocol is performed to prevent the seller obtaining the fingerprinted copy. Such a protocol is based on public-key cryptosystems because they assure only a buyer can decrypt a ciphertext though both of them can perform the enciphering operation. In order to achieve the asymmetric fingerprinting, a homomorphic property of public-key cryptosystems is applied.

2.1 Asymmetric Property

In order to achieve an asymmetric property, a homomorphic property of public-key cryptosystems is introduced in the fingerprinting protocols Pfitzmann & Sadeghi (1999). The homomorphic property enables a seller to obtain the ciphertext of fingerprinted copy by operating an encrypted fingerprint with an encrypted original content. Since the ciphertext is computed using a buyer's encryption key, only the buyer can decrypt it; hence, only he can obtain the fingerprinted copy.

The homomorphic property of public-key cryptosystems is often applied for cryptographic protocol as operations that can be performed without revealing the plain value. If an operation on a ciphertext space results in an operation on the message space, the cryptosystem is homomorphic, and principally the former operation is multiplication and the latter is one of three operations, *"addition, multiplication, exclusive or"*, in public-key cryptosystems.

Let $E(M)$ be a ciphertext of a message M. The homomorphic property satisfies the following equation:

$$g(E(M_1), E(M_2)) = E(f(M_1, M_2)), \tag{1}$$

where $g(\cdot)$ and $f(\cdot)$ is one of the operations, *addition, multiplication, XOR,* etc., which is related to the applied cryptosystem and the embedding algorithm (Most public-key cryptosystems select multiplication for $g(\cdot)$). If M_1 is regarded as a digital content and M_2 as a fingerprint, the fingerprint can be embedded in the content without decryption by multiplying those ciphertexts. Since they are calculated using buyer's public encryption-key, the fingerprinted copy is decrypted only by the buyer, hence the asymmetric property is satisfied. The embedding operation based on the homomorphic property is basically performed for each element of fingerprint information which will be composed of bit-sequence or spread spectrum sequence, hence each element is separately embedded in its corresponding position. Thus, M_1 is not the entire content, but one of the components like the frequency elements to be fingerprinted by a watermarking technique. Note that in watermarking techniques Katzenbeisser & Petitcolas (2000) for digital images, it is advisable to embed information in the frequency components for both the robustness and perceptual quality. When the vector representation of M_1 is given by $\{m_{1,1}, m_{1,2}, m_{1,3}, \ldots\}$, the ciphertext is also represented as $E(M_1) = \{E(m_{1,1}), E(m_{1,2}), E(m_{1,3}), \ldots\}$. As the consequence, the detail of Eq.(1) is given by

$$g(E(m_{1,i}), E(m_{2,i})) = E(f(m_{1,i}, m_{2,i})), \ (i = 1, 2, 3, \ldots). \tag{2}$$

The multiplicative property of RSA scheme Rivest et al. (1978) is applied to embed a fingerprint in Memon & Wong (2001), the homomorphism of a bit commitment scheme based on the quadratic residues Brassard et al. (1988) is exploited Pfitzmann & Sadeghi (1999; 2000), and the additive homomorphic property of public-key cryptosystem such as Okamoto-Uchiyama encryption scheme Okamoto & Uchiyama (1998) and Paillier cryptosystem Paillier (1999) is utilized in Kuribayashi & Tanaka (2005). In these schemes, to convince a seller that a transmitted ciphertexts really contains his fingerprinting information, zero-knowledge interactive protocol (ZKIP) must be performed, which is easily constructed using the applied public-key cryptosystem. Such characteristic is necessary for the security reason and the anonymity of a buyer is achieved.

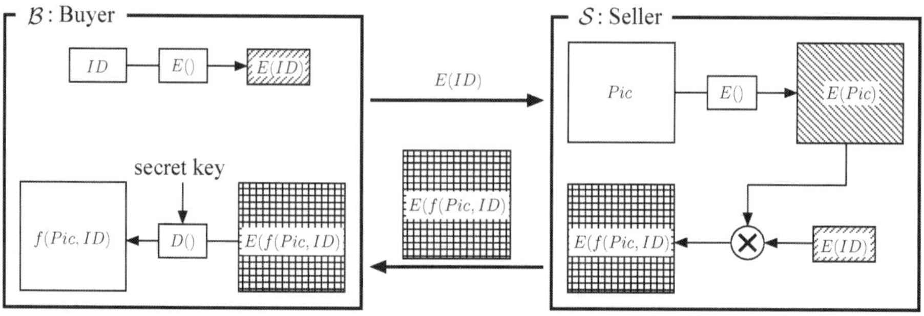

Fig. 1. The flow of the asymmetric fingerprinting protocol.

2.2 Asymmetric Fingerprinting Protocol Based on Bit Commitments

In the asymmetric fingerprinting scheme, a buyer and a seller jointly embed a fingerprint. First, the buyer encrypts a fingerprint and sends it to the seller. Then the seller verifies that the received ciphertext is made from the real fingerprint, and embeds it in his encrypted copy by multiplying those ciphertexts. Finally, the buyer receives the encrypted and fingerprinted copy and decrypts it. After the protocol, only the buyer gets the fingerprinted copy without disclosing his identity. The model of asymmetric fingerprinting protocol is described in Fig.1. A concept of an anonymous fingerprinting protocol was first presented in Pfitzmann & Waidner (1997), and the fingerprinting system composed of several protocols was presented Pfitzmann & Sadeghi (1999), which security was further improved in Pfitzmann & Sadeghi (2000). There are three parties, buyer $\mathcal{B}$, seller $\mathcal{S}$, and registration center $\mathcal{RC}$. First, $\mathcal{RC}$ generates a pair of keys, secret key and public key, and distributes the latter to all participants of the system. When $\mathcal{B}$ begins a trade to a seller $\mathcal{S}$, first $\mathcal{B}$ must register at $\mathcal{RC}$. And then $\mathcal{B}$ withdraws a digital coin which includes an identify proof $W = proof(id)$ of his identity(fingerprint), *id*, and its signature which can be verified using the $\mathcal{RC}$'s public key and can assure the legitimacy of the buyer. In *Fingerprinting Protocol*, $\mathcal{B}$ encrypts his fingerprint and sends to $\mathcal{S}$. Then using a zero-knowledge proof, $\mathcal{B}$ proves that the contents of the ciphertext is equivalent to that of W. After $\mathcal{S}$ is convinced the validity of the ciphertext, he encrypts his image, and multiplies the received ciphertext and the ciphertext of his image to embed the fingerprint in his image based on a homomorphic property. In order to prove that the ciphertext really includes the fingerprint without revealing the plain value, two kinds of bit commitment schemes are applied. One is based on the discrete logarithm assumption, and the other is on the quadratic residues Brassard et al. (1988) which security depends on the p-subgroup assumption and quadratic residues assumption, respectively. The commitment schemes BC_{DL} and BC_{RQ} are described as follows.

BC_{DL}: Let p be a large prime, and g and h be the generators. The commitment $com_{DL}(b,r)$ of a bit b is calculated using a random number r as follows.

$$com_{DL}(b,r) = g^b h^r \pmod{p} \tag{3}$$

BC_{QR}: Let p and q be large primes, and $n = pq$. The commitment $com_{QR}(b,r)$ is obtained by the following equation.

$$com_{QR}(b,r) = (-1)^b r^2 \pmod{n} \tag{4}$$

Here, it is remarkable that the committed value b of BC_{DL} is not only binary, it can take an integer of (Z/pZ). When W is calculated based on BC_{DL}, namely $W = com_{DL}(id,r) = g^{id}h^r \bmod p$, then it is difficult for a seller to embed directly the value of id using the commitment. Because of the characteristic of the commitment scheme, the recovery of the committed value is generally impossible. So instead of W, the commitment of each information bit of $id = \sum w_j 2^j$, which is calculated by $com_{QR}(w_j,r_j)$, is applied for embedding. For a certain bit $X_i \in \{0,1\}$ of digital contents, $\mathcal{S}$ computes the commitment $com_{QR}(X_i,r_i)$, and multiplies $com_{QR}(w_j,r_j)$ to it.

$$com_{QR}(X_i,r_i) \cdot com_{QR}(w_j,r_j) = (-1)^{X_i w_j}(r_i r_j)^2 \pmod{n} \tag{5}$$

It is noticed that if $X_i w_j$ is 0, the result is quadratic residue, otherwise, it is quadratic non-residue. The knowledge of two primes p and q allow $\mathcal{B}$ to compute the value $X_i w_i \bmod 2$ using the Jacobi Symbol while $\mathcal{S}$ can not determine that it is quadratic residue or not. So the security is based on the difficulty of factoring $n = pq$.
Before the above computation, $\mathcal{B}$ must certify that the values $com_{QR}(w_j,r_j)$ of the commitments are equivalent to that of W. Using BC_{DL}, $\mathcal{B}$ convinces $\mathcal{S}$ by zero-knowledge interactive protocol that the committed value of $com_{DL}(id,r)$ is equivalent to that of $com_{QR}(id,r)$. After the above protocol, only $\mathcal{B}$ can decrypt the fingerprinted copy and $\mathcal{S}$ can obtain the proof of the communication which can be used later if $\mathcal{B}$ illegally redistributes the copy.
The function $f(\cdot)$ in the homomorphic property of BC_{QR} is *exclusive or* operation. Based on the property, an encrypted fingerprint can be embedded in the encrypted copy, but the enciphering rate is extremely small because the commitment can contain only one-bit message in $\log_2 n$-bit ciphertext, where n is composed of two large primes such that the bit-length of n should be more than 1024. Therefore, the enciphering rate of this method is more than $1/1024$.

2.3 Unbinding Problem

It is also desirable for the fingerprinting protocol to solve the unbinding problem such that the relation between fingerprint information and a specific transaction performed by a buyer and a seller. In the elementary fingerprinting protocol Memon & Wong (2001), fingerprint information to be embedded is not well considered, which is merely related to user's information such as name, address, phone number, e-mail address, etc.. When a seller finds an illegal copy and detects the corresponding buyer by extracting the fingerprint, he will go to court with the collected proofs. A malicious seller, however, frames the detected buyer by embedding the obtained fingerprint into the other contents which are more expensive than the detected one what he really sold to the buyer. Therefore, once a seller obtains such a fingerprint, it is possible for him to transplant it into another much expensive contents so that he can get compensated more.
In Lei et al. (2004), a fingerprint is binded with a common agreement (ARG) by producing the signature of a trusted watermark certification authority ($\mathcal{WCA}$), and the transaction of digital contents is uniquely associated with a log file. For anonymity of buyers, a digital certification authority ($\mathcal{CA}$) is introduced in the fingerprinting protocol. A buyer $\mathcal{B}$ first randomly selects a key pair $(pk_{\mathcal{B}}, sk_{\mathcal{B}})$, where $pk_{\mathcal{B}}$ and $sk_{\mathcal{B}}$ are the public and secret keys of public-key

cryptosystem, respectively. He sends $pk_{\mathcal{B}}$, which is a pseudonym associated with $\mathcal{B}$, to $\mathcal{CA}$ in order to get an anonymous certificate $Cert_{\mathcal{CA}}(pk_{\mathcal{B}})$. When $\mathcal{B}$ makes an order to a seller $\mathcal{S}$, he checks the validity of $Cert_{\mathcal{CA}}(pk_{\mathcal{B}})$. Then $\mathcal{S}$ asks $\mathcal{WCA}$ to generate a unique watermark W for the current transaction between $\mathcal{B}$ and $\mathcal{S}$. The protocol between the buyer $\mathcal{B}$ and seller $\mathcal{S}$ is summarized below (the detail is referred to Lei et al. (2004)).

1. $\mathcal{B}$ selects one-time key pair $(pk^\star, sk^\star)$ and generates its certificate $Cert_{pk_{\mathcal{B}}}(pk^\star)$ using the public key $pk_{\mathcal{B}}$. After making a common agreement ARG, $\mathcal{B}$ calculates a digital signature $Sign_{pk^\star}(ARG)$ using the one-time public key $pk^\star$. $\mathcal{B}$ sends $pk_{\mathcal{B}}$, $pk^\star$, $Cert_{\mathcal{CA}}(pk_{\mathcal{B}})$, $Cert_{pk_{\mathcal{B}}}(pk^\star)$, ARG, and $Sign_{pk^\star}(ARG)$ to $\mathcal{S}$.
2. If the validity of the received items is verified, $\mathcal{S}$ generates a watermark V and embeds into contents X. The watermark is reference information to retrieve this sale record from illegally distributed copy; hence it could be omitted if the seller wants to avoid the degradation of quality. Then, $\mathcal{S}$ send $Cert_{pk_{\mathcal{B}}}(pk^\star)$, ARG, $Sign_{pk^\star}(ARG)$, and $X^{(V)}$ to $\mathcal{WCA}$.
3. Upon receiving the items, $\mathcal{WCA}$ verifies the validity of the certificate and signature, and reject the transaction if any of them is invalid. Otherwise, using $X^{(V)}$ it generates a unique and robust watermark W as fingerprint information which is specific to this transaction. Then, it computes $E_{pk^\star}(W)$, $E_{pk_{\mathcal{WCA}}}(W)$, and $Sign_{\mathcal{WCA}}(E_{pk^\star}(W), pk^\star, Sign_{pk^\star}(ARG))$, and sends them back to $\mathcal{S}$.
4. When $\mathcal{S}$ receives the response, the embedding operation in encrypted domain is performed by computing

$$E_{pk^\star}(X^{(W,V)}) = E_{pk^\star}(X^{(V)}) \oplus E_{pk^\star}(W), \tag{6}$$

   where $\oplus$ implies the embedding operation based on the homomorphic property. Then, $\mathcal{S}$ delivers $E_{pk^\star}(X^{(W,V)})$ to $\mathcal{B}$.
5. After decrypting the received $E_{pk^\star}(X^{(W,V)})$, $\mathcal{B}$ obtains the watermarked copy $X^{(W,V)}$.

Where $E_{pk}(\cdot)$ is an enciphering function using a public key pk. The flow of the transaction is summarized in Fig.2.
The signature $Sign_{\mathcal{WCA}}(E_{pk^\star}(W), pk^\star, Sign_{pk^\star}(ARG))$ explicitly binds W and ARG, which, in turn, uniquely specifies a particular digital content X, so it is impossible for $\mathcal{S}$ to transplant the watermark from an illegal copy to other contents.

3. Asymmetric Fingerprinting Protocol Based on Additive Homomorphism

The idea of the protocol Kuribayashi & Tanaka (2005) is to exploit the public-key cryptosystem with additive homomorphic property such as the Okamoto-Uchiyama encryption scheme Okamoto & Uchiyama (1998) and Paillier cryptosystem Paillier (1999) for anonymous fingerprinting.

3.1 Public-Key Cryptosystem with Additive Homomorphism

After Goldwasser-Micali's scheme Goldwasser & Micali (1984) based on quadratic residuosity, Benaloh's homomorphic encryption function, originally designed for electronic voting and relying on prime residuosity, prefigured the first attempt to exploit the plain resources of this theory. Okamoto and Uchiyama significantly extended the enciphering rate by investigating

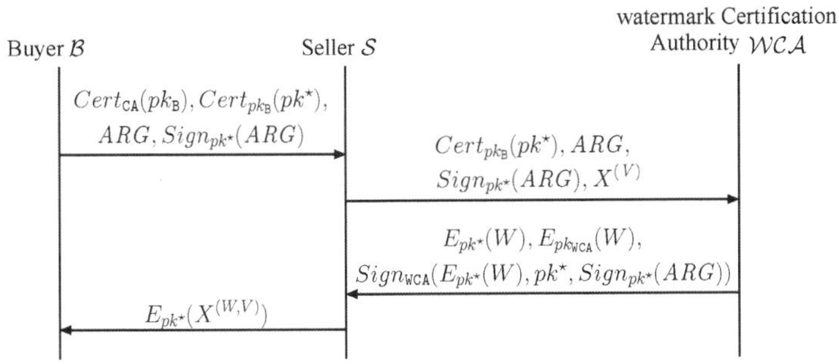

Fig. 2. The transaction of the fingerprinting protocol.

two different approaches: residuosity of smooth degree in Z^*_{pq} and residuosity of prime degree p in $Z^*_{p^2q}$, respectively. Here, we review the cryptosystem and enumerate the properties of the enciphering function.

Let p and q be two large primes ($|p| = |q| = \ell_p$ bits) and $N = p^2q$. Choose $g \in_R (Z/NZ)$ randomly such that the order of $g_p = g^{p-1} \bmod p^2$ is p, where $g.c.d.(p, q-1) = 1$ and $g.c.d.(q, p-1) = 1$. Let $h = g^N \bmod N$. Here a public key pk is (N, g, h, ℓ_p) and a secret key sk is (p, q). The cryptosystem, based on the exponentiation mod$N$, is constructed as follows.

Encryption: Let m $(0 < m < 2^{\ell_p - 1})$ be a plaintext. Selecting a random number $r \in_R (Z/NZ)$, a ciphertext is given by

$$C = g^m h^r \pmod N. \tag{7}$$

Decryption: Calculate first $C_p = C^{p-1} \bmod p^2$ and then

$$m = \frac{L(C_p)}{L(g_p)} \pmod p, \tag{8}$$

where

$$L(x) = \frac{x-1}{p}. \tag{9}$$

We denote the encryption function $E_{pk}(m, r)$ and decryption function $D_{sk}(C)$. Three important properties of the scheme are given by the following P1, P2 and P3.

P1. It has an additive homomorphic property : if $m_1 + m_2 < p$,

$$E_{pk}(m_1, r_1) \cdot E_{pk}(m_2, r_2) = E_{pk}(m_1 + m_2, r_1 + r_2) \pmod N. \tag{10}$$

P2. It is semantically secure if the following assumption, *i.e.* p-subgroup assumption, is true: $E_{pk}(0, r) = h^r \bmod N$ and $E_{pk}(1, r') = gh^{r'} \bmod N$ is computationally indistinguishable, where r and r' are uniformly and independently selected from $\in_R (Z/NZ)$.

P3. Anyone can change a ciphertext, $C = E_{pk}(m, r)$, into another ciphertext, $C' = Ch^{r'} \bmod N$, while preserving the plaintext of C (*i.e.*, $C' = E_{pk}(m, r'')$), and the relationship between C and C' can be concealed.

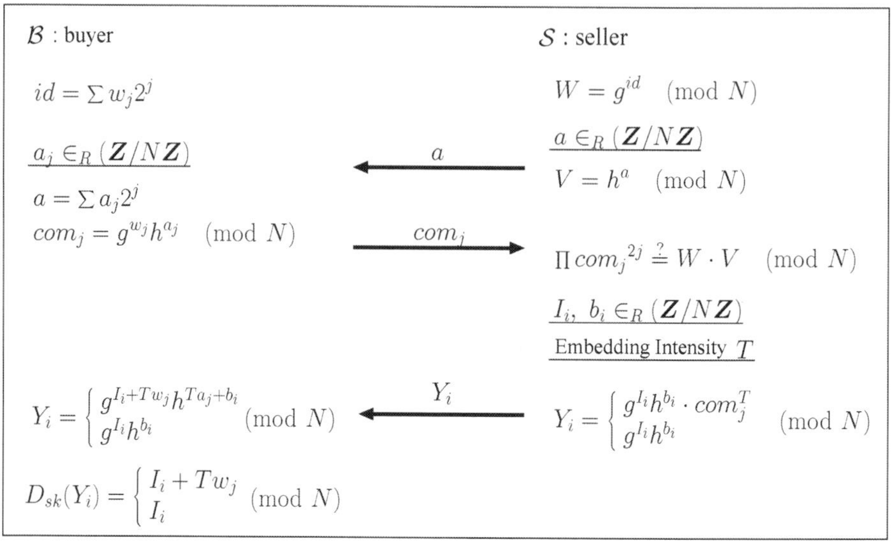

Fig. 3. Fingerprinting protocol based on additive homomorphism.

Although the enciphering rate of Paillier cryptosystem Paillier (1999), which has the similar structure to Okamoto-Uchiyama encryption scheme, is higher, it requires more computations. So the selection of the scheme is dependent on the applied system. For convenience, the cryptosystem in the protocol is represented by Okamoto-Uchiyama encryption scheme; the approach can be easily translated to the Paillier cryptosystem, the readers are recommended to check the original paper Paillier (1999).

3.2 Main Protocol

The fingerprinting protocol is executed between a buyer $\mathcal{B}$ and a seller $\mathcal{S}$. $\mathcal{B}$ commits his identity(fingerprint), $id = \sum w_j 2^j$ $(0 \leq j \leq \ell - 1)$ to $\mathcal{S}$ the enciphered form, com_j, where the values of w_j are binary. Then, $\mathcal{S}$ encrypts his image X_i $(0 \leq i \leq L)$ and multiplies it to the received com_j. We assume that $\mathcal{B}$ has already registered at a center $\mathcal{RC}$, and sent $\mathcal{S}$ the coin which includes a fingerprint and its signature. For simplicity, $W = g^{id} \bmod N$ is regarded as a commitment of *id*. Under the assumption, the fingerprinting protocol is given as follows (indicated in Fig.3).

[*Fingerprinting Protocol*]

Step 1. $\mathcal{S}$ generates a random number $a(2^\ell < a < N)$ and sends it to $\mathcal{B}$.

Step 2. $\mathcal{B}$ decomposes a into ℓ random numbers $a_j \in_R (Z/NZ)$ to satisfy the following equation.

$$a = \sum_{j=0}^{\ell-1} a_j 2^j \tag{11}$$

Where the values of a_1 to $a_{\ell-1}$ are selected randomly under the condition,

$$\sum_{j=1}^{\ell-1} a_j 2^j < a, \tag{12}$$

and a_0 is calculated as follows.

$$a_0 = a - \sum_{j=1}^{\ell-1} a_j 2^j \tag{13}$$

A bit commitment of each w_j is calculated as

$$\begin{aligned} com_j &= g^{w_j} h^{a_j} \pmod N, & (14)\\ &= E_{pk}(w_j, a_j) \pmod N, & (15) \end{aligned}$$

and sent to $\mathcal{S}$.

Step 3. To verify the commitment, $\mathcal{S}$ calculates

$$V = h^a \pmod N, \tag{16}$$

and makes sure that the following equation can be satisfied.

$$\prod_j com_j{}^{2^j} \stackrel{?}{=} W \cdot V \pmod N \tag{17}$$

Step 4. $\mathcal{S}$ generates L random numbers $b_i \in_R (Z/NZ)$ and embedding intensity T of even number. Then, in order to get the encrypted and fingerprinted image, $\mathcal{S}$ calculates

$$Y_i = \begin{cases} g^{X_i} h^{b_i} \cdot com_j^T \pmod N & \text{marking position} \\ g^{X_i} h^{b_i} \pmod N & \text{elsewhere} \end{cases} \tag{18}$$

and sends it to $\mathcal{B}$

Step 5. Since the received Y_i is rewritten as

$$Y_i = \begin{cases} g^{(X_i + Tw_j)} h^{Ta_j + b_i} \pmod N & \text{marking position} \\ g^{X_i} h^{b_i} \pmod N & \text{elsewhere,} \end{cases} \tag{19}$$

$\mathcal{B}$ can decrypt Y_i to get the plaintext.

$$D_{sk}(Y_i) = \begin{cases} X_i + Tw_j \pmod p & \text{marking position} \\ X_i \pmod p & \text{elsewhere} \end{cases} \tag{20}$$

On the deciphered message, if $w_j = 1$, then X_i has been increased, and if $w_j = 0$, then nothing has done to X_i.

Remark 1: If we regard w_j as a message and a_j as a random number, then com_j is represented by $E_{pk}(w_j, a_j)$ and com_j^T by $E_{pk}(Tw_j, Ta_j)$ because

$$\begin{aligned} com_j^T &= (g^{w_j}h^{a_j})^T \pmod N \\ &= g^{Tw_j}h^{Ta_j} \pmod N \\ &= E_{pk}(Tw_j, Ta_j). \end{aligned} \tag{21}$$

In many watermarking schemes, the embedding procedure is performed by an addition of watermark signal, namely a watermark is added to or subtracted from pixel values or frequency components with a certain intensity. Therefore, the additive homomorphism is suitable for such watermark schemes. In Eq.(18), $g^{X_i}h^{b_i} = E_{pk}(X_i, b_i)$ is regarded as $\mathcal{S}$'s enciphered image, and then from the property P1 Y_i at the marking position is rewritten as

$$\begin{aligned} Y_i &= E_{pk}(X_i, b_i) \cdot E_{pk}(Tw_j, Ta_j) \\ &= E_{pk}(X_i + Tw_j, Ta_j + b_i) \end{aligned} \tag{22}$$

If $\mathcal{S}$ uses X_i as a pixel value directly, the above operation can be applied easily. Considering about the robustness against attack such as lossy compression and filtering operation, etc., the transformed domain is generally more resilience for such attacks.
In the fingerprinting protocol $\mathcal{B}$ may be able to forge his identity as he has not proved that the values of w_j $(0 \le j \le \ell - 1)$ are binary. Even if they are not binary, Eq.(17) can be satisfied choosing them suitably. Then a malicious buyer may try to find the embedding position by setting the values adaptively. To solve the problem, a zero-knowledge interactive protocol has been introduced to prove that a commitment contains binary value, the procedure, called *binary proof*, is clearly described in Kuribayashi & Tanaka (2005).

3.3 Modified Fingerprinting Protocol

We consider the size of the message being encrypted, where the bit length of a message is revealed as the public key ℓ_p of Okamoto-Uchiyama encryption scheme. Since X_i and T are much smaller than $2^{\ell_p - 1} (< p)$ and the ciphertext is three times as large as p, the enciphering rate is still low. To exploit the message space effectively, the size of message to be encrypted should be modified as large as $2^{\ell_p - 1}$.
Let m_i be

$$m_i = \begin{cases} X_i + Tw_j & markingposition \\ X_i & elsewhere, \end{cases} \tag{23}$$

and ℓ_m be the maximum bit-length of m_i. Since ℓ_m is much smaller than ℓ_p, the message can be replaced by

$$M_{i'} = \sum_{t=0}^{\gamma-1} m_{i'\gamma+t} 2^{\ell_m t}, \qquad 0 \le i' \le L/\gamma - 1, \tag{24}$$

where

$$\gamma = \left\lceil \frac{\ell_p}{\ell_m} \right\rceil. \tag{25}$$

It is illustrated in Fig.4. If the ciphertext of the message $M_{i'}$ is calculated by $\mathcal{S}$ using com_j and X_i in the fingerprinting protocol, the enciphering rate becomes at most $1/3$ in theory.
In order to perform the above operations, the fingerprinting protocol of Step 4 and Step 5 presented in the fingerprinting protocol is changed as follows.

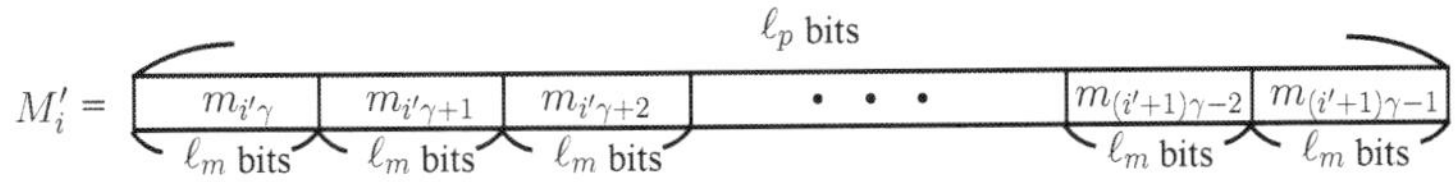

Fig. 4. Composition of the message $M_{i'}$.

[*Modified Fingerprinting Protocol*]

Step 4. In order to get the encrypted and fingerprinted image y_i, $\mathcal{S}$ calculates

$$y_i = \begin{cases} g^{X_i} \cdot com_j^T \pmod{N} & \text{marking position} \\ g^{X_i} \pmod{N} & \text{elsewhere.} \end{cases} \tag{26}$$

To synthesize some y_i in one ciphertext $Y_{i'}$, the following operation is performed using a random number $b_{i'} \in_R (Z/NZ)$.

$$Y_{i'} = \left(\prod_t (y_{i'\gamma+t})^{2^{\ell_m t}}\right) \cdot h^{b_{i'}} \pmod{N} \tag{27}$$

Step 5. $\mathcal{B}$ decrypts the received $Y_{i'}$ to obtain $M_{i'}$. Since he knows the bit-length ℓ_m of m_i, he can decompose $M_{i'}$ into the pieces, and finally he can get the fingerprinted image.

Remark 3: From Eqs.(23)-(26) and the property P3, Eq.(27) is expressed by

$$\begin{aligned} Y_{i'} &= \left(\prod_t g^{m_{i'\gamma+t}2^{\ell_m t}}\right) \cdot h^r \pmod{N} \\ &= g^{\sum m_{i'\gamma+t}2^{\ell_m t}} h^r \pmod{N} \\ &= g^{M_{i'}} h^r \pmod{N} \\ &= E_{pk}(M_{i'}, r). \end{aligned} \tag{28}$$

If the Okamoto-Uchiyama encryption scheme is secure and the bit-length of $M_{i'}$ is less than ℓ_p, $\mathcal{B}$ can decrypt $Y_{i'} = E(M_{i'}, r)$. Here, in Eqs.(27) and (28) several pieces $m_{i'\gamma+t}$ of fingerprinted image that compose $M_{i'}$ are encrypted in one ciphertext $E(M_{i'}, r)$, though each piece is encrypted in the original scheme. Therefore, $M_{i'}$ should retain a special data structure described by Eq.(24). If $\mathcal{S}$ changes the data structure, $\mathcal{B}$ can not decompose it into the correct pieces $m_{i'\gamma+t}$, and then he can claim the fact. Hence, with the knowledge of data structure $\mathcal{B}$ can decompose the decrypted message $M_{i'}$ into $m_{i'\gamma+t}$, and finally get the fingerprinted image. Furthermore, as $M_{i'}$ is simply produced by composing several pieces of $m_{i'\gamma+t}$, $\mathcal{B}$ can not derive any information about original image from the decrypted message.

Assume that the size of fingerprint is ℓ bits, and the fingerprint is embedded in the frequency components of an image where the number of components is L and each component is expressed by $\ell_{\overline{m}}$ bits. Then the total amount of plain data of digital contents is $\ell_{\overline{m}}L$. In Pfitzmann & Sadeghi (1999) and Pfitzmann & Sadeghi (2000), the modulus n is a composite of two large primes. Since only one bit is encrypted when bit commitment schemes are used, each bit of the frequency components must be encrypted, thus the total amount of encrypted data is $\ell_{\overline{m}}L \log_2 n$ bits. On the other hand, the modulus of the fingerprinting protocol with additive homomorphism is $N(= p^2q,\ 3\ell_p$ bits). In the original scheme, the amount of encrypted

conventional	original	modified
$1/3\ell_p$	$\ell_{\overline{m}}/3\ell_p$	$1/3$

Table 1. Enciphering rate.

data is $L\log_2 N(= 3\ell_p L)$ bits as each component is encrypted. In the modified scheme, it is $(L\log_2 N)/\gamma\,(\simeq 3\ell_{\overline{m}}L)$ bits, because from Eq.(25) there are at most L/γ messages $M_{i'}$ to be encrypted, since $\ell_m \simeq \ell_{\overline{m}}$. Here, if $\log_2 n \simeq \log_2 N = 3\ell_p$, the enciphering rates are indicated in Table 1. Since the enciphering rate of Paillier cryptosystem is $1/2$, the protocol can achieve the rate if the cryptosystem is applied instead of Okamoto-Uchiyama encryption scheme.

4. Collusion Resilience

In a fingerprinting scheme, each watermarked copy is slightly different, hence, malicious users will collect their copies in order to remove/alter the watermark. For an improperly designed fingerprint, it is possible to gather a small coalition of colluders and sufficiently attenuate each of colluders' fingerprint to produce a pirated copy with no detectable traces. Thus, it is important to model and analyze collusion, and to design fingerprints that can resist the collusion attack.

There are several types of collusion attacks that may be used against fingerprinting system. One method is to average fingerprinted copies, which is an example of the linear collusion attack. Another collusion attack involves users cutting out portions of each fingerprinted copy and pasting them together to form a pirated copy. Other attacks may employ nonlinear operations, such as taking the maximum or median of signal values of individual copies. As the countermeasure of collusion attack, a number of works on designing fingerprints have been proposed. One approach generates mutually independent sequences, *e.g.* spread spectrum sequence, for assigning users as their fingerprints, the other approach encodes fingerprint information considering the distances among fingerprint codes.

On the former approach, spread spectrum sequences which follow a normal distribution are assigned to users as fingerprints. The origin of the spread spectrum watermarking scheme is Cox's method Cox et al. (1997) that embeds the sequence into frequency components of digital image and detects it using a correlator. Since normally distributed values allow the theoretical and statistical analysis of the method, modeling of a variety of attacks have been studied. Studies in Zhao et al. (2005) have shown that a number of nonlinear collusions such as interleaving attack can be well approximated by averaging collusion plus additive noise. So far, many variants of the spread spectrum watermarking scheme are based on the Cox's method.

Let W be a watermark signal composed of ℓ elements $w_i \in N(0,1), (0 \le i < \ell)$ and each of them is embedded into selected DCT coefficient $X_i, (0 \le i < \ell)$ based on the following equation,

$$X_i^W = X_i(1 + \alpha w_i), \tag{29}$$

where $N(0,1)$ is a normal distribution with mean 0 and variance 1, and α is an embedding strength. At the detector side, we determine which SS sequence is present in a test image by evaluating the similarity of sequences. From the suspicious copy, a sequence $\tilde{W}$ is detected by calculating the difference of the original image, and its similarity with W is obtained as follows.

$$\mathrm{sim}(W, \tilde{W}) = \frac{W \cdot \tilde{W}}{\sqrt{\tilde{W} \cdot \tilde{W}}}, \tag{30}$$

If the similarity value exceeds a threshold, the embedded sequence is regarded as W.
At the detection, DCT coefficients of test image are subtracted from those of original image, and then the correlations with every candidates of watermark signal are computed. Thus, non-blind and informed watermarking scheme can be applied. In fingerprinting techniques, the original content may be available at a detection because a seller is assumed as the author, or a sales agent who knows it. A simple, yet effective collusion attack is to average some variants of copy because when c copies are averaged, the similarity value calculated by Eq.(30) results in shrinking by a factor of c, which will be roughly $\sqrt{\ell}/c$ Cox et al. (1997). Even in this case, we can detect the embedded watermark and identify the colluders by using an appropriately designed threshold.
Chen et al. Chen & Wornel (2001) showed that additive spread spectrum watermarking, in general, not good choices for embedding a bit-sequence, and, as an alternative, they introduced a new class of embedding strategies, which is referred to as "quantization index modulation (QIM)". In the study, they presented that dither modulation is a practical implementation of QIM that exhibits many of the attractive performance properties of QIM. The convenient structure of dither modulation, which is easily combined with error-correction coding, allows the system designer to achieve different rate distortion-robustness trade-offs by tuning parameters such as the quantization step size. It is also suitable for fingerprinting system by encoding fingerprint information by collusion-secure code. Thus, the combination of the QIM watermarking and collusion-secure code can provide a good fingerprinting system.
Aiming at the extraction of a fingerprint bit-sequence, the QIM watermarking is implemented in Kuribayashi & Tanaka (2005) and its variants are employed in Prins et al. (2007). In Swaminathan et al. (2006), the capability of the QIM based fingerprinting system is investigated, and the results show that one variant, which is called the spread transform dither modulation (STDM), retains an advantage under blind detection. Under non-blind detection, which is a reasonable assumption in fingerprinting system, there is still a performance gap with the spread spectrum method. It is noted that, in Yacobi (2001), the traceability is further improved by combining a spread spectrum embedding like Cox's method.
Assume that the bit-length of the message space is ℓ_M and that of each watermarked frequency components is ℓ_m. Generally, ℓ_M is much larger than ℓ_m. In order to exploit the message space effectively, dozens of watermarked frequency components are packed in one message in Kuribayashi & Tanaka (2005), hence, the enciphering rate is almost equivalent to that of an applied cryptosystem by suitably designing the message space of a ciphertext. From the viewpoint of enciphering rate, the modification of QIM method implemented in Prins et al. (2007) is not a good choice, and the improvement of the robustness against attacks is still inferior to the spread spectrum method. The adaption of fingerprinting code further restricts the scalability of the QIM based fingerprinting system because of the long code-length.

5. How to Implement Spread Spectrum Watermarking on Encrypted Domain

Despite the simple structure of the QIM watermarking, the exploitation of fingerprinting code prevents the usability for various kinds of digital contents. We note that one major drawback of the conventional methods Kuribayashi & Tanaka (2005) Prins et al. (2007) is the long code-length of the fingerprinting code. Alternatively, the spread spectrum watermarking technique Cox et al. (1997) is implemented on the fingerprinting protocol based on the homomorphic property of public-key cryptosystem in this section. Hereafter, for simplicity, the embedding of the reference information V, which is introduced in Lei et al. (2004), and a random number used for the encryption are omitted in the protocol.

The embedding operation in Eq.(29) can be easily performed using the additive homomorphic property of public-key cryptosystems such as Okamoto-Uchiyama encryption scheme Okamoto & Uchiyama (1998) and Paillier cryptosystem Paillier (1999). Remember that Eq.(22) is composed of two operations; multiplication and addition for $g(\cdot)$ and $f(\cdot)$, respectively. Since the multiplication is realized by the iteration of addition, the embedding operation is represented by the multiplication and exponentiation. Suppose that an original image is composed of L pixels and is represented by the DCT selected coefficients $X_i, (0 \le i < \ell)$ and the remain ones $X_i, (\ell \le i < L)$, and a watermark signal is represented by $w_i, (0 \le i < \ell)$. Then, the embedding operation of Eq.(29) is executed in the encrypted domain as follows.

$$E_{pk}(X_i(1+\alpha w_i)) = E_{pk}(X_i) \cdot E_{pk}(w_i)^{\alpha X_i} \tag{31}$$

The above operation can be directly applied for the operation $\oplus$ in Eq.(6). Here, it is noticed that a watermark signal and DCT coefficients are generally represented by real value and they must be rounded to integer before the encryption. If such parameters are directly rounded to the nearest integers, it may result in the loss of information. Hence, they should be scaled before rounding-off. In addition, a negative number should be avoided considering the property of a cryptosystem because it is represented by much longer bit-sequence under the finite field of applied cryptosystem, which affects the other packed ones described in Eq.(27). Hence, a rounding operation that maps real value into positive integer is required.

At first, we show the operation concerning to a watermark signal $W = \{w_0, w_1, w_2, \ldots, w_{\ell-1}\}$. Since the ciphertext of W is computed by a watermark certification authority $\mathcal{WCA}$, the enciphering operation is performed previously sent to a seller $\mathcal{S}$. A constant value p_w is added to each element of watermark signal $w_i, (0 \le i < \ell)$ to make the value positive. Then, it is scaled by a factor of s_w in order to keep the degree of precision, and it is quantized to $\overline{w}_i$. Such operations are formalized by the following one equation;

$$\overline{w}_i = int(s_w(w_i + p_w)),\ 0 \le i < \ell \tag{32}$$

where $int(a)$ outputs the nearest integer from a real value a. After the operation, $\mathcal{WCA}$ encrypts $\overline{W} = \{\overline{w}_0, \overline{w}_1, \overline{w}_2, \ldots, \overline{w}_{\ell-1}\}$ using a public key pk, and the ciphertexts $E_{pk}(\overline{W}) = \{E_{pk}(\overline{w}_0), E_{pk}(\overline{w}_1), E_{pk}(\overline{w}_2), \ldots, E_{pk}(\overline{w}_{\ell-1})\}$, p_w, and s_w are sent to $\mathcal{S}$. It is noted that $E_{pk}(\overline{W})$ corresponds to $E_{pk^*}(W)$ in Fig.2, and the corresponding ciphertext of $E_{pk_{\mathcal{WCA}}}(\overline{W})$ is also sent to $\mathcal{S}$.

Next, $\mathcal{S}$ performs the rounding operation to DCT coefficients $X_i, (0 \le i < \ell)$ as follows. A constant value p_x is added to each DCT coefficient, and then scaled by $s_w s_x$. By quantizing it, the rounded DCT coefficient $\overline{X}_i$ is obtained.

$$\overline{X}_i = int(s_w s_x(X_i + p_x)),\ 0 \le i < \ell \tag{33}$$

For the control of rounding operation of each DCT coefficient, the watermark strength α is modified to $\overline{\alpha}_i$;

$$\overline{\alpha}_i = int(s_x \alpha |X_i|),\ 0 \le i < \ell \tag{34}$$

Using the above items, $\mathcal{S}$ embeds $\overline{w}_i$ into $\overline{X}_i$ for $0 \le i < \ell$ based on the additive homomorphic property of public cryptosystem as follows.

$$E_{pk}(\overline{X}_i) \cdot E_{pk}(\overline{w}_i)^{\overline{\alpha}_i} = E_{pk}(\overline{X}_i + \overline{\alpha}_i \overline{w}_i) \tag{35}$$

Since the plain value of the ciphertext $E_{pk}(\overline{X}_i + \overline{\alpha}_i\overline{w}_i)$ is

$$\overline{X}_i + \overline{\alpha}_i\overline{w}_i = s_w s_x (X_i + p_x) + s_x \alpha |X_i| s_w (w_i + p_w), \tag{36}$$
$$= s_w s_x \big((X_i + \alpha w_i |X_i|) + (p_x + \alpha |X_i| p_w)\big), \tag{37}$$

the scaling factor $s = s_w s_x$ and the adjustment factor $p = p_x + \alpha|X_i|p_w$ are necessary to calculate the actual watermarked DCT coefficients $X_i + \alpha w_i |X_i|$. Therefore, these two parameters s and p are sent to $\mathcal{B}$ as well as $E_{pk}(\overline{X}_i + \overline{\alpha}_i\overline{w}_i)$. It is noticed that the remained DCT coefficients $X_i, (\ell \le i < L)$ should be sent to $\mathcal{B}$. In order to keep the secrecy of the embedding position, they must be encrypted before delivery. Without loss of generality, the rounding operation for those coefficients are given by

$$\overline{X}_i = int(s_x s_w (X_i + p_x + \alpha |X_i| p_w)), \ \ell \le i < L, \tag{38}$$

and the ciphertexts $E_{pk}(\overline{X}_i)$ are sent with $E_{pk}(\overline{X}_i + \overline{\alpha}_i\overline{w}_i)$ to $\mathcal{B}$. Namely, the ciphertexts of a watermarked image $E_{pk}(\overline{X}^W)$, which is corresponding to $E_{pk^*}(X^{(W,V)})$ in Fig.2, is composed of those ones.

$$E_{pk}(\overline{X}^W) = \begin{cases} E_{pk}(\overline{X}_i + \overline{\alpha}_i\overline{w}_i) & 0 \le i < \ell \\ E_{pk}(\overline{X}_i) & \ell \le i < L \end{cases} \tag{39}$$

After the decryption of the received ciphertexts $E_{pk}(\overline{X}^W)$, $\mathcal{B}$ divides the results by a factor of s, and then subtracts p as the post-processing operation. At the embedding position, the ciphertexts are $E_{pk}(\overline{X}_i + \overline{\alpha}_i\overline{w}_i)$ and the post-processing operation outputs the fingerprinted coefficients $X_i + \alpha w_i |X_i|$ as follows;

$$\frac{D_{sk}(E_{pk}(\overline{X}_i + \overline{\alpha}_i\overline{w}_i))}{s} - p = X_i + \alpha w_i |X_i|, \ 0 \le i < \ell, \tag{40}$$

where $D_{sk}(\cdot)$ is a deciphering function using a secret key sk. At the other position, the ciphertexts are $E_{pk}(\overline{X}_i)$ and $\mathcal{B}$ obtains X_i after the post-processing operation.

$$\frac{D_{sk}(E_{pk}(\overline{X}_i))}{s} - p = X_i, \ \ell \le i < L. \tag{41}$$

It is remarkable that the embedding position is kept secret from $\mathcal{B}$, the classification of the above operations is difficult. The diagram of the interactive protocol is shown in Fig.5.

In Eq.(22), the watermarked coefficient X_i^W is composed of two terms; X_i and $\alpha w_i X_i$. Since w_i is encrypted at the center $\mathcal{WCA}$ prior to the embedding operation at $\mathcal{S}$, X_i and w_i are rounded separately. Considering the post-processing at $\mathcal{B}$, the scaling factors s_w, s_x, and the compensation factor p should be constant. Here, we assume that a constant value is uniformly added to real values which are w_i and X_i to make it positive. Then, $\mathcal{B}$ must subtract the interference term related to both X_i and w_i, which requires additional communication costs. If the adjustment factor p is varied with respect to X_i, the amount of information to be sent to $\mathcal{B}$ from $\mathcal{S}$ becomes very large. In order to avoid it, we set p a constant value by controlling the value p_x. Even if p and α is known, to obtain X_i is still informationally difficult because of three unknown parameters p_x, p_w, and X_i for a given one equation $p = p_x + \alpha|X_i|p_w$. As the consequence, the secrecy of the original DCT coefficients is assured.

Notice that if the size of scaling factors s_w and s_x is increased, the proposed scheme can simulate the original Cox's method more precisely. From the viewpoint of enciphering rate, however, these factors should be small. Referring to the modified fingerprinting protocol, the

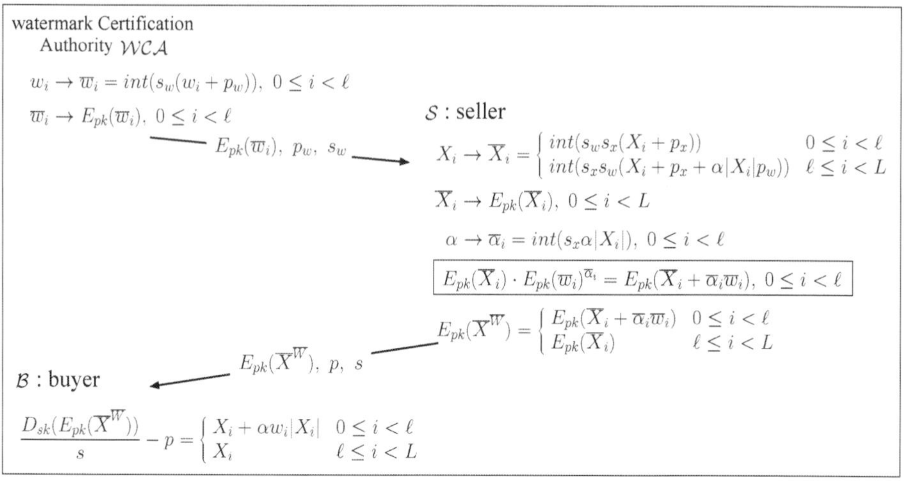

Fig. 5. The procedure of fingerprinting protocol to embed the spread spectrum watermark.

bit-length of a watermarked coefficient $\overline{X}_i^W = \overline{X}_i + \overline{\alpha}_i \overline{w}_i$, which is represented by a constant bit-length ℓ_x, is much smaller than that of message space in cryptosystems such as Okamoto-Uchiyama encryption scheme and Paillier cryptosystem, and some of $\overline{X}_i^W$ should be packed in one message $\overline{M}$;

$$\overline{M} = \overline{X}_i^W || \overline{X}_{i+1}^W || \cdots || \overline{X}_{i+\xi-1}^W, \tag{42}$$

where ξ is the number of packed coefficients and is dependent on s_w and s_x. Such a packing operation is easily performed by computing the $\ell_x t$-th power of $E_{pk}(\overline{X}_{i+t}^W)$;

$$E_{pk}(\overline{M}) = \prod_{t=0}^{\xi-1} \left(E_{pk}(\overline{X}_{i+t}^W) \right)^{\ell_x t} \tag{43}$$

The appropriate size of s_w and s_x are explored by implementing on a computer and evaluating the simulated performance. It is worth mentioning that the enciphering rate of Paillier cryptosystem approaches asymptotically 1 using the extension of the cryptosystem Damgård & Jurik (2001) and then more data can be packed in one ciphertext. Although the works in Fouque et al. (2003); Orlandi et al. (2007) can encode rational numbers by a limited precision, they are not suitable for the packing operation.

6. Simulation Results

Since the basic algorithm of our scheme is Cox's scheme with a limited precision, we evaluate the degradation of image quality by PSNR, and the detected correlation values compared with the original values. If the results are similar, we regard that the performance is not degraded. In our simulation, a standard gray-scaled image "lena" of 256×256 pixels is used. The length of watermark signal W is $\ell = 1000$ and the embedding intensity is $\alpha = 0.1$. Even if p_w and

p_x are added, the values of w_i and x_i might be negative. In such a case, the values are simply rounded to 0.

The comparison of PSNR and correlation values for the watermarked image which is not distorted by attacks are shown in Fig.6 and Fig.7, respectively. The PSNR of original Cox's scheme is 34.93 [dB] and the correlation value is 31.91, which are drawn by dot line in the figures. From the figures, we can see that the performance is asymptotically reaching the original value according to the increase of the scaling factors s_w and s_x. As the basic algorithm is Cox's scheme with a limited precision, we can regard that the performance is not degraded when the detected correlation values are similar.

One of the important characteristic in the spread spectrum watermarking technique is the orthogonality of each watermark signal because of the robustness against collusion attack. It is well-known that the original scheme retains the robustness with a dozen of colluders. Under averaging collusion with 5 users, the average similarity value of original scheme is 13.64, and the proposed one is shown in Fig.8. The robustness against the combination of collusion attack and JPEG compression are compared, which results are shown in Fig.9. From the results, the degradation of performance from the original scheme is very slight, and it does not affect the robustness against attacks. It is noted that the scaling factors s_w and s_x are closely related to the degradation of performance. It is better to increase the value of these parameters, for example $s_w \geq 2^3$ and $s_x \geq 2^3$, but we have to consider the communication costs because the bit-length to represent the watermarked DCT coefficient $\overline{X}_i + \overline{\alpha}_i \overline{w}_i$ is increased according to the size of s_w and s_x, which degrades the coding rate of such information. For other images, "aerial", "baboon", "barbala", "f16", "girl", and "peppers", the similar results are derived with the above parameters as shown in Table 2 and 3. The attenuation of PSNR value from the original one is at most 0.1%, that of the correlation value is at most 0.3%, and under averaging collusion the attenuation is less than 1%. As the consequence, recommended parameters are $s_w = 2^3$ and $s_x = 2^3$ from the simulation results.

When we use the above recommended parameters, the value of $\overline{X}_i^W$ can be represented by 20 bits (the range must be within $[0, 2^{20}]$ if $s_w = s_x = 2^3$). For the security reason, the bit-length of a composite $n = pq$ for the modulus of Paillier cryptosystem should be no less than 1024 bits. When $|n| = 1024$, an 1024-bit message is encrypted to an 2048-bit ciphertext. Under the above condition, the number of watermarked DCT coefficients in one ciphertext is at most 51 ($= \lfloor 1024/20 \rfloor$). Since the number of DCT coefficients are $65536 = 256 \times 256$, the number of ciphertexts is 1286 ($= \lfloor 65536/51 \rfloor$) and the total size of the ciphertexts is about 2.5MB, which is about 40 times larger than the original file size 66KB. In case the packing is not performed, the total size is more than 128MB. Therefore, we can conclude that the proposed method efficiently implements the Cox's spread spectrum watermarking scheme in the asymmetric fingerprinting protocol.

7. Conclusion

In this chapter, we investigated an asymmetric fingerprinting protocol with additive homomorphism and a method for implementing watermarking technique in an encrypted domain for assuring the asymmetric property of fingerprinting system. We developed the commitment scheme utilized to achieve the asymmetric property, and enhance the enciphering rate by applying Okamoto-Uchiyama encryption scheme for the cryptographic protocol that retains additive homomorphism. In order to contain information in one ciphertext as much as possible, the large message space is effectively partitioned by multiplexing each fingerprinted and encrypted component of an image.

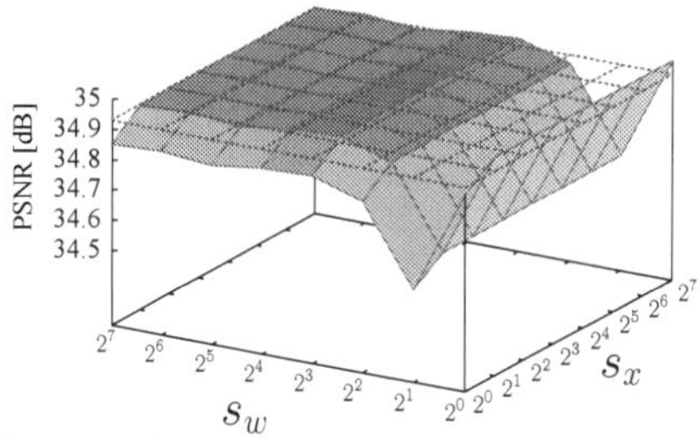

Fig. 6. The image quality for the scaling values s_w and s_x, where that of original scheme is 34.93 [dB] depicted by dot lines.

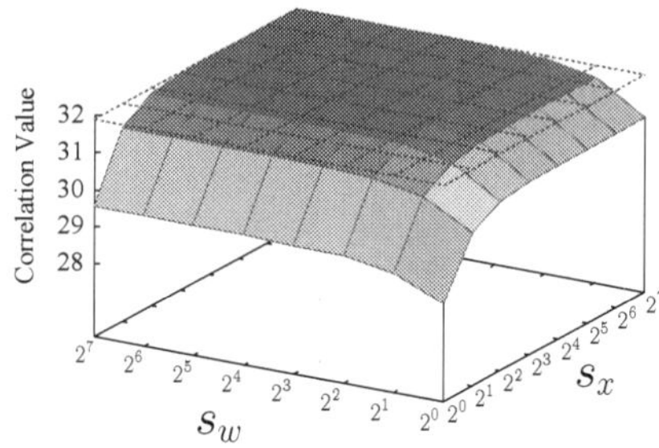

Fig. 7. The correlation values for the scaling values s_w and s_x, where that of original scheme is 31.90 depicted by dot lines.

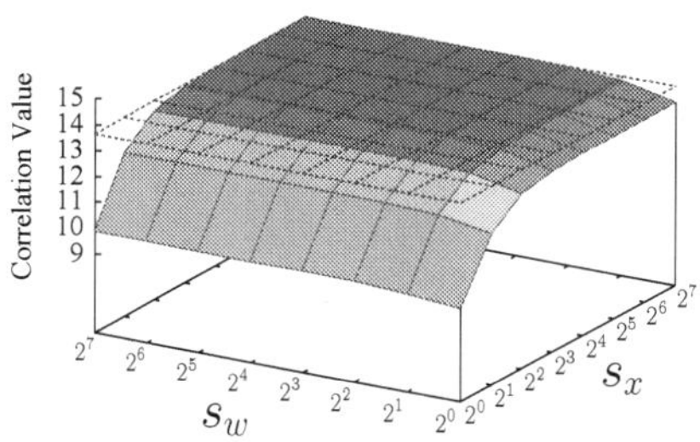

Fig. 8. The average correlation value after averaging collusion attack for the scaling values s_w and s_x.

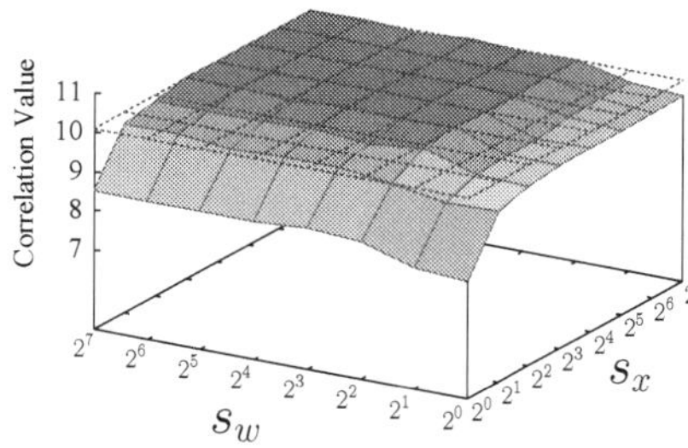

Fig. 9. The average correlation value after averaging collusion attack and JPEG compression with quality 35% for the scaling values s_w and s_x, where the average value of original scheme is 10.10.

We proposed a new of approaches for collaborating the proposed asymmetric fingerprinting protocol and watermarking technique. In the conventional implementation, the QIM watermarking is applied to the fingerprinting protocol exploiting the quantization procedure that truncates a real value to integer, which is unavoidable process to apply the public-key cryptosystem based on the algebraic property of integer. In the method, fingerprint information must be coded by a fingerprinting code to be robust against collusion attack. It also causes another issues such that the applicable contents are limited to huge contents like movie because of the long code-length. In this chapter, we implemented the spread spectrum watermarking to be applicable for various kinds of contents. After exploring the fundamental properties of signals in an encrypted domain, a fingerprint sequence is scaled up in order not to attenuate the signal energy by quantization. Moreover, the effects of rounding operation that maps a real value into a positive integer are formulated, and an auxiliary operation to obtain a watermarked image is presented. From our simulation results, the identification capability of our algorithm is quite similar to the original spread spectrum watermarking scheme, hence we can simulate the scheme on the cryptographic protocol with a limited precision.

	aerial	baboon	barbala	f16	girl	lena	peppers
original	36.34	34.96	34.61	35.59	35.49	34.96	34.48
proposed	36.35	34.95	34.61	35.59	35.48	34.95	34.48

Table 2. The degradation of the image quality when $s_w = s_x = 2^3$.

		aerial	baboon	barbala	f16	girl	lena	peppers
No attack	original	31.91	31.91	31.91	31.91	31.87	31.91	31.91
	proposed	31.87	31.82	31.85	31.85	31.79	31.84	31.85
Collusion	original	13.66	13.64	13.65	13.65	13.54	13.64	13.65
	proposed	13.61	13.50	13.54	13.57	13.40	13.54	13.55
Collusion	original	11.60	9.14	8.95	9.74	9.01	10.10	10.27
+ JPEG 35%	proposed	11.56	9.18	8.91	9.73	9.18	10.06	10.16

Table 3. The degradation of the correlation values when $s_w = s_x = 2^3$.

8. References

Boneh, D. & Shaw, J. (1998). Collusion-secure fingerprinting for digital data, *IEEE Trans. Inf. Theory* **44**(5): 1897–1905.

Brassard, G., Chaum, D. & Crepeau, C. (1988). Minimum disclosure proofs of knowledge, *Journal of Computer and System Sciences* **37**: 156–189.

Chen, B. & Wornel, G. W. (2001). Quantization index modulation: a class of provably good methods for digital watermarking and information embedding, *IEEE Trans. Inform. Theory* **47**(4): 1423–1443.

Cox, I. J., Kilian, J., Leighton, F. T. & Shamson, T. (1997). Secure spread spectrum watermarking for multimedia, *IEEE Trans. Image Process.* **6**(12): 1673–1687.

Damgård, I. & Jurik, M. (2001). A generalisation, a simplification and some applications of paillier's probabilistic public-key system, *Proc. of PKC '01*, Vol. 1992 of *LNCS*, Springer-Verlag, pp. 119–136.

Fouque, P. A., Stern, J. & Wackers, G. J. (2003). Cryptocomputing with rationals, *Proc. of Finalcial Cryptography*, Vol. 2357 of *LNCS*, Springer-Verlag, pp. 136–146.

Goldwasser, S. & Micali, S. (1984). Probabilistic encryption, *JCSS* **28**(2): 270–299.

Katzenbeisser, S. & Petitcolas, F. A. P. (2000). *Information hiding techniques for steganography and digital watermarking*, Artech house publishers.

Kuribayashi, M. & Tanaka, H. (2005). Fingerprinting protocol for images based on additive homomorphic property, *IEEE Trans. Image Process.* **14**(12): 2129–2139.

Lei, C., Yu, P., Tsai, P. & Chan, M. (2004). An efficient and anonymous buyer-seller watermarking protocol, *IEEE Trans. Image Process.* **13**(12): 1618–1626.

Memon, N. & Wong, P. W. (2001). A buyer-seller watermarking protocol, *IEEE Trans. Image Process.* **10**(4): 643–649.

Okamoto, T. & Uchiyama, S. (1998). A new public-key cryptosystem as secure as factoring, *Advances in Cryptology – EUROCRYPT'98*, Vol. 1403 of *LNCS*, Springer-Verlag, pp. 308–318.

Orlandi, C., Piva, A. & Barni, M. (2007). Oblivious neural network computing via homomorphic encryption, *EURASIP J. Inform. Security* **2007**(9).

Paillier, P. (1999). Public key cryptosystems based on degree residuosity classes, *Advances in Cryptology – EUROCRYPT'99*, Vol. 1592 of *LNCS*, Springer-Verlag, pp. 223–238.

Pfitzmann, B. & Sadeghi, A. (1999). Coin-based anonymous fingerprinting, *Advances in Cryptology – EUROCRYPT'99*, Vol. 1592 of *LNCS*, Springer-Verlag, pp. 150–164.

Pfitzmann, B. & Sadeghi, A. (2000). Anonymous fingerprinting with direct non-repudiation, *Advances in Cryptology – ASIACRYPT'2000*, Vol. 1976 of *LNCS*, Springer-Verlag, pp. 401–414.

Pfitzmann, B. & Schunter, M. (1996). Asymmetric fingerprinting, *Advances in Cryptology – EUROCRYPT'96*, Vol. 1070 of *LNCS*, Springer-Verlag, pp. 84–95.

Pfitzmann, B. & Waidner, M. (1997). Anonymous fingerprinting, *Advances in Cryptology – EUROCRYPT'97*, Vol. 1233 of *LNCS*, Springer-Verlag, pp. 88–102.

Prins, J. P., Erkin, Z. & Lagendijk, R. L. (2007). Anonymous fingerprinting with robust QIM watermarking techniques, *EURASIP J. Inform Security* **2007**(8).

Rivest, R. L., Shamir, A. & Adleman, L. (1978). A method for obtaining digital signatures and public key cryptosystems, *Commun. ACM* **21**(2): 120–126.

Staddon, J. N., Stinson, D. R. & Wei, R. (2001). Combinatiorial properties of frameproof and traceability codes, *IEEE Trans. Inform. Theory* **47**(3): 1042–1049.

Swaminathan, A., He, S. & Wu, M. (2006). Exploring QIM based anti-collusion fingerprinting for multimedia, *Proc. of SPIE, SPIE Conference on Security, Watermarking and Steganography*, p. 60721T.

Tardos, G. (2003). Optimal probabilistic fingerprint codes, *Proc. 35th ACM Symp. Theory of Comp.*, pp. 116–125.

Trappe, W., Wu, M., Wang, Z. J. & Liu, K. J. R. (2003). Anti-collusion fingerprinting for multimedia, *IEEE Trans. Signal Process.* **51**(4): 1069–1087.

Wang, Z. J., Wu, M., Trappe, W. & Liu, K. J. R. (2004). Group-oriented fingerprinting for multimedia forensics, *EURASIP J. Appl. Signal Process.* **2004**(14): 2142–2162.

Wang, Z. J., Wu, M., Zhao, H. V., Trappe, W. & Liu, K. J. R. (2005). Anti-collusion forensics of multimedia fingerprinting using orthogonal modulation, *IEEE Trans. Image Process.* **14**(6): 804–821.

Wu, M., Trappe, W., Wang, Z. J. & Liu, K. J. R. (2004). Collusion resistant fingerprinting for multimedia, *IEEE Signal Processing Mag.* pp. 15–27.

Yacobi, Y. (2001). Improved boneh-shaw content fingerprinting, *Proc. CT-RSA*, Vol. 2020 of *LNCS*, Springer-Verlag, pp. 378–391.

Zhao, H. V., Wu, M., Wang, Z. J. & Liu, K. J. R. (2005). Forensic analysis of nonlinear collusion attacks for multimedia fingerprinting, *IEEE Trans. Image Process.* **14**(5): 646–661.

Zhu, Y., Feng, D. & Zou, W. (2005). Collusion secure convolutional spread spectrum fingerprinting, *Proc. IWDW2005*, Vol. 3710 of *LNCS*, Springer-Verlag, pp. 67–83.

11

Semiparametric curve alignment and shift density estimation: ECG data processing revisited

T. Trigano[1], U. Isserles[3], T. Montagu[2] and Y. Ritov[3]
[1]*Shamoon College of Engineering, Ashdod Campus, Department of Electrical Engineering, 77141, Ashdod, Israel*
[2]*CEA-LIST, Laboratory of Stochastic Processes and Spectra, CEA-Saclay, 91191 Gif-sur-Yvette, France*
[3]*Hebrew University of Jerusalem, Department of Statistics, Mount Scopus, Israel*

Abstract

We address in this contribution a problem stemming from functional data analysis. Assuming that we dispose of a large number of shifted recorded curves with identical shape, the objective is to estimate the time shifts as well as their distribution. Such an objective appears in several biological applications, for example in ECG signal processing. We are interested in the estimation of the distribution of elapsed durations between repetitive pulses, but wish to estimate it with a possibly low signal-to-noise ratio, or without any knowledge of the pulse shape. This problem is solved within a semiparametric framework, that is without any knowledge of the shape. We suggest an M-estimator leading to two different algorithms whose main steps are as follows: we split our dataset in blocks, on which the estimation of the shifts is done by minimizing a cost criterion, based on a functional of the periodogram. The estimated shifts are then plugged into a standard density estimator. Some theoretical insights are presented, which show that under mild assumptions the alignment can be done efficiently. Results are presented on simulations, as well as on real data for the alignment of ECG signals, and these algorithms are compared to the methods used by practitioners in this framework. It is shown in the results that the presented method outperforms the standard ones, thus leading to a more accurate estimation of the average heart pulse and of the distribution of elapsed times between heart pulses, even in the case of low Signal-to- Noise Ratio (SNR).

1. Introduction

1.1 Description of the problem

Due to the improvements of electronic apparatus and registration systems, it is more and more common place to collect sets of curves or other functional observations. Such registration is often followed by a processing operation, since they tend to represent the same repeated phenomenon. In this contribution the problem of curve registration and alignment from a semiparametric point of view is addressed. More specifically, we assume that we dispose of

M registered curves, each of which being described by the model given in Equation (1.1):

$$y_m(t) = s(t - \theta_m) + \sigma\varepsilon_m(t),\ m = 0 \ldots M \tag{1.1}$$

where s is a curve of interest, θ_m is an unknown shift parameter distributed according to some probability density function f_θ, σ is a real positive number and ε_m is a standard Gaussian white noise process. We are interested in the estimation of the curve s and of the shifts $\{\theta_m, m = 0 \ldots M\}$ or, when the number of curves M is large, in the estimation of the shift distribution f_θ. Such a problem appears frequently in functional data analysis (FDA) applications, and we refer to Silveman & Ramsay (2005) and Ferraty & Vieu (2006) for examples and case studies related to this issue. In the framework described by the latter equation, the knowledge of the translation parameter θ, and more specifically of its distribution, can be used to determine the inner variability of a given cluster of curves. Several papers (see Ramsay (1998), Ramsay & Li (1998), Ronn (2001), Gasser & Kneip (1995),Kneip & Gasser (1992)) focus on this specific model for many different applications in signal processing for biology. For example, in neuroscience, neurons emit randomly electrical pulses which are recorded by an electrode. Biologists, in many applications, are interested in the estimation of the inter-spike interval, that is, either the estimation of the durations of elapsed time between two electrical pulses, or the estimation of its distribution. As stated in Johnson (1996), it is interesting to model the observed electrical signal as the sample path of a renewal process. We can find in recent contributions (see Pouzat et al. (2004) and Delescluse & Pouzat (2006)) the usefulness of the ISI for spike sorting. In those applications, it is often easy to segment roughly the signal such that we retain only one pulse into each segment, however the realignment of the obtained curves are mainly based in either alignment of the main structural information of the curves (e.g. the zeros, as in Gasser & Kneip (1995); see Kneip & Gasser (1992) for a description of available tools to characterize curves structural information), either in the knowledge of the shape of a standard electrical pulse, as in Ramsay (1998) or Ramsay & Li (1998) (in that case, the problem is often called *template matching*, see Lewicki (1998) and references therein). However, both approaches are sensitive to the level of noise, and some recordings are sometimes too noisy to authorize a satisfactory realignment of the curves. We are therefore interested in finding a method of estimation robust enough in relation to the noise level.

1.2 The curve alignment and estimation from a statistical point of view

The problem of the estimation of the shift parameter θ has been investigated in numerous statistical publications, and this according to two different approaches. The main contributions is this topic focus on the case of a finite number of curves, and provide asymptotic results when the number of sample points tend to infinity. For example, Dalalyan et al. (2006) studied the case of two shifted curves, and proposed a penalized Maximum Likelihood Estimator approach, whereas Gamboa et al. (2007) suggested a semiparametric joint estimation procedure in the case of J curves (J being a fixed number). Some functional data analysis techniques have also been described in Ramsay (1998) and Ramsay & Li (1998), and the authors generally assume that the shift can be expressed as a warping function which has to be estimated. The methods described in Gasser & Kneip (1995) and Kneip & Gasser (1992) are based on template matching procedures; for example, the latter suggested to estimate the sets of the local maxima of s, and to align the different curves accordingly. It shall be noticed that template matching approaches give indeed good results when the curve s is regular enough and the noise variance σ is small; however, they fail when the common shape s shows higher variability or in the case of low SNR. In the case of a finite number of curves, Lavielle & Levy-Leduc

(2005) suggested a semiparametric approach for the estimation of the period of a laser signal, thus following the lead of Ritov (1989).
Another way of looking at the same model has also been proposed: instead of fixing the number of observed curves, it is interesting to make this number tend to infinity and to look at the obtained asymptotics. The first paper dealing with the estimation with a large number of curves can be found in Ritov (1989), and has received a larger attention in the last years. For example, Castillo (2006) and Castillo & Loubes (2007) propose to relate to the nonlinear inverse problem methods and derive estimates based on the works of Dalalyan et al. (2006), whereas Ronn (2001) suggested a nonparametric maximum likelihood estimator approach. More recently, Bigot et al. (2008) and Bigot & Gadat (2008) investigated the estimation of the shape s for an identical model, and suggested a wavelet approach which leads to a near-optimal (in the minimax sense) estimator of the shape. However, their assumption is that the shift distribution f_θ is fully known, thus enabling a deconvolution step in order to compute a nonparametric estimator of s.

1.3 Curve alignment for ECG data

In this contribution we focus more specifically on the analysis of ECG signals. In recordings of the heart electrical activity, at each cycle of contraction and release of the heart muscle, we get a characteristic P-wave, which depicts the depolarization of the atria, followed by a QRS-complex stemming from the depolarization of the ventricles and a T-wave corresponding to the repolarization of the heart muscle. We refer to (Guyton & Hall, 1996, Chapter 12) for an in-depth description of the heart cycle. A typical ECG signal is shown in Figure 1.
Different positions of the electrodes, transient conditions of the heart, as well as some malfunctions and several perturbations (baseline wander, power-line interference, additional electromyographic signal)Fotiadis et al. (2006); Sarnmo & Laguna (2006), can alter the shape of the signal. We aim to situations in which the heart electrical activity remains regular enough in the sense that the shape of each cycle remains approximately repetitive, so that after prior segmentation of our recording, the above model still holds. This preliminary segmentation can be done, for example, by taking segments around the easily identified maxima of the QRS-complex, as it can be found in Gasser & Kneip (1995). It is therefore of interest to estimate the shift parameters θ_m in (1.1). These estimates can be used afterwards for a more accurate estimation of the heart rate distribution. In normal cases, such estimation can be done accurately by using the common FDA method (e.g. by using only the above prior segmentations). However, when the activity of the heart is more irregular, a more precise alignment can be helpful. This happens for example in cases of cardiac arrhythmia, whose identification can be easier if the heart cycles are accurately aligned. Among interpretations deduced from ECG data, some are based on the so called "signal averaged ECG" (SAECG). SAECG is routinely used in clinics for late potential detection, various heart diseases and arrhythmia detections, as mentioned in Cain et al. (1996), and more specifically for ventricular tachycardia and late potential detection (see e.g. Nava et al. (2000), Rodriguez et al. (2000)). Analysis of the SAECG signal is usually performed by using standard wavelet decomposition Englund et al. (1998). As mentioned in the cited contributions, SAECG is simply a signal averaging technique used to improve the signal-to-noise ratio, since clinicians assume that the ECG waveform is invariant and that the background noise is uncorrelated. Moreover a timing reference (i.e. a landmark) is set at the peak R of the QRS complex (since it is easily detectable) allowing averaging without distortion. This method is to relate to Kneip & Gasser (1992), where the authors chose several landmarks instead of one. We argue that this is actually a crucial point since jitter of

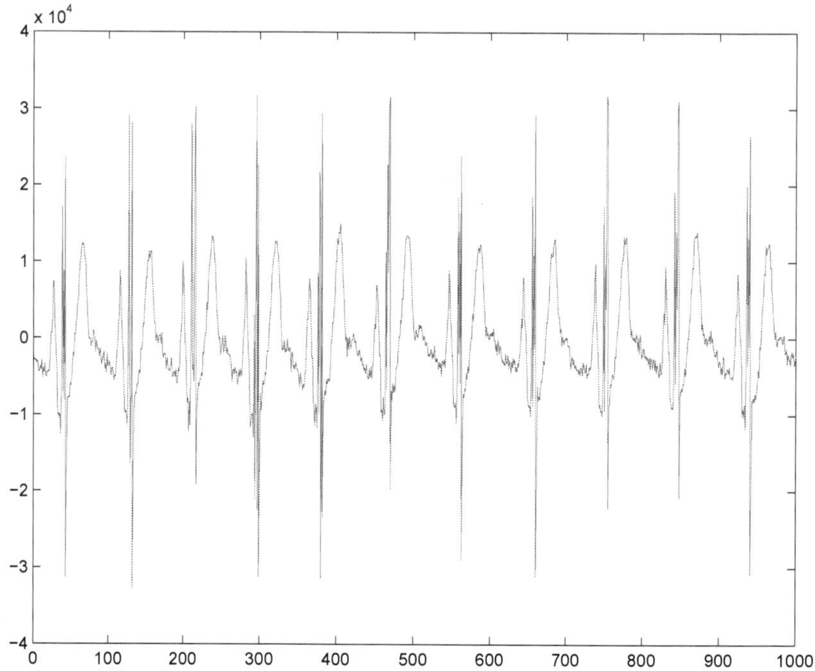

Fig. 1. Typical ECG signal of an healthy subject (arbitrary units).

this temporal reference would distort the resulting SAECG. The proposed method leads to an estimation of the mean cycle by averaging the segments after an alignment according to an estimated θ_j. Additional benefits for a more proper alignment can be found in many other measurements done by cardiologists.

1.4 Chapter organization

This chapter is organized as followed: Section 2 describes the derivation of the shift estimators and the density estimate. Roughly speaking, the estimation of the shifts is based on an M-estimation procedure with a cost function connected to the spectral density of the signal, and we suggest a plug-in estimation for the shift density; This leads to two different algorithms for curve alignment which are described in the end of the section. Some theoretical aspects are described in Section 3. Eventually, Section 4 is dedicated to results on simulations (in order to compare the performances of the two shifts algorithms) and real datasets, and discusses the influence of the standard perturbations which appear in ECG signal processing in the described algorithms.

2. Methodology

We present in this section the main assumptions used in the rest of the chapter and the derivation of the proposed estimator.

2.1 Main assumptions

We assume that after getting an electrical signal such as the one described in Figure 1, a preliminary segmentation is done so that we relate only to the model described in the introduction. We can therefore assume that we have observed sampled noisy curves on a finite time interval $[0, T]$. Each of these curves has being shifted randomly by some random variable θ. A typical curve is expressed in 1.1 and the number of curves is denoted by M. Assuming that the preliminary segmentation has been done efficiently and that each segmented curve has a whole single repetition of the signal, the following assumptions can be done:

(H-1) The distribution of the shift θ (denoted by f_θ) and the shape s both have finite support, respectively $[0, T_\theta]$ and $[0, T_s]$. We also assume that $s \neq 0$ on $[0, T_s]$ and that the derivative s' is bounded.

(H-2) $T_\theta + T_s < T$; that is, we assume that the shape is fully observed in the all the recorded curves.

As mentioned in Ritov (1989), this is equivalent to consider observations on a circle and setting $T = 2\pi$. Therefore, T will be chosen equal to 2π without any loss of generality. We also assume that there is no dependency between the shifts and the additional noise, that is:

(H-3) The random variables $\{\theta_l,\ l = 0 \dots M\}$ are independent and identically distributed, and are in addition independent from $\{\varepsilon_l,\ l = 0 \dots M\}$.

2.2 Description of the shift estimation procedure

In this section, we present a method for the semiparametric curve alignment. This method can be used as a first step for a nonparametric estimation of the shift density, by following the methodology described in Castillo (2006): first provide an estimate for the shifts, using in their example the methodology of Dalalyan et al. (2006), and then plug the obtained values into a standard kernel estimate. We propose an M-estimator to retrieve the shifts, in which the shape information is considered as a nuisance parameter and the shifts are estimated jointly. A similar approach appeared for example in Vimond (2008) leading to another estimator with good asymptotic properties. In another contribution, Gamboa et al. (2007) proposed a semiparametric method for the shifts, with applications to traffic forecasting. This M-estimate, based on a criterion function related to Fourier coefficients, has been shown to be consistent and asymptotically normal as the number of Fourier coefficients increases. However, in this contribution, we chose to focus on the asymptotic properties as the number of curves increases (of course, we also assume that the number of sampling points is large enough, since the M-estimation might lead to inconsistent results otherwise). This approach is explained by the fact that we have in practice little control on the sampling frequency, whereas obtaining a larger dataset of curves is easier.

Following the method of Castillo (2006), we propose to plug M estimates of shifts into a kernel estimate. Consequently, we need to estimate the sequence $\{\theta_l,\ l = 0 \dots M\}$. One important difference, compared to the previously cited works, is that we choose to estimate blocks of parameters jointly instead of one at a time. We therefore split our dataset of curves in N blocks of $K + 1$ curves each, as indicated in Figure 2. Observe that the curve y_0 is included in each block, since we wish to align each curve accordingly to y_0 ; consequently, it shall be assumed in the rest of the chapter that $\theta_0 = 0$. The interest of splitting the dataset of curves into blocks is double: it reduces the variance of the estimators of the shifts by estimating them jointly, and also provides smooth cost functions for the optimization procedure detailed in this section. Indeed, since the recorded signals are based on the same curve s, the average of the

Power Spectral Densities is close to the Power Spectral Density of the average curve provided the shifts are known and have been corrected. This idea will be the cornerstone of the M-estimation procedure proposed in this contribution. We thus estimate jointly the sequence of

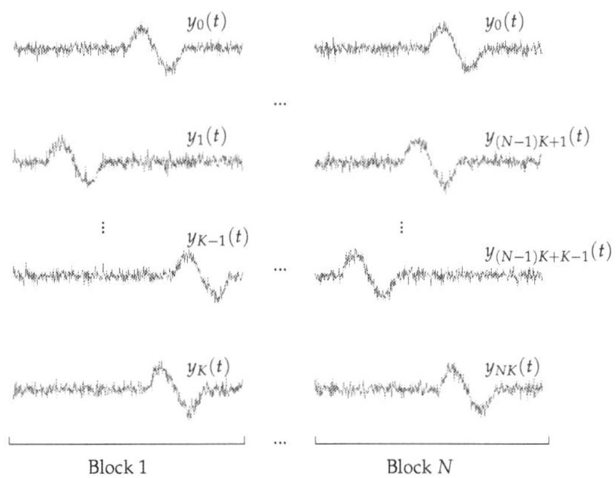

Fig. 2. Split of the curves dataset

vectors $\{\boldsymbol{\theta_m},\ m = 1 \dots N\}$, where for all integer m

$$\boldsymbol{\theta_m} \triangleq (\theta_{(m-1)K+1}, \dots, \theta_{m\,K}). \tag{2.1}$$

The estimation of $\{\boldsymbol{\theta_m},\ m = 1 \dots N\}$ is achieved by minimizing N cost functions, which are now detailed. Let us denote by S_y the squared modulus of the Fourier Transform of a given continuous curve y, that is for all ω:

$$S_y(\omega) \triangleq \left| \int_0^{2\pi} y(t)\mathrm{e}^{-i\omega t}\, dt \right|^2 .$$

This quantity is of interest, since it remains invariant by shifting. For each integer $m = 1 \dots N$, we define the weighted mean of K curves translated by some correction terms $\mathbf{ff_m} \triangleq (\alpha_{(m-1)K+1}, \dots, \alpha_{mK})$:

$$\bar{y}_m(t; \boldsymbol{\alpha_m}) \triangleq \frac{1}{K + \lambda(K)} \left(\lambda(K) y_0(t) + \sum_{k=(m-1)K+1}^{mK} y_k(t + \alpha_k) \right) . \tag{2.2}$$

where $\lambda(K)$ is a positive number which depends on K, and is introduced in order to give more importance to the reference curve y_0. In the rest of the paper, we shall write λ instead of $\lambda(K)$ in order to avoid cumbersome notations . We now consider the following function:

$$\frac{1}{M+1} \sum_{k=0}^{M} S_{y_k} - S_{\bar{y}_m} . \tag{2.3}$$

The function described in (2.3) represents the difference between the mean of the Power Spectral Densities and the Power Spectral Density of the mean curve. Observe that (2.3) tends to a constant if the curves used in (2.2) are well aligned, that is when $\boldsymbol{\alpha_m}$ is close to $\boldsymbol{\theta_m}$. Since the observed curves are sampled, we will approximate the integral of S_y by its Riemann sum, that is we shall use

$$\hat{S}_y(k) = \left| \frac{1}{n} \sum_{m=1}^{n} y(t_m) e^{-\frac{2i\pi mk}{n}} \right|^2$$

as an estimator of S_y; that is, the Discrete Fourier Transform (DFT) of a sampled curve $\{y(t_m),\ m = 1 \dots n\}$ will be used in practice instead of the actual Fourier transform of a curve y. The following cost criterion is then introduced and should be minimized in order to reshift all curves into the n-th block:

$$C_m(\boldsymbol{\alpha_m}) \triangleq \frac{1}{M+1} \sum_{k=0}^{M} \hat{S}_{y_k} - \hat{S}_{\bar{y}_m(\cdot;\boldsymbol{\alpha_m})} \cdot \tag{2.4}$$

The M-estimator of $\boldsymbol{\theta_m}$, denoted by $\hat{\boldsymbol{\theta}}_{\boldsymbol{m}}$, is therefore given by

$$\hat{\boldsymbol{\theta}}_{\boldsymbol{m}} \triangleq \operatorname{Arg\,min}_{\boldsymbol{\alpha}_m \in [0;2\pi]^K} \|C_m(\boldsymbol{\alpha_m})\|_2^2 \tag{2.5}$$

Remark 1. *It can be noticed that all blocks of $K+1$ curves have one curve y_0 in common. We chose to build the blocks of curves as described in order to address the problem of identifiability. Without this precaution, replacing the solution of (2.5) by $\hat{\boldsymbol{\theta}} + c + 2k\pi,\ k \in \mathbb{Z}$ and s by $s(\cdot - c)$ would let the cost criterion invariant. Adding curve y_0 as a referential allows to estimate $\boldsymbol{\theta} - \theta_0$, thus avoiding the non-identifiability of the model.*

In order to define the criterion function, we chose to split the set of observed curves in N blocks of $K+1$ curves. Indeed, this is not useful if the spectral information is fully known. However, since we observe noisy curves, and since we did not assume any knowledge on the spectral information, the functions S_y have to be estimated. A well known nonparametric estimator is the periodogram, which has been extensively studied (see e.g. Chonavel (2000) and references therein). This estimator is known to be asymptotically unbiased, but its variance does not tend to 0 in the general case; moreover, the pointwise estimation leads to uncorrelated estimated values, therefore the periodogram provides an estimate of the power spectral density of a process with many irregularities, regardless of the regularity of the true power spectrum. A good way to reduce the variance of this estimator is given by the averaged periodogram (or Bartlett's method), based on the mean of several periodogram estimators, thus the necessity of splitting the dataset. We refer to Chonavel (2000) for a more detailed description of this method.

It is interesting to compare the cost function introduced in (2.5) to the estimator introduced in Gamboa et al. (2007). In their contribution, they introduce additional weights to smooth the constrast function, for a fixed number of curves J. More precisely, they propose to estimate $\{\hat{\theta}_j,\ j = 1 \dots J\}$ the minimum of the following criterion function:

$$M_n(\alpha_1, \dots, \alpha_J) = \frac{1}{J} \sum_{j=1}^{J} \sum_{l=-\frac{n-1}{2}}^{\frac{n-1}{2}} \delta_l^2 \left| e^{i\alpha_j l} d_{jl} - \frac{1}{J} \sum_{m=1}^{J} e^{i\alpha_m l} d_{ml} \right|^2, \tag{2.6}$$

where $\{\delta_l,\ l \in \mathbb{Z}\}$ is real sequence such that $\sum_l \delta_l^2 < \infty$ and $\sum_l \delta_l^4 < \infty$, and d_{jl} is the l-th discrete Fourier coefficient associated to the j-th curve. This is to relate to Welch's method to reduce the variance of the periodogram, and makes sense since the number of curves in Gamboa et al. (2007) is assumed to be fixed. The asymptotics is then provided as the number of samples per curve tends to infinity. Similarly, the method proposed in Castillo (2006) leads to similar smoothing, since the shifting step is done by re-aligning one curve at a time, without using the fact that in the case of shift density estimation, the number of curves is assumed to be big. We argue that the method of averaged periodogram may be preferred for simplicity to weighted periodogram for variance reduction, since we only have one parameter to tune.

2.3 Description of the algorithmic procedures

2.3.1 Curve alignment with respect to a reference curve

Following the derivation of the M-estimator, the first algorithm for curve alignment is pretty straightforward: the dataset is split in blocks which include the reference curve and an optimization procedure (e.g. a conjugate gradient descent) is then performed on each block. The reference curve is by default the first one. The standard plug-in estimate is then used to estimate the density. The procedure is summarized in Algorithm 1.

Algorithm 1 Alignment procedure w.r.t. a reference curve **(A1)**

INPUTS: input curves $y_0, \dots, y_M$ where y_0 is the reference curve and parameters K, λ
OUTPUTS: Shift estimators - $\{\hat{\theta}_j, j = 1 \dots M\}$

Compute the average of the curves periodograms $\bar{S} = \dfrac{1}{M+1} \sum_{j=0}^{M} \hat{S}_{y_j}$.

Split the curve dataset into N blocks of $K+1$ curves, each of them including y_0.

for $m = 1 \dots N$ **do**

$$\bar{y}_m(t; \boldsymbol{\alpha_m}) \triangleq \frac{1}{K+\lambda} \left(\lambda y_0(t) + \sum_{j=(m-1)K+1}^{mK} y_j(t + \alpha_k) \right)$$

Define $C_m(\boldsymbol{\alpha_m}) \triangleq \bar{S} - \hat{S}_{\bar{y}_m(\cdot;\boldsymbol{\alpha_m})}$

Compute $\hat{\boldsymbol{\theta}}_m = \text{Arg}\min_{\boldsymbol{\alpha} \in [0;2\pi]^K} \|C_m(\boldsymbol{\alpha_m})\|_2^2$, where $\hat{\boldsymbol{\theta}}_m \triangleq \{\hat{\theta}_{(m-1)K+1}, \dots, \hat{\theta}_{mK}\}$

end for

Return $\{\hat{\theta}_j, j = 1 \dots M\}$

Algorithm **(A1)** is somehow problematic, since it involves the choice of a reference curve y_0 and giving it more importance.This may lead to a bad estimation of the shifts between curves, in the case of very noisy curves (when σ is for example of the same order of magnitude than the signal), since the noise is also magnified in the process. In order to address this issue, it is possible to use another algorithm described in 2.3.2.

2.3.2 A two-stage algorithm for curve alignment and shift density estimation

The two stage algorithm (denoted by **(A2)** in the rest of the chapter) can be described as follows: the dataset is split into N blocks of K curves, and the reference curve y_0 is not included in the blocks. The algorithm primarily performs alignment of the curves within each block. An average of the aligned curves of each block is calculated after this first step. The set of average curves is eventually aligned by similar means. The final shift estimator of each curve is the sum of the shift estimator of the curve among the curves of its block and the shift of the

averaged curve of that block; thus with the two stage algorithm the reference curve is unnecessary. This is the main advantage of a two-stage algorithm, since choosing a reference curve with possibly low SNR leads to significant alignment errors.
The two-stage procedure **(A2)** is summarized in Algorithm 2. In the first stage, estimation of the vector of shifts as in (2.1) is done for each block separately. Since we discard the reference curve y_0, the average of curves in blocks $m \in \{1,\ldots,N\}$ translated by some correction terms $\mathbf{ff_m} \triangleq (\alpha_{(m-1)K+1},\ldots,\alpha_{mK})$, is equal to

$$\bar{y}_m(t;\boldsymbol{\alpha_m}) \triangleq \frac{1}{K}\left(\sum_{k=(m-1)K+1}^{mK} y_k(t+\alpha_k)\right).$$

A cost function is then defined as it was for algorithm **(A1)**:

$$C_m(\boldsymbol{\alpha_m}) \triangleq \frac{1}{M+1}\sum_{k=0}^{M} \hat{S}_{y_k} - \hat{S}_{\bar{y}_m(\cdot;\boldsymbol{\alpha_m})}, \tag{2.7}$$

and the first stage ends by the computation of the M-estimator which minimizes the cost function defined in (2.7). At this stage we obtain the shift estimates $\{\tilde{\boldsymbol{\theta}}_{\boldsymbol{m}}, m = 1\ldots N\}$. At the second stage an average of the aligned curves within each block is calculated, and we align the averaged curves. That is, the average curve is

$$\bar{y}_m(t) \triangleq \frac{1}{K}\left(\sum_{k=(m-1)K+1}^{mK} y_k(t+\tilde{\theta}_k)\right),$$

and for a given correction term $\beta \triangleq (\beta_1,\ldots,\beta_N)$ the mean of translated average curves is

$$\bar{y}(t;\beta) \triangleq \frac{1}{N+1}\left(\sum_{k=1}^{N} \bar{y}_k(t+\beta_k)\right).$$

The second cost function for alignment between averaged curves is therefore

$$C(\beta) \triangleq \frac{1}{M+1}\sum_{k=0}^{M} \hat{S}_{y_k} - \hat{S}_{\bar{y}(\cdot;\beta)}$$

An M-estimator is now calculated for the shifts among blocks

$$\vartheta \triangleq \operatorname{Arg\,min}_{\beta\in[0;2\pi]^N} \|C(\beta)\|_2^2 .$$

Finally the estimator for the shift of y_l is the sum of the estimator obtained at the first stage of **(A2)** for this curve and the estimator obtained at the second stage for the averaged curve of the block y_l belongs to, that is:

$$(\hat{\boldsymbol{\theta}}_{\boldsymbol{m}})_k = \vartheta_m + (\tilde{\boldsymbol{\theta}}_{\boldsymbol{m}})_k, m = 1\ldots N, k = 1\ldots K.$$

Algorithm 2 Two-stage alignment procedure**(A2)**

INPUTS: input curves $y_1, \dots, y_M$ and size of each block K
OUTPUTS: Shift estimators - $\{\hat{\theta}_j, j = 1 \dots M\}$
Split the curve dataset into N blocks of K curves.
Compute the average of the curves periodograms $\bar{S} = \frac{1}{M}\sum_{j=1}^{M} \hat{S}_{y_j}$
for $m = 1 \dots N$ **do**
Define $\bar{y}_m(t; \boldsymbol{\alpha_m}) \triangleq \frac{1}{K}\left(\sum_{j=(m-1)K+1}^{mK} y_j(t + \alpha_j)\right)$
Define $C_m(\boldsymbol{\alpha_m}) \triangleq \bar{S} - \hat{S}_{\bar{y}_m(\cdot;\boldsymbol{\alpha_m})}$
Compute $\tilde{\boldsymbol{\theta}}_{\boldsymbol{m}} = \text{Arg}\min_{\boldsymbol{\alpha} \in [0;2\pi]^K} \|C_m(\boldsymbol{\alpha_m})\|_2^2$, where $\tilde{\boldsymbol{\theta}}_{\boldsymbol{m}} = \{\tilde{\theta}_{(m-1)K+1}, \dots, \tilde{\theta}_{mK}\}$
Compute $\bar{y}_m(t) \triangleq \frac{1}{K}\left(\sum_{k=(m-1)K+1}^{mK} y_k(t + \tilde{\theta}_k)\right)$
end for
Define $\bar{y}(t; \beta) \triangleq \frac{1}{N+1}\left(\sum_{j=1}^{N} \bar{y}_j(t + \beta_k)\right)$
Define $C(\beta) \triangleq \bar{S} - \hat{S}_{\bar{y}(\cdot;\beta)}$
Compute $\hat{\vartheta} = \text{Arg}\min_{\boldsymbol{\alpha} \in [0;2\pi]^K} \|C(\beta)\|_2^2$
for $m = 1 \dots N$ **do**
for $i = 1 \dots K$ **do**
$(\hat{\boldsymbol{\theta}}_{\boldsymbol{m}})_i = \hat{\vartheta}_m + (\tilde{\boldsymbol{\theta}}_{\boldsymbol{m}})_i$
end for
end for
Return $\hat{\boldsymbol{\theta}}_{\boldsymbol{1}}, \dots, \hat{\boldsymbol{\theta}}_{\boldsymbol{N}}$.

3. Theoretical properties

We provide in this section some theoretical results about the cost functions obtained in the latter section. In order to prove the efficiency of the method, it is indeed necessary to check that all cost functions have global minima at the actual shifts. We also have to verify that, provided the number of curves is large enough, the cost functions are smooth enough so that the optimization can be done efficiently. The presented results hold for the algorithm **(A1)**, though they can be easily extended to each stage of **(A2)**.

3.1 Expansion of a cost function

Recall that the total number of curves is $M = NK + 1$, where N is the number of blocks and K is the number of curves in each block. The first curve y_0 is a common reference curve for all blocks. We denote by $c_s(k)$ the discrete Fourier transform (DFT) of s taken at point k,

$$c_s(k) \triangleq \frac{1}{n}\sum_{m=1}^{n} s(t_m)e^{-\frac{2i\pi mk}{n}},$$

and by $f_{k,l}$ the DFT of y_l taken at point k:

$$f_{k,l} \triangleq \frac{1}{n} \sum_{m=1}^{n} y_l(t_m) e^{-\frac{2i\pi mk}{n}} .$$

Using this notation, relation (1.1) becomes in the Fourier domain for all $k = -\frac{n-1}{2} \dots \frac{n-1}{2}$ and $l = 0 \dots M$:

$$\begin{aligned} f_{k,l} &= e^{-ik\theta_l} \frac{1}{n} \sum_{m=1}^{n} s(t_m + \epsilon_l) e^{-\frac{2i\pi mk}{n}} + \frac{\sigma}{\sqrt{n}} (V_{k,l} + iW_{k,l}) \\ &= e^{-ik\theta_l} c_s(k) + O(\|s'\|_\infty n^{-1}) + \frac{\sigma}{\sqrt{n}} (V_{k,l} + iW_{k,l}) , \end{aligned} \tag{3.1}$$

where in the latter equation ϵ_l a constant such that $|\epsilon_l| < \pi n^{-1}$, and s' is the first derivative of s which we assumed to be bounded. This error term which results from the sampling operation is purely deterministic, and is further on neglected since it is not expected to induce shift estimation errors greater than the length of a single bin (i.e. n^{-1}). The sequences $\left\{V_{k,l},\ k = -\frac{n-1}{2} \dots \frac{n-1}{2}\right\}$ and $\left\{W_{k,l},\ k = -\frac{n-1}{2} \dots \frac{n-1}{2}\right\}$ are independent and identically distributed with same standard multivariate normal distribution $\mathcal{N}_n(0, I_n)$. We now compute the cost function C_m associated with block m:

$$\begin{aligned} \|C_m(\boldsymbol{\alpha_m})\|_2^2 &= \sum_{k=0}^{n-1} (A_M(k) - B_m(k, \boldsymbol{\theta_m}))^2 \\ &+ \sum_{k=0}^{n-1} (B_m(k, \boldsymbol{\theta_m}) - B_m(k, \boldsymbol{\alpha_m}))^2 \\ &+ 2 \sum_{k=0}^{n-1} (B_m(k, \boldsymbol{\theta_m}) - B_m(k, \boldsymbol{\alpha_m})) (A_M(k) - B_m(k, \boldsymbol{\theta_m})) , \end{aligned} \tag{3.2}$$

where $A_M(k)$ is the first term of the right hand side of (2.4) and $B_m(k, \boldsymbol{\alpha_m})$ is the second term of the right hand side of (2.4), both taken at point k. Each term of the latter equation is expanded separately. We get that

$$\begin{aligned} A_M(k) &= |c_s(k)|^2 + \frac{\sigma^2}{(M+1)n} \sum_{l=0}^{M} \left(V_{k,l}^2 + W_{k,l}^2\right) \\ &+ \frac{2\sigma \mathrm{Re}(c_s(k))}{(M+1)\sqrt{n}} \sum_{l=0}^{M} (V_{k,l} \cos(k\theta_l) - W_{k,l} \sin(k\theta_l)) \\ &- \frac{2\sigma \mathrm{Im}(c_s(k))}{(M+1)\sqrt{n}} \sum_{l=0}^{M} (V_{k,l} \sin(k\theta_l) + W_{k,l} \cos(k\theta_l)) . \end{aligned} \tag{3.3}$$

The last two terms of (3.3) converge almost surely to 0 as M tends to infinity, according to Assumption (H-3) and the law of large numbers. Moreover, the sum of the second term is distributed according to a χ^2 distribution with $M+1$ degrees of freedom. Thus, the term $A_M(k)$ tends to $|c_s(k)|^2 + 2n^{-1}\sigma^2$ as $M \to \infty$. We now focus on the expansion of the terms associated to $\|C_1(\boldsymbol{\alpha_1})\|_2^2$, since all other cost functions may be expanded in a similar manner up to a change of index. The first curve of each block is the reference curve, which is considered to be invariant and thus has a known associated shift $\alpha_0 = \theta_0 = 0$. We obtain

$$B_1(k, \boldsymbol{\alpha_1}) = \left| \frac{1}{\lambda + K} \left[\lambda (c_s(k) + \frac{\sigma}{\sqrt{n}} (V_{k,0} + \mathrm{i} W_{k,0})) + \sum_{l=1}^{K} \left(\mathrm{e}^{\mathrm{i}k(\alpha_l - \theta_l)} c_s(k) + \frac{\sigma}{\sqrt{n}} \mathrm{e}^{\mathrm{i}k\alpha_l} (V_{k,l} + \mathrm{i} W_{k,l}) \right) \right] \right|^2 ,$$

thus, if we define the sequence $\{\lambda_m, m = 0 \dots K\}$ such that $\lambda_0 \triangleq \lambda$ and $\lambda_m \triangleq 1$ otherwise:

$$\begin{aligned}
& B_1(k, \boldsymbol{\alpha_1}) \\
&= \frac{|c_s(k)|^2}{(\lambda+K)^2} \sum_{l,m=0}^{K} \lambda_l \lambda_m \mathrm{e}^{\mathrm{i}k(\alpha_l - \theta_l - \alpha_m + \theta_m)} \\
&+ \frac{\sigma^2}{n(\lambda+K)^2} \sum_{l,m=0}^{K} \lambda_l \lambda_m \{ \mathrm{e}^{\mathrm{i}k(\alpha_l - \alpha_m)} \times \\
&\quad [V_{k,l} V_{k,m} + W_{k,l} W_{k,m} + \mathrm{i}(V_{k,l} W_{k,m} - W_{k,l} V_{k,m})] \} \\
&+ \frac{\sigma c_s(k)}{\sqrt{n}(\lambda+K)^2} \sum_{l,m=0}^{K} \lambda_l \lambda_m \mathrm{e}^{\mathrm{i}(\alpha_l - \theta_l - \alpha_m)} (V_{k,m} - \mathrm{i} W_{k,m}) \\
&+ \frac{\sigma c_s^*(k)}{\sqrt{n}(\lambda+K)^2} \sum_{l,m=0}^{K} \lambda_l \lambda_m \mathrm{e}^{\mathrm{i}k(\theta_m + \alpha_l - \alpha_m)} (V_{k,l} + \mathrm{i} W_{k,l})
\end{aligned} \tag{3.4}$$

We now can study the behavior of the cost function, as the number of curves tend to infinity. The functional $\|C_1(\boldsymbol{\alpha_1})\|_2^2$ can be split into a noise-free part, that is a term without random variables V or W, and a random noisy part.

3.2 Decomposition of the cost function into a noise-free part and a noisy part

Recall that the noise-free part of $\|C_1(\boldsymbol{\alpha_1})\|_2^2$ neither depends on $\left\{ V_{k,l},\ k = -\frac{n-1}{2} \dots \frac{n-1}{2} \right\}$ nor $\left\{ W_{k,l},\ k = -\frac{n-1}{2} \dots \frac{n-1}{2} \right\}$), and is denoted further by $D_1(\boldsymbol{\alpha_1})$. This term is equal to:

$$D_1(\boldsymbol{\alpha_1}) = \sum_{k=0}^{n-1} |c_s(k)|^4 \left| \left| \frac{1}{K+\lambda} \sum_{m=0}^{K} \lambda_m \mathrm{e}^{\mathrm{i}k(\alpha_m - \theta_m)} \right|^2 - 1 \right|^2 \tag{3.5}$$

Details of the calculations can be seen in Trigano et al. (2009). Note that due to (3.5), D_1 has a unique global minimum which is attained when $\alpha_m = \theta_m$, for all $m = 1 \dots K$, that is the actual shift value. We now provide two quantitative results about algorithm **(A1)**. Their demonstrations can be also found in Trigano et al. (2009).

Proposition 1. *Let $\{\eta(K,\lambda),\ K \geq 0\}$ be a sequence such that $\eta(K,\lambda) \to 0$ as $K \to +\infty$ for all λ, and let α be a real positive number. Assume that for all $k = 0 \dots n-1$:*

$$\left| \frac{1}{(K+\lambda)} \sum_{m=0}^{K} \lambda_l \exp\left(\mathrm{i}k\left(\theta_m - \alpha_m\right)\right) \right| > 1 - \eta(K,\lambda),$$

then there exists two positive constants γ, and K_0 such that, for $K \geq K_0$, there is a constant $c(K,\lambda)$ such that the number of curves whose alignment error with respect to $\theta - c(K,\lambda)$ is bigger than $\eta(K,\lambda)^\alpha$, denoted by $\#\{m = 1 \ldots K : |\alpha_m - \theta_m - c(K,\lambda)| > \eta(K,\lambda)^\alpha\}$ is bounded as follows:

$$\#\{m : |\alpha_m - \theta_m - c(K,\lambda)| > \eta(K,\lambda)^\alpha\} \leq \gamma(K+\lambda)\eta(K,\lambda)^{1-2\alpha}$$

Proposition 1 can be intuitively interpreted as follows: provided the optimization procedure is effective enough, if the number of curves in each block is large enough, most curves will tend to align, but not necessarily with respect to the reference curve y_0. Consequently, the weighting factor λ is introduced in order to "force" all the curves in a block to align with respect to y_0, and the following proposition holds:

Proposition 2. *Assume that λ is an integer, and that*

$$\gamma\eta(K,\lambda)^{1-2\alpha} \leq \frac{\lambda}{K+\lambda}.$$

Then, under the assumption of Proposition 1, we get that $|c(K,\lambda)| < \eta(K,\lambda)^\alpha$

In other words, when choosing $\lambda(K)$ such that

$$\lambda(K) \to +\infty, \quad \frac{\lambda(K)}{K} \to 0 \text{ as } K \to \infty,$$

it is possible to obtain estimates very close to the actual shifts. In order to check that the optimization procedure can indeed be done effectively, we need the noisy part of the cost function to be small under the same conditions.
We now study the noisy part of $\|C_1(\boldsymbol{\alpha}_1)\|_2^2$. Recall that due to Equation (3.2), the noisy part of $\|C_1(\boldsymbol{\alpha}_1)\|_2^2$ stems from terms of the form $A_M(k) - B_1(k,\boldsymbol{\theta}_1)$ and $B_1(k,\boldsymbol{\theta}_1) - B_1(k,\boldsymbol{\alpha}_1)$. It is then possible to show the following proposition:

Proposition 3. *Assume that $K \to \infty$, $\lambda \to \infty$ and that $\lambda/K \to 0$, and let ε be any positive number. Let us denote by $R(k)$ the noisy part associated to $B_1(k,\boldsymbol{\theta}_1) - B_1(k,\boldsymbol{\alpha}_1)$; we get under these assumptions that*

$$A_M(k) - B_1(k,\boldsymbol{\theta}_1) = \frac{2\sigma^2}{n} + O_{\mathbb{P}}(n^{-1}K^{-1/2})$$

and

$$R(k) = O_{\mathbb{P}}(n^{-1}K^{-1/2+\varepsilon}) + O_{\mathbb{P}}(n^{-1})$$

Proposition 3 is of importance, since it shows that under the assumptions that each block contains a large number of curves, and that the weighting factor λ is important but negligible with respect to K, the cost function $\|C_1(\boldsymbol{\alpha}_1)\|^2$ reduces to $D_1(\boldsymbol{\alpha}_1)$ plus a constant term, which means that the minimum of $\|C_1(\boldsymbol{\alpha}_1)\|^2$ is with high probability close to the minimum of $D_1(\boldsymbol{\alpha}_1)$. In practice, a typical choice of the weighting parameter would be $\lambda = K^\beta$, with $0 < \beta < 1$, and verifies all the assumptions of the previous propositions.

4. Applications

We present in this section the results obtained by the presented algorithms, both for simulated and real data. In our simulations, the shape s is created according to a model used in neuroscience, namely the Hodgkin-Huxley model (see Johnson (1996) and references therein), and measure the performances of the shift alignment procedures by using the MISE (Mean Integrated Squared Error) criterion; more specifically, the shifts $\{\theta_m, m = 0 \dots M\}$ are drawn accordingly to a known probability distribution, then estimated by means of the previously described algorithms and, as a measure of performance, the MISE of the obtained plug-in density estimates proposed in the end of Section 2 is computed.
We first investigate the choice of the tuning parameters of the algorithm **(A1)**, that the number of curves in each block K and the weighting parameter λ, and discuss the influence of these values in the obtained density estimator, for different choices of σ^2. We then investigate the performances of the algorithms **(A1)** and **(A2)**, and how they compare to two standard methods:

- The alignment method with respect to the local extrema, as proposed in Gasser & Kneip (1995) (we denote this algorithm by **(A3)**, and
- a measure of fit based on the squared distance between the average pulse and the shifted pulses leading, which is often used by practitioners and is described in Silveman & Ramsay (2005) (this algorithm is denoted by **(A4)**.

It shall be seen that from the point of view of the shift density estimation, the algorithm **(A1)** outperforms the others.
We then apply the presented algorithms for the computation of the SAECG ; the real ECG data have been taken from the MIT-BIH database, and we present the obtained results for three different types of ECG recordings:

- recordings stemming from a normal heart
- recordings from a patient suffering of cardiac arrhythmia
- recordings of noise-stress tests, that is with a lower SNR.

4.1 Results on simulated data

4.1.1 Experimental protocol

Simulated data are created accordingly to the discrete model 1.1 and we compute the estimators for different values of the parameters K, λ and σ^2. For each curve, we sample in order to get 512 points equally spaced on the interval $[0; 2\pi]$. We make the experiment with s simulated according to the Hodgkin-Huxley model of a neural response. The shifts are drawn accordingly to a normal distribution $\mathcal{N}(0, 32^2)$, and $\theta_0 = 0$.

4.1.2 Results

We study the influence of the parameter K and λ empirically by providing the MISE of the plug-in density estimates for different values of K, λ and σ^2, with $N = 100$. In all these experiments, the value of the weighting parameter λ is chosen accordingly to K, that is $\lambda = K^{0.9}$. The numerical values of the MISE are provided for all algorithms in Table 1.
It shall be observed that the algorithm **(A1)** outperforms the other algorithms in most of the cases, except the case of extremely low SNR. We now present graphical results obtained by means of **(A1)**, **(A2)**, **(A3)** and **(A4)**, in the case of high SNR, which can be obtained for example

		K=10	K=20	K=30	K=50	K=100
$\sigma^2 = 0$	**(A1)**	0.0305	0.0228	0.0198	0.0153	0.0106
	(A2)	0.0407	0.0357	0.0372	0.0372	0.0375
	(A3)	0.0306	0.0234	0.0199	0.0156	0.0109
	(A4)	0.0316	0.0248	0.0227	0.0174	0.0136
$\sigma^2 = 10^{-4}$	**(A1)**	0.0312	0.0218	0.0183	0.0156	0.0121
	(A2)	0.0399	0.0383	0.0362	0.0364	0.0364
	(A3)	0.0325	0.0232	0.0212	0.0183	0.0158
	(A4)	0.0322	0.0219	0.0192	0.0168	0.0126
$\sigma^2 = 10^{-2}$	**(A1)**	0.0296	0.0218	0.0172	0.0143	0.0120
	(A2)	0.0410	0.0383	0.0384	0.0371	0.0355
	(A3)	0.0306	0.0232	0.0192	0.0172	0.0143
	(A4)	0.0303	0.0219	0.0182	0.0155	0.0125
$\sigma^2 = 1$	**(A1)**	0.0326	0.0274	0.0248	0.0255	0.0288
	(A2)	0.0460	0.0407	0.0374	0.0381	0.0395
	(A3)	0.0547	0.0806	0.0514	0.0553	0.0741
	(A4)	0.0510	0.0450	0.0414	0.0393	0.0370

Table 1. MISE of the density estimates obtained for different values of the noise variance σ^2 and number of curves in each block K, for a fixed value of $\lambda = K^{0.9}$

by choosing $\sigma = 0.01$, and in the case of low SNR, which can be obtained by fixing $\sigma = 0.1$. Two typical curves are presented in both cases in figure (3).

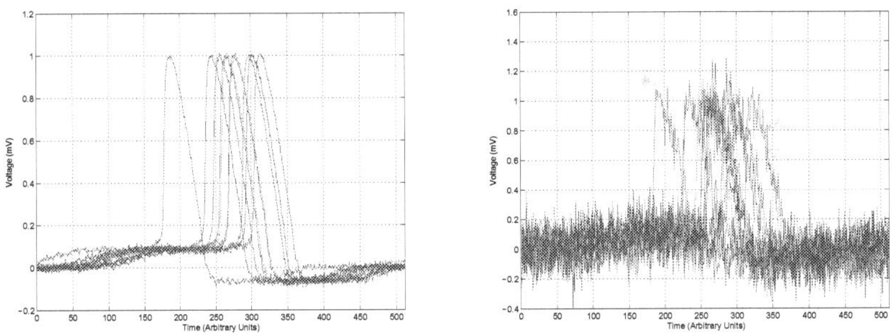

(a) High SNR ($\sigma^2 = 10^{-6}$) (b) Low SNR ($\sigma^2 = 10^{-2}$)

Fig. 3. Ten typical curves for different SNR values.

Results are presented for the four algorithms and for these specific choices of σ in figure (4) and figure(5).

Eventually, a graphical comparison of the actual shift distribution and its plug-in density estimate is presented in figure (6), and the results with a weighting parameter λ too small is given in figure (7).

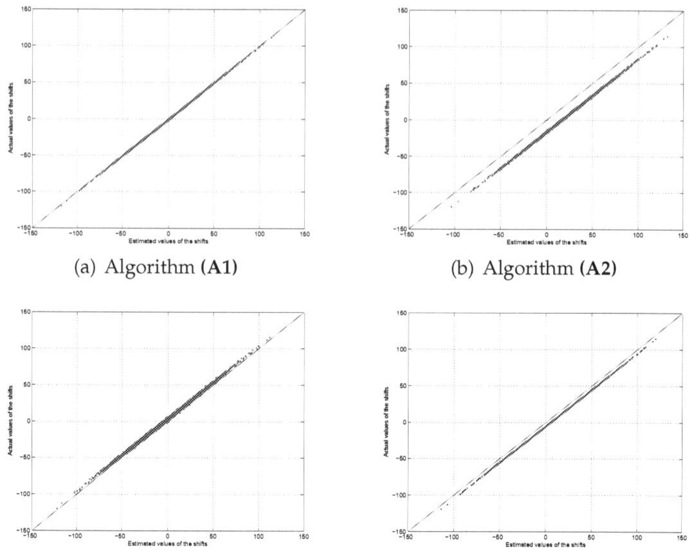

(a) Algorithm **(A1)** (b) Algorithm **(A2)**

(c) Algorithm **(A3)** (d) Algorithm **(A4)**

Fig. 4. Results of the curve alignment procedures for $K = 30$, $N = 100$, $\lambda = K^{0.9}$, $\sigma^2 = 10^{-6}$.

4.1.3 Discussion

The graph obtained in figure (7) well illustrates Proposition 1. In this graph, we observe that in each separate block the curves are well aligned, since for each block plotting the actual values of the shifts versus their estimated values gives lines with slope 1. However, they do not align with respect to the location of the reference curve, due to a weighting parameter λ too small. Taking a larger λ allows to address this problem, as it can be seen in figure (4(a)) and figure (5(a)). From the obtained results of Table 1, it can be observed that the algorithm **(A1)** outperforms the others, from the point of view of density estimation. This algorithm is also robust to the noise level σ, as it can be seen from figure (4(a)), figure (5(a)) and the results displayed in Trigano et al. (2008).

Not surprisingly, the algorithm **(A2)** is well suited for alignment (e.g. in order to compute the average signal), but is less adapted for density estimation, since the curves do not align accordingly to the reference curve, as stated in Proposition 1. This means that, provided the expectation of f_θ is known, the algorithm **(A2)** would give results close to **(A1)**. The two-step algorithm should be preferred for example in the case of very low SNR, where each curve is very noisy so that there is no good choice available for a reference curve y_0. Indeed, when comparing the results of **(A1)** and **(A2)** for $\sigma^2 = 0.01$ and $\sigma^2 = 1$, we can see that the MISE degradation is less important for **(A2)** than for **(A1)**.

The method described in Gasser & Kneip (1995), from which the algorithm **(A3)** is derived, is based on the features of the curves s, and is less effective when the noise level is important. This can be observed from figure (5(d)) and the results given in Table 1 for the highest values of σ^2. This is predictable, since any method which relies on a preliminary smoothing of

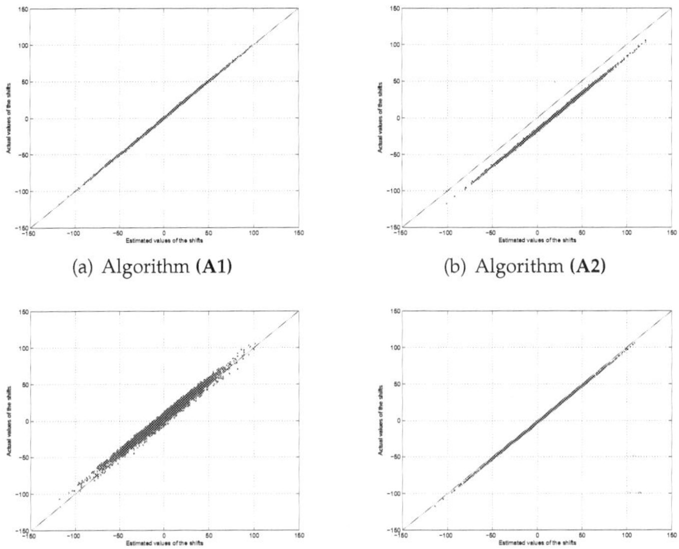

(a) Algorithm **(A1)** (b) Algorithm **(A2)**

(c) Algorithm **(A3)** (d) Algorithm **(A4)**

Fig. 5. Results of the curve alignment procedures for $K = 30$, $N = 100$, $\lambda = K^{0.9}$, $\sigma^2 = 10^{-2}$.

the curves and an alignment with respect to the maxima of the curve would lead to a more important error than a semiparametric approach if the SNR is low. However, **(A3)** competes relatively well with **(A1)** in the case of high SNR, and may be preferred for simplicity in that case. Nevertheless, since **(A1)** performs an efficient alignment both for high and low values of σ^2, since this parameter introduces only a constant term in the cost functions C_n, which can be omitted in the optimization procedure. We may argue that the main advantage of **(A1)** lies in its generality, and that it should be used for example when the SNR is unknown.

Eventually, it can be observed that **(A4)**, which relates to FDA methods described in Silveman & Ramsay (2005), is relatively efficient, provided the total number of curves is large enough. The MISE results as well as figures (4(c)) and (5(c)) indicate that this method is well fitted for curve alignment. However, a degradation of the performances can be noticed for the lowest values of K. This makes intuitively sense, since a small value of K indicates that only a few curves are used to compute the average signal at each iteration of **(A4)**. Therefore, the alignment w.r.t. the average signal yields a larger MISE. This appears e.g. in figure (4(c)), where a slight bias between the actual shifts and their estimators can be observed. Consequently, the algorithm **(A4)** gives results quite similar to **(A1)**, but requires one block of $N \times K$ curves to compare well to **(A1)**, which leads to significantly longer computational times.

From the theoretical point of view, the good performances of **(A1-2)** with respect to **(A3-4)** can be explained by the study of another M-estimate proposed in Gamboa et al. (2007) for curve alignment, which gives further insight in the comparison with the state-of-the-art method. Indeed, (Gamboa et al., 2007, Theorem 2.1) shows that a statistically consistent alignment can be obtained only when filtering the curves and aligning the low-frequency information.

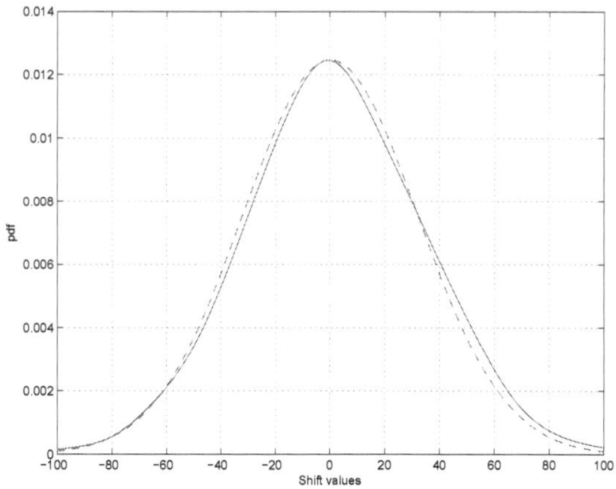

Fig. 6. Comparison between the true shift density (dotted red) and its plug-in estimate (blue).

Therefore, an approach based on the spectral information is more susceptible to achieve good alignment by comparison to the method of Silveman & Ramsay (2005).

4.2 Results on real ECG data

We now wish to compare our method to the state-of-the-art for the alignment of heart cycles, in order to estimate the average signal. We provide the study of the signal presented in figure (1), which was obtained from the MIT-BIH database, and is a recorded signal stemming from both a healthy (figure (8) and (10)) and arrhythmic heart (figure (12)).

4.2.1 Experimental protocol

In order to obtain a series of heart cycles, we first make a preliminary segmentation using the method of Gasser & Kneip (1995), namely alignment according to the local maxima of the heart cycle. We then apply our method, and compare it to the alignment obtained by comparing the mean curve to a shifted curve one at a time. We took in this example $K = 30$ and $\lambda = 10$ for 3 iterations.

4.2.2 Results

We present on the following figures results obtained by algorithms **(A1-4)** on three different data sets from the MIT-BIH database. Figure (8) show results obtained on (very) noisy ECG. At first sight, all four methods seem to perform equally well regarding P and T waves. However, zoomed QRS patterns on figure (9) show that alignment procedures **(A1)** and **(A2)** give better results. Indeed, the black mean curve is smoother (jitter is reduced) than the one obtained with the two other methods, reflecting that alignment is achieved in a better way. On the contrary, mean curves obtained by algorithms **(A3)** and **(A4)** are less satisfactory since they are less temporally concentrated ; Moreover, the average curves obtained in that case show several local maxima, which is far from the standard shape of the QRS complex (indeed, we are expecting to find one single mode in this part of the signal, as given by the algorithms **(A1)** and **(A2)**.

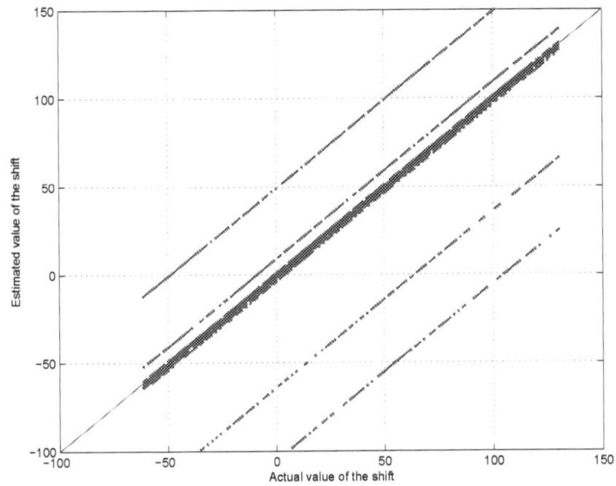

Fig. 7. Results of the shift estimation **(A1)** for $K = 200$, $N = 30$, $\lambda = 10$, $\sigma^2 = 10^{-1}$.

Figure (10) show results obtained with actual power-line interference and baseline shifting. On this data set, algorithm **(A2)** is outperformed by the 3 others as revealed by figure (11(b)). In this case, **(A3)** and **(A4)** perform well since maxima are. Note that **(A1)** mean curve is slightly smoother than **(A3)** and **(A4)** ones.

Figure (12) and (13) show alignment of an arrhythmic data set. These data are typically encountered in routine clinical use and contain ECG with very various waveforms and artifacts. **(A3-A4)** clearly achieve alignment according to maxima. Jitter is high in this case, since the shape of the curve can significantly vary from one pulse to another. Consequently, the mean curve does not reflect this variability. Such behavior from **(A3-A4)** could be expected, since one underlying assumption is that the curve shape s is made of peaked common noise-free patterns. By contrast, **(A1-A2)** achieve better alignment since the resulting jitter is comparatively reduced and the corresponding mean curve smoother. The shape variability is intrinsically taken into account by the way of periodogram coefficients.

4.3 Discussion

Results presented in the previous paragraph show clearly different behaviors of alignment procedure. Algorithms **(A1)** and **(A2)** fully take into account all frequencies composing curves including the different noise contributions, such as low frequencies representing baseline variations or more localized ones such as power-line interference. By contrast, **(A3)** and **(A4)** are based on curve maxima meaning only high frequencies. When these maxima are perturbed by noise or distorted by intrinsic curve change (such as arrhythmic ECG), the corresponding mean curve does not reflects such perturbations. We believe that it makes our periodogram-based alignment methods more robust to the classical ECG perturbations.

5. Conclusion

In this contribution several methods of curve alignment for repeated events were introduced and investigated; this led to plug-in estimate of the density of elapsed times between events. Their performances were presented both on simulations and real ECG, and compared to the

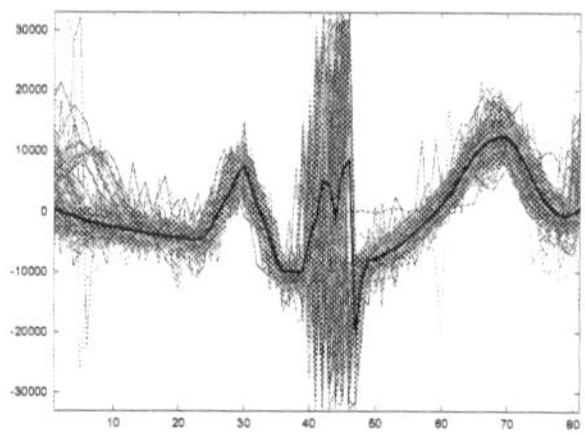

(a) Algorithm **(A1)**

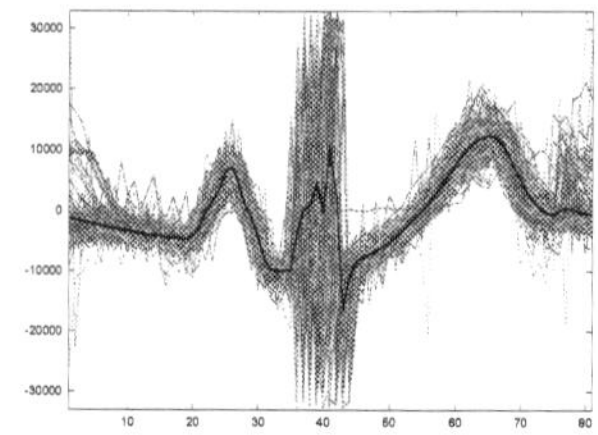

(b) Algorithm **(A2)**

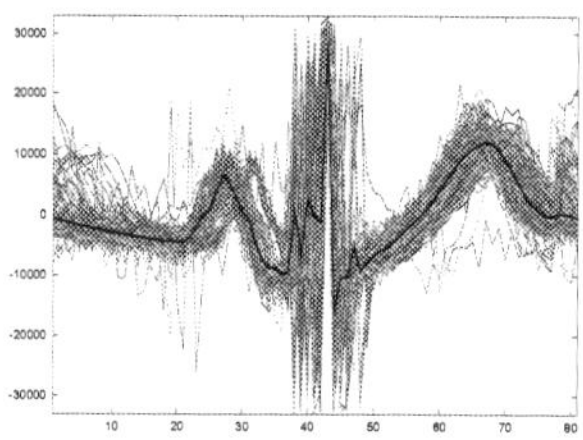

(c) Algorithm **(A3)**

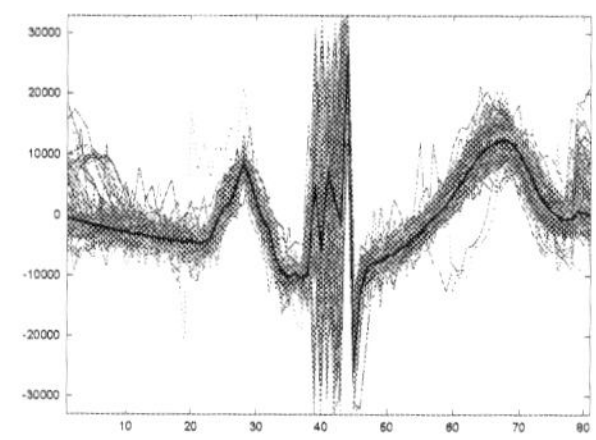

(d) Algorithm **(A4)**

Fig. 8. Results of the curve alignment procedures on real ECG for $K = 30$, $N = 10$, $\lambda = K^{0.9}$.

well-known shift correction methods based on the alignment with respect to the local extrema (which is the standard method used in the ECG signal processing framework). It is shown that the algorithms which are based on a semiparametric approach outperform the methods based on an FDA approach. The suggested algorithms provides excellent results, whether the SNR is high or low. On real ECG data, the proposed algorithms gives good results for the computations of the SAECG, and seem according to the experiments extremely robust to distortions such as power-line interference, baseline wander or variability of the pulse shapes. Further results on the rates of convergences of the density estimator and the applicability of the method for the detection of heart diseases should appear in future contributions.

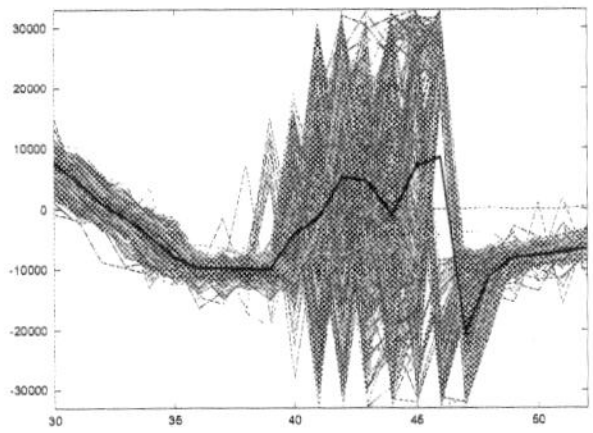

(a) Algorithm **(A1)**

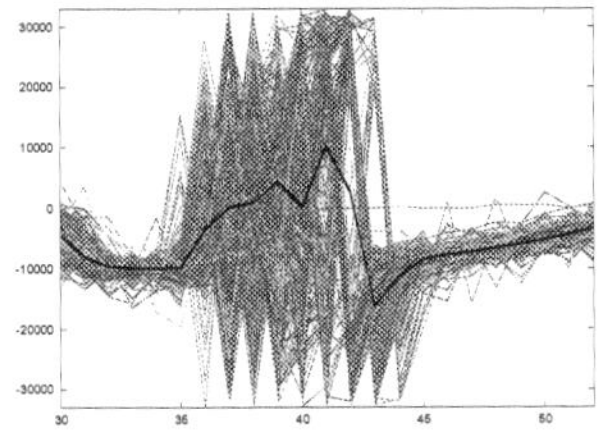

(b) Algorithm **(A2)**

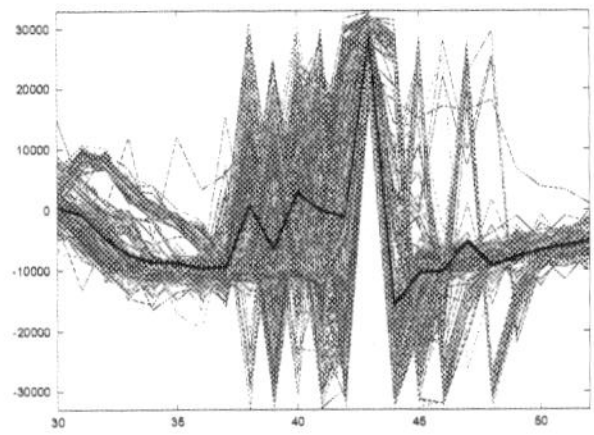

(c) Algorithm **(A3)**

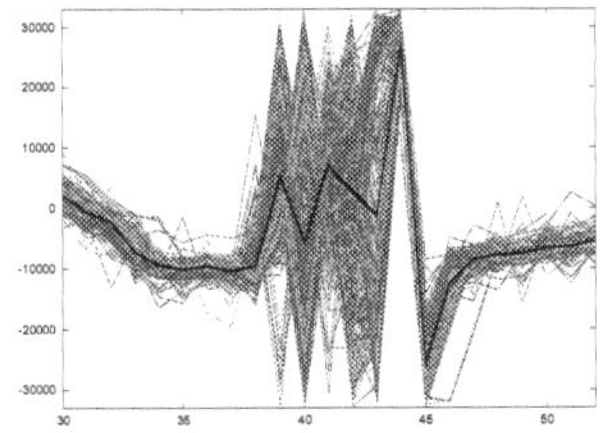

(d) Algorithm **(A4)**

Fig. 9. Zoom on figure (8) on each aligned QRS region.

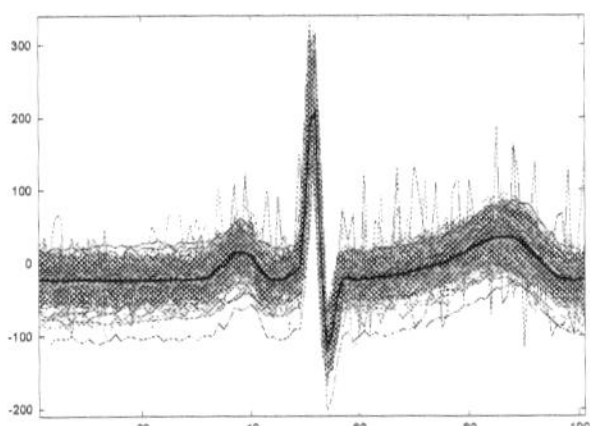

(a) Algorithm **(A1)**

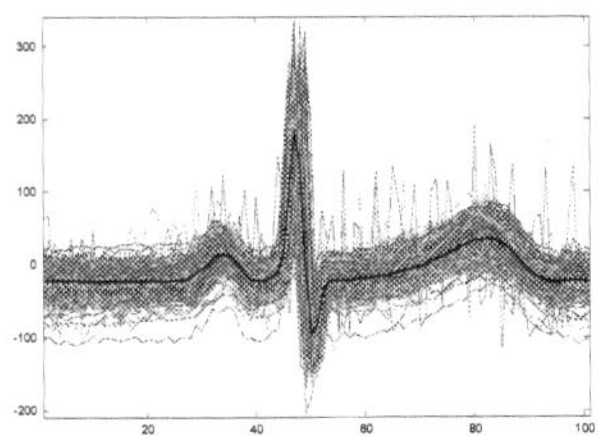

(b) Algorithm **(A2)**

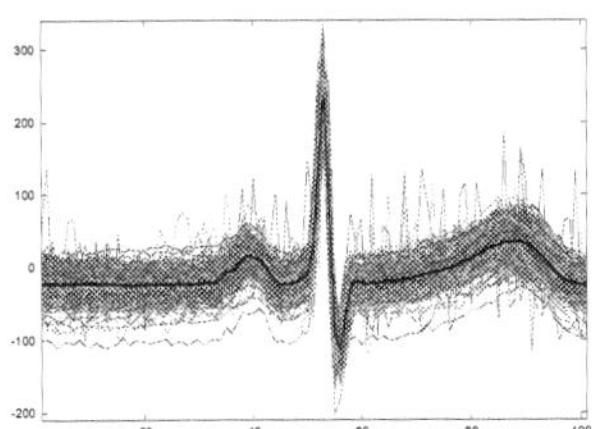

(c) Algorithm **(A3)**

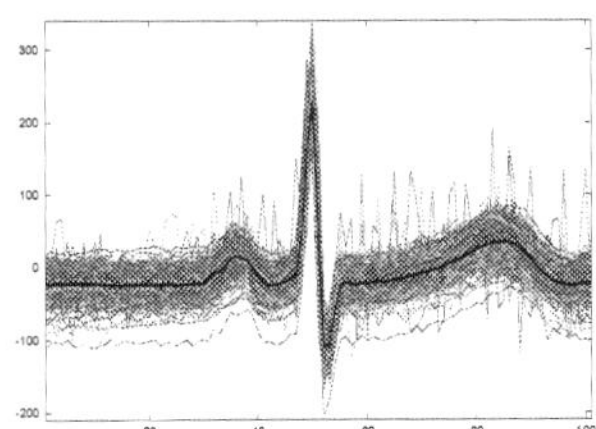

(d) Algorithm **(A4)**

Fig. 10. Results of the curve alignment procedures on real ECG for $K = 30$, $N = 10$, $\lambda = K^{0.9}$.

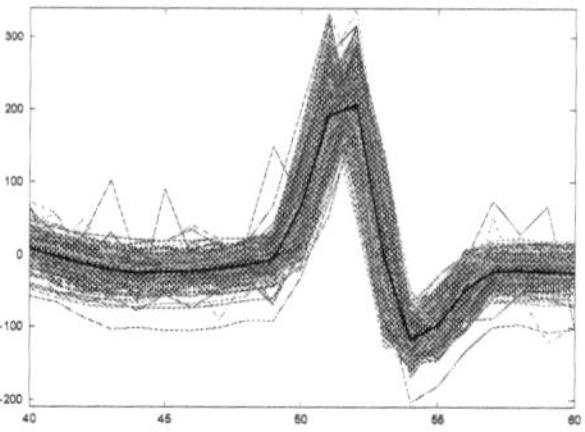

(a) Algorithm **(A1)**

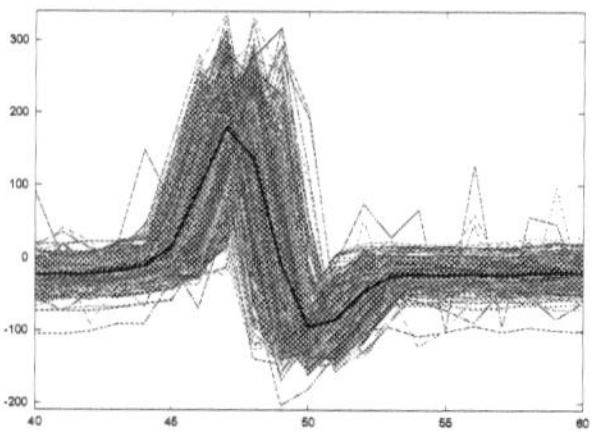

(b) Algorithm **(A2)**

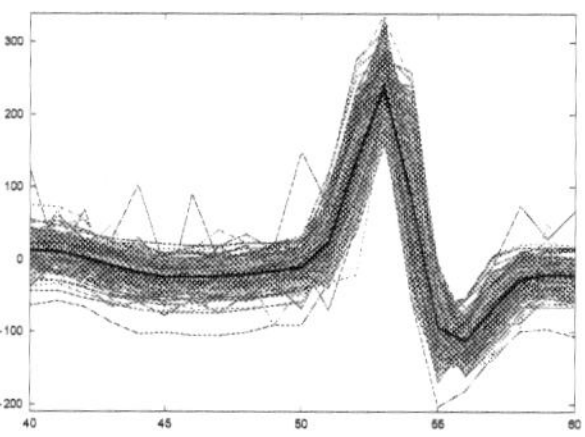

(c) Algorithm **(A3)**

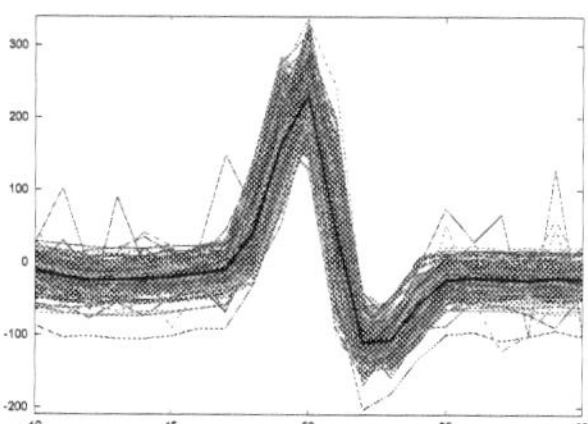

(d) Algorithm **(A4)**

Fig. 11. Zoom of figure (10) on each aligned QRS region.

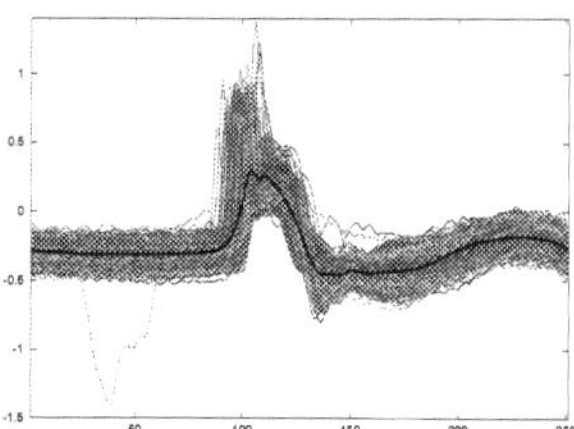

(a) Algorithm **(A1)**

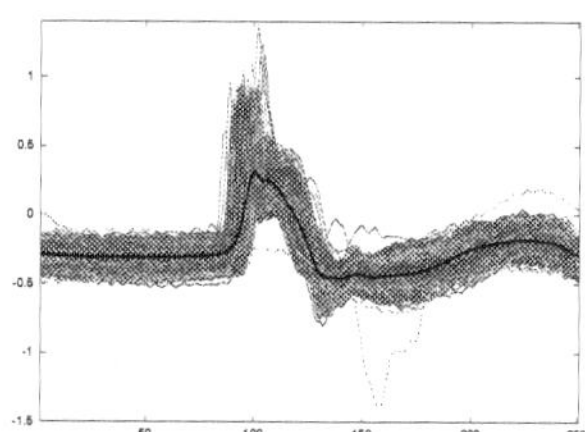

(b) Algorithm **(A2)**

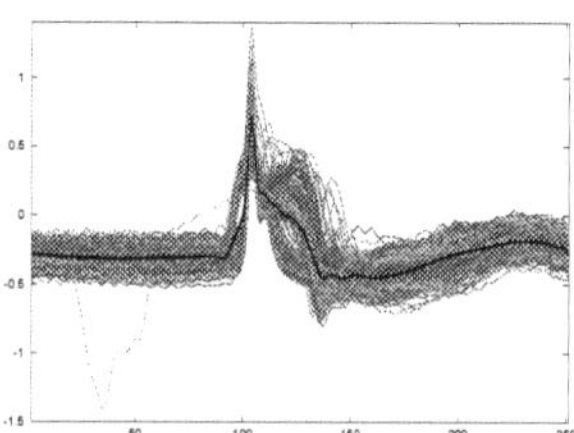

(c) Algorithm **(A3)**

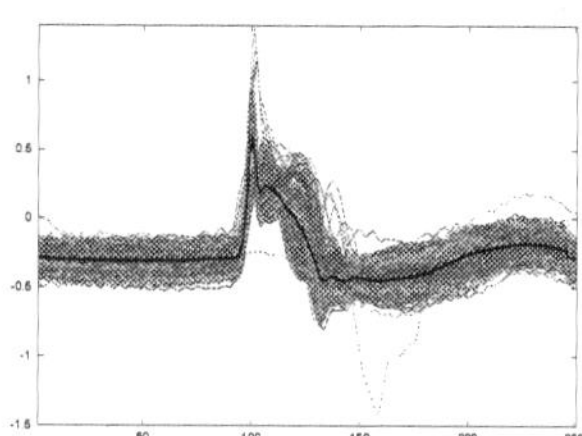

(d) Algorithm **(A4)**

Fig. 12. Results of the curve alignment procedures on real arrhythmic ECG for $K = 30$, $N = 10$, $\lambda = K^{0.9}$.

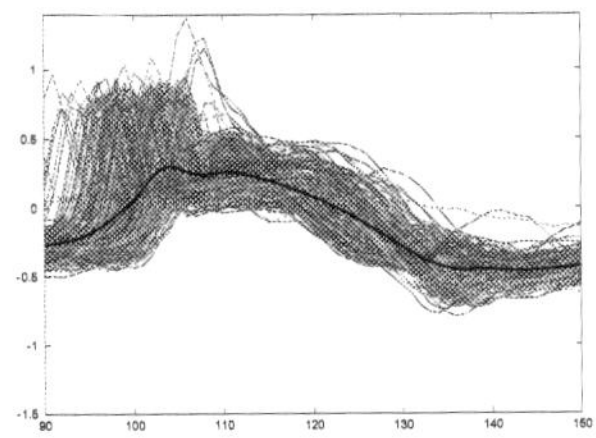

(a) Algorithm **(A1)**

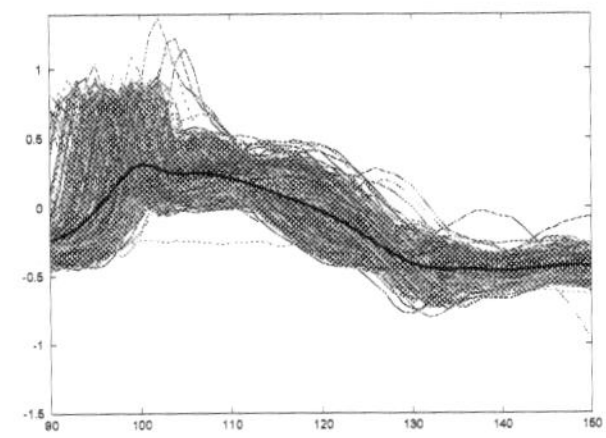

(b) Algorithm **(A2)**

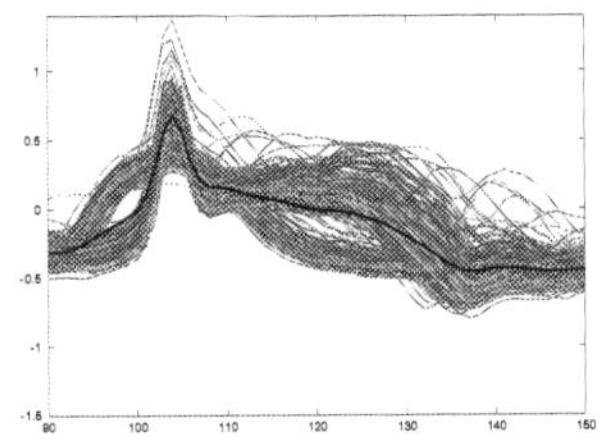

(c) Algorithm **(A3)**

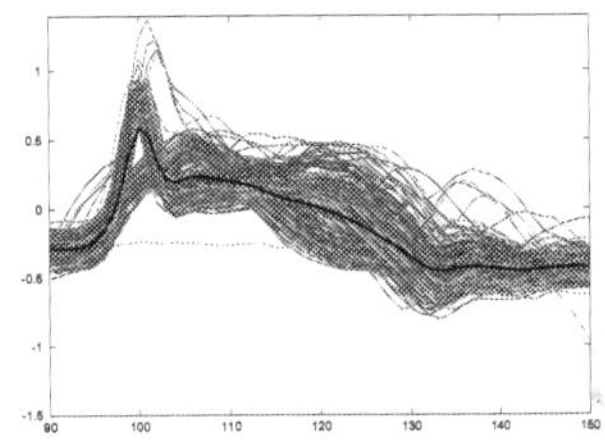

(d) Algorithm **(A4)**

Fig. 13. Zoom on figure (12) on each aligned QRS region.

6. References

Bigot, J. & Gadat, S. (2008). An Inverse Problem Point of View for Adaptive Estimation in a Shifted Curves Model, *Submitted* .

Bigot, J., Loubes, J.-M. & Vimond, M. (2008). Semiparametric Eestimation of Shifts on Compact Lie Groups for Image Registration, *Submitted* .

Cain, M., Anderso, J., Arnsdorf, M., Mason, J., Scheinman, M. & Waldo, A. (1996). Signal-Averaged Electrocardiography, *Journal of American College of Cardiology* **27**(1): 238–249.

Castillo, I. (2006). *Estimation semi-paramétrique à l'ordre 2 et applications*, PhD thesis, Université Paris XI.

Castillo, I. & Loubes, J.-M. (2007). Estimation of the Law of Random Shifts Deformation, *submitted to Pattern Analysis, Statistical Modelling and Computational Learning* .

Chonavel, T. (2000). *Statistical Signal Processing*, Springer.

Dalalyan, A. S., Golubev, G. K. & Tsybakov, A. B. (2006). Penalized maximum likelihood and semiparametric second-order efficiency, *Ann. Statist.* **34**(1): 169–201.

Delescluse, M. & Pouzat, C. (2006). Efficient Spike Sorting of Multi-State Neurons Using Inter-Spike Intervals Information, *Technical report*, CNRS UMR 8118.

Englund, A., Hnatkova, K., Kulakowski, P., Elliot, P., McKenna, W. & Malik, M. (1998). Wavelet decomposition analysis of the signal averaged electrocardiogram used for risk stratification of patients with hypertrophic cardiomyopathy, *European Heart Journal* **19**: 1383–1390.

Ferraty, F. & Vieu, P. (2006). *Nonparametric Functional Data Analysis: Theory and Practice*, Springer series in Statistics, 1 edn, Springer.

Fotiadis, D., Likas, A., Michalis, L. & Papaloukas, C. (2006). *Encyclopedia of Biomedical Engineering*, Wiley, chapter Electrocardiogram (ECG): (Automated Diagnosis).

Gamboa, F., Loubes, J.-M. & Maza, E. (2007). Semiparametric Estimation of Shifts Between Curves, *Elec. Journ. of Statist.* **1**: 616–640.

Gasser, T. & Kneip, A. (1995). Searching for structure in curve sample, *J. Am. Statist. Ass.* **90**(432): 1179–1188.

Guyton, A. & Hall, J. E. (1996). *Textbook of Medical Physiology*, 9 edn, W. H. Saunders.

Johnson, D. H. (1996). Point process models of single-neuron discharges, *Journal of Computational Neuroscience* **3**(4): 275–299.

Kneip, A. & Gasser, T. (1992). Statistical tools to analyze data representing a sample of curves, *Ann. Statist.* **20**(3): 1266–1305.

Lavielle, M. & Levy-Leduc, C. (2005). Semiparametric estimation of the frequency of unknown periodic functions and its application to laser vibrometry signals, *IEEE Trans. Signal Processing* **53**(7): 2306– 2314.

Lewicki, M. S. (1998). A Review of Methods for Spike Sorting: the Detection and Classification of Neural Action Potentials., *Network: Computation in Neural Systems* **9**(4): R53–R78.

Nava, A., Folino, F., Bauce, B., Turrini, P., Buja, G., Daliento, L. & Thiene, G. (2000). Signal-averaged electrocardiogram in patients with arrythmogenic right ventricular cardiomyopathy and ventricular arrythmias, *European Heart Journal* **21**: 58–65.

Pouzat, C., Delescluse, M., Viot, P. & Diebolt, J. (2004). Improved Spike-Sorting by Modeling Firing Statistics and Burst-Dependent Spike Amplitude Attenuation: a Markov Chain Monte Carlo Approach, *Journal of Neurophysiology* **91**: 2910–2928.

Ramsay, J. O. (1998). Estimating smooth monotone functions, *J. R. Statist. Soc. B* **60**(2): 365–375.

Ramsay, J. O. & Li, X. (1998). Curve registration, *J. R. Statist. Soc. B* **60**(2): 351–363.

Ritov, Y. (1989). Estimating a Signal with Noisy Nuisance Parameters, *Biometrika* **76**(1): 31–37.

Rodriguez, B., Jané, R. & Brooks, D. (2000). Ventricular Tachycardia Risk Detection using Wavelet Decompostion of the Signal Averaged ecg, *Computers in Cardiology* **27**: 731–734.

Ronn, B. (2001). Nonparametric Maximum Likelihood Estimation for Shifted Curves, *J. R. Statist. Soc. B* **63**(2): 243–259.

Sarnmo, L. & Laguna, P. (2006). *Encyclopedia of Biomedical Engineering*, Wiley, chapter Electrocardiogram (ECG)Signal Processing.

Silveman, B. W. & Ramsay, J. (2005). *Functional Data Analysis*, Springer Series in Statistics, 2 edn, Springer.

Trigano, T., Isserles, U. & Ritov, Y. (2008). Semiparametric shift estimation for alignment of ecg data, *Proceedings of the EUSIPCO Signal Processing Conference.*

Trigano, T., Isserles, U. & Ritov, Y. (2009). Semiparametric curve alignment and shift density estimation with applications to ecg data, *in revision for IEEE Transactions in Signal Processing* **arXiV preprint**: 0807.1271v3.

Vimond, M. (2008). Efficient Estimation for Homothetic Shifted Regression Models, *To appear in Annals of Statistics* .

12

Spatial prediction in the H.264/AVC FRExt coder and its optimization

Simone Milani
Dept. of Information Engineering, University of Padova
Italy

1. Introduction

Intra-only video coding is a widely used coding method in professional and surveillance video applications. This fact is partly due to its ease of editing and partly due to the significant amount of computational complexity required by motion estimation, which results hard to adopt in real-time video systems. In the H.264/AVC standardization process (Richardson, 2003) the compression performance of Intra coding was significantly improved by the adoption of spatial prediction in Intra frames, which have permitted the H.264/AVC coder to obtain a higher compression gain with respect to the previous coding standards, like JPEG2000 (Cho et al., 2007). The pixels of the current block are predicted using the reconstructed pixels of neighboring blocks interpolated along different orientations, which result closely related to the characteristics of the image correlation (Cappellari and Mian, 2004). In the first version of the H.264/AVC standard (Joint Video Team, 2002), the spatial prediction is limited to either blocks of 4×4 pixels or whole macroblocks (MBs) of 16×16 pixels. In the FRExt extension of the standard (Joint Video Team, 2004), blocks of 8×8 pixels are considered too. As a consequence, the computational complexity of an exhaustive rate-distortion optimization significantly increases because of the number of different partitioning modes and prediction directions. In order to overcome this problem, a wide variety of complexity reduction strategies, together with the introduction of novel hardware accelerators, have been proposed in literature.

Pan et al. (2005) propose a fast Intra prediction algorithm that extracts the image features using Sobel edge operators and chooses the predictor according to their statistics. In a similar way, the approaches by Pan et al. (2004) and by Ryu and Kim (2007) extract the directional features of each frame and use them to estimate the most probable prediction modes. The solutions proposed by Xin et al. (2004) and by Jeong and Kwon (2007) evaluate the distortion produced by prediction in the transform domain, while (Kim et al., 2006a) suggest extracting jointly the features of each block from both pixels and transform coefficients. In addition, temporal correlation existing between adjacent frames can be used too, as it is shown by Xin and Vetro (2006).

Many approaches employ early-termination decision in order to reduce the amount of computation (Lorás and Amiel, 2005). This makes the computational complexity significantly vary according to the processed video sequence (see the strategy proposed by Yong-dong et al. (2004) as an example where the relative reduction of coding time varies from 40% to 70%), and therefore, an *a priori* estimation of the resulting cost is not possible. At the same time, the

performance of the algorithm varies according to the coded sequence like in the case of the approach by Kalva and Christodoulou (2007) where a machine learning algorithm is used to select the best prediction mode among a reduced set of candidates.
With respect to these methods, the design of a complexity reduction strategy that permits controlling the amount of required computation provides several advantages, such as

- the possibility of adapting the algorithm to devices with different computational capabilities and power supply;
- an accurate estimation of the autonomy of battery-powered coding devices;
- the possibility of enabling power saving configurations that gradually reduce the computational complexity (at the cost of a worse rate-distortion optimization) according to the remaining battery charge.

The solution presented in the following computes for each 4×4 prediction mode the probability that it minimizes the cost function with respect to the other ones. According to this probability distribution, the algorithm elects a limited set of modes (the most probable ones) as possible *"best-mode"* candidates and computes the cost function for each of them. The probability estimation is performed using a low-cost Belief-Propagation (BP) strategy that exploits the statistical dependence among adjacent blocks. In the end, the algorithm checks whether it is worth merging the blocks together or not.
In the following, Section 2 will describe the Intra prediction process in the H.264/AVC FRExt coder and the related complexity problems. Section 3 presents how different solutions try to cope with the computational issue by designing appropriate low-complexity Intra prediction strategies. Then, Section 4 will present the proposed algorithm that estimates the best-mode probability for each prediction orientation from the previous coding results. The estimated probability distribution permits computing a reduced set of candidate modes. In second step, the algorithm chooses whether it is worth merging blocks together or not. Experimental results, presented in Section 5, will show that the performance of the algorithm compares well with other solutions, and in addition, that the computational complexity can be controlled by increasing or decreasing the number of candidate modes. Final conclusions will be drawn in Section 6.

2. The Intra coding mode in the H.264/AVC FRExt standard

Like many of the previously-proposed video coders (ISO/IEC JTC1, 2001; ITU-T, 1995; ITU-T and ISO/IEC JTC1, 1994), the H.264/AVC standard adopts a hybrid coding scheme that combines traditional transform coding with a predictive coding approach (see Fig. 1). The adoption of low-complexity integer transform decreases the compression efficiency of the transformation procedure for the sake of a lower computational complexity; it is possible to compensate this decrement in the coding gain by predicting the input signal from pixels belonging to the previous frames or to the previously-coded blocks.
The input video frames captured by the camera are partitioned into macroblocks of 16×16 pixels, and each macroblock can be divided into blocks of 4×4 or 8×8 pixels which can be predicted according to the chosen coding mode. For Inter macroblocks (i.e. temporally predicted macroblocks), from the previously-coded frames the coder selects a predictor block that approximates well the current one and identifies it using a motion vector (MV). This selection is performed via a motion search process, which considers all the blocks whose coordinates lie within a given search window and chooses the one that minimizes a given distortion metric. As for Intra macroblocks, the current block is predicted using the neighboring pixels

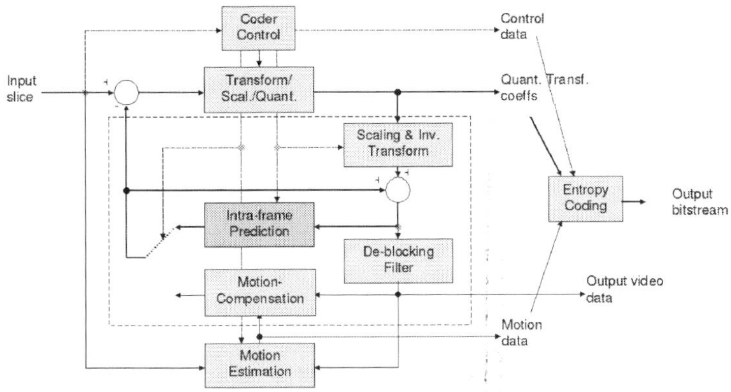

Fig. 1. Block diagram of the H.264/AVC coder.

belonging to previously-coded blocks and interpolating their values according to a set of linear equations. The residual signal after prediction is then transformed and quantized into a set of integer coefficients whose values are converted into a binary bit stream. The size of the adopted integer transform can be either 4×4 or 8×8 depending on the chosen macroblock partitioning. Since the adopted transforms are not orthonormal, the quantization unit needs to compensate this fact by rescaling the quantization steps for the different coefficients depending on the spatial frequencies. As a consequence, the set of quantization steps associated to a given distortion level is referenced using the Quantization Parameter QP, which assumes integer values in the range $[0\ 51]$ and is exponentially proportional to the quantization step according to the equation

$$\Delta = K_{i,j}\, 2^{QP/6} \tag{1}$$

where $K_{i,j}$ is a rescaling factor that depends on the spatial frequencies (i, j) and on the adopted quantization matrix. Then the block of coefficients is dequantized, inversely- transformed, and summed to the corresponding predictor block in order to reconstruct the coded signal. In the following, the chapter will be focused on the spatial Intra prediction.

Since the earliest stages of its standardization process, the Intra coding mode of the H.264/AVC codec has been characterized by block-based spatial prediction. The pixels in the current block are predicted from the neighboring ones according to a spatial predictor which is chosen among a set of possible standardized candidates (see Fig. 2 as an example for the `Intra4x4` mode).

More precisely, each candidate predictor is computed from the neighboring pixels of the upper and the left macroblocks interpolated along an assigned spatial directions. The H.264/AVC standard defines a finite set of directions whose number can vary from 4 up to 9 according to the coding mode of the block. At first, two Intra coding modes were defined, named `Intra4x4` and `Intra16x16` respectively. The first one performs spatial prediction on blocks of 4×4 pixels and has a set of 9 candidate predictors (reported in Fig. 2), while the second one predicts a whole macroblock of 16×16 pixels choosing one predictor among a set of 4 (see Fig. 3). As for the Chroma component, only 4 modes were standardized defining an Intra prediction on 8×8 blocks. With the extension of the coding standard (H.264/AVC FRExt), a novel `Intra8x8` mode was introduced using 9 possible candidates on Luma blocks of 8×8 pixels (Joint Video Team, 2004). Experimental results (Cappellari and Mian, 2004) have shown that the performance of spatial prediction coding in the H.264/AVC coder depends on the efficiency of the chosen directional predictor in modelling the characteristics of the signal. Given the Intra macroblock coding mode M ($M =$ `Intra4x4`, `Intra8x8`, `Intra16x16`), the default Intra coding strategy implemented in the reference H.264/AVC coder tests for the current block all the possible predictor blocks associated to the set of available prediction modes and chooses the mode m that minimizes the Lagrangian cost function

$$L(m) = D(m) + \lambda\ R(m). \tag{2}$$

The value $R(m)$ is the bit rate needed to code the current mode m in the bit stream, $D(m)$ is the distortion metric, and λ is a Lagrange multiplier that weights the influence of both distortion and bit rate in the cost function (Sullivan and Wiegand, 1998). In finding the best prediction mode, the distortion $D(m)$ is measured using the Sum of Absolute Differences (SAD) between the predicted block and the original one in order to limit the required computational complexity. Since the best prediction mode m for the current 4×4 block is strongly correlated with the modes chosen for the spatially-neighboring blocks, in the H.264/AVC standard the bit rate $R(m)$ is coded after estimating the most probable prediction mode according to the modes of the upper and left blocks (Joint Video Team, 2004). The same rate distortion strategy is adopted to find the best Intra macroblock coding mode M, where the distortion metric $D(M)$ is the Sum of the Squared Differences (SSD) between the original macroblock and the reconstructed one in place of the SAD. Depending on the adopted distortion metric (SAD or SSD), the value of the parameter λ is linearly or quadratically proportional to the adopted quantization step. The derivation process of the parameter λ for the reference H.264/AVC coder is reported in a work by Wiegand and Girod (2001), where λ is set to

$$\lambda = 0.85\ 2^{QP/6} \text{ when using SAD and } \lambda = 0.85\ 2^{QP/3} \text{ when using SSD.} \tag{3}$$

The distortion metric in eq (2) permits choosing the coding mode that could be slightly suboptimal in terms of distortion but requires a lower amount of bits.
In the following, the chapter will give a more detailed description about each prediction mode, how it is chosen, and how it is coded in the bit stream.

2.1 Spatial prediction on 4×4 blocks

The baseline Intra coding mode defined within the H.264/AVC standard is the `Intra4x4` mode, which partitions the macroblock into 4×4-pixels blocks and chooses for each block a spatial predictor out from a set of 9 possible standardized candidates. In Figure 2 all the 9 possible modes are reported (for a detailed description including the formulas to estimate the pixel values of each predictor see the standard release by Joint Video Team 2004). Note that each mode is associated to an identification number that is closely related to its average best-mode probability, i.e. the probability of being chosen as best prediction mode for the current block. As a consequence, vertical and horizontal modes, which are the most frequently adopted prediction orientations, are assigned to the numbers 0 and 1. Since the best prediction mode m for the current 4×4 block is strongly correlated with the modes chosen for the spatially-neighboring blocks, in the H.264/AVC standard the bit rate $R(m)$ is coded after estimating the most probable prediction mode according to the modes of the upper and left blocks (see Joint Video Team (2004)). The variable `most_probable_mode` is defined as the minimum between the modes of the neighboring upper and the left blocks. Whenever estimating

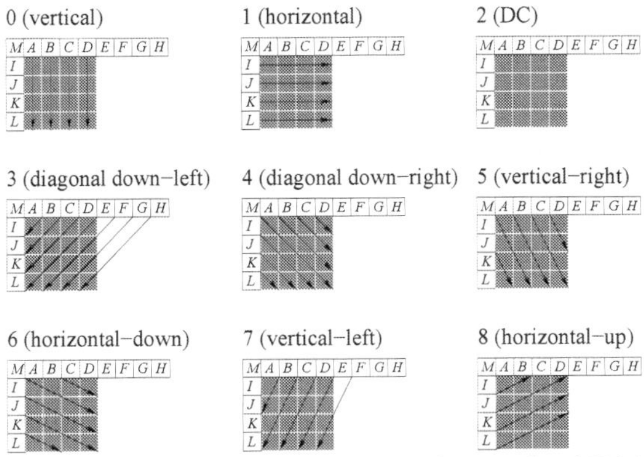

Fig. 2. Possible predictors for `Intra4x4` macroblock coding mode of H.264/AVC standard.

the best prediction mode m for the current block, the parameter $R(m)$ is equal to 1 or 4 since the coder at first signals with one bit whether the chosen mode equals `most_probable_mode` or not. In case m and `most_probable_mode` differs, the coder requires 3 additional bits to signal the correct predictors.

2.2 Spatial prediction on 16×16 blocks

The adoption of spatial predictions on 4×4 blocks imply that the video coder has to specify 16 prediction modes for each `Intra4x4` macroblocks with a consequent waste of coded bits. In addition, during the standardization process of the H.264/AVC architecture, preliminary experimental results had shown that spatial orientation of neighboring blocks does not change wherever the image is highly stationary (uniform regions). In these situations, the same results had also shown that performing spatial prediction on wider blocks proved to be more effective since a reduced number of prediction modes need to be specified. As a consequence, the H.264/AVC video coding standard was enabled with the additional `Intra16x16` coding mode, which predicts the whole macroblock using the pixels of the upper and the left macroblocks lying along the borders. In this case, 4 possible orientations were defined and, after performing the 4×4 integer transform on each residual block within the macroblock, an additional 4×4 Hadamard transform is applied on the DC coefficients (Joint Video Team, 2004). Figure 3 reports a graphic representation of the possible Intra prediction modes. Anyway, the extension of the H.264/AVC standard to other applications and video formats brought the need of defining an additional Intra prediction mode operating on the intermediate 8×8 blocks.

2.3 Spatial prediction on 8×8 blocks

Initially conceived for video communication and video streaming applications on low bandwidth channels, the standard H.264/AVC was successively extended to the transmission and storage of high definition video. As a drawback, the 4×4 integer transform was no more suitable for wider video formats, and therefore, an additional 8×8 integer transform was included in the standard. In addition, experimental results showed that performing the block-based spatial prediction on 8×8 blocks proved to be effective for a wide number of mac-

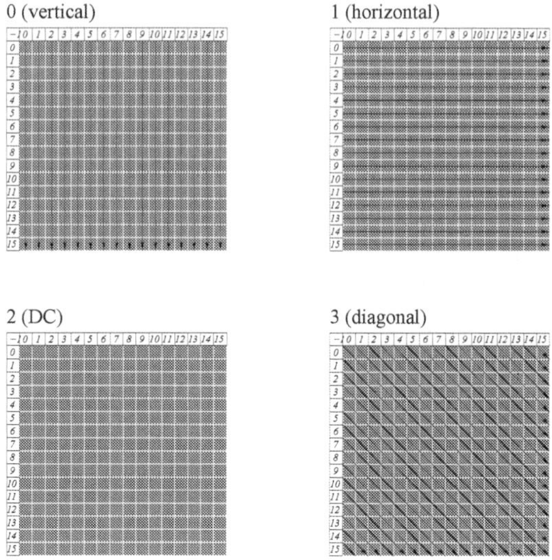

Fig. 3. Possible predictors for `Intra16x16` macroblock coding mode of H.264/AVC standard.

roblocks. As a result, the `Intra8x8` coding mode was introduced within the standard as an additional feature which has to be included in all the decoders implementing the highest profiles (Joint Video Team, 2004). The Intra prediction on 8×8 blocks has 9 different prediction orientations similar to those defined for the 4×4 blocks. In this case, the neighboring pixels are initially smoothed by a low-pass Finite Impulse Response (FIR) filter and then used to generate the predictor blocks. The coding strategy for the prediction mode is the same for the mode `Intra4x4` (see Fig. 4). In this case, the variable `most_probable_mode` can be computed from neighboring 4×4 blocks too (see the standard draft by Joint Video Team, 2004 for more details).

2.4 Spatial prediction on chrominance blocks

For input video signals in the YUV 4:2:0 format, which is the main format supported by the standard H.264/AVC (however, other formats are supported), every macroblock of luminance pixel is associated to two 8×8 pixel blocks in the U and V components respectively. Spatial prediction is also performed on these blocks considering neighboring pixels from the upper and the left macroblock. In this case, the characteristics of the chrominance signals do not require a wide range of possible predictor modes to perform an effective spatial prediction, and therefore, only 4 modes are defined within the standard similar to those defined for the `Intra16x16` mode despite the fact that the indexing is changed (see Fig. 3).

The default Intra coding algorithm tests all these possible choice and chooses the one that provides the best rate-distortion performance in terms of the metric of eq. (2). In the following we will present some solutions that permit obtaining a coding efficiency comparable to that of the extensive method and require a limited computational complexity.

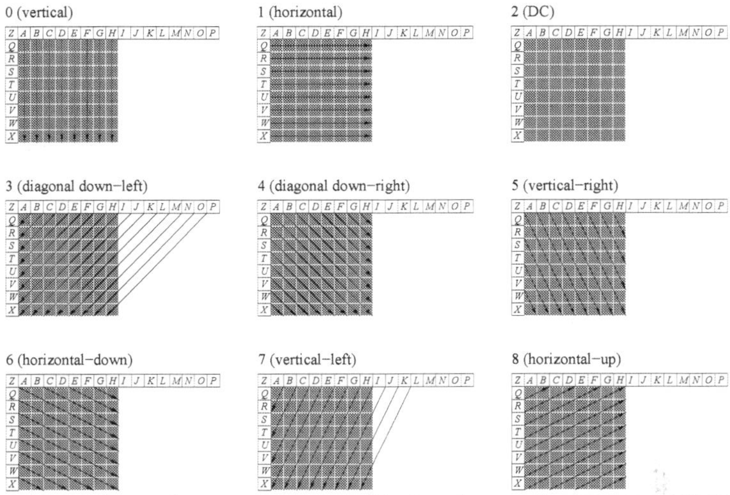

Fig. 4. Possible predictors for `Intra8x8` macroblock coding mode of H.264/AVC FRExt standard.

3. Overview of the existing Fast Intra Prediction methods

Most of the fast Intra coding algorithms reduce the computational complexity by identifying the spatial orientation of the current block and selecting an appropriate set of candidate modes without performing a complete testing of all the possible predictors (Pan et al., 2005). At the same time, these algorithms select the MB partitioning (`Intra4x4` or `Intra16x16`) that suits better to the current macroblock. Many methods rely on early termination solution, where the best predictor search is terminated before testing all the available modes whenever the resulting distortion is lower than a given threshold. Other solutions analyze the characteristics of the block to be coded in order to identify the most suitable prediction mode. These methods test the different predictors according to a hierarchical order or process the input block using some edge detection operators to create a set of possible candidate modes. The outcomes of these operations are used to infer the spatial orientations of the block to be coded and identify, as a consequence, the associated prediction mode. In most of the solutions presented in literature, the number of tested modes or operations depend on the characteristics of the input video signal, and as a consequence, the required computational complexity varies without permitting an *a priori* estimation. In the following some of these methods are shortly presented.

3.1 Fast Intra Prediction using edge detection operators

Since the efficiency of the spatial prediction relies on identifying accurately the orientation of the spatial correlation, many approaches try to infer this feature from the coded video signal using some edge detection operators. One of the first approaches that perform fast Intra prediction estimation was proposed by Pan et al. (2005). When evaluating the `Intra4x4` mode, the input 4×4 block is processed using vertical and horizontal Sobel operators, and the outcoming values are stored in a histogram with 9 bins associated to the different modes.

These values are used to estimate a set $\mathcal{M}$ of possible candidate modes. The mode with the highest probability, together with the two modes that result the closest to it and the DC prediction mode, is included in $\mathcal{M}$. Then, the algorithm chooses the predictor that obtains the lowest value in the cost function. As for the `Intra16x16` mode, only the most probable mode and the DC mode are considered reducing the number of tested modes from 4 to 2. When coding the 8×8 chrominance blocks, the most probable modes are estimated for both the U and V components from the orientation histograms and included in $\mathcal{M}$, together with the DC mode.

A similar approach is adopted in another work by the same authors (Pan et al., 2004), where an average edge directional field is computed for each 4×4 block in order to identify the dominant spatial orientation. The quadratic values of the Sobel operators are averaged within the current block in order to estimate the dominant spatial direction and the related coherence value.

A different approach is proposed by Yong-dong et al. (2004), which generates a subsampled version of the current 4×4 block and computes vertical and horizontal edge detection operators. According to the absolute values and the signs of these, different sets of candidate predictors (with different numbers of modes included) are generated and tested. In this way it is possible to save about 60 % of the computational complexity on average, but the actual saving depends on the chosen quantization parameter QP.

Other approaches approximate the distortion measure using alternative metrics, which either requires a lower complexity or proves to be more effective in identifying the orientation of the current block. The approach proposed by Kim et al. (2006b) evaluates a group of SAD metrics on a reduced set of pixels which are located close to the borders of each block. A possible alternative is presented by Jeong and Kwon (2007) where the orientation of the block is found computing a distortion metric on the relevant transform coefficients of the current block.

3.2 Fast Intra Prediction using hierarchical search

Another set of solution proposed in literature rely on the possibility that a tested prediction mode is very likely to be the best one whenever the associated distortion value is lower than a discriminating threshold. As a consequence, these solutions aim at finding the mode order that places the most probable best candidates first.

The approach by Lu and Yin (2005) tests the available prediction modes and coding options according to a predefined order. More precisely, the `Intra16x16` mode is considered at first, and the coding strategy tests the DC mode checking whether the associated cost function has a lower value with respect to fixed discriminating threshold. In case the cost is higher, vertical and horizontal modes are tested as well; otherwise, the `Intra16x16` coding process is finished (*early termination*). The `Intra4x4` is then tested considering DC, vertical, and horizontal modes at the beginning. In case the cost function for the `Intra16x16` mode is lower than a given threshold no additional `Intra4x4` prediction modes are considered.[1] Otherwise, the algorithm tests the remaining prediction orientations that are closer to the best mode between the vertical and the horizontal ones. The presence of early termination decision does not allow an accurate *a priori* estimation of the required computational cost.

In a similar way, the solution designed by Lorás and Amiel (2005) tests the vertical and the horizontal directions first, and according to whether the vertical or the horizontal orientation is better, it chooses the following set of modes to test. The same policy is applied to the new

[1] Early termination for the DC mode is evaluated also in this case.

candidate modes following a tree-ordered refinement policy of the Intra prediction for the current block.
Another hierarchical solution was proposed by Kalva and Christodoulou (2007), where the modes are tested following an adaptive tree structure that is modified using a machine learning algorithm.

3.3 Fast Intra Prediction using parametric models

Among the strategies that reduce the required computational complexity, a separate mention has to be done for those strategies that aim at achieving a lower computational cost the coding performance of the rate-distortion optimization algorithm proposed within the standard (Wiegand and Girod, 2001). The rate and the distortion of the final coded block are estimated using some parametric models. This class of algorithms compute some low-complexity metrics that characterize the features of the original signal, and use them to estimate the final coded bit rate and the associated distortion, whose calculation requires a significant amount of operations.
The approach proposed by Kim et al. (2006a) estimates the possible results of the rate-distortion optimization algorithm from the SAD metric computed on the pixel blocks and on the blocks obtained after a Hadamard transform (in this case the SAD is called SATD). The SAD and the SATD values permit identifying the prediction mode that is the most likely to be the best one. In a similar way, the strategy by Kim et al. (2003) infers a statistical model for the current block from the SATD values.
Unfortunately, many of these solutions adopt early termination strategies that make the required computational complexity vary. In the following we will present an optimization approach that permits controlling the amount of calculation with deterministic accuracy. In this way, it is possible to configure the algorithm in a flexible way according to the desired computational complexity.

4. A low-complexity Belief Propagation based Intra prediction strategy

The approach proposed by Milani (2008) reduces the set of tested candidate modes according to a probability estimation strategy, which is based on a Belief Propagation algorithm. This solution can be divided into three parts. At first, the algorithm estimates the most probable orientations for the current block. The estimated probabilities are used to generate a set of candidate predictors, and the best prediction mode is found by coding the current MB using the `Intra4x4` mode. In the following, the 4×4 blocks are fused into either 8×8 blocks or a whole 16×16-pixels macroblock according to their orientations. The following sections will present the three phases in detail.

4.1 Probability estimation for the best candidate modes

4.1.1 Estimation of orientations for 4×4 blocks

Assuming that the $M_0 \times 1$ array $\mathbf{p}(x,y) = [p_m(x,y)]$ $(m = 0, \ldots, M_0 - 1)$ groups the probabilities $p_m(x,y)$ that the mode m is the best mode for the block at coordinates (x,y) (with M_0 the total number of candidate modes), it is possible to write the elements of $\mathbf{p}(x,y)$ as follows

$$p_m(x,y) = \mathbf{p}^T(x,y-1)\; Q^m(x,y)\; \mathbf{p}(x-1,y), \tag{4}$$

where $Q^m(x,y) = [q^m_{i,j}(x,y)]$ is an $M_0 \times M_0$ matrix. The value $q^m_{i,j}(x,y)$ represents the conditional probability that mode m is the best mode for the current block at (x,y) given that i and

j are the best modes for blocks at coordinates $(x, y-1)$ and $(x-1, y)$ respectively. However, it may happen that only a smaller set $\mathcal{M}$ of M candidate modes ($M < M_0$) are available for the block at (x, y), and therefore, the probabilities $p_{m'}(x, y)$ are 0 for $m' \notin \mathcal{M}$. This is the case of blocks placed at positions where some reference pixels are not available because of the frame boundaries or the block coding order (e.g. upper-right pixels can not be used since the corresponding neighboring block has not been coded yet). The same candidate modes reduction is found for all the blocks whenever the H.264/AVC coder adopts a fast intra prediction algorithm that tests only a selected set of candidates to constrain the computational complexity. This candidate modes reduction affects the best-mode probability array, which can be replaced with the relation

$$\tilde{\mathbf{p}}(x, y) = P_M(x-1, y)\, \mathbf{p}(x, y) \tag{5}$$

where $P_M(x, y)$ is a singular projection matrix that sets to 0 some elements of $\mathbf{p}(x, y)$ according to which candidate modes are available.
As a consequence, the best-mode statistics for the current block at position (x, y) can be estimated propagating the best-mode probability of previous blocks via the equation

$$\begin{aligned} \tilde{p}_m(x, y) &= \mathbf{p}^T(x, y-1)\, P_M^T(x, y-1)\, Q^m(x, y)\, P_M(x-1, y)\, \mathbf{p}(x-1, y) \\ &= \tilde{\mathbf{p}}^T(x, y-1)\, Q^m(x, y)\, \tilde{\mathbf{p}}(x-1, y) \end{aligned} \tag{6}$$

(which is a modified version of eq. (4)), and projecting the array $\mathbf{p}(x, y)$ onto the subspace of allowed modes using equation (5). The resulting array $\tilde{\mathbf{p}}(x, y)$ differs from the original estimate $\mathbf{p}(x, y)$ of eq. (4) because of the approximation introduced by the projection and leads to a different set $\tilde{\mathcal{M}} \neq \mathcal{M}$ of candidate modes. As a possible drawback, the chosen predictor could not match accurately the orientation of the local correlation either because the optimal mode is not included in the set $\tilde{\mathcal{M}}$ or because all the required neighboring pixels are not available and the most appropriate predictor can not be adopted. The finally chosen mode $\tilde{m}$ could result sub-optimal for the current block and is going to affect the accuracy of probability estimation for the following adjacent blocks. It is possible to mitigate this effect by adopting a Belief-Propagation (BP) strategy that refines the statistics for each block.

4.1.2 The Belief-Propagation procedure for spatial orientations of 4×4 blocks

Before coding the block at the coordinates (x, y), the mode estimation routine propagates through a BP procedure the information about the best modes for the upper and left blocks found during the coding operations (see Figure 5 for a graphic example). These modes are denoted here with $\tilde{m}(x, y-1)$ and $\tilde{m}(x-1, y)$ respectively. According to this, the coding routine estimates a probability mass function (pmf) $\tilde{\mathbf{p}}(x, y)$ for the current block via equation (6), where

$$\begin{aligned} \tilde{p}_m(x-1, y) &= \begin{cases} 0 & m \neq \tilde{m}(x-1, y) \\ 1 & m = \tilde{m}(x-1, y) \end{cases} \\ \tilde{p}_m(x, y-1) &= \begin{cases} 0 & m \neq \tilde{m}(x, y-1) \\ 1 & m = \tilde{m}(x, y-1). \end{cases} \end{aligned} \tag{7}$$

According to the values of $\tilde{\mathbf{p}}(x, y)$, all the possible prediction modes are sorted in decreasing probability order, and the most probable ones are included in the set $\mathcal{M}$ according to the criteria that will be described in Section 4.2.

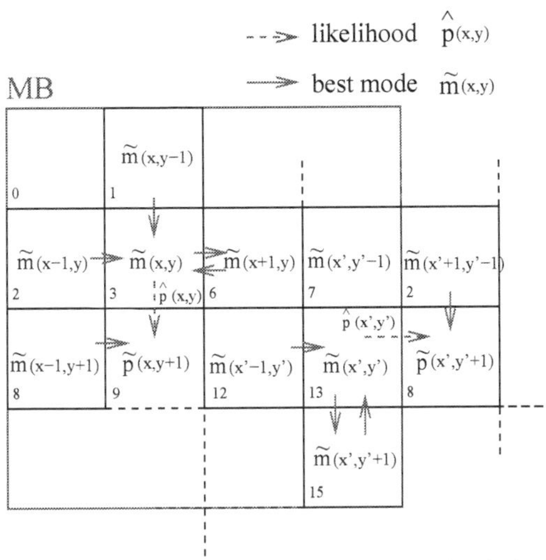

Fig. 5. Probability propagation according to the implemented Belief Propagation approach. Some message passing propagates hard information (solid arrows) regarding the chosen prediction modes, while others communicates likelihoods associated to the prediction mode of 4×4 blocks (dashed arrows).

After finding the mode that minimizes the cost function among the candidates in $\mathcal{M}$, the BP approach propagates this result to the previously coded blocks in order to refine the accuracy of the estimated mode probability (i.e. $\tilde{\mathbf{p}}(x,y-1)$ and $\tilde{\mathbf{p}}(x-1,y)$). The array $\tilde{\mathbf{p}}(x,y)$, whose elements are reported in eq. (7), is replaced by a *"soft"* best mode estimation $\hat{\mathbf{p}}(x,y)$ (a likelihood) computed using a reversed version of equation (4)

$$\hat{\mathbf{p}}(x,y) = \tilde{\mathbf{p}}^T(x,y-1)\ Q^{m,r}(x,y)\ \tilde{\mathbf{p}}(x+1,y). \tag{8}$$

The new arrays $\hat{\mathbf{p}}(x,y)$ affect the estimated mode probability distribution for the following blocks and improve the compression performance of the fast Intra coding algorithm. As an example, the elements for the probability array $\tilde{\mathbf{p}}(x,y+1)$ of block 9 in Fig. 5 are obtained via eq. (6) replacing the array $\tilde{\mathbf{p}}(x,y-1)$ with $\hat{\mathbf{p}}(x,y-1)$.
Experimental results have proved that the refinement step performed using equation (8) does not change the arrays $\tilde{\mathbf{p}}(x,y)$ in such a way that the order of candidate modes is altered. However, the likelihood estimate for the prediction mode $\tilde{m}(x,y)$ proves to be significant in the computation of the number of candidate modes as it will be explained in Subsection 4.2.1. Moreover, the best prediction modes found for `Intra4x4` coding are used to characterize the best-mode probability of prediction modes for bigger blocks in case the rate-distortion algorithm has chosen to merge the 4×4 blocks together, as it will be described in Section 4.4. In the estimation routine, the arrays $\tilde{\mathbf{p}}(x,y)$ and $\hat{\mathbf{p}}(x,y)$ are approximated using a finite set $\mathcal{P}$ of 100 pmfs, which has been obtained from an extensive set of training sequences via an LBG iterative classification (Gersho and Gray, 1991). In this procedure the distortion metric to

minimize is the Jensen-Shannon divergence between $\tilde{\mathbf{p}}(x,y)$ and $\hat{\mathbf{p}} \in \mathcal{P}$

$$JSD\left(\tilde{\mathbf{p}}(x,y)\|\hat{\mathbf{p}}\right) = \frac{1}{2}D\left(\tilde{\mathbf{p}}(x,y)\|\hat{\mathbf{p}}\right) + \frac{1}{2}D\left(\hat{\mathbf{p}}\|\tilde{\mathbf{p}}(x,y)\right) \tag{9}$$

where $D\left(\tilde{\mathbf{p}}(x,y)\|\hat{\mathbf{p}}\right)$ is the Kullback-Leibler divergence

$$D\left(\tilde{\mathbf{p}}(x,y)\|\hat{\mathbf{p}}\right) = \sum_{m=0}^{8} \tilde{\mathbf{p}}_m(x,y) \log\left(\frac{\tilde{\mathbf{p}}_m(x,y)}{\hat{\mathbf{p}}_m}\right). \tag{10}$$

The conditional probability matrix $Q_m(x,y)$ is a linear combination of arrays $\hat{\mathbf{p}} \in \mathcal{P}$, and the probability array $\tilde{\mathbf{p}}(x,y)$ at position (x,y) is updated after each iteration of the BP procedure using a Finite State Machine (FSM), where each state is related to an element of $\mathcal{P}$. In this way, it is possible to obtain an adaptive estimation of the probability for each prediction mode with limited computational complexity and memory area.

4.1.3 Estimation of probable spatial orientations for 8×8 blocks

After the optimization algorithm has chosen to merge together 4×4 blocks into 8×8 blocks, the coder estimates an `Intra8x8` best-mode probability distribution $\mathbf{p}^{8\times 8}$ according to the previously found `Intra4x4` modes. The adopted approach estimates three different mode probability distribution $\mathbf{p}^{8\times 8,i}$, $i = v,h,d$, which are dependent on the best Intra prediction modes of vertical, horizontal and diagonal couples of 4×4 blocks respectively (see Figure 6). Using the same notation of equation (4), it is possible to write $\mathbf{p}^{8\times 8,i} = [p_m^{8\times 8,i}]$, $i = v,h,d$ and $m = 0,\ldots,8$, as

$$\begin{aligned} p_m^{8\times 8,v} &= \tilde{\mathbf{p}}^T(x,y)\; F_m^{8\times 8,v}\; \tilde{\mathbf{p}}(x,y+1) \\ p_m^{8\times 8,h} &= \tilde{\mathbf{p}}^T(x,y)\; F_m^{8\times 8,h}\; \tilde{\mathbf{p}}(x+1,y) \\ p_m^{8\times 8,d} &= \tilde{\mathbf{p}}^T(x,y)\; F_m^{8\times 8,d}\; \tilde{\mathbf{p}}(x+1,y+1) \end{aligned} \tag{11}$$

where $\tilde{\mathbf{p}}(x,y)$ represents the chosen prediction mode (as defined in equation (7)) and $F_m^{8\times 8,i}$, $i = v,h,d$, is the conditional probability matrix of 8×8 Intra prediction mode m given the vertical, horizontal, and diagonal couples of 4×4 modes. In this way, `Intra8x8` best-mode probability estimation relies on the results of `Intra4x4` coding which has already been performed on the current macroblock.

4.2 Estimation of the set of candidates

4.2.1 Computation of the most probable prediction modes

After estimating the probability array $\tilde{\mathbf{p}}(x,y)$, the coding routine has to identify those modes that are more likely to be the best prediction mode for the current 4×4 block. The number of candidate modes M is usually set to the average value $\overline{M}$, but can vary according to the characteristics of the probability distribution identified by $\tilde{\mathbf{p}}(x,y)$. In fact, experimental data show that the entropies of distributions $\tilde{\mathbf{p}}(x,y)$ vary, and therefore, the mode probability distributions with a lower entropy only needs a reduced number of candidates.

Named $\text{ß} = [\text{ß}_\mathbf{m}]$ the average mode probability array, M is chosen in such a way that

$$\begin{array}{c} \sum_{m=0}^{M-1} S_m(\tilde{\mathbf{p}}(x,y)) \leq \sum_{m=0}^{\overline{M}-1} S_m\left(\text{ß}(\mathbf{x},\mathbf{y})\right) \\ \sum_{m=0}^{M} S_m(\tilde{\mathbf{p}}(x,y)) > \sum_{m=0}^{\overline{M}-1} S_m\left(\text{ß}(\mathbf{x},\mathbf{y})\right) \end{array} \tag{12}$$

where $S_m(\cdot) : [0,1]^9 \rightarrow [0,1]$ is an ordering function that returns the m-th value of the input array in decreasing order. The value $\overline{M}$ reports the average number of modes to be tested for each block and permits controlling the computational complexity. In this way it is possible to provide the same probability of finding the best prediction mode with a limited sets of candidates to all the 4×4 blocks of the image. This equalization permits saving some computational complexity without affecting the coding performance of the algorithm.

As it was mentioned in Subsection 4.1.2, the refinement provided by either $\tilde{\mathbf{p}}(x, y+1)$ or $\tilde{\mathbf{p}}(x+1, y)$ permits a better estimate of the probabilities related to the candidate modes of the current block. This improvement does not lead to a change in the order of modes but could modify the number of candidates that is considered for the current 4×4 block since it affects equation (12). Experimental results have shown that the refinement brought by the Belief-Propagation strategy leads to a reduction of the coding time with respect to the case when forward message passing is allowed only (see the solid-line arrows in Fig. 5). The same approach is adopted to estimate the set of candidate modes for `Intra8x8` as it will be described in Subsection 4.3.

4.2.2 Further reduction of the possible candidates (DD algorithm)

According to the probability values of $\tilde{\mathbf{p}}(x,y)$, the M most probable modes are included in the set $\mathcal{M}$ of candidates. Whenever the entropy associated with $\tilde{\mathbf{p}}(x,y)$ is high, it is possible that the set $\mathcal{M}$ includes modes with orthogonal spatial orientations. This fact is mainly due to the transient period in the probability estimation process, which may require several iteration before converging to an accurate estimate of mode statistics. Therefore, a further reduction of the candidate modes can be obtained by estimating whether horizontal or vertical modes are dominant in the distribution $\tilde{\mathbf{p}}(x,y)$ and eliminating the dominated modes (Dominated Deletion - DD). The number of orientations in the set $\mathcal{M}$ which are close to the vertical one is compared with the number of candidate modes which have a spatial orientation close to the horizontal one. In case one of them prevails, the modes of the other type are deleted from the set $\mathcal{M}$.

This additional improvement proves to be quite effective whenever the image orientation statistics has changed, and the array $\tilde{\mathbf{p}}(x,y)$ estimated by the algorithm does not provide a sufficiently-accurate approximation of the real pmf yet. Therefore, the estimated set $\mathcal{M}$ could include some candidate modes which are orthogonal to the other ones since they could be probable candidates in the neighboring region. The DD elimination algorithm prevents this transient phase from reducing the effectiveness of the algorithm and speeds up the best intra-prediction estimation process.

However, this elimination procedure has to be constrained in order to avoid an excessive reduction of the candidate sets whenever the statistics of prediction orientations is not clearly biased on either vertical or horizontal directions. In order to avoid the deletion of probable candidate modes, the DD algorithm is performed only for modes greater than 4 whenever the number of dominated modes is greater than a certain threshold value T. In the setting

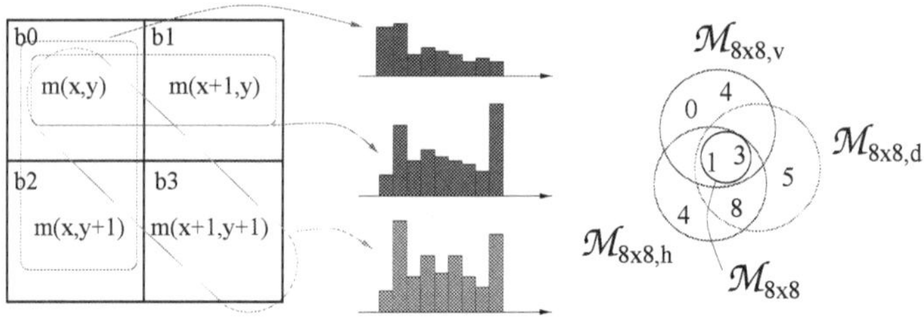

Fig. 6. Merging operation for 4×4 blocks.

operation of the fast intra algorithm, the parameter T can be varied in order to increase or decrease the cardinality of $\mathcal{M}$ according to the desired computational complexity.
Experimental results reported in Section 5 will underline its contribution in the overall performance of the fast intra prediction procedure.

4.3 Computation of the candidates for 8×8 blocks

In case the coding mode `Intra8x8` is enabled, the fast intra prediction algorithm has to estimate the most appropriate prediction modes for the current 8×8 block from the results of `Intra4x4` mode. The transcoding algorithm reported by Bialkowski et al. (2004) chooses the most frequently used prediction direction, but in case the estimated 4×4 orientations prove to be nonuniform within the same 8×8 block, a better performance can be obtained testing a set $\mathcal{M}_{8\times8}$ of different candidates. A procedure similar to that of Subsection 4.2.1 is adopted in order to estimate the sets of candidate $\mathcal{M}_{8\times8}$ for the current 8×8 block from $\mathbf{p}^{8\times8,i}$, $i = v, h, d$. Each mode probability distribution $\mathbf{p}^{8\times8,i}$ infers a different set $\mathcal{M}_{8\times8,i}$, $i = v, h, d$, of candidate modes which is obtained in the same way of the set of M possible candidate modes for `Intra4x4` blocks. In case the set $\mathcal{M}_{8\times8}$ obtained from the intersection of the sets

$$\mathcal{M}_{8\times8} = \mathcal{M}_{8\times8,v} \cap \mathcal{M}_{8\times8,h} \cap \mathcal{M}_{8\times8,d} \quad (13)$$

is not empty, the coding algorithm merges the 4×4 blocks into a 8×8 block and tests the predictors included in the set $\mathcal{M}_{8\times8}$ looking for the one that minimizes the cost function.
As for the `Intra16x16` coding, all the four possible predictions are tested since the estimation of the best mode probability for the 16×16 block from the best `Intra4x4` modes is not trivial. The same choice is adopted to spatially predict the chrominance components U and V.

4.4 Estimation of best macroblock partitioning for Intra prediction

After finding the best mode for each 4×4 block in the current MB, the coding routine tests whether it is better to use bigger blocks. In a first step the algorithm checks whether it is possible to merge together the 4×4 blocks into blocks of 8×8 pixels. In case the orientations of each 4×4 block are the same or close, the merging of separate blocks results convenient with respect to the `Intra4x4` block partitioning since a reduced number of predictors needs to be coded in the transmitted bit stream.
In order to detect these configurations, the encoder estimates the orientation differences $d(\tilde{m}(x,y), \tilde{m}(x+i, y+j))$ $(i, j = 0, 1)$ between vertical, horizontal and diagonal couples of 4×4 blocks (see Figure 6) within the current 8×8 block. The metric $d(\tilde{m}(x,y), \tilde{m}(x',y'))$ is computed as follows

$$d(\tilde{m}(x,y), \tilde{m}(x',y')) = \left| \angle\tilde{m}(x,y) - \angle\tilde{m}(x',y') \right| \quad (14)$$

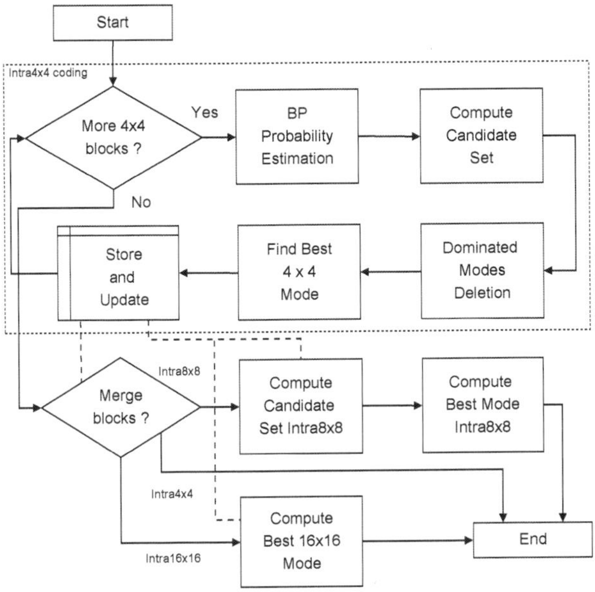

Fig. 7. Block diagram for the general Fast Intra algorithm.

where $\angle m$ denotes the angle associated to the spatial orientation of mode m. If the average difference

$$\overline{d} = \frac{d(\tilde{m}(x,y),\tilde{m}(x+1,y))}{3} + \frac{d(\tilde{m}(x,y),\tilde{m}(x,y+1))}{3} + \frac{d(\tilde{m}(x,y),\tilde{m}(x+1,y+1))}{3} \tag{15}$$

is lower than $40°$, the 4×4 blocks at (x,y), $(x+1,y)$, $(x,y+1)$, and $(x+1,y+1)$ could be merged into one block of 8×8 pixels. In case the condition on $\overline{d}$ is verified for all the 8×8, the `Intra8x8` coding mode is enabled. Moreover, the encoding routine tests whether it is worth merging the 8×8 blocks into one common 16×16 prediction block considering the `Intra4x4` modes for the blocks at the border of 8×8 blocks. In case the average absolute difference between the orientations of 4×4 blocks lying at the borders of 8×8 blocks is lower than $40°$, the `Intra16x16` prediction mode is chosen for the current macroblock. In this way, the wider block partitioning modes are tested only in case the orientations for the 4×4 blocks are approximately uniform, otherwise either 4×4 or 8×8 partitioning is preferred.
The whole fast Intra coding procedure is depicted in the block diagram of Fig. 7 and can be summarized by the following pseudo-code:

Test `Intra4x4` coding mode
for each 4×4 block in the current macroblock **do**
    compute $\tilde{\mathbf{p}}(x,y)$
    compute M and create the set $\mathcal{M}$
    test all the modes in $\mathcal{M}$ an
end for

check if it is worth merging the 4 × 4 blocks into bigger blocks as described in the current Section
if `Intra8x8` is to be enabled **then**
    for each 8 × 8 block in the current macroblock **do**
        compute $\tilde{\mathbf{p}}^{8\times 8,i}$, $i = v, h, d$
        compute $\mathcal{M}_{8\times 8}$ and find the best mode
    end for
end if
if `Intra16x16` mode is to be enabled **then**
    find the best prediction mode
end if
choose the MB Intra coding mode that minimize the total cost function.

Experimental results will show that this choice leads to good performance with respect to other proposed solutions.

5. Experimental results

In order to test the efficiency of the presented algorithm, different sequences were coded with different quantization parameter values and enabling different Intra coding modes. The proposed Intra coding strategy was implemented into the JM10.1 software. In the tests the adopted parameter setting is the same of the paper by Pan et al. (2005), coding different sequences with only Intra frames and $QP = 28, 32, 36, 40$. At first the performance of `Intra4x4` and `Intra16x16` modes only was evaluated, comparing the computational complexity, the PSNR value, and the coded bit rate of the presented solution with those provided by the full-complexity rate-distortion optimization algorithm implemented in the reference software. Experimental data show that the PSNR vs. rate curves of the two methods are quite close (see Figure 8). It is possible to notice that coding performance in terms of rate-distortion optimization is related to the target number $\overline{M}$ of candidate modes, which can vary according to the available computational resources or the remaining power supply.
Table 1 reports the PSNR loss, together with the rate increment and the complexity reduction, for the proposed approach with respect to the reference software (with `Intra8x8` mode disabled). The presented algorithm is able to reduce the coding time of approximately 63% with respect to the JM exhaustive approach with an average rate increment lower than 5% and a PSNR loss of 0.16 dB ($\overline{M} = 6$ and $T = 2$). The DD algorithm described in Subsection 4.2.2 makes possible to improve the relative coding time reduction of an additional 13% (compare results for $\overline{M} = 6$ and $T = 2$ with results for $\overline{M} = 6$ without DD).
The reported data also show that the rate-distortion performance is slightly better than that of the approaches by Pan et al. (2005) and by Yong-dong et al. (2004). The bottom part of Table 1 reports the results for the algorithm proposed by Pan et al. (2005). Equalizing the rate increment, the performance of the proposed algorithm with $\overline{M} = 7$ and $T = 2$ permits reducing the PSNR loss of 0.04 dB and improving the coding time saving of approximately 2%. Despite this slight improvement, the real advantage of the proposed approach relies on the possibility of forecasting the computational complexity required by coding operations. Table 2 reports the range of variation for the saved coding time of different fast Intra coding algorithms and different configurations. It is possible to notice that the computational complexity does not significantly vary according to the input sequence, since the maximum deviation of time sav-

(M,T)	Sequence	Δ Bits (%)	Δ PSNR	Δ Time (%)
(5,2)	container (qcif)	10.42	−0.18	−72.24
	news (qcif)	9.42	−0.23	−72.44
	coastguard (qcif)	8.04	−0.18	−71.55
	bus (cif)	6.22	−0.21	−70.50
	tempete (cif)	4.55	−0.30	−69.42
average		7.73	−0.22	−71.23
(6,2)	container (qcif)	5.35	−0.14	−62.56
	news (qcif)	5.79	−0.16	−62.46
	coastguard (qcif)	3.55	−0.14	−62.64
	bus (cif)	2.15	−0.16	−63.64
	tempete (cif)	4.95	−0.22	−63.00
average		4.36	−0.16	−62.86
(6,3)	container (qcif)	5.32	−0.14	−59.95
	news (qcif)	5.68	−0.15	−60.43
	coastguard (qcif)	3.67	−0.14	−60.48
	bus (cif)	2.15	−0.16	−63.64
	tempete (cif)	4.95	−0.22	−63.00
average		4.35	−0.16	−61.50
(7,2)	container (qcif)	3.77	−0.13	−58.98
	news (qcif)	4.55	−0.16	−57.85
	coastguard (qcif)	2.14	−0.13	−59.21
	bus (cif)	2.11	−0.14	−58.19
	tempete (cif)	4.61	−0.19	−57.88
average		3.44	−0.15	−58.42
(7,3)	container (qcif)	3.60	−0.12	−55.18
	news (qcif)	4.50	−0.14	−54.14
	coastguard (qcif)	2.19	−0.12	−55.25
	bus (cif)	2.13	−0.13	−54.83
	tempete (cif)	4.57	−0.18	−54.36
average		3.40	−0.14	−54.75
6 without DD	container (qcif)	5.64	−0.08	−50.43
	news (qcif)	4.96	−0.09	−47.79
	coastguard (qcif)	3.64	−0.09	−51.10
	bus (cif)	2.73	−0.10	−49.41
	tempete (cif)	5.05	−0.13	−50.07
average		4.40	−0.10	−49.76
Pan *et al.*	container (qcif)	3.69	−0.23	−56.36
	news (qcif)	3.90	−0.29	−55.34
	coastguard (qcif)	2.36	−0.11	−55.03
	bus (cif)	3.85	−0.10	−58.12
	tempete (cif)	3.51	−0.23	−57.70
average		3.46	−0.19	−56.51

Table 1. Experimental results with `Intra8x8` disabled and only Intra frames.

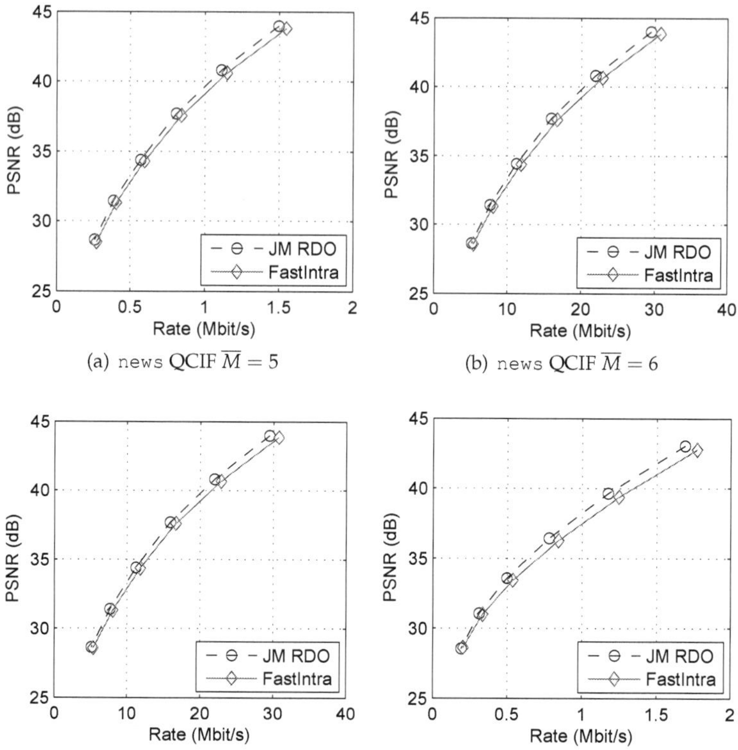

(a) news QCIF $\overline{M} = 5$

(b) news QCIF $\overline{M} = 6$

(c) news QCIF $\overline{M} = 7$

(d) silent QCIF $\overline{M} = 5$

Fig. 8. PSNR vs. rate for only Intra coded sequences with different target number $\overline{M}$ of candidates (`Intra4x4` mode only).

ing from its average with $\overline{M} = 7$ and $T = 2$ is 0.79% while it is equal to 5.81% for the algorithm of Pan *et al.* and 30.38% for the solution proposed by Yong-dong et al. (2004).

Moreover, it is possible to tune the parameters of the fast estimation algorithm in order to vary the required computational complexity and the rate-distortion performance. The results reported in Table 1 show that reducing the parameter $\overline{M}$ by 1 permits a decrement of the computational complexity between 4.44% and 8.37%.

In addition, Table 3 reports some experimental results obtained enabling the `Intra8x8` coding mode too. In this case the average performance does not significantly change, but the complexity reduction results slightly more variable because of the increased number of coding modes. Note also that the computational saving increases since the rate-distortion optimization process becomes more complex as the mode `Intra8x8` is added, and therefore, the adoption of fast method for Intra prediction proves to be an effective strategy in the coding process.

Algorithm	E [ΔTime (%)]	range for ΔTime (%)
BP $\overline{M} = 5$ $T = 2$	−71.23	[−72.44, −69.42]
BP $\overline{M} = 6$ $T = 3$	−61.50	[−63.64, −59.95]
BP $\overline{M} = 7$ $T = 2$	−58.42	[−59.21, −57.85]
Pan *et al.* Pan et al. (2005)	−59.57	[−65.38, −55.03]
Yong-dong *et al.* Yong-dong et al. (2004)	−60.38	[−68.70, −40.30]

Table 2. Experimental results of different algorithms for only Intra mode.

$(\overline{M}, T)$	Sequence	Δ Bits (%)	Δ PSNR	Δ Time (%)
(6,3)	container (qcif)	5.93	−0.14	−66.97
	news (qcif)	6.40	−0.19	−64.63
	coastguard (qcif)	5.09	−0.18	−66.51
	bus (cif)	3.42	−0.20	−63.69
	tempete (cif)	5.66	−0.22	−61.78
	average	5.30	−0.18	−64.72
(7,2)	container (qcif)	4.27	−0.13	−62.76
	news (qcif)	5.34	−0.17	−59.49
	coastguard (qcif)	3.40	−0.16	−62.37
	bus (cif)	3.12	−0.17	−59.73
	tempete (cif)	4.99	−0.20	−58.02
	average	4.23	−0.17	−60.47

Table 3. Experimental results with `Intra8x8` enabled and only Intra frames.

Final tests were devoted to evaluate the impact of the BP-based fast Intra prediction on the complexity of the overall coding process. To this purpose, the performance of the proposed fast intra algorithm was evaluated enabling Inter coding modes. In this case, the Intra coding is applied while coding Intra frames in order to find which is the best coding mode for the current macroblock (see the rate-distortion optimization routine of H.264/AVC by Joint Video Team (2004)). Table 4 reports the coding results for GOP of 100 frames with structure IP. . .P. It is possible to notice that the proposed method improves the results of the algorithm by Pan *et al.* both in terms of rate-distortion performance (we obtained lower rate increment and quality decrement for $\overline{M} = 6$) and of complexity reduction (the proposed approach permits an average 25.88% reduction in the coding time with respect to the 23.57% reduction of the algorithm by Pan et al. (2005)). For the sake of completeness, Table 5 reports the results for GOP IP. . .P and `Intra8x8` mode enabled. In this case the reduction of computational time saving approximately varies from 6.25% to 7.4% with respect to the approach with `Intra8x8` disabled (see Table 4) since the proposed algorithm significantly mitigates the computational load of the rate-distortion optimization routine (compare the results for $\overline{M} = 6$ and $T = 3$).

6. Conclusions

The chapter has described the block-based spatial prediction strategy adopted within the H.2634/AVC FRExt standard and stated the problem of enabling a low-complexity Intra coding on mobile devices. An overview of different techniques has been presented underlying the characteristics of each solution and the required complexity. Since most of the proposed solutions permit obtaining a varying computational savings which depends on the characteristics of the coded signal, the focus is centered on finding a fast Intra coding strategy that

(M,T)	Sequence	Δ Bits (%)	Δ PSNR	Δ Time (%)
(6,3)	container (qcif)	1.19	−0.04	−25.00
	news (qcif)	1.00	−0.05	−25.70
	coastguard (qcif)	0.03	−0.01	−27.00
	bus (cif)	0.23	−0.01	−26.88
	tempete (cif)	0.44	−0.01	−23.82
average		0.58	−0.02	−25.68
(7,2)	container (qcif)	0.74	−0.02	−18.67
	news (qcif)	0.79	−0.06	−19.14
	coastguard (qcif)	0.03	−0.01	−20.26
	bus (cif)	0.11	−0.00	−23.16
	tempete (cif)	0.38	−0.01	−22.20
average		0.41	−0.02	−20.69
Pan *et al.*	container (qcif)	1.80	−0.08	−20.78
	news (qcif)	1.23	−0.07	−23.11
	coastguard (qcif)	0.50	−0.02	−21.20
	bus (cif)	0.32	−0.01	−26.05
	tempete (cif)	0.81	−0.03	−26.72
average		0.93	−0.04	−23.57

Table 4. Experimental results with `Intra8x8` disabled GOP IP...P.

permits controlling the amount of tested modes (and, as a consequence, the required amount of calculation). The chapter presents a coding strategy that identifies a set of probable candidates calculating their best-mode probability. The probability estimates are obtained via Belief Propagation strategy that relies on the statistical dependence existing between spatially neighboring blocks. At the same time, the presented algorithm tries to identify the macroblock partitioning mode that better suits the current macroblock according to the coding results of the `Intra4x4` mode. Experimental results compare different algorithms and show that the Belief Propagation based strategy obtains a significant saving in terms of coding time (approximately 62%) with a negligible decrement of the PSNR value and a small average increment (less than 5.14%) in the bit rate. Moreover, the presented strategy permits an accurate control on the encoding complexity, which does not significantly vary depending on the input

(M,T)	Sequence	Δ Bits (%)	Δ PSNR	Δ Time (%)
(6,3)	container (qcif)	1.25	−0.04	−31.59
	news (qcif)	1.05	−0.07	−30.78
	coastguard (qcif)	0.22	−0.01	−32.10
	bus (cif)	0.25	−0.01	−33.70
	container (qcif)	1.25	−0.04	−31.59
average		0.80	−0.03	−31.95
(7,2)	container (qcif)	0.72	−0.04	−27.64
	news (qcif)	0.97	−0.07	−27.32
	coastguard (qcif)	0.15	−0.01	−27.95
	bus (cif)	0.17	−0.01	−30.02
	container (qcif)	0.72	−0.04	−27.64
average		0.55	−0.04	−28.11

Table 5. Experimental results with `Intra8x8` enabled GOP IP...P.

video sequence and can be tuned according to the power supply level and to the available computational resources.

Acknowledgements

Part of the work was done in collaboration with Luca Celetto of STMicroelectronics, Agrate Brianza (MI), Italy.

7. References

J. Bialkowski, A. Kaup, and K. Illgner, "Fast transcoding of intra frames between H.263 and H.264," in *Proc. of the 2004 IEEE International Conference on Image Processing (ICIP 2004)*, Singapore, Oct. 24 – 27, 2004, pp. 1151–1154.

L. Cappellari and G. A. Mian, "Analysis of joint predictive-transform coding for still image compression," *Signal Processing*, vol. 84, no. 11, pp. 2097–2114, Nov. 2004.

S. Cho, Z. Bojković, D. Milovanović, J. Lee, and J.-J. Hwang, "Image quality evaluation: Jpeg 2000 versus intra-only h.264/avc high profile," *Facta universitatis - series: Electronics and Energetics*, vol. 20, no. 1, pp. 71 – 84, Apr. 2007.

A. Gersho and R. M. Gray, *Vector Quantization and Signal Compression*. Norwell, MA, USA: Kluwer Academic Publisher, 1991.

ISO/IEC JTC1, "Coding of Audio-Visual Objects - Part 2: Visual," *ISO/IEC 14 496-2 (MPEG-4 Visual version 1), Apr. 1999; Amendment 1 (version 2), Feb. 2000; Amendment 4 (streaming profile), Jan. 2001*, Jan. 2001.

ITU-T, "Video Coding for Low Bitrate Communications, Version 1," ITU-T Recommendation H.263, 1995.

ITU-T and ISO/IEC JTC1, "Generic Coding of Moving Pictures and Associated Audio Information-Part 2: Video," ITU-T Recommendation H.262-ISO/IEC 13 818-2 (MPEG-2), 1994.

J. Jeong and D. N. Kwon, "DCT Based Fast 4X4 Intra-Prediction Mode Selection," in *Proc. of* 4th *IEEE Consumer Communications and Networking Conference (CCNC 2007)*, Las Vegas, NV, Jan. 11 – 13, 2007, pp. 332 – 335.

Joint Video Team, "Version 3 of H.264/AVC," in *Joint Video Team (JVT) of ISO/IEC MPEG & ITU-T VCEG (ISO/IEC JTC1/SC29/WG11 and ITU-T SG16 Q.6)*, 12th *Meeting*, Redmond, WA, USA, Jul. 17 – 23, 2004.

——, "Joint final committee draft (JFCD) of joint video specification (ITU-T Rec. H.264 | ISO/IEC 14496-10 AVC)," in *Joint Video Team (JVT) of ISO/IEC MPEG & ITU-T VCEG (ISO/IEC JTC1/SC29/WG11 and ITU-T SG16 Q.6)*, 4th *Meeting*, Klagenfurt, Germany, Jul. 2002. [Online]. Available: ftp://ftp.imtc-files.org/jvt-experts/2002_07_Klagenfurt/{JVT-D157.zip%}

H. Kalva and L. Christodoulou, "Using Machine Learning for Fast Intra MB Coding in H.264," in *Proc. of the SPIE-VCIP 2007*, San Jose, CA, USA, Feb. 2007, pp. 65 082U–1 – 65 082U–4.

C. Kim, H.-H. Shih, and C.-C. J. Kuo, "Fast H.264 intra-prediction mode selection using joint spatial and transform domain features," *Journal of Visual Communication and Image Representation*, vol. 17, no. 2, pp. 291–310, Apr. 2006.

C.-S. Kim, Q. Li, and C.-C. J. Kuo, "Fast Intra-Prediction Model Selection for H.264 Codec," in *SPIE International Symposium ITCOM 2003*, Orlando, FL, USA, Sep. 2003.

J. Kim, K. Jeon, and J. Jeong, "H.264 intra mode decision for reducing complexity using directional masks and neighboring modes," in *Proc. of* 4th *IEEE Consumer Communications and Networking Conference (CCNC 2007)*, vol. 4319, Las Vegas, NV, Dec. 10 – 13, 2006, pp. 959 – 968.

F. Lorás and J.-C. Amiel, "Method for finding the prediction direction in intraframe video coding," International Patent WO 2005/088979, Paris, FR, Jan. 2005.

X. Lu and P. Yin, "Fast intra mode prediction for an H.264 encoder," Princeton, NJ, USA, Oct. 2005.

S. Milani, "A Belief-Propagation based fast Intra coding algorithm for the H.264/AVC FRExt coder," in *Proc. of the 16th European Signal Processing Conference (EUSIPCO 2008)*, Lausanne, Switzerland, Aug. 25 – 28, 2008.

F. Pan, X. Lin, S. Rahardja, K. P. Lim, and Z. G. Li, "A directional field based fast Intra mode decision algorithm for H.264 video coding," in *Proc. of 2004 IEEE International Conference on Multimedia and Expo (ICME 2004)*, Taipei, Taiwan, Jun. 27 – 30, 2004, pp. 1147–1150.

F. Pan, X. Lin, S. Rahardja, K. P. Lim, Z. G. Li, D. Wu, and S. Wu, "Fast mode decision algorithm for intraprediction in H.264/AVC video coding," *IEEE Trans. Circuits Syst. Video Technol.*, vol. 15, no. 7, pp. 813–822, Jul. 2005.

I. E. G. Richardson, *H.264 and MPEG-4 Video Compression.* John Wiley and Sons, Sep. 2003.

J.-S. Ryu and E.-T. Kim, "Fast Intra coding method of H.264 for video surveillance system," *International Journal of Computer Science and Network Security (IJCSNS)*, vol. 7, no. 10, pp. 76–81, Oct. 2007.

G. J. Sullivan and T. Wiegand, "Rate-Distortion Optimization for Video Compression," *IEEE Signal Processing Mag.*, pp. 74–90, Nov. 1998.

T. Wiegand and B. Girod, "Parameter Selection in Lagrangian Hybrid Video Coder Control," in *Proc. of International Conference on Image Processing, ICIP 2001*, Thessaloniki, Greece, Oct. 2001.

J. Xin and A. Vetro, "Fast mode decision for Intra-only H.264/AVC coding," in *Proc. of the 2006 Picture Coding Symposium (PCS 2006)*, Beijing, China, Apr. 24 – 26, 2006.

J. Xin, A. Vetro, and H. Sun, "Efficient macroblock coding-mode decision for H.264/AVC video coding," in *Proc. of* 24th *Picture Coding Symposium (PCS 2004)*, San Francisco, CA, USA, Dec. 15 – 17, 2004.

Z. Yong-dong, D. Feng, and L. Shou-xun, "Fast 4×4 Intra-prediction mode selection for H.264," in *Proc. of 2004 IEEE International Conference on Multimedia and Expo (ICME 2004)*, Taipei, Taiwan, Jun. 27 – 30, 2004, pp. 1151–1154.

13

Detection of Signals in Nonstationary Noise via Kalman Filter-Based Stationarization Approach

Hiroshi Ijima* & Akira Ohsumi**,***
** Wakayama University*
*** University of Miyazaki*
Japan

1. Introduction

Needless to say, the signal detection is one of the most important problems in the signal processing area for a long time, and a great deal of investigations has been done up to the present time. Most of the conventional approaches are based on the (binary) hypothesis-testing, and treat the corrupting (additive) noise as a stationary random process because stationary process is rather easy to handle and moreover its (invariant) statistical parameters can be readily calculated under the ergodic hypothesis. However, it will be no doubt that the actual random noise such as environmental noise is considered to be nonstationary because its statistical properties are not always unchanged but vary according to underlying physical circumstances.
Thus the problem of detecting signals in nonstationary random noise is the more important. For such problem, several interesting methods have been proposed. For example, Haykin (1996) and Haykin & Bhattacharya (1997) treat this problem and proposed a method named the modular learning strategy which incorporates such three fundamental blocks as time-frequency analysis, feature extraction and pattern classification. Also, Haykin & Thomson (1998) proposed an adaptive detector based on learning for the detection of the target signal buried in nonstationary background noises.
Philosophically different from their method, the authors have proposed an approach to the signal detection in nonstationary random noise, a new method of stationarization of the observation noise. The key of the approach is to convert the nonstationary random noise to a stationary one, and this procedure was named as stationarization of the observation data.
In Ijima, Okui & Ohsumi (2005) and Ijima, Ohsumi & Okui (2006), the signal detection is performed by testing the stationarized observation data whether there is some non-stationarized portion or not, based on the KM_2O-Langevin equation (which is the AR model with time-varying coefficients). If there exists such a portion in the data, the existence of a signal is decided. Related to the signal detection, the stationarization approach is also used in Ijima,

* Faculty of Education, Wakayama University, Sakaedani, Wakayama 640-8510, Japan;
e-mail: ijima@center.wakayama-u.ac.jp
** Graduate School of Engineering, University of Miyazaki, Kibana, Gakuen, Miyazaki, 889-2192, Japan
*** Presently, Professor Emeritus of Kyoto Institute of Technology; e-mail: akiraspika@nifty.com

Ohsumi & Yamaguchi (2006) to estimate the time-delay of signals in nonstationary random noise, incorporated with the Wigner distribution-based maximum likelihood estimation.
In this paper the signal detection problem is investigated using the stationarization approach to nonstationary data. The model of the corrupting noise is given by an ARMA(p,q) model with unknown time-varying coefficients. These coefficient parameters are estimated from the (original) observation data by the Kalman filter.

2. Problem Statement

Let $\{y(k)\}$ be the (scalar) observation data taken at sampling time instant t_k $(k = 1,2,\cdots)$, and assume that it can be expressed as

$$y(k) = s(k) + n(k) \quad (k = 1,2,\cdots), \tag{1}$$

where $s(\cdot)$ is a signal to be detected, whose form is surely known, and is assumed to exist in a brief interval if it exists; and $n(\cdot)$ is the nonstationary random noise. In consequence, the observation data $\{y(k)\}$ becomes nonstationary, but its trend time series is assumed to be removed by the process

$$y(k) = \Delta^d Y(k), \tag{2}$$

where $Y(k)$ is the original data received by the receiver; $\Delta Y(k) = Y(k) - Y(k-1)$; and d indicates the order.
In this paper the random noise $n(k)$ is assumed to be given as the output of ARMA(p, q) model with time-varying coefficient parameters:

$$n(k) + \sum_{i=1}^{p} \alpha_i(k) n(k-i) = \sum_{j=1}^{q} \beta_j(k) w(k-j) + w(k), \tag{3}$$

where $w(\cdot)$ is the white Gaussian noise with zero-mean and variance parameter σ^2; $\{\alpha_i(\cdot)\}$ and $\{\beta_j(\cdot)\}$ are slowly and smoothly varying parameters to be specified.
Then our purpose is to propose a method of detecting the signal $s(k)$ from the noisy observation data $\{y(k)\}$.
The procedure taken in this paper is as follows:
(i) First, based on the noise model (3), coefficient functions $\{\alpha_i(\cdot)\}$ and $\{\beta_j(\cdot)\}$ are estimated using Kalman filter from the observation data $\{y(k)\}$.
(ii) Using the estimates $\{\hat{\alpha}_i(\cdot)\}$ and $\{\hat{\beta}_j(\cdot)\}$ obtained in (i), the observation data $y(k)$ is modified to become stationary. This procedure is called the *stationarization of observation data.*
(iii) Using the stationarized observation data $\hat{y}(k)$, the signal detection is based on the model

$$\hat{y}(k) = \hat{s}(k) + w(k), \tag{4}$$

where $\hat{s}(k)$ is the modified signal. Equation (4) is familiar in the conventional signal detection problem where the noise is stationary.

3. Stationarization of Observation Data

Recalling the assumption that the duration of the signal $s(k)$ is short, neglect the signal in the observation data and consider the signal-free case, i.e., $y(k) = n(k)$, then the observation data $y(k)$ is expressed by (1) and (3) as follows:

$$y(k) = -\sum_{i=1}^{p} \alpha_i(k) y(k-i) + \sum_{j=1}^{q} \beta_j(k) w(k-j) + w(k). \tag{5}$$

In order to estimate the time-varying parameters $\{\alpha_i(k)\}$ and $\{\beta_j(k)\}$ in (5), suppose that they change from step $k-1$ to k under random effects $\{e.(k)\}$. Define vectors

$$x(k) = \begin{bmatrix} -\alpha_1(k) \\ \vdots \\ -\alpha_p(k) \\ \beta_1(k) \\ \vdots \\ \beta_q(k) \end{bmatrix}, \quad v(k) = \begin{bmatrix} -e_1(k) \\ \vdots \\ -e_p(k) \\ e_{p+1}(k) \\ \vdots \\ e_{p+q}(k) \end{bmatrix}. \tag{6}$$

Then, $\{\alpha_i(k)\}$ and $\{\beta_j(k)\}$ are subject to the dynamics,

$$x(k+1) = x(k) + v(k), \tag{7}$$

where $\{e.(k)\}$ are assumed to be Gaussian with zero-means and variances $\tau_1^2, \cdots, \tau_{p+q}^2$. Then, Eq. (5) is expressed formally as

$$y(k) = H(k)x(k) + w(k) \tag{8}$$

in which $H(k)$ is given by

$$H(k) = [y(k-1), \cdots, y(k-p), w(k-1), \cdots, w(k-q)]. \tag{9}$$

At this stage it should be noted that the matrix $H(k)$ consists of the (unmeasurable) past noise sequence $\{w(\cdot)\}$. To remedy this inadequate situation, we resort to replace it by

$$\hat{H}(k) = [y(k-1), \cdots, y(k-p), \nu_m(k-1), \cdots, \nu_m(k-q)] \tag{10}$$

in which $\{\nu_m(\cdot)\}$ is the sequence modified from the innovation sequence $\nu(\cdot)$ as

$$\nu_m(\ell) = c(\ell)\,\nu(\ell) \quad (\ell = k-q, k-q+1, \cdots, k-1), \tag{11}$$

where

$$\nu(\ell) = y(\ell) - \hat{H}(\ell)\hat{x}(\ell|\ell-1) \tag{12}$$

and

$$c(\ell) = \left[1 + \frac{1}{\sigma^2}\hat{H}(\ell)P(\ell|\ell-1)\hat{H}^T(\ell)\right]^{-\frac{1}{2}}. \tag{13}$$

Here, $\hat{x}(\ell|\ell-1)$ and $P(\ell|\ell-1)$ are the one-step prediction and its covariance matrix computed by Kalman filter for the past interval.

It is a simple exercise to show that the statistical properties of $\nu_m(\cdot)$ is the same as that of $w(\cdot)$, i.e., $E\{\nu_m(k)\} = 0$ and $E\{|\nu_m(k)|^2\} = \sigma^2$ (for proof, see Appendix). Then, instead of (8) we have the expression,

$$y(k) = \hat{H}(k)x(k) + w(k)\,. \tag{14}$$

The procedure for computing $\hat{H}(k)$ is stated as follows:
(i) *Preliminaries*: Assume for the past $k(<0)$ that $\{\nu_m(-1), \nu_m(-2), \cdots, \nu_m(-q)\}$ are set appropriately (may be set all zero), and preassign $\hat{x}(0|-1)$, $\hat{P}(0|-1)$ and $\hat{H}(0)$ as initial values. Then, at time k $(k = 0, 1, 2, \cdots)$
(ii) *Computation of* $\nu(\ell)$ *and* $c(\ell)$: Compute the innovation $\nu(\ell)$ and coefficient $c(\ell)$ by (12) and (13) using $\hat{H}(\ell) = [y(\ell-1), \cdots, y(\ell-p), \nu_m(\ell-1), \cdots, \nu_m(\ell-q)]$.
(iii) *Computation of* $\nu_m(\ell)$: Compute $\nu_m(\ell)$ by (11) using $\nu(\ell)$ and $c(\ell)$ obtained in the previous step.
Repeat Steps (ii) and (iii) for $\ell = k-q, k-q+1, \cdots, k-1$ to obtain $\hat{H}(k)$. In computing (12) and (13), $\hat{x}(\ell|\ell-1)$ and $P(\ell|\ell-1)$ are computed by the Kalman filter (e.g., Jazwinski, 1970):

$$\hat{x}(\ell+1|\ell) = \hat{x}(\ell|\ell) \tag{15}$$

$$\hat{x}(\ell|\ell) = \hat{x}(\ell|\ell-1) + K(\ell)\nu(\ell), \tag{16}$$

$$K(\ell) = \frac{1}{\hat{H}(\ell)P(\ell|\ell-1)\hat{H}^T(\ell) + \sigma^2} P(\ell|\ell-1)\hat{H}^T(\ell) \tag{17}$$

$$P(\ell+1|\ell) = P(\ell|\ell) + Q \tag{18}$$

$$P(\ell|\ell) = P(\ell|\ell-1) - K(\ell)\hat{H}(\ell)P(\ell|\ell-1), \tag{19}$$

where $Q = \mathrm{diag}\,\{\tau_1^2, \cdots, \tau_{p+q}^2\}$.
Thus, the estimates of the coefficient parameters $\{\alpha_i(k)\}$ and $\{\beta_j(k)\}$ are obtained by the Kalman filter constructed for (7) and (14) (whose form is the same as (15)-(19) replacing ℓ by the present k). Under the basic assumption that the coefficient parameters vary slowly and smoothly, they can be treated like constants in an interval I_k around the current time k. Write them as $\hat{\alpha}_{ik}$ and $\hat{\beta}_{jk}$ in I_k. Replacing the past $\{w(k-j)\}$ in (5) by the statistically equivalent sequence $\{\nu_m(k-j)\}$, define the sequence $\hat{y}(k)$ by

$$\hat{y}(k) := y(k) + \sum_{i=1}^{p} \hat{\alpha}_{ik} y(k-i) - \sum_{j=1}^{q} \hat{\beta}_{jk} \nu_m(k-j). \tag{20}$$

Then, we have the following adequate approximation for (5),

$$\hat{y}(k) = w(k) \tag{21}$$

which implies that the sequence $\{\hat{y}(k)\}$ is stationary because $w(k)$ is the stationary white noise.

4. Signal Detection

After obtained the estimates of coefficient parameters, the observation process (14) may be written using estimates as

$$y(k) = \hat{H}(k)\hat{x}(k|k) + w(k) \tag{22}$$

or

$$y(k) + \sum_{i=1}^{p} \hat{\alpha}_{ik} y(k-i) = \sum_{j=1}^{q} \hat{\beta}_{jk} v_m(k-j) + w(k). \tag{23}$$

Now, let us revive the signal $s(k)$ in the observation data. To do this, replace $\{y(k)\}$ formally by $\{y(k) - s(k)\}$ in (23) to obtain

$$y(k) + \sum_{i=1}^{p} \hat{\alpha}_{ik} y(k-i) = \left[s(k) + \sum_{i=1}^{p} \hat{\alpha}_{ik} s(k-i) \right] + \sum_{j=1}^{q} \hat{\beta}_{jk} v_m(k-j) + w(k) \tag{24}$$

or

$$\hat{y}(k) = \hat{s}(k) + w(k), \tag*{(4)$_{\text{bis}}$}$$

where $\hat{y}(k)$ has the same form as (20) and

$$\hat{s}(k) = s(k) + \sum_{i=1}^{p} \hat{\alpha}_{ik} s(k-i). \tag{25}$$

Note that $(4)_{\text{bis}}$ is familiar to us as the mathematical model for the detection problem of signals in *stationary* noise (e.g., Van Trees, 1968).

Now, consider the binary hypotheses: H^1: $\hat{y}(k) = \hat{s}(k) + w(k)$, and H^0: $\hat{y}(k) = w(k)$, and let $\hat{Y}_k$ be the stationarized observation data taken up to k, $\hat{Y}_k = \{\hat{y}(\ell), \ell = 1, 2, \cdots, k\}$. Since the additive noise $w(k)$ is white Gaussian sequence with zero-mean and variance σ^2, the likelihood-ratio function $\Lambda(k) = p\{\hat{Y}_k | H^1\} / \hat{Y}_k | H^0\}$ is evaluated as follows:

$$\Lambda(k) = \frac{\prod_{\ell=1}^{k} (2\pi)^{-\frac{1}{2}} \exp\left\{ -\frac{\{\hat{y}(\ell) - \hat{s}(\ell)\}^2}{2\sigma^2} \right\}}{\prod_{\ell=1}^{k} (2\pi)^{-\frac{1}{2}} \exp\left\{ -\frac{\hat{y}^2(\ell)}{2\sigma^2} \right\}}. \tag{26}$$

We use rather its logarithmic form,

$$\begin{aligned} L(k) &:= \ln \Lambda(k) \\ &= \frac{1}{\sigma^2} \sum_{\ell=1}^{k} \hat{s}(\ell)\hat{y}(\ell) - \frac{1}{2\sigma^2} \sum_{\ell=1}^{k} \hat{s}^2(\ell) \end{aligned} \tag{27}$$

as the signal detector.

5. Simulation Studies

In this section, we provide a typical set of several simulation results to demonstrate the proposed method.

(i) *Experiment* 1.

The top of Fig.1 depicts a sample path of the observation data $\{Y(k)\}$ generated by calculating the output of the ARMA(4, 1)-model:

$$n(k) = -\sum_{i=1}^{4} \alpha_i(k)n(k-i) + \beta(k)w(k-1) + w(k)\,.$$

Time-varying coefficients $\{\alpha_i(k)\}$ and $\beta(k)$ are set as

$$\alpha_1(k) = -1.24\sin(0.002k - 0.95),\ \alpha_2(k) = 0.38 - 2\cos(0.004k - 1.89)$$
$$\alpha_3(k) = \alpha_1(k), \quad \alpha_4(k) = 1, \quad \beta(k) = 1.5.$$

The bottom of Fig.1 shows a signal embedded in the observation data around $k = 300$ given by

$$s(\ell) = 12\,e^{-2.78\ell^2}\sin(1.26\ell),$$

where $\ell = k - 300$. Figure 2 depicts trend-removed data and stationarized data $\hat{y}(k)$. The trend was removed by setting $d = 1$. For the Kalman filter (15)~(19), the parameters are set

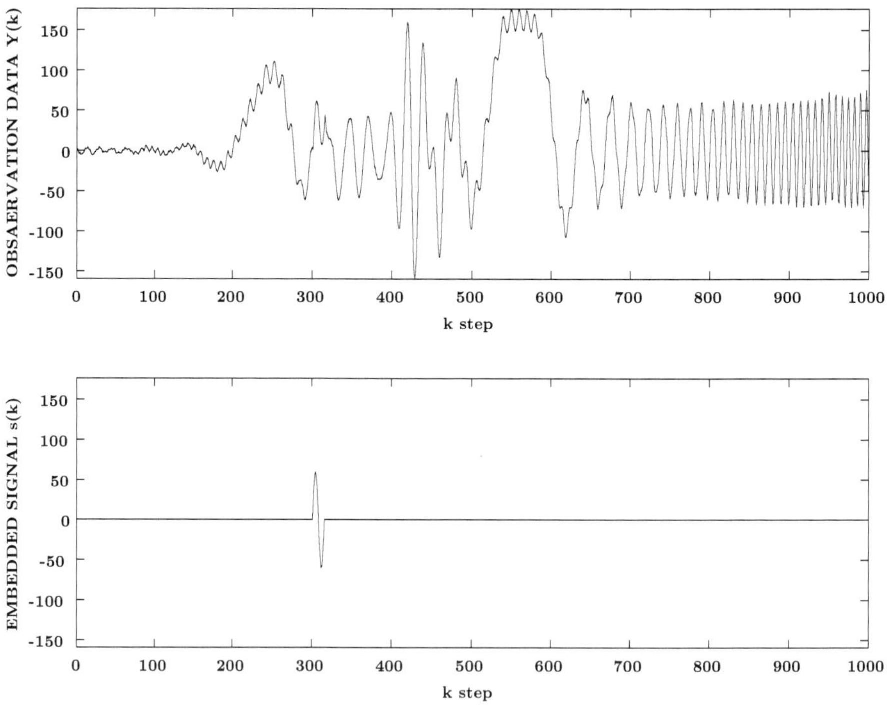

Fig. 1. A sample path of the observation data $Y(k)$ (top) and the embedded signal $s(k)$ (bottom).

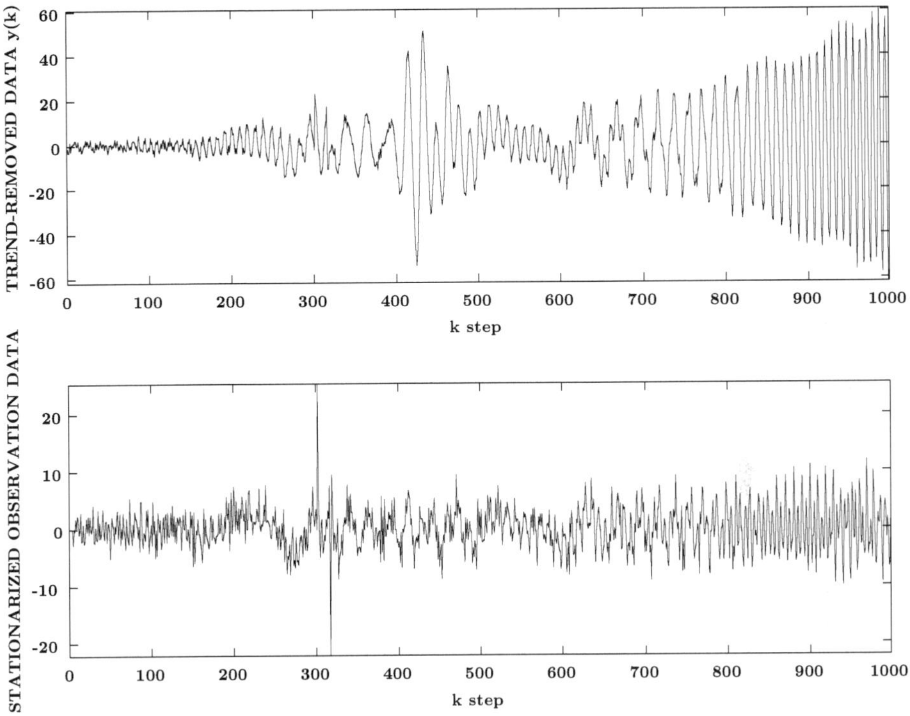

Fig. 2. The trend-removed data $y(k)$ (top) and the stationarized observation data $\hat{y}(k)$ (bottom).

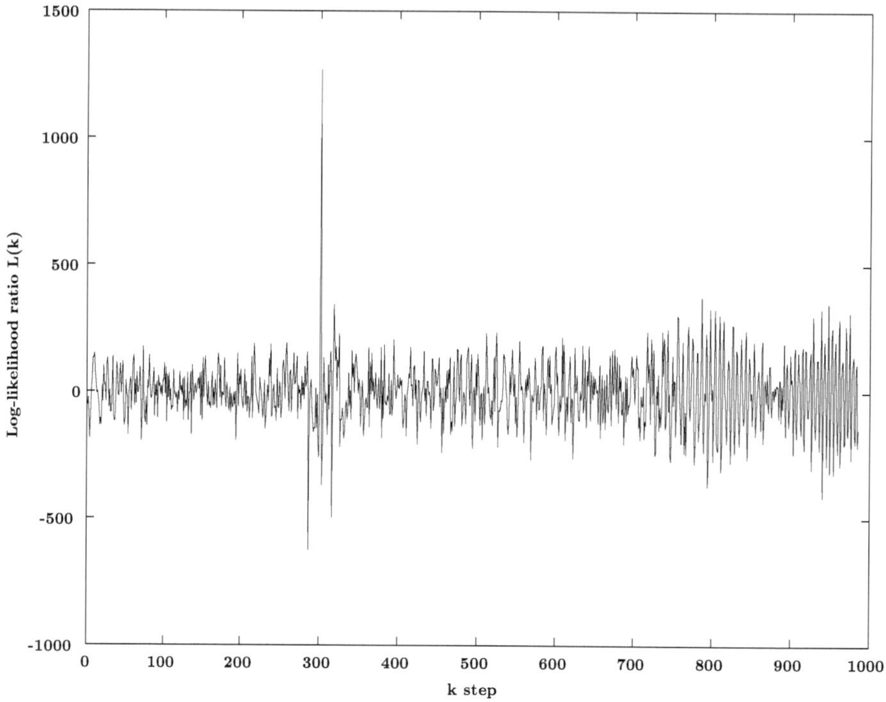

Fig. 3. Log-likelihood function $L(k)$.

as $Q = \text{diag}\{0.05, 0.05, 0.05, 0.05, 0.05\}$ and $\sigma^2 = 40$. It should be noted that from Fig. 2 the observation data is well stationarized and that even in this figure the signal emerges from the background noise.

Figure 3 shows the result of signal detection by the current log-likelihood ratio function $L(k)$. Clearly, it exhibits a salient peak around the true time instant $k = 300$ and this shows the existence of the signal.

(ii) *Experiment* 2.

Efficacy of the signal detector proposed in this paper is also tested for the pulse signal.

Figure 4 depicts observation data and embedded three pulses. Random noise $n(k)$ is generated by the same manner of previous simulation with same coefficients $\alpha_i(k)$ and $\beta(k)$. As a signals $s(k)$, a train of pulses with same magnitude is considered:

$$s(k) = \begin{cases} 20 & \text{for } D_i \le k < D_i + 5 \;\; (i = 1, 2, 3) \\ 0 & \text{otherwise,} \end{cases}$$

where $D_1 = 200$, $D_2 = 500$, $D_3 = 800$.

Figure 5 depicts trend-removed data and stationarized data $\hat{y}(k)$. The trend was also removed by setting $d = 1$. The parameters of Kalman filter are set as the same of previous experiment. Figure 6 shows the result of signal detection. Clearly, log-likelihood ratio function $L(k)$ has large value around each time when each pulse exists. Thus the signal detection is well succeeded.

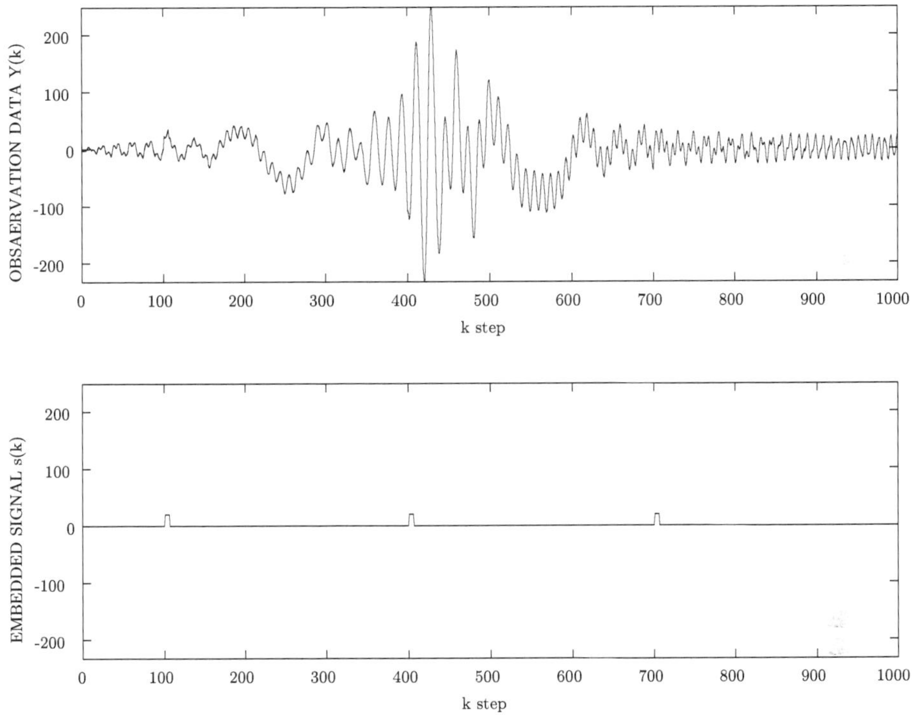

Fig. 4. A sample path of the observation data $Y(k)$ (top) and the pulse signal $s(k)$ (bottom).

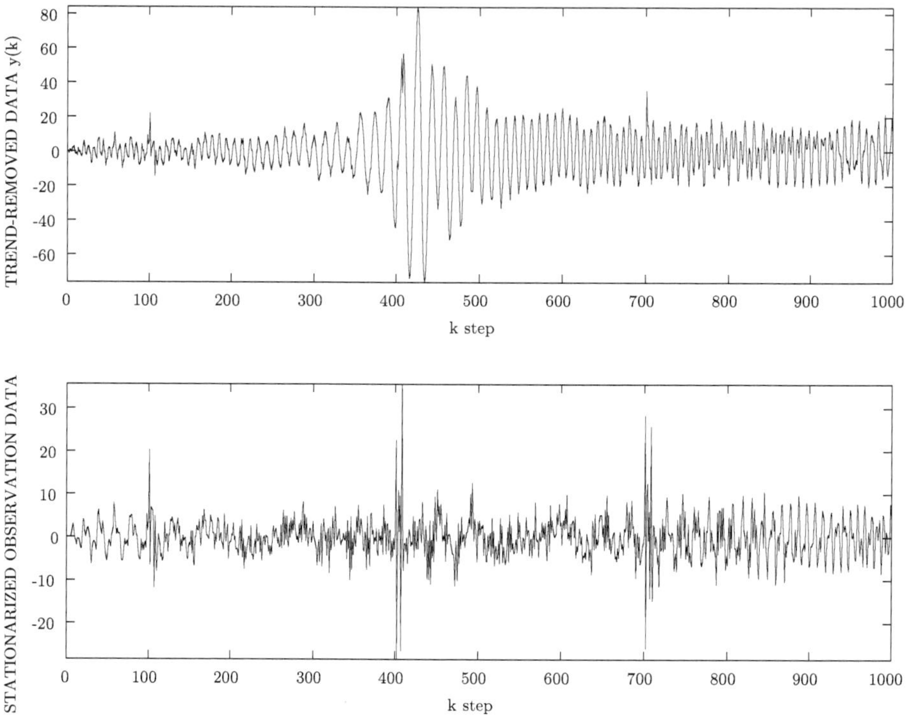

Fig. 5. The trend-removed data (top) and the stationarized observation data $\hat{y}(k)$ (bottom).

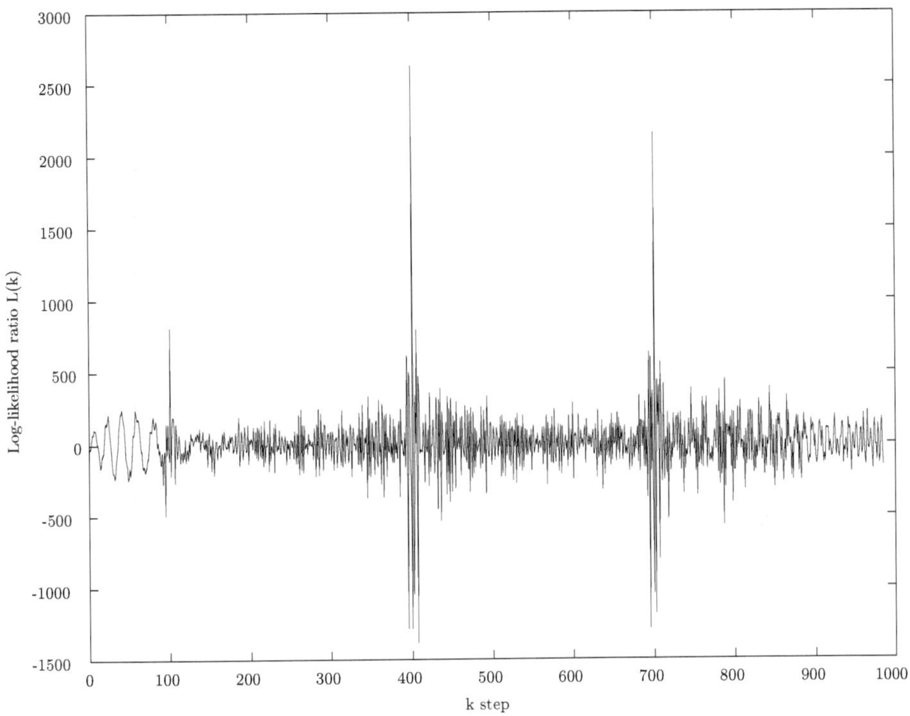

Fig. 6. Log-likelihood function $L(k)$.

6. Conclusion

The efficacy of the proposed signal detection method based on the stationarization of nonstationary observation data has been confirmed by simulation studies. The key to use the Kalman filter to estimate the coefficient parameters of the ARMA noise model is laid on the replacement of the unobservable past noise sequence by the equivalent (modified) innovation sequence which is observation data-measurable. The stationarization of a nonstationary data as introduced in this paper will have potential ability to treat the nonstationary noise or observation data in the signal processing.

Appendix. *Proof of Statistical Equivalence Between $\{w(k)\}$ and $\{\nu_m(k)\}$*

The mean of the modified innovation sequence $\nu_m(k)$ is clearly zero. Indeed,

$$\begin{aligned} \mathcal{E}\{\nu_m(k)\} &= c(k)\mathcal{E}\{\nu(k)\} \\ &= c(k)\mathcal{E}\{y(k) - \hat{H}(k)\hat{x}(k|k-1)\}. \end{aligned}$$

Here, recalling that $y(k)$ is given by the form (14), we have

$$
\begin{aligned}
&= c(k)[\hat{H}(k)\mathcal{E}\{x(k) - \hat{x}(k|k-1)\} + \mathcal{E}\{w(k)\}] \\
&= c(k)\hat{H}(k)\mathcal{E}\{\mathcal{E}\{x(k) - \hat{x}(k|k-1)|Y_{k-1}\}\} \\
&= c(k)\hat{H}(k)\mathcal{E}\{\mathcal{E}\{x(k)|Y_{k-1}\} - \hat{x}(k|k-1)\} \\
&= 0,
\end{aligned}
$$

where $Y_{k-1} = \{y(\ell), 0 \le \ell \le k-1\}$.
Next, the variance of $v_m(k)$ is evaluated as follows:

$$
\begin{aligned}
\mathcal{E}\{v_m^2(k)\} &= c^2(k)\mathcal{E}\{v^2(k)\} \\
&= c^2(k)\mathcal{E}\{[\hat{H}(k)[x(k) - \hat{x}(k|k-1)] + w(k)]^2\} \\
&= c^2(k)[\hat{H}(k)\mathcal{E}\{[x(k) - \hat{x}(k|k-1)][x(k) - \hat{x}(k|k-1)]^T\}\hat{H}^T(k) + \mathcal{E}\{w^2(k)\}] \\
&= c^2(k)[\hat{H}(k)P(k|k-1)\hat{H}^T(k) + \sigma^2].
\end{aligned}
$$

If we select $c(k)$ as (13), the variance of $v_m(k)$-sequence becomes σ^2 which is just the variance of $\{w(k)\}$.
(Q.E.D.)

7. References

Haykin, S. (1996). Neural networks expand SP's horizons. *IEEE Signal Processing Mag.*, Vol.13, No.2, pp.24-29

Haykin, S. & Bhattacharya, T. K. (1997). Modular learning strategy for signal detection in a nonstationary environment. *IEEE Trans. Signal Processing*, Vol.45, No.6, pp.1619-1637

Haykin, S. & Thomson, D. J. (1998). Signal detection in a nonstationary environment reformulated as an adaptive pattern classification problem. *Proc. of the IEEE*, Vol.86, No.11, pp.2325-2344

Ijima, H., Ohsumi, A. & Okui, R. (2006). A method of detection of signals corrupted by nonstationary random noise via stationarization of the data, *Trans. IEICE, Fundamentals of Electronics, Communications and Computer Sciences*, Vol. J89-A, No.6, pp.535-543 (in Japanese)

Ijima, H., Ohsumi, A. & Yamaguchi, S. (2006). Nonlinear parametric estimation for signals in nonstationary random noise via stationarization and Wigner distribution, *Proc. 2006 Int. Symp. Nonlinear Theory and its Applic.* (*NOLTA 2006*), Bologna, Italy, pp.851-854

Ijima, H., Okui, R. & Ohsumi, A. (2005). Detection of signals is nonstationary random noise via staionarization and stationary test, *Proc. IEEE Workshop on Statistical Signal Processing* (*SSP'05*), Bordeaux, France, Paper ID 68

Jazwinski A. H. (1970). *Stochastic Processes and Filtering Theory*, Academic Press, New York

Van Trees, H. L. (1968). *Detection, Estimation, and Modulation Theory*, Part I, John Wiley

14

Direct Design of Infinite Impulse Response Filters based on Allpole Filters

Alfonso Fernandez-Vazquez and Gordana Jovanovic Dolecek
Department of Electronics
INAOE, Puebla, Mexico
P.O. Box 51 and 216, 72000
Tel/Fax: +52 222 2470517
afernan@ieee.org, gordana@inaoep.mx

This chapter presents a new framework to design different types of IIR filters based on the general technique for maximally flat allpole filter design. The resulting allpole filters have some desired characteristics, i.e., desired degree of flatness and group delay, and the desired phase response at any prescribed set of frequency points. Those characteristics are important to define the corresponding IIR filters. The design includes both real and complex cases.
In that way we develop a direct design method for linear-phase Butterworth-like filters, using the same specification as in traditional analog-based IIR filter design. The design includes the design of lowpass filters as well as highpass filters. The designed filters can be either real or complex. The design of liner-phase two-band filter banks is also discussed.
Additionally, we discussed the designs of some special filters such as Butterworth-like filters with improved group delay, complex wavelet filters, and fractional Hilbert transformers.
Finally, we addressed a new design of IIR filters based on three allpass filters. As a result we propose a new design of lowpass filters with a desired characteristic based on the complex allpole filters.
Closed form equations for the computation of the filter coefficients are provided. All design techniques are illustrated with examples.

1. Introduction

The design of allpole filters has been attractive in the last years due to some promising applications, like the design of allpass filters (Chan et al., 2005; Lang, 1998; Pun & Chan, 2003; Selesnick, 1999; Zhang & Iwakura, 1999), the design of orthogonal and biorthogonal IIR wavelet filters (Selesnick, 1998; Zhang et al., 2001; 2000; 2006), the design of complex wavelets (Fernandes et al., 2003), the design of half band filters (Zhang & Amaratunga, 2002), the filter bank design (Kim & Yoo, 2003; Lee & Yang, 2004; Saramaki & Bregovic, 2002), the fractional delay filter design (Laakso et al., 1996), the fractional Hilbert transform (Pei & Wang, 2002), notch filters (Joshi & Roy, 1999; Pei & Tseng, 1997; Tseng & Pei, 1998), among others. The majority of the methods use some approximation of the desired phase in the least square sense and minimax sense.
The allpole filters with maximally flat phase response characteristic have been specially attractive due to promising applications, like the design of IIR filters (Selesnick, 1999), the design

of orthogonal and biorthogonal IIR wavelet filters (Selesnick, 1998; Zhang et al., 2001; 2000; 2006), the design of complex wavelets (Fernandes et al., 2003), the design of half band filters (Zhang & Amaratunga, 2002), the fractional delay filter design (Laakso et al., 1996) and the fractional Hilbert transform design (Pei & Wang, 2002).
This chapter presents a new design of real and complex allpole filters with the given phase, group delay, and degree of flatness, at any desired set of frequency points. The main motivation of this work is to get some new promising cases related with the applications of maximally flat allpole filters. In that way, using the proposed extended allpole filter design, we introduced some new special cases.
The rest of the chapter is organized as follows. Section 2 establishes the general equations for maximally flat real and complex allpole filters. The discussion of the proposed design is given in Section 3 for both, real and complex cases. Different special cases of the general allpole filter design is discussed in Section 4. Finally, Section 5 presents some applications of the proposed allpole filter design, i.e., linear-phase Butterworth-like filter, Butterworth-like filters with improved group delay, complex wavelet filters, fractional Hilbert transformers, and new IIR filters based on three allpass filters.

2. Equations for Maximally Flat Allpole Filter

We derive here equations for real and complex allpole filters both of order N, delay τ, and degree of flatness K, at a given set of frequency points.
We consider that an allpole filter of order N is given by,

$$D(z) = \frac{\alpha}{F(z)}, \tag{1}$$

where α is a complex constant with unit magnitude, z is the complex variable, and $F(z)$ is a polynomial of degree N,

$$F(z) = 1 + \sum_{n=1}^{N} f_n z^{-n}. \tag{2}$$

In general, the filter coefficients f_n , $n = 1, \ldots, N$, are complex, i.e., $f_n = f_{\mathrm{R}n} + \mathrm{j} f_{\mathrm{I}n}$ where $f_{\mathrm{R}n}$ and $f_{\mathrm{I}n}$ are the real and imaginary parts of f_n, respectively. Obviously, if $f_{\mathrm{I}n} = 0$, we obtain real coefficients.
The phase responses of $D(z)$ and $F(z)$ are related by

$$\phi_{\mathrm{D}}(\omega) = \phi_\alpha - \phi_{\mathrm{F}}(\omega), \tag{3}$$

where ϕ_α is the phase of α, and $\phi_{\mathrm{D}}(\omega)$ and $\phi_{\mathrm{F}}(\omega)$ are the phases of $D(z)$ and $F(z)$, respectively. The corresponding group delay is the negative derivative of the phase, as shown in (4).

$$G(\omega) = -\frac{\mathrm{d}\phi_{\mathrm{D}}(\omega)}{\mathrm{d}\omega} = \frac{\mathrm{d}\phi_{\mathrm{F}}(\omega)}{\mathrm{d}\omega}. \tag{4}$$

The conditions for the maximally flat group delay at the desired frequency point ω are

$$G(\omega) = \tau \tag{5a}$$

$$G^{(p)}(\omega) = 0, \qquad p = 1, \ldots, K, \tag{5b}$$

where τ is the desired group delay, K is the degree of flatness, and $G^{(p)}(\omega)$ indicates the pth derivative of $G(\omega)$.

By performing the Fourier transform, equation (2) can be written as

$$F(e^{j\omega}) = \left[F(e^{j\omega})F^*(e^{j\omega})\right]^{1/2} e^{j\phi_F(\omega)}, \tag{6}$$

where $F^*(e^{j\omega})$, is the complex conjugate of $F(e^{j\omega})$.
Using (4) and (6) the corresponding group delay $G(\omega)$ can be expressed as

$$G(\omega) = \frac{d\phi_F(\omega)}{d\omega} = \Im\left\{\frac{F^{(1)}(e^{j\omega})}{F(e^{j\omega})}\right\}, \tag{7}$$

where $F^{(1)}(e^{j\omega})$ is the first derivative of $F(e^{j\omega})$ and $\Im\{\cdot\}$ indicates the imaginary part of $\{\cdot\}$.
Combining (5) and (7), we arrive at

$$\Im\left\{\frac{F^{(1)}(e^{j\omega})}{F(e^{j\omega})}\right\} = \tau, \tag{8a}$$

$$\Im\left\{\frac{d^k}{d\omega^k}\left\{\frac{F^{(1)}(e^{j\omega})}{F(e^{j\omega})}\right\}\right\} = 0, \qquad l = 1, \ldots, K. \tag{8b}$$

The Fourier transform (6) can be rewritten as,

$$F(e^{j\omega}) = \sum_{n=0}^{N}\Big(f_{Rn}\cos(\omega n) + f_{In}\sin(\omega n)\Big) + j\sum_{n=1}^{N}\Big(f_{In}\cos(\omega n) - f_{Rn}\sin(\omega n)\Big). \tag{9}$$

Substituting (9) into (8), we find that that the conditions given in (8) result in the following set of linear equations:

$$\sum_{n=1}^{N}(n+\tau)^k\cos(\omega n + \phi_\alpha - \phi_D(\omega))f_{Rn}$$
$$+\sum_{n=1}^{N}(n+\tau)^k\sin(\omega n + \phi_\alpha - \phi_D(\omega))f_{In} = -\tau^k\cos(\phi_D(\omega) - \phi_\alpha),\ k \text{ odd}, \tag{10a}$$

$$\sum_{n=1}^{N}(n+\tau)^k\sin(\omega n + \phi_\alpha - \phi_D(\omega))f_{Rn}$$
$$-\sum_{n=1}^{N}(n+\tau)^k\cos(\omega n + \phi_\alpha - \phi_D(\omega))f_{In} = \tau^k\sin(\phi_D(\omega) - \phi_\alpha),\ k \text{ even}. \tag{10b}$$

Equations (10a) and (10b) are the general set of equations, which includes desired phases, group delays and degrees of flatness at given frequency points for both real and complex cases.
Notice that for each frequency point ω_l, we have $K_l + 2$ equations (see (10)) and $2N$ unknown coefficients. A consistent set of linear equations (10) is obtained if the following condition is satisfied,

$$N = \left(\frac{K_1}{2}+1\right) + \left(\frac{K_2}{2}+1\right) + \cdots + \left(\frac{K_L}{2}+1\right), \tag{11}$$

where L is the number of frequency points.

3. Description and discussion of the proposed allpole filter design

We describe the design procedure based on general equations for the allpole filter proposed in Section 2

The parameters of the design are the constant α, the number L, the corresponding frequency values ω_l, $l = 1, \dots, L$, phase values $\phi_D(\omega_l)$, $l = 1, \dots, L$, group delays $\tau(\omega_l)$, $l = 1, \dots, L$, and degrees of flatness K_l, $l = 1, \dots, L$.

For the real case, i.e., $f_{In} = 0$ and α is a real constant, the relations (10a) and (10b) become

$$\sum_{n=1}^{N} (n+\tau)^k \cos(\omega n - \phi_D(\omega)) f_n = -\tau^k \cos(\phi_D(\omega)), \quad k \text{ odd}, \tag{12a}$$

$$\sum_{n=1}^{N} (n+\tau)^k \sin(\omega n - \phi_D(\omega)) f_n = \tau^k \sin(\phi_D(\omega)), \quad k \text{ even}. \tag{12b}$$

Similarly, the condition (11), for the real case becomes

$$N = (K_1 + 2) + (K_2 + 2) + \cdots + (K_L + 2)\,. \tag{13}$$

The algorithm is described in the following steps:

Step 1. Compute the order of the allpole filter N, using (13) for the real case, and (11) for the complex case.

Step 2. Substitute the frequencies $\omega_l, l = 1, \dots, L$, group delays $\tau(\omega_l)$ and phases $\phi_D(\omega_l)$ into (12), for the real case, or (10), for the complex case.

Step 3. Calculate the filter coefficients f_n solving the resulting set of equations.

The following example illustrates the design of real allpole filter $D(z)$, ($\alpha = 1$) using three desired frequency points, $L = 3$.

Example 1. The design parameters are shown in Table 1.

l	ω_l	$\phi_D(\omega_l)$	$\tau(\omega_l)$	K_l
1	$\pi/5$	$\pi/3$	3	5
2	$\pi/2$	$\pi/4$	3	7
3	$4\pi/5$	$\pi/5$	4	4

Table 1. Design parameters in Example 1, using $L = 3$ and $\alpha = 1$.

Step 1. From (13), the estimated value of N is 22.

Step 2. We substitute the frequencies ω_l, group delays $\tau(\omega_l)$ and phases $\phi_D(\omega_l)$, $l = 1, \dots, 3$ into (12).

Step 3. Solving the resulting linear equations, we get the filter coefficients f_n.

Figure 1a shows the corresponding group delay, while the phase response is presented in Fig. 1b. The desired phases at $\omega = \pi/5, \omega = \pi/2$ and $\omega = 4\pi/5$ are also indicated in Fig. 1b.

The following example illustrates the complex case.

Example 2. We design the complex allpole filter with characteristics given in Table 2.

Step 1. The order N of the allpole filter is 13 (see (11)).

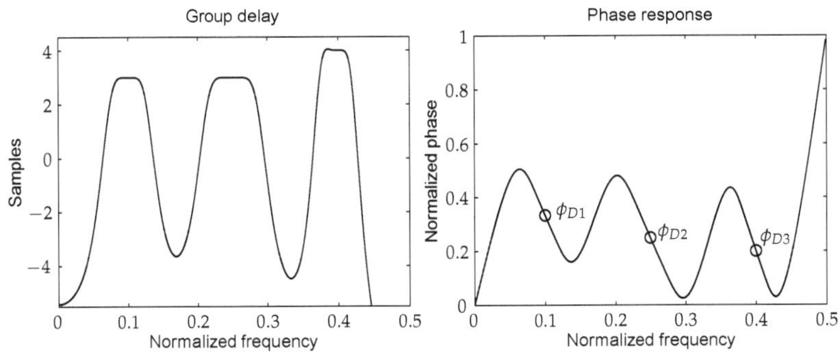

(a) (b)

Fig. 1. Phase response and group delay of the designed real allpole filter in Example 1.

l	ω_l	$\phi_D(\omega_l)$	$\tau(\omega_l)$	K_l
1	$\pi/3$	$\pi/6$	$1/2$	8
2	$4\pi/5$	$-\pi/20$	$1/2$	6
3	$8\pi/5$	$-3\pi/20$	$1/2$	6

Table 2. Design parameters in Example 2. The value L is 3 and $\alpha = 1$.

Step 2. Using (10a) and (10b), we obtain the set of linear equations with 26 unknowns coefficients; 13 for $f_{\mathrm{R}n}$ and 13 for $f_{\mathrm{I}n}$.

Step 3. Solving the resulting set of equations, we get the coefficients of the complex allpole filter.

Figure 2 illustrates the phase response and group delay of the designed allpole filter.

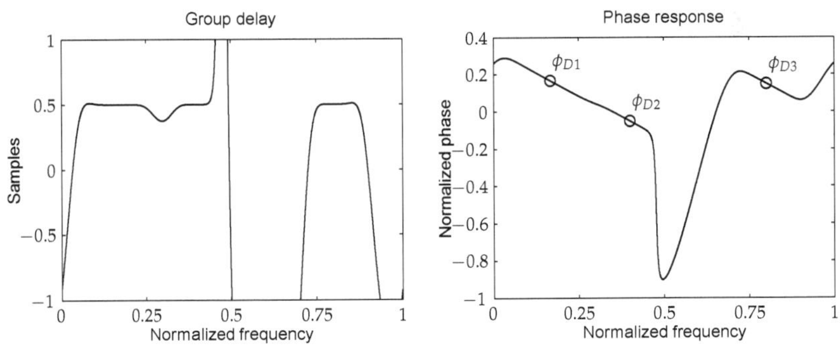

(a) (b)

Fig. 2. Group delay and phase response of the complex allpole filter $D(z)$ in Example 2.

3.1 Relationships between allpole filters and allpass filters

We consider the relations between allpole filters of order N and allpass filters.
An allpass filter $A(z)$ is related with an allpole filter as follows (Selesnick, 1999),

$$A(z) = z^{-N}\frac{D(z)}{\widetilde{D}(z)} = z^{-N}\frac{\alpha\widetilde{F}(z)}{\alpha^* F(z)}, \tag{14}$$

where $\widetilde{D}(z)$ is the paraconjugate of $D(z)$, that is, it is generated by conjugating the coefficients of $D(z)$ and by replacing z by z^{-1}.
The phase $\phi_A(\omega)$ of $A(z)$ can be expressed as

$$\phi_A(\omega) = -\omega N + 2\phi_D(\omega), \tag{15}$$

where the desired phase $\phi_D(\omega)$ is given by

$$\phi_D(\omega) = \frac{\phi_A(\omega) + \omega N}{2}. \tag{16}$$

From (15), the group delay of the complex allpass filter $\tau_A(\omega)$ is given by

$$\tau_A(\omega) = N + 2\tau(\omega), \tag{17}$$

where $\tau(\omega)$ is the group delay of $D(z)$.
Using (17), it follows

$$\tau(\omega) = \frac{\tau_A(\omega) - N}{2}. \tag{18}$$

It is well known that the structures based on allpass filters exhibit a low sensitivity to the filter quantization and a low noise level (Mitra, 2005). Therefore, the relationship (14), between allpass and allpole filters, gives the possibility to use efficient allpass structures in the proposed design.

4. Promising special cases

The proposed allpole filters have desired phases, group delays and degrees of flatness at a specified set of frequency points. In this section we introduce some new special cases of the proposed design (10), which are used for the design of complex allpole filters, complex wavelet filters, and linear-phase IIR filters.

4.1 First order allpole filters

Using (12), the filter coefficient f_{R1} is computed as follows:

$$f_{R1} = \frac{\sin(\phi_{D_1})}{\sin(\omega_1 - \phi_{D_1})}, \tag{19}$$

where ϕ_{D_1} is the desired phase at $\omega = \omega_1$.
To ensure the stability of the allpole filter, we have

$$\tan(2\phi_{D_1}) > \frac{1 - \cos(2\omega_1)}{\sin(2\omega_1)}. \tag{20}$$

Similarly for the complex case, the filter coefficient f_1 is

$$f_1 = \frac{\sin(\phi_\alpha - \phi_{D_2})e^{j(\omega_1+\phi_\alpha-\phi_{D_1})} - \sin(\phi_\alpha - \phi_{D_1})e^{j(\omega_2+\phi_\alpha-\phi_{D_2})}}{\sin(\omega_1 - \omega_2 + \phi_{D_2} - \phi_{D_1})}, \tag{21}$$

where ϕ_{D_1} and ϕ_{D_2} are the phases of the allpole filter at the desired frequency points $\omega = \omega_1$ and $\omega = \omega_2$, respectively. The stability of the allpole filter is satisfied if the following equation holds

$$\tan(\phi_{D_2} - \phi_\alpha) < \frac{\cos(\omega_1 - \omega_2 + \phi_\alpha - \phi_{D_1}) - |\cos(\phi_{D_1} - \phi_\alpha)|}{\sin(\omega_1 - \omega_2 + \phi_\alpha - \phi_{D_1}) + \sin(\phi_{D_1} - \phi_\alpha)}. \tag{22}$$

4.2 Second order allpole filter

We consider the following two cases.

Case 1. For $\omega = \omega_1$, we specify the desired phase ϕ_{D_1} and group delay τ. Substituting these conditions into the general equations (12), the resulting filter coefficients are

$$f_{R1} = -\frac{(\tau+1)\sin(2\omega_1) - \sin(2\omega_1 - 2\phi_{D_1})}{(\tau+1)\sin\omega_1 - \sin(\omega_1 - \phi_{D_1})\cos(2\omega_1 - \phi_{D_1})}, \tag{23}$$

$$f_{R2} = \frac{\tau\sin\omega_1 + \sin(\phi_{D_1})\cos(\omega_1 - \phi_{D_1})}{(\tau+1)\sin\omega_1 - \sin(\omega_1 - \phi_{D_1})\cos(2\omega_1 - \phi_{D_1})}. \tag{24}$$

Additionally, the condition for the stability of the allpole filter is

$$\tau > -1 + \frac{|\sin(2\omega_1 - 2\phi_{D_1})|}{2\sin\omega_1}. \tag{25}$$

Case 2. For two phases ϕ_{D_1} and ϕ_{D_2} at the frequencies ω_1 and ω_2, the filter coefficients are

$$f_{R1} = \frac{\sin(2\omega_1 - \phi_{D_1})\sin(\phi_{D_2}) - \sin(\phi_{D_1})\sin(2\omega_2 - \phi_{D_2})}{\sin(\omega_2 - \phi_{D_2})\sin(2\omega_1 - \phi_{D_1}) - \sin(\omega_1 - \phi_{D_1})\sin(2\omega_2 - \phi_{D_2})}, \tag{26}$$

$$f_{R2} = \frac{\sin(\phi_{D_1})\sin(\omega_2 - \phi_{D_2}) - \sin(\omega_1 - \phi_{D_1})\sin(\phi_{D_2})}{\sin(\omega_2 - \phi_{D_2})\sin(2\omega_1 - \phi_{D_1}) - \sin(\omega_1 - \phi_{D_1})\sin(2\omega_2 - \phi_{D_2})}. \tag{27}$$

Furthermore, the stability of the allpole filter is guaranteed if the equation

$$\tan(\omega_1 - \phi_{D_1}) < -\frac{\sin\omega_1 \sin\omega_2 \tan(\omega_2 - \phi_{D_2})}{\cos\omega_1\cos\omega_2 - 1 + |\cos\omega_1 - \cos\omega_2|} \tag{28}$$

is satisfied.

4.3 Complex Thiran allpole filters

We generalize the result proposed by Thiran (Thiran, 1971), for the design of real allpole filters that are maximally flat at $\omega = 0$, to include both the real and complex cases. The required design specifications are the order of the allpole filter N, group delay $\tau(\omega)$ at $\omega = 0$, τ_0, degree of flatness K, and the phase value ϕ_α.

Consequently, the allpole filter must satisfy:

- $\mathcal{A}.1$ The degree of flatness at $\omega = 0$ is K, where K can be either $2N-2$ or $2N-3$.
- $\mathcal{A}.2$ The phase value $\phi_D(\omega)$ is equal to zero at $\omega = 0$.

4.3.1 Degree of flatness $K = 2N - 2$

Substituting conditions $\mathcal{A}.1$ and $\mathcal{A}.2$ into the set of equations (10), we compute the complex coefficients as follows

$$f_n = (-1)^n \binom{N}{n} \frac{2(2\tau_0 + 1)_{n-1}}{(2\tau_0 + N + 1)_n} \left(\tau_0 + n e^{\mathrm{j}(\phi_\alpha - \pi/2)} \sin \phi_\alpha \right), \tag{29}$$

where $n = 1, \ldots, N$, the binomial coefficient is given by

$$\binom{N}{n} = \frac{N!}{n!(N-n)!}, \tag{30}$$

and the Pochhammer symbol $(x)_m$ indicates the rising factorial of x, which is defined as (Andrews, 1998),

$$(x)_m = \begin{cases} (x)(x+1)(x+2)\cdots(x+m-1) & m > 0, \\ 1 & m = 0. \end{cases} \tag{31}$$

The expression in (29) is the extension of the result proposed in (Thiran, 1971), which includes both real and complex cases. If ϕ_α is 0 or π, the imaginary coefficients are zero, and the result is a real allpole filter, consistent with (Thiran, 1971). For $\phi_\alpha = \pm\pi/2$, the filter is a real allpole filter (this case is not included in (Thiran, 1971)). For all other phase values, the imaginary coefficients are strictly non-zero, i.e., the filter is complex.

4.3.2 Degree of flatness $K = 2N - 3$

In this case, in order to get a degree of flatness $K = 2N - 3$, we set $f_{\mathrm{I}N} = 0$. Consequently, the filter coefficients are

$$f_n = (-1)^n \binom{N}{n} \frac{2(2\tau_0 + 1)_{n-1}}{(2\tau_0 + N + 1)_n} \left(\tau_0 + n + n \frac{(n-N)e^{\mathrm{j}\phi_\alpha} \cos \phi_\alpha}{2\tau_0 + N} \right), \tag{32}$$

where $n = 0, \ldots, N$.

In contrast with (32), to obtain a different solution, we now set $f_{\mathrm{R}N} = 0$. Therefore, we have

$$f_n = (-1)^n \binom{N}{n} \frac{2(2\tau_0 + 1)_{n-1}}{(2\tau_0 + N + 1)_n} \left(\tau_0 + n - \frac{n e^{\mathrm{j}\phi_\alpha}}{N \cos \phi_\alpha} \left(\tau_0 + n + \frac{(N-n)(\tau_0 + N\cos^2 \phi_\alpha)}{2\tau_0 + N} \right) \right), \tag{33}$$

where $n = 0, \ldots, N$.

We illustrate the design with one example.

Example 3. The desired phase ϕ_α, and the group delay τ_0 at $\omega = 0$, are $-\pi/6$, and $7/3$, respectively. The order N of the filter is 5.

We compute the corresponding filter coefficients using (29), (32), and (33). The resulting group delays of $D(z)$ are shown in Fig. 3a, while the phase responses of the designed filters are shown in Fig. 3b.

4.4 Complex allpole filter with flatness at $\omega = 0$ and $\omega = \pi$

Now, we present the design of complex allpole filters of order N (any positive integer) with flatness at $\omega = 0$ and $\omega = \pi$.

The design conditions are: (More detailed explanation is given in Section 5.1.)

$\mathcal{B}.1$ The phase response of $D(z)$ is flat at the frequency points $\omega = 0$ and $\omega = \pi$ with group delays $\tau(0) = \tau(\pi) = -N/2$.

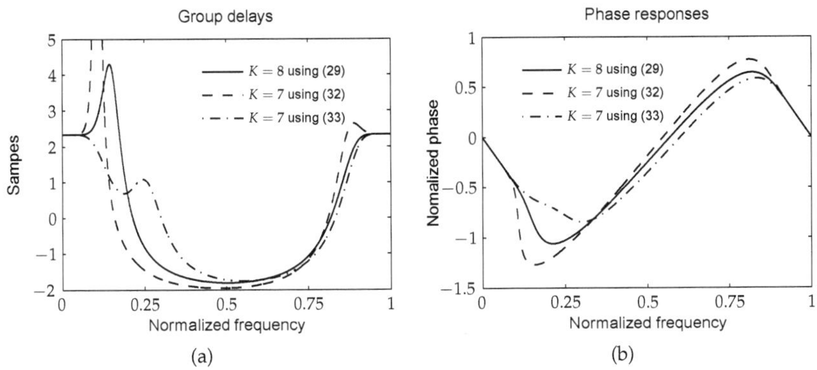

Fig. 3. Group delays and phase responses of the complex allpole filters in Example 3.

$\mathcal{B}$.2 The degree of flatness at these frequency points is the same, i.e., $K = N - 2$.

$\mathcal{B}$.3 The phase values of the allpole filter $\phi_D(\omega)$ at $\omega = 0$ and $\omega = \pi$, are 0 and $\pi(2N + (2l+1))/4$, respectively, where l is an integer.

$\mathcal{B}$.4 The desired phase value $\phi_D(\omega)$ at the given frequency $\omega = \omega_\mathrm{p}$ is ϕ_p, i.e., $\phi_\mathrm{p} = \phi_D(\omega_\mathrm{p})$.

Substituting conditions $\mathcal{B}$.1–$\mathcal{B}$.4 into (10a) and (10b) and solving the resulting set of linear equations, we arrive at

$$f_n = \begin{cases} \binom{N}{n} & n \text{ even,} \\ \binom{N}{n}\left(\sqrt{2}\mathrm{e}^{\mathrm{j}(2\phi_\alpha + \frac{\pi}{4})} - \mathrm{j}\right) & n \text{ odd,} \end{cases} \tag{34}$$

where

$$\phi_\alpha = \angle\left\{-\mathrm{j} - 1 - (-1)^{\lceil N/2 \rceil}\left(\cot\left(\phi_\mathrm{p} - \frac{\omega_\mathrm{p} N}{2}\right) - 1\right)\tan^N\left(\frac{\omega_\mathrm{p}}{2}\right)\right\}, \tag{35}$$

and $\angle\{\cdot\}$ indicates the angle of $\{\cdot\}$, while $\lceil\cdot\rceil$ stands for the floor function.

Next example illustrates the proposed design where the parameters of the design are the filter order N and the phase value ϕ_p at the frequency point ω_p.

Example 4. We design a complex allpole filter using the following specifications: the order of the allpole filter is $N = 7$ and the phase value $\phi_D(\omega)$ at ω_p is 1.2π, where $\omega_\mathrm{p} = 0.3\pi$.

The group delay and phase response of the designed filter are presented in Fig. 4a and 4b, respectively.

4.4.1 Closed form equations for the singularities of the allpole filter

In the following, we consider the computation of the poles of $D(z)$.

Using (34), we obtain the z-transform of the denominator of $D(z)$ defined in (1) as,

$$F(z) = \sum_{n \text{ even}} \binom{N}{n} z^{-n} + (\sqrt{2}\mathrm{e}^{\mathrm{j}(2\phi_\alpha + \pi/4)} - \mathrm{j}) \sum_{n \text{ odd}} \binom{N}{n} z^{-n}. \tag{36}$$

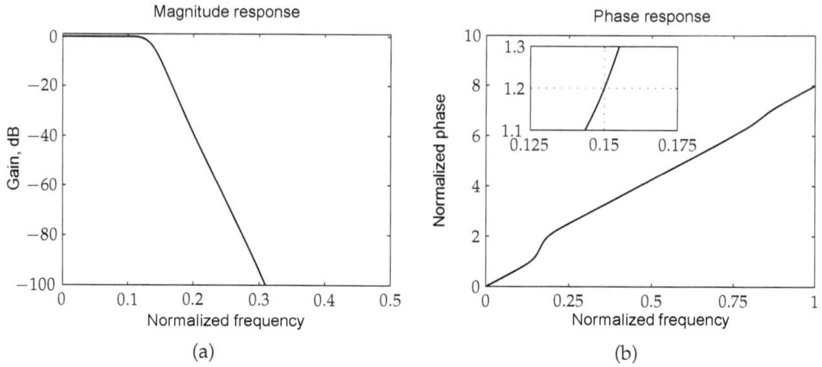

Fig. 4. Group delay and phase response and of the complex allpole filter in Example 4.

After some computations, we get

$$F(z) = \frac{e^{j\phi_\alpha}}{\sqrt{2}} \left[(\cos\phi_\alpha - \sin\phi_\alpha)(1+z^{-1})^N - (j-1)\sin\phi_\alpha (1-z^{-1})^N \right]. \tag{37}$$

Therefore, the corresponding poles are

$$p_k = \frac{\gamma_k + 1}{\gamma_k - 1}, \tag{38}$$

where $k = 0, \ldots, N-1$, and

$$\gamma_k = \left(\frac{\sqrt{2}}{1 - \cot\phi_\alpha} \right)^{\frac{1}{N}} e^{-j\frac{8k+1}{4N}\pi}. \tag{39}$$

4.5 Complex allpole filters with flatness at $\omega = 0$, and $\omega = \pm\omega_r$

In this section, we design a complex allpole filter with the following characteristics:

$\mathcal{C}.1$ The order N is even.

$\mathcal{C}.2$ The allpole filter has flat group delay at the frequency points $\omega = 0$, $\omega = -\omega_r$, and $\omega = \omega_r$. The degrees of flatness are $K_1(\omega = 0) = N-2$, $K_2(\omega = \pm\omega_r) = N/2 - 2$. The group delay at those frequency points is $\tau(0) = \tau(\pm\omega_r) = -N/2$.

$\mathcal{C}.3$ The desired allpole phase value $\phi_D(\omega)$ at the given frequency $\omega = \omega_p$ is ϕ_p, i.e., $\phi_p = \phi_D(\omega_p)$.

$\mathcal{C}.4$ The phase values of the allpole filter $\phi_D(\omega)$ at $\omega = 0$, $\omega = -\omega_r$, and $\omega = \omega_r$ are 0, $\pi/3 + \omega_r N/2$, and $\pi/3 - \omega_r N/2$, respectively.

Substituting conditions $\mathcal{C}.1$–$\mathcal{C}.4$ into (10a) and (10b) and solving the resulting set of linear equations, we have

$$f_n = (-1)^n \left[\binom{N}{n} - \frac{4e^{j\phi_\alpha}}{\sqrt{3}} \binom{N/2}{n} c_{N,n}(\omega_r) \cos(\phi_\alpha + \pi/6) \right], \tag{40}$$

where $n = 0, \ldots, N/2$,

$$\phi_\alpha = \angle \left\{ \sqrt{3} R_\mathrm{p} \cot(\phi_\mathrm{p} - \omega_\mathrm{p} N/2) + 1 + \mathrm{j}\sqrt{3}(R_\mathrm{p} + 1) \right\}, \tag{41}$$

and

$$R_\mathrm{p} = \frac{-2^{N-1} \sin^N \left(\frac{\omega_\mathrm{p}}{2}\right)}{c_{N,N/2}(\omega_\mathrm{r}) + 2C_N(\omega_\mathrm{r}, \omega_\mathrm{p})}, \tag{42}$$

where

$$C_N(\omega_\mathrm{r}, \omega_\mathrm{p}) = \sum_{n=1}^{N/2-1} (-1)^{N/2+n} \binom{N/2}{n} c_{N,n}(\omega_\mathrm{r}) \cos\left((N/2 - n)\omega_\mathrm{p}\right). \tag{43}$$

The function $c_{N,n}(\omega_\mathrm{r})$ for different values of N is given in Table 3. Moreover, we have $c_{N,0}(\omega_\mathrm{r}) = 0$ and $f_n = f_{N-n}$.

Example 5. The desired design specification is as follows: the allpole filter order is equal to 8, $\omega_\mathrm{p} = 0.35\pi$, $\omega_\mathrm{r} = 0.75\pi$, and $\phi_\mathrm{p} = 1.5\pi$. The resulting group delay and phase response of the designed filter are shown in Fig. 5.

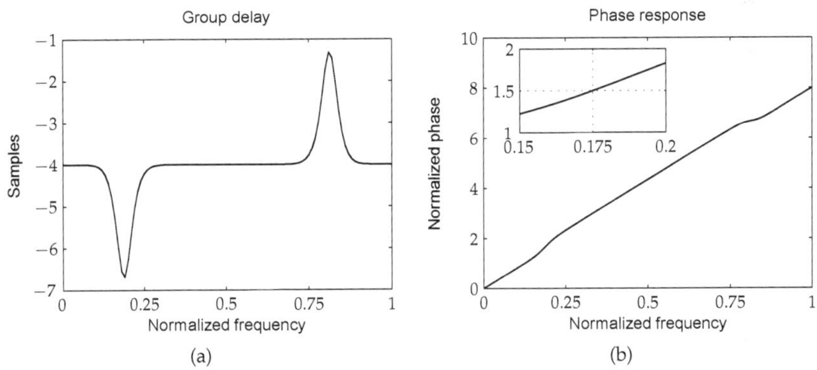

Fig. 5. Group delay and phase response and of the designed complex allpole filter in Example 5.

5. Design of IIR filters based on allpole filters

5.1 Direct design of linear-phase IIR Butterworth filters

A filter $H(z)$ has linear-phase if,

$$H(z) = cz^{-k}\widetilde{H}(z), \tag{44}$$

where $H(z)$ is not necessary causal, z^{-k} is the delay, the complex constant c has unit magnitude and $\widetilde{H}(z)$ is the paraconjugate of $H(z)$, that is, it is generated by conjugating the coefficients of $H(z)$ and by replacing z by z^{-1}.

It has been shown that causal Finite Impulse Response (FIR) filters can be designed to have linear-phase. However, Infinite Impulse Response (IIR) filters can have linear-phase property only in the noncausal case (Vaidyanathan & Chen, 1998), (the phase response is either zero or π). It has been recently shown that filters with the linear-phase property are useful in the filter

N	n	$c_{N,n}(\omega_r) = c_{N,N-n}(\omega_r)$
2	1	$1-\cos(\omega_r)$
4	1	$1-\cos(\omega_r)$
	2	$1-\cos(2\omega_r)$
6	1	$1-\cos(\omega_r)$
	2	$1-\cos(2\omega_r)$
	3	$10-9\cos(\omega_r)-\cos(3\omega_r)$
8	1	$1-\cos(\omega_r)$
	2	$1-\cos(2\omega_r)$
	3	$7-6\cos(\omega_r)-\cos(3\omega_r)$
	4	$17-16\cos(2\omega_r)-\cos(4\omega_r)$
10	1	$1-\cos(\omega_r)$
	2	$1-\cos(2\omega_r)$
	3	$6-5\cos(\omega_r)-\cos(3\omega_r)$
	4	$11-10\cos(2\omega_r)-\cos(4\omega_r)$
	5	$126-100\cos(\omega_r)-25\cos(3\omega_r)-\cos(5\omega_r)$
12	1	$1-\cos(\omega_r)$
	2	$1-\cos(2\omega_r)$
	3	$11/2-9/2\cos(\omega_r)-\cos(3\omega_r)$
	4	$9-8\cos(2\omega_r)-\cos(4\omega_r)$
	5	$66-50\cos(\omega_r)-15\cos(3\omega_r)-\cos(5\omega_r)$
	6	$262-225\cos(2\omega_r)-36\cos(4\omega_r)-\cos(6\omega_r)$
14	1	$1-\cos(\omega_r)$
	2	$1-\cos(2\omega_r)$
	3	$26/5-21/5\cos(\omega_r)-\cos(3\omega_r)$
	4	$8-7\cos(2\omega_r)-\cos(4\omega_r)$
	5	$143/3-35\cos(\omega_r)-35/3\cos(3\omega_r)-\cos(5\omega_r)$
	6	$127-105\cos(2\omega_r)-21\cos(4\omega_r)-\cos(6\omega_r)$
	7	$1761-1225\cos(\omega_r)-441\cos(3\omega_r)-49\cos(5\omega_r)-\cos(7\omega_r)$
16	1	$1-\cos(\omega_r)$
	2	$1-\cos(2\omega_r)$
	3	$5-4\cos(\omega_r)-\cos(3\omega_r)$
	4	$37/5-32/5\cos(2\omega_r)-\cos(4\omega_r)$
	5	$39-28\cos(\omega_r)-10\cos(3\omega_r)-\cos(5\omega_r)$
	6	$87-70\cos(2\omega_r)-16\cos(4\omega_r)-\cos(6\omega_r)$
	7	$715-490\cos(\omega_r)-196\cos(3\omega_r)-28\cos(5\omega_r)-\cos(7\omega_r)$
	8	$3985-3136\cos(2\omega_r)-784\cos(4\omega_r)-64\cos(6\omega_r)-\cos(8\omega_r)$

Table 3. Function $c_{N,n}(\omega_r)$ for different values of N.

bank design and the Nyquist filter design and different methods have been proposed for this design (Djokic et al., 1998; Powell & Chau, 1991; Surma-aho & Saramaki, 1999).

A linear-phase lowpass IIR filter $H(z)$ can be expressed in terms of complex allpass filters as (Zhang et al., 2001),

$$H(z) = \frac{1}{2}\left[A(z) + \widetilde{A}(z)\right], \tag{45}$$

where $A(z)$ is a complex allpass of order N (see (14)).

We can note that the filter defined in (45) satisfies the relation (44) if $k = 0$ and $c = 1$.

The main goal is to propose a new technique to design real and complex IIR filters with linear-phase, based on general design of Section 3, where the design specification is same as in traditional IIR filters design based on analog filters, i.e., the passband and stopband frequencies, ω_p and ω_s, the passband droop A_p, and the stopband attenuation A_s, shown in Fig. 6.

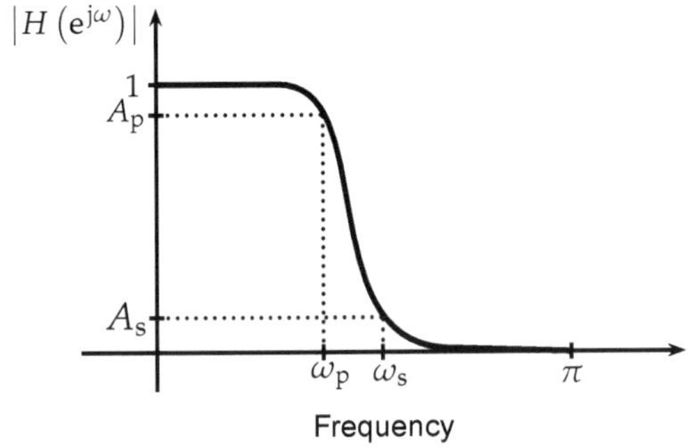

Fig. 6. Design parameters for low pass filter.

We relate the design of linear-phase IIR filter with allpass filter and in the next section we use the general approach to design the corresponding allpole filter.
First, we establish the conditions which the auxiliary complex allpass filters from (45) has to satisfy.
From (45), the magnitude response of $H(z)$ can be expressed as,

$$|H(e^{j\omega})| = \left|\cos\left(\phi_A(\omega)\right)\right|, \quad \text{for all } \omega. \tag{46}$$

The magnitude responses of $|H(e^{j\omega})|$ at $\omega = 0$, and $\omega = \pi$ are 1 and 0, respectively (see Fig. 6). Therefore, the values of $\phi_A(\omega)$ at these frequency points are 0 and $(2l+1)\pi/2$, respectively, where l is an integer. Since the magnitude response of $H(z)$ decreases monotonically, relation (46) can be rewritten as,

$$|H(e^{j\omega})| = \cos\left(\phi_A(\omega)\right), \quad 0 \le \omega \le \pi. \tag{47}$$

Note that $|H(e^{j\omega})|$ has a flat magnitude response at $\omega = 0$ and $\omega = \pi$, and that the filter $A(z)$ has a flat phase response at the same frequency points. As a consequence, the corresponding group delays $\tau_A(0)$ and $\tau_A(\pi)$ are equal to 0.
Considering the value A_p in dB we write

$$20\log_{10}|H(e^{j\omega})|_{\omega=\omega_p} = -A_p. \tag{48}$$

From (47) it follows,

$$\phi_{pA} = \phi_A(\omega_p) = \arccos\left(10^{-A_p/20}\right). \tag{49}$$

In summary, the conditions that the auxiliary complex allpass filter in (45) needs to satisfy are the following:

$\mathcal{D}.1$ The phase values of $\phi_A(\omega)$ at $\omega = 0$ and $\omega = \pi$ are 0 and $(2l+1)\pi/2$, respectively.

$\mathcal{D}.2$ The phase response of $A(z)$ is flat at $\omega = 0$ and $\omega = \pi$. Therefore, $\tau_A(0) = \tau_A(\pi) = 0$.

$\mathcal{D}.3$ The phase value $\phi_{\text{p}A}$ is controlled by A_p (see (49)).

In the following, we use the results from Section 3.1 and the Conditions $\mathcal{D}.1$–$\mathcal{D}.3$ in order to obtain the corresponding conditions for the allpole filter $D(z)$.

5.1.1 Design of flat linear-phase IIR filters based on complex allpole filters

We relate the allpass filter from (45) with the corresponding allpole filter.
Using (16) and the phase values $\phi_A(\omega)$ at $\omega = 0$ and $\omega = \pi$ (see Condition $\mathcal{D}.1$), we get $\phi(0) = 0$ and $\phi(\pi) = \pi(2N + (2l + 1))/4$.
Now, from (18) and Condition $\mathcal{D}.2$, we have $\tau(0) = \tau(\pi) = -N/2$.
Finally, the following relation is obtained using Condition $\mathcal{D}.3$ and (16),

$$\phi_D(\omega_\text{p}) = \phi_\text{p} = \frac{\arccos\left(10^{-A_\text{p}/20}\right) + \omega_\text{p} N}{2}. \tag{50}$$

As a consequence, the corresponding conditions that the allpole filter $D(z)$ has to satisfy are:

$\mathcal{E}.1$ The phase values of $D(z)$ at $\omega = 0$ and $\omega = \pi$ are 0 and $\pi(2N + (2l + 1))/4$, respectively.

$\mathcal{E}.2$ The group delay $\tau(\omega)$ of $D(z)$ at $\omega = 0$ and $\omega = \pi$ are $-N/2$.

$\mathcal{E}.3$ The phase value of $D(z)$ at ω_p, $\phi_D(\omega_\text{p})$, is given by (50).

For a filter having coefficients given in (34) the Conditions $\mathcal{E}.1$ and $\mathcal{E}.2$ are satisfied.
From the Condition $\mathcal{E}.3$ and (35), the corresponding value of $\phi_\alpha(N, \omega_\text{p}, A_\text{p})$ is equal to

$$\phi_\alpha(N, \omega_\text{p}, A_\text{p}) = \angle\left\{-\text{j} - 1 - (-1)^{\lceil N/2 \rceil} A_\text{p}{}' \tan^N\left(\frac{\omega_\text{p}}{2}\right)\right\}, \tag{51}$$

where

$$A_\text{p}{}' = \sqrt{\frac{10^{A_\text{p}/20} + 1}{10^{A_\text{p}/20} - 1}} - 1. \tag{52}$$

We note that the resulting allpole filter has a causal and an anticausal parts. The causal part can be implemented with the well known structures for allpass filters while the anticausal part can be implemented with the structures proposed in (Vaidyanathan & Chen, 1998).
The degree of flatness of the allpass filter $A(z)$ at $\omega = 0$ and $\omega = \pi$ is equal to $N - 2$. Based on this result it can be shown that we have $2N - 1$ null derivatives in the square magnitude response $|H(\text{e}^{\text{j}\omega})|^2$ at $\omega = 0$ and $\omega = \pi$.

5.1.2 Closed form equations for the singularities of $H(z)$

It follows from (37) and (45) that the transfer function $H(z)$ is given as,

$$H(z) = \frac{(1 + z^{-1})^N E(z)}{2z^{-N} F(z) \widetilde{F}(z)}, \tag{53}$$

where

$$E(z) = (1 - \sin(2\phi_\alpha))(1 + z^{-1})^N + ((\text{j} + 1) - (\text{j} - 1)) \sin\phi_\alpha (\cos(\phi_\alpha) - \sin(\phi_\alpha))(1 - z^{-1})^N. \tag{54}$$

We note that the transfer function $H(z)$ has N zeros at $z = -1$ and the other zeros are at (see (54)),

$$z_k = \frac{\beta_k + 1}{\beta_k - 1}, \tag{55}$$

where $k = 0, \ldots, N-1$, and the parameter β_k is given by,

$$\beta_k = \begin{cases} \left(2\frac{1-\cos(2\phi_\alpha)}{1-\sin(2\phi_\alpha)}\right)^{\frac{1}{2N}} e^{j\frac{2\pi}{N}k} & N \text{ even}, \\ \left(2\frac{1-\cos(2\phi_\alpha)}{1-\sin(2\phi_\alpha)}\right)^{\frac{1}{2N}} e^{j\frac{4k-1}{2N}\pi} & N \text{ odd}. \end{cases} \tag{56}$$

It is easily shown that the absolute values of z_k in (55), for even values of N, are always different than 1. However, there also exists one absolute value of z_k, for N odd, which is equal to 1, i.e., there is a zero on the unit circle. The corresponding frequency ω_0 is expressed as,

$$\omega_0 = \pi + 2\arctan\left(2\frac{1-\cos(2\phi_\alpha)}{1-\sin(2\phi_\alpha)}\right)^{\frac{1}{2N}}. \tag{57}$$

As a consequence, the frequency at which $H(e^{j\omega})$ is equal to -1 is given by

$$\omega_1 = \pi + 2\arctan\left(\frac{1}{2}\frac{1-\cos(2\phi_\alpha)}{1-\sin(2\phi_\alpha)}\right)^{\frac{1}{2N}}. \tag{58}$$

Finally, the transfer function $H(z)$ has $2N$ poles which are poles of the corresponding complex allpole filters $D(z)$ and $\widetilde{D}(z)$ (see Section 4.4.1).

5.1.3 Description of the algorithm

The proposed algorithm is described in the following steps:

Step 1. Estimate the order of the allpole filter using the following equation, which can be obtained by solving $\phi_\alpha(N, \omega_p, A_p) = \phi_\alpha(N, \omega_s, A_s)$,

$$N = \left\lfloor \frac{\log_{10}\left(\frac{A'_p}{A'_s}\right)}{\log_{10}\left(\frac{\omega_s'}{\omega_p'}\right)} \right\rfloor, \quad A_p' = \sqrt{\frac{10^{A_p/20}+1}{10^{A_p/20}-1}} - 1, \quad A_s' = \sqrt{\frac{10^{A_s/20}+1}{10^{A_s/20}-1}} - 1, \tag{59}$$

where $\lfloor \cdot \rfloor$ is the ceiling function.

Step 2. From the values N, ω_p and A_p, compute the phase value $\phi_\alpha(N, \omega_s, A_s)$, using (51).

Step 3. Using (34), compute the filter coefficients f_n.

Step 4. Calculate the filter coefficients of $H(z)$ using (45).

We illustrate the procedure with the following example.

Example 6. We design the IIR linear-phase lowpass filter with the passband and stopband frequencies $\omega_p = 0.25\pi$ and $\omega_s = 0.5\pi$, respectively. The passband droop is $A_p = 1$ dB, while the stopband attenuation is $A_s = 65$ dB.

Step 1. Using (59), we estimate $N = 10$. As a consequence, the filter $H(z)$ is real.

Step 2. We calculate the phase value $\phi_\alpha(N, \omega_s, A_s)$, to be $\phi_\alpha(N, \omega_s, A_s) = -0.749925\pi$.

Step 3. The filter coefficients f_n are computed from (34).

Step 4. We compute the coefficients of the designed filter $H(z)$. The magnitude response of the designed filter is given in Fig. 7.

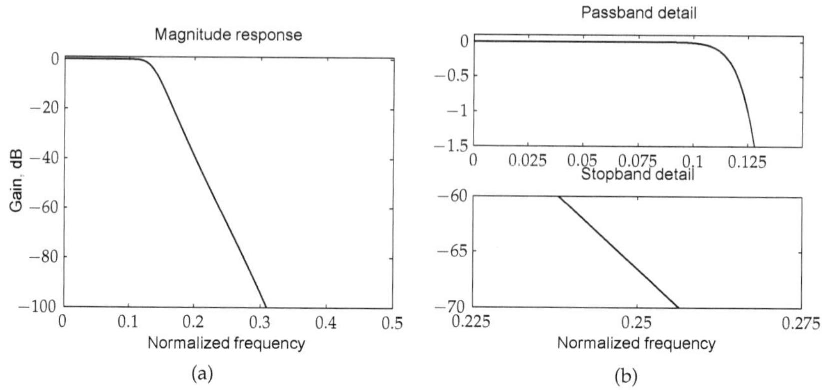

Fig. 7. Example 6.

5.1.4 Linear-phase IIR highpass filter design

Now, we extend the proposed algorithm for lowpass filter to highpass filter design.
Using the power-complementary property (Vaidyanathan et al., 1987), it can be shown that the corresponding complementary filter of $H(z)$, defined in (45), is given by

$$H_1(z) = \frac{1}{2j}\left[A(z) - \widetilde{A}(z)\right], \tag{60}$$

where $H_1(z)$ is a highpass filter.
Using (60), the phase value ϕ_{pA} is expressed as,

$$\phi_{pA} = \arcsin\left(10^{-A_p/20}\right). \tag{61}$$

Similarly, the phase value $\phi_\alpha(N, \omega_p, A_p)$ is given by,

$$\phi_\alpha(N, \omega_p, A_p) = \angle\left\{-(j+1)\cot^N\left(\frac{\omega_p}{2}\right) - \frac{2(-1)^{\lfloor N/2 \rfloor}}{A_p{}'}\right\}. \tag{62}$$

Finally, the filter coefficients of $H_1(z)$ are computed using (60).
The following example illustrates the procedure.
Example 7. The parameters of the design of the highpass filter are: the passband and stopband frequencies are $\omega_p = 0.75\pi$ and $\omega_s = 0.4\pi$, respectively. The stopband attenuation and passband droop are 50 dB and 1 dB, respectively.
The resulting filter order is equal to 6 and $\phi_\alpha(N, \omega_p, A_p) = -0.002569\pi$. The magnitude response, the passband and stopband details of the designed filter are shown in Fig. 8.

5.2 Direct design of linear-phase IIR filter banks

The modified two-band filter bank (Galand & Nussbaumer, 1984), is shown in Fig. 9. The analysis filter $H_0(z)$ and the synthesis filter $G_0(z)$ are lowpass filters, while the analysis filter $H_1(z)$ and the synthesis filter $G_1(z)$ are highpass filters. However, both the analysis and the synthesis filters are not causal. As a difference with traditional structure, in this structure

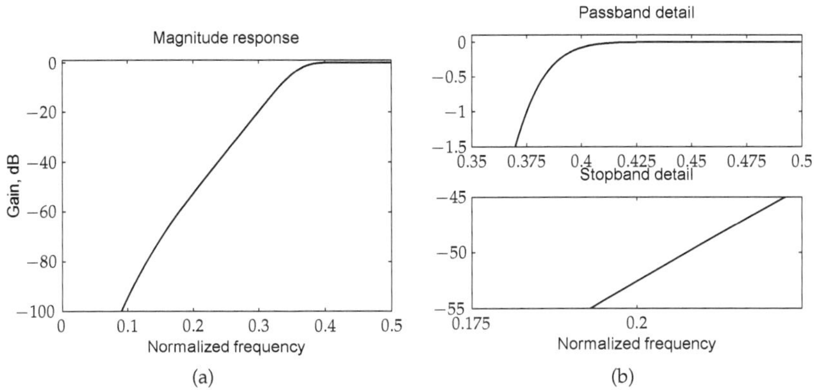

Fig. 8. Magnitude response of $H_1(z)$ in Example 7.

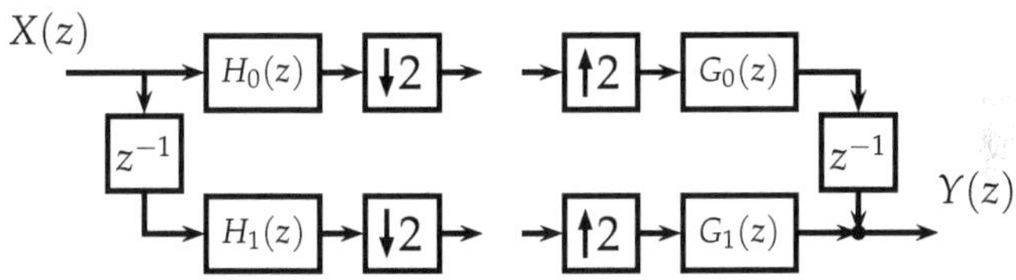

Fig. 9. Modified two-band filter bank.

there are two extra delays, one in the highpass analysis filter and another one in the lowpass synthesis filter (see Fig. 9).

The output $Y(z)$ is obtained using some multirate computations (Jovanovic-Dolecek, 2002), i.e.,

$$Y(z) = \frac{z^{-1}}{2}\left(X(z)\Big(G_0(z)H_0(z) + G_1(z)H_1(z)\Big) + X(-z)\Big(G_0(z)H_0(-z) - G_1(z)H_1(-z)\Big)\right). \tag{63}$$

The output of the filter bank (63) suffers from three types of errors, i.e., aliasing, amplitude distortion and phase distortion.

To avoid aliasing, the synthesis filters are related to the analysis filter $H_0(z)$ in the following form (Vaidyanathan et al., 1987),

$$G_0(z) = \widetilde{H}_0(z), \quad G_1(z) = H_0(-z), \tag{64}$$

where $\widetilde{H}_0(z)$ is the paraconjugate of $H_0(z)$ and $H_1(z) = \widetilde{H}_0(-z)$.

The amplitude and phase distortions are eliminated if the analysis filters are chosen to satisfy

$$H_0(z)\widetilde{H}_0(z) + H_0(-z)\widetilde{H}_0(-z) = 1. \tag{65}$$

From (65), the following relation holds,

$$|H_0(e^{j\omega})|^2 + |H_0(e^{j(\omega-\pi)})|^2 = 1. \tag{66}$$

The relationship between the passband frequency ω_p and stopband frequency ω_s of $H_0(z)$, is given by,

$$\omega_\mathrm{p} + \omega_\mathrm{s} = \pi. \tag{67}$$

Additionally, using (66) and (67) we have

$$10^{-A_\mathrm{p}/10} + 10^{-A_\mathrm{s}/10} = 1, \tag{68}$$

where A_p and A_s are the passband droop and the stopband attenuation in dB.
According to (Zhang et al., 2001), the analysis filters are given by,

$$H_0(z) = \frac{1}{2}\left[A(z) + \widetilde{A}(z)\right], \tag{69}$$

$$H_1(z) = \frac{1}{2\mathrm{j}}\left[A(z) - \widetilde{A}(z)\right], \tag{70}$$

where $A(z)$ is a complex allpass filter and $\widetilde{A}(z)$ is its paraconjugate.
From (69) and (70), we can see that the design of perfect reconstruction filter banks is reduced to the design of the complex allpass filter $A(z)$. In the following, we present one method for the modified two-band filter bank design based on the results obtained in Section 5.1.
The perfect reconstruction condition for the modified two-band IIR filter banks is established in (Vaidyanathan et al., 1987; Zhang et al., 2001), which implies that the poles of $H_0(z)$ and $H_1(z)$ must appear on the imaginary axis and in pairs $\mathrm{j}p$ and $1/\mathrm{j}p$, where p is a pole. From this condition, it follows that the filter coefficients given in (34) must be imaginary for even values of n (Vaidyanathan et al., 1987).
Consequently, the values of ϕ_α in (34) for an even N, must be

$$\phi_\alpha = \begin{cases} -\frac{7}{8}\pi & \text{for } \frac{N}{2} \text{ even,} \\ -\frac{3}{8}\pi & \text{for } \frac{N}{2} \text{ odd.} \end{cases} \tag{71}$$

Similarly, the values of ϕ_α when N is odd must be,

$$\phi_\alpha = \begin{cases} -\frac{3}{8}\pi & \text{for } \frac{N+1}{2} \text{ even,} \\ -\frac{7}{8}\pi & \text{for } \frac{N+1}{2} \text{ odd.} \end{cases} \tag{72}$$

5.2.1 Description of the algorithm

In the following, we describe the proposed algorithm for a linear-phase IIR filter banks. The IIR filters are real if N is even, otherwise they are complex.
The steps of the algorithm are described in the following

Step 1. Calculate the order N of the allpole filter using (68), (67) and (59). (Note that the filter $H_0(z)$ has order $2N$.)

Step 2. If N is even compute the filter coefficients (34) using (71), otherwise use (72).

We illustrate the method with the following examples.
Example 8. Stopband frequency ω_s of the analysis filter $H_0(z)$ is 0.65π, while the stopband attenuation A_s is 45 dB.

Step 1. From (68) and (67), it follows that $A_\mathrm{p} = 1.373381 \times 10^{-4}$ and $\omega_\mathrm{p} = 0.35\pi$. Using (59), the order of the complex allpole filter is 12. From (71), $\phi_\alpha = -\frac{7}{8}\pi$.

Step 2. We compute the filter coefficients using (34) and (71).

Figure 10a shows the corresponding magnitude responses of $H_0(z)$ and $H_1(z)$.

The following example illustrates the design of IIR filter banks using complex IIR filters. **Example 9.** We design the IIR filter bank with the following specifications $\omega_s = 0.75\pi$ and $A_s = 60$ dB for the analysis filter $H_0(z)$.

Step 1. The estimated value of N is 9 since $\omega_p = 0.25\pi$ and $A_p = 4.342946 \times 10^{-6}$. From (72), $\phi_\alpha = -\frac{3}{8}\pi$.

Step 2. Using (34) and (71), we compute the allpole filter coefficients.

The magnitude responses of $H_0(z)$ and $H_1(z)$ are shown in Fig. 10b. From Fig. 10b, (57), and (58), we note that both filters $H_0(z)$ and $H_1(z)$ have notch frequencies at $\omega_0 = 1.512254\pi$ and $\omega_1 = 1.487745\pi$, respectively.

In general, for N odd, both analysis filters have notch frequencies in the vicinity of $\omega = 3\pi/2$.

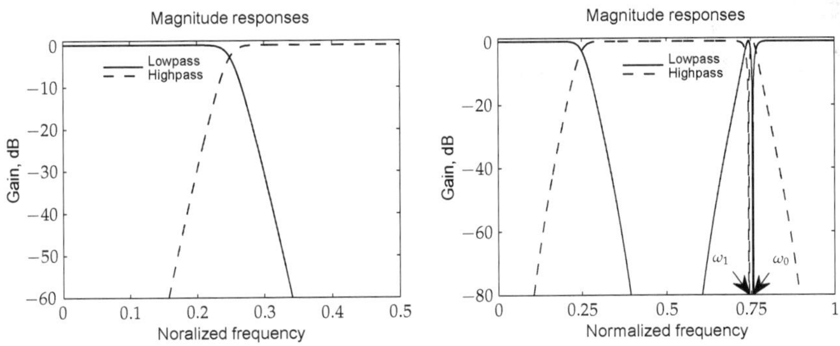

(a) Example 8 (b) Example 9

Fig. 10. Magnitude responses of the analysis filters in Examples 8 and 9.

5.3 Butterworth filters with an improved group delay

5.3.1 Linear-phase Butterworth filters

We relate the linear-phase Butterworth filter given in Section 5.1 with the corresponding stable and causal IIR filter.

We remember that a linear phase filter $H(z)$ can be expressed as

$$H(z) = cz^{-k}\widetilde{H}(z), \tag{73}$$

where z^{-k} is the delay, c is a rear or complex constant with unit magnitude and $\widetilde{H}(z)$ is the paraconjugate of $H(z)$.

Using $k = 0$ and $c = 1$, the linear-phase IIR filter $H(z)$ can be expressed as (Powell & Chau, 1991),

$$H(z) = H_c(z)\widetilde{H}_c(z). \tag{74}$$

where $H_c(z)$ is a causal and stable IIR filter. Consequently, the corresponding Fourier transform $H(e^{j\omega})$ is real and positive for all ω.

We note that the linear-phase filter $H(e^{j\omega})$ given in (53) takes both positive and negative values for N odd (see (58)). However, when N is even, the function $H(e^{j\omega})$ take only positives values. Therefore, the condition (74) is satisfied.
In the following we design the filter $H_cc(z)$ from (53).
From (53)–(54), it is easily shown that the polynomials $E(z)$ and $F(z)$ are symmetric for even values of N. Consequently, they can be expressed as,

$$E(z) = z^{-N/2} E_0(z) E_0(z^{-1}), \tag{75}$$

$$F(z) = z^{-N/2} F_0(z) F_0(z^{-1}), \tag{76}$$

where $E_0(z)$ and $F_0(z)$ are subfilters of $E(z)$ and $F(z)$, respectively.
From (75) and (76), the transfer function $H(z)$ (see (83)) can be rewritten as

$$H(z) = \frac{z^{-N/2}(1+z^{-1})^N E_0(z) E_0(z^{-1})}{2z^{-N} F_0(z)\widetilde{F}_0(z) F_0(z^{-1})\widetilde{F}_0(z^{-1})}. \tag{77}$$

Using (77) and (74), it follows

$$H_c(z) = \frac{(1+z^{-1})^{N/2} E_0(z)}{\sqrt{2} F_0(z)\widetilde{F}_0(z^{-1})}. \tag{78}$$

Therefore, the transfer function $H_c(z)$ has $N/2$ zeros at $z = -1$.
There exist many polynomials $E_0(z)$ and $F_0(z)$ satisfying (78). In order that $H_c(z)$ be stable, all zeros of $F_0(z)$ must be inside the unit circle. Moreover, it can be shown that for the given value of N, there exists

$$N_{\text{poly}} = 2^{\lfloor N/4 \rfloor}, \tag{79}$$

polynomials $E_0(z)$.
In the following example we design IIR filter $H(z)$ with linear-phase and the corresponding filter $H_c(z)$ using (77) and (78).
Example 10. We design an IIR filter $H(z)$ with the passband frequency, $\omega_p = 0.3\pi$, and passband droop, $A_p = 1$ dB. The allpole filter order is 8.
Consequently, $H(z)$ has 8 zeros at $z = -1$, while the remaining zeros z_k, $k = 0, \ldots, 7$, and poles p_k, $k = 0, \ldots, 2N-1$, are calculated using (55) and (38), respectively.
According to (79), there are four different polynomials for $E_0(z)$. The zeros of the first polinomial $E_0^{(1)}(z)$ are z_0, z_0^*, z_1, and z_1^*. Similarly, we can obtain the polynomials $E_0^{(l)}(z)$, $l = 2, 3, 4$, which shown in Table 4.

	$z_0, z_7 = 1/z_3 = z_0^*$	$z_1, z_6 = 1/z_2 = z_1^*$	$z_2, z_5 = 1/z_1 = z_2^*$	$z_3, z_4 = 1/z_0 = z_3^*$
$E_0^{(1)}(z)$	×	×		
$E_0^{(2)}(z)$	×		×	
$E_0^{(3)}(z)$		×		×
$E_0^{(4)}(z)$			×	×

Table 4. Different polynomials for $E_0(z)$.

The group delays of $H_c(z)$ for all $E_0^{(l)}(z)$, $l = 1, \ldots, 4$, are shown in Fig. 11.

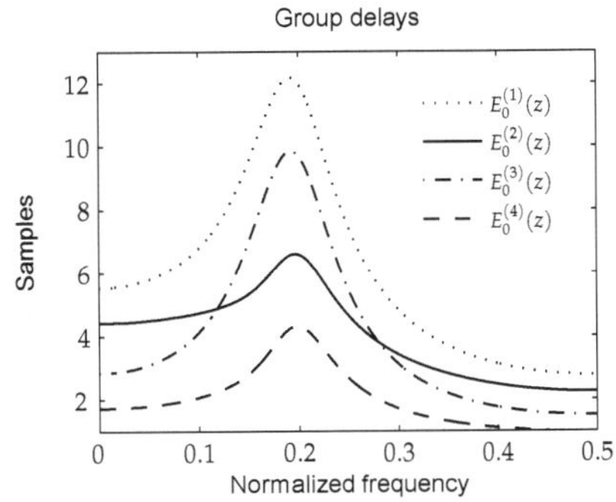

Fig. 11. Different group delays for the IIR filter $H_c(z)$ in Example 10.

We have different degrees of nonlinearity as illustrated in Fig. 11 for different $E_0^{(l)}$, $l = 1, \ldots, 4$. In this example, the group delay for $E_0^{(2)}(z)$ is more linear than the others. Therefore, for this example the best polynomial is $E_0^{(2)}(z)$.
The next issue is how to select in general case the best polynomial for $E_0(z)$.
Numerous examples indicate that it is necessary to satisfy the following two conditions:

1. The number of zeros of $H_c(z)$ inside and outside the unit circle, N_i and N_o, respectively, are related as

$$N_i \geq N_o, \tag{80}$$

where

$$N_o = \begin{cases} \left\lceil \frac{N}{2} \right\rceil & \text{if } \left\lceil \frac{N}{2} \right\rceil \text{ has the same parity of } N, \\ \left\lceil \frac{N}{2} \right\rceil - 1 & \text{if } \left\lceil \frac{N}{2} \right\rceil - 1 \text{ has the same parity of } N. \end{cases} \tag{81}$$

2. For each zero z_m inside, and each zero z_l outside of the unit circle, we have

$$\left| \frac{1}{z_l} \right| < |z_m|. \tag{82}$$

5.3.2 Description of the algorithm

The design parameters of the algorithm are passband and stopband frequencies, ω_p and ω_s, respectively, the passband droop A_p and the stopband attenuation A_s.
The algorithm has the following design steps:

Step 1. We estimate the order of the allpole filter $D(z)$ using results from Section 5.1,

$$N = \left\lfloor \frac{\log_{10}\left(\frac{A_p''}{A_s''}\right)}{\log_{10}\left(\frac{\omega_s'}{\omega_p'}\right)} \right\rfloor, \quad A_p'' = \sqrt{\frac{10^{A_p/10}+1}{10^{A_p/10}-1}} - 1, \quad A_s'' = \sqrt{\frac{10^{A_s/10}+1}{10^{A_s/10}-1}} - 1. \tag{83}$$

If the estimation filter order N is odd, increase it by one.

Step 2. Using the estimated value of N, we calculate the value of the phase $\phi_\alpha(N, \omega_p, A_p)$ as,

$$\phi_\alpha(N, \omega_p, A_p) = \angle\left\{-j - 1 - (-1)^{N/2} \tan^N\left(\frac{\omega_p}{2}\right) A_p''\right\}. \tag{84}$$

Step 3. Compute poles and zeros of $H_c(z)$ as indicated in the following

1. The zeros and poles of $H(z)$ are obtained using (55), (56), (38) and (39), respectively.
2. The N poles of $H(z)$, which are inside the unit circle, become poles of $H_c(z)$.
3. We select $N/2$ zeros of $H(z)$ which satisfy conditions (80)–(82) to be zeros of the filter $H_c(z)$ and the others $N/2$ zeros are at $z = -1$.

Step 4. Using the MATLAB function `poly.m`, we find the transfer function $H_c(z)$.

Example 11. We design the IIR filter with the following specifications: the passband and stopband frequencies are 0.25π and 0.55π, respectively; the passband droop and stopband attenuation are 1 dB and 50 dB, respectively.

Step 1. From (83), it follows that $N = 12$.

Step 2. Using the estimated value N and (84) we have, $\phi_\alpha(N, \omega_p, A_p) = -0.75\pi$.

Step 3. The resulting pole-zero pattern of $H_c(z)$ is shown in Fig. 12a.

Step 4. We compute the filter coefficients of the transfer function $H_c(z)$.

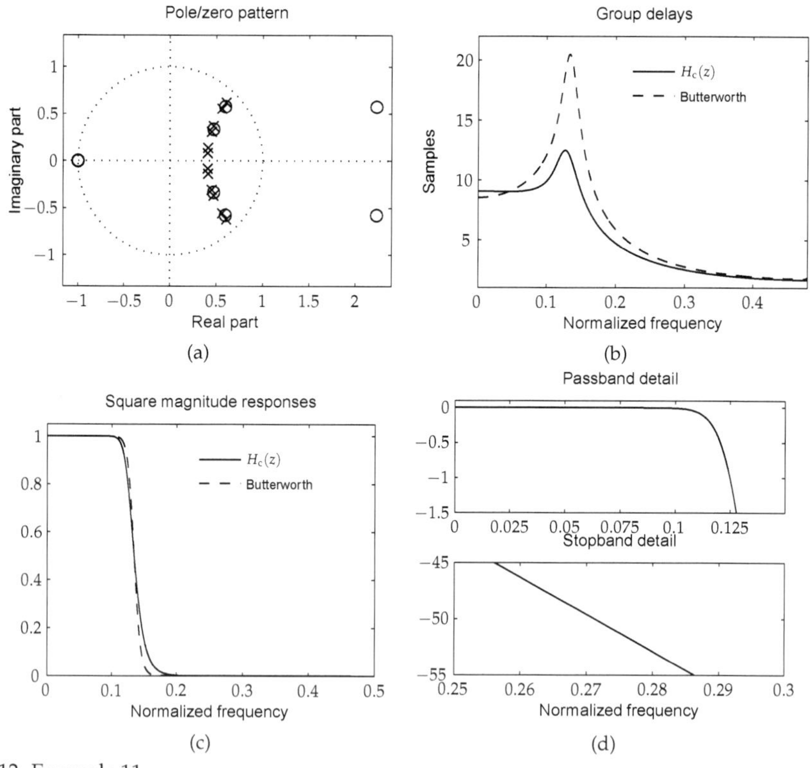

Fig. 12. Example 11.

The group delay of the designed filter is shown in Fig. 12b, while Figs. 12c and 12d present the magnitude response.
We compare our result with the traditional IIR Butterworth filter using the following specification: the filter order is equal to 12 and $\omega_c = 0.2689\pi$. Figure 12b and 12c show the group delays and magnitude responses of the Butterworth filter and the proposed one.
Notice that the proposed filter $H_c(z)$ has a better group delay than the traditional Butterworth filter.

5.4 Complex wavelet IIR filters

The main idea is to generalize the design of real IIR wavelets presented in (Phoong et al., 1995; Selesnick, 1998) and (Zhang et al., 2006) in a way that the complex case is also included. To this end we use the general approach for the complex allpole filter design from Section 4.3.
We generalize the result in (Selesnick, 1998), replacing the real allpass filter $A(z^{-2})$ with the complex allpass filter $\widetilde{A}(z^2)$, i.e.,

$$H_0(z) = \frac{1}{2}\left[A(z^2) + z^{-2M+1}\widetilde{A}(z^2)\right], \tag{85}$$

$$H_1(z) = \frac{1}{2}\left[A(z^2) - z^{-2M+1}\widetilde{A}(z^2)\right], \tag{86}$$

where $H_0(z)$ and $H_1(z)$ are lowpass and highpass filters, respectively, and M is arbitrary integer.
Knowing that $A(z) = 1/\widetilde{A}(z)$ (see (14)), it is easy to verify that $H_0(z)$ can be rewritten as,

$$H_0(z) = \frac{\widetilde{A}(z^2)}{2}\left[z^{-k} + A^2(z^2)\right], \tag{87}$$

where

$$k = 2M - 1. \tag{88}$$

Now, the problem to design complex filters (85) and (86) is reduced to the design of an allpass filter $A(z)$, which has the phase response equal to $-k\omega/4$ near to $\omega = 0$.
The group delay of $A(z)$ at $\omega = 0$ is equal to $k/4$. Then, the corresponding group delay $\tau_A(0)$ of $A(z)$ is expressed as,

$$\tau_{A0} = \frac{2M-1}{4}, \tag{89}$$

where $\tau_{A0} = \tau_A(0)$.
Using (17), the corresponding group delay of the complex allpole filter $D(z)$ is

$$\tau_0 = \frac{2M - 4N - 1}{8}. \tag{90}$$

The design of biorthogonal wavelet filter based on real allpass filter is proposed in (Phoong et al., 1995). The generalization of this result is written in the form

$$H_0(z) = \frac{1}{2}\left[z^{-2M} + z^{-1}A(z^2)\right], \tag{91}$$

$$H_1(z) = -A(z^2)H_0(z) + z^{-4M+1}, \tag{92}$$

where $A(z)$ is a complex allpass filter and M is any integer.

In this case, we first design the corresponding allpass filter $A(z)$ having the group delay at $\omega = 0$ equal to,

$$\tau_{A0} = \frac{2M-1}{2}. \tag{93}$$

The corresponding group delay τ_0 of $D(z)$ is given by, (See (17)),

$$\tau_0 = \frac{2M-2N-1}{4}. \tag{94}$$

Finally, the generalization of the orthogonal wavelet filters proposed in (Zhang et al., 2006) is given as,

$$H_0(z) = \frac{1}{2}\left[1 + z^{-2M+1}\widetilde{A}(z^2)\right], \tag{95}$$

$$H_1(z) = \frac{1}{2}\left[z^{-1} - z^{2M}A(z^2)\right]. \tag{96}$$

The group delays of the complex allpass filter $A(z)$ and allpole filter $D(z)$ at $\omega = 0$ are the same as for the filter (91) (see (93) and (94)).
We design the complex allpass filter $A(z)$ using complex Thiran allpole filter $D(z)$ given in Section 4.3, i.e.,

$$A(z) = z^{-N}\frac{D(z)}{\widetilde{D}(z)} == \frac{e^{j\phi_\alpha}}{e^{-j\phi_\alpha}} \frac{f_N^* + f_{N-1}^* z^{-1} + \cdots + z^{-N}}{1 + f_1 z^{-1} + \cdots + f_N z^{-N}}. \tag{97}$$

We can notice that by setting different values of the phase ϕ_α of the corresponding complex allpole filter $D(z)$, we can obtain different types of complex wavelet filters.
The following example illustrates the proposed method.
Example 12. We consider the design of complex wavelet filters using the methods proposed in (Selesnick, 1998), (Phoong et al., 1995) and (Zhang et al., 2006). We design a complex allpass filter of order $N = 6$, the phase value at $\omega = 0$ is equal to $\phi_\alpha = -\pi/5$, and delay $k = 1$. Therefore, according to (88), $M = 1$. Additionally, the degree of flatness K in this example is 9 and the filter coefficients are computed using (33).
Substituting the values of M and N into (90) and (94) we compute different group delays of the allpole filter $D(z)$. In particular, we denote the group delay of $D(z)$ based on equations (85) and that based on (86) as τ_1, and on (91) and (92) as τ_2. For the design based on (95) and (96) we have $\tau_3 = \tau_2$. The values of τ_1, τ_2 and τ_3 are -2.875, -2.75 and -2.75 samples, respectively. Substituting the values of τ_1 and τ_2 and the value of ϕ_α into (29), we compute the corresponding filter coefficients.
The magnitude responses of the complex wavelet filters based on (85) and (86) are shown in Fig. 13a, while the magnitude responses of the complex wavelet filters based on (91) and (92), and (95) and (96) are shown in Fig. 14b and 14c, respectively.

5.5 Fractional Hilbert transformers

Fractional Hilbert transform has applications in digital communications and signal processing (Pei & Yeh, 2000; Tseng & Pei, 2000). There exist different techniques for designing fractional Hilbert transformers (FHT) (Pei & Wang, 2002; Tseng & Pei, 2000). Here, we describe a direct method for the design of FHT. The method is based on the design of an allpass filter with desired characteristic.

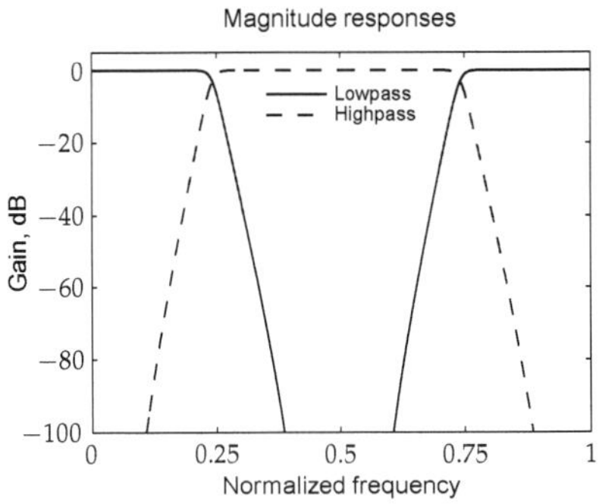

(a) Complex wavelets based on (Selesnick, 1998).

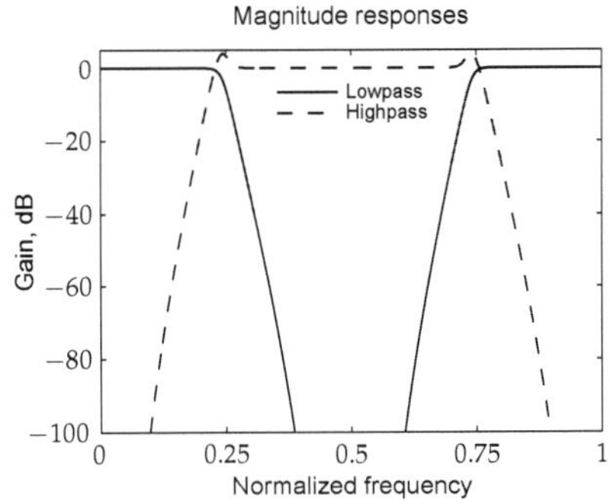

(b) Complex wavelets based on (Phoong et al., 1995).

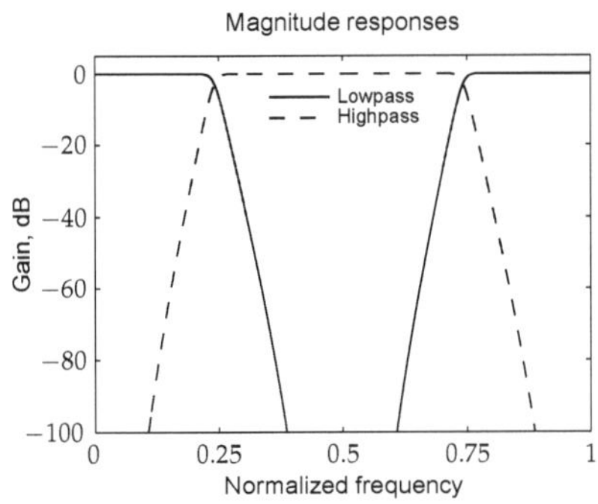

(c) Complex wavelets based on (Zhang et al., 2006).

Fig. 13. Magnitude response of the designed wavelet filters in Example 12.

The fractional Hilbert transformer is defined as (Pei & Wang, 2002),

$$H_\beta(\omega) = \begin{cases} e^{-j\frac{\beta\pi}{2}} & 0 \le \omega < \pi, \\ e^{j\frac{\beta\pi}{2}} & -\pi \le \omega < 0, \end{cases} \tag{98}$$

where β, satisfying $0 \le \beta \le 1$, is the fraction of the Hilbert transformer.
We can see from (98) that the magnitude response of $H_\beta(\omega)$ is 1 and the phase response is given by,

$$\angle H_\beta(\omega) = \begin{cases} -\frac{\beta\pi}{2} & 0 \le \omega < \pi, \\ \frac{\beta\pi}{2} & -\pi \le \omega < 0. \end{cases} \tag{99}$$

Therefore, the design of FHT is reduced to the design of an allpass filter $A(z)$ with the phase response given in (99). If the allpass filter has real coefficients, it is well known that, its phase response is an odd function of ω, (Mitra, 2005). Consequently, the allpass filter needs to satisfy (99) only $0 \le \omega < \pi$.

We use a second order allpass filter and $\omega = \pi/2$ to design the FHT. Therefore, for an stable allpass filter, the phase $\phi_A(\omega)$ and group delay $\tau_A(\omega)$ must be $-\ell\omega - \beta\pi/2$ and ℓ, respectively, where ℓ is a positive integer.
Consequently, from (16) and (18), the design parameters of the corresponding allpole filter are

$$\phi_D(\pi/2) = \frac{(2-\ell-\beta)\pi}{4}, \tag{100}$$

$$\tau(\pi/2) = \ell/2 - 1. \tag{101}$$

To ensure stability, from (25), we have

$$\ell > |\sin((\ell+\beta)\pi/2)|. \tag{102}$$

Substituting (100) and (101) into (23) and (24), we get

$$f_{R1} = \frac{2\sin((\ell+\beta)\pi/2)}{\ell+1-\cos((\ell+\beta)\pi/2)}, \tag{103}$$

$$f_{R2} = \frac{\ell-1+\cos((\ell+\beta)\pi/2)}{\ell+1-\cos((\ell+\beta)\pi/2)}. \tag{104}$$

Example 13. The design parameter for the fractional Hilbert transformer are $\beta = 0.2, 0.4, 0.6, 0.8, 1$ and $\ell = 2$. The resulting phase responses are shown in Fig. 14.

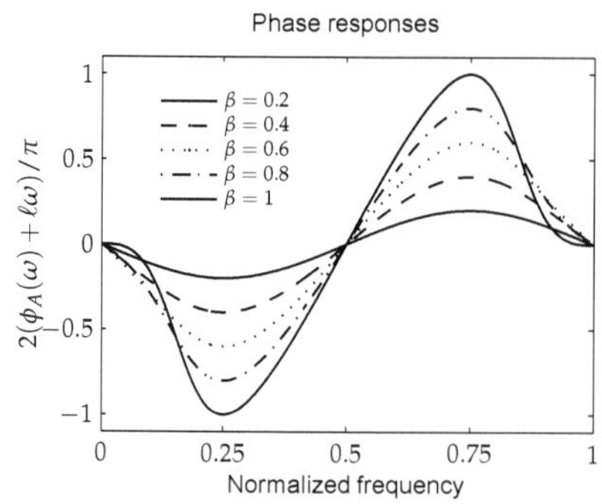

Fig. 14. Designed Fractional Hilbert transformers.

5.6 New design of IIR Butterworth-like filters based on three allpass filters

We address the magnitude approximation of real-valued lowpass Butterworth-like filters based on a new parallel connection of three allpass filters, that is, the proposed structure is composed by one real- and two complex-valued allpass filters. The design problem of lowpass filter is reduced further to design one complex-valued allpole filter with desired characteristics.
The proposed IIR filter is given by

$$H(z) = \frac{1}{3}\left[A_0(z) + A_1(z) + \widetilde{A}_1(z^{-1})\right]. \tag{105}$$

The allpass filters $A_0(z)$ and $A_1(z)$ must be stable in order that the filter $H(z)$ be stable.

We show that the problem of designing lowpass and stable IIR filter is reduced to designing a complex-valued allpole filter with desired characteristics.
At first, notice that (105) can be rewritten as

$$H(z) = \frac{A_0(z)}{3}\left[1 + A(z) + \widetilde{A}(z^{-1})\right], \tag{106}$$

where $A(z) = A_1(z)/A_0(z)$ is a complex allpass filter, which can have poles outside the unit circle due to the zeros of $A_0(z)$. The complex allpass filter is defined by (14).
In the following, some characteristics of $A(z)$ are described.
From (106), the corresponding magnitude response of $H(z)$ is

$$|H(e^{j\omega})| = \frac{1}{3}\left|1 + e^{j\phi_A(\omega)} + e^{-j\phi_A(-\omega)}\right|, \tag{107}$$

where $\phi_A(\omega)$ is the phase response of $A(z)$.
In order that $|H(e^{j\omega})|$ has the value 1 in the passband and the value 0 in the stopband (ideal case), the condition $\phi_A(\omega) = \phi_A(-\omega)$ must be satisfied, that is, the phase response must be an even function of ω.
Using this property, it follows that $A(z) = A(z^{-1})$. Consequently, the magnitude response $|H(e^{j\omega})|$ becomes

$$|H(e^{j\omega})| = \frac{1}{3}\left|1 + 2\cos\left(\phi_A(\omega)\right)\right|. \tag{108}$$

Considering the passband edge frequency ω_p and the attenuation in dB at this frequency point A_p. From (108) we define

$$\phi_{pA} = \cos^{-1}\left(\frac{3\cdot 10^{-A_p/20} - 1}{2}\right), \tag{109}$$

which gives the desired phase $\phi_A(\omega)$ at ω_p, i.e., $\phi_{pA} = \phi_A(\omega_p)$.
In order to achieve the condition $A(z) = A(z^{-1})$, the corresponding filter coefficients f_n, $n = 0, \ldots, N$, need to satisfy $f_n = f_{N-n}$, i.e., they must be a symmetric sequence. Generally, there are two cases that should be considered: N odd and N even. However, one can verify that N odd implies that at least one pole of $A(z)$ must be on the unit circle. As a consequence, in our design, we only consider the case where N is even.
Based on (108), We define the following properties for $A(z)$:

- $\mathcal{F}.1$ We select three frequency points where the phase response $\phi_A(\omega)$ is flat, i.e., $\omega = 0$ for the passband and $\omega = \pm\omega_r$ for the stopband. Furthermore, $\phi_A(0) = 0$ and $\phi_A(\pm\omega_r) = 2\pi/3$. This condition ensures that the filter $H(z)$ has flat magnitude response at $\omega = 0$ and $\omega = \omega_r$.
- $\mathcal{F}.2$ The group delay τ_A at $\omega = 0$ and $\omega = \omega_r$ is 0.
- $\mathcal{F}.3$ The phase value ϕ_{pA} is controlled by A_p (see (109)).

We relate the allpass filter $A(z)$ with the corresponding allpole filter.
Using (16) and the phase values $\phi_A(\omega)$ at $\omega = 0$ and $\omega = \pm\omega_r$ (see Condition $\mathcal{F}.1$), we get $\phi_D(0) = 0$ and $\phi_D(\pm\omega_r) = \pi/3 \pm \omega_r N/2$.
From (18) and Condition $\mathcal{F}.2$, we have $\tau(0) = \tau(\pm\omega_r) = -N/2$.

Finally, the following relation is obtained using Condition $\mathcal{F}$.3 and (16),

$$\phi_D(\omega_p) = \phi_p = \frac{\cos^{-1}\left(\frac{3\cdot 10^{-A_p/20}-1}{2}\right) + \omega_p N}{2}. \tag{110}$$

As a consequence, the allpole filter $D(z)$ has to satisfy the following conditions:

$\mathcal{G}$.1 The phase values of $D(z)$ at $\omega = 0$ and $\omega = \pm\omega_r$ are 0 and $\pi/3 \pm \omega_r N/2$, respectively.

$\mathcal{G}$.2 The group delay $\tau(\omega)$ of $D(z)$ at $\omega = 0$ and $\omega = \pm\omega_r$ are $-N/2$.

$\mathcal{G}$.3 The phase value of $D(z)$ at ω_p, $\phi_D(\omega_p)$, is given by (110).

For a filter having coefficients given in (40) the Conditions $\mathcal{G}$.1 and $\mathcal{G}$.2 are satisfied.
From the Condition $\mathcal{G}$.3 and (41), the corresponding value of ϕ_α becomes

$$\phi_\alpha(\omega_p, A_p, \omega_r) = \angle\left\{R_p {A_p}' + 1 + j\sqrt{3}(R_p + 1)\right\}, \tag{111}$$

where

$$ {A_p}' = \sqrt{\frac{1 + 3\cdot 10^{-A_p/20}}{1 - 10^{-A_p/20}}}. \tag{112}$$

In order to find the value ω_r and the order of the allpole filter N, we solve the following set of nonlinear equations:

$$\phi_\alpha(\omega_p, A_p, \omega_r) - \phi_\alpha(\pi, A_s, \omega_r) = 0, \tag{113}$$

$$\phi_\alpha(\omega_p, A_p, \omega_r) - \phi_\alpha(\omega_s, A_s, \omega_r) = 0. \tag{114}$$

Finally, we wish to find the allpass filters $A_0(z)$ and $A_1(z)$. First note that $F(z)$, the z-transform of f_n, can be rewritten as $F(z) = z^{-N/2}F_2(z^{-1})F_2(z)/\beta$, where $F_2(z)$ is a polynomial with all zeros inside the unit circle, i.e., $F_2(z) = 1 + f_{2,1}z^{-1} + \cdots + f_{2,N/2}z^{-N/2}$, and $\beta = f_{2,N/2}$. Accordingly, the corresponding allpass filters are expressed as,

$$A_0(z) = z^{-N}\frac{F_2(z^{-1})\widetilde{F}_2(z)}{\widetilde{F}_2(z^{-1})F_2(z)}, \quad A_1(z) = z^{-N}\frac{\alpha}{\alpha^*}\frac{\beta}{\beta^*}\frac{\widetilde{F}_2^2(z)}{F_2^2(z)}. \tag{115}$$

Example 14. We design the IIR filter based on three allpass filter using the following specification: $\omega_p = 0.3\pi$, $\omega_s = 0.55\pi$, $A_p = 0.5$ dB, and $A_s = 45$ dB.
From (111)–(114), it follows that $N = 6$, $\omega_r = 0.641272\pi$, and $\phi_\alpha(\omega_p, A_p, \omega_r) = 0.407889\pi$. Figure 15 shows the magnitude response of the designed IIR filter.

6. Conclusions

In this chapter, we have proposed a new general framework to designing real and complex allpole filters with given degree of flatness, and with phase and group delays at any desired set of frequency points. The filter coefficients are obtained by solving a set of linear equations. In the proposed allpole filter design, we can control the phase, group delay, and degree of flatness at different frequency points. Consequently, as demonstrated here, our proposal is useful for special IIR filter designs, i.e., linear-phase Butterworth-like filter, Butterworth-like filters with improved group delay, complex wavelet filters, fractional Hilbert transformers, and new IIR filters based on three allpass filters.

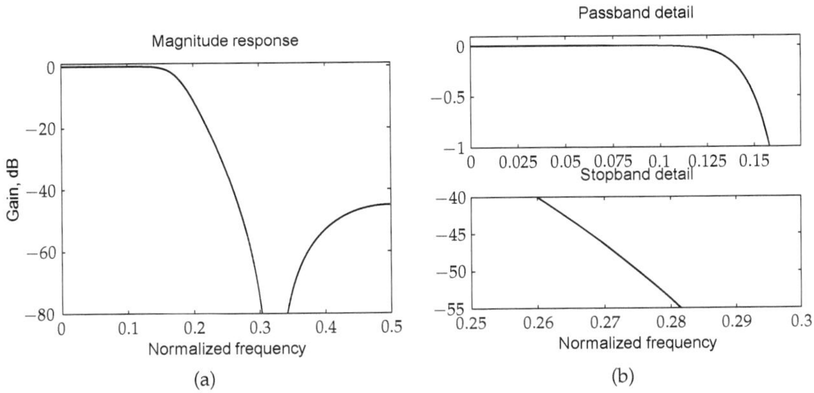

Fig. 15. Magnitude response of the designed IIR filter in Example 14.

Our approach is also useful for the direct design of causal Butterworth filters (Fernandez-Vazquez & Jovanovic-Dolecek, 2006) and higher order digital audio equalizers (Fernandez-Vazquez et al., 2007).

As a future work, we will turn our attention to other interesting applications of our proposed design.

7. Acknowledgments

This work was supported by CONACyT Mexico under Project 49640.

8. References

Andrews, L. C. (1998), *Special functions of mathematics for engineers*, second edn, Oxford University Press, SPIE Optical Press Engineering.

Chan, S., Chen, H. H. & Pun, K. S. (2005), 'The design of digital all-pass filter using second-order cone programming (SOCP)', *IEEE Trans. Circuits Syst. II* **52**(2), 66–70.

Djokic, B., Popovic, M. & Lutovac, M. (1998), 'A new improvement to the Powell and Chau linear phase IIR fitlers', *IEEE Trans. Signal Process.* **46**(6), 1685–1688.

Fernandes, F. C. A., Selesnick, I. W., Van-Spaendonck, R. L. C. & Burrus, C. S. (2003), 'Complex wavelet transform with allpass filters', *Signal Processing* **83**(5), 1689–1706.

Fernandez-Vazquez, A. & Jovanovic-Dolecek, G. (2006), 'A new method for the design of IIR filters with flat magnitude response', *IEEE Trans. Circuits Syst. I* **53**(8), 1761–1771.

Fernandez-Vazquez, A., Rosas-Romero, R. & Rodriguez-Asomoza, J. (2007), A new method for designing flat shelving and peaking filters based on allpass filters, *in* 'IEEE International Conference on Electronics, Communications and Computers (CONIELECOMP'07)', Vol. I, Cholula, Puebla, Mexico. Proceedings in CD.

Galand, C. R. & Nussbaumer, H. J. (1984), 'New quadrature mirror filter structures', *IEEE Trans. Acoust., Speech, Signal Process.* **32**(3), 522–531.

Joshi, Y. V. & Roy, S. D. (1999), 'Design of IIR multiple notch filters based on all-pass filters', *IEEE Trans. Circuits Syst. II* **46**(2), 134–138.

Jovanovic-Dolecek, G., ed. (2002), *Multirate Systems: Design and Applications*, Idea Group Publishing.

Kim, S. G. & Yoo, C. D. (2003), 'Highly selective M-channel IIR cosine-modulated filter banks', *IEE, Electronics Letters* **39**(20), 1478–1479.

Laakso, T. I., Välimäki, V., Karjalainen, M. & Laine, U. K. (1996), 'Splitting the unit delay', *IEEE Signal Process. Mag.* **13**(1), 30–60.

Lang, M. (1998), 'Allpass filter design and applications', *IEEE Trans. Signal Process.* **46**(9), 2505–2514.

Lee, J.-H. & Yang, Y.-H. (2004), 'Minimax design of two-channel nonuniform-division filterbanks using IIR allpass filters', *IEEE Trans. Signal Process.* **52**(11), 3227–3240.

Mitra, S. K. (2005), *Digital Signal Processing: A computer based approach*, third edn, Mc Graw Hill.

Pei, S.-C. & Tseng, C.-C. (1997), 'IIR multiple notch filter design based on allpass filter', *IEEE Trans. Circuits Syst. II* **44**(2), 133–136.

Pei, S.-C. & Wang, P.-H. (2002), Maximally flat allpass fractional Hilbert transformer, *in* 'Proc. IEEE Int. Symp. Circuits Syst. (ISCAS'02)', Vol. V, Scottsdale, Arizona, pp. 701–704.

Pei, S.-C. & Yeh, M.-H. (2000), 'Discrete fractional Hilbert transform', *IEEE Trans. Circuits Syst. II* **47**(11), 1307–1311.

Phoong, S.-M., Kim, C. W., Vaidynathan, P. P. & Ansary, R. (1995), 'A new class of two-channel biorthogonal filter banks and wavelets bases', *IEEE Trans. Signal Process.* **43**(3), 393–396.

Powell, S. R. & Chau, P. M. (1991), 'A technique for linear phase IIR filters', *IEEE Trans. Signal Process.* **39**(11), 2425–2435.

Pun, C. K. & Chan, S. C. (2003), The minimax design digital all-pass filters with prescribed pole radius constraint using semidefinite programming (SDP), *in* 'Proc. IEEE Int. Conf. Acoustics, Speech, Signal Processing (ICASSP'03)', Vol. VI, Hong Kong, China, pp. 413–416.

Saramaki, T. & Bregovic, R. (2002), *Multirate Systems and Filter Banks*, in Jovanovic-Dolecek (2002), chapter 2.

Selesnick, I. W. (1998), 'Formulas for orthogonal IIR wavelet filters', *IEEE Trans. Signal Process.* **46**(4), 1138–1141.

Selesnick, I. W. (1999), 'Low-pass filter realizable as all-pass sums: Design via a new flat delay filter', *IEEE Trans. Circuits Syst. II* **46**(1), 40–50.

Surma-aho, K. & Saramaki, T. (1999), 'A systematic technique for designing approximately linear phase recursive digital filters', *IEEE Trans. Circuits Syst. II* **46**(7), 956–963.

Thiran, J. P. (1971), 'Recursive digital filters with maximally flat group delay', *IEEE Trans. Circuit Theory* **CT–18**(6), 659–664.

Tseng, C.-C. & Pei, S.-C. (1998), 'Complex notch filter design using allpass filter', *IEE, Electronics Letters* **34**(10), 966–967.

Tseng, C.-C. & Pei, S.-C. (2000), 'Design and application of discrete-time fractional Hilbert transformer', *IEEE Trans. Circuits Syst. II* **47**(12), 1529–1533.

Vaidyanathan, P. P. & Chen, T. (1998), 'Structures for anticausal inverses and application in multirate filter banks', *IEEE Trans. Signal Process.* **46**(2), 507–514.

Vaidyanathan, P. P., Regalia, P. A. & Mitra, S. K. (1987), 'Design of doubly complementary IIR digital filters using a single complex allpass filter, with multirate applications', *IEEE Trans. Circuits Syst.* **34**(4), 378–389.

Zhang, X. & Amaratunga, K. (2002), 'Closed-form design of maximally flat IIR half-band filters', *IEEE Trans. Circuits Syst. II* **49**(6), 409–417.

Zhang, X. & Iwakura, H. (1999), 'Design of IIR digital allpass filters based on eigenvalue problem', *IEEE Trans. Signal Process.* **47**(2), 554–559.

Zhang, X., Kato, A. & Yoshikawa, T. (2001), 'A new class of orthonormal symmetric wavelet bases using a complex allpass filter', *IEEE Trans. Signal Process.* **49**(11), 2640–2647.

Zhang, X., Muguruma, T. & Yoshikawa, T. (2000), 'Design of orthogonal symmetric wavelet filter using real allpass filters', *Signal Processing* **80**(8), 1551–1559.

Zhang, X., Wang, W., Yoshikawa, T. & Takei, Y. (2006), 'Design of IIR orthogonal wavelet filter banks using lifting scheme', *IEEE Trans. Signal Process.* **54**(7), 2616–2624.

15

Robust Unsupervised Speaker Segmentation for Audio Diarization

Hachem Kadri[1], Manuel Davy[1] and Noureddine Ellouze[2]
[1]*LAGIS, UMR CNRS 8146 and INRIA SequeL Team*
France
[2]*Unité de Recherche Signal, Image et Reconnaissance de Formes*
Tunisia

1. Introduction

Audio diarization Reynolds & Carrasquillo (2005) is the process of partitioning an input audio stream into homogeneous regions according to their specific audio sources. These sources can include audio type (speech, music, background noise, ect.), speaker identity and channel characteristics. With the continually increasing number of larges volumes of spoken documents including broadcasts, voice mails, meetings and telephone conversations, diarization has received a great deal of interest in recent years which significantly impacts performances of automatic speech recognition and audio indexing systems. A subtype of audio diarization, where the speech segments of the signal are broken into different speakers, is speaker diarization Tranter & Reynolds (2006). It generally answers to the question "Who spoke when?" and it is divided in two modules: speaker segmentation and speaker clustering. The goal of speaker segmentation is finding the times when there is a change of speaker in the audio stream. Speaker clustering consists in merging speech segments, detected by the speaker segmentation step, related to a same speaker.
Recently, three main domains of application for speaker segmentation have received special attention Reynolds & Carrasquillo (2004):

- Broadcast news : Radio and TV programs with various kinds of programming, usually containing commercial breaks and music, over a single channel.
- Recorded meetings: meetings or lectures where multiple people interact in the same room or over the phone. Normally recordings are made with several microphones.
- Phone conversations: single channel recordings of phone conversations between two or more people.

Segmenting this types of audio stream in terms of speakers is useful in many application. In Automatic Speech Recognition (ASR) Moraru et al. (2003), for example, an initial segmentation is required in terms of homogeneous speech and non-speech regions. Having segmented speech regions, it is also often necessary to segment these further in terms of homogeneous speaker turns. In addition to improving ASR systems, speaker turn information can be helpful for speaker adaptation in rich transcription of videos and meetings Bonastre et al. (2000) and for content based audio classification and retrieval Hansen et al. (2005) which have a wide range of applications in the entertainment industry, audio archive management, surveillance, etc. Audio segmentation would also be an important tool in summarizing meetings, which has recently gained a lot of interest in the research community. For example, segmentation of the speech data in terms of speakers could help in efficient navigation through audio documents like meeting recordings Dielmann & Renals (2007); Jin & Schultz (2004). Using these segmentation queues, an interested user can directly access a particular segment of the speech made by a particular speaker.

1.1 Previous works

Recent research on audio segmentation mostly focused on four categories: energy based, model-based Kemp et al. (2000), metric-based Delacourt & Wellekens (2000), and information criterion-based approaches Cettolo & Vescovi (2003); Chen & Gopalakrishnan (1998); M.Cettolo & M.Federico (2000). Energy audio segmentation only detects change-points at silence segments, which generally are not directly connected with the acoustic changes of the audio signals. Model-based segmentation approach requires predefined audio classes and complete training data. The metric-based approach are not stable and need thresholds generally selected from experiments results. The information criterion-based scheme are proposed for evaluating models constructed by various estimation procedures when the specified family of probability distributions does not contain the distribution generating the data. The so-called Delta Bayesian information criterion (BIC) segmentation algorithm is widely employed in many studies Chen & Gopalakrishnan (1998). The BIC is intended to provide a measure of the weight of evidence favoring one model over another. According to previous research, the Delta-BIC is threshold-free and suitable for unknown acoustic conditions. However, this method, extremely computationally expensive, can introduce an estimation error due to insufficient data when the speaker turns are close to each other Huang & Hansen (2004). In order to minimize these effects, Delacourt Delacourt & Wellekens (2000)tested different metric criteria to associate them to the BIC criterion such as the Kullbach-Leibler distance, the similarity measure and the Generalized Likelihood Ratio measure (GLR). Still, this method encountered problems in case of short segments and requires also a high computation cost. On another issue, Zhou Zhou & Hansen (2000)recommends the use of the T^2−Statistic for metric-based segmentation in the aim to reduce this computation cost. However its technique, T^2−BIC, depends on many empiric parameters which affect the quality of the detection of speaker turns. In our previous work Kadri et al. (2006), we developed a hybrid segmentation algorithm called $DIS\_T^2\_BIC$ to improve the detection of speaker turns close to each others using a fixed threshold independent of the type of the audio stream with a low computation cost. Nevertheless all of these techniques suppose that the audio signal don't contains different acoustic changes and simultaneous speeches of two or more speakers and then find difficulties in segmenting streams containing background noise and overlapped speeches.

1.2 Contributions and Chapter organization

The main focus of this chapter is to introduce a new unsupervised speaker segmentation technique robust to different acoustic conditions. In most commonly used model selection segmentation techniques like BIC segmentation, the basic problem may be viewed as a two-class classification where the object is to determine whether N consecutive audio frames constitute a single homogeneous of frames W or two such windows: W_1 and W_2 with the boundary frame or change occurring at the ith frame. In order to detect if a speaker change occurred within a window of N frames, two models are built. One which represents the entire window by a Gaussian characterized by μ (mean) , Σ (variance) ; a second which represents the window up to the ith frame, W_1 with μ_1,Σ_1 and the remaining part, W_2, with a second Gaussian

μ_2,Σ_2. This representation using a gaussian process is not totally exact when the audio stream contains overlapped speeches and very short segments. To solve this problem, our proposed segmentation technique use the one class SVM and exponential family model to maximize the generalized likelihood ratio with any probability distribution of windows Kadri et al. (August 2008). Moreover, we use the discrete wavelet coefficient (DWC) to improve the detection of speaker changes in the presence of background noise. The use of these coefficient is suitable since our technique is insensitive to the dimension of acoustic features.
The remainder of this chapter is organized as follows. Section 2 details previous audio segmentation techniques based on BIC. Section 3 reviews the support vector machines approach and the exponential family model. The proposed speaker change detection method is illustrated in section 4. Experimental results are provided in Section 5. Section 6 concludes the paper with a summary and discussion.

2. Previous techniques: BIC based segmentation techniques

Model selection based speaker segmentation is proposed by Chen and Gopalakrishnan Chen & Gopalakrishnan (1998). Their method employs the bayesian information criterion as model selection criterion, illustrating several desirable properties such as robustness, threshold independence and optimality.

2.1 BIC Segmentation

BIC Chen & Gopalakrishnan (1998) is a model selection criterion penalized by the model complexity (amount of free parameters in the model). For a given acoustic segment X_i, the BIC value of a model M_i indicates how well the model fits the data, and is determined by:

$$BIC(X,M) = \log L(X_i, M_i) - \frac{\lambda}{2}\#(M_i) \cdot \log(N_i) \tag{1}$$

$\log L(X_i, M_i)$ is the log-likelihood of the data given the considered model, N_i is the number of frames in the considered segment, $\#(M_i)$ the number of free parameters to estimate in model M_i and λ is a free design parameter dependent on the data being modelled. λ determines the 'weight' applied to model parameters, theoretically 1, but tunable in practice. Given several different candidate models to explain a single dataset, the model with the largest BIC gives the best fit according to this criterion.
The BIC-based segmentation procedure is as follows: A sequence of d-dimensional audio feature vectors $X = x_i \in \mathbb{R}^d : i = 1, \ldots, N$ are modelled as independent draws from either one or two multivariate Gaussian distributions. The null hypothesis is that the entire sequence is drawn from a single distribution:

$$H_0 = \{x_1, \ldots, x_N\} \sim \mathcal{N}(\mu_0, \Sigma_0)$$

where $N(\mu, \Sigma)$ denotes a multivariate Gaussian distribution with mean vector μ and full covariance matrix Σ. The null hypothesis is compared to the hypothesis of having a segment boundary after sample t i.e. that the first t points are drawn from one distribution and that the remaining points come from a different distribution:

$$\begin{aligned} H_1 : \{x_1, \ldots, x_t\} &\sim \mathcal{N}(\mu_1, \Sigma_1) \\ \{x_{t+1}, \ldots, x_N\} &\sim \mathcal{N}(\mu_2, \Sigma_2) \end{aligned}$$

The difference in BIC scores between these two models is a function of the candidate boundary position t:

$$\Delta BIC(t) = \log(\frac{\mathcal{L}(X\backslash H_0)}{\mathcal{L}(X\backslash H_1)}) - \frac{\lambda}{2}\frac{d^2+3d}{2}\log(N) \quad (2)$$

where $\mathcal{L}(X\backslash H_0)$ is the likelihood of X under hypothesis H_0 etc., and $(d^2+3d)/2$ is the number of extra parameters in the two-model hypothesis H_1. When $\Delta BIC(t) > 0$, we place a segment boundary at time t, and then begin searching again to the right of this boundary and the search window size N is reset. If no candidate boundary t meets this criteria, the search window size is increased, and the search across all possible boundaries t is repeated. This continues until the end of the signal is reached.

2.2 T^2-BIC

T^2-BIC Zhou & Hansen (2000) is a variant of BIC segmentation technique which validates each speaker change point detected by Hotelling's T^2-statistic using the BIC criterion. Hotelling's T^2-statistic is a multivariate analogue of the square of the t-distribution Anderson (1985). The T^2-statistic is used when we wish to test if the mean of one normal population is equal to the mean of the other where the covariance matrices are assumed equal but unknown. In terms of segmentation Wegmann et al. (1999), the problem can be viewed as testing the hypothesis $H_0 : \mu_1 = \mu_2$ against the alternative $H_0 : \mu_1 \neq \mu_2$ where μ_1, μ_2 are, respectively, the means of two samples of the audio stream, one containing the frame $[1, b]$ and the second contains $[b, N]$. The likelihood ratio test is given by the following T^2-statistic:

$$T^2 = \frac{b(N-b)}{N}(\mu_1 - \mu_2)'\Sigma^{-1}(\mu_1 - \mu_2) \quad (3)$$

where Σ represent the common covariance matrix. The T^2 value defined in 3 can be considered as a distance measure of two samples. Obviously, the smaller the value of T^2, the more similar the two samples distributions. The T^2-BIC algorithm operates by fixing an analysis frame with L second length from the beginning of the parameterized audio stream and calculating the T^2 value in different points situated on this frame; the point that represents the highest value of T^2 is more probable to be a real speaker turns; then it can be validated by the BIC criterion. The T^2-BIC segmentation presents certainly some advantages. The selection, from the statistical criteria T^2, of a candidate speaker change permits to reduce computational costs. Thus, T^2-BIC offers a reduced calculation time compared to the BIC segmentation. Besides, this technique works with an automatic threshold and presents a low false alarm. However, T^2-BIC is not reliable for the segmentation of audio documents that contain speaker changes close to each other. In fact, it requires the use of a time delay τ Zhou & Hansen (2000) between two consecutive speaker turns which can lead missing some break points.

2.3 DIS_T^2_BIC

Like T^2-BIC, $DIS\_T^2\_BIC$ Kadri et al. (2006) is a speaker segmentation algorithm which process with a fixed threshold and low computation cost. It is proposed to improve speaker turns detection even they are close to each other. $DIS\_T^2\_BIC$ is based in a hybrid concept which is organized in two steps: the detection of most probable speaker turns and the validation of changes already detected. Speaker turns are detected by computing the value of T^2 between a pair of adjacent windows of the same size shifted by a fixed step along the whole parameterized speech signal. In the end of this procedure we obtain the curve of the variation of

T^2 in time. A speaker change point is characterized by the presence of a high value peak. To differentiate high peaks from low peaks, a fixed threshold is defined as below:

$$T^2 > \frac{(N-2)p}{N-p-1} F_{p,N-p-1}(\alpha) = T_0^2$$

where $F_{p,N-p-1}$ is the F-point for p and $N-p-1$ degrees of freedom with significance level α. A T^2 value lower than T_0^2 shows that the two samples are homogenous and consequently don't present a speaker change. So, break points can be detected by searching the local maxima of the T^2 curve that verify the criterion 2.3. The validation of already detected break points is made using the BIC criterion. Denote $\{T_1, ..., T_N\}$ as the set of speaker turns found in the first step, a ΔBIC value is computed for each pair of windows $[T_{i-1}, T_i]$ $[T_i, T_{i+1}]$. When this value is positive, a speaker turn is identified at time i. Otherwise, the point i is discarded from the candidate set, then the ΔBIC value is applied again for a larger pair of windows $[T_{i-1}, T_{i+1}]$ $[T_{i+1}, T_{i+2}]$. At this stage, when segments are large enough, BIC criterion gives better validation results since model estimation becomes more accurate. Detecting speaker changes from the curve of T^2 gives to $DIS\_T^2\_BIC$ the advantage to detect speaker turns close to each others and the use of the T^2-statistic criteria permits to reduce the computation cost and to have an automatic threshold decision independent of the type of the audio stream. However, like others BIC based segmentation technique, suppose that the audio signal don't contains different acoustic changes and simultaneous speeches of two or more speakers and then find difficulties to segment audio streams containing background noise and overlapped speeches.

3. Background information

This section provides a brief review of reproducing kernel Hilbert spaces, One-class Support Vector Machines and exponential families.

3.1 reproducing kernel Hilbert spaces Aronszajn (1950)

Let $\mathcal{X}$ be a set, and $\mathcal{H}$ be a Hilbert space included in the set of all functions on $\mathcal{X}$. The Hilbert space $\mathcal{H}$ is called reproducing kernel Hilbert space (RKHS) if the evaluation functional e_x : $\mathcal{H} \ni f \longmapsto f(x) \in \mathbb{R}$ is continuous on $\mathcal{H}$ for any $x \in \mathcal{X}$.

A function $k : \mathcal{X} \times \mathcal{X} \longrightarrow \mathbb{R}$ is a *positive kernel* if it is symmetric and for any points $x_1, ...x_n$ in $\mathcal{X}$ the matrix $(k(x_i, x_j))_{i,j}$ is positive semidefinite, i.e., for any sequence of scalar $\alpha_1, ...\alpha_n$ the inequality $\sum_{i,j=1}^{n} \alpha_i \alpha_j k(x_i, x_j) \geq 0$ is verified.

Using Riesz's theorem, If $\mathcal{H}$ is a RKHS on $\mathcal{X}$ then there exists a function $k(., x) \in \mathcal{H}$, called *reproducing kernel*, such that $e_x(f) = f(x) = \langle f(.), k(., x)\rangle_{\mathcal{H}}$, where $\langle\, ,\, \rangle_{\mathcal{H}}$ is the inner product of $\mathcal{H}$. The function $k(x, y)$ is a positive definite kernel, because it is symmetric from $k(y, x) = \langle k(., x), k(., y)\rangle_{\mathcal{H}} = \langle k(., y), k(., x)\rangle_{\mathcal{H}} = k(x, y)$, and positive definite from $\sum_{i,j} \alpha_i \alpha_j k(x_i, x_j) = \| \sum_i \alpha_i k(., x_i)\|_{\mathcal{H}}^2 \geq 0$.

In the other hand, it is known that for a positive definite kernel k on $\mathcal{X}$ there uniquely exists a Hilbert space $\mathcal{H}_k$ such that $\langle f(.), k(., x)\rangle_{\mathcal{H}_k} = f(x)$ holds for any $f \in \mathcal{H}_k$ and $x \in \mathcal{X}$. This propriety means that $\mathcal{H}_k$ is a RKHS with a reproduicing kernel k. given a RKHS $\mathcal{H}$ and its reproducing kernel $k(., x)$, because of the uniqueness of the reproducing kernel, we can conclude that the Hilbert space $\mathcal{H}_k$ constructed by k is identic to $\mathcal{H}$. So there is a bijection between the set of all possible RKHS and the set of all positive kernels.

3.2 One-Class SVM

The One-class approach was proposed by Schölkopf Smola & Shawe-Taylor (2000) and has been successfully aused for novetly detection. Davy & Godsill (2002) Davy et al. (2006) Desobry et al. (2005). 1-SVM distinguishes one class of data from the rest of the feature space given only a positive data set. Based on a strong mathematical foundation, 1-SVM draws a nonlinear boundary of the positive data set in the feature space using a parameter to control the noise in the training data and another one to control the smoothness of the boundary.
The 1-class SVM is a method that aims at learning a single class, by determining its contours. To explain 1-class SVM, we can begin by giving a kernel. A kernel $k(x,y)$ is a positive and symmetric function of two variables (for more details see [12]) lying in a Reproducing Kernel Hilbert Space with the scalar product:

$$\langle f,g\rangle_{\mathcal{H}} = \sum_{i=1}^{k}\sum_{j=1}^{l} f_i g_i k(x_i,y_j) \tag{4}$$

In this framework, the 1-class SVM problem with the sample $(x_i), i = 1,\dots,m$ is the solution of the following optimisation problem under constraints for $f \in H$:

$$\begin{cases} \min_{f,\rho,\xi} \frac{1}{2}\|f\|^2_{\mathcal{H}} + C\sum_{i=1}^{m}\xi_i - \rho \\ \text{s.t.} \quad f(x_i) > \rho - \xi_i \quad i = 1,\dots,m \\ \text{and} \quad \xi_i \geq 0, \quad i = 1,\dots,m \end{cases} \tag{5}$$

where C is a scalar that adjusts the smoothness of the decision function, ρ is a scalar called bias and ξ are slack variables. The dual formulation is:

$$\begin{cases} \max_{\alpha\in\mathbb{R}^m} \frac{-1}{2}\,\alpha^T K\alpha \\ \text{s.t.} \quad \alpha^T e = 1 \\ \text{and} \quad 0 < \alpha_i < C, \quad i = 1,\dots,m \end{cases} \tag{6}$$

where K is the kernel matrix $K_{ij} = k(x_i,x_j)$ and $e = [1,\dots,1]^T$. The 1-class SVM solution is then given by solving a quadratic optimization problem of dimension m under box constraints. The decision function is $D(x) = sign(f(x) - \rho)$. The input points are considered as part of the current class as long as the decision function is positive.

3.3 Exponential family

The exponential family covers a large number (and well-known classes) of distributions such as Gaussian, Multinomial and poisson. A general representation of a exponential family is given by the following probability density function:

$$p(x|\eta) = h(x)\, exp\{\eta^T T(x) - A(\eta)\} \tag{7}$$

where $h(x)$ is called the base density which is always ≥ 0,
η is the natural parameter,
$T(x)$ is the sufficient statistic vector
$A(\eta)$ is the cumulant generating function or the log normalizer.
The choice of $T(x)$ and $h(x)$ determines the member of the exponential family. Also we know that since this is a density function,

$$\int h(x)\, exp\{\eta^T T(x) - A(\eta)\}dx = 1 \tag{8}$$

then,

$$A(\eta) = \log \int \exp[\eta^T T(x)]h(x)dx \tag{9}$$

For a Gaussian distribution, $p(x|\mu,\sigma^2) = \frac{1}{\sqrt{2\pi}} \exp(\frac{\mu}{\sigma^2}x - \frac{1}{2\sigma^2}x^2 - \frac{\mu^2}{2\sigma^2} - log\sigma)$. In this case, $h(x) = \frac{1}{\sqrt{2\pi}}, \eta = [\frac{\mu}{\sigma^2}, \frac{-1}{2\sigma^2}]$ and $T(x) = [x, x^2]$. Thus, Gaussian distribution is included in the exponential family.

The density function of a exponential family can be written in the case of presence of an reproducing kernel Hilbert space $\mathcal{H}$ with a reproducing kernel k as :

$$p(x|\eta) = h(x)\ \exp\{\langle\eta(.), k(x,.)\rangle_{\mathcal{H}} - A(\eta)\} \tag{10}$$

with

$$A(\eta) = \log \int \exp\{\langle\eta(.), k(x,.)\rangle_{\mathcal{H}} h(x)dx \tag{11}$$

4. SVM based speaker segmentation

4.1 Speaker change detection using 1-class SVM and exponential family

Novetly change detection using SVM and exponential family is proposed by Canu and Smola Canu & Smola (2005) Smola (2004). Let $X = \{x_1, x_2, \ldots, x_N\}$ and $Y = \{y_1, y_2, \ldots, y_N\}$ two adjacent windows of acoustic feature vectors extracted from the audio signal ,where N is the number of data points in one window. Let Z denote the union of the contents of the two windows having $2N$ data points. The sequences of random variables X and Y are distributed according respectively to $\mathbb{P}x$ and $\mathbb{P}y$ distribution. We want to test if there exist a speaker turn after the sample x_N between the two windows. The problem can be viewed as testing the hypothesis $H_0 : \mathbb{P}_x = \mathbb{P}_y$ against the alternative $H1 : \mathbb{P}x \neq \mathbb{P}y$. H_0 is the null hypothesis and represents that the entire sequence is drawn from a single distribution, thus there not exist a speaker turn. While H_1 represents the hypothesis that there is a segment boundary after sample X_n. The likelihood ratio test of this hypotheses test is the following :

$$L(z_1, \ldots, z_{2N}) = \frac{\prod_{i=1}^{N} \mathbb{P}_x(z_i) \prod_{i=t+1}^{2N} \mathbb{P}_y(z_i)}{\prod_{i=1}^{2N} \mathbb{P}_x(z_i)} = \prod_{i=N+1}^{2N} \frac{\mathbb{P}_y(z_i)}{\mathbb{P}_x(z_i)} \tag{12}$$

since both densities are unknown the generalized likelihood ratio (GLR) has to be used :

$$L(z_1, \ldots, z_{2N}) = \prod_{i=N+1}^{2N} \frac{\widehat{\mathbb{P}}_y(z_i)}{\widehat{\mathbb{P}}_x(z_i)} \tag{13}$$

where $\hat{\mathbb{P}}_x$ and $\hat{\mathbb{P}}_y$ are the maximum likelihood estimates of the densities.

Assuming that both densities $\mathbb{P}_x$ and $\mathbb{P}_y$ are included in the generalized exponential family, thus it exists a reproducing kernel Hilbert space $\mathcal{H}$ embedded with the dot product $< \cdot, \cdot >_{\mathcal{H}}$ with a reproducing kernel k such that:

$$\mathbb{P}_x(z) = h(z)\ \exp\{\langle\eta_x(.), k(z,.)\rangle_{\mathcal{H}} - A(\eta_x)\} \tag{14}$$

and

$$\mathbb{P}_y(z) = h(z)\ \exp\{\langle\eta_y(.), k(z,.)\rangle_{\mathcal{H}} - A(\eta_y)\} \tag{15}$$

Using One class SVM and the exponential family, a robust approximation of the maximum likelihood estimates of the densities $\mathbb{P}_x$ and $\mathbb{P}_y$ can be written as:

$$\widehat{\mathbb{P}}_x(z) = h(z)\exp\left(\sum_{i=1}^{N}\alpha_i^{(x)}k(z,z_i) - A(\eta_x)\right) \tag{16}$$

$$\widehat{\mathbb{P}}_y(z) = h(z)\exp\left(\sum_{i=N+1}^{2N}\alpha_i^{(y)}k(z,z_i) - A(\eta_y)\right) \tag{17}$$

where $\alpha_i^{(x)}$ is computed by solving the one class SVM problem on the first half of the data (z_1 to z_N), while $\alpha_i^{(y)}$ is given by solving the one class SVM problem on the second half of the data (z_{N+1} to z_{2N}). Using these three hypotheses, the generalized likelihood ratio test is approximated as follows:

$$L(z_1,\ldots,z_{2N}) = \prod_{j=N+1}^{2N}\frac{\exp\left(\sum_{i=N+1}^{2N}\alpha_i^{(y)}k(z_j,z_i) - A(\eta_y)\right)}{\exp\left(\sum_{i=1}^{N}\alpha_i^{(x)}k(z_j,z_i) - A(\eta_x)\right)} \tag{18}$$

A speaker change in the frame z_n exist if :

$$L(z_1,\ldots,z_{2N}) > s_x \quad\Leftrightarrow\quad \sum_{j=N+1}^{2N}\left(\sum_{i=N+1}^{2N}\alpha_i^{(y)}k(z_j,z_i) - \sum_{i=1}^{N}\alpha_i^{(x)}k(z_j,z_i)\right) > s'_x \tag{19}$$

where s_x is a fixed threshold. Moreover, $\sum_{i=N+1}^{2N}\alpha_i^{(y)}k(z_j,z_i)$ is very small and can be neglect in comparison with $\sum_{i=1}^{N}\alpha_i^{(x)}k(z_j,z_i)$. Then a speaker turn is detected when :

$$\sum_{j=N+1}^{2N}\left(-\sum_{i=1}^{N}\alpha_i^{(x)}k(z_j,z_i)\right) > s'_x \tag{20}$$

4.2 Proposed speaker segmentation technique

In section 4.1, we show that a speaker changes exist if the condition defined by the equation (20) is verified. This speaker change detection approach can be interpreted like this: to decide if a speaker change exit between the two windows X and Y, we built an SVM using the data X as learning data, then Y data is used for testing if the two windows are homogenous or not.

On the other hand, since H_0 represent the hypothesis of $\mathbb{P}_x = \mathbb{P}_y$ the likelihood ratio test of the hypotheses test described in section 4.1 can be written like this:

$$L(z_1,\ldots,z_{2N}) = \frac{\prod_{i=1}^{N}\mathbb{P}_x(z_i)\prod_{i=t+1}^{2N}\mathbb{P}_y(z_i)}{\prod_{i=1}^{2N}\mathbb{P}_y(z_i)} = \prod_{i=1}^{N}\frac{\mathbb{P}_x(z_i)}{\mathbb{P}_y(z_i)} \tag{21}$$

Using the same gait, a speaker change has occurred if :

$$\sum_{j=1}^{N}\left(-\sum_{i=N+1}^{2N}\alpha_i^{(y)}k(z_j,z_i)\right) > s'_y \tag{22}$$

Experimental tests show that in some case is more appropriate when we use Y data for learning and X data for testing. Figure 1 presents the segmentation of an audio stream which presents four speaker changes. This audio stream is a sample of broadcast news extracted

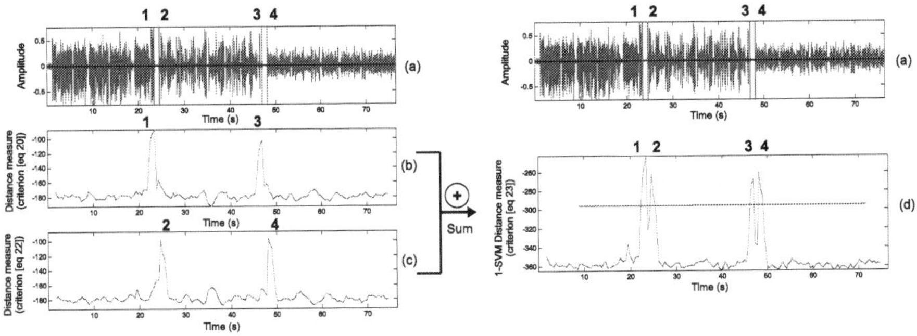

Fig. 1. Segmentation results of an audio stream extracted from NIST RT-02 broadcast news data using criteria defined by eq (20)(subplot b), eq (22)(subplot c) and eq (23)(subplot d).

from NIST RT-02 data. Figures (b) and (c) represent the result of segmentation using respectively (20) and (22). Using the criteria (20), we can detect only changes number 1 and 3 and using the criteria (22), we can detect only changes number 2 and 4. For these reason it is more appropriate to use the criterion described as follow:

$$\sum_{j=N+1}^{2N} \left(-\sum_{i=1}^{N} \alpha_i^{(x)} k(z_j, z_i)\right) + \sum_{j=1}^{N} \left(-\sum_{i=N+1}^{2N} \alpha_i^{(y)} k(z_j, z_i)\right) > S \tag{23}$$

In this case and as illustrated in figure 1, we can detect easily all speaker changes.

4.3 Our segmentation method

Our technique detects speaker turns by computing the distance detailed in equation (27) between a pair of adjacent windows of the same size shifted by a fixed step along the whole parameterized speech signal. In the end of this procedure we obtain the curve of the variation of the distance in time. The analysis of this curve shows that a speaker change point is characterized by the presence of a "significant" peak. A peak is regarded as "significant" when it presents a high value. So, break points can be detected easily by searching the local maxima of the distance curve that presents a value higher than a fixed threshold.

Algorithm 1: Speaker change detection algorithm

Step 0: Initialization

- initialize the interval $[a, b]$, $a = 0, b =$ SIZE_WINDOW

Step 1: Computing detection criterion

- Compute the distance measure $d1$ according to equation (20) with $[a, b/2]$ testing data and $[b/2 + 1, b]$ training data.
- Compute the distance measure $d2$ according to equation (22) with $[b/2 + 1, b]$ testing data and $[a, b/2]$ training data
- Compute the decision criterion $d = d1 + d2$
- a=$a + pas$ and $b = b + pas$; go to step 1

Step 2: speaker turns detection

- detecting peaks of d-curve, $p = p_i$
- decision:
  - if $d(p_i) > s$ a speaker change is detected,
  - if $d(p_i) < s$ no speaker change is detected,

5. Experiments

5.1 Data set

In order to evaluate 1-SVM-based segmentation method, experiments are based essentially on the segmentation of IDIAP meetings Corpus. This database contains two separate test sets sampled at 16 kHz. The first test set contains only single speaker segments without overlapping. However the second one contains a short overlap segment included at each speaker change. Further, to generalize our experiments, we used also other types of audio streams like broadcast news and telephone conversations. These audio streams are extracted from the Rich Transcription-04 MDE Training Data Speech corpus created by Linguistic Data Consortium (LDC). Description of the used datasets is presented below:

1. IDIAP meetings Moore (2002):
   - Test set 1: contains only single speaker segments without overlap segments. This test set groups nine files, each of them contains 10 speaker turns constructed in a random manner with segments duration varying from 5 to 20 seconds. The total test set duration was 20 minutes.
   - Test set 2: contains a short overlap segment included at each speaker change. The test set is formed by six files, each containing 10 single speaker segments (of between 5-17 seconds duration), interleaved with 9 segments of dual-speaker overlap (of between 1.5-5 seconds duration).
2. Broadcast news data: is composed of three approximately 10-minute excerpts from three different broadcasts. The broadcasts were selected from programs from NBC, CNN and ABC, all collected in 1998.
3. Telephone conversation: is composed of a 10-minute excerpt from a conversation between two switchboard operators.

5.2 Evaluation criteria

For evaluating the performance of the segmentation task, we use Type-I errors: precision (PRC) and Type-II errors: recall (RCL) was widely used in previous research Ajmera et al. (2004). Type-I errors occur if a true change is not spotted (missed alarm) within a certain window. Type-II errors occur when a detected change does not correspond to a true change in the reference (false alarm). Precision (PRC) and recall (RCL) are defined as below:

$$\text{PRC} = \frac{\text{number of correctly found changes}}{\text{Total number of changes found}} \tag{24}$$

$$\text{RCL} = \frac{\text{number of correctly found changes}}{\text{Total number of correct changes}} \tag{25}$$

(26)

In order to compare the performance of different systems, the F-measure is often used and is defined as

$$F = \frac{2.0 \times \text{PRC} \times \text{RCL}}{\text{PRC} + \text{RCL}} \tag{27}$$

The F-measure varies from 0 to 1, with a higher F-measure indicating better performance.

5.3 Audio features components

In the experiments, two kinds of feature vectors are proposed: MFCCs and DWCs. Mel frequency cepstral coefficients (MFCCs) are a short-time spectral decomposition of audio that convey the general frequency characteristics important to human hearing. We calculate MFCCs by using overlapping frames of 30 ms. The Discrete Wavelet Coefficients (DWCs) are computed by applying the Discrete Wavelet Transform (DWT) which provides a time-frequency representation of the signal. It was developed to overcome the short coming of the Short Time Fourier Transform (STFT), which can also be used to analyze non-stationary signals. While STFT gives a constant resolution at all frequencies, the Wavelet Transform uses multi-resolution technique by which different frequencies are analyzed with different resolutions. The DWT is computed by successive lowpass and highpass filtering of the discrete time-domain signal. This is called the Mallat algorithm or Mallat-tree decomposition Mallat (1998).

5.3.1 Mel frequency cepstral coefficient

MFCCs are a short-time spectral decomposition of audio that convey the general frequency characteristics important to human hearing. While originally developed to decouple vocal excitation from vocal tract shape for automatic speech recognition. In order to calculate MFCCs, the signal is first broken into overlapping frames, each approximately 25ms long, a time scale at which the signal is assumed to be stationary. The log-magnitude of the discrete Fourier transform of each window is warped to the Mel frequency scale, imitating human frequency and amplitude sensitivity. The inverse discrete cosine transform decorrelates these "auditory spectra" and the so called "high time" portion of the signal, corresponding to fine spectral detail, is discarded, leaving only the general spectral shape

5.3.2 Discrete Wavelet transform

The Wavelet Transform provides a time-frequency representation of the signal. It was developed to overcome the short coming of the Short Time Fourier Transform (STFT), which can also be used to analyze non-stationary signals. While STFT gives a constant resolution at all frequencies, the Wavelet Transform uses multi-resolution technique by which different frequencies are analyzed with different resolutions. The DWT is computed by successive lowpass and highpass filtering of the discrete time-domain signal. This is called the Mallat algorithm or Mallat-tree decomposition Mallat (1998). Its significance is in the manner it connects the continuous-time mutiresolution to discrete-time filters. In the figure, the signal is denoted by the sequence x[n], where n is an integer. The low pass filter is denoted by G0 while the high pass filter is denoted by H0. At each level, the high pass filter produces detail information, d[n], while the low pass filter associated with scaling function produces coarse approximations, a[n].

5.4 Results

Table 1 illustrates speaker segmentation experiments conducted on the various audio documents previously described and their corresponding results using 1-SVMs and $DIS\_T^2\_BIC$

approaches. Segmentation using 1-SVMs outperforms $DIS\_T^2\_BIC$ based segmentation technique for all the tested audio documents. The segmentation of the IDIAP meetings(1) using the two methods presents the highest value of precision and recall. In fact, opposite to other types of audio streams, this corpus contains long speech segments allowing good estimation of data. As presented in the table 1, the PRC and RCL values obtained with IDIAP meetings(1) increases respectively from 0.69 to 0.8 and from 0.68 to 0.79.

Audio	1-SVM method				$DIS\_T^2\_BIC$ method			
Streams	Features	RCL	PRC	F	Features	RCL	PRC	F
M. IDIAP1	39MFCC+DWC_5	0.8	0.79	0.79	13MFCC	0.69	0.68	0.68
M. IDIAP2	39MFCC+DWC_5	0.68	0.67	0.67	13MFCC	0.58	0.56	0.57
B. News	39MFCC+DWC_6	0.75	0.75	0.75	39MFCC	0.63	0.66	0.64
Tel. Conv	39MFCC+DWC_3	0.72	0.71	0.71	13MFCC	0.56	0.58	0.57

Table 1. Segmentation results using the proposed 1-SVM and $DIS\_T^2\_BIC$ methods.

The proposed method based on 1-SVMs allows the improvement of speaker change detection in audio streams which contain overlapping speeches. The improvement in the PRC and RCL values using IDIAP meetings(2) is more than 10% with respect to $DIS\_T^2\_BIC$ method. Generally, BIC based segmentation techniques detect a speaker change between two adjacent analysis windows. Each window is modelized by a gaussian distribution. This supposition is not true when the window contains overlapped speeches. In this case, it is more suitable to suppose that each window can be modelized by an exponential family.

Broadcast news segmentation results are enhanced by adding discrete wavelet coefficients to cepstral coefficients. The use of this kind of parametrization makes speaker changes detection possible in the presence of background noise. Further, deploying 1-SVMs permits to better put in evidence this characteristic since it is insensitive to the dimension of acoustic features. Also, the proposed method is more appropriate to detect speaker changes close each others. The F value obtained with the segmentation results of the telephone conversation is raised from 0.56 with $DIS\_T^2\_BIC$ method to 0.71 with 1-SVMS method.

6. Conclusion

In this chapter, we have proposed a new unsupervised detection algorithm based on 1-SVMs. This algorithm outperforms model-selection based detection methods. Using the exponential family model, we obtain a good estimation of the generalized Likelihood ratio applied on the known hypothesis test generally used in change detection tasks. By adding to cepstral coefficients the discrete wavelet coefficients. The use of this kind of parametrization permitted to detect speaker changes even in real-world conditions in which the environment and context are so complex that the segmentation results are often affected. The use of support vector machines permit to deal practically with this high dimensional acoustic features vector. Experimental results present higher precision and recall values than those obtained with $DIS\_T^2\_BIC$ technique, the increase of PRC and RCL values obtained with various kinds of audio streams is roughly over 10%.

7. References

Ajmera, J., McCowan, I. & Bourlard, H. (2004). Robust speaker change detection, *IEEE Signal-Processing Letters* pp. 649–651.

Anderson, T. (1985). *An introduction to multivariate statistical analysis*, John Wiley and Sons, New York, NY.

Aronszajn, N. (1950). Theory of reproducing kernels, *Trans. Amer. Math. Soc* .

Bonastre, J., Delacourt, P., Fredouille, C., Merlin, T. & Wellekens, C. (2000). A speaker tracking system based on speaker turn detection for nist evaluation, *ICASSP'00*, Istanbul, Turkey, pp. 1177–1180.

Canu, S. & Smola, A. (2005). Kernel methods and the exponential family, *ESANN'05*, Brugge, Belgium.

Cettolo, M. & Vescovi, M. (2003). Efficient audio segmentation algorithms based on the bic, *ICASSP 03*.

Chen, S. & Gopalakrishnan, P. (1998). Speaker, environment and channel change detection and clustering via the bayesian information criterion, *DARPA Broadcast News Transcription and Understanding Workshop*.

Davy, M., Desobry, F., Gretton, A. & Doncarli, C. (2006). An online Support Vector Machine for Abnormal Events Detection, *Signal Processing* **86**(8): 2009–2025.

Davy, M. & Godsill, S. (2002). Detection of Abrupt Spectral Changes using Support Vector Machines. An Application to Audio Signal Segmentation, *IEEE ICASSP*, Vol. 2, Orlando, USA, pp. 1313–1316.

Delacourt, P. & Wellekens, C. (2000). DISTBIC: a speaker based segmentation for audio data indexing, *Speech Communication* **32**: 111–126.

Desobry, F., Davy, M. & Doncarli, C. (2005). An online kernel change detection algorithm, *IEEE Transactions on Signal Processing* **53**(5).

Dielmann, A. & Renals, S. (2007). Automatic meeting segmentation using dynamic bayesian networks, *IEEE Transactions on MultiMedia* pp. 25–36.

Hansen, J., Huang, R., Zhou, B., Deadle, M., Deller, J., Gurijala, A., Kurimo, M. & Angkititraku, P. (2005). Speechfind: Advances in spoken document retrieval for a national gallery of the spoken word, *IEEE Trans. Speech Audio Process* pp. 712–730.

Huang, R. & Hansen, J. (2004). Advances in unsupervised audio segmentation for the broadcast news and ngsw corpora, *ICASSP*, pp. 741–744.

Jin, Q. & Schultz, T. (2004). Speaker segmentation and clustering in meetings, *INTERSPEECH'04* pp. 597–600.

Kadri, H., Davy, M., Rabaoui, A., Lachiri, Z. & Ellouze, N. (August 2008). Robust audio speaker segmentation using one class svms, *Europpean Signal Processing Conference, EUSIPCO'08*, Lausanne, Switzeland.

Kadri, H., Lachiri, Z. & Ellouze, N. (2006). Hybrid approach for unsupervised audio speaker segmentation, *Europpean Signal Processing Conference, EUSIPCO'06*, Florence, Italy.

Kemp, T., Schmidt, M., Westphal, M. & Waibel, A. (2000). Strategies for automatic segmentation of audio data, *ICASSP*, pp. 1423–1426.

Mallat, S. (1998). *A wavelet tour of signal processing*, Academic Press.

M.Cettolo & M.Federico (2000). Model selection criteria for acoustic segmentation, *ISCA Tutorial and Research Workshop ASR*.

Moore, D. (2002). The idiap smart meeting room, *IDIAPCOM 07*.

Moraru, D., Meignier, S., Besacier, L., Bonastre, J. & I.Magrin-Chagnolleau (2003). The elisa consortium approaches in speaker segmentation during the nist 2002 speaker recognition evaluation, *ICASSP'04* .

Reynolds, D. & Carrasquillo, T. (2004). The mit lincoln laboratories rt-04f diarization systems: Applications to broadcast audio and telephone conversations, *Fall 2004 Rich Transcription Workshop (RT04)*, Palisades, NY., USA.

Reynolds, D. & Carrasquillo, T. (2005). Approaches and applications of audio diarization, *ICASSP'05* .

Smola, A. (2004). Exponential families and kernels, *Technical report*, Berder summer school, http://users.rsise.anu.edu.au/ smola/teaching/summer2004/.

Smola, B. S. R. W. A. & Shawe-Taylor, J. (2000). Support vector method for novelty detection, *NIPS*, pp. 582–588.

Tranter, S. & Reynolds, D. (2006). An overview of automatic speaker diarization systems, *IEEE Transactions on Audio, Speech and Language Processing* pp. 1557–1565.

Wegmann, S., Zhan, P. & Gillick, L. (1999). Progress in broadcast news transcription at dragon systems, *ICASSP*, Phoenix, Arizona, USA.

Zhou, B. & Hansen, J. (2000). Unsupervised audio stream segmentation and clustering via the bayesian information criterion, *ICSLP*, Beijing, China, pp. 714–717.

16

New directions in lattice based lossy compression

Adriana Vasilache
Nokia Research Center
Finland

1. Introduction

One of the first articles that have addressed lattice quantizers in practical applications is the work of Sayood et al. (Sayood et al., 1984). The lattice quantization has been strongly stimulated by the articles of Conway and Sloane (Conway & Sloane, 1982), (Conway & Sloane, 1983) presenting fast algorithms for nearest neighbor search algorithms. The principal factors that have brought the lattices in the attention of the quantization community are:

- The lattices are uniformly distributed structures in the n-dimensional space, therefore they are immediately applicable as quantizer structures for uniform sources. This affirmation is based on the, now widely accepted, conjecture of Gersho (Gersho, 1979), stating that, when the rate is high, the optimal quantizer of a uniform source will have the partition cells all congruent to some polytope. This is equivalent to saying that the optimal quantizer of a uniform source is a tessellating[1] quantizer, i.e. it completely fills the space with copies of a same polytope. Gersho (Gersho, 1979) has shown that this polytope must have the lowest normalized second order moment for the considered space dimension.
- The asymptotic equipartition property, used in the context of source coding, suggests that in a high-dimensional space almost all points will lie in a region of high probability specified by the entropy of the source (Cover & Thomas, 1991). The region of high probability will have a shape dependent on the source (Fischer, 1989) (e.g. the hypersphere for the memoryless Gaussian source (Sakrison, 1968), the hyper-pyramid (hyper-octahedron) for the memoryless Laplacian source (Fischer, 1986)). The pdf of the points, f, being almost constant on that region of high probability, the formula under the high-rate assumption, for the point density of the optimal quantizer (Gersho, 1979) indicates, that the codebook should also be uniform in that region.
- The regular structure of a lattice VQ reduces considerably the memory requirements for the storage of the codebook.
- Fast nearest neighbor search algorithms exist for the lattices which are generally used as quantizers (Conway & Sloane, 1992).

State of the art speech codecs as AMR-WB+ (Ragot et al., 2004) and G.718 (Rämö et al., 2008) codec make use of its advantages. Audio coding methods based on lattice quantization have been as well proposed (Vasilache & Toukomaa, 2006).

---

[1] All the lattices form tessellations, but not all tessellations are obtained from lattices.

Most of the lattice based coding methods rely on fixed rate coding or on a semi-variable rate coding where the vector to be quantized is split in several sub-blocks for which the rate is variable, but the overall bit rate for the global vector is fixed (Ragot et al., 2004). There exist also variable rate encoding techniques of lattice codevectors. Most of these methods rely on the grouping of codevectors on classes such as leader classes or shells (Fischer, 1991), (Vasilache & Tabus, 2001) or apply directly entropy coding methods to the lattice codevector components (Zhao et al., 2007). However, the former method becomes less practical when the number of classes increases (with the increase of the bit rate and for some of the truncation shapes), while the latter is from the start less efficient than a direct entropy coding of the lattice vectors indexes, but obviously less complex.

We discuss in the present work a new approach for entropy encoding of lattice codevectors that can be applied for higher dimensional lattices without additional storage requirements and that allows parameterization of the lattice truncation size. The proposed method is based on the indexing method for lattice vectors that makes use of the product code indexing method. The presented approach is exemplified on rectagular truncation of lattices, where the number of leader classes is relatively high, but the shape of the truncation is accounted for through companding.

This work is presenting first several lattice definitions and terms, followed by a short description of the product code indexing that enables the key method of the work, the new entropy encoding of lattice vectors. The proposed method will be exemplified within an audio coding scheme that will be briefly presented prior to the results. Future research directions will be discussed and conclusions of the work will make the object of the last section.

2. Lattice quantization: terminology and definitions

2.1 Lattice definition

Geometrically, a lattice is an infinite regular array of points which uniformly fills the n-dimensional space.

Algebraically, an n-dimensional lattice Λ is a set of real vectors whose coordinates are integers in a given basis $\{b_i \in R^n\}_{i=1,n}$

$$\Lambda = \left\{ \mathbf{v} \in \mathbf{R}^n | \mathbf{v} = \sum_{i=1}^{n} \alpha_i b_i, \alpha_i \in \mathbf{Z} \right\}. \tag{1}$$

When used as fixed rate quantizer a lattice should be truncated to a finite number of points corresponding to the selected bit rate. Even if, in principle, for the variable bit rate case, when entropy coding is applied, the lattice can be considered infinite, for practical reasons (i.e. indexing algorithms and numerical aspects of entropy coding), a finite support for the lattice should be specified.

2.2 Lattice truncation

Generally, the lattice support, or truncation is defined by means of a norm $N(\mathbf{x})$ of the lattice points which should be less than a given value K:

$$\Lambda_K = \left\{ (\mathbf{x}) = (x_1, x_2, \ldots, x_n) \in \Lambda \ |N(\mathbf{x}) \leq K \right\}. \tag{2}$$

The truncation shape is spherical if N is the Euclidean norm, or pyramidal if the N is l_1, or rectangular if N is the maximum norm i.e. the maximum absolute value of the lattice vector components. Also other, more general norms, can be considered.

A generalization of the rectangular truncation is the truncation having different maximum absolute norms, $\{K_i\}_{i=1:n}$ along different dimensions

$$\Lambda_{K_i} = \left\{(\mathbf{x}) = (x_1, x_2, \ldots, x_n) \in \Lambda \ ||x_i| \leq K_i\right\}. \tag{3}$$

The generalization is exemplified in Fig. 1 for the lattice Z_2 with $K_1 = 3$ and $K_2 = 2$. The truncation includes all Z_2 points inside the smaller rectangle, as well as the points from the border.

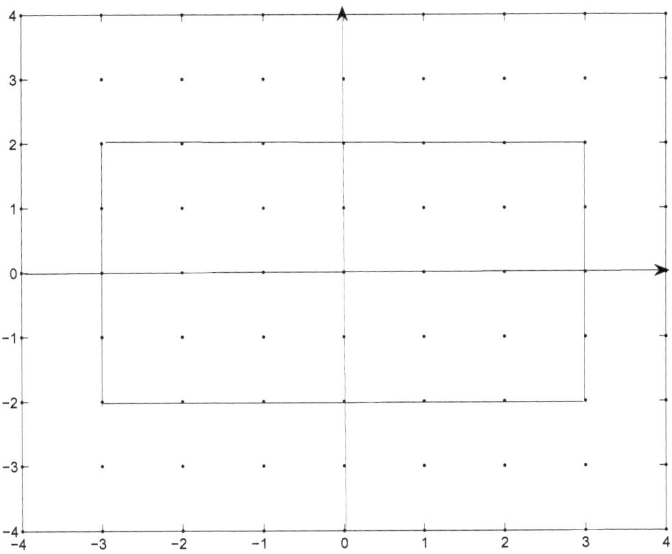

Fig. 1. Illustration of the generalized rectangular truncation of Z_2.

A given norm defines, in addition to the lattice truncation, the lattice shell, as the set of lattice points that have the same norm value, K:

$$\Lambda_K = \left\{(\mathbf{x}) = (x_1, x_2, \ldots, x_n) \in \Lambda \ |N(\mathbf{x}) = K\right\}. \tag{4}$$

Consequently, the lattice truncation can be seen as a union of lattice shells.

A division of the lattice into even finer sets is obtained starting from the definition of a leader vector and that of a leader class. A leader vector is a positive integer vector $\mathbf{v} = (v_m, ..., v_m, ..., v_i, ..., v_i, ..., v_1, ..., v_1)$ where $0 \leq v_1 < ... < v_i < ... < v_m$. The leader class of the leader vector $\mathbf{v}$ is the set of all the vectors obtained through signed permutations, with some possible constraints, of the vector $\mathbf{v}$. The leader class notion has been proposed originally in (Adoul, 1986), (Adoul & Barth, 1988).

Most of the lattices used for quantization can be defined as union of leader classes (Moureaux et al., 1998).

2.3 Counting lattice points

The use of lattice truncations as quantizers implies knowing the number of lattice codevectors inside the considered truncation. Following the definition of a lattice truncation as a union of shells, counting the lattice points reduces to finding expressions for the cardinality of a shell, i.e. the number of lattice points at a given distance from the origin, under the specified norm. The solution of this problem is given by the *theta* functions for ℓ_2 norm for many standard lattices in (Conway & Sloane, 1992). In (Solé, 1993) the *theta* functions have been generalized for the norm ℓ_p and in (Moureaux et al., 1995), (Barlaud et al., 1993) for weighted ℓ_2 norms. In (Vasilache et al., 1999) the *theta* series approach is used to count the lattice points on spherical (ℓ_2 norm) shells and generalized to pyramidal (ℓ_1 norm) shells.

A second method of counting the points from a truncated lattice is based on the notion of leader classes: from the definition of the leader class, the number of vectors belonging to that class can be easily deduced using polynomial coefficients (Moureaux et al., 1998), (Rault & Guillemot, 2001). This approach is also more appropriate for applications where the indexing of lattice points is also required. There exist other methods for counting the lattice points, but they will be treated in the section dedicated to the indexing of lattice points.

2.4 Indexing the vectors in truncated lattices

Several lattice enumeration techniques have been proposed over the years for different truncations and lattice types. One of the first papers to present an indexing algorithm for lattices was (Conway & Sloane, 1983), but it was restricted to Voronoi truncated lattices. Few years later, Fischer introduced the first enumeration technique on pyramid truncated lattice in (Fischer, 1986) which he subsequently generalized for weighted pyramids in Z_n (Fischer, 1989), (Fischer & Pan, 1995). This method, which we dub Fischer enumeration, is based on the iterative counting

$$N(l,k) = \sum_{i=-k}^{k} N(l-1, k-|i|) \tag{5}$$

where $N(l,k)$ is the number of vectors in the pyramidal shell of norm k of the lattice Z_l. $N(l,k)$ can be viewed as the number of ways l integer values can sum up in absolute value to k. For maximum efficiency, the numbers $N(k,l)$ must be stored, resulting in a table of size logarithmic in the codebook size. Alternatively, methods of deriving the values of $N(l,k)$ are presented in (Hung et al., 1998). A second type of indexing method, also based on an iterative counting of the points having a certain property has been presented in (Hung et al., 1998). There are four significant quantities of a codevector, which can be iteratively numbered, finally their juxtaposition forming a product code. These quantities are:

1. $D(s,l)$: the number of possible distinct distributions of s elements in l locations,
2. $S(s,k)$: the number of possible combinations of s non-zero elements that sum up to k (distinct additive partitions),
3. $B(s)$: the number of sign combinations for s non-zero elements.

In terms of a lattice codevector, s is the number of non-zero components of the l dimensional vector. The number of points for a given ℓ_1 norm k is thus given by (Hung et al., 1998)

$$N(l,k) = \sum_{s=1}^{m} B(s)D(s,l)S(s,k) = \sum_{s=1}^{m} 2^s \binom{l}{s} \binom{k-1}{s-1} \quad (6)$$

where m is the maximum number of non-zero elements in the lattice vectors included in truncation. The use of a product code enhances the error resilience over noisy channels, when compared to the original enumeration proposed by Fischer (Hung et al., 1998). These algorithms, as described in (Hung et al., 1998) apply mainly to Z_n lattices or D_n with pyramidal truncations. The product code of (Hung et al., 1998) can be generalized to spherical truncations, but with some additional storage requirements for the term $S(s,k)$ (Constantinescu, 2001).

In (Serra-Sagrista, 2000) combinatorial formulas like in (6) have been proposed for the A_n, D_n^* and D_n^+ lattices with pyramidal truncation. A generalization of Fischer's method to lattices derived from binary linear block codes through *Construction A* and *B* (Conway & Sloane, 1992) has been presented for pyramidal truncations in (Wang et al., 1998). This method has $O(nK)$ computational complexity, where n is the lattice dimension and K the truncation maximum ℓ_1 norm, and it is based on a Fischer type enumeration of pyramidal truncations of Z_n and of translated $2Z_n$.

An indexing technique based on the notion of leader vector of a lattice was developed in (Moureaux et al., 1998) for Z_n and D_n lattices. In (Vasilache & Tabus, 2002) a method based on leader vectors for lattices that can be defined as unions of leader classes (including Z_n, D_n, D_n^* and D_n^+ lattices) has been proposed. Rault and Guillemot (Rault & Guillemot, 2001) have presented an enumeration based on signed leaders or generated signed leaders valid for a large class of lattices (Z_n, A_n, D_n and D_n^{++}). The principle of the methods based on leaders, is to count the signed permutations generating the vectors in a leader class. The methods described in (Moureaux et al., 1998) and (Rault & Guillemot, 2001) are based on the lexicographical or inverse lexicographical order of vectors. The methods proposed in (Vasilache & Tabus, 2002) utilize also a second possible order of the vectors within a leader class, based on binomial coefficients.

3. Lattice entropy coding

Allowing variable bit rate encoding through entropy encoding brings substantial compression efficiency increase. Moreover, in the case of vector quantization, lattice vector quantization in particular, it is more efficient to entropy encode the codevector indexes than the codevector components.

This fact is illustrated in figures 2 and 3 where experimental compression performance in the rate-distortion plane is drawn for the lattices D_4 and D_8 respectively. The curve marked as "comp" corresponds to the case when the lattice codevector components are supposed to be entropy encoded, while the curve marked with "idx" corresponds to the case when the codevector indexes are supposed to be entropy encoded. The rate is assimilated to the entropy, to consider the best achievable case and the entropy values are estimated from the data. Zero mean Gaussian data with unitary variance is used for test. Also the curve corresponding to the Z_4/Z_8 lattice is depicted in the graphs, and as expected, for this lattice the rate-distortion curves are the same whether the entropy coding is applied to the components or to the indexes.

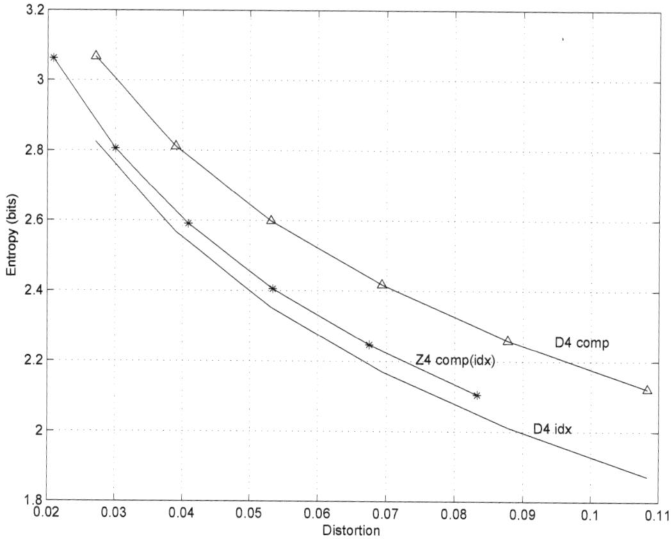

Fig. 2. Comparison of rate-distortion curves for Z_4 and D_4 lattice when the lattice vector components are entropy encoded ("comp") and when the lattice vector indexes are entropy encoded ("idx").

Ideally, the entropy coding of lattice codevectors should consider each codevector individually. However, the use of lattice codebooks is most usefull for high dimensions, where even for bit rates relatively small, the number of codevectors easily becomes large, making the individual consideration of each codevector impractical. Practical solutions to this problem have been the grouping of codevectors into sets (i.e. shells or leader classes) and entropy encoding of the index of the set while the vector index within the set is encoded using enumerative coding (Vasilache & Tabus, 2001), (Rault & Guillemot, 2001), (Moureaux et al., 1998), (Loyer et al., 2003). However, the large number of leader classes for some particular truncation shapes, makes their use less practical.

Another approach has been to entropy encode the lattice vector components (Zhao et al., 2007), but for lattices where there exist constraints relative to the values of a lattice vector (e.g. sum of components should be even) this approach is not very efficient with respect to the entropy coding of the lattice vector indexes.

3.1 Product code lattice codevector indexing

In (Hung et al., 1998) the use of a product code type index for pyramidal truncation, in which at least the sign bits were separated has been proposed and shown to have good error resilience performance.

Using a similar approach, the idea of a product code has been extended to spherical lattice truncations (Constantinescu, 2001) and to rectangular lattice truncations (Vasilache, 2007).

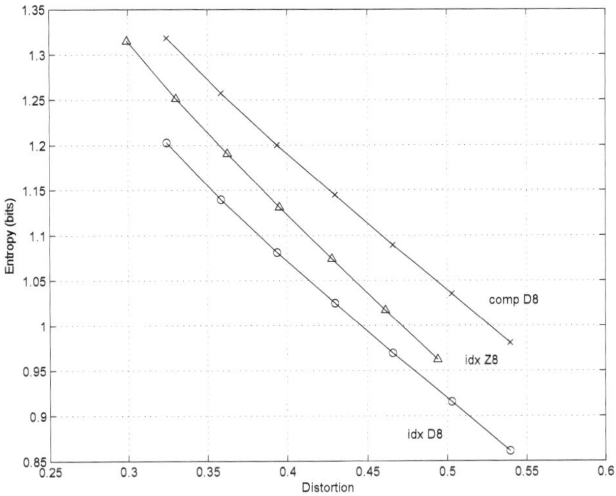

Fig. 3. Comparison of rate-distortion curves for Z_8 and D_8 lattice when the lattice vector components are entropy encoded ("comp") and when the lattice vector indexes are entropy encoded ("idx").

We propose in the present study the use of the product code indexing from (Vasilache, 2007) for the entropy coding of the lattice codevectors. The rectangular truncation uses the maximum absolute norm of a vector $\mathbf{y} = (y_1, y_2, ..., y_n) \in \mathbf{R}^n$ defined as

$$N(\mathbf{y}) = \max_{i=1:n}(|y_i|). \tag{7}$$

The idea of the product code is to extract different informational entities from the vector to be indexed and concatenate their respective codes. The information contained in the vector from a rectangular Z_n lattice truncation is represented by the following entities:

- The number of the significant (non zero) components (A);
- The number of maximum valued components (in absolute value) (B);
- The position of the maximum valued components within the lattice codevector (C);
- The values of the significant non-maximum components (D);
- The position of the significant non maximum values within the lattice codevector without the maximum valued components (E);
- The signs of the significant components (F).

The borders between the bits corresponding to different entities that form the index are not strict, except for the bits corresponding to the signs. The strict border of the sign bits is due to the fact that they are situated at an extreme of the index and the cardinality of the set describing all the sign combinations is a power of two. The indexing corresponds to the bits ordering | A / B / C / D / E | F |. The delimiter "|" represents a strict border.

3.1.1 Alternate approaches

There are more possible representations into information units. For instance, an equivalent representation can be (representation II):

- The number of the significant (non zero) components (A′);
- The number of maximum valued components (in absolute value) (B′);
- The position of the significant components within the lattice vector (C′);
- The position of the maximum valued components within the significant ones (D′);
- The values of the significant non-maximum components (E′);
- The signs of the significant components (F′)

or as representation III:

- The number of the significant (non zero) components (A″);
- The number of maximum valued components (in absolute value) (B″);
- The position of the maximum valued components within the lattice codevector (C″);
- The positions of the significant non-maximum values within the lattice codevector without the maximum components (D″);
- The values of the significant non-maximum components (E″);
- The signs of the significant components (F″).

3.2 Entropy coding based on product code lattice codevector indexing

The different informational entities extracted from the vector, can be also interpreted as means of classifying the vectors into different sets. The existence of several entities implies the division of all the vectors into sets, sub-sets and so forth. If the index corresponding to all or part of the set(sub-set) types are entropy encoded, an entropy code can be obtained for the initial lattice vector.

For instance, given the 4 dimensional vector (2 -3 0 -1), having maximum norm equal to 3, it has three significant components (A), one maximum valued component (B), index 1 for the position of the maximum valued component (C) and index 1 for the position of the non maximum valued components (E) (Vasilache, 2007). There are at least one and at most four significant values, therefore there are four possible symbols for the number of significant components, which can be entropy encoded. Furthermore, the number of maximum valued components can be entropy encoded, as well as the position indexes of the maximum valued components and so on.

There is a practical limit to the number of entities that can be entropy encoded, which is activated when the number of symbols for the considered entity becomes prohibitively large. For instance, for the encoding of the index of non-maximum significative values there are $(K-1)^{S-M}$ possible symbols, where S is the number of significative components and M the number of maximum components. For high truncation size (K) and/or high number of non-maximum significative values ($(S-M)$), this number becomes large and the probability of the index to be encoded very hard to model.

For small lattice codevector dimension the proposed lattice codevector entropy encoding method might become less efficient than the fixed rate encoding because there are more sources of inexact modelling.

3.2.1 Lattice truncation size parametrization

In the previously presented representations of the index, the lattice truncation size, given by its norm, is considered to be fixed. A more flexible approach for data with wide range of variation is obtained if the value of the current maximum is considered as side information that is entropy encoded.

3.2.2 Context entropy encoding of the index information units

The encoding of the information units should be done context based, because there is a strong correlation between the different units involved.

For instance, let's consider representation II, when the value of the maximum for each lattice codevector is transmitted as side information and the variables to be encoded (maximum value, number of significant components, number of maxima, position of significant components, position of maxima, index of non-maximum significant values, signs of significant components) are denoted respectively by

$$K, S, M, pS, pM, nM, sg.$$

Then the probability models for each variable are:

$$p(K), p(S|K), p(M|S,K), p(pS|S), p(pM|S,M), p(nM|S,M), p(sg).$$

For the first variables (K, S, M) their actual values are encoded. For pS and pM a position index specifying the location of l components out of n possible locations is created. A position vector $\mathbf{r} = (r_0, ..., r_{l-1}) \in 0, ..., n-1^l$, $r_0 < ... < r_{l-1}$ is created, which specifies the exact location of each of the l components. Since there are $\binom{n}{l}$ such vectors, they can be enumerated like binomial coefficients following the algorithm given by the next equations:

$$I_{pos}(l, n, \mathbf{r}) = \sum_{i=1}^{r_0} \binom{n-i}{l-1} + I_{pos}(n - r_0 - 1, l - 1, (r_1, ..., r_{l-1}) - r_0 - 1) \quad (8)$$

$$I_{pos}(l', 1, [i]) = i, \;\; 0 \leq i < l' \leq l. \quad (9)$$

The resulting index I_{pos} is the number to be encoded for pS and pM.

The index to be encoded for the values of non-maximum significant components is calculated as

$$I_{nM} = \sum_{i=1}^{S-M} (K-1)^{i-1}(y_i - 1) \quad (10)$$

where $y_i, i = 0, S - M - 1$ are the non-maximum significant values.

3.2.3 Bit rate calculation

Consider the n-dimensional vectors from the Z_n rectangular truncation of norm K. Any vector from this set can be represented on N_0 bits, where

$$N_0 = \lceil \log_2((2K+1)^n) \rceil. \quad (11)$$

If the entity corresponding to the number of significant values is entropy encoded on n_1 bits, the current vector from the set of vectors can be represented on N_1 bits instead of N_0, where

$$N_1 = n_1 + \left\lceil \log_2 \left(2^S \left(\binom{n}{1} \binom{n-1}{S-1} (K-1)^{S-1} + \binom{n}{2} \binom{n-2}{S-2} (K-1)^{S-2} + \ldots + \binom{n}{S} \right) \right) \right\rceil, \quad (12)$$

S is the number of significant components.

If the number of significant components is entropy encoded on n_1 bits, the number of maximum valued components is encoded on n_2 bits and the index of positions for the maximum valued components is encoded on n_3 bits, then the current vector from the set of vectors can be represented on N_3 bits, where

$$N_3 = n_1 + n_2 + n_3 + \left\lceil \log_2 \left(2^S \binom{n-M}{S-M} (K-1)^{S-M} \right) \right\rceil \quad (13)$$

where M is the number of maximum valued components whose position is already coded on n_3 bits.

If, in addition, the positions of the non-maximum significant values are entropy encoded on n_4 bits, then the current vector from the set of vectors can be represented on N_4 bits, where

$$N_4 = n_1 + n_2 + n_3 + n_4 + \left\lceil \log_2 \left((K-1)^{S-M} \right) \right\rceil + S. \quad (14)$$

4. Lattice quantization for audio coding

We exemplify the potential of the proposed method within an audio encoding algorithm. For the sake of completeness, we present briefly the overall audio encoding framework that uses rectangular lattice truncations for quantization. For a detailed description see (Vasilache & Toukomaa, 2006). The overall performance of the audio coding method is similar to the MPEG4-AAC for higher bitrates (128kbits/s down to 64kbits/s) and better than MPEG4-AAC for lower bitrates.

The global encoding framework is similar to the one used in the AAC. Within the bit pool mechanism, at each frame a given number of bits is available for the quantization of the modified discrete cosine transform (MDCT) coefficients grouped in several scale factor bands, according to the perceptual model. Roughly, only half of the coefficients are actually quantized, the coefficients corresponding to the higher frequencies being set to zero. The number of spectral coefficients, the number of scale factor bands and their lengths depend upon the sampling frequency of the input audio signal.

The normalized MDCT coefficients from each scale factor band i, are multiplied with b^{-s_i} and the result is further encoded. The encoding consists of companding the scaled coefficients and quantizing using a rectangular truncation of the lattice Z_n. The companding function is trained off-line.

The information to be encoded consists of the scale factor exponents $\{s_i\}$, the lattice codevector indexes, and side information providing the number of bits on which each index is represented. The maximum absolute value, i.e. the maximum norm of the scale factor band codevector, is used to calculate the number of bits on which the index of the scale factor band codevector is represented. We denote in the following $\{s_i\}$ by scales.

The scales are integers from a finite domain and they are entropy coded, same as the maximum norms of the lattice codevectors. The scale values are optimized such that the total

Name	Description
es01	Vocal (S. Vega)
es02	German male speech
es03	English female speech
sc01	Trumpet solo and orch.
sc02	Classical orch. music
sc03	Contemp. pop music
si01	Harpsichord
si02	Castanets
si03	Pitch pipe
sm01	Bagpipes
sm02	Glockenspiel
sm03	Plucked strings

Table 1. Test samples.

number of bits to encode a frame is within the available number of bits given by the bit pool mechanism. Since the maximum absolute norm of the lattice codevectors is encoded separately, the indexing of the lattice codevectors is done within the corresponding rectangular shell.

5. Results

We consider as test samples the 44.1kHz, mono samples presented in Table 1.
We have considered two encoding bit rates 32kbits/s and 48kbits/s for the audio codec from (Vasilache & Toukomaa, 2006). The number of bits for the quantized spectral coefficients is calculated according to the formulas from Equations 11 and 12. The difference between the average per frame number of bits N_1 and N_0 for all the spectral scale-factor bands is given numerically in percentages in Table 2. It corresponds to the case when the number of significant values is entropy encoded for all the scale-factor bands. The average codelength for n_1 is estimated based on the entropy. The absolute bit savings are not very significant yet.
However, when the first three entities (number of significant values, number of maximum valued components, and their position index) are entropy encoded, the bit savings become significant.
The difference between the average per frame number of bits N_3 and N_0 for all the spectral scale-factor bands is given numerically in Table 3. The number of bits for the quantized spectral coefficients are calculated according to the formulas from Equations 11 and 13.

File	BS32[%]	BS48[%]
es01	6.60	4.75
es02	8.00	5.62
es03	8.80	6.00
sc01	11.20	7.00
sc02	7.20	5.25
sc03	4.80	3.62
si01	5.40	2.75
si02	9.00	7.00
si03	10.60	6.75
sm01	7.40	4.00
sm02	8.40	5.25
sm03	4.80	3.25

Table 2. Bitrate savings, in percentage, when the number of significant values is entropy encoded.

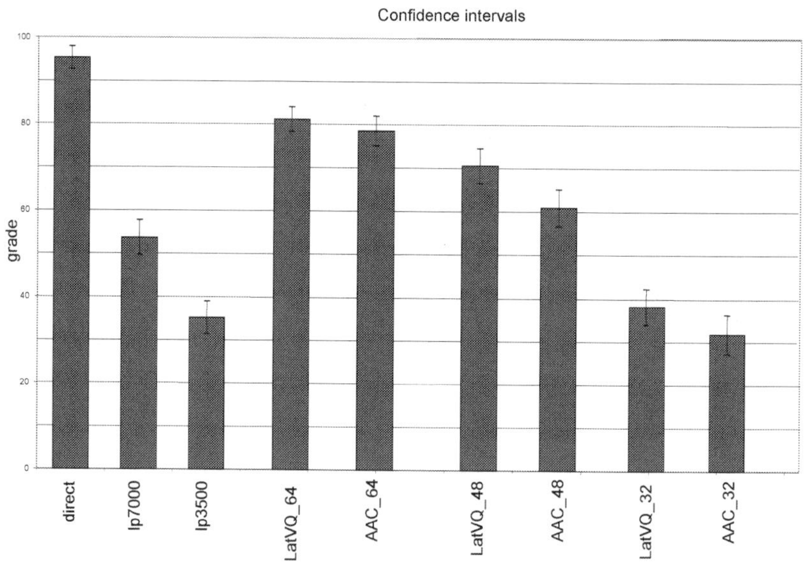

Fig. 4. Listening test results (Vasilache & Toukomaa, 2006)

Compared with the number of bits per frame available for spectral quantization only, in the fixed rate case, for the considered bitrates, the values in Table 3 give an average of 30% bitrate reduction without any loss of quality.
The method (labeled as 'LatVQ') without entropy coding was compared in (Vasilache & Toukomaa, 2006), against the quantization procedure from the MPEG4-AAC codec, in a MUlti Stimulus test with Hidden Reference and Anchor (MUSHRA) (BS.1534-1, 2003). A particularity of the AAC codec framework was the 11kHz bandwidth considered for quantization for

File	BS32[%]	BS48[%]
es01	70.20	53.12
es02	37.80	30.12
es03	49.20	36.62
sc01	34.80	21.75
sc02	60.20	48.75
sc03	76.60	63.87
si01	-21.80	-6.25
si02	-19.80	-0.75
si03	14.00	9.62
sm01	35.40	28.12
sm02	-0.80	-0.50
sm03	46.20	40.37

Table 3. Bit savings, in percentages, when the number of significant values, the number of maximum valued components, and their position index are entropy encoded.

all the bitrates. The files used in the tests are listed in Table 1. The files es01 and sm01 were used only in the training experiment and the remaining files were used in each of the three testing experiments. There were 11 expert listeners.

Since the addition of the proposed entropy coding does not change the quality of the LatVQ method, it means that the conditions LatVQ_48 and LatVQ_32 (Figure 4) should actually correspond to bitrates of approximately 30 % less than 48 kbits/s and 32 kbits/s respectively.

The proposed entropy encoded method was used in this case only for the scale-factor bands with dimensions up to 24, the higher dimensional ones generating too many symbols, at least for the position index of the maximum valued components. However, previous entropy coding methods of lattice vector indexes were generally on dimension 10 or lower (Vasilache & Tabus, 2001).

5.1 Further discussions

A very delicate matter related to the enumeration of lattice points is the error resilience over a noisy channel. Few papers (Hung et al., 1998), (Vasilache & Tabus, 2002), (Vasilache & Tabus, 2003) have dealt with the error resilience over the channel for lattice codebooks.

In (Hung et al., 1998) the channel error resilience is obtained through the use of product code based indexing while in (Vasilache & Tabus, 2003) lexicographical and binomial families of indexing methods are proposed, allowing the optimization of the indexing with respect to the channel distortion (or some other criterion) within a given family.

The proposed lattice coding, being an entropy encoding method, is on one side sensitive to channel errors but is has built-in error concealment mechanisms due to the dependencies existing between the information units that are encoded. In addition, extending the observations from (Vasilache, 2007), the proposed method can made scalable in bitrate through the control of the variables that are encoded, allowing thus an approximate representation of the original lattice codevector and the use of the corresponding bits for channel protection, for instance. The potential of this approach needs to be investigated through future studies.

Another potential direction of investigation is to study the time correlation of each information unit to be encoded, that should be easier to exploit than the time correlation of the lattice codevector indexes if it exists.

The method presented here can be applied wherever product code indexing is applicable (pyramidal or spherical truncations as well), but it is limited so far to Z_n, D_n, D_n^* and D_n^+ lattices.

6. Conclusion

We have presented a new method for entropy encoding of lattice codevectors. It is based on the lattice vector set partitioning generated by the product code indexes of such vectors. It can provide bitrate savings up to 30% within an audio coding scenario with respect to the fixed rate lattice quantization. In addition to the improved compression efficiency, the proposed method enables the use of lattice entropy encoding in higher dimensions.

7. References

Adoul, J.-P. (1986). La quantification vectorielle des signaux: approche algébrique, *Annales des Télécommunications* **41**(3-4): 158–177.

Adoul, J.-P. & Barth, M. (1988). Nearest neighbor algorithm for spherical codes from the leech lattice, *IEEE Transactions on Information Theory* **38**(5II): 1188–1202.

Barlaud, M., Solé, P., Moureaux, J. M., Antonini, M. & Gauthier, P. (1993). Elliptical codebook for lattice vector quantization, *Proceedings of the ICASSP 1993*, Minneapolis, USA, pp. 590–593.

BS.1534-1, I.-R. (2003). Method for the subjective assessment of intermediate quality level of coding systems.

Constantinescu, M. E. (2001). Lattice VQ for image compression, Internal report, Tampere University of Technology, Tampere, Finland.

Conway, J. H. & Sloane, N. J. A. (1982). Fast quantizing and decoding algorithms for lattice quantizers and codes, *IEEE Transactions on Information Theory* **IT-28**(2): 227–232.

Conway, J. H. & Sloane, N. J. A. (1983). A fast encoding method for lattice codes and quantizers, *IEEE Transactions on Information Theory* **37**(5): 820–824.

Conway, J. H. & Sloane, N. J. A. (1992). *Sphere Packings, Lattices and Groups*, Springer-Verlag, New York.

Cover, T. M. & Thomas, J. A. (1991). *Elements of Information Theory*, John Wiley & Sons, Inc.

Fischer, T. R. (1986). A pyramid vector quantizer, *IEEE Transactions on Information Theory* **IT-32**(4): 568–583.

Fischer, T. R. (1989). Geometric source coding and vector quantization, *IEEE Transactions on Information Theory* **35**(1): 137–144.

Fischer, T. R. (1991). Entropy-constrained geometric vector quantization for transform image coding, *Proceedings of ICASSP 1991*, Vol. 4, pp. 2269–2272.

Fischer, T. R. & Pan, J. (1995). Enumeration encoding and decoding algorithms for pyramid cubic lattice and trellis codes, *IEEE Transactions on Information Theory* **41**(6): 2056–2061.

Gersho, A. (1979). Asymptotically optimal block quantization, *IEEE Transactions on Information Theory* **IT-25**(4): 373–380.

Hung, A. C., Tsern, E. K. & Meng, T. H. (1998). Error-resilient pyramid vector quantization for image compression, *IEEE Transactions on Image Processing* **7**(10): 1373–1386.

Loyer, P., Moureaux, J. M. & Antonini, M. (2003). Lattice codebook enumeration for generalized Gaussian source, *IEEE Transactions on Information Theory* **49**(2).

Moureaux, J., Antonini, M. & Barlaud, M. (1995). Counting lattice points on ellipsoids: application to image coding, *Electronics letters* **31**(8): 1224–1225.

Moureaux, J. M., Loyer, P. & Antonini, M. (1998). Low complexity indexing method for Z_n and D_n lattice quantizers, *IEEE Transactions on Communications* **46**(12): 1602–1609.

Ragot, S., Bessette, B. & Lefebvre, R. (2004). Low-complexity multi-rate lattice vector quantization with application to wideband tcx speech coding at 32 kbit/s, *Proceedings of ICASSP 2004*, Vol. 1, Montreal, Canada.

Rämö, A., Toukomaa, H., Greer, S. C., Laaksonen, L., Stachurski, J., Ertan, A. E., Svedberg, J., Gibbs, J. & Vaillancourt, T. (2008). Quality evaluation of the g.ev-vbr speech codec, *Proceedings of ICASSP 2008*, Las Vegas, USA.

Rault, P. & Guillemot, C. (2001). Indexing algorithms for Z_n, A_n, D_n and D_n^{++} lattice vector quantizers, *IEEE Transactions on Multimedia* **3**(4): 395–404.

Sakrison, D. J. (1968). A geometric treatment of the source encoding of a Gaussian random variable, *IEEE Transactions on Information Theory* **IT-14**(3): 481–486.

Sayood, K., Gibson, J. D. & Rost, M. C. (1984). An algorithm for uniform vector design, *IEEE Transactions on Information Theory* **IT-30**(6): 805–814.

Serra-Sagrista, J. (2000). Enumeration of lattice points in ℓ_1 norm, *Information processing letters* **76**: 39–44.

Solé, P. (1993). Generalized theta functions for lattice vector quantization, *Proceedings of IEEE International Symposium on Information Theory*, pp. 174–174.

Vasilache, A. (2007). Indexing of lattice codevectors applied to error resilient audio coding, *Proceedings of the AES 30th International Conference*, Saariselkä, Finland.

Vasilache, A. & Tabus, I. (2001). Indexing and entropy coding of lattice codevectors, *Proceedings of ICASSP 2001*, Salt Lake City, Utah, USA.

Vasilache, A. & Tabus, I. (2002). LSF quantization with MSLLVQ for transmission over noisy channels, *Proceedings of EUSIPCO 2002*, Toulouse, France.

Vasilache, A. & Tabus, I. (2003). Robust indexing for lattices and permutation codes over binaty symmetric channels, *Signal Processing* **83**(7): 1467–1486.

Vasilache, A. & Toukomaa, H. (2006). Vectorial spectral quantization for audio coding, *Proceedings of ICASSP 2006*, Toulouse, France.

Vasilache, A., Vasilache, M. & Tabus, I. (1999). Predictive multiple-scale lattice VQ for LSF quantization, *Proceedings of ICASSP 1999*, Phoenix, Arizona, USA, pp. 657–660.

Wang, C., Cao, H. Q., Li, W. & Tzeng, K. K. (1998). Lattice labeling algorithms for vector quantization, *IEEE Transactions on Circuits and Systems for Video Technology* **8**(2): 206–220.

Zhao, D. Y., Samuelsson, J. & Nilsson, M. (2007). GMM-based entropy-constrained vector quantization, *Proceedings of ICASSP 2007*, Hawaii, USA.

17

Segmented Online Neural Filtering System Based On Independent Components Of Pre-Processed Information

Rodrigo Torres[1], Eduardo Simas Filho[1,2],
Danilo de Lima[1] and José de Seixas[1]
[1] *COPPE / Poli - Federal University of Rio de Janeiro, Brazil*
[2] *Federal Institute of Education, Science and Technology of Bahia, Brazil*

1. Introduction

Data filtering systems are used in different fields of research, aiming at isolating signals of interest from patterns related to a given background noise. Nowadays, in many complex applications, the input data space dimensionality is very high, as well as the incoming data rate. In this case, the difficulty of the input data stream analysis increases significantly. Also, the processing speed plays a critical role when the filtering system is envisaged for online operation. Finally, the signals of interest may rarely occur, forcing the experiment to keep running for a long period of time in order to acquire a reasonable amount of events for better measurement estimation.

In general, online filtering systems should have the following features:

- High detection efficiency for a low false alarm probability.
- Simplified software / hardware implementation.
- Flexibility in order to accomplish possible future requirements.
- Execution speed capable of meeting the desired time requirements.
- Robustness, in order to keep its filtering features through its lifetime of operation.

To cope with such high-input data dimension, feature extraction techniques may be applied in order to isolate the relevant information from the event data description, eventually reducing its dimension. For this, different data compaction techniques have been developed using expert information or / and stochastic processing. Pre-processing schemes based on signal decorrelation (linear or nonlinear) may even reduce the complexity of the classifier (signal against background) design. Finally, in the case where the available information is from a set of sensors, signal pre-processing might also be segmented, better exploiting the available local information.

Statistical processing can play a valuable role in the pattern recognition task, since it can provide better separation cuts than deterministic methods, specially for the case where the problem to be solved presents nonlinear characteristics. By using algorithms based on high-order statistics, it is possible to better estimate the bounds of each pattern, achieving higher detection efficiencies. In many applications, neural networks (Haykin, 2008) may play a role in signal classification. On the other hand, by reducing the classifier design complexity by means of signal pre-processing, it might be possible to restrict the nonlinear processing implemented by the neural network to perform slight adjustments to the linear signal classification. It may also be the case where signal classification can go linear (through a Fisher Discriminant) (Duda et al., 2004), as a result of a highly-efficient pre-processing scheme.

In the field of experimental high-energy physics, stringent conditions make signal processing a challenge, as there is often a large gap between the experiment requirements and the technology currently available, which forces the development of new technologies. This is particularly the case for modern particle collider experiments, in which particles are accelerated at high speed and put in collision route. Analyzing the resulting collisions products, one can probe deeper into the structure of matter (Perkins, 2000). One important aspect in particle collider experiments is that events of interest are typically very rare, since most of the produced events are from background noise. In addition, the fine-grained segmentation of the particle detectors placed around the collision points for the resulting interaction readout may produce up to terabytes per second of information. Therefore, an online filtering system must be applied for selecting only the interesting physics channels, while rejecting, as much as possible, the huge amount of background noise.

Presently, the Large Hadron Collider (LHC) at CERN (CERN, 2007) is the largest particle accelerator in the world. LHC has a total length of 27 km and will be colliding protons with 14 TeV at their center of mass, at a rate of 40 MHz and at a luminosity of $10^{34}cm^{-2}s^{-1}$ (Evans and Bryant, 2008). Multiple collision points occur around the LHC ring. Around each collision point, a detection laboratory is placed to analyze the sub-products of the collisions. Among such detectors ATLAS (The ATLAS Collaboration, 2008) is the largest one. It comprises multiple sub-detectors, such as tracking, calorimeter and muon detection systems. Due to the detector granularity, each collision produces ~1.5 MBytes of information, resulting in a total rate of ~60 TB/s of information. Therefore, an online filtering system is mandatory for proper ATLAS operation.

This chapter focuses on proposing an efficient data filtering strategy for operating at stringent conditions. It is based on a signal processing scheme that combines expert knowledge with stochastic signal processing techniques for data dimension reduction and relevant feature extraction. The classifier design that implements the final filtering operation (rejection / acceptance of incoming data) is evaluated in terms of complexity and efficiency. For this, the input nodes of the classifier are fed from pre-processed information. The proposed signal processing strategy will be applied in high-energy physics, using the ATLAS detector as a case study.

This chapter is organized as follows: Section 2 briefly describes the pre-processing methods used in the application. Then, in Section 3, the ATLAS filtering system will be explained, and the envisaged application is presented. In Section 4, the obtained results for such application are discussed. Finally, conclusions are derived in Section 5.

2. Signal Pre-Processing

The pre-processing techniques presented in this section focus on performing linear and nonlinear input variable decorrelation. This could make the relevant discrimination features more evident to the classifier, simplifying its design. Furthermore, depending on the power of the nonlinear decorrelation applied, the classifier could be simplified to the point of a simple linear discriminant.

2.1 Independent Component Analysis

Independent Component Analysis (ICA) is a multidimensional signal processing technique that searches for a linear transformation of the data, so that its essential structure becomes somehow more accessible (Hyvärinen et al., 2001). In ICA, the transformed variables are restricted to be statistically independent.

In the standard ICA model, the measured (observed) signals $x=[x_1,x_2,...,x_N]^T$ are considered to be generated through a linear combination of the independent (unobserved) signals $s=[s_1,s_2,...,s_N]^T$:

$$x_i = \sum_{j=1}^{N} a_{ij} s_j \rightarrow \mathbf{x}=\mathbf{As} \qquad (1)$$

where $i=1,...,N$ and $\boldsymbol{A}$ is the mixing matrix. The ICA model has been widely applied in a variety of signal processing tasks, see as reference (Choi et al., 2005) and (Moura et al., 2009). The purpose of ICA is to estimate the independent signals $\mathbf{s}$ and the mixing matrix $\boldsymbol{A}$ using only the observed data $\boldsymbol{x}$. This can be achieved through an inverse model:

$$\mathbf{y}=\mathbf{Wx}, \qquad (2)$$

where the coefficients of the estimated matrix $\boldsymbol{W}$ are obtained by considering that the components of $\boldsymbol{y}$ are statistically independent (or at least as much independent as possible).

There are some indeterminacies in the ICA model: the order of extraction of the independent components can change and scalar multipliers (positive or negative) may modify the estimated components. Fortunately these limitations are insignificant in most applications.

In some practical signal processing problems, the standard linear ICA model may not be able to properly describe the data. Considering a practical ICA application, both the mixing environment and the sensors may present some nonlinear behavior. Providing a more general formulation, the nonlinear independent component analysis (NLICA) model considers that the measured signals $\boldsymbol{x}$ are formed by a nonlinear instantaneous mixing model (Almeida, 2006):

$$\mathbf{x}=F(\mathbf{s}) \qquad (3)$$

where $F(.)$ is a $\boldsymbol{R}^N$ -> $\boldsymbol{R}^N$ nonlinear mapping (the number of sources is usually assumed to be equal to the number of observed signals). The purpose of NLICA is to estimate an inverse transformation $G(.)$ $\boldsymbol{R}^N$ -> $\boldsymbol{R}^N$:

$$\mathbf{y}=\mathrm{G}(\mathbf{x}) \qquad (4)$$

so that the components of y are statistically independent. If $G(.)=F^{-1}(.)$, the sources are perfectly recovered (Jutten and Karhunen, 2003).

A characteristic of the NLICA problem is that the solutions are non-unique (Jutten and Karhunen, 2003). If $\boldsymbol{u}$ and $\boldsymbol{v}$ are independent random variables, it is easy to prove that $f(\boldsymbol{u})$

and $g(v)$, where $f(.)$ and $g(.)$ are differentiable functions, are also independent. So, it is clear that, without imposing some restrictions, there is an infinite number of solutions for the inverse mapping G in a given application (the problem is ill-posed). Considering this, an unique solution for the nonlinear independent component analysis (NLICA) can not be achieved without some prior information on the mixing model or the sources. A complete investigation on the uniqueness of nonlinear ICA solutions can be found in (Hyvärinen and Pajunen, 1999). NLICA algorithms have recently been applied in different problems such as speech processing (Rojas et al., 2003), (Wei et al., 2006), image denoising (Haritopoulos et al., 2002), chemistry sensor array processing (Duarte et al., 2009).
The minimization of statistical dependence is a main concern for any ICA/NLICA algorithm, as it leads to the estimation of the mixing system (and consequently the independent components). In addition, ICA often requires some pre-processing for data compaction, especially for high-dimension input data space applications. These topics are briefly described in the next subsections. It is also summarized the JADE algorithm, which has been widely used for independent component estimation. Different NLICA approaches are also briefly reviewed.

2.1.1 Statistical Independence

Considering two random vectors v_1 and v_2, they are statistically independent if and only if (Papoulis and Pillai, 2002):

$$p_{\mathbf{v}_1,\mathbf{v}_2}(\mathbf{v}_1,\mathbf{v}_2) = p_{\mathbf{v}_1}(\mathbf{v}_1)p_{\mathbf{v}_2}(\mathbf{v}_2) \tag{5}$$

where $p_{v1}(v_1)$, $p_{v2}(v_2)$ are, respectively, the probability density function (pdf) of v_1 and v_2 and $p_{v1,v2}(v_1, v_2)$ is their joint pdf. In typical ICA problems, there is very little information on the source signals and so, the pdf estimation is a very difficult task. Considering this, alternative independence measures are usually applied during the search for independent components (Hyvärinen et al., 2001) (Cichocki and Amari, 2002). They are defined next for reference.

2.1.1.1 Nonlinear Decorrelation

Two zero-mean random variables (u_1 and u_2) are said to be (linearly) uncorrelated if their cross-correlation R_{u1u2} is zero (here, $E\{.\}$ is the expectation operator):

$$R_{u_1u_2} = E\{u_1u_2^T\} \tag{6}$$

Independent variables are uncorrelated, although, the reciprocal is not always true. Linear correlation is verified by second order statistics, while independence needs higher-order information too (requiring direct or indirect computation of higher-order moments).
Considering $g(u_1)$ and $f(u_2)$ absolutely integrable functions of u_1 and u_2, respectively, it can be proved that if Equation 7 holds for all possible $g(.)$ and $f(.)$, than u_1 and u_2 are independent

$$E\{g(u_1)f(u_2)\} = E\{g(u_1)\}E\{f(u_2)\} \tag{7}$$

By choosing $g(.)$ and $f(.)$ as nonlinear functions, high-order statistical information is (indirectly) accessed. The statistical independence measure provided by Equation 7 is usually called the nonlinear decorrelation between u_1 and u_2 (Cichocki and Unbehauen, 1996).

A practical limitation appears when trying to apply this measure in an ICA algorithm as it is not possible to check all integrable functions *g(.)* and *f(.)*. Thus estimates of the independent components are usually obtained while guaranteeing nonlinear decorrelation between a finite set of nonlinear functions (Cichocki and Unbehauen, 1996).

2.1.1.2 Higher-Order Statistics

Another principle that can be used to estimate the dependence of variables comes from the central limit theorem (McClave et al., 2008): "The sum of two random variables is always closer to a Gaussian distribution than the original variable distributions". As the measured signals (x) are considered to be a linear combination of independent sources (s), then the measured signals are closer to a Gaussian distribution than the original sources. Thus, the independent components can be obtained through maximization of non-gaussianity (Hyvärinen et al., 2001).

It is known that, for Gaussian random variables, the cumulants of orders higher than two are all zero. Considering this, non-gaussianity (and consequently independence) measures can be obtained by using high-order cumulants, such as the kurtosis K_4, which, for a zero-mean, unit-variance random variable u is defined through (Papoulis and Pillai, 2002):

$$K_4 = E\{u^4\} - 3\left[E\{u^2\}\right]^2 \tag{8}$$

2.1.1.3 Information Theoretic Measures

Alternative statistical independence measures can be obtained from information theory (Mackay, 2002). A basic definition in information theory is the entropy (*H(.)*), which, for a discrete random variable u, is defined as (Shannon, 1948):

$$H(u) = -\sum_i P(u = \kappa_i) \log P(u = \kappa_i) \tag{9}$$

Where κ1, κ2, ..., κ m are all the possible discrete values of u. is that the Gaussian variable has maximum entropy between the random variables of same variance (Hyvärinen et al., 2001). Considering this, entropy can be used as gaussianity measure.

The Negentropy *J(u)* of the random variable u is also applied in the ICA context:.

$$J(u) = H(u_{gauss}) - H(u) \tag{10}$$

where u_{gauss} is a Gaussian random variable with the same mean and variance of u. The advantage of using *J(u)*, instead of *H(u)*, is that it is always non-negative and zero when u is Gaussian. A problem with the computation of both *J(.)* and *H(.)* is the pdf estimation. To avoid this, approximations using high-order cumulants or non-polynomial functions are often applied (Murillo-Fuentes et al., 2004).

The Mutual Information $I(u_1, u_2, ..., u_m)$ between m random variables $u_1, u_2, ..., u_m$ is obtained through Equation 11.

$$I(u_1, u_2, \ldots, u_m) = \sum_{i=1}^{m} H(u_i) - H(\mathbf{v}) \tag{11}$$

It is known that the entropy of the vector v = [u_1, u_2, ..., u_m] is always smaller than the sum of $H(u_i)$, unless the variables are independent. So, minimization of mutual information leads to independence (Hyvärinen et al., 2001).

2.1.2 Signal Decorrelation

The standard ICA model assumes a mixing system where the number of sources and observed signals is the same. In a practical problem, this assumption may not be always true. When there exist more sources than sensors (observed signals), the problem is under-determined and the sources are only recovered approximately through algorithms derived for such situation (Syskind et al., 2006), (Natora et al., 2009). In the case where the number of sources (K) is smaller than the number of observed signals (N), the problem is over-determined and thus some signal compaction algorithm is needed to reduce signal dimensionality. With this purpose, Principal Component Analysis (PCA) is usually applied as a pre-processing for ICA algorithms. Principal Components for Discrimination (PCD) analysis (Caloba et al., 1995) has been introduced as an alternative to PCA, when ICA is applied to classification problems (Simas Filho et al., 2009b).

2.1.2.1 Principal Component Analysis

Principal Component Analysis (PCA) (Jolliffe, 2002) is a statistical signal processing technique that searches for a new representation of the input signals where the energy is concentrated on a small number of components. Using second-order statistics, PCA transformation searches for a vector basis for which the projections $y_i = w_i\, x_i$ of a zero-mean random vector $\boldsymbol{x}$ ($E\{x\}=0$) are uncorrelated and have maximum variance (i.e. composing an orthonormal basis).

The first principal direction w_1 can be computed through the maximization of

$$J_1^{PCA}(w_1) = E\{v^2\} = E\{(w_1 x)^2\} = w_1^T C_x w_1 \tag{12}$$

where Cx is the covariance matrix of x and $||w_1||=1$.

PCA transformation is very useful as a pre-processing for ICA as it eliminates second-order dependencies (correlation) between the signals, facilitating the search for independence.

2.1.2.2 Whitening

A zero-mean random vector z is said to be white if their components are uncorrelated and have unit variance (Hyvärinen et al., 2001). This implies that the covariance matrix (and also the correlation matrix) of z equals the identity matrix. Whitening is sometimes called sphering and is a slightly stronger operation than decorrelation. One popular method to perform whitening is the eigenvalue decomposition (EVD) of the covariance matrix (Strang,

2009). In this approach, considering $\boldsymbol{Z}$ the matrix whose columns are the unit-norm eigenvectors of the covariance matrix $\boldsymbol{C}_x$ of a random vector $\boldsymbol{x}$ and $\boldsymbol{D}$ the diagonal matrix of the eigenvalues of $\boldsymbol{C}_x$, the linear whitening transform $\boldsymbol{V}$ is given by:

$$\mathbf{V} = \mathbf{D}^{-1/2}\mathbf{Z}^T \tag{13}$$

2.1.2.3 Principal Components of Discrimination

Considering a classification problem, the purpose of PCD analysis is to determine the directions that maximize class separation (Caloba et al., 1995). Typically, PCD provides a higher compaction rate for classification problems with respect to PCA (Simas Filho et al., 2009b).

The PCD analysis can be performed through a Multilayer Perceptron (MLP) neural network (Haykin, 2008). For simplicity, considering binary discrimination, a network with a single hidden neuron, trained to maximize class discrimination, extracts the first discriminating component (see Fig. 1-a). By sequentially adding neurons to the hidden layer and restarting the training procedure, the next components are estimated. The hidden weights are trained only for the added neurons (highlighted synaptic lines in Fig. 1-b). The estimated weights from the previous steps are kept fixed, as they represent the directions of the principal components already extracted. The weights of the output layer are adjusted during the whole training procedure for optimal combination of principal components at each processing step. The PCD extraction continues up to the point where the classification efficiency does not improve significantly by adding more components.

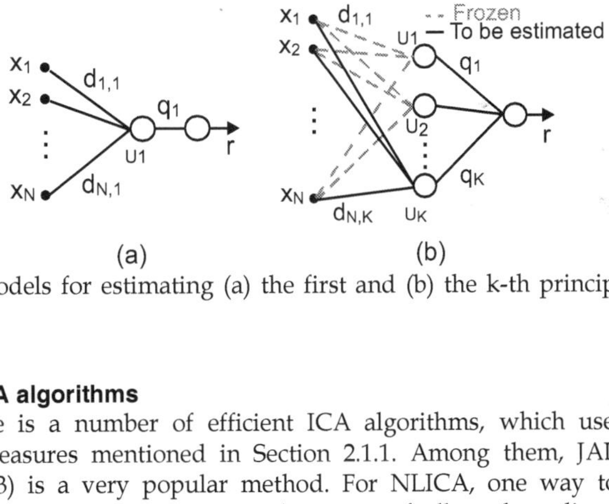

Fig. 1. Neural models for estimating (a) the first and (b) the k-th principal discriminating component.

2.1.3 ICA / NLICA algorithms

Nowadays, there is a number of efficient ICA algorithms, which use, in general, the independence measures mentioned in Section 2.1.1. Among them, JADE (Cardoso and Souloumiac, 1993) is a very popular method. For NLICA, one way to address the ill-posedness of the problem is to restrict the range of allowed nonlinearities, generating structural constrained models for the mixing system and thus unique solutions for the problem (Jutten and Karhunen, 2003). Among these models, we can mention the post-nonlinear (PNL) mixture, which has met a significant practical applicability (Almeida, 2006). There is also a method closely related to the NLICA problem, known as Local ICA, which introduces nonlinear transformations by clustering the dataset into groups of similar characteristics. After that, linear ICA is applied to data belonging to each cluster producing local independent components.

2.1.3.1 JADE

In JADE (Joint Approximate Diagonalization of Eigenmatrices) algorithm, second and fourth-order statistics are applied for independent component estimation through a tensorial approach. The second-order cumulant (i.e. the covariance matrix) is used to ensure that data are white (uncorrelated). Fourth-order information (through the fourth-order cumulant tensor matrix) produces an independence criterion.
Tensors are considered as a higher-dimensional generalization of matrices or linear operators (Michal, 2008). Cumulant tensors are matrices containing the cross-cumulants. Considering this, the second-order cumulant tensor is the covariance matrix and the fourth-order tensor (**T_4**) is formed by the fourth-order cross-cumulants $cum(u_i,u_j,u_k,u_l)$, which, for zero-mean random variables, is defined as:

$$cum\left(u_i,u_j,u_k,u_l\right)=E\left\{u_i,u_j,u_k,u_l\right\}-E\left\{u_i,u_j\right\}E\left\{u_k,u_l\right\}-E\left\{u_i,u_k\right\}E\left\{u_j,u_l\right\}-E\left\{u_k,u_j\right\}E\left\{u_i,u_l\right\} \quad (14)$$

The fourth-order cumulant tensor T_4 is a four-dimensional array, where, for each element $q_{ijkl}= cum(u_i,u_j,u_k,u_l)$, the indexes i ,j ,k ,l vary from 1 to N (where N is the number of signals). The fourth-order cumulant tensor contains all fourth-order information of the data.
JADE estimation criterion is derived through a procedure analogous to diagonalization of the covariance matrix, which produces signal decorrelation. As T_4 is a fourth-order counterpart of the covariance matrix, independence can be achieved by diagonalizing T_4, as for independent signals the unique non-zero fourth-order cross-cumulant appears when $i=j=k=l$. Analogous to the second-order case, diagonalization of the fourth-order tensor can be achieved through eigenvalue decomposition (EVD) (Strang, 2009).
Using tensorial methods for ICA is theoretically simple, but computing EVD of four-dimensional matrices by ordinary algorithms requires a very large amount of memory and may be computationally prohibitive in some cases. In order to avoid this limitation, methods like JADE were proposed in the literature. JADE algorithm searches for the matrix **W** that minimizes the sum of the squares of the non-diagonal elements of the output data of $T_4^{(y)}$ (where $T_4^{(y)}$ is the fourth-order cumulant tensor of the output data **y**).

2.1.3.2 Post-Nonlinear ICA

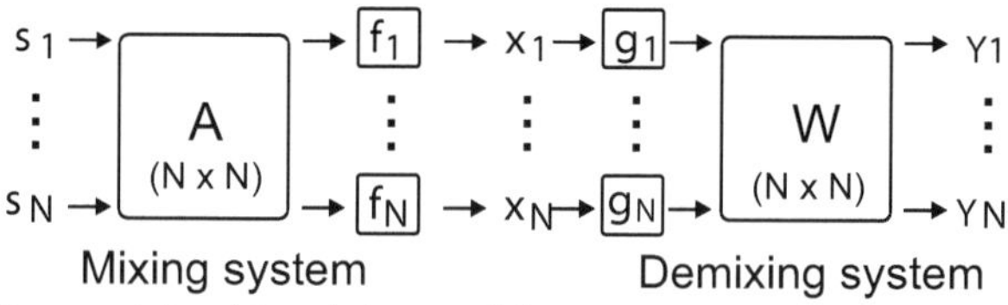

Fig. 2. Post-Nonlinear mixing/de-mixing model.

Post-Nonlinear (PNL) mixtures arise whenever, after a linear mixing process, the sensors present nonlinear behavior. The observed signals can be expressed as (Almeida, 2006):

$$x_i = f_i(\alpha_i) \tag{15}$$

where $\boldsymbol{\alpha}=\boldsymbol{As}$. As stated in Eq. 15, each observed signal x_i is obtained through component-wise nonlinear functions f_i applied to the linearly mixed signals $\boldsymbol{\alpha}_i$. The independent components are obtained by a mirror model:

$$y_i = \mathbf{W}_i g_i(x_i) \tag{16}$$

where $\boldsymbol{W}$ is the de-mixing matrix and g_i the inverse nonlinearity (see Fig. 2). The nonlinear functions are usually estimated through neural networks (MLP) and the de-mixing matrix by a linear ICA algorithm (Taleb and Jutten, 1999).

A limitation of the PNL algorithm is that the number of observed signals is assumed to be equal to the number of sources (square model). This prevents its application to high-dimensional data problems as both the number of parameters and the computational complexity increase exponentially with problem dimensionality.

In order to deal with high-dimensional data, a modified PNL model for the overdetermined case (when there exist more sensors N than sources K) was proposed in (Simas Filho et al., 2009a). As illustrated in Fig. 3, a linear block $\boldsymbol{B}$ is added to the standard PLN mixing model, allowing $K<N$. Coefficients of matrix $\boldsymbol{B}$ are estimated through signal compaction methods such as PCA and PCD, described in Section 2.1.2. The inverse (demixing) algorithm is thus described using a mirror model: $\boldsymbol{y}=\boldsymbol{W}\, G(\boldsymbol{Dx})$, where $\boldsymbol{y}$ are the estimated sources.

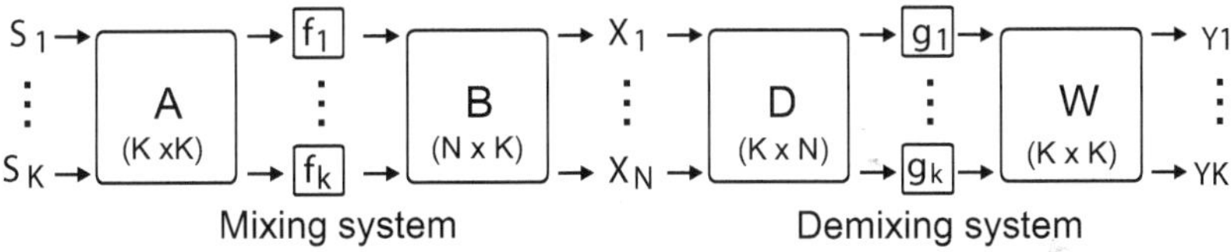

Fig. 3. Modified Post-Nonlinear mixing/de-mixing model.

2.1.3.3 Local ICA

Local ICA (Karhunen et al., 2000), (Jutten and Karhunen, 2003) can be viewed as a compromise between linear and nonlinear ICA. If the ICA model is used for feature extraction, better description of the data set can be obtained while exploring local characteristics. The purpose is to obtain better data representation when compared to linear ICA, while avoiding the high computational cost of the nonlinear models.

In Local ICA model (see Equation 17), a N-dimensional input space Q R^N is divided into a finite number of subsets Q_l, $l=1,\dots,L$, which satisfy:

$$Q_1 \cup Q_2 \cup \ldots \cup Q_L = Q \tag{17}$$

Clustering is responsible for the overall nonlinear representation. Linear ICA models are applied to data belonging to each cluster ($\boldsymbol{x}^{(l)}$) in order to estimate the local independent components $\mathbf{s}^{(l)}=\boldsymbol{B}^{(l)}\boldsymbol{x}^{(l)}$, where $\boldsymbol{B}^{(l)}$ is a local de-mixing matrix.

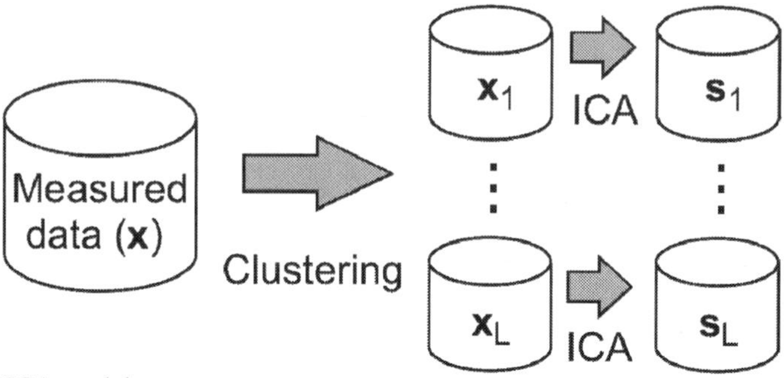

Fig. 4. Local ICA model.

3. The Application

As mentioned in Section 1, the LHC collision rate, together with ATLAS granularity, will result in a data stream of ~60 TB/s, requiring an efficient online filtering system for retrieving the interesting physics channels from dense background noise. This filtering system comprises three cascaded operation levels, applying successive cuts to the incoming data (Riu et al., 2008).

The first level (L1) will receive full data and will reduce the input event rate to ~75 kHz. The first level is responsible for marking the regions in the detector that have effectively been excited. These regions are known as *Region of Interest* - RoI, and will be the only information passed over to the second level analysis.

The second level (L2) will receive the regions of interest marked by the first level and will apply more specific analysis on them. For coping with an average processing time of 40 ms per event, a set of 500 off-the-shelf server processors will be employed, providing a multi-processed environment. The third and last filtering level, also known as Event Filter - EF, will take the final decision on events approved by the previous levels. A highly parallel processing environment composed by ~1600 off-the-shelf server processors will be employed for coping with an average processing time of 4 sec. At the end, a rate of ~200 Hz events will be recorded in mass storage devices for further offline analysis by the physicists.

One of the ATLAS main research goals is to experimentally prove the Higgs boson (Perkins, 2000). Being the Higgs boson highly unstable, it soon decays into more stable particles. Therefore, the physicists will prove its existence not by detecting the Higgs boson directly, but by analyzing its decaying signatures. It is known (Perkins, 2000) that some of such signatures produce electrons at their final state. Therefore, the identification of electrons is of great importance. On the other hand, during proton-proton collisions, a cascade of quark and anti-quark pairs can be produced, which quickly merge into more stable particles, producing a pattern known as jet. These jets may interact with the detector in a manner very similar to electrons, making the correct identification of electrons a tricky process.

Our analysis will focus on the electron / jet separation problem at the second level of the ATLAS filtering system, using calorimeter information. Calorimeters are total absorption detectors (Wigmans, 2000). Typically, they use a (passive) material (iron, lead, for instance) for absorbing entirely the energy of the incoming particle and sample the energy being deposited in the detector by using an active material (scintillating fibers, tiles, for instance).

Calorimeters play a major role in collider experiments as they provide fast response, their energy resolution improves with increasing energy, and they interact with charged and non-charged particles. In addition, they are highly-segmented detectors, so that it is possible to identify particle classes by their energy deposition profile.

The ATLAS calorimetry system is composed by two calorimeter sections (The ATLAS Collaboration, 2008). The electromagnetic (EM) calorimeter is responsible for detecting electrons, positrons and photons. The hadronic calorimeter (HD) is responsible for detecting hadrons (kaons, pions, etc) and it is placed on top of the electromagnetic calorimeter. Both detectors comprise 3 sequential layers with distinct granularity and depth, providing detailed information of incoming particles. The electromagnetic calorimeter has, in addition, a very thin layer in front of it, which is called the pre-sampler (PS). Fig. 5 displays the energy deposition profile for an electron interaction. A region of interest selected by the first-level filtering system amounts, in average, to 1,000 calorimeter cells.

Electrons have the property of depositing their energy in a very punctual way, differently from jets, which, for L2 data, tend to slightly spread their energy over multiple cells within a layer. Therefore, the relevant information relies not at the impact point center, but at its surrounding area. Aiming at exploiting this feature, a topological pre-processing based on ring sums has been tried by some L2 algorithms for data formatting (Torres et al., 2008). In this approach, the cell that samples the highest energy value (also known as the *hottest cell*) is considered the center of our region of interest in each calorimeter layer (seven in total). Then, a set of concentric rings are built around this hottest cell in a pattern similar to the one presented in Fig. 6. It can also be observed in Fig. 6 that, depending on the layer granularity, the rings might not close (incomplete) or even be composed only by strips. Finally, the cells belonging to a given ring are summed up, reducing the final event dimension, without jeopardizing their physics interpretation. This ring procedure is performed on a per layer basis, resulting, at the end, in a total of 100 rings, distributed as shown in Tab. 1.

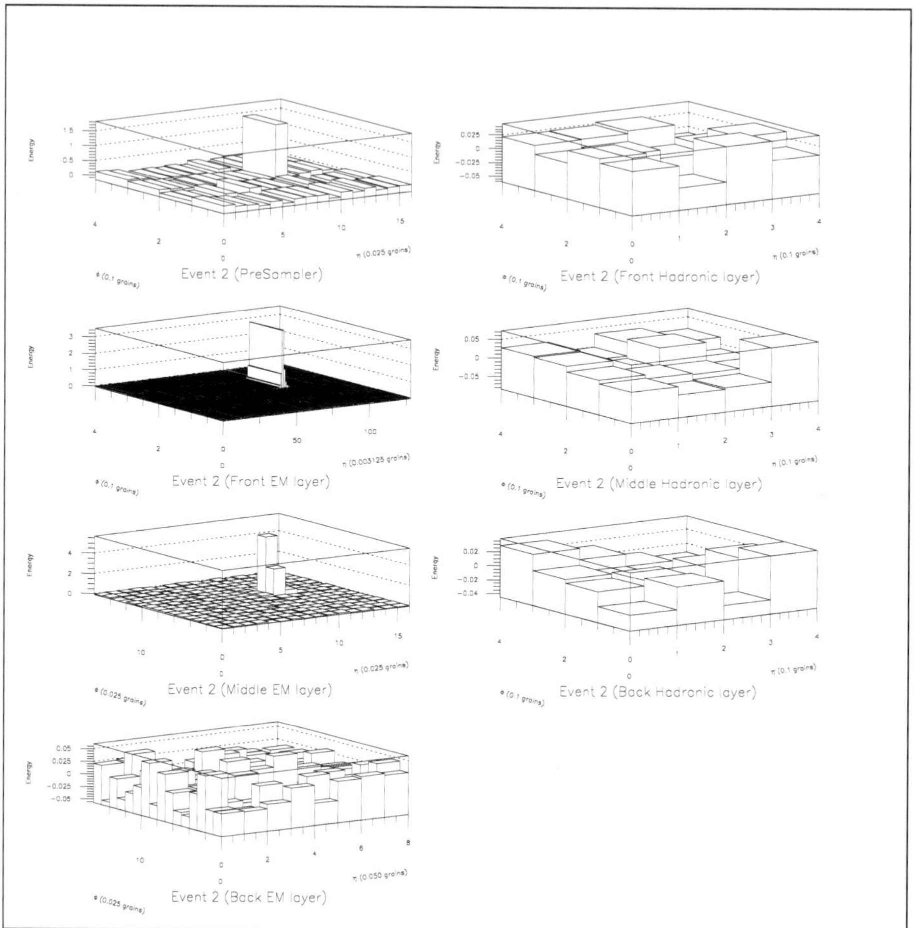

Fig. 5. Example of the segmented calorimeter information obtained from an incoming electron.

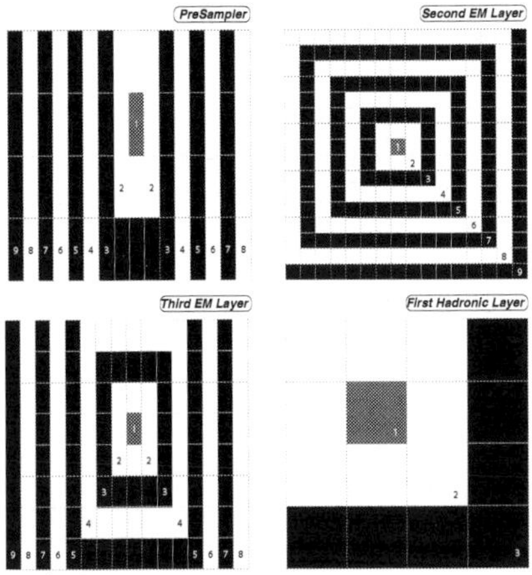

Fig. 6. Ring formatting for calorimetry.

Layer	PS	EM1	EM2	EM3	HD1	HD2	HD3	Total
Rings	8	64	8	8	4	4	4	100

Table 1. Number of rings in each calorimeter layer.

In the electron / jet separation problem, the dynamic range of the sampled energy is very large, therefore, an energy normalization procedure is applied, in order to focus, as much as possible, our analysis at the signal shape, rather than its energy nominal value, resulting in a steady detection efficiency over all the relevant energy spectrum. Also, since the relevant information from the discrimination point of view is known to be off-center, a sequential normalization is employed (dos Anjos et al., 2006). In this procedure, for each calorimeter layer, the normalized energy (E_N) of each ring is given by

$$E_{N_{l,i}} = \frac{E_{l,i}}{E_{tot_l} - \sum_{j=1}^{i-1} E_{l,j}} \tag{18}$$

where $E_{l,i}$ is the original energy of the i-th ring belonging to the l-th layer, and $E_{tot\ l}$ is the total sampled energy by the l-th layer. As a result, successively smaller attenuation factors are applied to the outer rings, but the normalization procedure is resilient enough to keep track of the signal-to-noise ratio, avoiding the amplification of irrelevant information.

4. Results

The available dataset was obtained through Monte Carlo simulation for proton-proton collisions and comprises approximately 470,000 electrons and 310,000 jet signatures. The simulation considers the detector characteristics and the first-level filtering operation. The available data set was approximately equally split into training, validation (stopping criterion for neural network training based on mean-squared error) and testing (performance evaluation) sets.

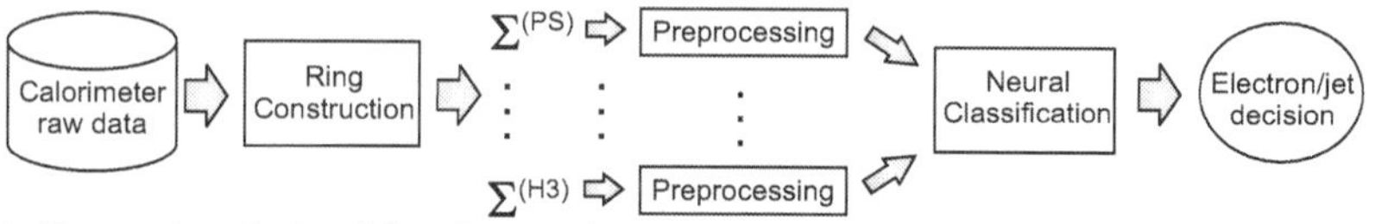

Fig. 7. - Processing chain of the electron/jet separation system.

It is shown in Fig. 7 the block diagram of the electron / jet discriminator. The raw calorimeter data is received and the topological processing based on ring sums is performed. Next, for the segmented case, the rings belonging to a given layer are pre-processed individually and the pre-processed event obtained for each layer is concatenated, generating a single input, which is propagated to the neural network for the pattern recognition. For the non-segmented case, the generated rings are concatenated prior to the pre-processing phase, so that the pre-processing is performed in all 100 rings at once. For the ICA based pre-processing, the JADE algorithm was used, and the clustering algorithm used by local ICA was the k-mean (Duda et al., 2004).
In this work, the Fisher Linear Discriminant (FLD) and supervised Multi-Layer Perceptron (MLP) neural classifiers (single hidden layer) (single hidden layer) were used to perform particle identification over calorimeter information. The neural networks were trained using the Resilient Backpropagation algorithm (Riedmiller and Braun, 1993). In order to compare the discrimination efficiency for the proposed classifiers, both the Receiver Operating Characteristics (ROC) and the SP index were applied. The ROC curve (Van Trees, 2003) shows how the detection probability P_D and false alarm probability P_F vary as the decision threshold changes. The SP index (dos Anjos et al., 2006) is computed through

$$SP = \frac{P_D + P_J}{2} \times \sqrt{(P_D \times P_J)} \tag{19}$$

where P_J is the efficiency for jets. The threshold value that maximizes the SP provides both high P_D and low P_F.

As mentioned in previous sections, the available calorimeter signatures are topologically pre-processed, generating 100 rings for an incoming event. Considering this, the discrimination system may benefit from signal compaction algorithms as they reduce redundant information and signal dimensionality. Here, compaction was performed through both Principal Component Analysis (PCA) and Principal Components for Discrimination (PCD), using segmented (layer-level) and non-segmented approaches. As the calorimeter system provides highly-segmented information, segmented processing tries to exploit subtle differences in electron and jet energy deposition profiles, which are available at the layer level.

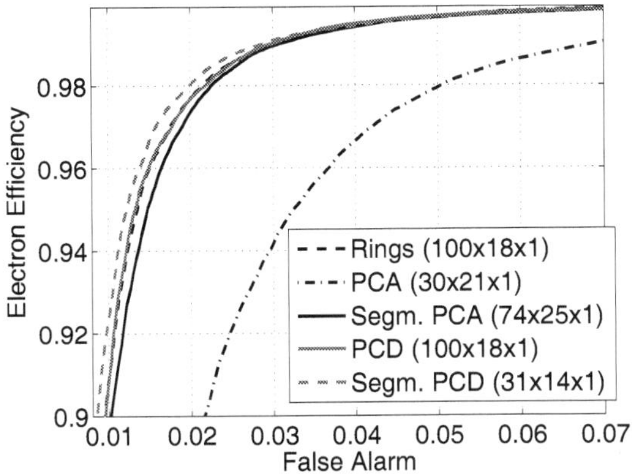

Fig. 8. ROC curves (and respective classifier topology) for segmented and non-segmented feature extraction through PCA and PCD.

Fig. 8 illustrates the discrimination performance for different methods in terms of ROC curves. It can be observed that the segmented approach outperforms the non-segmented one, for both PCA and PCD. It can also be seen that PCD usually presents lower false-alarm when compared to PCA (for the same detection probability) and achieves higher compaction rates (31 components for PCD against 74 components for PCA in segmented processing mode). This is a result of the compaction strategies, as in PCA the purpose is to maximize the energy projection and in PCD the objective is to optimize the discrimination capability of the components. Moreover, PCD uses nonlinear processing to estimate its components, which proves to be efficient in terms of discrimination performance. As it can be seen from Fig. 8, using only 31 components, the PCD performance is even better than processing 100 rings without any further pre-processing.

The (linear) Independent Component Analysis (ICA) model was without any further pre-processingalso applied to ring signals, either without pre-processing or combined with segmented and non-segmented PCA and PCD compaction schemes. Fig. 9 illustrates the ROC curves for different ICA-based discriminators. It can be observed that the segmented feature extraction provides slightly higher discrimination performance when independent components are estimated. Other benefit observed with ICA is that the classifier training procedure usually converges in very few iterations, in contrast to PCA and PCD based discriminators, which, in general, require a larger number of training steps. From Fig. 9, it is also interesting to observe that ICA could be the only pre-processing technique, as the nonlinear decorrelation it provides allows the neural network to perform slightly better in terms of discrimination efficiency.

Considering feature extraction through NLICA (using the modified PNL model) based on PCD projection, the nonlinearities which may arise are expected to be smooth. In a practical design, a calorimeter can exhibit small nonlinearities along the wide dynamic range it has to work on. In view of this, the neural networks used to estimate the inverse nonlinearities are restricted to have small number of hidden neurons and thus can only approximate smooth nonlinear functions. This also reduces the probability of reaching local minima during the training procedure.

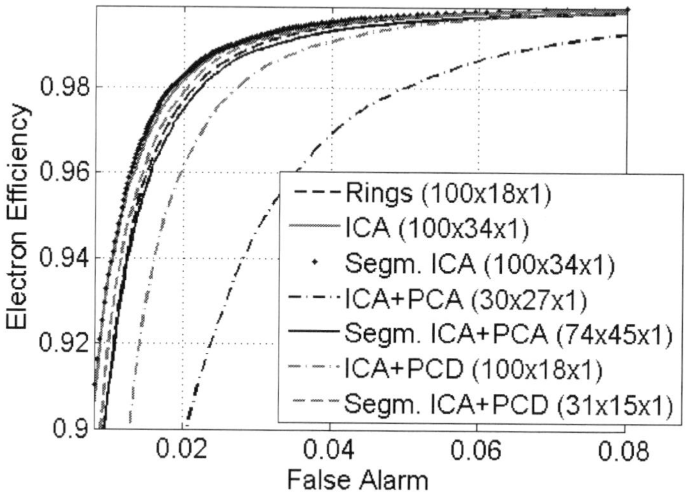

Fig. 9. ROC curves (and respective classifier topologies) for ICA-based discriminators.

In the Local ICA approach, the training data set was initially clustered into two clusters (as there are two possible classes for the incoming particles). As illustrated in Fig. 10, cluster 1 concentrates most of the electron signatures and cluster 2 the jets. After clustering, ICA and ICA with PCD pre-processing were both estimated for data belonging to each cluster. The classifiers were also trained locally, generating two ROCs (one for each cluster). A global optimization algorithm (Genetic Algorithm) (Haupt and Haupt, 2004) was used to search for the optimal combination of the local thresholds, which provides optimum global discrimination.

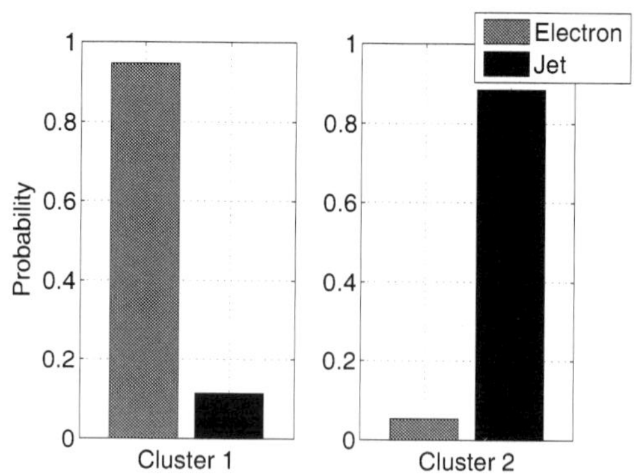

Fig. 10. Concentration of electrons and jets in each cluster for Local ICA pre-processing approach.

Fig. 11 illustrates the discrimination performance obtained through PNL and Local ICA approaches. It can be seen that, compared to the linear ICA model, PNL exhibits slightly poorer performance. On the other hand, Local ICA produces higher discrimination efficiency with respect to the other models when it is performed on PCD directions. For Local ICA, only the optimum point is shown in Fig. 11.

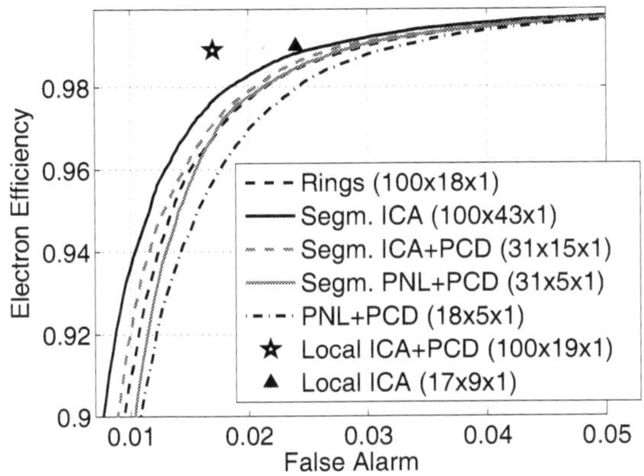

Fig. 11. ROC curves (and respective classifier topology) for NLICA and ICA discriminators.

A summary of the results achieved for each approach can be observed in Tab. 2, where the maximum SP value obtained for each approach is presented. Furthermore, Tab. 3 presents the false alarm probability for a fixed 97% electron detection efficiency.

The classifier complexity is shown in Tab. 4 for each approach. It can be depicted from this table that applying nonlinear decorrelation (PCD and ICA based algorithms) reduces the computational requirements for the classification task. The local ICA based on PCD projections not only achieves better classification efficiency, but it is also very efficient in terms of computational load (~33% reduction with respect to the rings only approach).

Approach	Non-segmented	Segmented
Rings	96.10	---
PCA	93.07	96.04
PCD	96.11	96.28
ICA	96.38	96.45
ICA + PCA	93.21	96.00
ICA + PCD	95.45	96.25
PNL + PCD	95.80	96.20
Local ICA	96.63	---
Local ICA + PCD	97.32	---

Table 2. Maximum SP (× 100) obtained for segmented and non-segmented approaches.

Approach	Non-segmented	Segmented
Rings	1.75	---
PCA	4.20	1.88
PCD	1.77	1.59
ICA	1.55	1.51
ICA + PCA	4.04	1.83
ICA + PCD	2.26	1.68
PNL + PCD	2.02	1.72
Local ICA	1.30	---
Local ICA + PCD	0.82	---

Table 3. False alarm probability (%) for a detection efficiency of 97%.

Approach	Non-segmented	Segmented
Rings	3636	---
PCA	4242	5050
PCD	3636	2828
ICA	6868	8686
ICA + PCA	5454	9090
ICA + PCD	200	3030
PNL + PCD	3934	6768
Local ICA	4438	---
Local ICA + PCD	2418	---

Table 4. Number of total floating point operations per approach.

In order to verify whether a linear classifier suffices, the pre-processed signals were used to feed a linear Fisher Discriminant (FLD), which is proved to be optimal linear discriminators (Duda et al., 2004). Fig. 12 provides a comparison between the discrimination performance obtained through linear (FLD) and nonlinear (MLP) classifiers. It can be seen that the nonlinear decorrelation introduced by ICA was able to improve the discrimination obtained through FLD, providing more separated patterns for different types of particles. Through the proposed pre-processing chain, the results of the linear classifier got closer to the ones obtained by the MLP. However, the nonlinear decorrelation provided by PCD and ICA were still not sufficient to discard a nonlinear classifier in order to achieve optimal detection efficiency. Tab. 5 and Tab. 6 summarize the detection efficiency comparison between linear Fisher and neural discriminants. An important issue is the computational cost, which, for a linear classifier, is much smaller (see Tab. 7) with respect to the nonlinear counterpart. This might be a striking advantage for online filtering.

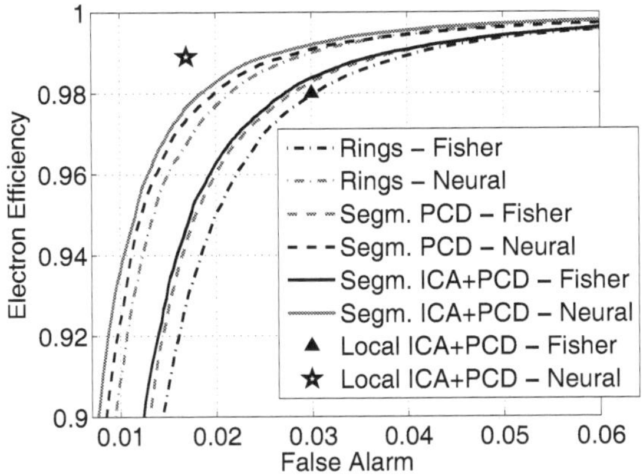

Fig. 12. ROC curves for the linear and neural discriminators.

Approach	Neural	Fisher
Rings	96.10	95.12
Segm. PCD	96.28	95.35
Segm. ICA + PCD	96.25	95.43
Local ICA + PCD	97.32	94.40

Table 5. Maximum SP (× 100) obtained for each approach considered for a linear classifier.

Approach	Neural	Fisher
Rings	1.75	2.50
Segm. PCD	1.59	2.29
Segm. ICA + PCD	1.68	2.22
Local ICA + PCD	0.82	3.00

Table 6. False alarm (%) for a detection efficiency of 97% for each approach considered for a linear classifier.

Approach	Neural	Fisher
Rings	3636	200
Segm. PCD	2828	200
Segm. ICA + PCD	3030	200
Local ICA + PCD	2418	700

Table 7. Number of total floating point operations per approach considered for a linear classifier.

5. Conclusions and Perspectives

Online data filtering in high-dimensional input data space finds application in multiple areas. Depending on the accumulated knowledge about the target problem, combining what is known by experts with high-order stochastic signal processing techniques is being shown to be an efficient design approach. Among the benefits, high signal compaction rates, relevant feature extraction and reduced computational load are often accomplished.
For a very demanding high-energy physics application, it was shown that we could benefit from topological pre-processing, which implements the expert part of the whole pre-processing scheme. Then, adding decorrelation techniques to the signal processing chain provided efficient feature extraction. For this, only 30% of the original data components were required. Further knowledge about the problem pointed out that the segmented signal processing was the right approach. In addition, the overall computational load could significantly be reduced, which was attractive due to the low processing time required by the target application.
Nonlinear independent component analysis achieved the best performance in this case study, which motivates further application investigations. A possibility is to implement it through SOM (Self-Organizing Maps) (Haykin, 2008). In detectors where the arising nonlinearities of practical designs are expected to be small deviations from the linear behavior, it would also be important to restrict the degrees of freedom of the nonlinear component extraction. The independent component analysis is also attractive in facing pile-up effects (Knoll, 1989), which typically decreases discrimination efficiencies in high event rate applications. There is plenty of room for algorithm development in high demanding application scenarios.

6. Acknowledgements

The authors would like to express their gratitude to CNPq, FINEP, CAPES, FAPERJ (Brazil) and CERN (Switzerland) for their financial support. We also thank the ATLAS collaboration at CERN for providing the simulated calorimeter data and for fruitful discussions concerning this work.

7. References

Almeida, L. B. (2006). *Nonlinear Source Separation*, Morgan and Claypool.

Caloba, L., Seixas, J. and Pereira, F. (1995). Neural discriminating analysis for a second-level trigger system, *Proceedings of the International Conference on Computing in High Energy Physics (CHEP95)*, Rio de Janeiro, Brazil.

Cardoso, J. F. and Souloumiac, A. (1993). Blind beamforming for non-gaussian signals, *IEEE Proceedings*- F 140(6): 362–370.

CERN (2007). European organization for nuclear research. URL: http://www.cern.ch

Choi, S., Cichocki, A., Park, H. and Lee, Y. (2005). Blind source separation and independent component analysis - a review, *Neural Information Processing - Letters and Reviews* 6(1).

Cichocki, A. and Amari, S. (2002). *Adaptive Blind Signal and Image Processing*, Willey.

Cichocki, A. and Unbehauen, R. (1996). Robust neural networks with on-line learning for blind identification and blind separation of sources, *IEEE Transactions on Circuits and Systems-I: Fundamental Theory and Applications* (11).

dos Anjos, A., Torres, R. C., Seixas, J. M., Ferreira, B. C. and Xavier, T. C. (2006). Neural triggering system operating on high resolution calorimetry information, *Nuclear Instruments and Methods in Physics Research* 559: 134–138.

Duarte, L. T., Jutten, C. and Moussaoui, S. (2009). Ion selective electrode array based on a bayesian nonlinear source separation method, in T. Adali, C. Jutten, J. Romano and A. Barros (eds), Independent Component Analysis And Signal Separation, 8th International Conference, *Lecture Notes In Computer Science*, Springer, Paraty, Brazil, pp. 662-669.

Duda, R. O., Hart, P. E. and Stork, D. G. (2004). *Pattern Classification*, 2nd ed, Wiley-Interscience.

Evans, L. and Bryant, P. (2008). LHC machine, *Journal of Instrumentation* (2008 JINST 3 S08001).

Haritopoulos, M., Yin, H. and Allinson, N. M. (2002). Image denoising using self-organizing map-based nonlinear independent component analysis, *Neural Networks* pp. 1085–1098.

Haupt, R. L. and Haupt, S. E. (2004). *Practical Genetic Algorithms*, 2nd ed,Wiley-Interscience.

Haykin, S. (2008). *Neural Networks and Learning Machines*, 3rd ed, Prentice Hall.

Hyvärinen, A., Karhunen, J. and Oja, E. (2001). *Independent Component Analysis*, John Wiley & Sons.

Hyvärinen, A. and Pajunen, P. (1999). Nonlinear independent component analysis: Existence and uniqueness results, *Neural Networks* 12(3): 429–439.

Jolliffe, I. T. (2002). *Principal Component Analysis*, 2nd ed, Springer.

Jutten, C. and Karhunen, J. (2003). Advances in nonlinear blind source separation, *Proceedings of the 4th Int. Symp. on Independent Component Analysis and Blind Signal Separation* (ICA2003) pp. 245–256.

Karhunen, J., Malaroiu, S. and Ilmoniemi, M. (2000). Local linear independent component analysis based on clustering, Int. *Journal of Neural Systems* 10: 439–451.

Knoll, G. F. (1989). *Radiation Detection and Measurement*, 2nd ed, John Wiley & Sons.

Mackay, D. J. C. (2002). *Information Theory, Inference and Learning Algorithms*, Cambridge University Press.

McClave, J. T., Sincich, T. and Mendenhall, W. (2008). *Statistics*, 11th ed, Prentice Hall.

Michal, A. D. (2008). *Matrix and Tensor Calculus With Applications to Mechanics, Elasticity and Aeronautics*, 1st ed, Dover.

Moura, N. N., Simas Filho, E. F. and Seixas, J. M. (2009). *Advances in Sonar Signal Processing*, In-Tech, Vienna, Austria, chapter Independent Component Analysis for Passive Sonar Signal Processing, pp. 91–110.

Murillo-Fuentes, J., Boloix-Tortosa, R., Hornillo-Mellado, S. and Zarzoso, V. (2004). Independent component analysis based on marginal entropy approximations, *Proceedings of the World Automation Congress* (16): 433–438.

Natora, M., Franke, F., Munk, M. and Obermayer, K. (2009). Bss of sparse overcomplete mixtures and application to neural recordings, in T. Adali, C. Jutten, J. Romano and A. Barros (eds), Independent Component Analysis And Signal Separation, 8th

International Conference, *Lecture Notes In Computer Science*, Springer, Paraty, Brazil, pp. 459–467.

Papoulis, A. and Pillai, S. U. (2002). *Probability, Random Variables, and Stochastic Processes*, 4th ed, McGraw-Hill.

Perkins, D. H. (2000). *Introduction to High Energy Physics*, 4th ed, Cambridge University Press.

Riedmiller, M. and Braun, H. (1993). A direct adaptive method for faster backpropagation learning: The RPROP algorithm, *Proceedings of the IEEE International Conference on Neural Networks*, San Francisco, CA, pp. 586–591.

Riu, I., Abolins, M., Adragna, et al. (2008). Integration of the trigger and data acquisition systems in ATLAS, *IEEE Transactions on Nuclear Science* 55(1): 106–112.

Rojas, F., Puntonet, C. G. and Rojas, I. (2003). Independent component analysis evolution based method for nonlinear speech processing, *Artificial Neural Nets Problem Solving Methods*, PT II 2687: 679–686.

Shannon, C. E. (1948). A mathematical theory of communication, *The Bell System Technical Journal* pp. 379–423.

Simas Filho, E. F., Seixas, J. M. and Caloba, L. P. (2009a). High-energy particle online discriminators based on nonlinear independent components, in T. Adali, C. Jutten, J. Romano and A. Barros (eds), Independent Component Analysis And Signal Separation, 8th International Conference, *Lecture Notes In Computer Science*, Springer, Paraty, Brazil, pp. 718–725.

Simas Filho, E. F., Seixas, J. M. and Caloba, L. P. (2009b). Optimized calorimeter signal compaction for an independent component based ATLAS electron/jet second-level trigger, *Proceedings of Science* - PoS ACAT08 102.

Strang, G. (2009). *Introduction to Linear Algebra*, 4th ed, Wellesley Cambridge Press.

Syskind, M., Wang, D. L., Larsen, J. and Kjem, U. (2006). Separating underdetermined convolutive speech mixtures, in J. Rosca, D. Erdogmus, J. C. Principe and S. Haykin (eds), Independent Component Analysis And Signal Separation, 8th International Conference, *Lecture Notes In Computer Science*, Springer, Charleston, USA, pp. 674–681.

Taleb, A. and Jutten, C. (1999). Source separation in post-nonlinear mixtures, *IEEE Transactions on Signal Processing* (47): 2807–2820.

The ATLAS Collaboration (2008). The ATLAS experiment at the CERN large hadron collider, *Journal of Instrumentation* (2008 JINST 3 S08003).

Torres, R. C., Seixas, J. M., dos Anjos, A. and Cunha, D. V. (2008). Online electron/jet neural high-level trigger over independent calorimetry information, *Proceedings of Science* PoS(ACAT)039: 1–15.

Van Trees, H. L. (2003). *Detection, Estimation, and Modulation Theory*, Part I, Wiley.

Wei, C., Khor, L. C., Woo, W. L. and Dlay, S. S. (2006). Post-nonlinear underdetermined ICA by bayesian statistics, in J. Rosca, D. Erdogmus, J. C. Principe and S. Haykin (eds), Independent Component Analysis And Signal Separation, 8th International Conference, *Lecture Notes In Computer Science*, Springer, Charleston, USA, pp. 773–780.

Wigmans, R. (2000). *Calorimetry: Energy Measurement In Particle Physics*, Oxford.

18

Practical Source Coding with Side Information

Lorenzo Cappellari
Dept. of Information Engineering, University of Padova
Italy

1. Introduction

The problem of coding the realizations of a random source when some other one, correlated with the former, is available at the decoder but *not* at the encoder goes under the name of *source coding with side information*. The minimum achievable transmission rates in this scenario were already found about thirty years ago by means of a random coding analysis. Practical coding schemes have been instead investigated only recently for enabling improved compression performance in sensor networks and computationally light and robust source coding in video applications.

Differently from the traditional source coding scenario, these schemes take advantage of both a *code* that is good for *channel coding* and a code that is good for *source coding*. Practical approaches where these two codes are *nested* have been shown to be asymptotically optimal, but schemes that use *independent* codes have also appeared that are easier to implement, in particular in the dual context of channel coding with side information at the encoder.

In the first half of this chapter we will review the main theoretical results regarding both this problem and, in general, the problem of *distributed source coding* (Section 2). The most important coding schemes that have appeared in literature for achieving the promises of the theoretical investigations are also described (Section 3); in particular, we discuss an approach based on the principle of *superposition* coding that we also show to be optimal.

The second half of this chapter is more focused on practical coding schemes. In Section 4 we give an original *factor graph*-based interpretation of the decoding algorithms used in the schemes for *lossless* reconstruction based on *turbo codes*. We also present a performance comparison between several of them. In Section 5 we discuss a solution to the *lossy* source coding problem with side information based on *continuous-valued syndromes*. In particular, this scheme embodies the superposition approach and uses independent channel and source codes. In order to broad the range of applications of this coding scheme, model-aided statistical decoding of continuous-valued syndromes is also proposed for the case of coding Markov sources. We compare the performance of this coding scheme against other systems both for the case of coding purely Gaussian sources and for the case of coding natural video sequences, both in the *discrete cosine transform* and in the *discrete wavelet transform* domain. We will conclude with a short discussion on the drawbacks of the proposed coding solutions and on the future research (Section 6).

Throughout the chapter, we use the following notation. The *random variable* (r.v.) X takes realizations x on the set $\mathcal{X}$ and has *probability mass function* $p(x)$. X^n is an n-dimensional random process with independent and identically distributed components; the realizations x^n are elements of $\mathcal{X}^n$. Matrices and random vectors are shown in bold face (e.g. $\mathbf{X}$). Alphabets are usually discrete. $P[\cdot]$ and $E[\cdot]$ denote the probability of an event and the expected value of a r.v., respectively; $\chi\{\cdot\}$ is the indicator function of an event. $H(\cdot)$, $H(\cdot|\cdot)$ and $I(\cdot;\cdot)$ denote entropy, relative entropy, and mutual information; $\mathcal{A}_\varepsilon^{(n)}$ is the (strongly) typical set over which n-dimensional processes distribute uniformly (Cover & Thomas, 2006). A variable $X \sim \mathcal{B}(p)$ is a Bernoulli r.v. that equals one with probability p; $H(p)$ is its entropy; addition of Bernoulli variables is defined over the group $GF(2)$. A variable $X \sim \mathcal{N}(\mu, \sigma^2)$ is a Gaussian r.v. with mean μ and variance σ^2. $a \circ b$ denotes function composition, $\cdot^T$ matrix transposition; the notation 2^{nR} usually means $\lfloor 2^{nR} \rfloor$. A *good* source/channel code is a code that achieves the rate-distortion/channel capacity function asymptotically with its length.

2. Problem Statement and Theoretical Results

Suppose that we want to map some environmental parameter, e.g. the temperature, over a certain space. Then, we place $m \geq 2$ temperature sensors across that space, and have each one communicate its measurement to a central unit; let X_i denote this measurement. Data compression is employed at each sensor node in order to save transmission power. It is likely that these measurements are somewhat correlated, i.e. that $H(X_1 X_2 \ldots X_m) < \sum_{i=1}^{m} H(X_i)$. According to classical information theory results (Shannon, 1948), at least $H(X_1 X_2 \ldots X_m)$ bits must be received by the central node for describing exactly all measurements. But this is achievable with traditional source coding means only if communication between the sensor nodes *is* possible. The problem of *distributed source coding* (DSC) refers to the scenario in which the sensor nodes *are not* allowed to communicate with each other.

Closely related to DSC is the problem of *source coding with side information (at the decoder)* (SCSI). Suppose that the $m-1$ measurements $X_2, X_3, \ldots, X_m$ are reconstructed at the central node upon receiving data from the respective $m-1$ sensor nodes. Again, the remaining sensor node is not allowed to communicate with any of them. Then, the decoder has knowledge about the *side information* (SI) $Y \triangleq (X_2, X_3, \ldots, X_m)$, which is correlated with measurement X_1, but unavailable at the respective sensor node.

Answers to questions regarding the minimum transmission rates needed in the DSC/SCSI problem for *lossless* or *lossy* (i.e. within a certain distortion) reconstruction have been mostly given and are summarized in the following. Coding schemes achieving these rates have been also inherently suggested while answering these questions, but they are in practice not useful. Luckily, more structured coding schemes have been investigated in literature that achieve the same performance, as described in Section 3.

2.1 Distributed Source Coding

Let $\mathbf{X}$ denote the source vector $(X_1, X_2, \ldots, X_m)$. A *code* of length n and rate $(R_1, R_2, \ldots, R_m)$ for the DSC problem consists of the following functions:

$$f_i \; : \; \mathcal{X}_i^n \to \left[1, 2^{nR_i}\right] , \quad i = 1, 2, \ldots, m , \tag{1}$$

$$g \; : \; \prod_{i=1}^{m} \left[1, 2^{nR_i}\right] \to \prod_{i=1}^{m} \mathcal{X}_i^n . \tag{2}$$

Its *probability of error*, once $p(\mathbf{x})$ is known, is defined as

$$P_e^{(n)} \triangleq P\left[g \circ (f_1, f_2, \ldots, f_m)\left(\mathbf{X}^n\right) \neq \mathbf{X}^n\right] , \tag{3}$$

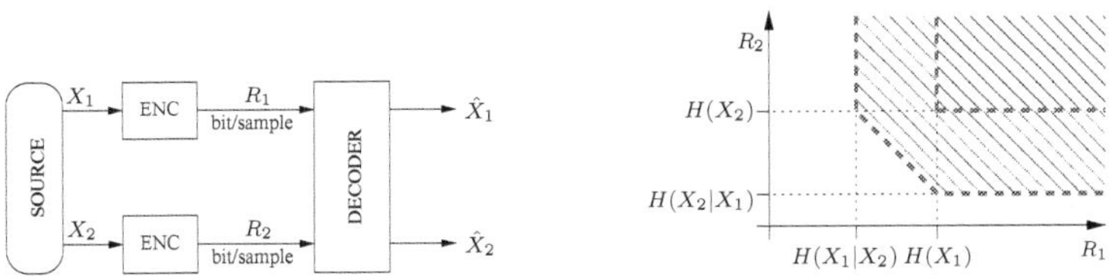

(a) scheme (b) achievable rate region

Fig. 1. Slepian-Wolf coding.

and the rate $(R_1, R_2, \ldots, R_m)$ is said to be *achievable* if there exist a sequence of codes at rate $(R_1, R_2, \ldots, R_m)$ such that $P_e^{(n)} \to 0$ as $n \to \infty$. The *achievable rate region* is the closure of the set of achievable rates.

Consider the DSC problem with two encoders ($m = 2$) shown in Fig. 1(a). The achievable rate region for this problem (Slepian & Wolf, 1973) is given by

$$R_1 \geq H(X_1|X_2)\,, \tag{4}$$

$$R_2 \geq H(X_2|X_1)\,, \tag{5}$$

$$R_1 + R_2 \geq H(X_1X_2)\,, \tag{6}$$

and is shown in Fig. 1(b). Each internal point (R_1, R_2) of this region is shown to be achievable. In particular it is shown that, among the *random partitionings* of the elements of $\mathcal{X}_i^n$ into 2^{nR_i} bins each, there exist at least one such that if

- $f_i(x_i^n)$ reveal the bin to which x_i^n belongs, and
- $g(j_1, j_2)$ returns the tuple[1] $(x_1^n, x_2^n) \in \mathcal{A}_\varepsilon^{(n)}$ with x_i^n belonging to the j_i-th bin of $\mathcal{X}_i^n$,

the code defined by these functions has asymptotically a negligible probability of error.

If $R_1 > H(X_1|X_2)$ and $R_2 > H(X_2|X_1)$, a coding scheme is indeed given for achieving a *sum rate* arbitrarily close to $H(X_1X_2)$, i.e. to the achievable rate when the two encoders *can* communicate with each other. However, this scheme is not practical because (i) no constructive procedures are given to find the needed code, and (ii) there is no structure to be exploited in order to evaluate the functions f_i and g without resorting to huge lookup tables. Similar results can be shown for jointly ergodic sources and for the case with $m > 2$ (Cover & Thomas, 2006).

2.2 Source Coding with Side Information

Assume that in Fig. 1(a) we have $R_2 > H(X_2)$. Then, by classical results, the decoder can already reconstruct X_2 without receiving any data from the first encoder. We may then wonder which is the minimum rate needed for reconstructing $X \triangleq X_1$ when the SI $Y \triangleq X_2$ is available at the decoder, as in Fig. 2(a). From the analysis of the DSC problem, it can be inferred that lossless reconstruction of X is possible at rates over $H(X|Y)$.

---

[1] More precisely, if there are no tuples or there is more than one that satisfies this property, g assigns a random tuple to (j_1, j_2). Similar strategies are also taken by the "theoretical" algorithms discussed in the following.

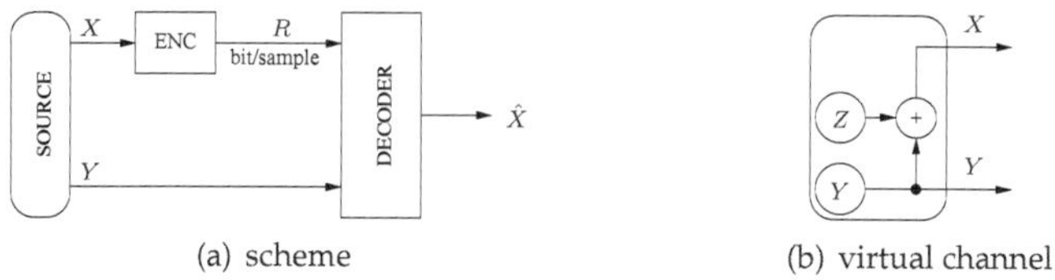

Fig. 2. Wyner-Ziv coding.

From a broader point of view, it is also interesting to investigate the rates needed for lossy reconstruction with SI. If $\hat{\mathcal{X}}$ is the set over which the reconstruction $\hat{X}$ of the source at the decoder takes values, a *(single-letter) distortion function* $d : \mathcal{X} \times \hat{\mathcal{X}} \to \mathbb{R}^+$ is usually defined that is extended to n-dimensional realizations by assuming (with an abuse of notation) $d(x^n, \hat{x}^n) \triangleq \frac{1}{n}\sum_{i=1}^{n} d(x_i, \hat{x}_i)$.
In the SCSI scenario, a *code* of length n and rate R consists of the following functions

$$f \; : \; \mathcal{X}^n \to \left[1, 2^{nR}\right] , \tag{7}$$

$$g \; : \; \left[1, 2^{nR}\right] \times \mathcal{Y}^n \to \hat{\mathcal{X}}^n . \tag{8}$$

Its *distortion*, once $p(x,y)$ is known, is defined as

$$D^{(n)} \triangleq E\left[d\left(X^n, g\left(f(X^n), Y^n\right)\right)\right] , \tag{9}$$

and the pair (R, D) is said to be *achievable* if there exist a sequence of codes at rate R such that $\lim_{n\to\infty} D^{(n)} \leq D$. The *rate-distortion region* is the closure of the set of these achievable pairs; the *rate-distortion function* $R^*(D)$ is the infimum of rates R such that the pair (R, D) is achievable.
The rate-distortion function for SCSI equals (Wyner & Ziv, 1976)

$$R^*(D) = \min_{p(u|x), p(\hat{x}|u,y)} I(X; U|Y) , \tag{10}$$

where the minimum[2] is taken over all variables U and $\hat{X}$ such that $Y \to X \to U$ and $X \to (U, Y) \to \hat{X}$ form a Markov chain, and $E[d(X, \hat{X})] \leq D$. It is interesting to note that the rate-distortion function when *both* the encoder and the decoder have access to the SI, i.e. $R_{X|Y}(D) = \min I(X; \hat{X}|Y)$ where the minimum is over all $p(\hat{x}|x,y)$ such that $E[d(X, \hat{X})] \leq D$ (Shannon, 1959), can be similarly expressed as

$$R_{X|Y}(D) = \min_{p(u|x), p(\hat{x}|u,y)} I(X; \hat{X}|Y) , \tag{11}$$

where the minimum is taken under the same conditions of equation (10) (Pradhan et al., 2003). Since $I(X;U|Y) \geq I(X;\hat{X}|Y)$, in general, $R^*(D) \geq R_{X|Y}(D)$, with equality if and only if at optimality in (11) $X \to (\hat{X}, Y) \to U$ forms a Markov chain.
The rate loss with respect to the case where also the encoder knows the side information is investigated in (Zamir, 1996). However, the Gaussian-quadratic scenario is an important

[2] The search can be limited to $p(\hat{x}|u,y) = \chi\{\hat{x} = h(u,y)\}$, where h is a deterministic function.

example in which $R^*(D) = R_{X|Y}(D)$. In particular, if $\mathcal{X} = \hat{\mathcal{X}} = \mathbb{R}$ and $d(x,\hat{x}) = (x-\hat{x})^2$, there are no losses if $(X,Y) \sim \mathcal{N}$ (Wyner & Ziv, 1976) and also if $X = Y + N$, with $N \sim \mathcal{N}$ independent from Y, which in turn can have *any* distribution (Pradhan et al., 2003).

In SCSI, the coding scheme used in the proof of achievability of all rates over $R^*(D)$ involves the *random generation* of a set $\mathcal{U}$ of $2^{nI(X;U)}$ codewords distributed according to $\prod_{i=1}^{n} p^*(u_i)$, where $p^*(u)$ is the marginal of the joint distribution achieving the minimum in (10), and the *random partitioning* of them into $2^{nI(X;U|Y)}$ bins; each bin contains approximately $2^{nI(Y;U)}$ elements. The encoder associates each x^n to the element $u^n \in \mathcal{U}$ such that $(x^n, u^n) \in \mathcal{A}_\varepsilon^{(n)}$, and sends the index j of the bin to which u^n belongs. The decoder looks for the element u^n in the j-th bin such that $(u^n, y^n) \in \mathcal{A}_\varepsilon^{(n)}$, and returns $\hat{x}_i = h^*(u_i, y_i)$, where $h^*(u,y)$ is the deterministic function achieving the minimum in (10). Note that the bins into which $\mathcal{U}$ is partitioned take the role of *good channel codes* for the channel between Y and U; in turn, $\mathcal{U}$ takes the role of a *good source code*, since via the function h it leads to a representation close to the source. Again, this scheme is practically useless.

In many cases the decoder has perfect knowledge about the SI. One may however wonder if it is possible to characterize a rate-distortion region assuming that both $X_1 = X$ and $X_2 = Y$ are independently encoded at finite rates R_1 and R_2 and jointly decoded into representations within distortions D_1 and D_2, respectively. In the general case, this rate region is currently still unknown and only inner and outer bounds have been found. Recently, the problem has been solved for the two-terminal Gaussian-quadratic case. We refer the interested reader to (Wagner et al., 2008) and to the references therein.

3. Structured Codes for Binning

In practice, in order to achieve the performance claimed by the theory there must exist *good structured* codes and feasible algorithms to search for *jointly typical codewords* over them. Transmission rates involved in the DSC/SCSI problem are also finite. Lossless reconstruction is therefore possible only when dealing with discrete source alphabets. All practical lossless coding schemes treat essentially the binary case, that is the most simple; on the other hand, the binary representation of a discrete r.v. can be always seen as a random vector with (correlated) binary entries. Lossy reconstruction is instead possible with both binary and continuous (real) variables; the Hamming distance

$$d_H(x,\hat{x}) \triangleq \begin{cases} 0, & x = \hat{x} \\ 1, & x \neq \hat{x} \end{cases} \tag{12}$$

and the quadratic distance $d(x,\hat{x}) \triangleq (x-\hat{x})^2$ are normally used as distortion function in the two cases, respectively. In the following we will review some of the practical coding schemes recently appeared in the literature for the DSC/SCSI problem.

3.1 Near Lossless Coding

In traditional binary lossless source coding there exist many *exactly* lossless codes with performance close to the Shannon bound. On the other side, practical codes for *binary channel coding* with rates close to the Shannon capacity bound, such as the turbo codes (Berrou & Glavieux, 1996), operate in a *near* lossless regime, i.e. with very low, but not zero, probability of error.

As observed in (Wyner, 1974), the problem of lossless SCSI is indeed a channel coding problem. Assume that the source and the SI are actually generated from two *independent* binary

sources Y and $Z \sim \mathcal{B}(p)$ as in Fig. 2(b); then, a *virtual "correlation" channel* exists between Y and X. This channel is a *(memoryless) binary symmetric channel* (BSC) for which *linear* codes and *closest neighbor search* algorithms are asymptotically shown to achieve capacity.
Let $\mathbf{H}$ be a *parity-check matrix* of a good (n,k) code $\mathcal{C}$ for the virtual channel. The code contains all binary vectors c^n whose *syndrome* $s^{n-k} \triangleq \mathbf{H}c^n$ is equal to zero, and partitions $\mathcal{X}^n$ into 2^{n-k} *cosets* (bins) of 2^k elements; elements in each coset $\mathcal{C}_s$ have a distinctive syndrome s^{n-k}. The code $\mathcal{C}$ can be used to reliably transmit information at its *code* rate $R_{\mathcal{C}} \triangleq k/n \approx C$ bit per channel use, where $C = 1 - H(Z)$ is the channel capacity (Cover & Thomas, 2006). The *decoding function* is defined by $f_{\mathcal{C}}(s^{n-k}) \triangleq \arg\min_{c^n \in \mathcal{C}_s} d_H(c^n, 0)$, and is such that $P[f(\mathbf{H}Z^n) \neq Z^n]$ is asymptotically negligible. Then, the code defined by (see equations (7) and (8))

$$f(x^n) = \mathbf{H}x^n , \tag{13}$$

$$g(s^{n-k}, y^n) = y^n + f_{\mathcal{C}}(s^{n-k} + \mathbf{H}y^n) \tag{14}$$

is a good *near* lossless code for the SCSI problem. In fact, its rate is $R = (n-k)/n = 1 - R_{\mathcal{C}} \approx H(Z) = H(X|Y)$, and

$$P[g(f(X^n), Y^n) \neq X^n] = P[Y^n + f_{\mathcal{C}}(\mathbf{H}Z^n) \neq X^n] \tag{15}$$

is asymptotically negligible.
Practically, the capacity of the BSC has been approached by turbo and *low density parity check* (LDPC) codes (MacKay, 1999). These codes have been successfully used in SCSI too. The evaluation of the syndrome in order to perform encoding is straightforward in the case of LDPC codes and very easy in the case of turbo codes. SCSI approaches based on turbo and LDPC codes are investigated in, among others, (Liveris et al., 2003; Roumy et al., 2007; Tu et al., 2005) and in (Liveris et al., 2002), respectively. In all cases the decoding function is very well approximated by means of iterative algorithms; we will give some more detail on these algorithms in Section 4.
With reference to Fig. 2(b), if $Y \sim \mathcal{B}(1/2)$, then it turns out that Z is independent from X too, such that a BSC is indeed also defined by $Y = X + Z$. SCSI approaches based on *systematic* turbo codes use this interpretation to show that if the $n-k$ *parity bits* relative to each encoded k-tuple are sent to the decoder, then near lossless performance is achieved since the SI is indeed a corrupted version of the systematic portion of a codeword (Aaron & Girod, 2002; Garcia-Frias & Zhao, 2001).
Under the same condition, a coding scheme based on syndromes was also devised for the two-terminal DSC problem that achieves all rates with the minimum sum rate. Let $\mathbf{G}$ and $\mathbf{H}$ be a *generator matrix* and a parity-check matrix of a good (n,k) code $\mathcal{C}$ for the virtual channel between $X_2 \triangleq Y$ and $X_1 \triangleq X$. Chose two subcodes $\mathcal{C}_1$ and $\mathcal{C}_2$ of $\mathcal{C}$ that admit generator matrices $\mathbf{G}_1$ and $\mathbf{G}_2$ constructed by taking $k_1 \leq k$ and the remaining $k_2 = k - k_1$ rows of $\mathbf{G}$, respectively. Each $c^n \in \mathcal{C}$ has a unique factorization into the sum of two codewords belonging to these two subcodes; denote with π_i the function that gives the codeword relative to code $\mathcal{C}_i$. Denote with $\mathbf{H}_i$ a parity-check matrix for the code $\mathcal{C}_i$, and with $t_i(s_i^{n-k_i})$ a deterministic function that gives an n-tuple of $\mathcal{C}_{is_i}$. Define the function

$$h(s_1^{n-k_1}, s_2^{n-k_2}) \triangleq \left(t_1(s_1^{n-k_1}) + t_2(s_2^{n-k_2})\right) + f_{\mathcal{C}}\left(\mathbf{H}\left(t_1(s_1^{n-k_1}) + t_2(s_2^{n-k_2})\right)\right) . \tag{16}$$

Then, the code defined by (see equations (1) and (2))

$$f_i(x_i^n) = \mathbf{H}_i x_i^n , \tag{17}$$

$$g_i(s_1^{n-k_1}, s_2^{n-k_2}) = t_i(s_i^{n-k_i}) + \pi_i \circ h(s_1^{n-k_1}, s_2^{n-k_2}) \tag{18}$$

has rate that satisfies $R_i \geq (n-k)/n \approx H(X_1|X_2) = H(X_2|X_1)$ and $R_1 + R_2 = (2n-k)/n = 2 - R_C \approx 1 + H(Z) = H(X_1 X_2)$, and

$$P[g_i(f_1(X_1^n), f_2(X_2^n)) \neq X_i^n] \tag{19}$$

is asymptotically negligible. This is a direct consequence of the fact that, if $c_i^n \in C_i$ is such that $t_i(\mathbf{H}_i x_i^n) = x_i^n + c_i^n$, $P[h(\mathbf{H}_1 X_1^n, \mathbf{H}_2 X_2^n) \neq C_1^n + C_2^n]$ is asymptotically negligible since $X_1 + X_2 \sim \mathcal{B}(p)$.

The scheme outlined above for encoding two sources was devised in (Pradhan & Ramchandran, 2005) and essentially tested using *convolutional* codes. Convolutional codes are used in (Pradhan & Ramchandran, 2003) too in the SCSI context. The extension to $m \geq 2$ sources is delineated in (Stanković et al., 2006), and it is shown to be optimal for *uniform* sources such that $\sum_{i=1}^{m} X_i \sim \mathcal{B}(p)$; tests conducted with more performing codes (e.g. turbo) show a very good performance.

3.2 Lossy Coding

In case of reconstruction within a certain distortion, the search for practical SCSI algorithms is more involved since both a good channel and a good source code are needed. In the seminal work (Zamir et al., 2002), it is shown that *nested* linear codes and *lattices* achieve the theoretical bounds in the binary-Hamming and in the Gaussian-quadratic case, respectively.

In practice, the suggested coding scheme requires that a *fine* linear/lattice code C_1 is used that is a good source code for the problem of coding the source without SI. Instead of sending to the decoder the index of the codeword that is the closest to the actual realization of the source (as in traditional source coding), the encoder sends the index of the coset to which this closest codeword belongs. The codewords of C_1 are in fact partitioned into cosets once a *coarse* linear/lattice subcode $C_2 \subset C_1$ is defined. If C_2 is a good channel code for the virtual channel between the SI and this closest codeword, then the decoder can reconstruct the latter with negligible probability of error, as shown in the previous section. From it, and using also the SI, an estimate of the source is eventually obtained. The theoretical bounds are achieved because, with good linear/lattice codes, (i) the closest codeword distributes as the variable $U^n \sim \prod_{i=1}^{n} p^*(u_i)$, (ii) at the decoder, once u^n is reconstructed, the distortion is minimized by implementing the function $h^*(u,y)$, and (iii) the number of cosets, i.e. the *nesting ratio* of the two codes is approximately $I(X;U|Y)$.

In lossless SCSI the virtual channel considered for channel code design is between Y and X; here, instead, it is between Y and U. But $Y \to X \to U$ forms a Markov chain, so the channel code must be actually more robust; this phenomenon is investigated in detail in (Zamir et al., 2002) under the name of *self-noise*.

In particular, in the binary-Hamming case ($Z \sim \mathcal{B}(p)$) optimality in (10) is achieved by $U = X + Q$ with $Q \sim \mathcal{B}(D)$ independent from X, and by $h^*(u,y) = u$ (see Fig. 3(a)). In practice, dithered quantization over a fine code guaranteeing distortion D achieves *almost* this U (Zamir & Feder, 1996), but with a coarse channel code that is *exponentially* good for the BSC $U = Y + Z_e$, where $Z_e \triangleq Z + Q \sim \mathcal{B}(p * D)$ with $p * D \triangleq p(1-D) + D(1-p)$, the recovery of U from the SI at the decoder is still successful (Zamir et al., 2002).

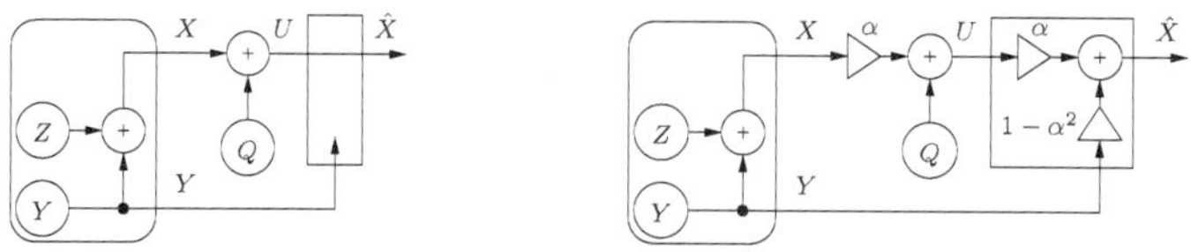

(a) binary-Hamming case (b) Gaussian-quadratic case

Fig. 3. Relations among the random variables involved in lossy SCSI at optimality: Y, Z and Q are independent Gaussian/Bernoulli random variables. U is not actually "sent" to the decoder, but rather reconstructed relying on the knowledge of Y.

In the Gaussian-quadratic case ($Z \sim \mathcal{N}(0, \sigma_z^2)$) optimality in (10) is achieved by $U = \alpha X + Q$ with $Q \sim \mathcal{N}(0, D)$ independent from X, and by $h^*(u, y) = \alpha u + (1 - \alpha^2)y$; $\alpha \triangleq \sqrt{1 - D/\sigma_z^2} < 1$ guarantees that (i) $h^*(u, y)$ gives the minimum mean square error estimate of X from Y and U, and (ii) $E[d(X, h^*(U, Y))] = D$ (see Fig. 3(b)). In this case, dithered quantization of αX over a fine lattice guaranteeing distortion D achieves *essentially* this U (Zamir & Feder, 1996)[3]; if the coarse sublattice is *exponentially* good for the *additive white Gaussian noise* (AWGN) channel $U = \alpha Y + Z_e$, where $Z_e \triangleq \alpha Z + Q \sim \mathcal{N}(0, \sigma_z^2)$, then U can be recovered from αY at the decoder (Zamir et al., 2002).

The nested coding approach outlined above, for which the existence of good *and* nested codes was actually showed in later papers, is surely more practical than random binning; practical implementations of the Gaussian-quadratic case are indeed investigated in (Liu et al., 2006; Servetto, 2007). However, there are still practical difficulties in its implementation due to the fact that good performance is achieved only asymptotically with the length n of the code. In practice, for finite n recovering of U is possible with the coarse code having a reduced code rate with respect to the one achieving optimality, not only because the *self-noise* (Q) actually introduced is not Bernoulli/Gaussian, but also because the nesting constraint does not permit to efficiently randomize the channel code. This leads to a rate loss with respect to the achievable rate, or, equivalently, to a distortion gap, which in particular increases for fixed n with the rate of the SCSI scheme. This phenomenon was observed in (Liu et al., 2006), and a scheme was proposed in which a second coding stage (based on schemes shown in the previous section) on top of nested quantization with finite n is used to losslessly send the coset index to the SI-aware decoder; the resulting scheme is probably the most performing appeared in literature.

Other practical schemes for lossy SCSI of continuous sources are based on the observation that once traditional (vector) quantization produces an index in a discrete domain, lossless SCSI means could be used to send this index to the decoder. In this way, a good source code and a good channel code are indeed individually designed. Channel codes that are essentially based on convolutional codes are used in (Pradhan & Ramchandran, 1999; 2003; 2005); more performing channel codes are used instead in (Yang et al., 2008), where the problem of lossy distributed coding of many sources is tackled as well. As a remark, note that even if this "separated" approach has indeed been shown to be optimal for the two-terminal Gaussian-quadratic case (Wagner et al., 2008), in general it is not.

[3] Note that, if $Y \sim \mathcal{N}$, $U' \triangleq \alpha U$ assumes the conditional distribution $p(u'|x)$ which minimizes $I(X; U')$ under distortion D (Cover & Thomas, 2006).

3.2.1 Superposition Coding

It should be clear that the joint design of good source/channel codes for the lossy SCSI/DSC problem is very hard. Coding schemes in which optimality is also achieved if the two codes are designed independently are then preferable since they are more practical. One such scheme has been proposed and investigated for the dual problem of *channel coding with side information (at the encoder)* (CCSI) and is briefly discussed in the following. The SCSI approach we propose in Section 5 is indeed dual to this approach; more details regarding this duality can be found in (Cappellari, 2009).

Consider the additive channel $X = \hat{X} + Y + Z$, where $\hat{X}$ is the input to the channel, Y is an *interference* known to the encoder (but not to the decoder) and independent from $\hat{X}$, Z is an unknown *noise* independent from $\hat{X}$ and Y, and X is the channel output. The goal is to transfer the maximum amount of information to the decoder once a *cost* constraint is given to $\hat{X}$; usually this constraint is given as $E[d(0, \hat{X})] \leq W$ where d is a distortion function. A *capacity-cost* function $C^*(W)$ is then defined that gives this maximum amount; in particular, it was evaluated (for the general, *non*-additive setting) in (Gel'fand & Pinsker, 1980).

A random coding scheme is suggested too as follows. Generate a set $\mathcal{U}$ of codewords distributed according to a suitable distribution $\prod_{i=1}^{n} p^*(u_i)$, and partition it into bins; associate each bin to a different message to be sent. The encoder selects the u^n in the desired bin such that $(u^n, y^n) \in \mathcal{A}_\varepsilon^{(n)}$ and inputs to the channel the codeword $\hat{x}_i = h^*(u_i, y_i)$, for a suitable choice of h^*. The decoder looks for the element u^n in $\mathcal{U}$ such that $(x^n, u^n) \in \mathcal{A}_\varepsilon^{(n)}$, and returns the message corresponding to the bin to which this element belongs. Now, the bins into which $\mathcal{U}$ is partitioned take the role of *good source codes*, since via the function h a codeword satisfying the cost constraint can be formed and transmitted; in turn, $\mathcal{U}$ takes the role of a *good channel code*.

In the additive setting, nested linear codes and lattices exist that achieve optimality both in case of binary-noise Hamming-cost and in case of Gaussian-noise quadratic-cost, respectively (Zamir et al., 2002). Nevertheless, optimality is also achieved with a *superposition* of two independent codes (Bennatan et al., 2006). In particular, a *coarse* code $\mathcal{C}_2$ which is a good source code with respect to the distortion constraint W is used by the encoder for selecting the codeword to be transmitted on the channel. The *fine* code $\mathcal{C}_1$ is generated as the sum of $\mathcal{C}_2$ and a code $\mathcal{C}_0$ which is a good channel code with respect to the noise Z, i.e. $\mathcal{C}_1 = \mathcal{C}_0 + \mathcal{C}_2$. With a proper generation of $\mathcal{C}_0$, $\mathcal{C}_1$ is partitioned into bins $c_0^n + \mathcal{C}_2$, for $c_0^n \in \mathcal{C}_0$, i.e. each $c_0^n \in \mathcal{C}_0$ is in one-to-one correspondence with a bin of $\mathcal{C}_1$. At the encoder the message is then selected in terms of a $c_0^n \in \mathcal{C}_0$. At the decoder a codeword of $\mathcal{C}_1$ plus some noise is received; upon decoding this signal over the sum of $\mathcal{C}_0$ and $\mathcal{C}_2$, the best estimate of c_0^n is declared as the received message. Details and implementation of this scheme with practical codes is discussed in (Bennatan et al., 2006).

In the lossy SCSI problem, let us in principle generate a *coarse* code $\mathcal{C}_2$ which is a good channel code with respect to the virtual channel between Y and U. Then, we generate $\mathcal{C}_0$ as a good source code for Z_e with respect to the distortion D, and obtain the *fine* code $\mathcal{C}_1 = \mathcal{C}_0 + \mathcal{C}_2$. In particular, in the binary case ($Z \sim \mathcal{B}(p)$) $\mathcal{C}_2$ and $\mathcal{C}_0$ are codes made of 2^{nR_2} and 2^{nR_0} codewords with distribution $\mathcal{B}(1/2)$ and $\mathcal{B}(q)$, respectively. The encoder looks for $c_0^n + c_2^n$ such that $(x^n, c_0^n + c_2^n) \in \mathcal{A}_\varepsilon^{(n)}$ and sends the index of c_0^n (in practice, dithered quantization can be employed); there is an encoder error if $d_H(x^n, c_0^n + c_2^n) > D$.

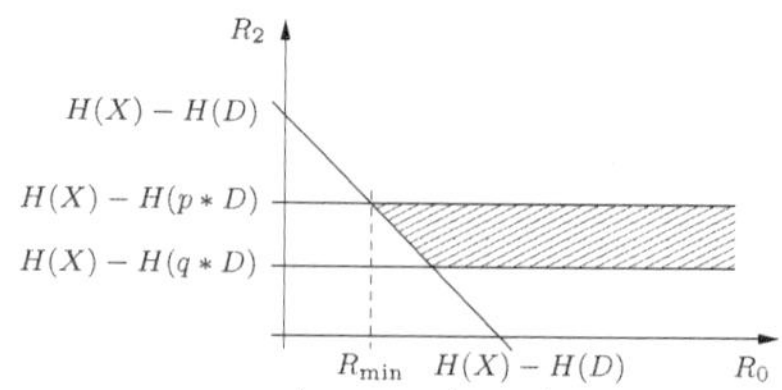

Fig. 4. Region in which there are no encoder nor decoder errors.

Theorem 1. *The probability of having an encoder error is negligible with $n \to \infty$ if*

$$\begin{aligned} R_2 &> H(X) - H(q * D) \quad (20) \\ R_0 + R_2 &> H(X) - H(D) . \quad (21) \end{aligned}$$

Sketch of proof: Asymptotically, x^n takes values on a set of $2^{nH(X)}$ elements, and for a fixed c_2^n, the code $\mathcal{C}_0 + c_2^n$ *covers* at most $2^{nH(q*D)}$ of them within distortion D. Hence, there must be at least $2^{nH(X)-nH(q*D)}$ codewords in code $\mathcal{C}_2$. Then, since each n-tuple approximates at most $2^{nH(D)}$ elements within Hamming-distortion D, the superposition code must provide at least $2^{nH(X)-nH(D)}$ codewords. Once we have these two conditions the probability that a typical $(c_0^n + c_2^n)$ is within distortion D approaches one. This may be proved with an argument similar to the one used in the standard proof of the achievability of the rate-distortion function (Cover & Thomas, 2006). If both given bounds are approached, the *test channel* between $C_0 + C_2$ and X is such that $X = C_0 + C_2 - Q$, with $Q \sim \mathcal{B}(D)$ independent from C_0 and C_2 (asymptotically); for rates over the bounds a lower distortion can be achieved.
The decoder looks for $c_2^n \in \mathcal{C}_2$ such that $(c_0^n + c_2^n, y^n) \in \mathcal{A}_\epsilon^{(n)}$ (in practice, a closest neighbor search is conducted), and reconstructs the source as $c_0^n + c_2^n$; there is a decoding error if c_2^n is not correctly recovered. But once c_0^n is known, the equivalent noise between Y and $C_2 = Y + Z + Q - C_0$ is distributed as Z_e. Hence, the following holds.

Theorem 2. *The probability of having a decoder error is negligible with $n \to \infty$ if*

$$R_2 < C_{p*D}(W) , \quad (22)$$

where $C_{p*D}(W) \triangleq H(W * p * D) - H(p * D) = H(X) - H(p * D)$ is the capacity of the BSC between Y and U, subject to a Hamming-cost constraint W such that $Y + Z + Q$ distributes as X (i.e. the balls related to codewords of $\mathcal{C}_2$ are packed *only over the space in which x^n lies).*

The closure of the rate region where there are no errors is shown in Fig. 4; it is not empty for any q such that $H(q * D) \geq H(p * D)$, and the minimum of R_0 approaches the rate-distortion function $R^*(D) = H(p * D) - H(D)$ for all distortions $0 \leq D \leq d_C < p$ (Wyner & Ziv, 1976).
In the Gaussian case ($Z \in \mathcal{N}(0, \sigma_z^2)$), $\mathcal{C}_0$ is generated from the distribution $\mathcal{N}(0, \sigma_q^2)$ and again the scale factor $\alpha = \sqrt{1 - D/\sigma_z^2}$ is used. If R_2 and $R_0 + R_2$ are high enough, dithered quantization of αX over the superposition of codes $\mathcal{C}_2$ and $\mathcal{C}_0$ leads asymptotically to the relation $\alpha X = C_0 + C_2 - Q$, with $Q \sim \mathcal{N}(0, D)$ independent from C_0 and C_2. At the decoder, which knows c_0^n, the channel between αY and C_2 satisfies $C_2 = \alpha Y + \alpha Z + Q - C_0$, i.e. it is Gaussian, with capacity $C(W) \triangleq (1/2)\log(1 + W/(\alpha^2\sigma_z^2 + D)) = (1/2)\log(1 + W/\sigma_z^2)$ under the quadratic cost constraint W. There are no decoding errors if the code rate R_2 is

below this capacity, and, again, the best estimate of the source at the decoder can be found by taking $\alpha(c_0 + c_2) + (1 - \alpha^2)y$. The minimum achievable rate can be in this case computed with a geometric argument: the goal is to *cover* the n-dimensional balls related to codewords of $\mathcal{C}_2$ with as least as possible balls of average quadratic-distortion D. But the quadratic-distortion of the formers cannot be smaller than σ_z^2 so that the minimum code rate of code $\mathcal{C}_0$, provided that $\sigma_q^2 + D \geq \sigma_z^2$, equals the rate-distortion function of the SCSI problem $R^*(D) = (1/2)\log(\sigma_z^2/D)$ (Wyner & Ziv, 1976).

Despite in principle the decoder/encoder for a CCSI problem can be used as the encoder/decoder of a dual SCSI problem (Pradhan et al., 2003), from a practical point of view CCSI and SCSI are very different. In CCSI source coding is done at the encoder; the code $\mathcal{C}_2$ must be structured such that exhaustive search can be employed in order to perform a closest neighbor search (e.g. be a trellis code). Channel decoding is done at the decoder, and both $\mathcal{C}_0$ and $\mathcal{C}_2$ should be performing channel codes for which a good algorithm approximating maximum likelihood search exist (e.g. turbo codes). In practice, no penalty is introduced in having $\mathcal{C}_2$ not very good from a channel coding perspective (Bennatan et al., 2006).

In SCSI channel decoding is done at the decoder; $\mathcal{C}_2$ should be a performing channel code for which a good algorithm approximating maximum likelihood search exist (e.g. turbo codes). Source coding is done at the encoder, and the code $\mathcal{C}_0 + \mathcal{C}_2$ must be structured such that exhaustive search can be employed in order to perform a closest neighbor search (e.g. be a trellis code). Unfortunately, there are currently no algorithms that perform similarly to a closest neighbor search over good codes for channel coding. Hence, in Section 5 we will actually rely on convolutional codes $\mathcal{C}_2$, paying in this case a penalty with respect to the theoretical bounds.

4. Practical Iterative Algorithms for Lossless Coding

Turbo codes are good practical channel codes, and hence are good tools for lossless (binary) SCSI. In the following we discuss the utilization of *standard* and *ready-available* turbo encoding and decoding algorithms for this problem. Differently from other contributions on this subject, we use the *factor graph*-based approach commonly taken in the LDPC-codes-related literature. For a useful tutorial article on factor graphs and *message-passing* algorithms, the reader is referred to (Kschischang et al., 2001). Under a *unified formulation*, we describe in principle the cases in which syndromes or parity bits are sent to the decoder, over binary or non-binary, lossless or lossy transmission channels, with binary or non-binary side information; more details can be found in (Cappellari & De Giusti, 2008).

4.1 Turbo Codes Review and the Parity-Based Approach

Turbo codes actually include different kinds of codes. In the most common case (*parallel concatenated convolutional codes*) they are *systematic* codes: in correspondence of a sequence of Nk outcomes from X ($\mathbf{x}$) the turbo encoder uses two systematic (n, k) *convolutional* codes to form two sequences of parity bits of $N(n-k) + z_t$ bits each[4] ($\mathbf{p}_0$ and $\mathbf{p}_1$), according to the following algorithm.

```
1: function TRBENC(x)
2:     p0 ← GETPARITY0(x)
3:     x' ← INTERLEAVE(x)
```

[4] The additional $z_t \ll N(n-k)$ bits are emitted while terminating the encoding into the zero state (*zero-tailing*).

$\mathbf{p}_1 \leftarrow$ GETPARITY$_1(\mathbf{x}')$
return $[\mathbf{x}, \mathbf{p}_0, \mathbf{p}_1]$
end function

Once $\mathbf{x}$ and $\mathbf{p}_i$ are sent over a channel, they are received as $\mathbf{r}$ and $\mathbf{r}_i$ respectively, and the turbo decoder aims to maximize $p_{\mathbf{r}\mathbf{r}_0\mathbf{r}_1}(\mathbf{x}) \propto l_{\mathbf{r}\mathbf{r}_0\mathbf{r}_1}(\mathbf{x})p(\mathbf{x})$.[5] The *maximum likelihood* (ML) decoding procedure is approximated by a message-passing algorithm on the factor graph of $l_{\mathbf{r}\mathbf{r}_0\mathbf{r}_1}(\mathbf{x})$. In particular, $l_{\mathbf{r}\mathbf{r}_0\mathbf{r}_1}(\mathbf{x})$ factorizes into $l_{\mathbf{r}}(\mathbf{x})l_{\mathbf{r}_0}(\mathbf{x})l_{\mathbf{r}_1}(\mathbf{x})$, and $l_{\mathbf{r}_i}(\mathbf{x}) = \sum_{\mathbf{p}_i} \chi_i(\mathbf{p}_i|\mathbf{x})l_{\mathbf{r}_i}(\mathbf{p}_i)$, where $\mathbf{p}_i$ are the *true* parity sequences and $\chi_i(\mathbf{p}_i|\mathbf{x})$ are the indicator functions that are unitary if and only if $\mathbf{p}_i$ is the parity of $\mathbf{x}$ (according to the i-th convolutional code, comprehensive of the interleaver for $i = 1$). The traditional decoding algorithm operates (on the factor graph of Fig. 5(a)) as follows, where the function FBA$_i(\cdot)$ computes the APP function relative to the i-th convolutional code, assuming $q(\mathbf{x})$ as the *prior* probability and using the *forward-backward algorithm* (Bahl et al., 1974). If the prior probability $p(\mathbf{x})$ is known, it can be absorbed into $l_{\mathbf{r}}(\mathbf{x})$ in order to implement *maximum a posteriori probability* (MAP) decoding.

function TRBDEC$(l_{\mathbf{r}}(\mathbf{x}), l_{\mathbf{r}_0}(\mathbf{p}_0), l_{\mathbf{r}_1}(\mathbf{p}_1), M)$
  $m \leftarrow 0, i \leftarrow 1$, initialize $q(\mathbf{x})$ ▷ Initialization
  repeat ▷ Turbo loop
    $m \leftarrow m + 1, i \leftarrow 1 - i$
    $ap^{(m)}(\mathbf{x}) \leftarrow$ FBA$_i(l_{\mathbf{r}}(\mathbf{x}), l_{\mathbf{r}_i}(\mathbf{p}_i), q(\mathbf{x}))$
    $q(\mathbf{x}) \leftarrow ap^{(m)}(\mathbf{x}) / [l_{\mathbf{r}}(\mathbf{x})q(\mathbf{x})]$
  until $m \geq M$
  return $ap^{(m)}(\mathbf{x})$
end function

The application of turbo codes to the SCSI problem $X = Y + Z$, with $Z \sim \mathcal{B}(p)$ and $Y \sim \mathcal{B}(1/2)$, is very straightforward. In particular, the parities are sent, and decoding is done by simply invoking TRBDEC$(l_{\mathbf{y}}(\mathbf{x}), l_{\mathbf{r}_0}(\mathbf{p}_0), l_{\mathbf{r}_1}(\mathbf{p}_1), M)$ (Aaron & Girod, 2002; Garcia-Frias & Zhao, 2001), where $l_{\mathbf{y}}(\mathbf{x}) = p_{Z^{Nk}}(\mathbf{x} - \mathbf{y})$ takes into account for the virtual channel statistics (see Fig. 5(a)). In addition, it is possible to jointly decode and estimate p with no performance loss (Garcia-Frias & Zhao, 2001). Since *puncturing* (i.e. bit removal) can be employed at the encoder before transmission (the decoder can take into account this fact by assuming uniform likelihoods in correspondence of the punctured bits), any rate $0 \leq R \leq \frac{2(n-k)}{k}$ is achievable.

4.2 Syndrome-Based Approach

A turbo code can be seen as a $(N(2n-k) + 2z_t, Nk)$ systematic *block* code whose *generator matrix* is $\mathbf{G} = [\mathbf{I}_{Nk}|\mathbf{P}_0|\mathbf{P}_1]$, where $\mathbf{P}_i$ is the $Nk \times [N(n-k) + z_t]$ *parity formation* matrix corresponding to the i-th convolutional code (comprehensive of the possible interleaver). If puncturing is employed (exclusively on the parity bits), then the equivalent generator matrix is $\mathbf{G}' = [\mathbf{I}_{Nk}|\mathbf{P}'_0|\mathbf{P}'_1]$, where $\mathbf{P}'_i$ is the $Nk \times s_i$ matrix obtained removing from $\mathbf{P}_i$ the columns corresponding to the punctured parity bits. Consequently,

$$\mathbf{H}' = \left[\begin{array}{c|c|c} \mathbf{P}'^T_0 & \mathbf{I}_{s_0} & \mathbf{0}_{s_0 \times s_1} \\ \hline \mathbf{P}'^T_1 & \mathbf{0}_{s_1 \times s_0} & \mathbf{I}_{s_1} \end{array}\right] \tag{23}$$

[5] Given two r.v. A and B, the *likelihood* and *a posteriori probability* (APP) functions will hereafter be denoted by $l_a(b) \triangleq p(a|b)$ and $p_a(b) \triangleq p(b|a)$ respectively.

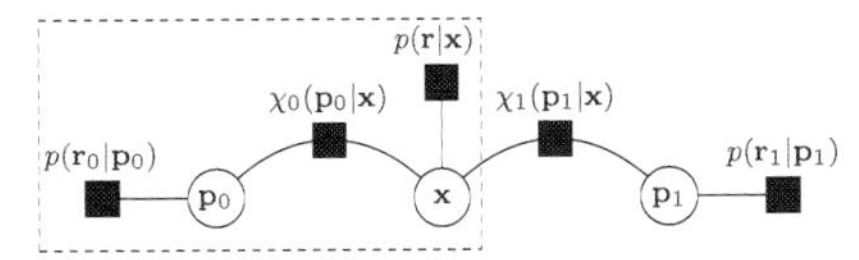

(a) parity-based approach (with $p(\mathbf{r}|\mathbf{x}) = p(\mathbf{y}|\mathbf{x})$)

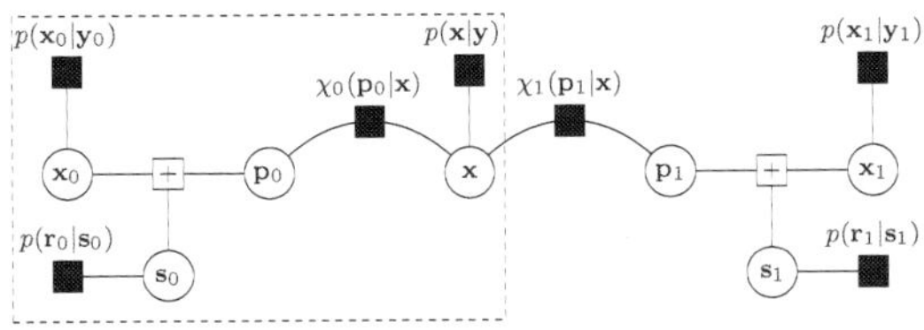

(b) syndrome-based approach

Fig. 5. Factor graphs representing the APP functions in the SCSI problem using turbo codes.

is a parity-check matrix of the turbo code. In correspondence of a sequence of $Nk + s_0 + s_1$ outcomes from X (partitioned into the three sub-sequences $\mathbf{x}$, $\mathbf{x}_0$, and $\mathbf{x}_1$ of length Nk, s_0, and s_1 respectively), the syndrome is obtained according to the following algorithm. Eventually, any rate $0 \le R \le \frac{2(n-k)}{2n-k} < 1$ bit/sample is achievable; for example, if $(2,1)$ constituent codes are employed, $0 \le R \le 2/3$ bit/sample.

```
function SYNENC(x, x0, x1)
    [x, p0, p1] ← TRBENC(x)
    for i ← 0, 1 do
        p ← PUNCTURE_i(p_i)
        s_i ← p + x_i
    end for
    return [s0, s1]
end function
```

We now directly tackle the problem of optimal MAP syndrome decoding, assuming that $\mathbf{s}_i$ are sent over a general channel and are received as $\mathbf{r}_i$. In particular, the decoding algorithm is derived from examining the factor graph of the APP function $p_{\mathbf{y}\mathbf{y}_0\mathbf{y}_1\mathbf{r}_0\mathbf{r}_1}(\mathbf{x}\mathbf{x}_0\mathbf{x}_1) \propto p_{\mathbf{y}\mathbf{y}_0\mathbf{y}_1}(\mathbf{x}\mathbf{x}_0\mathbf{x}_1) l_{\mathbf{r}_0\mathbf{r}_1}(\mathbf{x}\mathbf{x}_0\mathbf{x}_1)$. But $p_{\mathbf{y}\mathbf{y}_0\mathbf{y}_1}(\mathbf{x}\mathbf{x}_0\mathbf{x}_1)$ factorizes into $p_{\mathbf{y}}(\mathbf{x}) p_{\mathbf{y}_0}(\mathbf{x}_0) p_{\mathbf{y}_1}(\mathbf{x}_1)$; similarly $l_{\mathbf{r}_0\mathbf{r}_1}(\mathbf{x}\mathbf{x}_0\mathbf{x}_1) = l_{\mathbf{r}_0}(\mathbf{x}\mathbf{x}_0) l_{\mathbf{r}_1}(\mathbf{x}\mathbf{x}_1)$, and $l_{\mathbf{r}_i}(\mathbf{x}\mathbf{x}_i) = \sum_{\mathbf{s}_i} l_{\mathbf{r}_i}(\mathbf{s}_i) \sum_{\mathbf{p}_i} \chi_i(\mathbf{p}_i|\mathbf{x}) \chi_{\{\mathbf{p}_i + \mathbf{x}_i = \mathbf{s}_i\}}$, where $\mathbf{s}_i$ and $\mathbf{p}_i$ are the *true* syndrome sequences and the parity sequences from which they are computed respectively, and $\chi_{\{\mathbf{p}_i + \mathbf{x}_i = \mathbf{s}_i\}}$ is the indicator function of the condition in brackets. The corresponding factor graph of the APP function is shown in Fig. 5(b).

This factor graph is an extension without additional cycles of the factor graph relative to the parity-based approach. MAP decoding can be achieved by reusing the turbo decoding algorithm presented above; in particular, it is only necessary to form the correct input likelihoods to the function TRBDEC(·) and post-process the output APP function $ap(\mathbf{x})$, for example using the following algorithm (*hard syndrome decoding*).[6]

1: **function** HSYNDEC($p_{\mathbf{y}}(\mathbf{x}), p_{\mathbf{y}_0}(\mathbf{x}_0), p_{\mathbf{y}_1}(\mathbf{x}_1), l_{\mathbf{r}_0}(\mathbf{s}_0), l_{\mathbf{r}_1}(\mathbf{s}_1), M$)
2: **for** $i \leftarrow 0, 1$ **do** ▷ Pre-processing
3: $l_i(\mathbf{p}_i) \leftarrow \sum_{\mathbf{s}_i} l_{\mathbf{r}_i}(\mathbf{s}_i) \sum_{\mathbf{x}_i} p_{\mathbf{y}_i}(\mathbf{x}_i) \chi_{\{\mathbf{p}_i+\mathbf{x}_i=\mathbf{s}_i\}}$
4: **end for**
5: $ap(\mathbf{x}) \leftarrow$ TRBDEC($p_{\mathbf{y}}(\mathbf{x}), l_0(\mathbf{p}_0), l_1(\mathbf{p}_1), M$)
6: $\hat{\mathbf{x}} \leftarrow \arg\max_{\mathbf{x}} ap(\mathbf{x})$
7: $[\hat{\mathbf{x}}, \hat{\mathbf{p}}_0, \hat{\mathbf{p}}_1] \leftarrow$ TRBENC($\hat{\mathbf{x}}$)
8: **for** $i \leftarrow 0, 1$ **do** ▷ Post-processing
9: $\hat{\mathbf{x}}_i \leftarrow \arg\max_{\mathbf{x}_i} p_{\mathbf{y}_i}(\mathbf{x}_i) l_{\mathbf{r}_i}(\hat{\mathbf{p}}_i + \mathbf{x}_i)$
10: **end for**
11: **return** $[\hat{\mathbf{x}}, \hat{\mathbf{x}}_0, \hat{\mathbf{x}}_1]$
12: **end function**

Using the *log-likelihood ratio* and the *log-APP ratio* defined as

$$l_a \triangleq \log \frac{l_a(1)}{l_a(0)}, \qquad p_a \triangleq \log \frac{p_a(1)}{p_a(0)}, \tag{24}$$

the j-th factor computed by the pre-processing operation (line 3) is $l_{i,j} = l_{\mathbf{r}_{i,j}} * p_{\mathbf{y}_{i,j}}$, where the *log-likelihood ratio convolution* operator is defined as $l_1 * l_2 \triangleq \log \frac{e^{l_1}+e^{l_2}}{1+e^{l_1+l_2}}$. Post-processing (line 9) yields $\hat{\mathbf{x}}_{i,j} = \mathbf{r}_{i,j} + \hat{\mathbf{p}}_{i,j}$; maximization translates into thresholding.

The thresholding and parity formation operations permit the reutilization of the traditional turbo algorithms. Nevertheless, they prevent the computation of the correct messages across the nodes $\mathbf{p}_i$, so the hard syndrome decoding algorithm is not optimal. But if a *full* turbo decoding function FTRBDEC(·) is used that outputs the APP functions $ap(\mathbf{p}_i)$ for the parity bits as well, the post-processing can be improved as follows (*soft syndrome decoding*).

1: **function** SSYNDEC($p_{\mathbf{y}}(\mathbf{x}), p_{\mathbf{y}_0}(\mathbf{x}_0), p_{\mathbf{y}_1}(\mathbf{x}_1), l_{\mathbf{r}_0}(\mathbf{s}_0), l_{\mathbf{r}_1}(\mathbf{s}_1), M$)
2: **for** $i \leftarrow 0, 1$ **do** ▷ Pre-processing
3: $l_i(\mathbf{p}_i) \leftarrow \sum_{\mathbf{s}_i} l_{\mathbf{r}_i}(\mathbf{s}_i) \sum_{\mathbf{x}_i} p_{\mathbf{y}_i}(\mathbf{x}_i) \chi_{\{\mathbf{p}_i+\mathbf{x}_i=\mathbf{s}_i\}}$
4: **end for**
5: $[ap(\mathbf{x}), ap(\mathbf{p}_0), ap(\mathbf{p}_1)] \leftarrow$ FTRBDEC($p_{\mathbf{y}}(\mathbf{x}), l_0(\mathbf{p}_0), l_1(\mathbf{p}_1), M$)
6: **for** $i \leftarrow 0, 1$ **do** ▷ Post-processing
7: $ap'(\mathbf{x}_i) \leftarrow \sum_{\mathbf{s}_i} l_{\mathbf{r}_i}(\mathbf{s}_i) \sum_{\mathbf{p}_i} \frac{ap(\mathbf{p}_i)}{l_i(\mathbf{p}_i)} \chi_{\{\mathbf{p}_i+\mathbf{x}_i=\mathbf{s}_i\}}$
8: $ap(\mathbf{x}_i) \leftarrow p_{\mathbf{y}_i}(\mathbf{x}_i) ap'(\mathbf{x}_i)$
9: **end for**
10: **return** $[ap(\mathbf{x}), ap(\mathbf{x}_0), ap(\mathbf{x}_1)]$
11: **end function**

Now, in order to estimate $\mathbf{x}_{i,j}$ thresholding will be applied to $ap_{\mathbf{x}_{i,j}} = p_{\mathbf{y}_{i,j}} + l_{\mathbf{r}_{i,j}} * (ap_{\mathbf{p}_{i,j}} - l_{i,j})$, which is certainly more accurate than before. If the transmission channel is error-free

[6] The operations in the pre- and post-processing (that do not involve the punctured parity bits) are written in the most general fashion, but in practice they are *symbol-wise* operations between marginal functions.

(i.e. $|l_{\mathbf{r}_{i,j}}| = \infty$) it is easy to show that $ap_{\mathbf{x}_{i,j}}$ equals $ap_{\mathbf{p}_{i,j}}$ or $-ap_{\mathbf{p}_{i,j}}$ if $\mathbf{r}_{i,j}$ is 0 or 1 respectively, because in either case the contributions of $p_{\mathbf{y}_{i,j}}$ and $l_{i,j}$ cancel out; then, $\mathbf{x}_{i,j}$ can be again estimated by $\hat{\mathbf{x}}_{i,j} = \mathbf{r}_{i,j} + \hat{\mathbf{p}}_{i,j}$, where $\hat{\mathbf{p}}_{i,j}$ is the estimate of the corresponding parity bit obtained thresholding $ap_{\mathbf{p}_{i,j}}$ rather than the one obtained invoking the function TRBENC($\hat{\mathbf{x}}$). On the contrary, if the TC is not error-free $|l_{\mathbf{r}_{i,j}}| < \infty$, and hence $ap_{\mathbf{x}_{i,j}}$ must be actually computed in order to correctly estimate $\mathbf{x}_{i,j}$.

4.3 Experimental Results and Comparisons

A virtual channel has been simulated with $Y \sim \mathcal{B}(1/2)$ and $Z \sim \mathcal{B}(p)$, for different values of p; error-free transmission has been considered for comparison purposes with previous literature on this subject. Both parity- and syndrome-based approaches have been simulated. The turbo code uses two identical $(n,k) = (2,1)$, 16-state, systematic constituent codes with generator matrix $\mathbf{G}(D) = \left[1 \ \frac{1+D+D^2+D^4}{1+D^3+D^4}\right]$; $\lfloor LR \rfloor$ parity/syndrome bits are sent in correspondence to each data *frame* of $L = 2^{16} = 65536$ samples. Puncturing is performed such that rates R of $2/3$ or $1/2$ bit/samples are achieved. $2^{13} = 8192$ frames have been generated for each p, such that the average *bit error ratio* (BER) is eventually estimated over $2^{29} \simeq 5 \cdot 10^8$ bits. The decoding routines TRBDEC and SSYNDEC are set for a number of runs of the FBA algorithm M equal to 40.

Comparisons are given in Fig. 6, in which the BER is shown as a function of $H(p)$. When $R = 2/3$, the proposed method 65536-SSYNDEC outperforms the coding performance of the "SF+ISF" method given in (Tu et al., 2005). Despite the different syndrome formation procedure used in the latter (which does not rely on a standard turbo encoding engine), these two methods are very similar in the way they work. Hence, it is reasonable to think that the different performance is the result of better coding parameters (i.e. frame length, convolutional code, interleaver and puncturer). Despite the very large interleaver length, the "Syn. trellis" method proposed in (Roumy et al., 2007) has very poor performance, which is even worse than the performance of the parity-based method 65536-TRBDEC. When $R = 1/2$, the proposed method 65536-SSYNDEC has again a good performance, which are surpassed only by the LDPC-based systems reported in (Liveris et al., 2002) (which employ a longer frame size) and by the "P&C trellis" method proposed in (Liveris et al., 2003), which makes use of longer frames and of different 16-state constituent codes (specifically tailored for heavy data puncturing). Again, despite its smart formulation and very long frame size, the "Syn. trellis" method (Roumy et al., 2007) has very poor performance.

5. Continuous-Valued Syndromes for Lossy Coding

Traditional (discrete) syndromes of a linear code are good for lossless SCSI. In this section we discuss a coding method based on *continuous-valued* syndromes of a lattice for lossy SCSI of continuous sources with quadratic distortion (Cappellari & Mian, 2006b). This method embodies the superposition coding approach described in Section 3.2.1.

Consider a lattice $\Lambda \subset \mathbb{R}^n$. Being a subgroup of $\mathbb{R}^n$, it induces the partition of $\mathbb{R}^n$ into the cosets of $\mathbb{R}^n/\Lambda$. Each coset is uniquely identified by one of its elements; in particular we assume as *coset leader* of $L \in \mathbb{R}^n/\Lambda$ the element $l(L) \triangleq \arg\min_{\lambda \in L} d(\lambda, 0)$. We call *continuous-valued syndrome* (CVS) of $x^n \in \mathbb{R}^n$, relative to Λ, the element $s_\Lambda(x^n) \triangleq l(L)$ such that $x^n \in L$. If we define the *quantizer* $Q_\Lambda(x^n) \triangleq \arg\min_{\lambda \in \Lambda} d(x^n, \lambda)$ (with the further condition $\lambda + s_\Lambda(x^n) = x^n$ in case of ambiguity), the CVS satisfies $s_\Lambda(x^n) = x^n - Q_\Lambda(x^n)$.

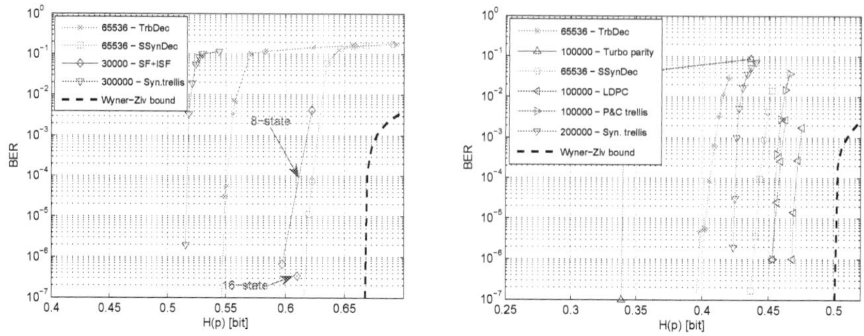

(a) $R = 2/3$ (b) $R = 1/2$

Fig. 6. Comparison between different SCSI methods. The label "SF+ISF" refers to the syndrome-based method in (Tu et al., 2005) (results for two different convolutional codes are shown); the label "Syn. trellis" refers to the syndrome-based method in (Roumy et al., 2007), where 16-state constituent codes are employed. The label "Turbo parity" refers to the parity-based method in (Aaron & Girod, 2002), that uses two $(5,4)$ 16-state constituent codes. The label "LDPC" refers to the syndrome-based method in (Liveris et al., 2002) (results relative to two irregular LDPC codes are shown); the label "P&C trellis" refers to the syndrome-based method in (Liveris et al., 2003) that uses 16-state constituent codes. The frame length is reported too.

We consider the additive virtual channel $X = Y + Z$. If $P[Q_\Lambda(Z^n) \neq 0]$ is asymptotically negligible (i.e. the realizations of Z^n lie in the *fundamental Voronoi region* of Λ), then $s_\Lambda(x^n)$ permits near lossless reconstruction at the decoder; in fact

$$x^n = y^n + z^n \overset{(1)}{=} y^n + s_\Lambda(z^n) \overset{(2)}{=} y^n + s_\Lambda\left(s_\Lambda(x^n) + s_\Lambda(-y^n)\right) , \tag{25}$$

where $^{(1)}$ holds with high probability and $^{(2)}$ follows from linear properties of the CVS. In practice, the reconstruction from $s_\Lambda(x^n)$ and y^n is obtained by a single quantization as

$$x^n = s_\Lambda(x^n) - Q_\Lambda\left(s_\Lambda(x^n) - y^n\right) . \tag{26}$$

Of course, we would need a channel with infinite capacity in order to transmit the CVS to the decoder. Hence, we assume that a quantized version $\hat{s}_{\beta\Lambda}(x^n)$ of the syndrome $s_{\beta\Lambda}(x^n)$, such that $S_{\beta\Lambda} = \hat{S}_{\beta\Lambda} - Q$ with Q independent from $\hat{S}_{\beta\Lambda}$, is actually transmitted by the encoder.[7] For $\beta \geq 1$, the realizations of Z^n and, reasonably, the ones of the *error* Q^n, lie in the fundamental Voronoi region of $\beta\Lambda$. The reconstruction, according to (25), satisfies

$$\begin{aligned} \tilde{x}^n &= y^n + s_{\beta\Lambda}\left(s_{\beta\Lambda}(x^n) + s_{\beta\Lambda}(q^n) + s_{\beta\Lambda}(-y^n)\right) = y^n + s_{\beta\Lambda}\left(z^n + q^n\right) & (27) \\ &= x^n + \left(q^n - Q_{\beta\Lambda}\left(z^n + q^n\right)\right) \triangleq x^n + \left(q^n + q^n_{ol}\right) , & (28) \end{aligned}$$

[7] If the Voronoi regions of $\beta\Lambda$ are asymptotically spherical, $\hat{S}_{\beta\Lambda}$ and Q exist that are approximately Gaussian.

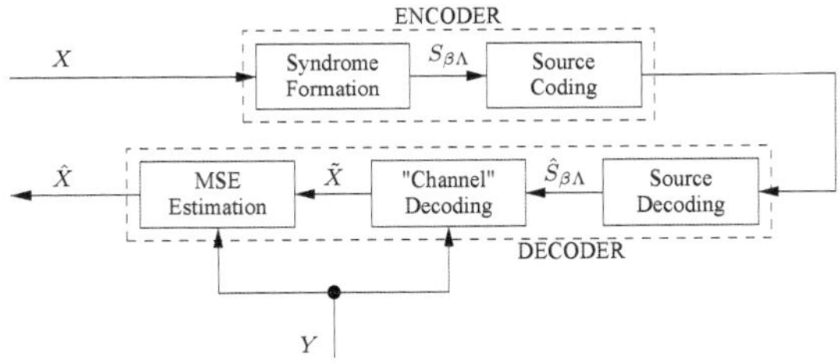

Fig. 7. Wyner-Ziv coding using continuous-valued syndromes.

where Q_{ol} is the *overload error*. If $Q_t \triangleq Q + Q_{ol}$ is independent from Y and Z (and the mean of all random variables is zero), $Y \to X \to \tilde{X}$ forms a Markov chain, such that the minimum mean square error *linear* estimate for X computed at the decoder is eventually given by

$$\hat{X} = \frac{\sigma_z^2}{\sigma_z^2 + \sigma_{q_t}^2}\tilde{X} + \frac{\sigma_{q_t}^2}{\sigma_z^2 + \sigma_{q_t}^2}Y\,, \tag{29}$$

and the achieved distortion D satisfies $1/D = 1/\sigma_z^2 + 1/\sigma_{q_t}^2$, where $\sigma_z^2 \triangleq E[Z^2]$ and $\sigma_{q_t}^2 \triangleq E[Q_t^2]$. This coding scheme is shown in Fig. 7.
For a fixed transmission rate R the best possible syndrome is sent, and the parameter β is experimentally tuned in order to minimize the variance of D. In theory, in the Gaussian case ($Z \sim \mathcal{N}(0, \sigma_z^2)$) with Λ being a good channel code for the virtual AWGN channel between Y and X, $\beta = 1/\alpha = 1/\sqrt{1 - D^*(R)/\sigma_z^2}$ guarantees that the rate-distortion function $R^*(D)$ is achieved ($D^*(R) = \sigma_z^2 2^{-2R}$ is its inverse). In fact, in this case, (i) since the syndrome distributes uniformly over the fundamental Voronoi region of $\beta\Lambda$ and Λ is a good channel code for the noise Z, $S_{\beta\Lambda} \sim \mathcal{N}(0, \beta^2\sigma_z^2)$, (ii) the minimum distortion in sending the syndrome at rate R is such that $E[Q^2] = \beta^2\sigma_z^2 2^{-2R} = \beta^2 D^*(R)$, (iii) since $\sigma_z^2 + E[Q^2] = \beta^2\sigma_z^2$ and $\beta\Lambda$ is a good channel code for an AWGN of power $\beta^2\sigma_z^2$, there is no overload error, i.e. $\sigma_{q_t}^2 = E[Q^2]$, (iv) $D = \sigma_z^2 E[Q^2]/(\sigma_z^2 + E[Q^2]) = E[Q^2]/\beta^2 = D^*(R)$.
A superposition of two codes is indeed used where the coarse code is the lattice code $\beta\Lambda$ and the additive code is the source code used for quantization of $S_{\beta\Lambda}$. The encoder is dual to the decoder of a *multiple access channel* problem that operates by *interference cancellation*: first, the codeword of the code with the lower code rate (the coarse one) is computed; then, this is subtracted from the source and the codeword to be transmitted to the decoder is formed according to the additive code. In practice, since we must be able to conduct an exact closest neighbor search on the coarse code, it cannot be a very performing channel code, i.e. we must cope in general with an overload error Q_{ol} (which corresponds to having a decoder error, as defined in Section 3.2.1). The parameter β permits to balance the contributions of the two errors. The higher is β, the lower is the overload error; but, for fixed transmission rate R, the higher is β, the higher is the variance of the *granular* error Q.

5.1 Experimental Results and Comparisons

We simulated the AWGN channel $X = Y + Z$ with a Gaussian input $Y \sim \mathcal{N}(0, \sigma_y^2 = 1)$ and a noise Z with various variances σ_z^2. We employ *trellis-coded quantization* (TCQ) based on the partition $a\mathbb{Z}/4a\mathbb{Z}$ for syndrome formation (Marcellin & Fisher, 1990), which defines the lattice

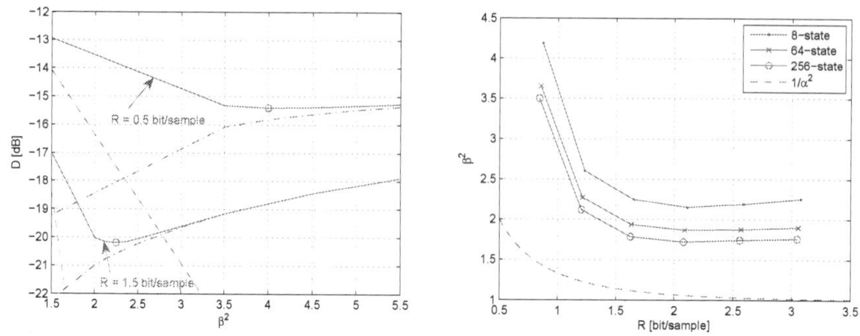

(a) effect on the errors

(b) optimum value

Fig. 8. Optimization of the volumetric parameter β^2.

Λ; the length of each input data frame is $n = 1000$; a is tuned such that the experimental second moment per dimension of the Voronoi regions of Λ equals σ_z^2. Any suitable source coding algorithm can be used to code the n-dimensional CVS; again, we employ TCQ, based on the partition $b\mathbb{Z}/4b\mathbb{Z}$ and on 8-state trellises. For each rate R, b is tuned such that the normalized volume of the Voronoi regions induced by this quantizer is 2^{2R} times less than the corresponding parameter of $\beta\Lambda$. Actually, in the following, R denotes the average entropy for describing the quantized syndrome, measured with the 2-supersets context-based method proposed in (Marcellin, 1994).

The effect of β^2 on the variances of the granular and of the overload error is shown in Fig. 8(a), for $\sigma_y^2/\sigma_z^2 = 14.0$ dB and at two different target rates. At low β^2, the total error (solid curves) is approximated by the overload error (dashed curves); at high β^2, the total error is approximated by the granular error (dot-dashed curves). The circles indicate the optimum value of β^2 and the corresponding distortion. The optimum β^2 does not depend on the variance ratio σ_y^2/σ_z^2 but only on the coding rate R of the system. In particular, this optimum is shown in Fig. 8(b) and it is decreasing with the rate. By increasing the number of states of the trellis, Λ gets closer to a good channel code and consequently β^2 decreases; for comparison, the figure also shows $1/\alpha^2$, i.e. the lower bound for β^2.

The experimental performance loss with respect to the *distortion-rate* function $D^*(R)$ is shown in Fig. 9(a). More precisely, the measurements are relative to a CVS-based system in which the TCQ used for syndrome quantization has been optimized with an algorithm adapted from (Chou et al., 1989). Similarly to the optimum value of β, the performance loss does not depend on σ_y^2/σ_z^2; for each rate, the value shown is the average over the various values of σ_z^2 (σ_y^2/σ_z^2 is in the range $9 \div 19$ dB). The error bars show the average of the 95 % confidence intervals; for each value of σ_z^2 the confidence interval is estimated over 5000 independent simulations. The experiments show that the performance of the proposed system is within $3 \div 4$ dB from the theoretical bound at rates between 0.5 and 3.0 bit/sample. A comparison is given in Fig. 9(b) against another practical SCSI system, namely the "DISCUS" system (Pradhan & Ramchandran, 2003). By simply choosing the right scaling factor a, tuned with respect to σ_z^2, the proposed system adapts to any correlation and gives the same performance loss, while the "DISCUS" system should be optimized for different correlations. This would not be an

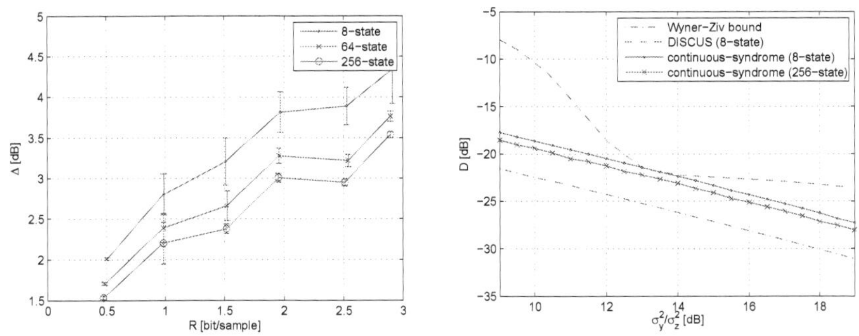

(a) performance loss (b) comparison

Fig. 9. Experimental performance of CVS-based SCSI.

easy task since it would involve the redesign of a source and of a channel code. Moreover, while only integer rates can be achieved by the "DISCUS" system, any rate can be achieved by SCSI based on CVS. This can be simply obtained by choosing the right value of b in case of syndrome coding with TCQ or using another ad-hoc source coding method for transmitting $S_{\beta\Lambda}$.

The proposed coding method turns out to be competitive with the SCSI methods in which the channel code component is a convolutional code; in addition, it allows for easy adaptation to the virtual channel statistics and to the desired transmission rate. More involved decoding algorithms for the actual case in which the virtual channel is not exactly known, and applications of this coding scheme in the video coding scenario have been proposed too and are briefly discussed in the following.

5.2 Iterative Algorithms for Unknown Virtual Channels

The factor graph approach used in Section 4 for lossless SCSI turns out to be useful for optimized CVS decoding too, in place of the simple operation given in (26). In particular, in (Cappellari, 2008) a factor graph-based decoding method is discussed for the case where the virtual channel statistics is *time-varying* and not exactly known at the encoder. More precisely, with the hypothesis of a negligible overload error such that $\tilde{X} \approx Y + \tilde{Z}$, where $\tilde{Z} \triangleq Z + Q$ is independent from Y, a doubly stochastic *hidden Markov model* (HMM) (Rabiner, 1989) is assumed for $\tilde{Z}$. The model has L states and the distribution corresponding to the j-th state is the *generalized Gaussian distribution* (GGD) $\mathcal{G}_\alpha(\mu_j, \sigma_j^2)$. The simulated n-dimensional realizations of Z^n are identified within another HMM with possibly different number of states and state variances in order to simulate a partial knowledge regarding the virtual channel; this information is used by the encoder and transmitted to the decoder (the required bit-rate is taken into account) for syndrome formation and decoding, respectively.

Since $\hat{S} = S + Q$ (we will omit subscripts for clarity) is with good approximation the syndrome corresponding to $\tilde{X} = X + Q$, $Y \to \tilde{X} \to \hat{S}$ forms a Markov chain, and optimal MAP decoding amounts to maximizing

$$f(\tilde{x}^n | y^n, \hat{s}^n) \propto f(\tilde{x}^n | y^n) f(\hat{s}^n | \tilde{x}^n) , \tag{30}$$

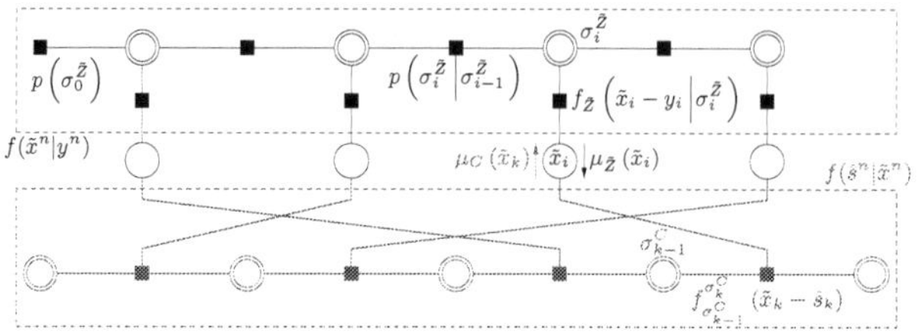

Fig. 10. Factor graph-based CVS decoding ($n = 4$).

where the terms $f(\tilde{x}^n|y^n) = f_{\tilde{Z}}(\tilde{x}^n - y^n)$ and $f(\hat{s}^n|\tilde{x}^n)$ take account of the virtual channel structure and of the syndrome formation algorithm, respectively. Once we define the *hidden state variables* $\sigma_i^{\tilde{Z}}$, the *state transition probabilities* $p\left(\sigma_i^{\tilde{Z}}\left|\sigma_{i-1}^{\tilde{Z}}\right.\right)$, and the *state probability densities* $f_{\tilde{Z}}(a|j) = \frac{\alpha/2}{\sqrt{2\Gamma(1/\alpha)^2\gamma_j^2}}\exp\left\{-\left(\frac{|a-\mu_j|}{\sqrt{2\gamma_j^2}}\right)^{\alpha}\right\}$, with $\gamma_j^2 \triangleq \sigma_j^2\Gamma(1/\alpha)/2\Gamma(3/\alpha)$, $f_{\tilde{Z}}$ is found by marginalizing

$$f_{\tilde{Z}}\left(z^n;\sigma^{\tilde{Z}}\right) = p\left(\sigma_0^{\tilde{Z}}\right) f_{\tilde{Z}}\left(z_0\left|\sigma_0^{\tilde{Z}}\right.\right)\prod_{i=1}^{m-1} p\left(\sigma_i^{\tilde{Z}}\left|\sigma_{i-1}^{\tilde{Z}}\right.\right) f_{\tilde{Z}}\left(z_i\left|\sigma_i^{\tilde{Z}}\right.\right). \tag{31}$$

The (TCQ-based) syndrome formation is instead a deterministic transformation, i.e. $f(\hat{s}^n|\tilde{x}^n)$ is a Dirac's delta function that, given $\tilde{x}^n$, reveals its syndrome. Equivalently, it is a delta function that reveals the event $\{\tilde{x}^n - \hat{s}^n \in \beta\Lambda\}$; by introducing the *trellis state variables* σ_k^C, $f(\hat{s}^n|\tilde{x}^n)$ is found marginalizing

$$f\left(\hat{s}^n;\sigma^C|\tilde{x}^n\right) = \prod_{k=0}^{m-1}\chi_{\sigma_{k-1}^C}^{\sigma_k^C}\sum_{b\in\mathcal{B}_{\sigma_{k-1}^C}^{\sigma_k^C}}\delta\left(\tilde{x}_k - \hat{s}_k - b\right), \tag{32}$$

where χ_j^l and $\mathcal{B}_j^l$ are the indicator function and the set of reconstruction values relative to the transition from state j to l, respectively.
In order to increase the independence between the information about $\tilde{X}$ brought by Y and by $\hat{S}$, the syndrome formation algorithm is operated on a randomly scrambled version of x^n, such that the actual factor graph used in CVS decoding is similar to the one sketched in Fig. 10. At the m-th iteration, *model messages* $\mu_{\tilde{Z}}^{(m)}(\tilde{x}_i)$ and *code messages* $\mu_C^{(m)}(\tilde{x}_k)$ are exchanged between the upper and the lower part of the factor-graph and viceversa, until they converge to a fixed value. The final estimate $\hat{x}^n$ for x^n is given by

$$\hat{x}_i = \arg\max_{\tilde{x}_i} f(\tilde{x}_i|y^n)f(\hat{s}^n|\tilde{x}_i). \tag{33}$$

We report some experimental results for the case where $Y \sim \mathcal{N}(0, \sigma_y^2 = 1)$ and Z is a 3-state Gaussian Markov process ($\alpha = 2$). The distortion-rate function obtained with traditional ML

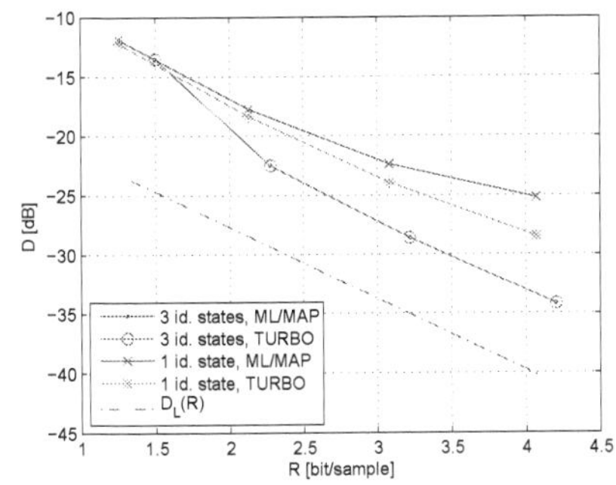

Fig. 11. Experimental results for factor graph-based CVS decoding; $D_L(R)$ is an estimate of the theoretical distortion-rate function of the considered SCSI problem.

decoding, with MAP decoding (i.e. considering only one iteration in the decoding process), and with TURBO decoding (i.e. at convergence) are measured. The syndrome is uniformly quantized and entropy coded for transmission at the decoder; 1000 sequences of $n = 1000$ samples each are generated. If the encoder has knowledge about the virtual channel statistics (i.e. the same model is artificially used for hidden state identification[8]), the TURBO decoding algorithm does not perform any better than the MAP decoding algorithm, that in turn was shown to perform like the ML decoding (at least in the Gaussian case). If a single-state HMM is used for hidden state identification (i.e. the encoder only knows the average variance of Z), the MAP decoding performs again like the ML decoding, but TURBO decoding leads to about one order of magnitude less reconstruction errors, which translate into an up to 3 dB decrease of the mean error variance (see Fig. 11) at bit-rates $R = 3 \div 4$ bit/sample.

5.3 Video Coding Applications

Traditional video coding standards, e.g. H.264/AVC (ITU-T & ISO/IEC: JTC1/SC29/WG11, 2007), are based on *predictive* coding for exploiting the high temporal correlation between adjacent frames. This implies that (i) the algorithms used during encoding are computationally heavy with respect to the ones used at the decoder, and (ii) the coded representation is very sensible to possible packet losses on the transmission channel. To alleviate these problems, in order to permit effective video encoding and transmission on wireless and battery-operated devices, several research groups have recently explored SCSI-based methods for video compression. A review on these methods can be found in (Girod et al., 2005).

In practice, a frame is encoded assuming that some adjacent frames are already available as SI at the decoder. Hence, (i) the encoding algorithm is more light since it does not exploit the *inter-frame* correlation, and (ii) packet losses are not so bad as long as several adjacent frames are stored at the decoder that can be used as SI.

The CVS method has been applied to video coding in (Cappellari, 2007; Cappellari & Mian, 2006a). In particular, it has been tested in both the *discrete cosine transform* (DCT) and the *discrete wavelet transform* (DWT) domain. In both cases, every other frame is sent as an *intra-frame* (without referencing any adjacent frame); the remaining ones are sent as inter-frames. The decoder performs *motion compensated interpolation* for each couple of consecutive intra-frames

[8] There may be still uncertainties about the *actual* hidden states.

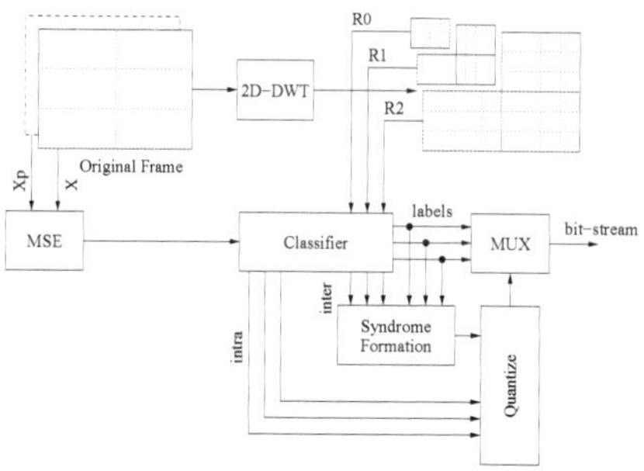

(a) DWT-domain encoder

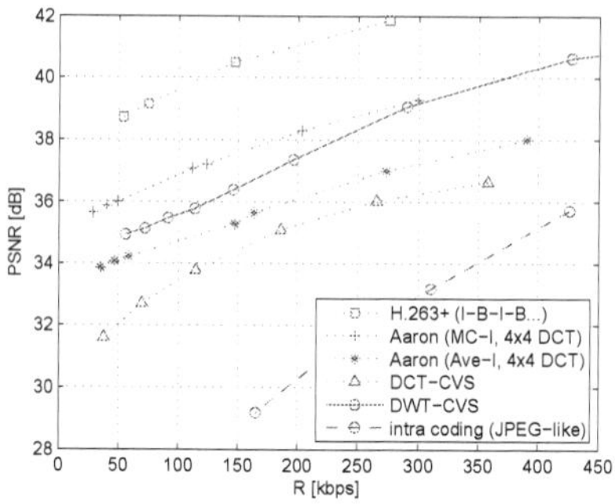

(b) performance comparison

Fig. 12. Scheme of the proposed DWT-domain CVS-based video coding method and performance of different video codecs, averaged on the first 100 frames of the sequence foreman (QCIF resolution) at 25 frames per second (data relative to intra frames are not taken into account).

in order to construct the SI for decoding the inter-frame between them. In the DCT case, inter-frames are partitioned into 8×8 blocks of *pixels* and the DCT coefficients corresponding to the lower spatial frequencies of each block form the signal to be coded relying on co-positioned coefficients of the SI; the remaining coefficients are sent in intra mode. In the DWT case (see Fig. 12(a)), the DWT coefficients are classified into the classes intra, inter, and *skip*, for coefficients that are expected to have little, medium and high correlation with the co-positioned coefficients of the SI, respectively. Intra coefficients are sent in intra mode, no information is sent for the skip coefficients (the corresponding SI is taken directly as reconstruction), and the remaining ones form the signal to be coded using SI.

Classification and correlation estimation are in both cases performed using the block-based MSE between the inter-frame to be coded and the previous one. These estimates are used for proper TCQ-based syndrome formation and decoding. Syndromes are quantized with an *embedded* uniform quantizer, such that *quality scalable* reconstruction is achieved at the decoder. The typical performance of the proposed coders is shown in Fig. 12(b) and compared with results from (Aaron et al., 2004); the average *peak signal-to-noise ratio* (PSNR) is reported as a function of the average transmission rate. The DWT-CVS coder outperforms both the DCT-CVS coder and one of the coders (Ave-I) from (Aaron et al., 2004), while being very close to the other solution (MC-I). The superiority of this (turbo code-based) method is probably due to the utilization of a feedback channel between decoder and encoder for estimation of the actual SI-source correlation. This solution is very good for this purpose, but also highly unpractical with respect to correlation estimation at the encoder only.

6. Conclusion and Future Research

In this chapter, we presented the SCSI problem and discussed several practical solutions. Our main contribution is the coding method based on continuous-valued syndromes, which is an embodiment of the theoretically optimal superposition coding approach. We showed that this coding method is very practical due to the separation between channel and source coding.

In particular, we showed that it can be quite performing in the actual scenarios, where for example the actual source-SI correlation is not exactly known and/or very complex, as in the case of video coding.
In practice, despite its optimality, the superposition coding approach for SCSI suffers some performance loss because there are currently no efficient algorithms for source coding over codes with a "random structure". Indeed, a good channel code should be used as coarse code, but all good channel codes have this "random structure" (e.g. turbo codes rely on random interleaving). Convolutional codes are less performing but are still the best ones for which a good closest neighbor search algorithm exists. In the future, it may be possible that message-passing algorithms will be developed that permit quantization over *sparse* codes that are good for channel coding; some effort in this direction is discussed in (Ciliberti et al., 2005; Martinian & Yedidia, 2003).
In the near future, we plan to be more concerned with the problem of correlation estimation in the actual SCSI scenarios. In fact, all SCSI schemes proposed in literature are usually investigated under the hypothesis of a toy virtual channel $Y = X + Z$ in which the statistics of Z is known at the encoder and at the decoder. But in practice the source-SI correlation is not known and is more complex, so that by using these simple assumptions we incur into some performance degradation. For example, the performance of the SCSI-based video coders is still under the one of the traditional coders, at least in the scenarios with no losses on the transmission channel. We hope that our investigative efforts into statistical model aided decoding could be eventually used towards improving the efficacy of SCSI-based coding not only in video coding applications, but also in several other practical cases.

7. References

Aaron, A. & Girod, B. (2002). Compression with side information using turbo codes, *Proc. of IEEE Data Compression Conf.*, pp. 252–261.

Aaron, A., Rane, S., Setton, E. & Girod, B. (2004). Transform-domain Wyner-Ziv codec for video, *Proc. Visual Commun. and Image Proc. (VCIP-2004)*, San Jose, CA, USA.

Bahl, L., Cocke, J., Jelinek, F. & Raviv, J. (1974). Optimal decoding of linear codes for minimizing symbol error rate, *IEEE Trans. Inf. Theory* **20**(2): 284–287.

Bennatan, A., Burshtein, D., Caire, G. & Shamai, S. (2006). Superposition coding for side-information channels, *IEEE Trans. Inf. Theory* **52**(5): 1872–1889.

Berrou, C. & Glavieux, A. (1996). Near optimum error correcting coding and decoding: turbo-codes, *IEEE Trans. Commun.* **44**(10): 1261–1271.

Cappellari, L. (2007). Wavelet-domain distributed video coding based on continuous-valued syndromes, *Proc. of European Signal Process. Conf. (EUSIPCO)*, Poznań, Poland, pp. 1422–1426.

Cappellari, L. (2008). Statistical model-aided decoding of continuous-valued syndromes for source coding with side information, *Proc. of European Signal Process. Conf. (EUSIPCO)*, Lausanne, Switzerland.

Cappellari, L. (2009). On superposition coding for the Wyner-Ziv problem.
URL: *http://arxiv.org/pdf/0904.0879*

Cappellari, L. & De Giusti, A. (2008). Binary data compression with and without side information at the decoder: the syndrome-based approach using off-the-shelf turbo codecs.
URL: *http://arxiv.org/pdf/0902.0562*

Cappellari, L. & Mian, G. A. (2006a). An algorithm for intra-frame video coding based on continuous-valued syndromes, *Conf. Rec. of 40th IEEE Asilomar Conf. on Signals, Syst. and Comput.*, Pacific Grove, CA, U.S.A., pp. 1090–1094.

Cappellari, L. & Mian, G. A. (2006b). A practical algorithm for distributed source coding based on continuous-valued syndromes, *Proc. of European Signal Process. Conf. (EUSIPCO)*, Florence, Italy.

Chou, P. A., Lookabaugh, T. & Gray, R. M. (1989). Entropy-constrained vector quantization, *IEEE Trans. Acoust., Speech, Signal Process.* **37**(1): 31–42.

Ciliberti, S., Mezard, M. & Zecchina, R. (2005). Message passing algorithms for non-linear nodes and data compression.
URL: *http://arxiv.org/pdf/cond-mat/0508723*

Cover, T. M. & Thomas, J. A. (2006). *Elements of Information Theory*, John Wiley & Sons, Inc., Hoboken, NJ, USA.

Garcia-Frias, J. & Zhao, Y. (2001). Compression of correlated binary sources using turbo codes, *IEEE Commun. Lett.* **5**(10): 417–419.

Gel'fand, S. & Pinsker, M. (1980). Coding for channel with random parameters, *Probl. Contr. Inf. Theory* **9**(1): 19–31.

Girod, B., Aaron, A. M., Rane, S. & Rebollo-Monedero, D. (2005). Distributed video coding, *Proc. IEEE* **93**(1): 71–83.

ITU-T & ISO/IEC: JTC1/SC29/WG11 (2007). Advanced video coding for generic audiovisual services, ITU-T Recommendation H.264, ISO/IEC 14496-10 (MPEG-4 AVC). (including SVC extension).

Kschischang, F. R., Frey, B. J. & Loeliger, H.-A. (2001). Factor graphs and the sum-product algorithm, *IEEE Trans. Inf. Theory* **47**(2): 498–519.

Liu, Z., Cheng, S., Liveris, A. D. & Xiong, Z. (2006). Slepian-Wolf coded nested lattice quantization for Wyner-Ziv coding: High-rate performance analysis and code design, *IEEE Trans. Inf. Theory* **52**(10): 4358–4379.

Liveris, A. D., Xiong, Z. & Georghiades, C. N. (2002). Compression of binary sources with side information at the decoder using LDPC codes, *IEEE Commun. Lett.* **6**(10): 440–442.

Liveris, A. D., Xiong, Z. & Georghiades, C. N. (2003). Distributed compression of binary sources using conventional parallel and serial concatenated convolutional codes, *Proc. of IEEE Data Compression Conf.*, pp. 193–202.

MacKay, D. (1999). Good error-correcting codes based on very sparse matrices, *IEEE Trans. Inf. Theory* **45**(2): 399–431.

Marcellin, M. W. (1994). On entropy-constrained trellis coded quantization, *IEEE Trans. Commun.* **42**(1): 14–16.

Marcellin, M. W. & Fisher, T. R. (1990). Trellis coded quantization of memoryless and Gauss-Markov sources, *IEEE Trans. Commun.* **38**(1): 82–93.

Martinian, E. & Yedidia, J. S. (2003). Iterative quantization using codes on graphs, *Proc. of 41st Annual Allerton Conf. on Commun., Control and Comput.*, pp. 1317–1326.

Pradhan, S. S., Chou, J. & Ramchandran, K. (2003). Duality between source coding and channel coding and its extension to the side information case, *IEEE Trans. Inf. Theory* **49**(5): 1181–1203.

Pradhan, S. S. & Ramchandran, K. (1999). Distributed source coding using syndromes (DISCUS): design and construction, *Proc. of IEEE Data Compression Conf.*, pp. 158–167.

Pradhan, S. S. & Ramchandran, K. (2003). Distributed source coding using syndromes (DISCUS): design and construction, *IEEE Trans. Inf. Theory* **49**(3): 626–643.

Pradhan, S. S. & Ramchandran, K. (2005). Generalized coset codes for distributed binning, *IEEE Trans. Inf. Theory* **51**(10): 3457–3474.

Rabiner, L. R. (1989). A tutorial on hidden Markov models and selected applications in speech recognition, *Proc. IEEE* **77**(2): 257–286.

Roumy, A., Lajnef, K. & Guillemot, C. (2007). Rate-adaptive turbo-syndrome scheme for slepian-wolf coding, *Conf. Rec. of 41st IEEE Asilomar Conf. on Signals, Syst. and Comput.*, pp. 545–549.

Servetto, S. D. (2007). Lattice quantization with side information: Codes, asymptotics, and applications in sensor networks, *IEEE Trans. Inf. Theory* **53**(2): 714–731.

Shannon, C. E. (1948). A mathematical theory of communication, *The Bell Syst. Tech. J.* **27**: 379–423, 623–656.

Shannon, C. E. (1959). Coding theorems for a discrete source with a fidelity criterion, *IRE Convention Record*, Vol. 4, pp. 142–163.

Slepian, D. & Wolf, J. K. (1973). Noiseless coding of correlated information sources, *IEEE Trans. Inf. Theory* **19**(4): 471–480.

Stanković, V., Liveris, A. D., Xiong, Z. & Georghiades, C. N. (2006). On code design for the Slepian-Wolf problem and lossless multiterminal networks, *IEEE Trans. Inf. Theory* **52**(4): 1495–1507.

Tu, Z., Li, J. & Blum, R. S. (2005). An efficient SF-ISF approach for the Slepian-Wolf source coding problem, *EURASIP J. Appl. Signal Process.* **2005**(6): 961–971.

Wagner, A. B., Tavildar, S. & Viswanath, P. (2008). Rate region of the quadratic gaussian two-encoder source-coding problem, *IEEE Trans. Inf. Theory* **54**(5): 1938–1961.

Wyner, A. D. (1974). Recent results in the Shannon theory, *IEEE Trans. Inf. Theory* **20**(1): 2–10.

Wyner, A. D. & Ziv, J. (1976). The rate-distortion function for source coding with side information at the decoder, *IEEE Trans. Inf. Theory* **22**(1): 1–10.

Yang, Y., Stanković, V., Xiong, Z. & Zhao, W. (2008). On multiterminal source code design, *IEEE Trans. Inf. Theory* **54**(5): 2278–2302.

Zamir, R. (1996). The rate loss in the Wyner-Ziv problem, *IEEE Trans. Inf. Theory* **42**(6): 2073–2084.

Zamir, R. & Feder, M. (1996). On lattice quantization noise, *IEEE Trans. Inf. Theory* **42**(4): 1152–1159.

Zamir, R., Shamai, S. & Erez, U. (2002). Nested linear/lattice codes for structured multiterminal binning, *IEEE Trans. Inf. Theory* **48**(6): 1250–1276.

19

Crystal-like Symmetric Sensor Arrangements for Blind Decorrelation of Isotropic Wavefield

Nobutaka Ono and Shigeki Sagayama
The University of Tokyo
JAPAN

1. Introduction

Sensor array technique has been widely used for measuring various types of wavefields such as acoustic waves, mechanical vibrations, and electromagnetic waves (1). A common goal of array signal processing is estimating locations of sources or separating source signals based on multiple observations. For obtaining efficient spatial information, the geometrical arrangement of sensors is one of the significant issues in this field. An uniform linear array is the most popular and fundamental one (2; 3), and suiting with purposes, various types of arrays have been considered such as circular, planar, cross-shaped, cylindrical, and spherical arrays.
In this chapter, we discuss the sensor arrangements from a new viewpoint: correlation between channels. Generally, multiply-observed signals have correlation each other, and it becomes larger especially in a small-sized array. In the case, observed signals themselves are not efficient representation due to redundancy between channels. Although they are uncorrelated by appropriate basis transformation, which is corresponding to the diagonalization of the covariance matrix, it depends on the observed wavefield.
However, in isotropic wavefield, there exist special geometrical sensor arrangements, and observed signals by them are commonly uncorrelated by a fixed basis transform. The significances of isotropic wavefield decorrelation are as follows.

- If there is no a priori knowledge to wavefield, the isotropic assumption is simple and natural. It means spatial stationarity.
- It is well known that Fourier coefficients of a temporally stationary periodic signal are uncorrelated each other. The isotropic wavefield decorrelation can be considered as a spatial version of it and decorrelated components represent something like *spatial spectra*.
- The decorrelated representation are also useful for encoding because redundancy between channels is removed.
- It can be applied for several kinds of estimation methods in isotropic noise field such as power spectrum estimation (4), noise reduction (5), and inverse filtering (6).
- The isotropy assumption can be valid even if wavefield is disturbed by sensor array itself. Suppose that microphone array is mounted on a rigid sphere. Although the rigid sphere disturbs acoustic field, due to the symmetry of sphere, the isotropy is still hold.

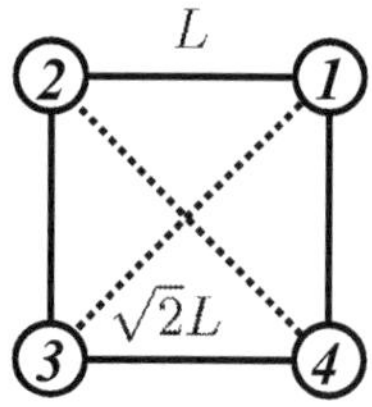

Fig. 1. Square

Although our main concern lies on microphone array, this technique can be applied for different kinds of wavefield sensing. In the following, we mathematically discuss possible sensor arrangements for blind decorrelation.

2. Problem Formulation

Let's consider isotropic wavefield is observed by M sensors. Let $x_m(t)$ be a signal observed by the mth sensor, $X_m(\omega)$ be its Fourier transform, and $\boldsymbol{X}(\omega) = (X_1(\omega)\ X_2(\omega)\ \cdots\ X_M(\omega))^t$ be the vector representation, respectively, where ^{t} denotes transpose operation. The isotropic assumption leads: 1) the power spectrum is the same on each sensor, and 2) the cross spectrum is determined by only a distance between sensors. Under them, by normalizing diagonal elements to unit, the covariance matrix $V(\omega)$ of the observation vector $\boldsymbol{X}(\omega)$ is represented as

$$V(\omega) = E[\boldsymbol{X}(\omega)\boldsymbol{X}(\omega)^h] = \begin{pmatrix} 1 & \Gamma(r_{12},\omega) & \cdots & \Gamma(r_{1n},\omega) \\ \Gamma(r_{21},\omega) & 1 & \cdots & \Gamma(r_{2n},\omega) \\ \vdots & \vdots & \ddots & \vdots \\ \Gamma(r_{n1},\omega) & \Gamma(r_{n2},\omega) & \cdots & 1 \end{pmatrix}, \tag{1}$$

where $E[\cdot]$ denotes expectation operation, ^{h} denotes Hermite transpose, r_{ij} is the distance between sensor i and j, and $\Gamma(r,\omega)$ represents the spatial coherence function of the wavefield (3). Under the isotropic assumption, $V(\omega)$ is a symmetry matrix since $r_{ij} = r_{ji}$. Then, there exist an orthogonal matrix U for diagonalizing $V(\omega)$. Our goal here is to find special sensor arrangements and corresponding unitary matrices U such that $U^t V(\omega) U$ is constantly diagonal for any coherence function $\Gamma(r,\omega)$. We call this kind of decorrelation *blind decorrelation* because we don't have to know each element of $V(\omega)$ and the diagonalization matrix U is determined by only sensor arrangements. For simplicity, we hereafter omit ω and represents the covariance matrix of the observation vector by just V.
Intuitively, it seems to be impossible since a diagonalization matrix U generally depends on the elements of V. But suppose that four sensors are arrayed at vertices of a square. There are only two distances among the vertices in a square: one is the length of a line L, another is the length of a diagonal $\sqrt{2}L$. Then, numbering sensors circularly shown in Fig. 1 and letting $a = \Gamma(L,\omega)$ and $b = \Gamma(\sqrt{2}L,\omega)$, the covariance matrix is represented as the following form

$$V = \begin{pmatrix} 1 & a & b & a \\ a & 1 & a & b \\ b & a & 1 & a \\ a & b & a & 1 \end{pmatrix} \tag{2}$$

for any ω and any coherence function $\Gamma(r,\omega)$. Since it is a circulant matrix, it is diagonalized by the fourth order DFT matrix Z_4 or its real-valued version $\tilde{Z}_4$ defined by

$$\tilde{Z}_4 = \begin{pmatrix} \frac{1}{2}\cos\frac{2\pi\cdot 0\cdot 0}{4} & \frac{1}{\sqrt{2}}\cos\frac{2\pi\cdot 1\cdot 0}{4} & \frac{1}{\sqrt{2}}\sin\frac{2\pi\cdot 1\cdot 0}{4} & \frac{1}{2}\cos\frac{2\pi\cdot 2\cdot 0}{4} \\ \frac{1}{2}\cos\frac{2\pi\cdot 0\cdot 1}{4} & \frac{1}{\sqrt{2}}\cos\frac{2\pi\cdot 1\cdot 1}{4} & \frac{1}{\sqrt{2}}\sin\frac{2\pi\cdot 1\cdot 1}{4} & \frac{1}{2}\cos\frac{2\pi\cdot 2\cdot 1}{4} \\ \frac{1}{2}\cos\frac{2\pi\cdot 0\cdot 2}{4} & \frac{1}{\sqrt{2}}\cos\frac{2\pi\cdot 1\cdot 2}{4} & \frac{1}{\sqrt{2}}\sin\frac{2\pi\cdot 1\cdot 2}{4} & \frac{1}{2}\cos\frac{2\pi\cdot 2\cdot 2}{4} \\ \frac{1}{2}\cos\frac{2\pi\cdot 0\cdot 3}{4} & \frac{1}{\sqrt{2}}\cos\frac{2\pi\cdot 1\cdot 3}{4} & \frac{1}{\sqrt{2}}\sin\frac{2\pi\cdot 1\cdot 3}{4} & \frac{1}{2}\cos\frac{2\pi\cdot 2\cdot 3}{4} \end{pmatrix} \quad (3)$$

$$= \begin{pmatrix} 1/2 & 1/\sqrt{2} & 0 & 1/2 \\ 1/2 & 0 & 1/\sqrt{2} & -1/2 \\ 1/2 & -1/\sqrt{2} & 0 & 1/2 \\ 1/2 & 0 & -1/\sqrt{2} & -1/2 \end{pmatrix} \quad (4)$$

such as

$$\tilde{Z}_4^t V \tilde{Z}_4 = \begin{pmatrix} 2a+b+1 & 0 & 0 & 0 \\ 0 & -b+1 & 0 & 0 \\ 0 & 0 & -b+1 & 0 \\ 0 & 0 & 0 & -2a+b+1 \end{pmatrix}. \quad (5)$$

This diagonalization can be performed at any frequency ω because $\tilde{Z}_4$ is independent of a and b. It means the following basis-transformed observations:

$$y_1(t) = x_1(t) + x_2(t) + x_3(t) + x_4(t) \quad (6)$$
$$y_2(t) = x_1(t) - x_3(t) \quad (7)$$
$$y_3(t) = x_2(t) - x_4(t) \quad (8)$$
$$y_4(t) = x_1(t) - x_2(t) + x_3(t) - x_4(t) \quad (9)$$

are uncorrelated each other in any isotropic field. The problem we concern here is a generalization of it.

If $U^t V U$ is diagonalized as

$$U^t V U = \begin{pmatrix} \gamma_1 & 0 & \cdots & 0 \\ 0 & \gamma_2 & \cdots & 0 \\ \vdots & \vdots & \ddots & \vdots \\ 0 & 0 & \cdots & \gamma_M \end{pmatrix}, \quad (10)$$

V is represented as

$$V = U \begin{pmatrix} \gamma_1 & 0 & \cdots & 0 \\ 0 & \gamma_2 & \cdots & 0 \\ \vdots & \vdots & \ddots & \vdots \\ 0 & 0 & \cdots & \gamma_M \end{pmatrix} U^t. \quad (11)$$

Then, for blind decorrelation, one of the necessary conditions is that V is represented by only M parameters $(\gamma_1 \cdots \gamma_M)$ at most. It means there should exist at most M kinds of distances between sensors. Generally, when sensor arrangement has some symmetry, the number of kinds

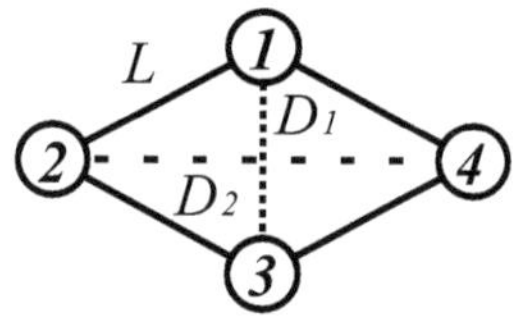

Fig. 2. Argyle

of distances between sensors is smaller. But what kind of symmetry the sensor arrangement should have for blind decorrelation is not trivial. For instance, suppose an argyle arrangement shown in Fig. 2. An argyle is one of symmetrical shapes and there are three kinds of distances among sensors. In arranging sensors shown in Fig. 2, the covariance matrix has the following form:

$$V = \begin{pmatrix} 1 & a & b & a \\ a & 1 & a & c \\ b & a & 1 & a \\ a & c & a & 1 \end{pmatrix}. \tag{12}$$

Despite of the symmetry of argyle, there are no matrices U for diagonalizing V in eq. (12) independent of a, b and c. It can be easily checked as the following (7). V in eq. (12) is decomposed as

$$V = I + aP_1 + bP_2 + cP_3 \tag{13}$$

where I is an identity matrix and

$$P_1 = \begin{pmatrix} 0 & 1 & 0 & 1 \\ 1 & 0 & 1 & 0 \\ 0 & 1 & 0 & 1 \\ 1 & 0 & 1 & 0 \end{pmatrix}, \tag{14}$$

$$P_2 = \begin{pmatrix} 0 & 0 & 1 & 0 \\ 0 & 0 & 0 & 0 \\ 1 & 0 & 0 & 0 \\ 0 & 0 & 0 & 0 \end{pmatrix}, \tag{15}$$

$$P_3 = \begin{pmatrix} 0 & 0 & 0 & 0 \\ 0 & 0 & 0 & 1 \\ 0 & 0 & 0 & 0 \\ 0 & 1 & 0 & 0 \end{pmatrix}. \tag{16}$$

For diagonalizing V by an unitary matrix U independently of a, b and c, it is necessary that P_1, P_2 and P_3 have to be jointly diagonalized, which is equivalent to the condition that P_1, P_2 and P_3 are commutative each other. However,

$$P_1P_2 - P_2P_1 = \begin{pmatrix} 0 & 1 & 0 & 1 \\ -1 & 0 & -1 & 0 \\ 0 & 1 & 0 & 1 \\ -1 & 0 & -1 & 0 \end{pmatrix}, \tag{17}$$

which means P_1 and P_2 are not commutative. Therefore, there are no matrices U to jointly diagonalize P_1 and P_2. More rigorous mathematical discussion is described in (7).

Note that the finding possible sensor arrangements for blind decorrelation includes two kinds of problems. One is what a matrix represented by several parameters is diagonalized independently of the values of the parameters, and the other is whether a corresponding sensor arrangement to the matrix exists or not. For example,

$$V = \begin{pmatrix} 1 & a & a & a & a \\ a & 1 & a & a & a \\ a & a & 1 & a & a \\ a & a & a & 1 & a \\ a & a & a & a & 1 \end{pmatrix} \tag{18}$$

is diagonalized by the DFT matrix Z_5 independently of a since V in eq. (18) is a kind of circulant matrix. However, eq. (18) means that each different pair of five sensors has the same distance, which cannot be realized in 3-D space.

3. Crystal Arrays

3.1 Necessary Condition

First, we begin with the following lemma.

Lemma 1. *A necessary condition for V defined by eq. (1) to be diagonalized by an unitary matrix U for any function $\Gamma(r,\omega)$, is that a set of distances from the sensor i to others: $\{r_{i1}, r_{i2}, \cdots, r_{in}\}$ is identical for any i.*

Proof: If V is diagonalized by an unitary matrix U without dependence on $\Gamma(r,\omega)$, the matrix I_n, of which all elements are identical to 1, is also diagonalized by U since I_n is obtained by letting $\Gamma(r,\omega) = 1$. Then, V and I_n are commutative. From (i,j) element of $VI_n = I_nV$, we see that

$$\sum_{k=1}^{n} \Gamma(\omega, r_{ik}) = \sum_{k=1}^{n} \Gamma(\omega, r_{jk}) \tag{19}$$

has to be an identical equation of r_{ij}s. It means that a distance set: $\{r_{ij} | j = 1, 2, \cdots n\}$ must be identical for any i. ■

A square arrangement surely satisfies Lemma 1 since a set of distances from the sensor i to others is represented as $\{0, L, L, \sqrt{2}L\}$, which is identical to any i ($i = 1,2,3,4$). While, in an argyle arrangement, a set of distances is $\{0, L, L, D_1\}$ from the sensor 1, and it is $\{0, L, L, D_2\}$ from the sensor 2. Thus, an argyle arrangement does't satisfy Lemma 1.

Lemma 1 directly gives a necessary condition of sensor arrangements for the blind decorrelation, but it is not a sufficient condition. Actually, there exist arrangements which satisfies Lemma 1 but cannot be used for the blind decorrelation. An example is shown in Fig. 3. The shape is obtained by merging vertices of two triangles with the same center and a different angle in the same plane, denoted as a bi-triangle.

In a bi-triangle arrangement, there are four kinds of distances between sensors: a short and a long line, and two kind of diagonals. The corresponding covariance matrix V is represented by

$$V = \begin{pmatrix} 1 & a & a & b & c & d \\ a & 1 & a & d & b & c \\ a & a & 1 & c & d & b \\ b & d & c & 1 & a & a \\ c & b & d & a & 1 & a \\ d & c & b & a & a & 1 \end{pmatrix}. \tag{20}$$

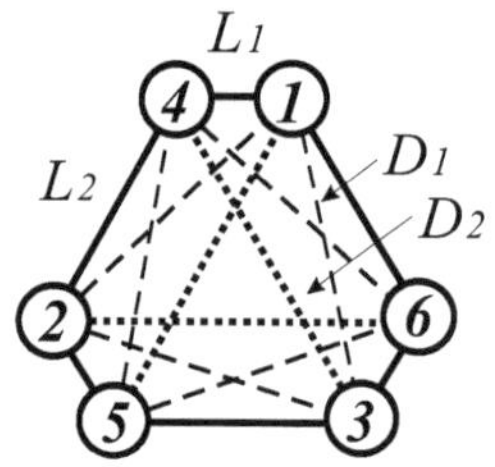

Fig. 3. Bi-triangle

This arrangement obviously satisfies Lemma 1 since a set of distances from a sensor to others is identically represented as $\{0, L_1, L_2, L_2, D_1, D_2, D_2\}$, but there is no matrices for diagonalizing U in eq. (20).

Although it is not straightforward from lemma 1 to a specific sensor arrangement, we have found five classes of sensor arrangements for blind decorrelation up to now (4; 8). According to the geometrical resemblance with crystals, we call them *crystal arrays*.

3.2 Five classes of crystal arrays

1) Regular polygons

Let *circ* denote a circulant matrix as

$$\mathrm{circ}(1, a, b) = \begin{pmatrix} 1 & a & b \\ b & 1 & a \\ a & b & 1 \end{pmatrix}. \tag{21}$$

In arraying sensors on vertices of a n-sided regular polygon, circularly numbering them as shown in Fig. 4 yields a circulant $V = \mathrm{circ}(1\ a_1\ a_2 \cdots a_2\ a_1)$. As well known, it is diagonalized by n-th order DFT matrix Z_n (9). Note that as a matrix to diagonalize V, we can choose a real-valued version of Z_n as shown in eq. (4), instead of Z_n itself, which leads simple basis transform in time domain discussed in section 2.

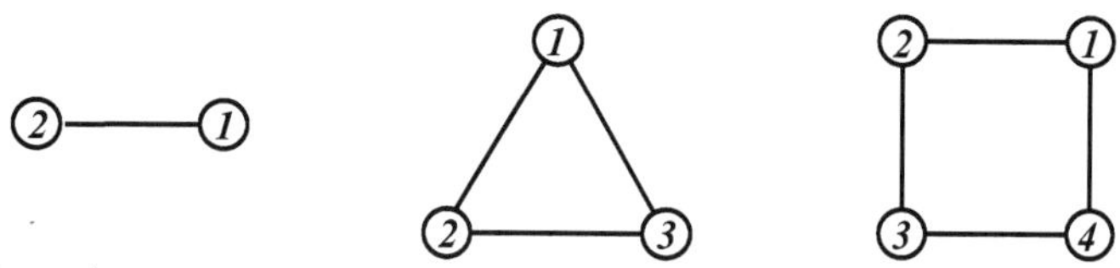

Fig. 4. Regular polygons

2) Rectangular

The second class consists of only a rectangular. Under numbering sensors as shown in Fig. 5, V has a block-circulant structure as

$$V = \begin{pmatrix} F_1 & F_2 \\ F_2 & F_1 \end{pmatrix}, \tag{22}$$

where F_1 and F_2 are 2×2 circulant matrices. It is diagonalized by $U = Z_2 \otimes Z_2$.

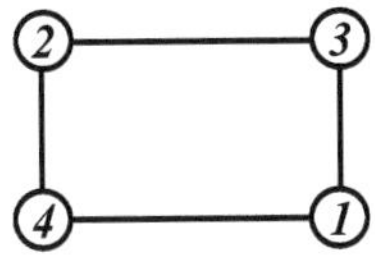

Fig. 5. Rectangular

3) Regular polygonal prisms

The regular polygonal prism arrangement is given by merging vertices of two parallel n-sided polygons with the same center axis. As the rectangular case, V has a block-circulant structure as

$$V = \begin{pmatrix} F_1 & F_2 \\ F_2 & F_1 \end{pmatrix}, \tag{23}$$

where F_1 and F_2 are $n \times n$ circulant matrices. It is diagonalized by

$$U = Z_n \otimes Z_2 = \begin{pmatrix} Z_n & Z_n \\ Z_n & -Z_n \end{pmatrix}. \tag{24}$$

The two parallel n-sided polygon may have a certain different angle, which yields a twisted prism as shown in Fig. 6. In $n = 2$, any angles are allowable, which the matrix structure is invariant for. In $n \geq 3$, only the rotation with π/n is allowable, where V becomes simply circular by alternative numbering in the top and the bottom n-sided polygon as shown in Fig. 6.

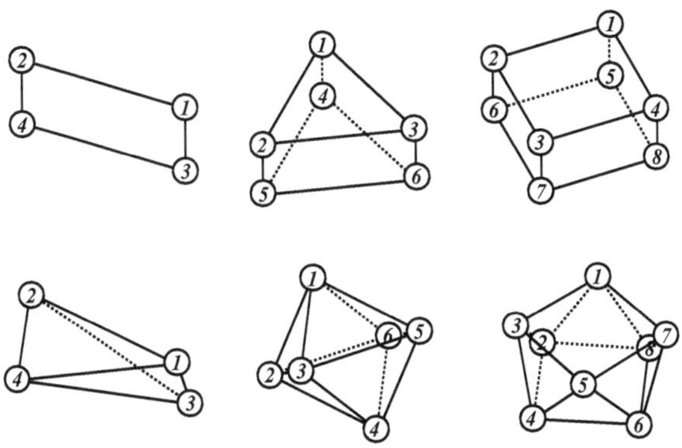

Fig. 6. Regular polygonal prisms (upper) and their twisted versions (lower)

4) Rectangular solid

In related to a rectangular, a rectangular solid forms another class. By numbering sensors shown in Fig. 7, V has the following structure:

$$V = \begin{pmatrix} F_1 & F_2 & F_3 & F_4 \\ F_2 & F_1 & F_4 & F_3 \\ F_3 & F_4 & F_1 & F_2 \\ F_4 & F_3 & F_2 & F_1 \end{pmatrix}, \tag{25}$$

where F_i $(i = 1, 2, 3, 4)$ are 2×2 circulant matrices. V itself is not circulant but it has recursively circulant structure. Hence, it is diagonalized by $U = Z_2 \otimes Z_2 \otimes Z_2$.

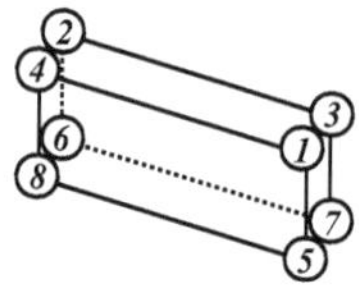

Fig. 7. A rectangular solid

5) Regular polyhedrons

As well known, there are only five polyhedrons in a 3D space: tetrahedron, octahedron, hexahedron, icosahedron, and dodecahedron, and they form the last class. From the viewpoint of the covariance matrix form, the tetrahedron is a special case of a twisted 2-sided polygonal prism, while the octahedron and the hexahedron are a special case of twisted 3-sided and 4-sided polygonal prisms, respectively. The most difficult cases are given by the icosahedron and the dodecahedron arrangements.

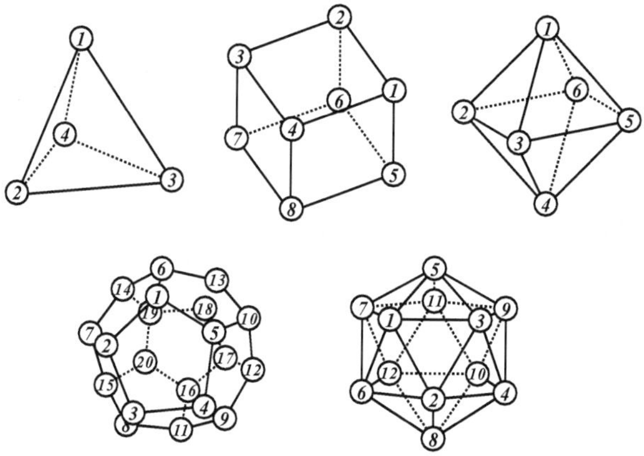

Fig. 8. Polyhedrons

An icosahedron has twenty equilateral triangular faces. Let two opposed triangles be the top and the bottom faces. Then, all vertices lie in four parallel planes. Numbering vertices circularly in the top plane, and then, from the top to the bottom in order as shown in Fig. 8, we have

$$V = \begin{pmatrix} F_1 & F_2 & F_3 & F_4 \\ F_2 & F_5 & F_6 & F_3 \\ F_3 & F_6 & F_5 & F_2 \\ F_4 & F_3 & F_2 & F_1 \end{pmatrix}, \tag{26}$$

where

$$F_1 = \mathrm{circ}(1\ a\ a), \quad F_2 = \mathrm{circ}(b\ a\ a), \tag{27}$$
$$F_3 = \mathrm{circ}(a\ b\ b), \quad F_4 = \mathrm{circ}(c\ b\ b), \tag{28}$$
$$F_5 = \mathrm{circ}(1\ b\ b), \quad F_6 = \mathrm{circ}(c\ a\ a). \tag{29}$$

Unlike the other cases, V doesn't have the circulant structure. Taking into consideration that 1) F_i $(1 \le i \le 6)$ is diagonalized by Z_3 (the 3rd order DFT matrix) and 2) the block structure is different between the first, fourth columns and the second, third columns, we assume that U has the following form:

$$U = \begin{pmatrix} Z_3 & Z_3 & Z_3 & Z_3 \\ Z_3P_3 & Z_3Q_3 & -Z_3R_3 & -Z_3S_3 \\ Z_3P_3 & Z_3Q_3 & Z_3R_3 & Z_3S_3 \\ Z_3 & Z_3 & -Z_3 & -Z_3 \end{pmatrix}, \tag{30}$$

where P_3, Q_3, R_3, and S_3 are diagonal matrices. Eq. (30) yields

$$Z^H V Z = \begin{pmatrix} K_1 & A & O & O \\ A & K_2 & O & O \\ O & O & K_3 & B \\ O & O & B & K_4 \end{pmatrix}, \tag{31}$$

where K_i $(1 \le i \le 4)$ are diagonal matrices with the size of 3×3 and

$$\begin{aligned} A &= (G_1 + G_2Q_3 + G_3Q_3 + G_4) + P_3(G_2 + G_5Q_3 + G_6Q_3 + G_3) \\ &\quad + P_3(G_3 + G_6Q_3 + G_5Q_3 + G_2) + (G_4 + G_3Q_3 + G_2Q_3 + G_1), \end{aligned} \tag{32}$$
$$\begin{aligned} B &= (G_1 - G_2S_3 + G_3S_3 - G_4) - R_3(G_2 - G_5S_3 + G_6S_3 - G_3) \\ &\quad + R_3(G_3 - G_6S_3 + G_5S_3 - G_2) - (G_4 - G_3S_3 + G_2S_3 - G_1), \end{aligned} \tag{33}$$

$$G_1 = \mathrm{diag}(1+2a\ \ 1-a\ \ 1-a), \tag{34}$$
$$G_2 = \mathrm{diag}(2a+b\ \ b-a\ \ b-a), \tag{35}$$
$$G_3 = \mathrm{diag}(a+2b\ \ a-b\ \ a-b), \tag{36}$$
$$G_4 = \mathrm{diag}(2b+c\ \ c-b\ \ c-b), \tag{37}$$
$$G_5 = \mathrm{diag}(1+2b\ \ 1-b\ \ 1-b), \tag{38}$$
$$G_6 = \mathrm{diag}(2a+c\ \ c-a\ \ c-a), \tag{39}$$

where *diag* denote a diagonal matrix as

$$\mathrm{diag}(a, b, c) = \begin{pmatrix} a & 0 & 0 \\ 0 & b & 0 \\ 0 & 0 & c \end{pmatrix}. \tag{40}$$

From A=0, we have

$$2(1+c)(1+p_1q_1) + 2(a+b)(2+3(p_1+q_1)+2p_1q_1) = 0, \tag{41}$$
$$2(1+c-a-b)(1+p_2q_2) = 0, \tag{42}$$
$$2(1+c-a-b)(1+p_3q_3) = 0, \tag{43}$$

where p_i and q_i $(i = 1,2,3)$ are diagonal components of P_3 and Q_3, respectively. For satisfying them for any aĄCbĄCand c, there are ambiguities on determining p_2, q_2, p_3, q_3 since the conditions for them are only $p_2q_2 = p_3q_3 = 1$, Determining them the most simply, we choose

$$p_1 = p_2 = p_3 = 1, \tag{44}$$
$$q_1 = q_2 = q_3 = -1. \tag{45}$$

While, $B = 0$ yields

$$2(1-c)(1+r_1s_1) + 2(a-b)(2-(r_1+s_1)-2r_1s_1) = 0, \tag{46}$$
$$2(1-c)(1+r_2s_2) - 2(a-b)(1-2(r_2+s_2)-r_2s_2) = 0, \tag{47}$$
$$2(1-c)(1+r_3s_3) - 2(a-b)(1-2(r_3+s_3)-r_3s_3) = 0, \tag{48}$$

where r_i and s_i $(i = 1,2,3)$ are diagonal components of R_3 and S_3, respectively. In the same way as p_i and q_i, we have

$$r_1s_1 = -1, \quad r_1 + s_1 = 4, \tag{49}$$
$$r_2s_2 = -1, \quad r_2 + s_2 = 1, \tag{50}$$
$$r_3s_3 = -1, \quad r_3 + s_3 = 1. \tag{51}$$

Solving them,

$$r_1 = \gamma_+^2 + \gamma_+, \qquad s_1 = \gamma_-^2 + \gamma_-, \tag{52}$$
$$r_2 = r_3 = \gamma_+, \qquad s_2 = s_3 = \gamma_-, \tag{53}$$

where r_i and s_i $(i = 1,2,3)$ are diagonal components of R_3 and S_3, respectively, and

$$\gamma_+ = (1+\sqrt{5})/2, \quad \gamma_- = (1-\sqrt{5})/2. \tag{54}$$

Consequently,

$$P_3 = \mathrm{diag}(1\ 1\ 1), \tag{55}$$
$$Q_3 = -\mathrm{diag}(1\ 1\ 1), \tag{56}$$
$$R_3 = \mathrm{diag}(\gamma_+^2 + \gamma_+\ \ \gamma_+\ \ \gamma_+), \tag{57}$$
$$S_3 = \mathrm{diag}(\gamma_-^2 + \gamma_-\ \ \gamma_-\ \ \gamma_-), \tag{58}$$

in eq. (30) gives us U to diagonalize eq. (26).
By the similar numbering to the icosahedron shown in Fig. 8, V in the dodecahedron has the same block structure as eq. (26) where

$$F_1 = \mathrm{circ}(1\ a\ b\ b\ a), \quad F_2 = \mathrm{circ}(a\ b\ c\ c\ b), \tag{59}$$
$$F_3 = \mathrm{circ}(d\ c\ b\ b\ c), \quad F_4 = \mathrm{circ}(e\ d\ c\ c\ d), \tag{60}$$
$$F_5 = \mathrm{circ}(1\ b\ d\ d\ b), \quad F_6 = \mathrm{circ}(e\ c\ a\ a\ c). \tag{61}$$

The form of U is also the same structure as eq. (30), just replacing the subscript 3 by 5, where

$$P_5 = \mathrm{diag}(1\ \gamma_-^2\ \gamma_+^2\ \gamma_+^2\ \gamma_-^2), \tag{62}$$
$$Q_5 = -\mathrm{diag}(1\ \gamma_+^2\ \gamma_-^2\ \gamma_-^2\ \gamma_+^2), \tag{63}$$
$$R_5 = \mathrm{diag}(\gamma_+^2 + \gamma_+\ \ \gamma_+\ \ \gamma_+\ \ \gamma_+\ \ \gamma_+), \tag{64}$$
$$S_5 = \mathrm{diag}(\gamma_-^2 + \gamma_-\ \ \gamma_-\ \ \gamma_-\ \ \gamma_-\ \ \gamma_-). \tag{65}$$

4. Conclusions

In this paper, we discussed geometrical sensor arrangements for the blind decorrelation of isotropic wavefield. Based on a necessary condition, we showed specific five classes of sensor arrangements: 1) regular polygons, 2) rectangular, 3) regular polygonal prisms, 4) rectangular solid, and 5) polyhedrons, the first two of which have two dimensional, and other three have three dimensional geometries, respectively. Specific orthogonal matrices corresponding to the sensor arrangements are also derived.

Finding all possible sensor arrangements for blind decorrelation is still an open problem and we are investigating the relationship with the group theory in mathematics, especially, *a point group* (10).

5. References

[1] P. S. Naidu, *Sensor Array Signal Processing*, CRC Press, 2001.

[2] D. H. Johnson and D. E. Dudgeon, *Array signal processing: Concepts and Techniques*, Prentice Hall, 1993.

[3] M. Brandstein and D. Ward, *Microphone arrays*, Springer-Verlag, 2001.

[4] H. Shimizu, N. Ono, K. Matsumoto, and S. Sagayama, "Isotropic noise suppression on power spectrum domain by symmetric microphone array," *Proc. WASPAA*, pp. 54–57. Oct. 2007.

[5] N. Ito, N. Ono, and S. Sagayama, "A blind noise decorrelation approach with crystal arrays on designing post-filters for diffuse noise suppression," *Proc. ICASSP*, pp. 317–320, Mar. 2008.

[6] A. Tanaka and M. Miyakoshi, "Joint estimation of signal and noise correlation matrices and its application to inverse filtering," *Proc. ICASSP*, pp. 2181–2184, Apr. 2009.

[7] A. Tanaka, M. Miyakoshi, and N. Ono, "Analysis on Blind Decorrelation of Isotropic Noise Correlation Matrices Based on Symmetric Decomposition," *Proc. SSP*, Sep., 2009. (to appear)

[8] N. Ono, N. Ito, and S> Sagayama, "Five Classes of Crystal Arrays for Blind Decorrelation of Diffuse Noise," *Proc. SAM*, pp. 151–154, Jul. 2008.

[9] G. Golub and C. Van Loan, *Matrix computations*, Johns Hopkins University Press, 1996.

[10] S. Sternberg, *Group theory and physics*, Cambridge University Press, 1994.

20

Phase Scrambling for Image Matching in the Scrambled Domain

Hitoshi Kiya and Izumi Ito
Graduate School of System Design, Tokyo Metropolitan University
6-6 Asahigaoka, Hino-shi, Tokyo, Japan

1. Introduction

In recent years, signal matching has been required in many fields. A number of matching methods have been developed, and an appropriate method should be selected for each application in order to obtain the desired performance (1)(2). Phase-only correlation (POC), phase correlation or PHAse Transform (PHAT) (3)-(17), which is referred to herein as POC, is a phase-based correlation that is used for various applications, such as delay estimation (3)(4), motion estimation (5), registration (6)(7), video detection (8)(9), and biometrics authentication (10)(11). Phase-only correlation with Fourier transform was developed as PHAT in sound/sonar processing literature (3), and POC with discrete Fourier transform was proposed by Kuglin and Hines (12). The concept of POC is based on the fact that the information related to the displacement of two signals resides in the phase of the cross spectrum. Combining POC with various techniques, such as interpolation and curve fitting, provides highly accurate estimation (13)-(17). In special cases, the normalized cross spectrum corresponds to the product of the signs of discrete cosine transform (DCT) coefficients. Previously, we derived this relationship mathematically and proposed DCT sign phase correlation (DCT-SPC) based on this relationship (18). DCT-SPC is a phase-based correlation and has properties that are similar to those of POC.

Images, particularly in the fields of biometrics, medicine, and surveillance camera require extreme security in order to avoid the risk of identity theft and invasion of privacy (19). Generally, encrypting and scrambling are used to protect information (20) (21). However, these protected images require decrypting or descrambling before image matching. In other words, neither POC nor DCT-SPC can be directly applied to conventional encrypted and scrambled images. Based on privacy concerns, secure multi-party techniques were applied to vision algorithms such as Blind Vision in (22). However, in (22), neither the registration nor the estimation of the geometric relationship between two images was discussed.

In this chapter, for POC and DCT-SPC, we present phase-scrambled signals and a matching method that can be directly applied to phase-scrambled signals without descrambling. The presented methods are motivated by secure data management. The phase scrambling distorts only the phase information, which contains significant information of signals. Phase scrambling protects against the exposure of the information in the signal. Synchronized phase scrambling yields the relationship between non-scrambled signals. Therefore, POC and DCT-SPC can be directly applied to phase-scrambled signals. Moreover, the presented scrambling

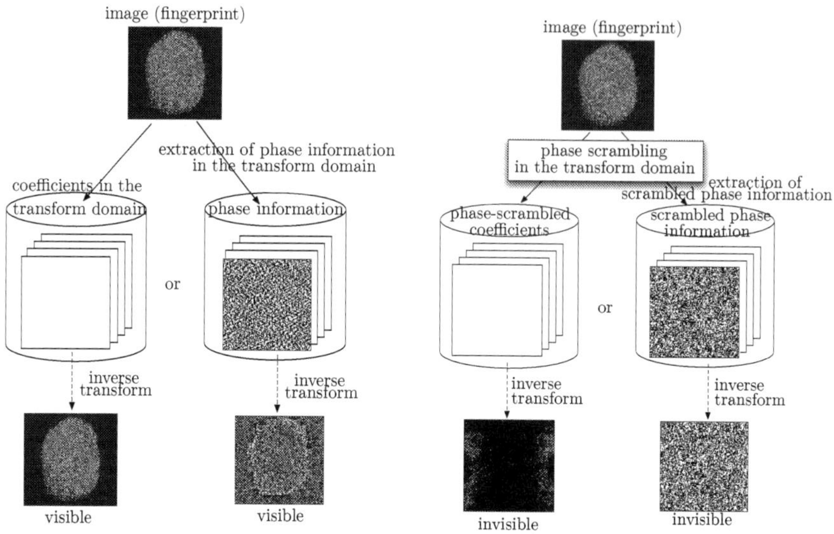

(a) conventional templates (b) secure templates by phase scrambling.

Fig. 1. Stored templates for phase-based correlation. (a) Conventional templates: If the templates in a database were to be stolen, information about the original images would be vulnerable. (b) Secure templates: A template is stored in either a phase-scrambled coefficients form or a scrambled phase information form in order to guarantee secure data management. Phase scrambling prevents templates from putting at risk the information about the original images.

has no effect on image matching. That is, the same accuracy is obtained from phase-scrambled signals without descrambling (23)(24).

This chapter is organized as follows. In Section 2, we describe the motivations and important considerations of the present study. In Section 3, POC and DCT-SPC are explained. In Section 4, the phase-scrambled signals and image matching for POC are described. We explain the reason why the POC between phase-scrambled signals has the same accuracy as that between the non-scrambled signals. In Section 5, the sign phase-scrambled signals and image matching for DCT-SPC are described. In Section 6, various simulations are presented for the purpose of confirming the effectiveness and appropriateness of the scrambled signals and image matching. Finally, Section 7 concludes this chapter.

2. Image matching between visually protected images

Image matching for authentication requires several templates that have been registered previously. Generally, the management of these templates requires a great deal of labor. Countermeasures to prevent theft and refusal of cross-references [1] are required. Phase-based correlation uses the phase information of signals. Specifically, POC and DCT-SPC require the phase

[1] Templates registered in a particular system being diverted to another system without the permission of a registrant.

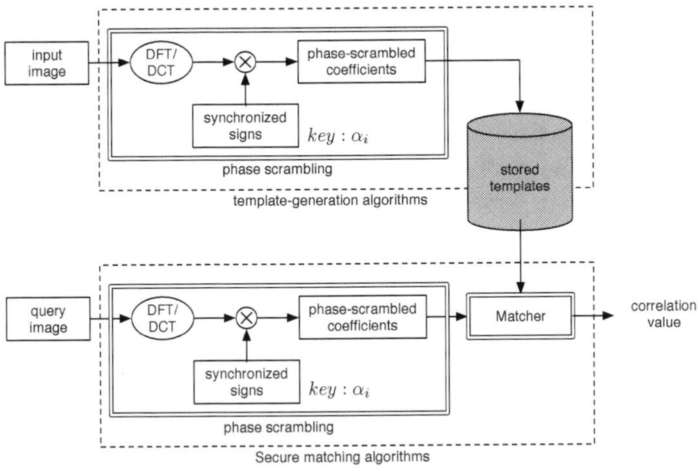

Fig. 2. Model of template-generation and matching algorithms for secure data management

factors of DFT coefficients (DFT phase factors) and the signs of DCT coefficients (DCT signs) respectively, for translation estimation. In addition, both correlations require the magnitude of DFT coefficients for rotation and scaling estimation (6). When the effect of rotation and scaling are small and can be ignored, only phase information is used for matching. Therefore, the conventional template for phase-based correlation is stored in either the coefficients in the transformed domain or in a phase information form. If the template stored in the coefficients were to be stolen, the information in the original signal may be compromised. Even in the case of the templates stored in the phase information form, the information in the original signal may be exposed by the inverse transform of the phase information, as shown in Fig. 1 (a). In addition, neither the templates stored in the coefficients form nor the phase information form is considered for cross-referencing. Moreover, the templates stored in either the coefficients form or the phase information form may be modified or removed. Alternately, new templates may be introduced to the database. In order to address these problems, we focus on secure data management.

In this chapter, we present phase-scrambled signals and a matching method for these signals using POC and DCT-SPC. The presented method is motivated by the need to guarantee secure data management. The template is stored in either phase-scrambled coefficients or a scrambled phase information form, as shown in Fig. 1 (b), and the complete information about the original signal is protected by phase scrambling. In addition, the templates are used for image matching without descrambling. Synchronized scrambling by the same key allows estimation of the translated, rotated, and scaled values between an image and the template by phase-based correlation. Desynchronized scrambling using different keys prevents cross-referencing of templates, thereby guaranteeing secure data management. Note that, in the presented method, phase scrambling has no effect on matching using POC and DCT-SPC. That is, the estimation value between the phase-scrambled signals is obtained with the same accuracy as that between non-scrambled signals.

3. Phase-based correlation

Two phase-based correlations, POC and DCT-SPC, are explained. Single-dimensional notation is used for the sake of brevity. Let $\mathbb{C}$, $\mathbb{R}$, and $\mathbb{Z}$ denote the sets of complex, real, and integer numbers, respectively.

3.1 Phase-only correlation (POC)

Let the N-point DFT of the N-point real signal $g_i(n)$, $(i = 1,2)$ $(n = 0,1,\cdots N-1)$ be $G_i(k)$, $(k = 0,1,\cdots,N-1)$. $G_i(k)$ is expressed in polar form as

$$G_i(k) = |G_i(k)|e^{j\theta_{ik}} \tag{1}$$

$$= |G_i(k)|\phi_{G_i}(k) \tag{2}$$

where $j = \sqrt{-1}$. The quantities $|G_i(k)|$ and θ_{ik} are the magnitude and phase, respectively. $\phi_{G_i}(k) = e^{j\theta_{ik}}$ is referred to as the phase factor.
The normalized cross spectrum is given as

$$R_\phi(k) = \phi_{G_1}(k) \cdot \phi^*_{G_2}(k), \tag{3}$$

where $\phi^*_{G_2}(k)$ denotes the complex conjugate of $\phi_{G_2}(k)$.
The POC is defined as the inverse DFT of $R_\phi(k)$ in (10)-(12), i.e.,

$$r_\phi(n) = \frac{1}{N}\sum_{k=0}^{N-1} R_\phi(k)W_N^{-nk}, \quad n=0,1,\cdots,N-1, \tag{4}$$

where W_N denotes $e^{-j2\pi/N}$. The integer displacement value between signals is estimated using (4).

3.2 DCT sign phase correlation (DCT-SPC)

Let the N-point DCT of the N-point real signal $g_i(n)$ be $G_{iC}(k)$. The DCT-II is defined as

$$G_{iC}(k) = \sqrt{\frac{2}{N}}C_k \sum_{n=0}^{N-1} g_i(n)\cos\left(\frac{\pi(n+1/2)k}{N}\right) \tag{5}$$

where

$$C_k = \begin{cases} 1/\sqrt{2}, & k=0 \\ 1, & k \neq 0 \end{cases}. \tag{6}$$

$G_{iC}(k)$ is expressed as the absolute value, $|G_{iC}(k)|$, and the sign, $\sigma_{Gi}(k)$, i.e.,

$$G_{iC}(k) = |G_{iC}(k)|\sigma_{Gi}(k). \tag{7}$$

The DCT sign product is given as

$$R_\sigma(k) = \sigma_{G_1}(k) \cdot \sigma_{G_2}(k), \quad k=0,1,\cdots,N-1, \tag{8}$$

where $\sigma_{G_i}(k)$ is the sign of $G_{iC}(k)$. If $G_{iC}(k)$ is zero, $\sigma_{G_i}(k)$ is replaced by zero. DCT-SPC is defined in (18) as

$$r_\sigma(n) = \frac{1}{N}\sum_{k=0}^{N-1} K_k R_\sigma(k)\cos\left(\frac{\pi nk}{N}\right), \quad n=0,1,\cdots,N-1 \tag{9}$$

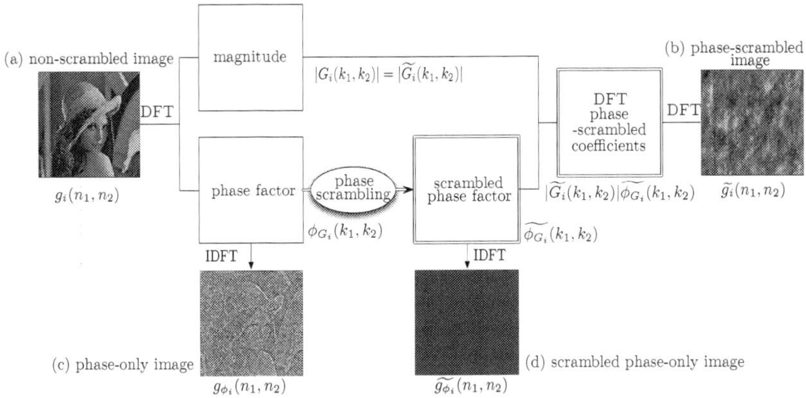

Fig. 3. Images derived from a non-scrambled image and their relationships: The non-scrambled image is composed of the magnitude $|G_i(k_1,k_2)|$ and the phase factor $\phi_{G_i}(k_1,k_2)$, while the phase-scrambled image is composed of the magnitude $|\widetilde{G}_i(k_1,k_2)|$, which is identical to $|G_i(k_1,k_2)|$, and the scrambled phase factor $\widetilde{\phi_{G_i}}(k_1,k_2)$.

where K_k is the weight, which is generally given as

$$K_k = (C_k)^2. \tag{10}$$

The integer displacement value is estimated using (9). The advantages of DCT-SPC over POC are computational complexity and memory complexity, because the DCT-SPC uses only the DCT signs to estimate translation between signals. The translation with non-integer numbers can be estimated by DCT-SPC with fitting function as well as POC (25).

4. Phase-scrambled signals and matching using POC

4.1 Template-generation and matching algorithms for secure data management

Figure 2 shows a model of the template-generation and matching algorithms. In the template-generation algorithms, either the DFT or the DCT coefficients of an input image are calculated and multiplied by the synchronized signs in order to generate the phase-scrambled coefficients. Either the phase-scrambled coefficients or the scrambled phase information, which is extracted from the phase-scrambled coefficients, is stored as a template in a database. In the secure matching algorithms, when a query image, which is not scrambled, is input, the DFT or the DCT coefficients of the query image are calculated and multiplied by the synchronized signs to generate the phase-scrambled coefficients. The matcher executes phase-based correlation between the phase-scrambled coefficients and templates.

In this section, we explain scrambled signals for POC and an image-matching method using POC. We demonstrate that scrambling has no effect on the accuracy of matching.

4.2 Phase-scrambled signals

Let us first consider scrambling of the N-point signal $g_i(n)$ for POC. First, N-point signs, $s_{\alpha_i}(k)$, are generated in random order by a random number generator with a key, α_i, i.e.,

$$s_{\alpha_i}(k) \in \{1, -1\} \tag{11}$$
$$k = 0, 1, \cdots, N-1. \tag{12}$$

In this chapter, the key corresponds to a seed that initializes the random number generator. Multiplying the DFT coefficients, $G_i(k)$, of $g_i(n)$ by the N-point signs, $s_{\alpha_i}(k)$, yields the scrambled DFT coefficients $\widetilde{G}_i(k)$; i.e.,

$$\widetilde{G}_i(k) = G_i(k) \cdot s_{\alpha_i}(k) \tag{13}$$
$$= G_i(k) \cdot e^{-j(s_{\alpha_i}(k)-1)\pi/2}$$
$$= |G_i(k)| e^{j\theta_{ik}} e^{-j(s_{\alpha_i}(k)-1)\pi/2} \tag{14}$$

where $s_{\alpha_i}(k) = e^{-j(s_{\alpha_i}(k)-1)\pi/2}$. $\widetilde{G}_i(k)$ is expressed in polar form as

$$\widetilde{G}_i(k) = |\widetilde{G}_i(k)| e^{j\widetilde{\theta_{ik}}}. \tag{15}$$

Comparing (14) and (15) yields the relationship between the non-scrambled coefficients and the phase-scrambled coefficients:

$$|\widetilde{G}_i(k)| = |G_i(k)| \tag{16}$$

and

$$\widetilde{\theta_{ik}} = \begin{cases} \theta_{ik} + \pi, & s_{\alpha_i}(k) = -1 \\ \theta_{ik}, & s_{\alpha_i}(k) = 1 \end{cases} . \tag{17}$$

We can conclude that scrambling has no effect on the magnitude. Therefore, the phase-scrambled coefficients $\widetilde{G}_i(k)$ are expressed in terms of the DFT magnitude, $|G_i(k)|$, of the original signal and the scrambled phase factor, $\widetilde{\phi_{G_i}}(k)$, as

$$\widetilde{G}_i(k) = |G_i(k)| \widetilde{\phi_{G_i}}(k). \tag{18}$$

The phase-scrambled signal $\widetilde{g}_i(n)$ is the inverse transform of the phase-scrambled coefficients:

$$\widetilde{g}_i(n) = \frac{1}{N} \sum_{k=0}^{N-1} \widetilde{G}_i(k) W_N^{-nk}. \tag{19}$$

Let us consider the two-dimensional version of the signals as images. Figure 3 shows the limited images derived from a non-scrambled image $g_i(n_1, n_2)$, the DFT coefficients of which are $G_i(k_1, k_2) = |G_i(k_1, k_2)| \phi_{G_i}(k_1, k_2)$. The phase-scrambled image $\widetilde{g}_i(n_1, n_2)$ protects the visual information of the non-scrambled image, as shown in Fig. 3 (b). The DFT magnitude of the non-scrambled image and that of the phase-scrambled image are identical. The phase factor of the non-scrambled image and that of the phase-scrambled image are different. The phase-only image $g_{\phi_i}(n_1, n_2)$, as shown in Fig. 3 (c), which is derived from the phase factors of the non-scrambled image, exposes information about the non-scrambled image, whereas the

scrambled phase-only image $\widetilde{g}_i(n_1, n_2)$, as shown in Fig. 3 (d), protects the visual information about the non-scrambled image.
These limited images are expressed as follows:

$$g_{\phi_i}(n_1, n_2) = \frac{1}{N^2}\sum_{k_1=0}^{N-1}\sum_{k_2=0}^{N-1} \phi_{G_i}(k_1, k_2) W_N^{-n_1 k_1} W_N^{-n_2 k_2}. \tag{20}$$

$$\widetilde{g}_i(n_1, n_2) = \frac{1}{N^2}\sum_{k_1=0}^{N-1}\sum_{k_2=0}^{N-1} |G_i(k_1, k_2)| \widetilde{\phi_{G_i}}(k_1, k_2) W_N^{-n_1 k_1} W_N^{-n_2 k_2}. \tag{21}$$

$$\widetilde{g_{\phi_i}}(n_1, n_2) = \frac{1}{N^2}\sum_{k_1=0}^{N-1}\sum_{k_2=0}^{N-1} \widetilde{\phi_{G_i}}(k_1, k_2) W_N^{-n_1 k_1} W_N^{-n_2 k_2}. \tag{22}$$

where $\widetilde{\phi_{G_i}}(k_1, k_2)$ denotes the scrambled-phase factor.
The phase-scrambled signal and the phase-scrambled coefficients are the space domain representation and the frequency domain representation, respectively. In the following sections, we generally do not distinguish the phase-scrambled signal from the phase-scrambled coefficients, except where confusion may occur. We refer to the phase-scrambled coefficients as the phase-scrambled signal for one-dimensional expression or the phase-scrambled image for two-dimensional expression.

4.3 Matching using POC between phase-scrambled signals

From (3), the normalized cross spectrum, $\widetilde{R_\phi}(k)$, between $\widetilde{\phi_{G_1}}(k)$ and $\widetilde{\phi_{G_2}}(k)$ is given as

$$\begin{aligned}\widetilde{R_\phi}(k) &= \widetilde{\phi_{G_1}}(k) \cdot \widetilde{\phi^*_{G_2}}(k) \\ &= s_{\alpha_1}(k) \cdot \phi_{G_1}(k) \cdot s^*_{\alpha_2}(k) \cdot \phi^*_{G_2}(k)\end{aligned} \tag{23}$$

where, if the same key is used, i.e., $s_{\alpha_1}(k) = s_{\alpha_2}(k)$, for any k, then

$$s_{\alpha_1}(k) \cdot s^*_{\alpha_2}(k) = s_{\alpha_1}(k) \cdot s_{\alpha_2}(k) = 1 \tag{24}$$

and

$$\widetilde{R_\phi}(k) = R_\phi(k). \tag{25}$$

If the keys are different, i.e., $\alpha_1 \neq \alpha_2$, then $\widetilde{R_\phi}(k) \neq R_\phi(k)$. We conclude that the normalized cross spectrum of phase-scrambled signals and that of non-scrambled signals are identical if the key is the same, and we can therefore obtain the estimation values with the same accuracy.

4.4 Scrambling and image matching steps for POC

4.4.1 Scrambling

Scrambling proceeds as follows:

Step 1 The DFT coefficients are calculated from an image.

Step 2 The signs $s_{\alpha_i}(k)$ are generated by a key α_i.

Step 3 The DFT coefficients are multiplied by the signs according to (13).

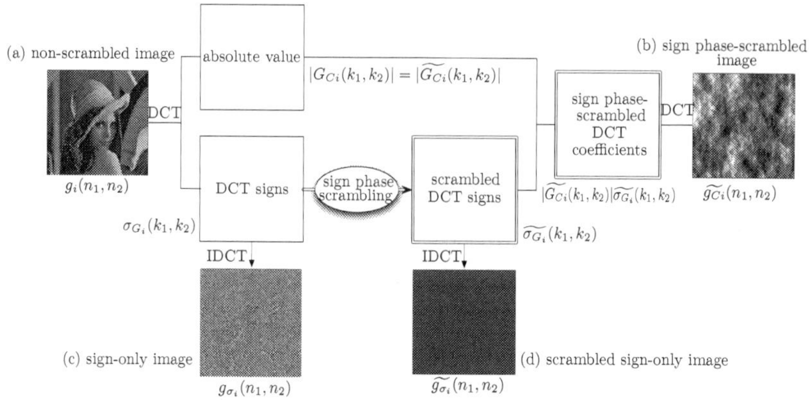

Fig. 4. Images derived from a non-scrambled image and their DCT relationships: The non-scrambled image is composed of the absolute value $|G_C(k_1,k_2)|$ of DCT coefficients and the DCT signs $\sigma_{G_i}(k_1,k_2)$, while the sign phase-scrambled image is composed of the absolute value $|\widetilde{G_{Ci}}(k_1,k_2)|$, which is identical to $|G_{Ci}(k_1,k_2)|$, and the scrambled DCT signs $\widetilde{\sigma_{G_i}}(k_1,k_2)$.

4.4.2 Image matching for translation

Image matching using POC for estimating translation between a query and a template is accomplished according to the following steps:

Step 1 The query is scrambled by the signs that are used for scrambling of the template.

Step 2 The DFT phase factors are extracted.

Step 3 The normalized cross spectrum is calculated using (3).

Step 4 The inverse DFT is applied to the result of Step 3 using (4).

Scrambling has no effect on the accuracy of image matching, because the effect of scrambling is canceled when the normalized cross spectrum is calculated.

4.4.3 Image matching for rotation and scaling

The DFT magnitude is used for the estimation of the rotated and scaled values between images (6). The phase scrambled method does not distort the DFT magnitude. Therefore, the DFT magnitude can be directly used for estimation. The steps for phase-scrambled images are the same as those for non-scrambled images.

5. Sign phase-scrambled signals and DCT-SPC

In this section, we explain sign phase-scrambled signals and their matching for DCT-SPC. The DCT signs express the phases of signals in the transform domain (18). We show that scrambling has no effect on the accuracy of image matching.

5.1 Sign phase-scrambled signal

Let us consider sign phase scrambling of $g_i(n)$ for DCT-SPC. Multiplying $s_{\alpha_i}(k)$ in (17) by $G_{Ci}(k)$ yields the sign phase-scrambled DCT coefficients, $\widetilde{G_{Ci}}(k)$, i.e.,

$$\begin{aligned}\widetilde{G_{Ci}}(k) &= G_{Ci}(k) \cdot s_{\alpha_i}(k) \\ &= |G_{Ci}(k)|\sigma_{G_i}(k) \cdot s_{\alpha_i}(k) \quad (26)\\ &= |\widetilde{G_{Ci}}(k)|\widetilde{\sigma_{G_i}}(k) \quad (27)\end{aligned}$$

where the quantities $|\widetilde{G_{Ci}}(k)|$ and $\widetilde{\sigma_{G_i}}(k)$ are the absolute value and sign, respectively. Combining (26) and (27) gives the quantitative relationships between the sign phase-scrambled DCT coefficients, $\widetilde{G_{Ci}}(k)$, and the non-scrambled DCT coefficients, $G_{Ci}(k)$:

$$|\widetilde{G_{Ci}}(k)| = |G_{Ci}(k)| \quad (28)$$

and

$$\widetilde{\sigma_{G_i}}(k) = \sigma_{G_i}(k) \cdot s_{\alpha_i}(k). \quad (29)$$

Therefore, the sign phase-scrambled DCT coefficient, $\widetilde{G_{Ci}}(k)$, is expressed in terms of the absolute value, $|G_{Ci}(k)|$, of the non-scrambled signal and the scrambled DCT sign, $\widetilde{\sigma_{G_i}}(k)$, as

$$\widetilde{G_{Ci}}(k) = |G_{Ci}(k)|\widetilde{\sigma_{G_i}}(k) \quad (30)$$

The sign phase-scrambled signal is the inverse transform of the sign phase-scrambled DCT coefficients, i.e.,

$$\widetilde{g_{C_i}}(n) = \sqrt{\frac{2}{N}} \sum_{k=0}^{N-1} C_k |G_{C_i}(k)| \widetilde{\sigma_{G_i}}(k) \cos\left(\frac{\pi(n+\frac{1}{2})k}{N}\right). \quad (31)$$

The sign phase-scrambled signals are real numbers. The DCT-SPC uses the DCT signs, which are extracted from the transform of the sign phase-scrambled signals.

Figure 4 shows the images derived from a non-scrambled image, as shown in Fig. 4 (a), and the relationships between these images. As shown in Fig. 4 (b), the sign phase-scrambled image protects the information about the non-scrambled image. The DCT signs of the non-scrambled image and that of the sign phase-scrambled image are different. The sign-only image, as shown in Fig. 4 (c), which is derived from the DCT signs of the non-scrambled image, exposes the information of the non-scrambled image, while the scrambled sign-only image, as shown in Fig. 4 (d), protects the information about the non-scrambled image.

5.2 Matching using DCT-SPC between sign-scrambled signals

In the case of the sign phase-scrambled DCT coefficients, the DCT sign product is also invariant if the same key is used. From (8), the DCT sign product, $\widetilde{R_\sigma}(k)$, between $\widetilde{\sigma_{G_1}}(k)$ and $\widetilde{\sigma_{G_2}}(k)$ is given as

$$\widetilde{R_\sigma(k)} = \widetilde{\sigma_{G_1}}(k) \cdot \widetilde{\sigma_{G_2}}(k). \quad (32)$$

From (8),

$$\widetilde{R_\sigma(k)} = \sigma_{G_1}(k)s_{\alpha_1}(k) \cdot \sigma_{G_2}(k)s_{\alpha_2}(k). \quad (33)$$

If the same key is used, we obtain the same result under scrambling, i.e.,

$$\widetilde{R_{\sigma}}(k) = R_{\sigma}(k). \tag{34}$$

If the keys are different, the result is $\widetilde{R_{\sigma}}(k) \neq R_{\sigma}(k)$. This can help prevent illegal use of the image matching.
We can thus conclude that there is no effect of scrambling on registration accuracy.

5.3 Scrambling and image matching steps for DCT-SPC

5.3.1 Sign phase scrambling

Scrambling proceeds as follows:

Step 1 The DCT coefficients are calculated from an image.

Step 2 The signs $s_{\alpha_i}(k)$ are generated by a key α_i.

Step 3 The DCT coefficients are multiplied by the signs $s_{\alpha_i}(k)$ according to (26).

5.3.2 Image matching for translation

Image matching using DCT-SPC for estimating translation between a query and a template is accomplished according to the following steps:

Step 1 The query is scrambled by the signs that are used for scrambling of the template.

Step 2 The DCT signs are extracted.

Step 3 The DCT sign product is calculated using (8).

Step 4 The inverse transform is applied to the result of Step 3 using (9).

Scrambling does not affect the accuracy of image matching, because the effect of scrambling is canceled when the DCT sign product is calculated.

6. SIMULATION

6.1 Translation (synchronized phase scrambling)

Translation estimation experiments were performed using non-scrambled images and synchronized phase-scrambled images. Figure 5 shows the test images: (a) is a 256×256 non-scrambled image, (b) is the shifted image of (a) by 20 pixels in both the horizontal and vertical directions, and (c) and (d) are the phase-scrambled images of (a) and (b), respectively. Note that the phase-scrambled images were generated with the same key, which initializes the random number generator, i.e., $\alpha_1 = \alpha_2$, $s_{\alpha_1}(k) = s_{\alpha_2}(k)$, for any k. We refer to the use of the same key as synchronized phase scrambling. We executed POC between the two non-scrambled images, (a) and (b), and POC between the two phase-scrambled images, (c) and (d), as shown in Fig. 5. Figure 6 shows that the POC surface between phase-scrambled images in (21) was the same as the POC surface between non-scrambled images in the case of synchronized phase scrambling. Phase scrambling has no effect on the accuracy of image matching.
We also performed DCT-SPC between the two non-scrambled images and DCT-SPC between the corresponding sign phase-scrambled images. Note that the sign phase-scrambled images were generated using the same key. Figure 7 shows the DCT-SPC surface between sign phase-scrambled images and that between non-scrambled images. Sign phase scrambling was confirmed to have no effect on the accuracy of image matching.

We also confirmed the estimation of translation with subpixel accuracy. The same accuracy was obtained for phase-scrambled images as that for non-scrambled images. (Details are omitted due to space limitations.)

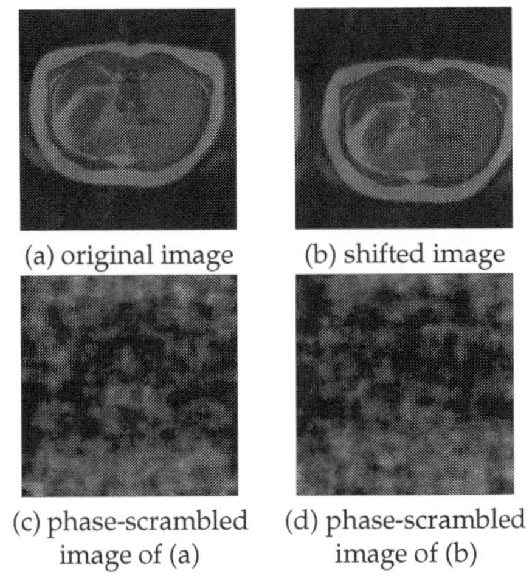

Fig. 5. Test images (256 × 256): (a) is the original image, and (b) is the shifted image of (a). (c) and (d) are the phase-scrambled images of (a) and (b), respectively.

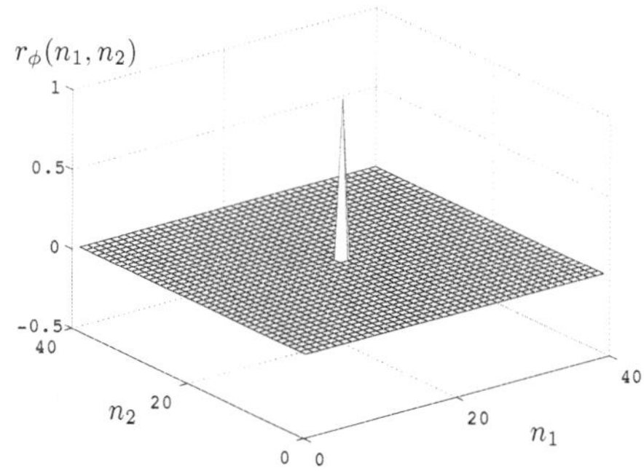

(a) non-scrambled image

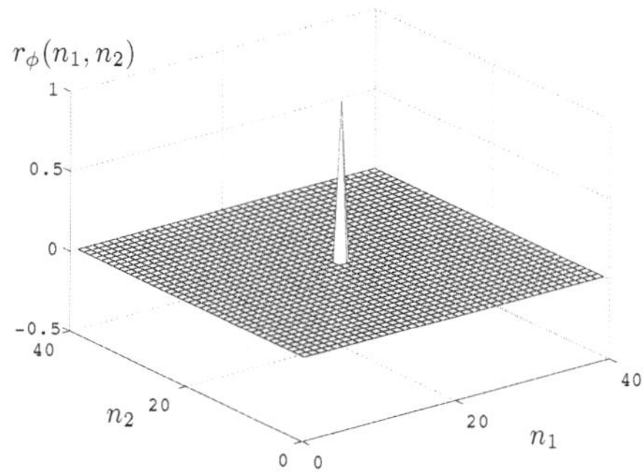

(b) scrambled image with the same key, $\alpha_1 = \alpha_2$

Fig. 6. Estimation of translation using POC: (a) is the POC surface between the non-scrambled images, and (b) is the POC surface between the phase-scrambled images. (a) and (b) are identical, and an acute peak appears at the location expressing the translational displacement.

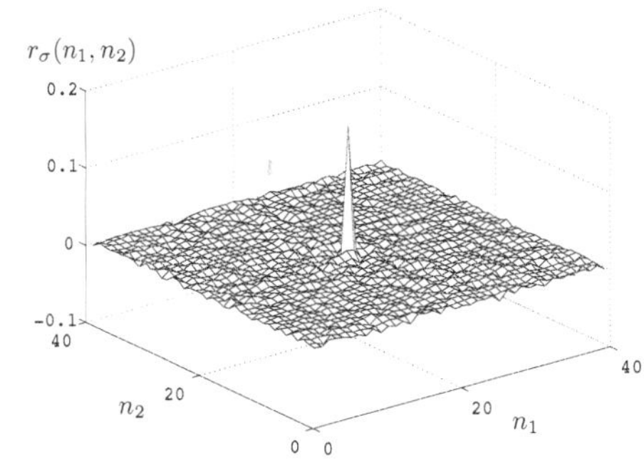

(a) non-scrambled image

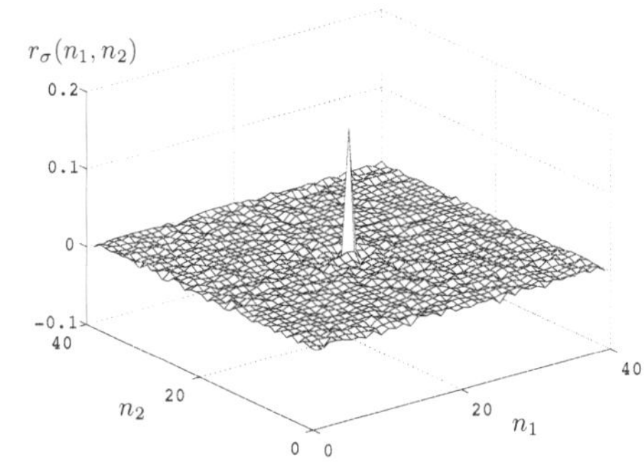

(b) scrambled image with the same key, $\alpha_1 = \alpha_2$

Fig. 7. Estimation of translation using DCT-SPC: (a) is the DCT-SPC surface between the non-scrambled images, and (b) is the DCT-SPC surface between the sign phase-scrambled images. (a) and (b) are identical, and an acute peak appears at the location expressing the translational displacement.

6.2 Effect of noise on image matching (synchronized phase scrambling)

Figure 8 shows the effect of noise on image matching. The test image is shown in Fig. 5 (a), and the shifted image is shown in Fig. 5 (b). First, the noise, which consisted of Gaussian random numbers with zero mean and a standard deviation of 25, was added to the shifted image in the space domain. Figure 8 (a) shows the POC surface between the image and the shifted image with noise. Compared with Fig. 6 (a), the effect of noise on the POC surface is clear.

Next, we scrambled these two images and performed POC. Figure 8 (b) shows the results. We confirmed that (a) and (b) in Fig. 8 were identical. We can conclude that scrambling has no effect on image matching.

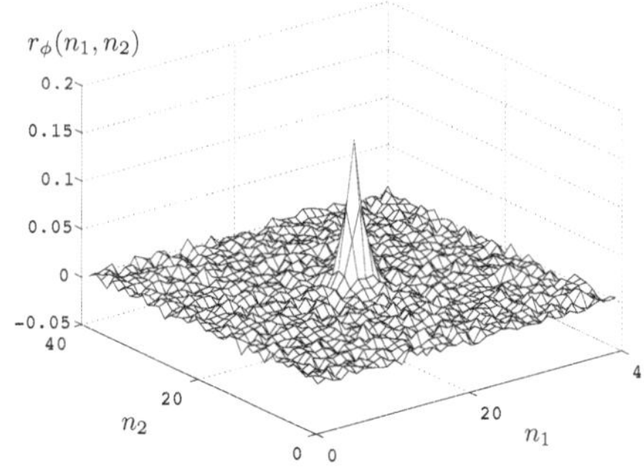

(a) POC between the non-scrambled image and the non-scrambled shifted image with noise

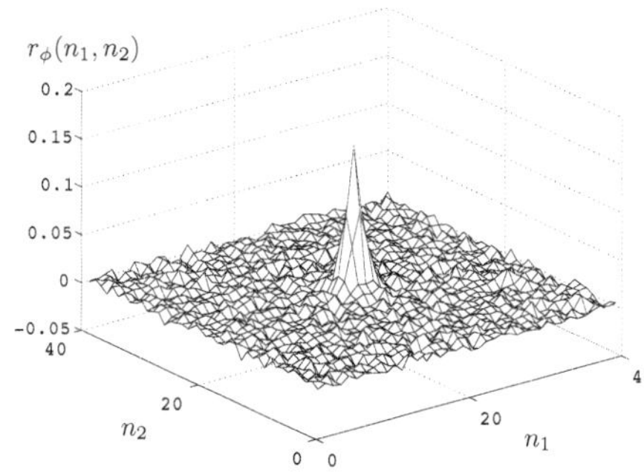

(b) POC between the phase-scrambled image and the phase-scrambled shifted image with noise

Fig. 8. POC with noise: Gaussian random number with zero mean and a standard deviation of 25. (a) and (b) are identical.

6.3 Translation (desynchronized phase scrambling)

Translation estimation experiments were performed between the desynchronized phase-scrambled images and desynchronized sign phase-scrambled images. That is, the phase-scrambled images were generated with different keys, i.e., $\alpha_1 \neq \alpha_2$. The sign phase-scrambled images were also generated with different keys, i.e., $\alpha_1 \neq \alpha_2$. Figure 9 shows both the POC surface between phase-scrambled images and the DCT-SPC surface between sign phase-scrambled images. A distinct peak expressing the translational displacement did not appear on either the POC surface and the DCT-SPC surface. The properties of phase-scrambled images with different keys provides a countermeasure against cross-referencing.

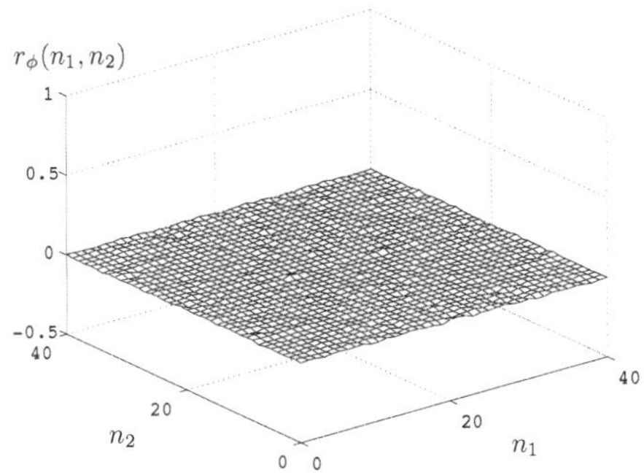

(a) POC with different key $\alpha_1 \neq \alpha_2$

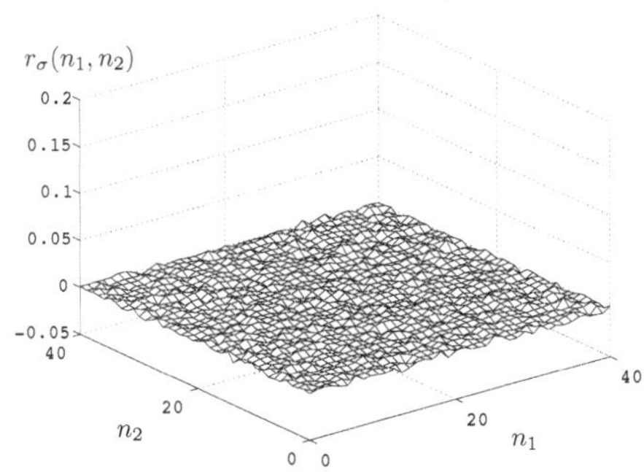

(b) DCT-SPC with different key $\alpha_1 \neq \alpha_2$

Fig. 9. Estimation of translation with different key, $\alpha_1 \neq \alpha_2$ (a) is the POC surface between phase-scrambled images with different keys, (b) is the DCT-SPC surface between sign phase-scrambled images with different keys. A distinct peak expressing the translational displacement did not appear in (a) or (b).

6.4 Rotation and Scaling

Rotated and scaled values are generally estimated using the DFT magnitude. This is based on the fact that the DFT magnitude contains information related to the rotated and scaled values, which are independent of translation. Note that the log-polar transform is applied to the DFT magnitude in order to reduce the rotated and scaled values to vertical and horizontal translations, respectively (6).

The rotated and scaled values between two images, as shown in Fig. 10, were estimated under two conditions: non-scrambling and phase scrambling with the same key. We confirmed that the POC surface between phase-scrambled images with the same key and that between non-scrambled images were identical. This result is trivial, however, because the presented phase scrambling does not distort the DFT magnitude, as shown in (16).

The phase scrambling does not affect the image matching, and we can perform image matching without descrambling.

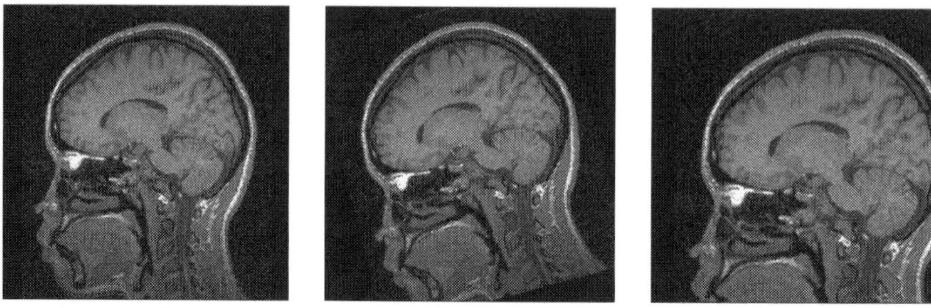

(a) original image (b) rotated image, angle: 15°. (c) scaled image, scale factor: 1.2

Fig. 10. Estimation of the rotated and scaled values. Log-polar transform is used to reduce rotated and scaled values to translational values (6).

7. Conclusion

The presented scrambling enables image matching using invisible images. In addition, image matching between phase-scrambled images is performed with the same accuracy as that between non-scrambled images. We have explained how to generate phase-scrambled signals that protect the information in the original image and demonstrated that the presented synchronized phase-scrambling maintains the relative relationship between two signals mathematically. We have shown that the presented scrambling is applicable to both DFT and DCT coefficients, and therefore secure image matching for phase-based correlation is achieved.
In particular, DCT-SPC is closely related to the image compression method. Application of the presented scrambling in areas such as image communications and image compression appears promising.
In the presented scrambling, the management of keys depends on desired systems. Meanwhile, for visual protection, there is one-time key based phase scrambling which does not require the management of keys (26; 27).

8. References

[1] B. V. K. V. Kumar, A. Mahalanobis and R. Juday, *Correlation pattern recognition*, Cambridge University Press. UK, Nov. 2005

[2] C. H. Chen and P. S. P. Wang, *Hand book of pattern recognition and computer vision (3rd edition)*, World Scientific Publishing. 2005

[3] C. H. Knapp and G. C. Carter, "The generalized correlation method for estimation of time delay," *IEEE trans. Acoust., Speech, Signal Process.*, vol. ASSP-24, no. 4, Aug. 1976

[4] O. S. Jahromi and P. Aarabi, "Theory and design of multirate sensor array," *IEEE trans. Signal Process.*, vol. 53, no. 5, May 2005

[5] C. A. Wilson and J. A.Theriot, "A correlation-based approach to calculate rotation and translation of moving cells," *IEEE Trans. Image Process.*, vol. 15, no. 7, pp. 1939–1951, July 2006

[6] Q. Chen, M. Defrise, and F. Deconinck, "Symmetric phase-only matched filtering of Fourier-Mellin transforms for image registration and recognition," *IEEE Trans. Pattern Anal. Mach. Intell.*, vol. 16, no. 2, pp. 1156–1168, Dec. 1994

[7] B. S. Reddy and B. N. Chatterji, "An FFT-based technique for translation, rotation, and scale-invariant image registration," *IEEE Trans. Image Process.*, vol. 5, no. 8, pp. 1266-1271, Aug. 1996
[8] O. Urhan, M. K. Güllü, and S. Ertürk, "Modified phase-correlation based robust hard-cut detection with application to archive Film," *IEEE Trans. Circuits Syst. Video Technol.*, vol. 16, no. 6, pp. 753–770, June 2006
[9] T. Vlachos, "Cut detection in video sequences using phase correlation," *IEEE Signal Process. Lett.*, vol. 7, no. 7, pp. 173–175, Jul. 2000
[10] K. Ito, A. Morita, T. Aoki, T. Higuchi, H. Nakajima, and K. Kobayashi, "A fingerprint recognition algorithm using phase-based image matching for low-quality Fingerprints," in *Proc. IEEE Int. Conf. Image Process.*, vol. 2, pp. 33–36, Sept. 2005
[11] K. Miyazawa, K. Ito, T. Aoki, K. Kobayashi, and H. Nakajima, "An efficient iris recognition algorithm using phase-based image matching," in *Proc. IEEE Int. Conf. Image Process.*, vol. 2, pp. 49–52, Sept. 2005
[12] C. D. Kuglin and D. C. Hines, "The phase correlation image alignment method," in *Proc. Int. Conf. Cybernetics and Society*, pp. 163–165, Sept. 1975
[13] M. Balci and H. Foroosh, "Subpixel estimation of shifts directly in the Fourier domain," *IEEE Trans. Image Process.*, vol. 15, no. 7, pp. 1965–1972, July 2006
[14] H. Foroosh and M. Balci, "Sub-pixel registration and estimation of local shifts directly in the Fourier domain," in *Proc. IEEE Int. Conf. Image Process.*, vol. 3, pp. 1915–1918, Oct. 2004
[15] H. Foroosh, J. Zerubia, and M. Berthod, "Extension of phase correlation to sub-pixel registration," *IEEE Trans. Image Process.*, vol. 11, no. 3, pp. 188-200, Mar. 2002
[16] W. S. Hoge, "A subspace identification extension to the phase correlation method," *IEEE Trans. Med. Imag.*, vol. 22, no. 2, pp. 277-280, Feb. 2003
[17] P. Thévenaz. U. E. Ruttimann, and M. unser, "A pyramidal approach to subpixel registration based on intensity," *IEEE Trans. Image Process.*, vol. 7, no. 1, pp. 27-41, Jan. 1998
[18] I. Ito and H. Kiya, "DCT sign-only correlation with application to image matching and the relationship with phase-only correlation," in *Proc. IEEE Int. Conf. Acoust., Speech Signal Process.*, vol. 1, pp. 1237-1240, Apr. 2007
[19] A. K. Jain, A. Ross, and S. Pankanti, "Biometrics: A tool for information security," *IEEE Trans. Inf. Forensics Security*, vol. 1, no. 2, pp. 125–143, June 2006
[20] M. Fujiyoshi, W. Saitou, O. Watanabe, and H. Kiya, "Hierarchical encryption of multimedia contents for access control," in *Proc. IEEE Int. Conf. Image Process.*, pp. 1977–1980, Oct. 2006
[21] K. Kuroiwa, M. Fujiyoshi, and H. Kiya, "Codestream domain scrambling of moving objects based on DCT sign-only correlation for motion JPEG movies, " in *Proc. IEEE Int. Conf. Image Process.*, vol. V, pp. 157–160, Sept. 2007
[22] S. Avidan and M. Butman, "Blind Vision," in *Proc. ECCV 2006*, Part III, LNCS 3953, pp. 1–13, Springer-Verlag, 2006
[23] H. Kiya and I. Ito, "Image matching between scrambled images for secure data management," in *Proc. EURASIP* 16th *European Signal Process. Conf.*, Aug. 2008
[24] I. Ito and H. Kiya, "A new class of image registration for guaranteeing secure data management," in *Proc. 2008 IEEE Int. Conf. Image Process.*, pp. 269–272, Oct. 2008
[25] I. Ito and H. Kiya, "Multiple-peak model fitting function for DCT sign phase correlation with non-integer shift precision," in *Proc. 2009 IEEE Int. Conf. Acoustics, Speech and Signal Process.*, pp. 449–452, Apr. 2009.

[26] I. Ito and H. Kiya, "Image matching between visually protected images with one-time key based phase scrambling," in *Proc. EURASIP* 17th *Europian Signal Processing Conf.*, pp. 1314-1318, Aug. 2009.
[27] I. Ito and H. Kiya, "One-time key based phase scrambling for phase-only correlation between visually protected images," EURASIP Journal on Information Security, to be published.

21

Fast Algorithms for Inventory Based Speech Enhancement

Robert M. Nickel and Tomohiro Sugimoto
Department of Electrical Engineering
Bucknell University
Lewisburg, PA 17837
robert.nickel@bucknell.edu

Xiaoqiang Xiao
Department of Electrical Engineering
The Pennsylvania State University
University Park, PA 16802
xxx106@psu.edu

1. Introduction

A significant number of the algorithms that are currently employed in commercially available single-channel speech enhancement products are *waveform filtering* based methods. Waveform filtering implies that an appropriately chosen filter[1] is applied to the incoming noisy speech data in order to change or smooth the shape the resulting filtered waveform. The objective of the filtering is usually to either improve the *perceptual quality* of the output -or- to improve the *recognition rate* of a subsequently used speech recognition system. Prominent examples of waveform processing are the Wiener filtering extensions proposed by McAulay & Malpass (1980) and Ephraim & Malah (1984). Other examples include schemes that employ wavelets by Hu & Loizou (2004) and modifications of the iterative Wiener filter and the Kalman filter by Mouchtaris et al. (2007). Also related are the spectral subtraction method developed by Boll in 1979 (see the text by Deller et al. (1993)) and its powerful extension, the *multiband spectral subtraction* described in the text by Loizou (2007).

The success of many waveform filtering based methods is due to their relative (computational) simplicity and robustness. A disadvantage of filtering based methods, however, is that they are never able to completely remove the noise. They are usually aiming to achieve a reasonable tradeoff between a desired reduction of the noise and an undesired but inadvertent distortion of the targeted signal.

The search for a denoising paradigm that, at least in theory, allows for potentially "perfect" enhancement has motivated many researchers to study model based denoising methods. In model based denoising a parametric model for a speech signal (which may be deterministic or stochastic in nature) is used instead of a general waveform model. A popular choice

[1] The employed filters are typically linear but potentially time-variant.

for a speech model in this context is the *harmonic plus noise model* (HNM) which was studied amongst others by Zavarehei et al. (2007). Related is also the work by Zhao & Kleijn (2007) on the modelling and estimation of speech and noise gains via hidden Markov models. Codebooks of linear predictive coefficients and their employment for speech denoising within a maximum-likelihood framework were studied by Srinivasan et al. (2006). A minimum mean square error approach for denoising that relies on a combined stochastic and deterministic speech model was studied by Hendriks et al. (2007).

The model based speech denoising method discussed in this chapter was proposed by Xiao et al. (Aug. 2008) and (Apr. 2009). It is inspired by the increasing success of *inventory based speech synthesis systems* as discussed in a review paper by O'Shaughnessy (2007). In this work it is assumed that speaker enrollment and noise enrollment are feasible. The speaker enrollment procedure provides training data that can be appropriately clustered and used as an inventory for a "clean" speech signal model. The inventory based denoising is supported by a statistical analysis of the speech signal under clean and noisy conditions.

One of the disadvantages of this method in comparison to other model based approaches is its high computational complexity. The procedure requires, in its originally proposed form, a very large number of floating point multiplications. The bottleneck of the procedure can be found in correlation operations that need to be carried out over large data records. In this chapter we are describing a modification of the original approach that incorporates a *fast algorithm* for the denoising stage. The proposed method substantially reduces the amount of necessary multiplications via the employment of a set of number theoretic transforms (NTTs, Blahut (1987)). Number theoretic transforms allow the computation of correlations in fixed-point arithmetic with a substantial reduction in multiplications. However, NTTs come generally at the expense of reduced computational accuracy due to the required signal quantization. We present an approach that balances a dramatic reduction in computational complexity with only a very slight reduction in perceptual denoising performance.

The chapter is divided into two main sections. Section 2 provides a summary of the proposed denoising paradigm. A full and detailed description of the method is beyond the scope of this chapter. The interested reader will find it in the two papers by Xiao et al. (Aug. 2008) and (Apr. 2009). Section 3 focuses explicitly on the parts of the procedure that can be improved with a fast algorithm.

2. The Denoising Paradigm

The method proposed by Xiao et al. (Apr. 2009) can be divided into three main tasks: (i) a system training task, (ii) the signal preprocessing task, and (iii) the signal denoising task. The main contribution of this work can be found in the modification of the signal denoising task. For the reader's convenience, however, we are providing a cursory overview of the entire system in this section. The description follows closely in structure and notation with that of the original paper by Xiao et al. (Apr. 2009). Many key details, however, are omitted here. The interested reader may want to consult the original paper for a comprehensive presentation.

The system training task consists of the development of a *speech waveform inventory*, two *mel-frequency cepstral coefficient* (MFCC) codebooks (under clean and noisy conditions), and a *hidden Markov model* (HMM). The HMM is used to model the codeword transition statistics under clean and noisy conditions. The system training task is discussed in some greater detail in section 2.1.

The procedures of the signal preprocessing task are adjusted according to the expected noise type. Three different noise types are considered in the original paper. They are white

noise, colored noise, and non-stationary noise. No preprocessing is performed in the case of white noise. Stationary colored noise requires preprocessing with a *prewhitening filter*. Non-stationary noise is preprocessed with a combination of a short-time power spectral estimator (via *harmonic tunnelling*, Ealey et al. (2001)) and subsequent *Wiener filtering*.
Lastly, the speech denoising task combines the results of the preprocessing with the results of a *state sequence computation* from the trained HMM as described in section 2.1. Suitable sections from the speech inventory are chosen through an *inventory unit selection scheme* and are then concatenated to form the targeted denoised speech signal (see section 2.2). The inventory unit selection scheme constitutes the computational bottleneck of the procedure. Most other components of the method have a computational complexity that is comparable to that of other model based methods. The complexity of the inventory unit selection scheme, however, dominates the overall processing requirement by an order of magnitude. The fast processing algorithm presented in this work focuses therefore exclusively on the inventory unit selection. It is comprehensively described in section 3.
Throughout this chapter we are using a mathematical notation that is consistent with the one introduced in the paper by Xiao et al. (Apr. 2009). At the *denoising* stage we assume that we observe a signal $x[n]$ which consists of speech $s[n]$ that is uttered by the enrolled speaker and is distorted by zero mean additive noise $v[n]$, i.e. $x[n] = s[n] + v[n]$. At the *training* stage we use $\hat{s}[n]$ to, similarly, denote the *speaker enrollment data*. System training is done off-line from speaker-specific pre-recorded *clean* training signals. For simplicity we assume that all training records of speech are concatenated into one long training sequence $\hat{s}[n]$.
An accurate description of the enhancement procedure requires the definition of speech *units* or *frames*. We represent a unit as a vector of N successive samples of a signal:

$$\mathbf{s}_n = [\ s[n-L]\ \ s[n-L+1]\ \ \dots\ \ s[n-L+N-1]\ ]^{\mathrm{T}}. \tag{1}$$

Note that in section 3 we employ signal segments of a different length, i.e. segments with a processing block-length of K (with $K > N$, see equations (10) and (11)). The amount of overlap between adjacent frames is controlled by a step size L. If i denotes a unit (or frame) index then the associated vector is written as $\mathbf{s}_{iL}$. Symbols $\mathbf{x}_n$, $\mathbf{v}_n$, and $\hat{\mathbf{s}}_n$ are defined analogously to equation (1). Symbol $\mathbb{S}$ is used to denote our *speech-waveform-unit inventory*. Set $\mathbb{S}$ consists of all clean training data frames $\hat{\mathbf{s}}_n$ ($\forall n$, i.e. with a step size of one) with the exception of data frames that are entirely silent. Data frames are considered entirely silent if the total frame energy falls below a certain minimal level.
The fundamental paradigm behind the considered denoising method is quite simple: find a mapping $\mathbf{x}_{iL} \rightarrow \hat{\mathbf{s}}_{n(i)}$ that associates a specific inventory frame $\hat{\mathbf{s}}_{n(i)}$ to every observed noisy frame $\mathbf{x}_{iL}$. The complexity of the method arises from the fact that this mapping is generally not fixed, but time-variant and context dependent. A resulting denoised signal $\tilde{s}[n]$ is obtained by "concatenating" the found frames $\hat{\mathbf{s}}_{n(i)}$ via a *sinusoidal model* based resynthesis technique. The employed resynthesis technique is similar to the one described in the text by Quatieri (2002). Please refer to the original paper by Xiao et al. (Apr. 2009) for the details.

2.1. System Training and State Sequence Estimations

The system training stage is used to achieve two separate goals: (1) to provide the denoising procedure with an *inventory* of available speech units and (2) to generate a *hidden Markov model* that describes transition statistics within the inventory. An illustration of the inventory design procedure is shown in figure 1. All inventory elements $\hat{\mathbf{s}}_n$ that belong to a similar *phonemic*

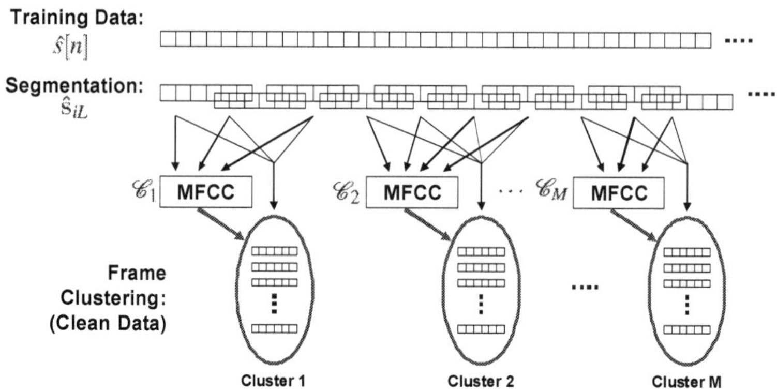

Fig. 1. An illustration of the data clustering method used by the denoising procedure by Xiao et al. (Apr. 2009). Training data is segmented, MFCC coefficients are extracted, and frames with "similar" coefficient vectors are lumped into one of $M = 50$ inventory clusters.

function[2] are grouped into the same cluster. The purpose of the grouping is to be able to study the statistical properties of the group as a whole and then apply a resulting statistical description in the denoising process. The procedure requires the construction of two *mel-frequency cepstral coefficient* (MFCC) codebooks: a clean MFCC codebook $\mathcal{C} = \{\mathcal{C}_1, \mathcal{C}_2, \ldots, \mathcal{C}_M\}$ and a noisy MFCC codebook $\widehat{\mathcal{C}} = \{\widehat{\mathcal{C}}_1, \widehat{\mathcal{C}}_2, \ldots, \widehat{\mathcal{C}}_M\}$. The codebooks contain the average of the MFCC vectors of all clean/noisy inventory units within a respective cluster. The details of the clustering procedure and the inventory design are omitted here. Please consult the paper by Xiao et al. (Aug. 2008) for a comprehensive description. An illustration of the noisy codebook design procedure is shown in figure 2. To maintain compatibility with the notation introduced in Xiao et al. (Aug. 2008) we will refer to the resulting cluster sets of inventory vectors $\hat{\mathbf{s}}_n$ with $\mathbb{K}_k$ for $k = 1, 2, \ldots M$.

Given the clean and noisy MFCC codebook vectors for each inventory cluster it becomes possible to estimate the cluster transition statistics for the given speaker. An illustration of the considered statistical description after Xiao et al. (Aug. 2008) is shown in figure 3. We use $\hat{\mathbf{s}}_n \rightarrow k$ to indicate the cluster membership of inventory frame $\hat{\mathbf{s}}$ with cluster k. Similarly, we define $\hat{\mathbf{x}}_{iL} \rightarrow j$ to indicate that the incoming noisy frame $\hat{\mathbf{x}}_{iL}$ is vector quantized via the noisy codebook $\widehat{\mathcal{C}}$ into cluster j. With a simple counting process we can estimate the first-order temporal *state transition probabilities*, i.e.

$$P_{k,j} = \text{Prob}[\ \hat{\mathbf{s}}_{(i+1)L} \rightarrow j \,|\, \hat{\mathbf{s}}_{iL} \rightarrow k\,]. \tag{2}$$

Similarly, we can convert our sequence of noisy training frames $\hat{\mathbf{x}}_{iL}$ into an *observation code sequence*. Again, with a counting process we can estimate the noise induced *observation probabilities* jointly from our clean and noisy training data:

$$Q_{k,j} = \text{Prob}[\ \hat{\mathbf{x}}_{iL} \rightarrow j \,|\, \hat{\mathbf{s}}_{iL} \rightarrow k\,]. \tag{3}$$

[2] We are using the term *phonemic function* in reference to a general, function carrying unit of a language. The group *may* or *may not* match with an actual *phoneme* defined for that language.

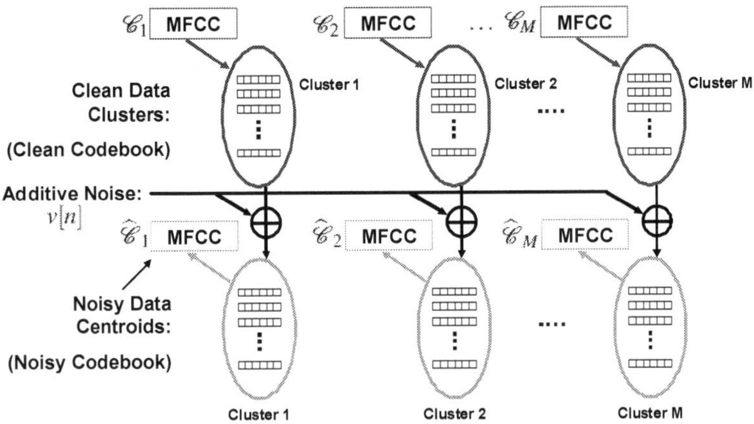

Fig. 2. An illustration of the generation of the noisy MFCC codebook as proposed by Xiao et al. in (Aug. 2008) and (Apr. 2009). Training noise is added to the elements of the clean inventory. The noisy MFCC codebook arises from the average of the MFCC vectors computed from the respective distorted signals within each clean cluster.

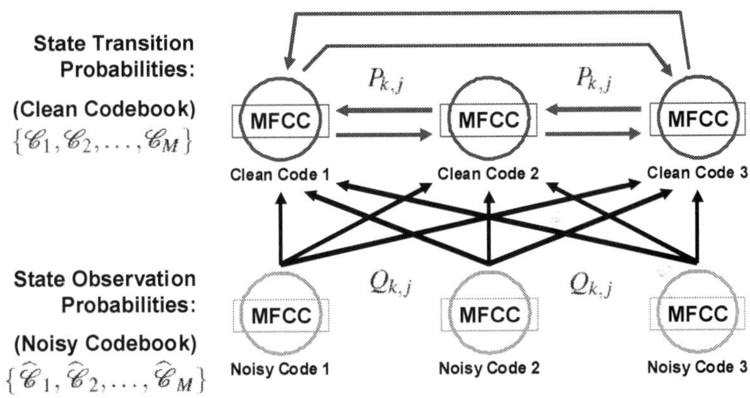

Fig. 3. An illustration of the statistical description of the considered cluster membership after Xiao et al. (Aug. 2008). The observation of a "noisy" code is statistically related to the "true" cluster membership of the underlying clean signal segment.

The transition probabilities $P_{k,j}$ and $Q_{k,j}$ are both used in the denoising process. The statistical description enables us to define an "optimal" sequence $k_{opt}(i)$ of cluster memberships for incoming testing frames $\mathbf{x}_{iL}$. The sequence is optimal in the sense that the "most likely" inventory element $\hat{\mathbf{s}}_{n(i)}$ to represent the denoised frame for $\mathbf{x}_{iL}$ is found in set $\mathbb{K}_{k_{opt}(i)}$. Again, the details of how to find the sequences $k_{opt}(i)$ are omitted. A comprehensive description is found in the paper by Xiao et al. (Aug. 2008).

2.2. Speech Denoising

After completion of the described system training we can begin to denoise new incoming signals $x[n]$. The denoising procedure can be broken down into 4 separate steps: (1) the estimation of the "optimal" cluster membership sequence $k_{opt}(i)$ (as discussed in the previous section), (2) the preprocessing, i.e. prewhitening, of the noisy signal $x[n]$, (3) the identification of the best match for each $\mathbf{x}_{iL}$ in $\mathbb{K}_{k_{opt}(i)}$, i.e. the *intra cluster frame matching*, and (4) the "concatenation" of the resulting inventory frames to resynthesize the targeted denoised signal.
As indicated in the previous section, we will omit the details of the $k_{opt}(i)$-sequence estimation. Sequence $k_{opt}(i)$ can be computed fast and efficiently via the *Viterbi algorithm*, as described in the paper by Xiao et al. (Aug. 2008). We also omit most of the details of the data preprocessing, as they have been comprehensively described in the same paper. We will, however, briefly describe the underlying principles of the *intra cluster frame matching* since it is the target of the proposed fast algorithm described in section 3.
In a first step we define a similarity measure between a noisy frame $\mathbf{x}_{iL}$ and an inventory element $\hat{\mathbf{s}}_n$. The choice of the similarity measure proposed in the paper by Xiao et al. (Apr. 2009) was guided by fundamental detection theory. If we are assuming a maximum likelihood criterion and if the additive noise $\mathbf{v}_{iL}$ is independent white Gaussian noise then a correlation detector should be used (see Poor (1994)). Since the power of the training frame and the testing frame may be significantly different a power normalization was proposed as well. The resulting similarity measure becomes

$$\sigma(\mathbf{x}_{iL}, \hat{\mathbf{s}}_n) = \frac{\mathbf{x}_{iL}^{\mathrm{T}} \hat{\mathbf{s}}_n}{\sqrt{\|\mathbf{x}_{iL}\|^2 - V^2} \cdot \|\hat{\mathbf{s}}_n\|}, \tag{4}$$

in which $\sqrt{\|\mathbf{x}_{iL}\|^2 - V^2}$ represents the estimated power of the underlying clean speech $s[n]$. If $\mathbf{v}_{iL}$ contains colored noise then a prewhitening filter is used before the correlation detector. With $\mathbf{h}_w$ denoting the impulse response of the prewhitening filter we obtain

$$\acute{\sigma}(\mathbf{x}_{iL}, \hat{\mathbf{s}}_n) = \frac{(\mathbf{x}_{iL} * \mathbf{h}_w)^{\mathrm{T}} (\hat{\mathbf{s}}_n * \mathbf{h}_w)}{\sqrt{\|\mathbf{x}_{iL} * \mathbf{h}_w\|^2 - V_w^2} \cdot \|\hat{\mathbf{s}}_n * \mathbf{h}_w\|}, \tag{5}$$

where we use $V_w^2 = \mathrm{E}\{(\mathbf{v}_n * \mathbf{h}_w)^{\mathrm{T}}(\mathbf{v}_n * \mathbf{h}_w)\}$ to denote the variance of the prewhitened noise. A discussion of the non-stationary noise case is omitted here since it is effectively using the same similarity measure as the colored noise case.
After the generation of an appropriate similarity measure between an incoming noisy frame $\mathbf{x}_{iL}$ (or $\tilde{\mathbf{x}}_{iL}$) and an inventory element $\mathbf{s}_n$ we can define an optimal intra cluster match $\hat{\mathbf{s}}^{(i,k)}$ via

$$\hat{\mathbf{s}}^{(i,k)} = \arg\max_{\hat{\mathbf{s}}_n \in \mathbb{K}_k} \sigma(\mathbf{x}_{iL}, \hat{\mathbf{s}}_n). \tag{6}$$

In a last step we need to resynthesize our targeted signal. First, we are replacing each frame $\mathbf{x}_{iL}$ with the inventory frame $\hat{\mathbf{s}}^{(i,k_{opt}(i))}$, i.e. $\mathbf{x}_{iL} \rightarrow \hat{\mathbf{s}}^{(i,k_{opt}(i))}$, and second, we reconcatenate the resulting frames via a *sinusoidal model expansion* similar to the one proposed by Quatieri (2002). The reconcatenation with the sinusoidal model is important to minimize phase incompatibilities at the frame boundaries.
The performance of the proposed method was evaluated by Xiao et al. (Apr. 2009) with experiments over a subset of the `CMU_ARCTIC` database from the Language Technologies Institute at Carnegie Mellon University[3]. Data processing was conducted at a sampling rate of 8 kHz

[3] The corpus is available at <http://www.festvox.org/cmu_arctic>.

and with a segment length of $N = 160$ samples and a step size of $L = 80$ samples. The targeted signal-to-noise ratio was 10 dB. The quality of the resulting denoised speech was assessed with the *Perceptual Evaluation of Speech Quality*[4] (PESQ) measure. For white noise Xiao et al. reported an improvement of up to 1.06 points on the PESQ scale. For colored noise an improvement of up to 0.87 points was reported. The performance of the presented method compared favorably with other state-of-the-art denoising methods.

3. Fast Processing Methods

As mentioned earlier, the bottleneck of the proposed denoising procedure, in terms of computational complexity, can be found in the maximization of equations (4) and (5) as expressed in equation (6). In the experiments conducted by Xiao et al. (Apr. 2009) training sets of around 1 hour in length were used. If we operate at a sampling rate of 8 kHz and with a number of $M = 50$ clusters then we can expect to have around $500 \cdot 10^3$ to $600 \cdot 10^3$ samples per cluster. For the denoising of each incoming frame we need to correlate a vector of length 160 with the entire data set contained in the cluster targeted by $k_{opt}(i)$. The resulting computational complexity per frame is therefore huge, if no fast computational procedures are involved.
For the remainder of this section we will discuss methods that can dramatically reduce the computational complexity of the maximization implied in equation (6). In a first step we are moving to a slightly simplified similarity measure since for a fixed $\mathbf{x}_{iL}$ the terms $\sqrt{\|\mathbf{x}_{iL}\|^2 - V^2}$ and $\sqrt{\|\mathbf{x}_{iL} * \mathbf{h}_w\|^2 - V_w^2}$ remain unchanged and can therefore be dropped from the computation:

$$\tilde{\sigma}(\mathbf{x}, \hat{\mathbf{s}}_n) = \frac{\mathbf{x}^{\mathrm{T}} \cdot \hat{\mathbf{s}}_n}{\|\hat{\mathbf{s}}_n\|}. \tag{7}$$

Similarity measure (5) can be modified accordingly. The respective result for equation (5) is obtained by substituting $\mathbf{x}_{iL} * \mathbf{h}_w$ and $\hat{\mathbf{s}}_n * \mathbf{h}_w$ into equation (7).
The fast computation of (7) for all frames in a given cluster (as expressed in equation (6)) is accomplished in three steps:

1. Quantization of the elements in $\mathbf{x}$ and $\hat{\mathbf{s}}_n$.
2. Computation of $\mathbf{x}^{\mathrm{T}} \cdot \hat{\mathbf{s}}_n$ with an overlap-add based convolution procedure via number theoretic transforms (NTTs).
3. Recursive computation of $\|\hat{\mathbf{s}}_n\|$ and $\tilde{\sigma}(\mathbf{x}, \hat{\mathbf{s}}_n)$.

We begin by applying a uniform scalar quantizer (see Sayood (1996)) to all elements of our (possibly preprocessed) incoming frame $\mathbf{x}$ and the elements of our inventory vectors $\hat{\mathbf{s}}_n$. The quantizer is designed to assign a unique integer between $-J$ and $+J$ ($J \in \mathbb{N}$) to every value in $\mathbf{x}$ and $\hat{\mathbf{s}}_n$. An optimal choice of J is dependent on three things: (1) the employed frame length N, (2) the statistics of our training data, and (3) the parameters of the employed number theoretic transforms. Good choices for J are discussed in section 3.3.
For simplicity of notation we assume for the remainder of this section that symbols $\mathbf{x}$ and $\hat{\mathbf{s}}_n$ and the associated signals $x[n]$ and $\hat{s}[n]$ are *quantized* versions of the original signals, i.e. all elements of these signals and vectors are integers in the range $-J \ldots +J$. It is important to emphasize that we are *not* operating with this kind of quantized data in *other* components of the proposed method, especially in the step $\mathbf{x}_{iL} \rightarrow \hat{\mathbf{s}}^{(i,k_{opt}(i))}$ during the target signal resynthesis where we want to use the original inventory data and not the quantized one.

[4] The PESQ measure, an ITU recommendation, is aiming to asses the *subjective quality* of speech. Please refer to the text by Loizou (2007) for the details.

3.1. Preliminary Computations and Notation

Before we delve into the fast computation of $\mathbf{x}^{\mathrm{T}} \cdot \hat{\mathbf{s}}_n$ it is beneficial to first briefly discuss an efficient way to compute the term $\|\hat{\mathbf{s}}_n\|$ in (7). For notational convenience we introduce the shifted inventory signal $s'[n] = \hat{s}[n-L+N-1]$ and its square $\varsigma[n] = s'[n] \cdot s'[n]$. We can use $\varsigma[n]$ as an input to the following recursive system with output $\xi[n]$:

$$\xi[n] = \xi[n-1] + \varsigma[n] - \varsigma[n-N]. \tag{8}$$

Term $\|\hat{\mathbf{s}}_n\|$ is then obtained from $\|\hat{\mathbf{s}}_n\| = \sqrt{\xi[n]}$. The computation of $\|\hat{\mathbf{s}}_n\|$ therefore requires one multiplication, two additions[5], and one square root operation (table lookup) per sample. A major step in simplifying the computation of $\mathbf{x}^{\mathrm{T}} \cdot \hat{\mathbf{s}}_n$ is obtained from recognizing that the inner product in (7) is equivalent to a convolution operation (indicated with symbol $*$):

$$\mathbf{x}^{\mathrm{T}} \cdot \hat{\mathbf{s}}_n = \sum_{k=0}^{N-1} [\mathbf{x}]_{N-k} \cdot \hat{s}[n-k+N-L-1] = [\mathbf{x}]_{N-k} * s'[n]. \tag{9}$$

We use the notation $[\mathbf{x}]_k$ to indicate the kth element of vector $\mathbf{x}$ with $[\mathbf{x}]_k = 0$ if $k < 1$ and $k > N$. The convolution of equation (9) is further broken down by segmenting $s'[n]$ into segments of length R. The segments are zero padded to arrive at a processing block-length of K samples:

$$\mathbf{s}'_k = [\ s'[kR]\ \ s'[kR+1]\ \ \ldots\ \ s'[kR+R-1]\ \ \underbrace{0\ 0\ \ldots\ 0}_{K-R}\ ]^{\mathrm{T}}. \tag{10}$$

Similarly we are defining a time-reversed and zero padded input signal vector $\mathbf{x}'$ as:

$$\mathbf{x}' = [\ [\mathbf{x}]_N\ \ [\mathbf{x}]_{N-1}\ \ \cdots\ \ [\mathbf{x}]_2\ \ [\mathbf{x}]_1\ \ \underbrace{0\ 0\ \ldots\ 0}_{K-N}\ ]^{\mathrm{T}}. \tag{11}$$

The convolution operation can then be performed via number theoretic transforms (NNTs, see Blahut (1987)). The details of the proposed NTT operation are described in section 3.2. If we assume that we have access to the output vector $\mathbf{y}'_k = \mathrm{NTTConv}\{\mathbf{x}', \mathbf{s}'_k\}$ of the proposed K-point NTT convolution of $\mathbf{x}'$ and $\mathbf{s}'_k$ then the inner product in equation (9) becomes:

$$\mathbf{x}^{\mathrm{T}} \cdot \hat{\mathbf{s}}_n = \textstyle\sum_k [\mathbf{y}'_k]_{n+1-kR}. \tag{12}$$

The overlap and add method implied in equation (12) requires $(K-R)$ additions for each block of length K, plus the operations necessary for NTTConv.

3.2. Number Theoretic Transforms

Number theoretic transforms can be used for efficient computations of convolutions if the underlying data is, as indicated earlier, discretized or quantized (see Blahut (1987)). NTTs generally operate in *finite fields* or *Galois fields*. The order p of the field is typically a prime number, in which case all operations within the field (addition, subtraction, multiplication, and division) are executed via a *modulo-p* arithmetic (see Blahut (1987)).
Not all number theoretic transforms are necessarily well suited for the development of fast algorithms. NTTs of a certain subclass, known as *Fermat NTTs*, however, have properties that make them superior to the commonly used *fast Fourier transform* (FFT, see Proakis & Manolakis

[5] We are counting subtractions and additions as the same since they share roughly the same computational complexity.

(1996)) in computing convolutions within a fixed-point arithmetic. The advantage of such NTTs are that: (1) an NTT can be implemented in real-valued arithmetic (i.e. it does not require an underlying complex number representation), and (2) many of the multiplications required for the computation simplify to *shift* operations if the underlying processing hardware is utilizing binary number representations.

NTTs have, however, three important limitations that render their practical implementation significantly less flexible than that of the FFT: (1) the processing block length K is tied to (i.e. not independent of) the order p of the underlying number representation, (2) NTTs only exist for a very limited number of combinations of K and p, and (3) internal overflow errors during convolution computations cannot be detected and/or flagged. A general discussion of all of these problems is beyond the scope of this book chapter. The interested reader may consult the literature, especially the text by Blahut (1987), for a detailed discussion. We will address the three issues above only within the context of the proposed denoising scheme.

Out of the general set of possible combinations for K and p we found that $K = 1024$ and $p = 2^{16} + 1$ (Fermat prime) are quite well suited for the proposed algorithm. We begin by considering a general integer vector $\mathbf{v} = [\ v_1\ v_2\ \ldots\ v_K\ ]^T$ of length K. More specifically, we assume that all elements v_k of $\mathbf{v}$ are integers between $-\frac{p-1}{2}$ and $+\frac{p-1}{2}$. Furthermore, we define the following warping operation:

$$\text{warp}\{v_k\} = \begin{cases} v_k & \text{if } v_k \geq 0 \\ v_k + p & \text{if } v_k < 0. \end{cases} \tag{13}$$

The notation $\tilde{\mathbf{v}} = \text{warp}\{\mathbf{v}\}$ refers to an application of the warp-function on vector $\mathbf{v}$ on an element-by-element basis. We also require the following dewarping mapping:

$$\text{dewarp}\{\tilde{v}_k\} = \begin{cases} \tilde{v}_k & \text{if } \tilde{v}_k \leq \frac{p-1}{2} \\ \tilde{v}_k - p & \text{if } \tilde{v}_k > \frac{p-1}{2}. \end{cases} \tag{14}$$

Again, $\mathbf{v} = \text{dewarp}\{\tilde{\mathbf{v}}\}$ refers to an application of the dewarp-function on vector $\tilde{\mathbf{v}}$ on an element-by-element basis. Given the parameters $K = 1024$ and $p = 2^{16} + 1$ we arrive at the following definition for the employed NTT:

$$\tilde{\mathbf{V}} = \text{NTT}\{\tilde{\mathbf{v}}\} \quad \text{such that} \quad [\tilde{\mathbf{V}}]_{k+1} = \sum_{i=0}^{1023} \omega^{ik}\,[\tilde{\mathbf{v}}]_{i+1} \bmod p \quad \text{for} \quad k = 0 \ldots 1023. \tag{15}$$

Number ω must be chosen such that $\omega^{1024} \bmod p = 1$. There are a number of values ω that satisfy this conditions. Not all choices, however, are well suited for the design of a fast algorithm. It is possible to apply the *radix-two Cooley-Tukey divide-and-conquer* approach (see Blahut (1987)) to equation (15). With the special choice of $\omega = 18990$ we obtain:

$$[\tilde{\mathbf{V}}]_{32k'+k''} = \sum_{i'=0}^{31} 2^{i'k'} \left[\omega^{i'k''} \sum_{i''=0}^{31} 2^{i''k''}\,[\tilde{\mathbf{v}}]_{i'+32i''} \right] \bmod p \quad \text{for} \quad k', k'' = 0 \ldots 31. \tag{16}$$

It is, therefore, possible to divide the 1024-point NTT from equation (15) into two sets of 32 sub-NTTs of length 32 each and one set of 1024 multiplications with $\omega^{i'k''}$. Furthermore, the 32-point sub-NTTs can be computed *without any multiplications* since a multiplication with a power-of-two number is equivalent to a *shift operation* if the underlying processing hardware

operates on a binary number system. A detailed analysis of equation (16) reveals that equation (15) can be computed with roughly 1024 multiplications, 5120 additions, and 5120 shift operations.
An important aspect of the computations in equations (16) and (15) is the modulo reduction of order p. Given the standard approach to modulo reductions one might suspect that each reduction comes at the cost of an integer division. In the given case of $p = 2^{16} + 1$, however, it becomes possible to reduce the complexity of a modulo reduction to that of an addition, if the underlying processing hardware operates on a binary number system. To that end, we can group adjacent bits in our underlying number representation into blocks of 16. All blocks with bits higher than 16 are shifted down to line up with the least significant bit and then added block-by-block with an alternating sign. The details of the implementation are readily found in the literature (see also Blahut (1987)). Due to the cyclic nature of the $p = 2^{16} + 1$ reduction it is possible to build the require modulo operation directly into the hardware of the employed multiplier, adder, and shifting units. We, therefore, do not count modulo operations separately in our complexity analysis.
The computation of convolutions via NTTs requires us to also consider the inverse NTT. Similarly to equation (15) we define:

$$\tilde{\mathbf{v}} = \mathrm{NTT}^{-1}\{\tilde{\mathbf{V}}\} \quad \text{such that} \quad [\tilde{\mathbf{v}}]_{k+1} = K^{-1} \sum_{i=0}^{1023} \omega^{-ik} \, [\tilde{\mathbf{V}}]_{i+1} \mod p \qquad \text{for} \quad k = 0 \ldots 1023. \tag{17}$$

Note that (K^{-1}) represents the integer with the property $(K^{-1}) \cdot K \bmod p = 1$. The inverse NTT can also be computed via the *radix-two Cooley-Tukey divide-and-conquer* approach:

$$[\tilde{\mathbf{v}}]_{32k'+k''} = K^{-1} \cdot \sum_{i'=0}^{31} 2^{-i'k'} \left[\omega^{-i'k''} \sum_{i''=0}^{31} 2^{-i''k''} \, [\tilde{\mathbf{V}}]_{i'+32i''} \right] \mod p \qquad \text{for} \quad k', k'' = 0 \ldots 31. \tag{18}$$

The computational complexity of the NTT and the inverse NTT are therefore the same, except we have an additional set of 1024 multiplications with K^{-1} in the case of the inverse NTT. We will see in section 3.3 though that the scaling with K^{-1} can be omitted when we apply the inverse NTT to our proposed fast computation procedure.
We are now in the position to define the computation of $\mathbf{y}'_k$ as used in equation (12). The operation requires two warping operation, one dewarping operation, two NTTs, and one inverse NTT:

$$\mathbf{y}'_k = \mathrm{NTTConv}\{\mathbf{x}', \mathbf{s}'_k\} = \mathrm{dewarp}\{\mathrm{NTT}^{-1}\{\mathrm{NTT}\{\mathrm{warp}\{\mathbf{x}'\}\} \odot \mathrm{NTT}\{\mathrm{warp}\{\mathbf{s}'_k\}\}\}\}, \tag{19}$$

in which $\odot$ denotes element-by-element-wise vector multiplication.

3.3. Complexity Analysis and Perfomance

A successful implementation of the fast algorithm proposed in the previous two sections requires a careful definition of our quantization granularity[6] J. If J is too big then we are likely to receive too many (undetectable) overflow errors in the NTT based convolution operation.

[6] Note that the effective number of quantization levels for our data is given by $2J + 1$.

The resulting intra cluster frame matching becomes unreliable and the perceptual quality of the proposed denoising method suffers. If we pick J too small then the effective quantization granularity of our data becomes too coarse. Again, the resulting intra cluster frame matching becomes unreliable and the perceptual quality is reduced.

In experiments over the same data set that was used in the original performance analysis by Xiao et al. (Aug. 2008) we found that the error count in the intra cluster frame matching procedure remained relatively unaffected by the number of employed quantization levels if the number did not drop significantly below 60, i.e. $2J + 1 \geq 60$. Similar experiments revealed that we receive virtually no overflow errors in our procedure[7] if $J \leq 35$. A recommended range for J is therefor between 30 and 35.

To maximize the efficiency of the proposed NTT based convolution it is best to pick $K = N + R - 1$. With a processing block-length K of 1024 and a frame length N of 160 we obtain $R = 865$.

To obtain reasonably normalized numbers for the computational complexity of different solution approaches for equation (6) we decided to reference all operation counts to an equivalent count for each inventory sample. A direct, brute force, computation of equation (6) requires 320 multiplications/sample and 318 additions/sample. We technically also require one division/sample and one square-root-operation/sample. The division and the square root, however, are a part of all considered algorithms and are therefore omitted in the overall counts.

For comparison we consider the proposed fast convolution approach with a conventional *radix-two fast Fourier transform* (FFT) instead of the proposed NTT. A 1024-point FFT requires 9216 complex multiplications and 10240 complex additions[8] (see Blahut (1987)). Each complex multiplication can be evaluated with 3 real multiplications and 5 real additions. We, therefore, obtain 27648 real multiplications and 56320 real additions. The disadvantage of a complex arithmetic of the FFT is partially alleviated by the fact that we can typically process two FFTs with real imputs with a single FFT with complex inputs (see Proakis & Manolakis (1996)). Operations are consequently cut in half and we obtain as a final count for a 1024-point FFT 13824 (real) multiplications and 28160 (real) additions. The FFT equivalent of equation (19) can be evaluated on-line with one 1024-point FFT, one 1024-point inverse FFT and 1024 complex multiplications. Note that we only need one FFT to compute (19) on-line since the corresponding FFTs of our inventory $\hat{s}[n]$ can be precomputed off-line. Furthermore, we do not need to consider the additional scaling factor of $\frac{1}{K}$ in the inverse FFT since the scaling becomes immaterial in the subsequent maximum search. Furthermore, we receive an additional number of $K - R = N - 1 = 1023$ additions due to the overlap and add procedure from equation (12).

In summary, we require $2 \times 13824 + 3 \times 1024 = 30720$ multiplications and $2 \times 28160 + 5 \times 1024 + 1023 = 62463$ additions to compute the required 1024-point convolution with an FFT based approach. The convolution operation has to be repeated every $R = 865$ samples. On a per-sample count we obtain 35.52 multiplications/sample and 72.22 additions/sample. Technically we need to also add in the one multiplication/sample and the two additions/sample for the separate computation of $||\hat{\mathbf{s}}_n||$.

[7] Assuming $N = 160$, $K = 1024$, and $p = 2^{16} + 1$.

[8] The complexity analysis presented here may slightly differ from complexity computations from other sources. The main differences in computation counts are usually due to differences in how trivial multiplications are considered. We decided to include the count of trivial multiplications for the FFT as well as the NTT.

The computation of a 1024-point NTT after section 3.2 requires 1024 multiplications, 5120 additions, and 5120 shift operations. Similarly to the computations for the FFT we require $2 \times 1024 + 1024 = 3072$ multiplications, $2 \times 5120 + 1023 = 11263$ additions, and $2 \times 5120 = 10240$ shift operations to compute the required 1024-point convolution with an NTT based approach. Again, the convolution operation has to be repeated every $R = 865$ samples. On a per-sample count we obtain 3.56 multiplications/sample, 13.03 additions/sample, and 11.84 shifts/sample. Considering also the one multiplication/sample and the two additions/sample for the separate computation of $\|\hat{\mathbf{s}}_n\|$ we obtain a total tally of 4.56 multiplications/sample, 15.03 additions/sample, and 11.84 shifts/sample for the proposed approach.

4. Conclusions

We presented a *fast algorithm* for the correlation computations that are required for the inventory based speech enhancement method proposed by Xiao et al. (Apr. 2009). The correlation computations are used in the inventory unit selection scheme of the enhancement procedure. They present a significant computational bottleneck for this method. The computational complexity of the inventory unit selection scheme would dominate the overall processing requirement of the method by an order of magnitude if no fast algorithms were employed.
The fast computation procedure proposed in this chapter is able to dramatically reduce the computational complexity of the proposed method without significantly affecting its enhancement performance. The number of multiplications per inventory sample required for the processing can be reduced from around 36.52 for a conventional FFT based method down to around 4.56 for the proposed NTT based method. The proposed approach is thus significantly faster than conventional computation methods.

5. References

Blahut, R. E. (1987). *Fast Algorithms for Digital Signal Processing*, Addison-Wesley.

Deller, J. R., Proakis, J. G. & Hansen, J. H. (1993). *Discrete-Time Processing of Speech Signals*, Macmillan, New York.

Ealey, D., Kelleher, H. & Pearce, D. (2001). Harmonic tunnelling: tracking non-stationary noises during speech, *Proceedings of EUROSPEECH* pp. 437–440.

Ephraim, Y. & Malah, D. (1984). Speech enhancement using a minimum mean square error short-time spectral amplitude estimator, *IEEE Transactions on Acoustics, Speech, and Signal Processing* **32**: 1109–1121.

Hendriks, R. C., Heusdens, R. & Jensen, J. (2007). An MMSE estimator for speech enhancement under a combined stochastic/deterministic speech model, *IEEE Transactions on Audio, Speech and Language Processing* **15**(2): 406–415.

Hu, Y. & Loizou, P. C. (2004). Speech enhancement based on wavelet thresholding the multitaper spectrum, *IEEE Transactions on Speech and Audio Processing* **12**(1): 59–67.

Loizou, P. C. (2007). *Speech Enhancement, Theory and Practice*, CRC-Press.

McAulay, R. J. & Malpass, M. L. (1980). Speech enhancement using a soft-decision noise suppression filter, *IEEE Transactions on Acoustics, Speech, and Signal Processing* **ASSP-28**(2): 137–145.

Mouchtaris, A., Van der Spiegel, J., Mueller, P. & Tsakalides, P. (2007). A spectral conversion approach to single-channel speech enhancement, *IEEE Transactions on Audio, Speech and Language Processing* **15**(4): 1280–1193.

O'Shaughnessy, D. (2007). Modern methods of speech synthesis, *IEEE Circuits and Systems Magazine* **7**(3): 6–23.

Poor, H. V. (1994). *An Introduction to Signal Detection and Estimation*, Springer-Verlag.

Proakis, J. G. & Manolakis, D. G. (1996). *Digital Signal Processing – Principles, Algorithms, and Applications*, 3rd edn, Prentice Hall, Upper Saddle River, New Jersey 07458.

Quatieri, T. F. (2002). *Discrete-Time Speech Signal Processing: Principles and Practice*, Prentice Hall.

Sayood, K. (1996). *Introduction to Data Compression*, Morgan Kaufman.

Srinivasan, S., Samuelsson, J. & Kleijn, W. B. (2006). Codebook driven short-term predictor parameter estimation for speech enhancement, *IEEE Transactions on Audio, Speech, and Language Processing* **14**(1): 163–176.

Xiao, X., Lee, P. & Nickel, R. M. (Apr. 2009). Inventory based speech enhancement for speaker dedicated speech communication systems, *Proceedings of ICASSP*, Taipei, Taiwan, pp. 3877–3880.

Xiao, X., Lee, P. & Nickel, R. M. (Aug. 2008). Inventory based speech denoising with hidden Markov models, *Proceedings of EUSIPCO*, Lausanne, Switzerland.

Zavarehei, E., Vaseghi, S. & Yan, Q. (2007). Noisy speech enhancement using harmonic-noise model and codebook-based post-processing, *IEEE Transactions on Audio, Speech, and Language Processing* **15**(4): 1194–1203.

Zhao, D. Y. & Kleijn, W. B. (2007). HMM-based gain modeling for enhancement of speech in noise, *IEEE Transactions on Audio, Speech, and Language Processing* **15**(3): 882–892.

22

Compression of microarray images *

António J. R. Neves and Armando J. Pinho
Signal Processing Lab, DETI/IEETA, University of Aveiro
Portugal

1. Introduction

DNA microarrays have become a tool of paramount importance in the study of gene function, regulation, and interaction across large numbers of genes, and even entire genomes (Hegde et al., 2000; Moore, 2001). Microarray experiments generate pairs of 16 bits per pixel grayscale images (see Fig. 1, for an example). These images, which may require several tens of megabytes in order to be stored or transmitted, are analyzed by software tools that extract relevant information, such as the intensity of the spots and the background level. This information is then used for evaluating the expression level of individual genes (Hegde et al., 2000; Moore, 2001).

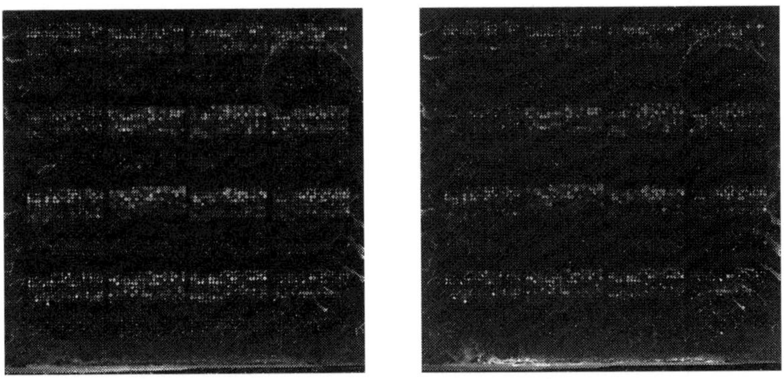

(a) Green channel (b) Red channel

Fig. 1. Example of a pair of images (1041 × 1044 pixels) that results from a microarray experiment.

The common approach for microarray compression has been based on image analysis for spot finding (griding followed by segmentation) with the aim of separating the microarray image data into different streams based on pixel similarities (Adjeroh et al., 2006; Faramarzpour and Shirani, 2004; Faramarzpour et al., 2003; Hua et al., 2003; 2002; Jörnsten et al., 2003; 2002a; Lonardi and Luo, 2004; Zhang et al., 2005). Once separated, the streams are compressed together with the segmentation information. A potential drawback of these segmentation based

*This work was supported in part by the FCT (Fundação para a Ciência e Tecnologia).

approaches is that different spot placements (e.g., non-rectangular) might compromise their performance. In fact, although initially the rectangular packing was the organization used for spot placement in microarrays, other non-rectangular packings have also been proposed (see Fig. 2).

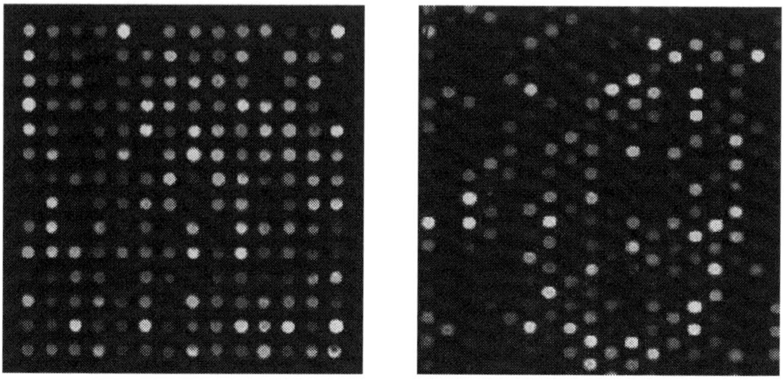

(a) Rectangular packing (b) Orange packing

Fig. 2. Different spot packing: (a) Rectangular packing; (b) Orange packing (sample image from `http://microarray1k.aecom.yu.edu/`). Note that these images are not related. They serve just for illustrating different spot placements.

Although initially most of the specialized techniques for microarray image compression considered the lossy approach as a reasonable possibility (Faramarzpour and Shirani, 2004; Hua et al., 2003; 2002; Jörnsten et al., 2003; 2002a), the most recent methods address mainly reversible techniques (Faramarzpour et al., 2003; Lonardi and Luo, 2004; Zhang et al., 2005). Keeping the original images allows future re-analysis by possibly better algorithms. In fact, the analytic methods that are used for extracting information from the images are continuously being improved (Kothapalli et al., 2002; Leung and Cavalieri, 2003; Sasik et al., 2004). Also, as with other biomedical related data, legal issues might play a key role when choosing between maintaining or deleting the original data.

Recently, we have investigated methods for compressing microarray images that do not require spot segmentation. This new approach is based on arithmetic coding that is driven by image-dependent multi-bitplane finite-context models. Basically, the image is compressed on a bitplane basis, going from the most significant to the least significant bitplane. The finite-context model used by the arithmetic encoder uses (causal) pixels from the bitplane under compression and also pixels from the bitplanes already encoded. To our knowledge, this technique is currently the best one available in terms of compression efficiency of microarray images (Neves and Pinho, 2009).

In this chapter, we start by describing the most important techniques for the lossless compression of microarray images that have been proposed in the literature. Then, we present a set of experiments that have been performed with the aim of providing a reference regarding the performance of standard image coding techniques, namely, lossless JPEG2000, JBIG and JPEG-LS, when applied to the lossless compression of microarray images. We proceed with the description of an image-independent multi-bitplane finite-context approach and we continue with the image-dependent version. Finally, we present experimental results that illustrate the compression performance of the several approaches and we draw some conclusions.

2. Compression techniques for microarray images

In this section, we present the most important methods for compression of microarray images, namely, the works of Jörnsten et al. (2003), Hua et al. (2002), Faramarzpour et al. (2003), Lonardi and Luo (2004) and Zhang et al. (2005). Although all the methods presented in this section address the microarray compression problem using different approaches, some of the processing steps are common and similar to the ones depicted in Fig. 3.

All the methods start by segmenting the microarray images into *regions of interest* (ROIs) containing the spot and some surrounding background. Some methods go even further, separating the spot area from the background. However, the segmentation algorithm used in each method is different.

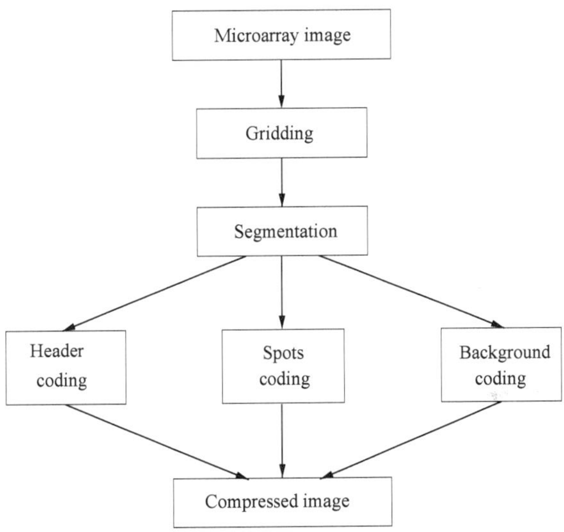

Fig. 3. The common processing steps of the compression methods presented in this section.

Through segmentation, it is possible to encode the spots and background separately. This is explicitly done in the works of Hua et al. (2003; 2002); Jörnsten et al. (2003); Jörnsten and Yu (2000; 2002); Jörnsten et al. (2002a;b); Lonardi and Luo (2004), and more implicilty in the work of Faramarzpour and Shirani (2004); Faramarzpour et al. (2003), because, in this case, the separation between the spot area and the background is performed only when the sequence is entropy encoded.

Almost all available methods have also a lossy compression version. These methods remove what is considered to be noise or redundant. Although this step sounds obvious, the question is "What should be considered noise or redundant?" Note that, in the context of microarray images, the background is very important for noise estimation, because the bias due to noise can be estimated and removed in the calculation of the gene expression level of each spot.

The technique proposed by Jörnsten et al. (2003) is characterized by a first stage devoted to griding and segmentation. Using the approximate center of each spot, a seeded region growing is performed for segmenting the spots. The segmentation map is encoded using chain-coding, whereas the interior of the regions are encoded using a modified version of the LOCO-I algorithm (LOw COmplexity LOssless COmpression for Images, the algorithm behind the JPEG-LS coding standard), named SLOCO. Besides lossy-to-lossless capability, Jörnsten's technique allows partial decoding by means of independently encoded image blocks.
Hua et al. (2002) presented a transform-based coding technique. Initially, a segmentation is performed using the Mann-Whitney algorithm and the segmentation information is encoded separately. Due to the thresholding properties of the Mann-Whitney algorithm, the griding stage is avoided. Then, a modified EBCOT (Embedded Block Coding with Optimized Truncation) (Taubman and Marcellin, 2002) for handling arbitrarily shaped regions is used for encoding the spots and background separately, allowing lossy-to-lossless coding of background only (with the spots encoded in lossless mode) or both background and spots.
The compression method proposed by Faramarzpour et al. (2003) starts by locating and extracting the microarray spots, isolating each spot into an individual ROI. A spiral path is adjusted to each of these ROIs, such that its center coincides with the center of mass of the spot. The idea is to transform the ROI into an one-dimensional signal with minimum entropy. Then, predictive coding is applied along this path, with a separation between residuals belonging to the spot area and those belonging to the background area.
Lonardi and Luo (2004) proposed lossless and lossy compression algorithms for microarray images (MicroZip). The method uses a fully automatic griding procedure, similar to that of Faramarzpour's method, for separating spots from the background (which can be lossy compressed). Through segmentation, the image is split into two streams: foreground and background. Then, for entropy coding, each stream is divided into two 8 bit sub-streams and arithmetic encoded, with the option of being previously processed by a Burrows-Wheeler transform.
The method proposed by Adjeroh et al. (2006); Zhang et al. (2005) is based on PPAM (Prediction by Partial Approximate Matching). PPAM is an image compression algorithm which extends the PPM text compression algorithm, considering the special characteristics of natural images (Zhang et al., 2005). Initially, the microarray image is separated into background and foreground. Then, for each of these two components, the pixel representation is separated into its most significant and least significant parts. To compress the data, the most significant part is first processed by an error prediction scheme. The residuals are then encoded by the PPAM context model and encoder. The least significant part is encoded directly by the PPAM encoder and the segmentation information is saved without compression.

3. Standard image compression methods

JBIG, JPEG-LS and JPEG2000 are state-of-the-art standards for coding digital images. They have been developed with different goals in mind, being JBIG more focused on bi-level imagery, JPEG-LS dedicated to the lossless compression of continuous-tone images and JPEG2000 designed with the aim of providing a wide range of functionalities.
The JBIG standard (Joint Bi-level Image Experts Group) was issued in 1993 by ISO/IEC (International Organization for Standardization / International Electrotechnical Commission) and ITU-T (Telecommunication Standardization Sector of the International Telecommunication Union) for the progressive lossless compression of binary and low-precision gray-level images (typically, having less than 6 bits per pixel). The major advantages of JBIG over other

existing standards, such as FAX Group 3/4, are its capability of progressive encoding and its superior compression efficiency (Hampel et al., 1992; ISO/IEC, 1993; Netravali and Haskell, 1995; Salomon, 2000). The core of JBIG is an adaptive context-based arithmetic encoder, relying on 1024 contexts when operating in sequential mode or on low resolution layers of the progressive mode, or 4096 contexts when encoding high resolution layers. More recently, a new version, named JBIG2, has been published (ISO/IEC, 2000b), introducing additional functionalities to the standard, such as multipage document compression, two modes of progressive compression, lossy compression and differentiated compression methods for different regions of the image (e.g., text or halftones) (Salomon, 2000).

JPEG-LS was developed by the Joint Photographic Experts Group (JPEG) with the aim of providing a low complexity lossless image standard that could be able to offer better compression efficiency than lossless JPEG (ISO/IEC, 1999; Taubman and Marcellin, 2002; Weinberger et al., 2000). Part 1 of this standard was finalized in 1999. The core of JPEG-LS is based on the LOCO-I algorithm, that relies on prediction, residual modeling and context-based coding of the residuals. Most of the low complexity of this technique comes from the assumption that prediction residuals follow a two-sided geometric probability distribution and from the use of Golomb codes which are known to be optimal for this kind of distributions. Besides lossless compression, JPEG-LS also provides a lossy mode where the maximum absolute error can be controlled by the encoder. This is known as near-lossless compression or L_∞-constrained compression.

From the three image coding standards addressed in this section, JPEG2000 is the most recent one (ISO/IEC, 2000a; Taubman and Marcellin, 2002). Part 1 was published as an International Standard in the year 2000. It is based on wavelet technology and EBCOT coding of the wavelet coefficients, providing very good compression performance for a wide range of bitrates, including lossless coding. Moreover, JPEG2000 allows the generation of embedded code streams, meaning that from a higher bitrate stream it is possible to extract lower bitrate instances without the need for re-encoding. This property is of fundamental importance for progressive transmission, for example, over slow communication channels.

These three standard image encoders cover a great variety of coding approaches. In fact, whereas JPEG2000 is transform based, JPEG-LS relies on predictive coding, and JBIG relies on context-based arithmetic coding. This diversity in coding engines might be helpful for drawing conclusions regarding the appropriateness of each of these technologies for the case of microarray image compression.

3.1 Compression performance of the standards

Before trying to develop new compression methods, it is always useful to find out how existing compression standards behave on the class of images of interest. Therefore, for performing that assessment, we collected microarray images from three different publicly available sources: (1) 32 images that we refer to as the Apo AI set and which have been collected from `http://www.stat.berkeley.edu/users/terry/zarray/Html/index.html` (this set was previously used by Jörnsten et al. (2003); Jörnsten and Yu (2002)); (2) 14 images forming the ISREC set which have been collected from `http://www.isrec.isb-sib.ch/DEA/module8/P5_chip_image/images/`; (3) three images previously used to test MicroZip (Lonardi and Luo, 2004), which were collected from `http://www.cs.ucr.edu/~yuluo/MicroZip/`.

JBIG compression was obtained using version 1.6 of the JBIG Kit package[1], with sequential coding (-q flag). JPEG2000 lossless compression was obtained using version 5.1 of the JJ2000 codec with default parameters (lossless compression)[2]. JPEG-LS coding was obtained using version 2.2 of the SPMG JPEG-LS codec with default parameters[3]. For additional reference, we also give compression results using the popular compression tool GZIP (version 1.2.4).
Table 1 shows the compression results, in number of bits per pixel (bpp), where the first group of images corresponds to the Apo AI set, the second to the ISREC set and the third one to the MicroZip image set. Image size ranges from 1000×1000 to 5496×1956 pixels, i.e., from uncompressed sizes of about 2 megabytes to more than 20 megabytes (all images have 16 bits per pixel). The average results presented take into account the different sizes of the images, i.e., they correspond to the total number of bits divided by the total number of image pixels.

Image set	Gzip	JPEG2000	JBIG	JPEG-LS
APO_AI	12.711	11.063	10.851	10.608
ISREC	12.464	11.366	10.925	11.145
Microzip	11.434	9.515	9.297	8.974
Average	**12.273**	**10.653**	**10.393**	**10.218**

Table 1. Compression results, in bits per pixel (bpp), using lossless JPEG2000, JBIG and JPEG-LS. For reference, results are also given for the popular compression tool GZIP.

The total average results show that gains of about 13.2%, 15.3% and 16.7%, in relation to GZIP compression, are attained respectively for lossless JPEG2000, JBIG and JPEG-LS, showing the superiority of image coding techniques over general purpose data compression methods in the task of compressing images. The average results by image set show that JPEG-LS provides the highest compression in the case of the Apo AI and MicroZip images, whereas JBIG gives the best results for the ISREC set. Lossless JPEG2000 is always slightly behind these two. It is interesting to note that the set for which JBIG gave the best results is also the one requiring more bits per pixel for encoding.

3.1.1 Sensitivity to noise

It has been noted by Jörnsten et al. (2003) that, in general, the eight least significant bitplanes of cDNA microarray images are close to random and, therefore, incompressible. Since this fact may result in some degradation in the compression performance of the encoders, we decided to address this problem and to study the effect of noisy bitplanes in the compression performance of the standards.
To perform this evaluation, we separated the images into a number p of most significant bitplanes and $16 - p$ least significant bitplanes. Whereas the p most significant bitplanes have been sent to the encoder, the $16 - p$ least significant bitplanes have been left uncompressed. This means that the bitrate of a given image is the sum of the bitrate generated by encoding the p most significant bitplanes plus the $16 - p$ bits concerning the bitplanes that have been left uncompressed.

[1] `http://www.cl.cam.ac.uk/~mgk25/jbigkit/`.
[2] `http://jj2000.epfl.ch`.
[3] The original website of this codec, `http://spmg.ece.ubc.ca`, is currently unavailable. However, it can be obtained from `ftp://www.ieeta.pt/~ap/codecs/jpeg_ls_v2.2.tar.gz`.

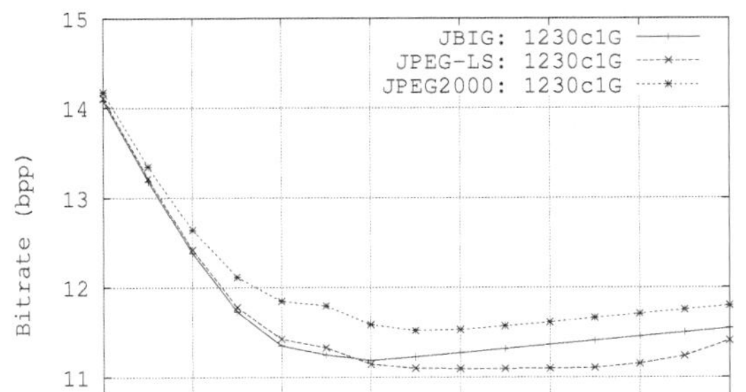

Fig. 4. Influence of noisy bitplanes in the performance of the standard encoding methods. The the curves indicate the bitrate obtained when only a given number p of the most significant bitplanes are sent to the encoder, whereas the other $16 - p$ bitplanes are left uncompressed.

Image set	JPEG2000		JBIG		JPEG-LS	
	8 bp	Best	8 bp	Best	8 bp	Best
Apo_AI	10.940	10.790	10.510	10.507	10.523	10.433
ISREC	11.100	10.954	10.607	10.583	10.838	10.713
MicroZip	9.918	9.321	9.506	9.030	9.588	8.912
Average	**10.661**	**10.376**	**10.224**	**10.073**	**10.302**	**10.026**

Table 2. Average compression results, in bits per pixel (bpp), when a number of bitplanes is left uncompressed. The columns labeled "8 bp" provide results for the case where only the 8 most significant bitplanes have been encoded and the 8 least significant bitplanes have been left uncompressed. The column named "Best" contains the results for the case where the separation of most and least significant bitplanes has been optimally found.

Figure 4 depicts bitrate curves, as a function of p, for two different images, "1230c1G" and "array1". As can be observed, the best bitrate is generally not met when compressing all 16 bitplanes, but instead when some of the least significant bitplanes are left uncompressed. However, the value of the optimum value of p, p_{opt}, varies not only from image to image, but also from one encoder to the other. In fact, for the Apo AI set, which is characterized by the most regular value of p_{opt}, JBIG is the encoder with the highest value of p_{opt} (around 8), then comes lossless JPEG2000 (around 10) and, finally, JPEG-LS (around 13). This result is not surprising, since JBIG encodes the bitplanes independently. Therefore, without being able to get information from other bitplanes, it is natural that JBIG starts considering bitplanes as "noise" earlier than the other encoders. Moreover, this can also be the justification for its better performance in the ISREC set, because it is the most noisy.
Table 2 compares average results for the three set of images regarding two situations: (1) the image is divided into the eight most significant bitplanes (which are encoded) and the eight least significant bitplanes (which are left uncompressed); (2) the optimum value of p is determined for each image. From this table, and comparing with the Table 1, we can see that, in fact, this splitting operation can provide some additional compression gains. The best results attained provided improvements of 3.1%, 2.6% and 1.9% respectively for JBIG, lossless JPEG2000 and JPEG-LS.
However, finding the right value for p may require as many as 16 iterations of the compression phase in order to find it. Moreover, from the results shown in Table 2, we can see that a simple separation of the bitplanes in an upper and lower half may improve the compression in some cases (Apo AI and ISREC image sets), but may also produce the opposite result (MicroZip image set).

3.1.2 Lossy-to-lossless compression

From the point of view of compression efficiency, and taking into account the results presented in Table 1, JPEG-LS is the overall best lossless compression method, followed by JBIG and lossless JPEG2000. The difference between JPEG-LS and lossless JPEG2000 is about 4.1% and between JPEG-LS and JBIG is only 1.7%. However, the better compression performance provided by JPEG-LS can be overshadowed by a potentially important functionality provided by the other two standards, which is progressive, lossy-to-lossless, transmission.
In the case of lossless JPEG2000, this functionality is basically a by-product of the multi-resolution wavelet technology used in its encoding engine and also due to a strategy of encoding the information in layers (Taubman and Marcellin, 2002). In the case of JBIG, this property comes from two different sources. On one hand, images with more that one bitplane are encoded using a bitplane-by-bitplane coding approach. This provides a kind of progressive transmission, from most to least significant bitplanes, where the precision of the pixels is improved for each added bitplane. Moreover, this technique produces a reduction of the L_∞ error by a factor of two for each additional bitplane. On the other hand, JBIG permits the progressive transmission of each bitplane by progressively increasing its spatial resolution (ISO/IEC, 1993; Salomon, 2000). However, the compression results that we present in Table 1 do not take into account the additional overhead implied by this encoding mode of JBIG (we used the -q flag of the encoder, which disables this mode).
In Fig. 5, we present rate-distortion curves for two images, "1230c1G" and "array1", obtained with the lossless JPEG2000 and JBIG coding standards, and according to two error metrics: L_2-norm (root mean squared error) and L_∞-norm (maximum absolute error). Regarding the L_2-norm, we observe that lossless JPEG2000 provides slightly better rate-distortion results for

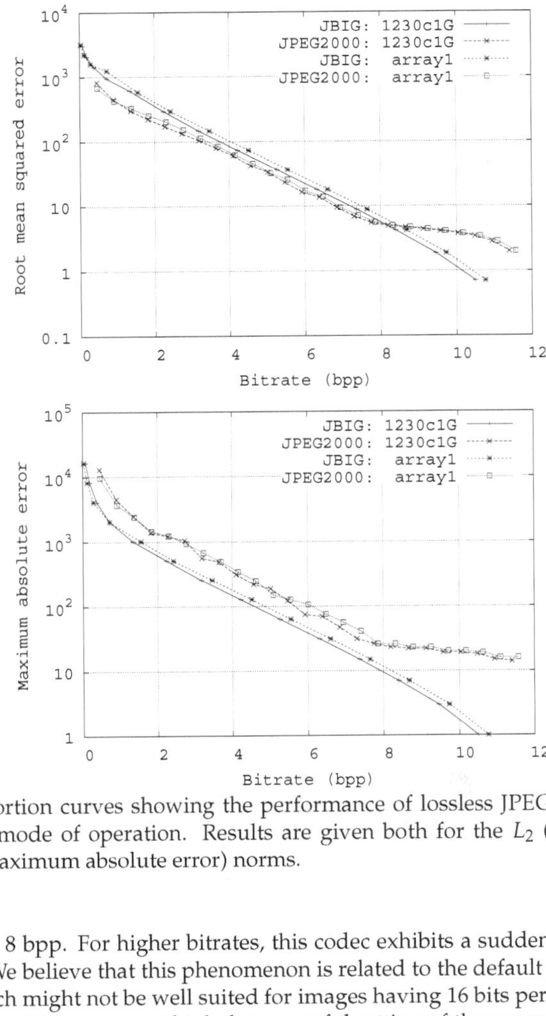

Fig. 5. Rate distortion curves showing the performance of lossless JPEG2000 and JBIG in a lossy-to-lossless mode of operation. Results are given both for the L_2 (root mean squared error) and L_∞ (maximum absolute error) norms.

bitrates less than 8 bpp. For higher bitrates, this codec exhibits a sudden degradation of the rate-distortion. We believe that this phenomenon is related to the default parameters used by the encoder, which might not be well suited for images having 16 bits per pixel, such as those of the microarrays. Moreover, we think that a careful setting of these parameters may lead to improvements in the rate-distortion of JPEG2000 for bitrates higher than 8 bpp, although we consider this tuning a problem that is beyond the scope of this work.

With respect to the L_∞-norm, we observe that JBIG is the one with the best rate-distortion performance. In fact, due to its bitplane-by-bitplane approach, it guarantees an exponential and upper bounded decrease of the maximum absolute error. The upper bound of the error is given by $2^{(16-p)} - 1$, where p is the number of bitplanes already decoded. Contrarily, lossless JPEG2000 cannot guarantee such bound, which may be a major drawback in some cases. Finally, we note that the sudden deviation of the lossless JPEG2000 curves around bitrates of 8 bpp is probably related to the same problem pointed out earlier for the case of the L_2-norm.

3.2 Conclusions

The main objective of this section was to provide a set of comprehensive results regarding the lossless compression of microarray images by state-of-the-art image coding standards, namely, lossless JPEG2000, JBIG and JPEG-LS. In order to facilitate future comparisons by other researchers, we collected a total of 49 microarray images available from the Internet. We believe that the development of specialized compression techniques should be supported by a preliminary study of the performance provided by well established methods and, particularly, by those that are standards. Only after making such study it is possible to be in a comfortable position for arguing about the relevance of some specialized technique.

From the experimental results obtained, we conclude that JPEG-LS gives the best lossless compression performance. However, it lacks lossy-to-lossless capability, which may be a decisive functionality if remote transmission over possibly slow links is a requirement. Complying to this requirement we find JBIG and lossless JPEG2000, lossless JPEG2000 being the best considering rate-distortion in the sense of the L_2-norm and JBIG the most efficient when considering the L_∞-norm. Moreover, JBIG is consistently better than lossless JPEG2000 regarding lossless compression ratios. Also, JBIG is the method that can benefit most from a correct separation of most significant bitplanes that are encoded and least significant bitplanes that are left uncompressed (it gained 3.1%), and it is also the coding technique that, due to the bitplane-by-bitplane coding, can search for the optimum point of separation on-the-fly. In fact, this can be done by monitoring the bitrate resulting from the compression of each bitplane, and stop doing compression when this value is over 1 bpp. As a final conclusion, and according to what we presented in this section, it is our opinion that the technology behind JBIG seems to be the most appropriate for microarray image coding.

4. Compression of microarray images using finite-context models and arithmetic coding

4.1 Finite-context models

The core of the methods proposed in the remainder of this chapter consists of an adaptive finite-context model followed by arithmetic coding. A finite-context model (see Fig. 6) of an information source assigns probability estimates to the symbols of an alphabet $\mathcal{A}$, according to a conditioning context computed over a finite and fixed number, M, of past outcomes (order-M finite-context model) (Rissanen, 1983; Rissanen and Langdon, Jr., 1981; Sayood, 2000). At time t, we represent these conditioning outcomes by $c^t = x_{t-M+1}, \ldots, x_{t-1}, x_t$. The number of conditioning states of the model is $|\mathcal{A}|^M$, dictating its complexity (or model cost). In our case, $\mathcal{A} = \{0, 1\}$ and, therefore, $|\mathcal{A}| = 2$.

In practice, the probability that the next outcome, x_{t+1}, is "0" is obtained using the estimator

$$P(x_{t+1} = 0|c^t) = \frac{n(0, c^t) + \delta}{n(0, c^t) + n(1, c^t) + 2\delta}, \quad (1)$$

where $n(s, c^t)$ represents the number of times that, in the past, the information source generated symbol $s \in \mathcal{A}$ having c^t as the conditioning context. The parameter $\delta > 0$, besides allowing fine tuning the estimator, avoids generating zero probabilities when a symbol is encoded for the first time. In our case, we used $\delta = 1$, which corresponds to Laplace's estimator (it can be seen as an initialization of all counters to one). The counters are updated each time a symbol is encoded. Since the context template is causal, the decoder is able to reproduce the same probability estimates without needing additional information.

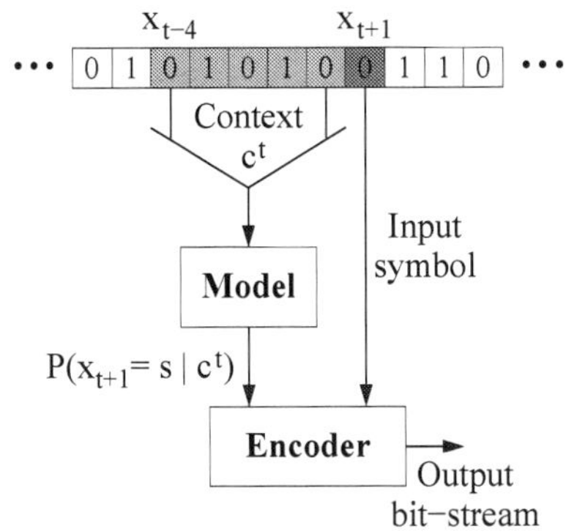

Fig. 6. Finite-context model: the probability of the next outcome, x_{t+1}, is conditioned by the M last outcomes. In this example, $M = 5$.

Context, c^t	$n(0,c^t)$	$n(1,c^t)$	$n(0,c^t)+n(1,c^t)$
00000	23	41	64
00001	16	6	22
00010	19	30	49
00011	34	42	76
00100	36	17	53
⋮	⋮	⋮	⋮
11111	8	2	10

Table 3. Simple example illustrating how finite-context models are implemented. The rows of the table represent a probability model at a given instant t. In this example, the particular model that is chosen for encoding a symbol depends on the last five encoded symbols (order-5 context).

Table 3 shows an example of how a finite-context is typically implemented. In this example, an order-5 finite-context model is presented. Each row represents a probability model that is used to encode a given symbol according to the last encoded symbols (five in this example). Therefore, if the last symbols were "00010", i.e., $c^t = 00010$, then the model communicates the following probability estimates to the arithmetic encoder: $P(0|00010) = 19/49$ and $P(1|00010) = 30/49$.

The block denoted "Encoder" in Fig. 6 is an arithmetic encoder. It is well known that practical arithmetic coding generates output bit-streams with average bitrates almost identical to the entropy of the model (Bell et al., 1990; Salomon, 2000; Sayood, 2000). In our case, the theoretical bitrate average (entropy) of the model after encoding N symbols is given by

$$H_N = -\frac{1}{N}\sum_{t=0}^{N-1} \log_2 P(x_{t+1} = s|c^t) \quad \text{bps,} \tag{2}$$

where "bps" stands for "bits per symbol". Since we are dealing with images, instead of using the generic "bps" measure we use "bpp", which stands for "bits per pixel". Recall that the entropy of any sequence of two symbols is limited to 1 bps, a value that is achieved when the symbols are independent and equally likely.

4.2 Image-independent contexts

In Section 3, we presented a study of the compression performance of three image coding standards in the context of microarray image compression: JPEG2000, JBIG and JPEG-LS. Since they rely on three different coding technologies, we were able not only to evaluate the performance of each of these standards, but also to collect hints regarding what might be the best coding technology regarding microarray image compression. In that study, we concluded that from the three technologies evaluated (predictive coding in the case of JPEG-LS, transform coding in the case of JPEG2000 and context-based arithmetic coding in the case of JBIG), the technology behind JBIG seemed to be the most promising. In fact, JPEG-LS provided the highest compression, closely followed by JBIG. However, unlike JPEG2000 and JBIG, it does not provide lossy-to-lossless capabilities, a characteristic that might be of high interest, specially in the case where remote databases have to be accessed using transmission channels of reduced bandwidth. Moreover, with JBIG, the image bitplanes are compressed independently, suggesting the existence of some room for improvement.

Motivated by these observations, we developed a compression method for microarray images which is based on the same technology as JBIG but that, unlike JBIG, exploits inter-bitplane dependencies, providing coding gains in relation to JBIG (Neves and Pinho, 2006). Designing contexts that gather information from more than one bitplane (multi-bitplane contexts) is not just a matter of joining more bits to the context, because for each new bit added the memory required doubles. Moreover, there is the danger of running into the context dilution problem, due to the lack of sufficient data for estimating the probabilities. Therefore, this extension to multi-bitplane contexts must be done carefully.

The method proposed by Neves and Pinho (2006) was inspired by EIDAC (Yoo et al., 1998), a compression method that has been used with success for coding images with a reduced number of intensities (simple images). The images are compressed on a bitplane basis, from the most to the least significant bitplane. The causal finite-context model that drives the arithmetic encoder uses pixels both from the bitplane currently being encoded and from the bitplanes already encoded. As encoding proceeds, the average bitrate obtained after encoding each bitplane is monitored. If, for some bitplane, the average bitrate exceeds one bit per pixel, then the encoding process is stopped and the remaining bitplanes are saved without compression. The encoding procedure is outlined in Fig. 7.

The context modeling part of EIDAC was designed mainly with the aim of compressing images with eight bitplanes or less, implying, at most, 19 bits of context. A straightforward extension to images with 16 bitplanes would require contexts of 27 bits, i.e., at least $2 \times 2^{27} = 2^{28}$ counters. Essentially, the technique proposed by Neves and Pinho (2006) differs from EIDAC in three aspects: (1) it was designed taking into account the specific nature of the images, keeping the size of the contexts limited to 21 bits; (2) it does not use the histogram packing procedure proposed for EIDAC because, generally, microarray images have dense intensity histograms; (3) it implements a rate-control mechanism that avoids producing average bitrates of more than one bit per pixel in bitplanes that are too noisy (this is a common characteristic of the least significant bitplanes of microarray images (Jörnsten et al., 2003)).

As we mentioned before, choosing the context template for a multi-bitplane image is a critical task, requiring tradeoffs involving aspects such as the maximum size of the context, the problem of context dilution and the placement of the context bits such that the maximum informa-

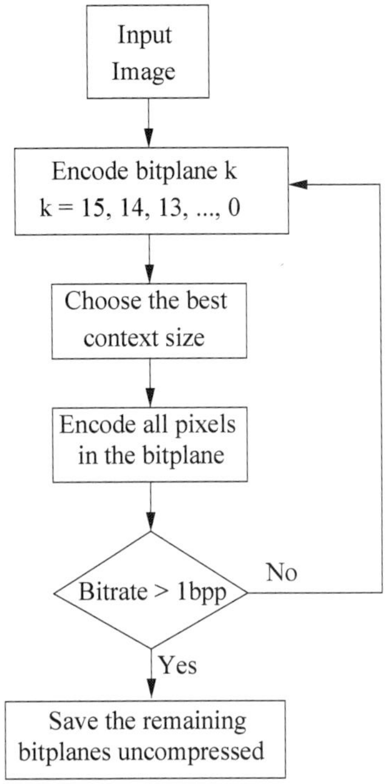

Fig. 7. Encoding procedure of the method proposed by Neves and Pinho (2006). The choice of the context shape is based on Fig. 8. Note that, being a bitplane based encoder, it is possible to monitor the bitrate used to encode each bitplane.

tion can be collected. This work was done in (Neves and Pinho, 2006) mainly using a trial and error procedure, leading to the image-independent context configuration displayed in Fig. 8. Note that, when encoding the eight least significant bitplanes, the finite-context model is only formed with pixels from the higher numbered bitplanes. This specific context configuration together with the rate-control mechanism avoids the degradation in compression rate when there are bitplanes that are close to random and, therefore, are almost incompressible.

Although being able to provide state-of-the-art compression results, the method proposed in (Neves and Pinho, 2006) could be improved. In fact, due to its image-independent nature, and despite being designed for a specific type of images (microarrays), the context configuration depicted in Fig. 8 resulted from a complicated process that tried to balance the inevitable particularities among the images. From the point of view of a single image, this context configuration might seem overkill, i.e., a smaller context might suffice. However, it is needed for satisfying the ensemble of images. This observation motivated the image-dependent context-modeling approach that we describe in the next section.

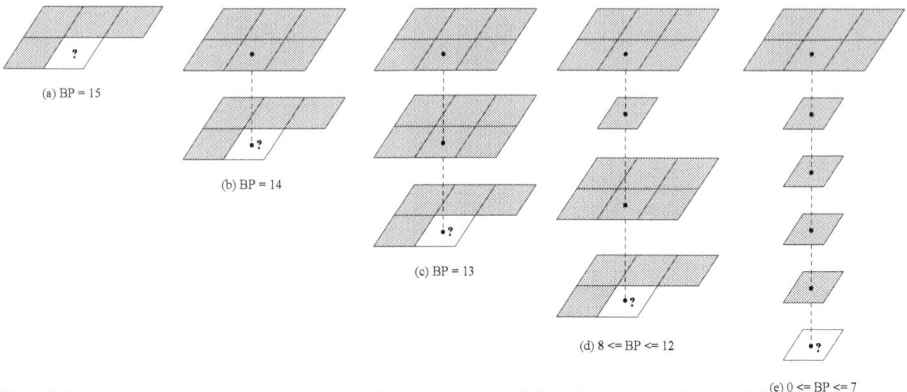

Fig. 8. Image-independent context configuration used in (Neves and Pinho, 2006) at five different compression stages: (a) when encoding the most significant bitplane (four bits of context); (b) when encoding the second most significant bitplane (ten bits of context); (c) when encoding the third most significant bitplane (16 bits of context); (d) from the fourth until the eighth most significant bitplanes (17–21 bits of context); (e) the eight least significant bitplanes (13–20 bits of context). Context positions falling outside the image at the image borders are considered as having zero value.

5. Image-dependent finite-context models

Instead of using the image-independent context model presented in Fig. 8, the algorithm that we describe in this section tries to find the "best" context configuration to encode the current bitplane, based on the templates depicted in Fig. 9. The test of all possible context configurations is a hard task, virtually impossible, due to the huge number of possibilities. To overcome this drawback, we developed a greedy approach that we explain next.

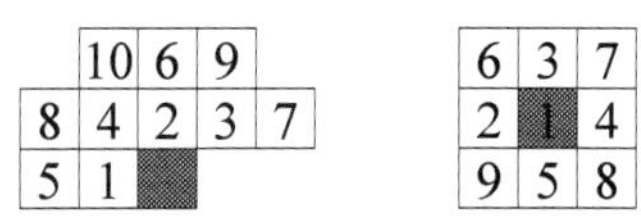

(a) (b)

Fig. 9. (a) The template used for growing the context at the level of the bitplane currently being encoded; (b) The template used for growing the context corresponding to the bitplanes already encoded.

Before encoding a bitplane, p, the algorithm constructs an appropriate context configuration through an iterative process (note that bitplanes are numbered from 0, the least significant bitplane, to 15, the most significant bitplane). In each iteration, an additional context bit is tested in each of the $16 - p$ possible locations, one in each of the $16 - p$ context bitplanes that are available. In a given context bitplane, the additional bit can only be inserted in position k of the corresponding template displayed in Fig. 9 if all positions $i < k$ belong already to the best context configuration found so far. This means that the part of the context belonging to a given bitplane can grow only according to the pixel numbering shown in Fig. 9. The template

in Fig. 9(a) is used for the context bitplane p, whereas the template in Fig. 9(b) applies to the remaining context bitplanes, i.e., from bitplane $p+1$ to bitplane 15.
After performing an iteration, the new context bit is assigned to the position where the largest improvement in the compression performance of bitplane p occurred. If none of the possible $16-p$ context bit positions were able to improve the compression, then the search stops and the context configuration found so far is used for encoding the bitplane p. Otherwise, a new context bit is tested. This iterative process proceeds while the new context bit is able to improve the compression performance of bitplane p or until the maximum context depth is reached. For the results presented in this section, we used a maximum of 20 context bits. Figure 10 presents an example of the context configuration obtained with this process for some of the bitplanes of the image "1230c1G" (APO_AI image set).
The configuration of the context bits for a particular bitplane, p, can be communicated to the decoder using approximately $4(16-p)$ bits. Note that the maximum number of context bits per context bitplane is less that 16 (see Fig. 9) and, therefore, can be represented in four bits. Hence, the total overhead regarding the image-dependent contexts is just some tens of bytes. The algorithm is outlined next.

```
bestCtx := 0-order context;
bestRate := rate for encoding bitplane
 with 0-order context;
do
  improved := FALSE;
  for p := bitplane to be encoded, 15
    if p = bitplane to be encoded
      add bit according to Fig. 9(a);
    else
      add bit according to Fig. 9(b);
    end
    rate := rate for encoding bitplane
     using current context;
    if rate < bestRate
      bestCtx := current context;
      bestRate := rate;
      improved := TRUE;
    end
    remove bit added above;
  end
while size of bestCtx < 20 AND improved
```

Being a greedy approach, it is not guaranteed that the optimum is found. In fact, as can be seen, for each context bitplane the context can only grow according to a predefined order which is given by the pixel numbering associated to the templates of Fig. 9. This limits the number of degrees of freedom of the search process, reducing the probability of finding the optimum configuration, but, on the other hand, also allowing running this procedure in a reasonable time.
In order to further accelerate the process of choosing these image-dependent contexts, and due to the highly structured nature of microarray images, we developed another version of the algorithm where only a small region of the image is used for constructing the contexts. Using this faster approach, the results obtained for a region of 256×256 pixels have been slightly worse. However, we verified a significant reduction in the time spent. In a 2 GHz Pentium 4 computer with 512 MBytes of memory, the MicroZip test set (three images totaling

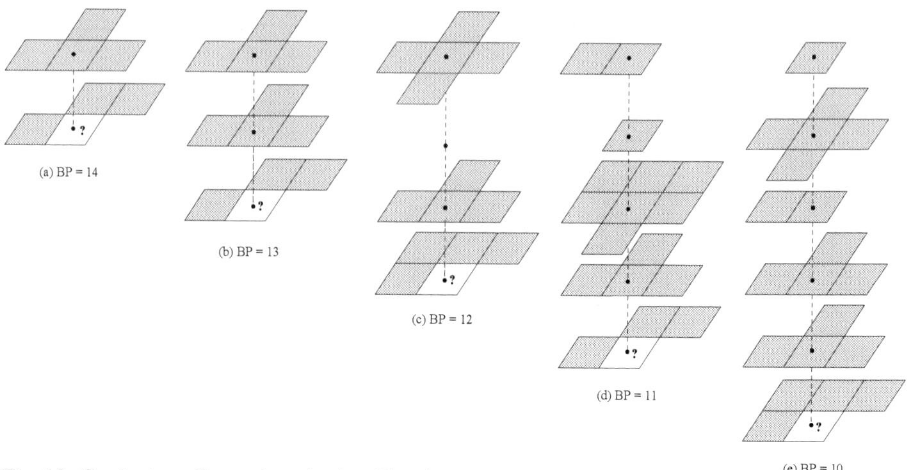

Fig. 10. Context configuration obtained by the proposed method in five different bitplanes of the image "1230c1G": (a) when encoding bitplane 14 (seven bits of context); (b) when encoding bitplane 13 (11 bits of context); (c) when encoding bitplane 12 (13 bits of context); (d) when encoding bitplane 11 (17 bits of context); (e) when encoding bitplane 10 (20 bits of context). Context positions falling outside the image at the image borders are considered as having zero value.

approximately 21 million pixels) required about 220 minutes to compress when the whole image was used to performed the search. When we used a region of 256 × 256 pixels, it required approximately 6 minutes to compress the MicroZip test set (about 2 minutes more than the image-independent approach). These three images have sizes of 1916 × 1872, 5496 × 1956 and 3625 × 1929 pixels. Decoding is faster, because the decoder does not have to search for the best context: that information is embedded in the bitstream.

6. Experimental results

Table 4 shows the average compression results, in bits per pixel, for the three sets of images described previously (see Section 3). In this table, we present experimental results of both the image-independent and the image-dependent approaches. We also include results obtained with SPIHT (Said and Pearlman, 1996)[4] and EIDAC (Yoo et al., 1998).
Comparing with the results presented in Table 1, we can see that the fast version of the image-dependent method (indicated as "256 × 256" in the table) is 6.3% better than JBIG, 4.7% better than JPEG-LS and 8.6% better than lossless JPEG2000. It is important to remember that JPEG-LS does not provide progressive decoding, a characteristic that is intrinsic to the image-dependent multi-bitplane finite-context method and also to JPEG2000 and JBIG. From the results presented in Table 4, it can also be seen that using an area of 256 × 256 pixels in the center of the image for finding the context, instead of the whole image, leads to a small degradation in the performance (about 0.3%), showing the appropriateness of this approach.

[4] SPIHT codec from `http://www.cipr.rpi.edu/research/SPIHT/` (version 8.01).

Image set	SPIHT	EIDAC	Image independent	Image-dependent	
				256×256	Full
APO_AI	10.812	10.543	10.280	10.225	10.194
ISREC	11.098	10.446	10.199	10.198	10.158
MicroZip	9.198	8.837	8.840	8.667	8.619
Average	**10.378**	**10.005**	**9.826**	**9.741**	**9.708**

Table 4. Average compression results, in bits per pixel, using SPIHT, EIDAC, the image-independent and the image-dependent methods. The "256 × 256" column indicates results obtained with a context model adjusted using only a square of 256 × 256 pixels at the center of the microarray image, whereas "Full" indicates that the search was performed in the whole image. The average results presented take into account the different sizes of the images, i.e., they correspond to the total number of bits divided by the total number of image pixels.

Table 5 confirms the performance of the image-dependent method relatively to two recent specialized methods for compressing microarray images: MicroZip (Lonardi and Luo, 2004) and Zhang's method (Adjeroh et al., 2006; Zhang et al., 2005). As can be observed, the image-dependent multi-bitplane finite-context method provides compression gains of 9.1% relatively to MicroZip and 6.2% in relation to Zhang's method, on a set of test images that has been used by all these methods.

Images	MicroZip	Zhang	Image independent	Image-dependent	
				256×256	Full
array1	11.490	11.380	11.105	11.120	11.056
array2	9.570	9.260	8.628	8.470	8.423
array3	8.470	8.120	7.962	7.717	7.669
Average	**9.532**	**9.243**	**8.840**	**8.667**	**8.619**

Table 5. Compression results, in bits per pixel, using two specialized methods, MicroZip and Zhang's method, the image-independent method and the image-dependent method. The "256 × 256" column indicates results obtained with a context model adjusted using only a square of 256 × 256 pixels at the center of the microarray image, whereas "Full" indicates that the search was performed in the whole image.

Figure 11 shows, for three different images, the average number of bits per pixel that are needed for representing each bitplane. As expected, this value generally increases when going from most significant bitplanes to least significant bitplanes. For the case of images "`Def661Cy3`" and "`1230c1G`", it can be seen that the average number of bits per pixel required by the eight least significant bitplanes is close to one, as pointed out by Jörnsten et al. (2003). However, image "`array3`" shows a different behavior. Because this image is less noisy, the compression algorithm is able to exploit redundancies even in lower bitplanes. This is done without compromising the compression efficiency of noisy images, due to the mechanism that monitors and controls the average number of bits per pixel required for encoding each bitplane.

The maximum number of context bits that we allowed for building the contexts was limited to 20. Since the coding alphabet is binary, this implies, at most, $2 \times 2^{20} = 2\,097\,152$ counters that can be stored in approximately 8 MBytes of computer memory. In a 2 GHz Pentium 4

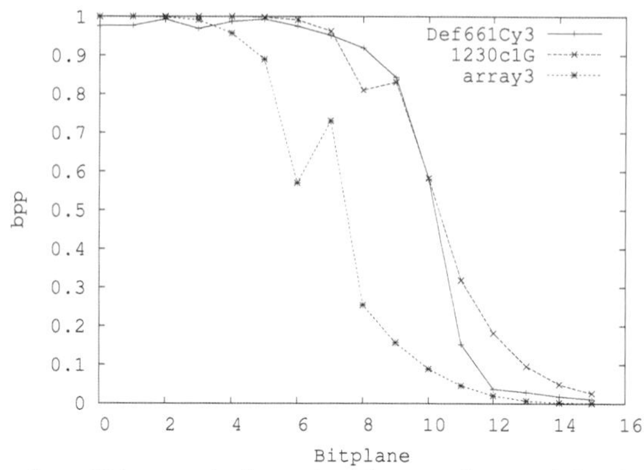

Fig. 11. Average number of bits per pixel required for encoding each bitplane of three different microarray images (one from each test set).

computer with 512 MBytes of memory, the image-dependent algorithm required about six minutes to compress the MicroZip test set (note that this compression time is only indicative, because the code has not been optimized for speed). Decoding is faster, because the decoder does not have to search for the best context. Just for comparison, the codecs of the compression standards took approximately one minute to encode the same set of images.

7. Conclusions

The use of microarray expression data in state-of-the-art biology has been well established. The widespread adoption of this technology, coupled with the significant volume of data generated per experiment, in the form of images, has led to significant challenges in storage and query-retrieval. In this work, we have studied the problem of coding this type of images.

We presented a set of comprehensive results regarding the lossless compression of microarray images by state-of-the-art image coding standards, namely, lossless JPEG2000, JBIG and JPEG-LS. From the experimental results obtained, we conclude that JPEG-LS gives the best lossless compression performance. However, it lacks lossy-to-lossless capability, which may be a decisive functionality if remote transmission over possibly slow links is a requirement. Complying to this requirement we find JBIG and lossless JPEG2000, lossless JPEG2000 being the best considering rate-distortion in the sense of the L_2-norm and JBIG the most efficient when considering the L_∞-norm. Moreover, JBIG is consistently better than lossless JPEG2000 regarding lossless compression ratios.

Motivated by these findings, we have developed efficient methods for lossless compression of microarray images, allowing progressive, lossy-to-lossless decoding. These methods are based on bitplane compression using image-independent or image-dependent finite-context models and arithmetic coding. They do not require griding and/or segmentation as most of the specialized methods that have been proposed do. This may be an advantage if only compression is sought, since it reduces the complexity of the method. Moreover, since they do not require griding, they are robust, for example, against layout changes in spot placement.

The results obtained by the multi-bitplane context-based methods have been compared with the three image coding standards and with two recent specialized methods: MicroZip and Zhang's method. The results obtained show that these new methods have better compression performance in all image test sets used.

8. References

Adjeroh, D., Y. Zhang, and R. Parthe (2006, February). On denoising and compression of DNA microarray images. *Pattern Recognition 39*, 2478–2493.

Bell, T. C., J. G. Cleary, and I. H. Witten (1990). *Text compression*. Prentice Hall.

Faramarzpour, N. and S. Shirani (2004, March). Lossless and lossy compression of DNA microarray images. In *Proc. of the Data Compression Conf., DCC-2004*, Snowbird, Utah, pp. 538.

Faramarzpour, N., S. Shirani, and J. Bondy (2003, November). Lossless DNA microarray image compression. In *Proc. of the 37th Asilomar Conf. on Signals, Systems, and Computers, 2003*, Volume 2, pp. 1501–1504.

Hampel, H., R. B. Arps, C. Chamzas, D. Dellert, D. L. Duttweiler, T. Endoh, W. Equitz, F. Ono, R. Pasco, I. Sebestyen, C. J. Starkey, S. J. Urban, Y. Yamazaki, and T. Yoshida (1992, April). Technical features of the JBIG standard for progressive bi-level image compression. *Signal Processing: Image Communication* 4(2), 103–111.

Hegde, P., R. Qi, K. Abernathy, C. Gay, S. Dharap, R. Gaspard, J. Earle-Hughes, E. Snesrud, N. Lee, and J. Q. (2000, September). A concise guide to cDNA microarray analysis. *Biotechniques 29*(3), 548–562.

Hua, J., Z. Liu, Z. Xiong, Q. Wu, and K. Castleman (2003, September). Microarray BASICA: background adjustment, segmentation, image compression and analysis of microarray images. In *Proc. of the IEEE Int. Conf. on Image Processing, ICIP-2003*, Volume 1, Barcelona, Spain, pp. 585–588.

Hua, J., Z. Xiong, Q. Wu, and K. Castleman (2002, October). Fast segmentation and lossy-to-lossless compression of DNA microarray images. In *Proc. of the Workshop on Genomic Signal Processing and Statistics, GENSIPS*, Raleigh, NC.

ISO/IEC (1993, March). *Information technology - Coded representation of picture and audio information - progressive bi-level image compression*. International Standard ISO/IEC 11544 and ITU-T Recommendation T.82.

ISO/IEC (1999). *Information technology - Lossless and near-lossless compression of continuous-tone still images*. ISO/IEC 14495–1 and ITU Recommendation T.87.

ISO/IEC (2000a). *Information technology - JPEG 2000 image coding system*. ISO/IEC International Standard 15444–1, ITU-T Recommendation T.800.

ISO/IEC (2000b). *JBIG2 bi-level image compression standard*. International Standard ISO/IEC 14492 and ITU-T Recommendation T.88.

Jörnsten, R., W. Wang, B. Yu, and K. Ramchandran (2003). Microarray image compression: SLOCO and the effect of information loss. *Signal Processing 83*, 859–869.

Jörnsten, R. and B. Yu (2000, March). Comprestimation: microarray images in abundance. In *Proc. of the Conf. on Information Sciences*, Princeton, NJ.

Jörnsten, R. and B. Yu (2002, July). Compression of cDNA microarray images. In *Proc. of the IEEE Int. Symposium on Biomedical Imaging, ISBI-2002*, Washington, DC, pp. 38–41.

Jörnsten, R., B. Yu, W. Wang, and K. Ramchandran (2002a, September). Compression of cDNA and inkjet microarray images. In *Proc. of the IEEE Int. Conf. on Image Processing, ICIP-2002*, Volume 3, Rochester, NY, pp. 961–964.

Jörnsten, R., B. Yu, W. Wang, and K. Ramchandran (2002b, October). Microarray image compression and the effect of compression loss. In *Proc. of the Workshop on Genomic Signal Processing and Statistics, GENSIPS*, Raleigh, NC.

Kothapalli, R., S. J. Yoder, S. Mane, and T. P. L. Jr (2002). Microarray results: how accurate are they? *BMC Bioinformatics 3*.

Leung, Y. F. and D. Cavalieri (2003, November). Fundamentals of cDNA microarray data analysis. *Trends on Genetics 19*(11), 649–659.

Lonardi, S. and Y. Luo (2004, August). Gridding and compression of microarray images. In *Proc. of the IEEE Computational Systems Bioinformatics Conference, CSB-2004*, Stanford, CA.

Moore, S. K. (2001, March). Making chips to probe genes. *IEEE Spectrum 38*(3), 54–60.

Netravali, A. N. and B. G. Haskell (1995). *Digital pictures: representation, compression and standards* (2nd ed.). New York: Plenum.

Neves, A. J. R. and A. J. Pinho (2006, October). Lossless compression of microarray images. In *Proc. of the IEEE Int. Conf. on Image Processing, ICIP-2006*, Atlanta, GA, pp. 2505–2508.

Neves, A. J. R. and A. J. Pinho (2009, February). Lossless compression of microarray images using image-dependent finite-context models. *IEEE Trans. on Medical Imaging 28*(2), 194–201.

Pinho, A. J. and A. J. R. Neves (2006, October). Lossy-to-lossless compression of images based on binary tree decomposition. In *Proc. of the IEEE Int. Conf. on Image Processing, ICIP-2006*, Atlanta, GA, pp. 2257–2260.

Rissanen, J. (1983, September). A universal data compression system. *IEEE Trans. on Information Theory 29*(5), 656–664.

Rissanen, J. and G. G. Langdon, Jr. (1981, January). Universal modeling and coding. *IEEE Trans. on Information Theory 27*(1), 12–23.

Said, A. and W. A. Pearlman (1996, June). A new, fast, and efficient image codec based on set partitioning in hierarchical trees. *IEEE Trans. on Circuits and Systems for Video Technology 6*(3), 243–250.

Salomon, D. (2000). *Data compression - The complete reference* (2nd ed.). Springer.

Sasik, R., C. H. Woelk, and J. Corbeil (2004, August). Microarray truths and consequences. *Journal of Molecular Endocrinology 33*(1), 1–9.

Sayood, K. (2000). *Introduction to data compression* (2nd ed.). Morgan Kaufmann.

Skodras, A., C. Christopoulos, and T. Ebrahimi (2001, September). The JPEG 2000 still image compression standard. *IEEE Signal Processing Magazine 18*(5), 36–58.

Taubman, D. S. and M. W. Marcellin (2002). *JPEG 2000: image compression fundamentals, standards and practice.* Kluwer Academic Publishers.

Weinberger, M. J., G. Seroussi, and G. Sapiro (2000, August). The LOCO-I lossless image compression algorithm: principles and standardization into JPEG-LS. *IEEE Trans. on Image Processing 9*(8), 1309–1324.

Yoo, Y., Y. G. Kwon, and A. Ortega (1998, November). Embedded image-domain adaptive compression of simple images. In *Proc. of the 32nd Asilomar Conf. on Signals, Systems, and Computers*, Volume 2, Pacific Grove, CA, pp. 1256–1260.

Zhang, Y., R. Parthe, and D. Adjeroh (2005, August). Lossless compression of DNA microarray images. In *Proc. of the IEEE Computational Systems Bioinformatics Conference, CSB-2005*, Stanford, CA.

Roundoff Noise Minimization for State-Estimate Feedback Digital Controllers Using Joint Optimization of Error Feedback and Realization

Takao Hinamoto, Keijiro Kawai, Masayoshi Nakamoto and Wu-Sheng Lu
Name-of-the-University-Company
Country

1. INTRODUCTION

Due to the finite precision nature of computer arithmetic, the output roundoff noise of a fixed-point IIR digital filter usually arises. This noise is critically dependent on the internal structure of an IIR digital filter [1],[2]. Error feedback (EF) is known as an effective technique for reducing the output roundoff noise in an IIR digital filter [3]-[5]. Williamson [6] has reduced the output roundoff noise more effectively by choosing the filter structure and applying EF to the filter. Lu and Hinamoto [7] have developed a jointly optimized technique of EF and realization to minimize the effects of roundoff noise at the filter output subject to l_2-norm dynamic-range scaling constraints. Li and Gevers [8] have analyzed the output roundoff noise of the closed-loop system with a state-estimate feedback controller, and presented an algorithm for realizing the state-estimate feedback controller with minimum output roundoff noise under l_2-norm dynamic-range scaling constraints. Hinamoto and Yamamoto [9] have proposed a method for applying EF to a given closed-loop system with a state-estimate feedback controller.

This paper investigates the problem of jointly optimizing EF and realization for the closed-loop system with a state-estimate feedback controller so as to minimize the output roundoff noise subject to l_2-norm dynamic-range scaling constraints. To this end, the problem at hand is converted into an unconstrained optimization problem by using linear-algebraic techniques, and then an iterative technique which relies on a quasi-Newton algorithm [10] is developed. With a closed-form formula for gradient evaluation and an efficient quasi-Newton solver, the unconstrained optimization problem can be solved efficiently. Our computer simulation results demonstrate the validity and effectiveness of the proposed technique.

Throughout the paper, $\boldsymbol{I}_n$ stands for the identity matrix of dimension $n \times n$, the transpose (conjugate transpose) of a matrix $\boldsymbol{A}$ is indicated by $\boldsymbol{A}^T$ $(\boldsymbol{A}^*)$, and the trace and ith diagonal element of a square matrix $\boldsymbol{A}$ are denoted by $\mathrm{tr}[\boldsymbol{A}]$ and $(\boldsymbol{A})_{ii}$, respectively.

2. ROUNDOFF NOISE ANALYSIS

Consider a stable, controllable and observable linear discrete-time system described by

$$\begin{aligned} \boldsymbol{x}(k+1) &= \boldsymbol{A}_o\boldsymbol{x}(k) + \boldsymbol{b}_o u(k) \\ y(k) &= \boldsymbol{c}_o\boldsymbol{x}(k) \end{aligned} \tag{1}$$

where $\boldsymbol{x}(k)$ is an $n \times 1$ state-variable vector, $u(k)$ is a scalar input, $y(k)$ is a scalar output, and $\boldsymbol{A}_o$, $\boldsymbol{b}_o$ and $\boldsymbol{c}_o$ are $n \times n$, $n \times 1$ and $1 \times n$ real constant matrices, respectively. The transfer function of the linear system in (1) is given by

$$H_o(z) = \boldsymbol{c}_o(z\boldsymbol{I}_n - \boldsymbol{A}_o)^{-1}\boldsymbol{b}_o. \tag{2}$$

If a regulator is designed by using the full-order state observer, we obtain a state-estimate feedback controller as

$$\begin{aligned} \tilde{\boldsymbol{x}}(k+1) &= \boldsymbol{F}_o\tilde{\boldsymbol{x}}(k) + \boldsymbol{b}_o u(k) + \boldsymbol{g}_o y(k) \\ &= \boldsymbol{R}_o\tilde{\boldsymbol{x}}(k) + \boldsymbol{b}_o r(k) + \boldsymbol{g}_o y(k) \\ u(k) &= -\boldsymbol{k}_o\tilde{\boldsymbol{x}}(k) + r(k) \end{aligned} \tag{3}$$

where $\tilde{\boldsymbol{x}}(k)$ is an $n \times 1$ state-variable vector in the full-order state observer, $\boldsymbol{g}_o$ is an $n \times 1$ gain vector chosen so that all the eigenvalues of $\boldsymbol{F}_o = \boldsymbol{A}_o - \boldsymbol{g}_o\boldsymbol{c}_o$ are inside the unit circle in the complex plane, $\boldsymbol{k}_o$ is a $1 \times n$ state-feedback gain vector chosen so that each of the eigenvalues of $\boldsymbol{A}_o - \boldsymbol{b}_o\boldsymbol{k}_o$ is at a desirable location within the unit circle, $r(k)$ is a scalar reference signal, and $\boldsymbol{R}_o = \boldsymbol{F}_o - \boldsymbol{b}_o\boldsymbol{k}_o$. The closed-loop control system consisting of the linear system in (1) and the state-estimate feedback controller in (3) is illustrated in Fig. 1.

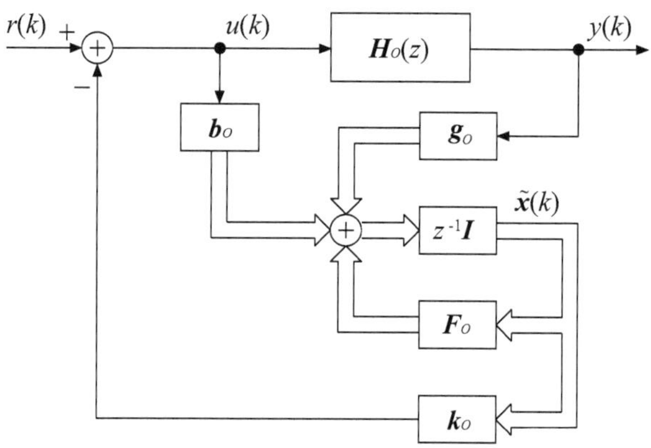

Fig. 1. The closed-loop control system with a state-estimate feedback controller.

When performing quantization before matrix-vector multiplication, we can express the finite-word-length (FWL) implementation of (3) with error feedback as

$$\begin{aligned} \hat{\boldsymbol{x}}(k+1) &= \boldsymbol{R}\,\boldsymbol{Q}[\hat{\boldsymbol{x}}(k)] + \boldsymbol{b}r(k) + \boldsymbol{g}y(k) + \boldsymbol{D}\boldsymbol{e}(k) \\ u(k) &= -\boldsymbol{k}\,\boldsymbol{Q}[\hat{\boldsymbol{x}}(k)] + r(k) \end{aligned} \tag{4}$$

where

$$\boldsymbol{e}(k) = \hat{\boldsymbol{x}}(k) - \boldsymbol{Q}[\hat{\boldsymbol{x}}(k)]$$

is an $n \times 1$ roundoff error vector and $\boldsymbol{D}$ is an $n \times n$ error feedback matrix. All coefficient matrices $\boldsymbol{R}$, $\boldsymbol{b}$, $\boldsymbol{g}$ and $\boldsymbol{k}$ are assumed to have an exact fractional B_c bit representation. The FWL state-variable vector $\hat{x}(k)$ and signal $u(k)$ all have a B bit fractional representation, while the reference input $r(k)$ is a $(B - B_c)$ bit fraction. The vector quantizer $Q[\cdot]$ in (4) rounds the B bit fraction $\hat{x}(k)$ to $(B - B_c)$ bits after completing the multiplications and additions, where the sign bit is not counted. It is assumed that the roundoff error vector $e(k)$ can be modeled as a zero-mean noise process with covariance $\sigma^2 I_n$ where

$$\sigma^2 = \frac{1}{12} 2^{-2(B-B_c)}.$$

It is noted that if the ith element of the roundoff error vector $e(k)$ is indicated by $e_i(k)$ for $i = 1, 2, \cdots, n$ then the variable $e_i(k)$ can be approximated by a white noise sequence uniformly distributed with the following probability density function:

$$p(e_i(k)) = \begin{cases} 2^{B-B_c} & \text{for } -\frac{1}{2}2^{-(B-B_c)} \le e_i(k) \le \frac{1}{2}2^{-(B-B_c)} \\ 0 & \text{otherwise} \end{cases}$$

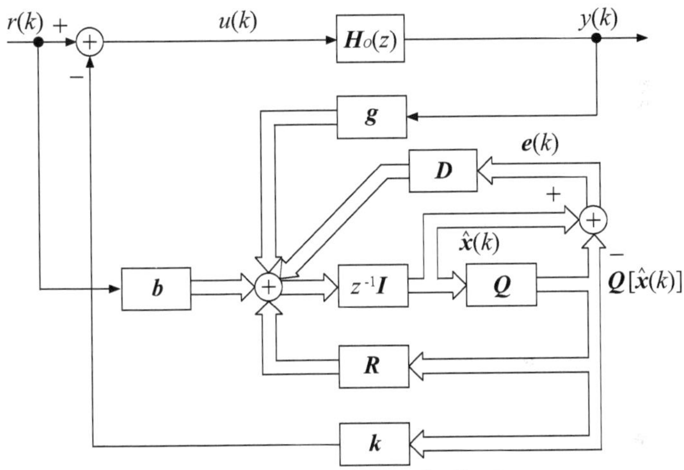

Fig. 2. A state-estimate feedback controller with error feedback.

The closed-loop system consisting of the linear system in (1) and the state-estimate feedback controller with error feedback in (4) is shown in Fig. 2, and is described by

$$\begin{aligned} \begin{bmatrix} x(k+1) \\ \hat{x}(k+1) \end{bmatrix} &= \overline{A} \begin{bmatrix} x(k) \\ \hat{x}(k) \end{bmatrix} + \overline{b} r(k) + \overline{B} e(k) \\ y(k) &= \overline{c} \begin{bmatrix} x(k) \\ \hat{x}(k) \end{bmatrix} \end{aligned} \tag{5}$$

where

$$\overline{A} = \begin{bmatrix} A_o & -b_o k \\ g c_o & R \end{bmatrix}, \qquad \overline{b} = \begin{bmatrix} b_o \\ b \end{bmatrix}$$

$$\overline{B} = \begin{bmatrix} b_o k \\ D - R \end{bmatrix}, \qquad \overline{c} = \begin{bmatrix} c_o & 0 \end{bmatrix}.$$

From (5), the transfer function from the roundoff error vector $e(k)$ to the output $y(k)$ is given by

$$G_D(z) = \overline{c}\,(zI_{2n} - \overline{A})^{-1}\overline{B}. \tag{6}$$

The output noise gain $J(D) = \sigma_{out}^2/\sigma^2$ is then computed as

$$J(D) = \mathrm{tr}[W_D] \tag{7}$$

with

$$W_D = \frac{1}{2\pi j}\oint_{|z|=1} G_D^*(z) G_D(z) \frac{dz}{z} \tag{8}$$

where σ_{out}^2 stands for the noise variance at the output. For tractability, we evaluate $J(D)$ in (7) by replacing R, b, g and k by R_o, b_o, g_o and k_o, respectively. Defining

$$S = \begin{bmatrix} I_n & 0 \\ I_n & -I_n \end{bmatrix}, \tag{9}$$

the transfer function in (6) can be expressed as

$$\begin{aligned} G_D(z) &= \overline{c}S(zI_{2n} - S^{-1}\overline{A}S)^{-1}S^{-1}\overline{B} \\ &= \overline{c}(zI_{2n} - \Phi)^{-1} \begin{bmatrix} b_o k_o \\ F_o - D \end{bmatrix} \\ &= c_o(zI_n - A_o + b_o k_o)^{-1} b_o k_o (zI_n - F_o)^{-1} \\ &\quad \cdot (zI_n - D) \\ &= \overline{c}(zI_{2n} - \Phi)^{-1} U (zI_n - D) \end{aligned} \tag{10}$$

where

$$\Phi = \begin{bmatrix} A_o - b_o k_o & b_o k_o \\ 0 & F_o \end{bmatrix}$$

$$U = \begin{bmatrix} 0 \\ I_n \end{bmatrix}.$$

It is noted that the stability of the closed-loop control system is determined by the eigenvalues of matrix $\overline{A}$ in (5), or equivalently, those of matrix Φ in (10). This means that neither of the roundoff error vector $e(k)$ and the error-feedback matrix D affects the stability.
Substituting (10) into matrix W_D in (8) gives

$$\begin{aligned} W_D = &(b_0 k_0)^T W_1 b_0 k_0 + (b_0 k_0)^T W_2 (F_0 - D) \\ &+ (F_0 - D)^T W_3 b_0 k_0 \\ &+ (F_0 - D)^T W_4 (F_0 - D) \end{aligned} \tag{11}$$

where

$$W = \Phi^T W \Phi + \overline{c}^T \overline{c}$$

$$W = \begin{bmatrix} W_1 & W_2 \\ W_3 & W_4 \end{bmatrix}.$$

Since W is positive semidefinite, it can be shown that there exists an $n \times n$ matrix P such that $W_3 = W_4 P$. In addition, (11) can be written by virtue of $W_2 = W_3^T$ as

$$\begin{aligned} W_D = &(F_0 + Pb_0k_0 - D)^T W_4 (F_0 + Pb_0k_0 - D) \\ &+ (b_0k_0)^T (W_1 - P^T W_4 P) b_0 k_0. \end{aligned} \tag{12}$$

Alternatively, applying z-transform to the first equation in (5) under the assumption that $e(k) = 0$, we obtain

$$\begin{bmatrix} X(z) \\ \hat{X}(z) \end{bmatrix} = (zI - \overline{A})^{-1} \overline{b} R(z) \tag{13}$$

where $X(z)$, $\hat{X}(z)$ and $R(z)$ represent the z-transforms of $x(k)$, $\hat{x}(k)$ and $r(k)$, respectively. Replacing R, b, k and g by R_o, b_o, k_o and g_o, respectively, and then using

$$S^{-1} \begin{bmatrix} X(z) \\ \hat{X}(z) \end{bmatrix} = (zI_{2n} - S^{-1}\overline{A}S)^{-1} S^{-1} \overline{b}$$

yields

$$\hat{X}(z) = X(z) = F(z) R(z) \tag{14}$$

where

$$F(z) = [zI_n - (A_o - b_o k_o)]^{-1} b_o.$$

The controllability Gramian K defined by

$$K = \frac{1}{2\pi j} \oint_{|z|=1} F(z) F^*(z) \frac{dz}{z} \tag{15}$$

can be obtained by solving the following Lyapunov equation:

$$K = (A_o - b_o k_o) K (A_o - b_o k_o)^T + b_o b_o^T. \tag{16}$$

3. ROUNDOFF NOISE MINIMIZATION

Consider the system in (4) with $D = 0$ and denote it by $(R, b, g, k)_n$. By applying a coordinate transformation $\hat{x}'(k) = T^{-1}\hat{x}(k)$ to the above system $(R, b, g, k)_n$, we obtain a new realization characterized by $(\tilde{R}, \tilde{b}, \tilde{g}, \tilde{k})_n$ where

$$\begin{aligned} \tilde{R} &= T^{-1} R T, & \tilde{b} &= T^{-1} b \\ \tilde{g} &= T^{-1} g, & \tilde{k} &= kT. \end{aligned} \tag{17}$$

For the system described by (17), the counterparts of W_i for $i = 1, 2, 3, 4$ are given by

$$\tilde{W}_i = T^T W_i T \tag{18}$$

and the corresponding output noise gain is given by

$$J(\boldsymbol{D},\boldsymbol{T}) = \mathrm{tr}[\tilde{\boldsymbol{W}}_D] \tag{19}$$

where $\tilde{\boldsymbol{W}}_D$ can be obtained referring to (11) as

$$\begin{aligned}\tilde{\boldsymbol{W}}_D = &\left[\boldsymbol{T}^{-1}(\boldsymbol{F}_0+\boldsymbol{P}\boldsymbol{b}_0\boldsymbol{k}_0)\boldsymbol{T}-\boldsymbol{D}\right]^T\\ &\cdot\boldsymbol{T}^T\boldsymbol{W}_4\boldsymbol{T}\left[\boldsymbol{T}^{-1}(\boldsymbol{F}_0+\boldsymbol{P}\boldsymbol{b}_0\boldsymbol{k}_0)\boldsymbol{T}-\boldsymbol{D}\right]\\ &+\boldsymbol{T}^T(\boldsymbol{b}_0\boldsymbol{k}_0)^T(\boldsymbol{W}_1-\boldsymbol{P}^T\boldsymbol{W}_4\boldsymbol{P})\boldsymbol{b}_0\boldsymbol{k}_0\boldsymbol{T}.\end{aligned}$$

In addition, (15) can be written as

$$\begin{aligned}\tilde{\boldsymbol{K}} &= \frac{1}{2\pi j}\oint_{|z|=1}\boldsymbol{T}^{-1}\boldsymbol{F}(z)\boldsymbol{F}^*(z)\boldsymbol{T}^{-T}\frac{dz}{z}\\ &= \boldsymbol{T}^{-1}\boldsymbol{K}\boldsymbol{T}^{-T}.\end{aligned} \tag{20}$$

As a result, the output roundoff noise minimization problem amounts to obtaining matrices $\boldsymbol{D}$ and $\boldsymbol{T}$ which jointly minimize $J(\boldsymbol{D},\boldsymbol{T})$ in (19) subject to the l_2-norm dynamic-range scaling constraints specified by

$$(\tilde{\boldsymbol{K}})_{ii} = (\boldsymbol{T}^{-1}\boldsymbol{K}\boldsymbol{T}^{-T})_{ii} = 1, \quad i = 1,2,\cdots,n. \tag{21}$$

To deal with (21), we define

$$\hat{\boldsymbol{T}} = \boldsymbol{T}^T\boldsymbol{K}^{-\frac{1}{2}}. \tag{22}$$

Then the l_2-norm dynamic-range scaling constraints in (21) can be written as

$$(\hat{\boldsymbol{T}}^{-T}\hat{\boldsymbol{T}}^{-1})_{ii} = 1, \quad i = 1,2,\cdots,n. \tag{23}$$

These constraints are always satisfied if $\hat{\boldsymbol{T}}^{-1}$ assumes the form

$$\hat{\boldsymbol{T}}^{-1} = \left[\frac{\boldsymbol{t}_1}{||\boldsymbol{t}_1||},\frac{\boldsymbol{t}_2}{||\boldsymbol{t}_2||},\cdots,\frac{\boldsymbol{t}_n}{||\boldsymbol{t}_n||}\right]. \tag{24}$$

Substituting (22) into (19), we obtain

$$\begin{aligned}J(\boldsymbol{D},\hat{\boldsymbol{T}}) = \mathrm{tr}&\left[\hat{\boldsymbol{T}}(\hat{\boldsymbol{A}}-\hat{\boldsymbol{T}}^T\boldsymbol{D}\hat{\boldsymbol{T}}^{-T})^T\hat{\boldsymbol{W}}_4\right.\\ &\left.\cdot(\hat{\boldsymbol{A}}-\hat{\boldsymbol{T}}^T\boldsymbol{D}\hat{\boldsymbol{T}}^{-T})\hat{\boldsymbol{T}}^T+\hat{\boldsymbol{T}}\hat{\boldsymbol{C}}\hat{\boldsymbol{T}}^T\right]\end{aligned} \tag{25}$$

where

$$\begin{aligned}&\hat{\boldsymbol{A}} = \boldsymbol{K}^{-\frac{1}{2}}(\boldsymbol{F}_0+\boldsymbol{P}\boldsymbol{b}_0\boldsymbol{k}_0)\boldsymbol{K}^{\frac{1}{2}}, \quad \hat{\boldsymbol{W}}_4 = \boldsymbol{K}^{\frac{1}{2}}\boldsymbol{W}_4\boldsymbol{K}^{\frac{1}{2}}\\ &\hat{\boldsymbol{C}} = \boldsymbol{K}^{\frac{1}{2}}(\boldsymbol{b}_0\boldsymbol{k}_0)^T(\boldsymbol{W}_1-\boldsymbol{P}^T\boldsymbol{W}_4\boldsymbol{P})\boldsymbol{b}_0\boldsymbol{k}_0\boldsymbol{K}^{\frac{1}{2}}.\end{aligned}$$

From the foregoing arguments, the problem of obtaining matrices $\boldsymbol{D}$ and $\boldsymbol{T}$ that minimize (19) subject to the scaling constraints in (21) is now converted into an unconstrained optimization problem of obtaining $\boldsymbol{D}$ and $\hat{\boldsymbol{T}}$ that jointly minimize $J(\boldsymbol{D},\hat{\boldsymbol{T}})$ in (25).

Let $\boldsymbol{x}$ be the column vector that collects the variables in matrix $\boldsymbol{D}$ and matrix $[\boldsymbol{t}_1, \boldsymbol{t}_2, \cdots, \boldsymbol{t}_n]$. Then $J(\boldsymbol{D}, \hat{\boldsymbol{T}})$ is a function of $\boldsymbol{x}$, denoted by $J(\boldsymbol{x})$. The proposed algorithm starts with an initial point $\boldsymbol{x}_0$ obtained from an initial assignment $\boldsymbol{D} = \hat{\boldsymbol{T}} = \boldsymbol{I}_n$. In the kth iteration, a quasi-Newton algorithm updates the most recent point $\boldsymbol{x}_k$ to point $\boldsymbol{x}_{k+1}$ as [10]

$$\boldsymbol{x}_{k+1} = \boldsymbol{x}_k + \alpha_k \boldsymbol{d}_k \tag{26}$$

where

$$\begin{aligned} \boldsymbol{d}_k &= -\boldsymbol{S}_k \nabla J(\boldsymbol{x}_k) \\ \alpha_k &= arg \left[\min_{\alpha} J(\boldsymbol{x}_k + \alpha \boldsymbol{d}_k) \right] \\ \boldsymbol{S}_{k+1} &= \boldsymbol{S}_k + \left(1 + \frac{\boldsymbol{\gamma}_k^T \boldsymbol{S}_k \boldsymbol{\gamma}_k}{\boldsymbol{\gamma}_k^T \boldsymbol{\delta}_k}\right) \frac{\boldsymbol{\delta}_k \boldsymbol{\delta}_k^T}{\boldsymbol{\gamma}_k^T \boldsymbol{\delta}_k} - \frac{\boldsymbol{\delta}_k \boldsymbol{\gamma}_k^T \boldsymbol{S}_k + \boldsymbol{S}_k \boldsymbol{\gamma}_k \boldsymbol{\delta}_k^T}{\boldsymbol{\gamma}_k^T \boldsymbol{\delta}_k} \\ \boldsymbol{S}_0 &= \boldsymbol{I}, \quad \boldsymbol{\delta}_k = \boldsymbol{x}_{k+1} - \boldsymbol{x}_k, \quad \boldsymbol{\gamma}_k = \nabla J(\boldsymbol{x}_{k+1}) - \nabla J(\boldsymbol{x}_k). \end{aligned}$$

Here, $\nabla J(\boldsymbol{x})$ is the gradient of $J(\boldsymbol{x})$ with respect to $\boldsymbol{x}$, and $\boldsymbol{S}_k$ is a positive-definite approximation of the inverse Hessian matrix of $J(\boldsymbol{x}_k)$. This iteration process continues until

$$|J(\boldsymbol{x}_{k+1}) - J(\boldsymbol{x}_k)| < \varepsilon \tag{27}$$

is satisfied where $\varepsilon > 0$ is a prescribed tolerance.

In what follows, we derive closed-form expressions of $\nabla J(\boldsymbol{x})$ for the cases where $\boldsymbol{D}$ assumes the form of a general, diagonal, or scalar matrix.

*1) Case 1: **D** Is a General Matrix:* From (25), the optimal choice of $\boldsymbol{D}$ is given by

$$\boldsymbol{D} = \hat{\boldsymbol{T}}^{-T} \hat{\boldsymbol{A}} \hat{\boldsymbol{T}}^T, \tag{28}$$

which leads to

$$J(\hat{\boldsymbol{T}}^{-T} \hat{\boldsymbol{A}} \hat{\boldsymbol{T}}^T, \hat{\boldsymbol{T}}) = \mathrm{tr}\left[\hat{\boldsymbol{T}} \hat{\boldsymbol{C}} \hat{\boldsymbol{T}}^T\right]. \tag{29}$$

In this case, the number of elements in vector $\boldsymbol{x}$ consisting of $\hat{\boldsymbol{T}}$ is equal to n^2 and the gradient of $J(\boldsymbol{x})$ is found to be

$$\begin{aligned} \frac{\partial J(\boldsymbol{x})}{\partial t_{ij}} &= \lim_{\Delta \to 0} \frac{J(\hat{\boldsymbol{T}}_{ij}) - J(\hat{\boldsymbol{T}})}{\Delta} \\ &= 2\boldsymbol{e}_j^T \hat{\boldsymbol{T}} \hat{\boldsymbol{C}} \hat{\boldsymbol{T}}^T \hat{\boldsymbol{T}} \boldsymbol{g}_{ij}, \qquad i,j = 1,2,\cdots,n \end{aligned} \tag{30}$$

where $\hat{\boldsymbol{T}}_{ij}$ is the matrix obtained from $\hat{\boldsymbol{T}}$ with a perturbed (i,j)th component, which is given by

$$\hat{\boldsymbol{T}}_{ij} = \hat{\boldsymbol{T}} + \frac{\Delta \hat{\boldsymbol{T}} \boldsymbol{g}_{ij} \boldsymbol{e}_j^T \hat{\boldsymbol{T}}}{1 - \Delta \boldsymbol{e}_j^T \hat{\boldsymbol{T}} \boldsymbol{g}_{ij}}$$

and $\boldsymbol{g}_{ij}$ is computed using

$$\boldsymbol{g}_{ij} = \partial \left\{ \frac{\boldsymbol{t}_j}{||\boldsymbol{t}_j||} \right\} / \partial t_{ij} = \frac{1}{||\boldsymbol{t}_j||^3} (t_{ij} \boldsymbol{t}_j - ||\boldsymbol{t}_j||^2 \boldsymbol{e}_i).$$

*2) Case 2: **D** Is a Diagonal Matrix:* Here, matrix $\boldsymbol{D}$ assumes the form

$$\boldsymbol{D} = \mathrm{diag}\{d_1, d_2, \cdots, d_n\}. \tag{31}$$

In this case, (25) becomes

$$J(D,\hat{T}) = \mathrm{tr}\left[\hat{T}M_d\hat{T}^T\right] \tag{32}$$

where

$$\begin{aligned} M_d = \hat{C} + \hat{A}^T\hat{W}_4\hat{A} + \hat{W}_4\hat{T}^T D^2\hat{T}^{-T} \\ -\hat{A}^T\hat{W}_4\hat{T}^T D\hat{T}^{-T} - \hat{W}_4\hat{A}\hat{T}^T D\hat{T}^{-T}. \end{aligned}$$

It follows that

$$\begin{aligned} \frac{\partial J(x)}{\partial t_{ij}} &= 2e_j^T\hat{T}M_d\hat{T}^T\hat{T}g_{ij}, \quad i,j = 1,2,\cdots,n \\ \frac{\partial J(x)}{\partial d_i} &= 2e_i^T(D\hat{T} - \hat{T}\hat{A}^T)\hat{W}_4\hat{T}^T e_i, \quad i = 1,2,\cdots,n. \end{aligned} \tag{33}$$

3) Case 3: D Is a Scalar Matrix: It is assumed here that $D = \alpha I_n$ with a scalar α. The gradient of $J(x)$ can then be calculated as

$$\begin{aligned} \frac{\partial J(x)}{\partial t_{ij}} &= 2e_j^T\hat{T}M_s\hat{T}^T\hat{T}g_{ij}, \quad i,j = 1,2,\cdots,n \\ \frac{\partial J(x)}{\partial \alpha} &= \mathrm{tr}\left[\hat{T}(2\alpha\hat{W}_4 - \hat{A}^T\hat{W}_4 - \hat{W}_4\hat{A})\hat{T}^T\right] \end{aligned} \tag{34}$$

where

$$M_s = (\hat{A} - \alpha I_n)^T\hat{W}_4(\hat{A} - \alpha I_n) + \hat{C}.$$

4. A NUMERICAL EXAMPLE

In this section we illustrate the proposed method by considering a linear discrete-time system specified by

$$A_o = \begin{bmatrix} 0 & 1 & 0 \\ 0 & 0 & 1 \\ 0.339377 & -1.152652 & 1.520167 \end{bmatrix}, \quad b_o = \begin{bmatrix} 0 \\ 0 \\ 1 \end{bmatrix}$$

$$c_o = \begin{bmatrix} 0.093253 & 0.128620 & 0.314713 \end{bmatrix}.$$

Suppose that the poles of the observer and regulator in the system are required to be located at $z = 0.1532, 0.2861, 0.1137$, and $z = 0.5067, 0.6023, 0.4331$, respectively. This can be achieved by choosing

$$k_o = \begin{bmatrix} 0.471552 & -0.367158 & 3.062267 \end{bmatrix}$$

$$g_o = \begin{bmatrix} -0.006436 & 3.683651 & 5.083920 \end{bmatrix}^T.$$

Performing the l_2-norm dynamic-range scaling to the state-estimate feedback controller, we obtain $J(\mathbf{0}) = 686.4121$ in (7) where $D = \mathbf{0}$. Next, the controller is transformed into the optimal realization that minimizes $J(\mathbf{0})$ in (7) under the l_2-norm dynamic-range scaling constraints. This leads to $J_{min}(\mathbf{0}) = 28.6187$. Finally, EF and state-variable coordinate transformation are applied to the above optimal realization so as to jointly minimize the output roundoff noise. The profiles of $J(x)$ during the first 20 iteration for the cases of D being a general, diagonal, and scalar matrix are depicted in Fig. 3.

*1) Case 1: **D** Is a General Matrix:* The quasi-Newton algorithm was applied to minimize (25). It took the algorithm 20 iterations to converge to the solution

$$D = \begin{bmatrix} 0.211191 & -3.078211 & -3.344596 \\ -1.321589 & 1.897308 & 3.243515 \\ 1.917916 & -1.890027 & -3.807473 \end{bmatrix}$$

$$T = \begin{bmatrix} -11.039974 & -43.683697 & -30.131793 \\ -3.231505 & 8.919473 & 9.118205 \\ 2.620911 & 6.462685 & 7.032260 \end{bmatrix}$$

and the minimized noise gain was found to be $J(\boldsymbol{D}, \hat{\boldsymbol{T}}) = 4.8823$. Next, the above optimal EF matrix $\boldsymbol{D}$ was rounded to a power-of-two representation with 3 bits after the binary point, which resulted in

$$D_{3bit} = \begin{bmatrix} 0.250 & -3.125 & -3.375 \\ -1.375 & 1.875 & 3.250 \\ 1.875 & -1.875 & -3.750 \end{bmatrix}$$

and a noise gain $J(\boldsymbol{D}_{3bit}, \hat{\boldsymbol{T}}) = 23.4873$. Furthermore, when the optimal EF matrix $\boldsymbol{D}$ was rounded to the integer representation

$$D_{int} = \begin{bmatrix} 0 & -3 & -3 \\ -1 & 2 & 3 \\ 2 & -2 & -4 \end{bmatrix},$$

the noise gain was found to be $J(\boldsymbol{D}_{int}, \hat{\boldsymbol{T}}) = 293.0187$.

*2) Case 2: **D** Is a Diagonal Matrix:* Again, the quasi-Newton algorithm was applied to minimize $J(\boldsymbol{D}, \hat{\boldsymbol{T}})$ in (25) for a diagonal EF matrix $\boldsymbol{D}$. It took the algorithm 20 iterations to converge to the solution

$$D = \text{diag}\{0.050638, -0.608845, -0.951572\}$$

$$T = \begin{bmatrix} 3.588878 & 0.735966 & 0.010417 \\ -2.457241 & 0.728171 & 0.556762 \\ 1.514232 & -2.058856 & 0.142204 \end{bmatrix}$$

and the minimized noise gain was found to be $J(\boldsymbol{D}, \hat{\boldsymbol{T}}) = 12.7097$. Next, the above optimal diagonal EF matrix $\boldsymbol{D}$ was rounded to a power-of-two representation with 3 bits after the binary point to yield $\boldsymbol{D}_{3bit} = \text{diag}\{0.000, -0.625, -1.000\}$, which leads to a noise gain $J(\boldsymbol{D}_{3bit}, \hat{\boldsymbol{T}}) = 12.7722$. Furthermore, when the optimized diagonal EF matrix $\boldsymbol{D}$ was rounded to the integer representation $\boldsymbol{D}_{int} = \text{diag}\{0, -1, -1\}$, the noise gain was found to be $J(\boldsymbol{D}_{int}, \hat{\boldsymbol{T}}) = 13.7535$.

*3) Case 3: **D** Is a Scalar Matrix:* In this case, the quasi-Newton algorithm was applied to minimize (25) for $\boldsymbol{D} = \alpha \boldsymbol{I}_3$ with a scalar α. The algorithm converges after 20 iterations to converge to the solution

$$D = -0.779678\, I_3$$

$$T = \begin{bmatrix} 3.252790 & -0.081745 & -0.198376 \\ -1.717225 & 1.220068 & -0.792487 \\ 0.546599 & -0.854316 & 2.295944 \end{bmatrix}$$

and the minimized noise gain was found to be $J(\boldsymbol{D}, \hat{\boldsymbol{T}}) = 16.2006$. Next, the EF matrix $\boldsymbol{D} = \alpha \boldsymbol{I}_3$ was rounded to a power-of-two representation with 3 bits after the binary point as well as

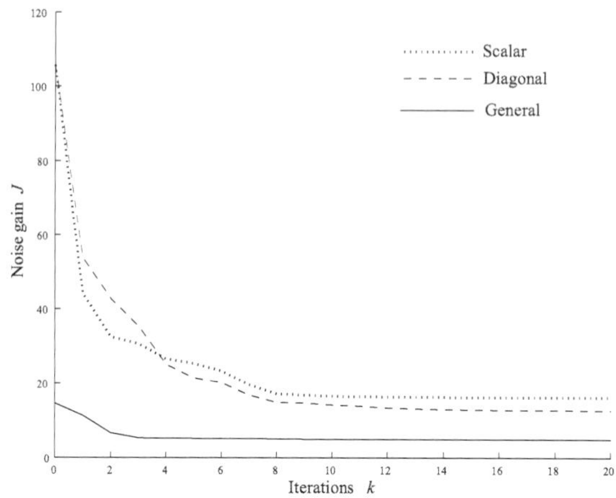

Fig. 3. Profiles of iterative noise gain minimization.

an integer representation. It was found that these representations were given by $D_{3bit} = \text{diag}\{0.750, 0.750, 0.750\}$ and $D_{int} = \text{diag}\{1, 1, 1\}$, respectively. The corresponding noise gains were obtained as $J(D_{3bit}, \hat{T}) = 16.2370$ and $J(D_{int}, \hat{T}) = 18.2063$, respectively.
The above simulation results in terms of noise gain $J(D, \hat{T})$ in (25) are summarized in Table 1. For comparison purpose, their counterparts obtained using the method in [9] are also included in the table, where the minimization of the roundoff noise was carried out using EF and state-variable coordinate transformation, but in a separate manner. From the table, it is observed that the proposed joint optimization offers improved reduction in roundoff noise gain for the cases of a scalar EF matrix and a diagonal EF matrix when compared with those obtained by using *separate* optimization. However, in the case of a general EF matrix, the optimal solution with infinite precision appears to be quite sensitive to the parameter perturbations.

Error-Feedback Scheme	Accuracy of D		
	Infinite Precision	3 Bit Quantization	Integer Quantization
$D = 0$ Separate	28.6187		
Scalar Separate [9]	20.1235	20.1810	26.0527
Scalar Joint	16.2006	16.2370	18.2063
Diagonal Separate [9]	16.4104	16.4547	17.4039
Diagonal Joint	12.7097	12.7722	13.7535
General Separate [9]	11.6352	11.7054	16.5814
General Joint	4.8823	23.4873	293.0187

Table 1. Noise gain $J(D, \hat{T})$ for different EF schemes.

More reduction of the noise gain might be possible by re-designing the coordinate transformation matrix T for the optimally quantized D.

5. CONCLUSION

The joint optimization problem of EF and realization to minimize the effects of roundoff noise of the closed-loop system with a state-estimate feedback controller subject to l_2-norm dynamic-range scaling constraints has been investigated. The probelm at hand has been converted into an unconstrained optimization problem by using linear algebraic techniques. An efficient quasi-Newton algorithm has been employed to solve the unconstrained optimization problem. The proposed technique has been applied to the cases where EF matrix is a general, diagonal, or scalar matrix. The effectiveness for the cases of a scalar EF matrix and a diagonal EF matrix compared with the existing method [9] has been illustrated by a numerical example.

6. References

C. T. Mullis and R. A. Roberts, "Synthesis of minimum roundoff noise fixed point digital filters," *IEEE Trans. Circuits Syst.*, vol. CAS-23, pp. 551-562, Sept. 1976.

S. Y. Hwang, "Minimum uncorrelated unit noise in state-space digital filtering," *IEEE Trans. Acoust. Speech, Signal Processing*, vol. ASSP-25, pp. 273-281, Aug. 1977.

W. E. Higgins and D. C. Munson, "Optimal and suboptimal error-spectrum shaping for cascade-form digital filters," *IEEE Trans. Circuits Syst.*, vol. CAS-31, pp. 429-437, May 1984.

T. I. Laakso and I. O. Hartimo, "Noise reduction in recursive digital filters using high-order error feedback," *IEEE Trans. Signal Processing*, vol. 40, pp. 1096-1107, May 1992.

P. P. Vaidyanathan, "On error-spectrum shaping in state-space digital filters," *IEEE Trans. Circuits Syst.*, vol. CAS-32, pp. 88-92, Jan. 1985.

D. Williamson, "Roundoff noise minimization and pole-zero sensitivity in fixed-point digital filters using residue feedback," *IEEE Trans. Acoust. Speech, Signal Processing*, vol. ASSP-34, pp. 1210-1220, Oct. 1986.

W.-S. Lu and T. Hinamoto, "Jointly optimized error-feedback and realization for roundoff noise minimization in state-space digital filters," *IEEE Trans. Signal Processing*, vol. 53, pp. 2135-2145, June 2005.

G. Li and M. Gevers, "Optimal finite precision implementation of a state-estimate feedback controller," *IEEE Trans. Circuits Syst.*, vol. CAS-37, pp. 1487-1498, Dec. 1990.

T. Hinamoto and S. Yamamoto, "Error spectrum shaping in closed-loop systems with state-estimate feedback controller," in *Proc. IEEE Int. Symp. Circuits Syst. (ISCAS'02)*, May 2002, vol. 1, pp. 289-292.

R. Fletcher, *Practical Methods of Optimization*, 2nd ed. New York: Wiley, 1987.

24

Signal processing for non-invasive brain biomarkers of sensorimotor performance and brain monitoring

Rodolphe J. Gentili, Hyuk Oh, Trent J. Bradberry,
Bradley D. Hatfield and José L. Contreras-Vidal
University of Maryland-College Park
USA

1. Introduction

Many endogenous and exogenous factors can affect the physiological, mental and behavioral states in humans. In order to identify such states, monitoring tools need to use biological indicators, or biomarkers, able to identify biological events and predict outcomes. These biomarkers can be divided into two categories.

The first category contains what we could call the "structural" biomarkers that are extracted from physiological structures and mainly defined at the genetic and/or molecular level (e.g., Berg, 2008; Dengler et al., 2007; Eleuteri et al., 2009; Isaac, 2008; Moura et al., 2008; Wei, 2009). For instance, the formation or consumption of certain molecules provide biomarkers to identify patients with moderate to severe forms of cardiac heart failure (Eleuteri et al., 2009; Isaac, 2008) while changes in cortisol level allow detection of an increased stress response (Armstrong & Hatfield, 2006). Similarly, other active molecules (e.g., C-reactive protein) are used as biomarkers of valvular heart disease (Moura et al., 2008) while cardiac troponins and N-type natriuretic peptides can be used in post-transplant patient surveillance (Dengler et al., 2007). Other examples of structural biomarkers aim to identify abnormalities in neural connectivity in the brain. For instance, the presence of certain molecules in venous blood or a damaged white matter provides potential predictors of risk of cerebral palsy (Dammann & Leviton, 2004, 2006; Kaukola et al., 2004). Also, genomic and proteomic biomarkers are able to define the risk of an individual to develop a neurodegenerative disease such as Parkinson's disease (Gasser, 2009), Alzheimer's disease (Berg, 2008; Wei, 2009) or amyotrophic lateral (Tuner et al., 2009) and multiple sclerosis (Wei, 2009).

The second category includes what we could call "functional" biomarkers that are further related to continuous measurements of body function throughout time in order to track physiological, mental and behavioral states (e.g., Georgopoulos et al., 2007; Hejjel & Gál, 2001; Hofstra et al., 2008). For instance, electro-cardiograms, heartbeat, and body temperature are possible functional biomarkers to determine stress level (Hejjel & Gál, 2001). Body temperature can be used to detect the phase of circadian rhythms (Hofstra et al.,

2008), and blood pressure can be employed to identify the chronic fatigue (Newton et al., 2009). Recently, it has been also suggested that measurements of the skin conductance was a better tool to monitor nociceptive stimulation and pain than heart rate and blood pressure (Storm et al., 2008).

Another important family of functional biomarkers includes status measurements of brain functions in order to monitor and interpret neural activity, identify specific neurological events and predict outcomes (e.g., Gentili et al., 2008; Guarracino, 2008; Hatfield et al., 2004; Irani et al., 2007; Tuner et al., 2009; van Putten et al., 2005; Williams & Ramamoorthy, 2007). These brain indicators, or brain biomarkers, can be derived from signals recorded by means of invasive acquisition techniques such as implantable microelectrodes arrays or electrocorticography (Schalk et al., 2008), or, alternatively, non-invasive techniques such as electroencephalography (EEG), magnetoencephalography (MEG), functional magnetic resonance imaging (fMRI) or emerging neuroimaging technologies such as functional near infrared spectroscopy (fNIRS) (Irani et al., 2007; Parasuraman & Rizzo, 2007). For instance, brain biomarkers derived from temporal or spectral EEG signals processing allow for the determination of anesthetic depth during pediatric cardiac surgery (Williams & Ramamoorthy, 2009). Other brain biomarkers derived from EEG, such as the brain symmetry index, permit the detection of seizure activity in the temporal lobe and can be, therefore, useful for epileptic monitoring needed in intensive care units (van Putten et al., 2005). Still using EEG analysis, it is also possible to detect a reduction of cerebral blood flow below a certain threshold (Guarracino et al., 2008). Other high-temporal resolution measurement techniques such as MEG have also been used to successfully classify respective groups of individuals subjected to multiple sclerosis, Alzheimer's disease, schizophrenia, Sjögren's syndrome, chronic alcoholism, facial pain and healthy controls (Georgopoulos et al., 2007). More recently, it has been shown that the fNIRS imaging technique, a relatively novel cerebral imaging tool, could provide information allowing the monitoring of brain oxygenation by measuring regional cerebral venous oxygen saturation (Guarracino et al., 2008).

These examples provided by medical, biomedical and bioengineering research fields illustrate how various brain monitoring tools are being developed intending to uncover structural or functional brain biomarkers for detection, prevention, prediction, and diagnosis of heart function, adverse neurological events and neural/neurodegenerative diseases. However, the research aiming to uncover functional brain biomarkers directly relevant for the restoration of cognitive-motor and/or sensorimotor functions (e.g., disabled populations, advanced aging) is still a relatively young research field. Indeed, although many assistive technologies aiming to restore cognitive-motor and sensorimotor functions are currently underway (e.g., neuroprosthetics (Cipriani et al., 2008; Wolpaw et al., 2007); exoskeletons (Carignan et al., 2008)), few brain monitoring tools related to sensorimotor integration are being developed. However, these bioengineering applications, such as the design of smart neuroprosthetics, require a deeper understanding of brain dynamics in ecological situations that involve human interaction with new tools and/or changing environments that guide learning and more generally shape motor behavior. Specifically, such monitoring tools aiming to assess the dynamic status of the brain necessitates the knowledge of brain biomarkers able to track brain dynamics in ecological situations where humans have to learn new tasks, to master novel tools and/or changing environments. These brain biomarkers should be preferably non-invasive (i.e., no surgical intervention needed), simple to record and analyze, simultaneously robust and sensitive to specific changes in brain function in natural situations. Such assessment in ecological situations requires non-invasive recording of the dynamic brain activity with a high temporal resolution (e.g., millisecond), which is well suited for EEG. Although some research efforts are underway (e.g., Deeny et al., 2003, 2009; Gentili et al., 2008, 2009a,b; Hatfield et al., 2004; Haufler et al., 2000; Kerick et al., 2004) to develop methods to provide non-invasive functional brain biomarkers able to track the brain status during sensorimotor performance; some questions and problems remain. For example, how accurately and efficiently can a cognitive-motor or sensorimotor state be inferred? What methods might provide robust brain biomarkers applicable on single-subject and single-trial bases? How can the signal processing techniques used in laboratory contexts to derive such biomarkers can be transferred successfully in real-time applications to ecological contexts? Although this manuscript does not purport to exhaustively answer these questions, some elements of response and possible problem-solving perspectives will be presented and discussed.

Therefore, the aims of this chapter are to provide the state-of-the-art of the research along with the main signal processing techniques related to functional non-invasive EEG/MEG brain biomarkers that allow tracking of cortical dynamics to assess the level of mastery of a sensorimotor task and the adaptation to novel tools or environments. It must be noted that, from a technical point of view, the methodological approaches presented here are also applicable to some (minimally) invasive techniques such as electrocorticography. However, when considering an invasive approach, in addition to the inherent risks and difficulties related to a surgical intervention, the whole scalp will not be likely covered by the recording device, creating limitations in terms of the regions of interest where potential biomarkers could be detected. Thus, we will mainly focus on non-invasive recording techniques that use a high-temporal resolution (EEG/MEG) with a particular emphasis on results obtained with EEG since this recording technique is portable and, thus, applicable in ecological situations. In Section 2, the main pre-processing methods employed to clean the EEG/MEG signals of artifacts will be explained along with the subsequent methodological approaches that allow for the computation of brain biomarkers. Specifically, Section 2 will focus on the spectral power and phase synchronization representing the two most classical univariate and multivariate non-invasive functional brain biomarkers of performance. In Section 3, the classical and the latest findings in this brain biomarker research field will be presented by emphasizing promising progress but also current limitations and possible solutions to overcome them. Section 4, will present how these brain biomarkers may provide important advances in bioengineering applications in ecological contexts such as the development of smart neuroprosthetics and brain monitoring techniques. Finally, we will summarize these results and suggest future research directions.

2. Signal Processing Methods

The aim of this second section is not to provide an exhaustive presentation of all the existing processing methods for EEG and MEG signals, but rather, to introduce some signal processing approaches for EEG and MEG signals to, first, pre-process the signal to remove artifacts and, then, to derive non-invasive functional brain biomarkers (e.g., based on spectral power and coherence) that are used to assess and track adaptation in cognitive-motor/sensorimotor performance in humans.

2.1 Pre-processing

During recording, EEG/MEG signals are generally corrupted with some undesirable artifacts such as body movements, muscular artifacts, eye movements, eye blinks, environmental noise or heart beat. These artifacts produce possible biases in the detection and interpretation of brain biomarkers that will be later derived from the EEG/MEG signals. Constraints placed on subjects to minimize these artifacts in a laboratory setting cannot be realistically expected in an ecological situation. Therefore, in order to remove such artifacts, pre-processing of the EEG/MEG signals may be a necessary and critical step (Georgopoulos et al., 2007). Although several signal processing methods are available, such pre-processing stage can be performed by using various methods such as Independent Component Analysis (ICA) and adaptive filtering.

2.1.1 Artifact removal using Independent Component Analysis

In many dynamical systems, the measurements are given as a set of mixed signals with noise. For example, in the same way conversations are recorded by a number of microphones in a crowded party, brain signals containing artifacts are measured through multiple EEG/MEG sensors. The information in each of the original signals can be analyzed as long as it is possible to identify the system corresponding to the source that emits these signals captured by a set of sensors. In this regard, blind source separation is a relevant method to approximately recover the original source signals from a set of observed mixed signals without any *a priori* knowledge about either the source signals or the mixing system. Regarding applications in biomedical signal processing, ICA is currently considered one of the most sophisticated statistical approaches for solving the general problem of blind source separation.

2.1.1.1 Basic assumptions of ICA

ICA is a linear transformation method to find estimated source signals (i.e., the independent components) while optimally demixing the mixed signals where independent components must satisfy the following conditions (Hyvärinen & Oja, 2000; Oja, 2004; Vaseghi, 2007; Vigário et al., 2000):

i) The independent components are non-Gaussian and statistically independent of the higher-order statistics (covariance and kurtosis).
ii) At most, no more than one independent component can be Gaussian.
iii) The dimension of the set of independent components does not exceed the number of sensors.

Moreover, three additional assumptions must be considered when ICA is applied to EEG/MEG signals (Hyvärinen et al., 2001):

iv) The existence of statistically independent components in EEG/MEG source signals is assumed.
v) The statistically independent components are instantaneously and linearly mixed at the sensors.
vi) The independent components and the mixing processes are supposed to be stationary.

Several versions of ICA exist. First, the simple ICA will be presented. Then, the two most popular ICA algorithms named Infomax ICA and FastICA will be reviewed.

2.1.1.2 Simple ICA algorithm

In the simple ICA algorithm, the unknown additive noise is excluded (Oja, 2004). Assume that the m dimensional observed signal (e.g., EEG/MEG) vector $\mathbf{x}(k)=[x_1(k),\ x_2(k),\ \cdots,\ x_m(k)]^T$ is given by a linear combination of the n dimensional source signal vector $\mathbf{s}(k)=[s_1(k),\ s_2(k),\ \cdots,\ s_n(k)]^T$ at each time sample k, that is:

$$x_i(k)=a_{i1}s_1(k)+a_{i2}s_2(k)+\cdots+a_{in}s_n(k), i=1, 2, \cdots, m. \tag{1}$$

In a more compact notation, Equation (1) can be rewritten as

$$\mathbf{x}(k)=\sum_{j=1}^{n}\mathbf{a}_j s_j(k)=\mathbf{A}\mathbf{s}(k) \tag{2}$$

where the matrix $\mathbf{A}=[\mathbf{a}_1,\ \mathbf{a}_2,\ \cdots,\ \mathbf{a}_n]$ is the mixing matrix, the indices n and m are the number of sensors and sources, respectively. The matrix A is a m x n matrix (generally m ≥ n but a common choice is m = n). Practically, both the mixing matrix and the source signal vector are unknown; however, we can estimate a demixing matrix $\mathbf{W}$ in order to obtain the estimation of a source signal vector $\hat{\mathbf{s}}(k)$ using three fundamental assumptions (from i) to iii); see section 2.1.1.1) for ICA previously mentioned such that:

$$\hat{\mathbf{s}}(k)=\mathbf{W}\mathbf{x}(k) \tag{3}$$

where ideally $\mathbf{W}=\mathbf{A}^{-1}$ and the elements of $\hat{\mathbf{s}}(k)$ are statistically independent.
Practically, several preprocessing strategies make ICA simpler and better conditioned (Hyvärinen & Oja, 2000). For example, the centering technique simplifies the ICA algorithms by subtracting the mean vector from the observed signal vector so as to make it a zero mean valued vector. On the other hand, whitening decreases the correlation among the observed signals by transforming the centered observed vector to have unit variance in all directions (Vigário, 2000).

2.1.1.3 Infomax ICA and FastICA

Among the various ICA algorithms that are available, Infomax ICA (Bell & Sejnowski, 1995) and FastICA (Hyvärinen, 1999) are the two most popular ones. They use different independence properties to obtain the independent components. Specifically, Infomax ICA minimizes the mutual information whereas FastICA maximizes the non-Gaussian nature. These two algorithms provide qualitatively and quantitatively similar results. However, FastICA is generally faster than Infomax ICA, but is subject to more variability than Infomax ICA especially when applied to removal of eye blink artifacts (Glass et al., 2004). Concerning Infomax ICA, this approach is unable to separate source signals with a sub-Gaussian distribution. Therefore, an extended version of Infomax ICA, named extended Infomax ICA, has been introduced to separate both sub-Gaussian and super-Gaussian distributions for the source signals (Lee et al., 1999).

2.1.1.4 Independent Components Analysis for artifact identification and removal from EEG and MEG signals

ICA has been recently applied to the analysis of biomedical signals mostly acquired from EEG and MEG. In these applications, it is essential to associate each independent component with the neurophysiological nature of the phenomenon (e.g., event-related brain dynamics, steady-state brain activity, etc.) in order to identify them. In many cases, ICA algorithms have been successfully applied to EEG and MEG in order to identify and remove artifacts such as cardiac, ocular, or muscular activities from the neurophysiological activities of interest (the computational steps of these algorithms are illustrated in Fig.1), since the nature of the artifact sources is different from those of the actual brain activity related sources in terms of anatomical, physiological, and statistical considerations.

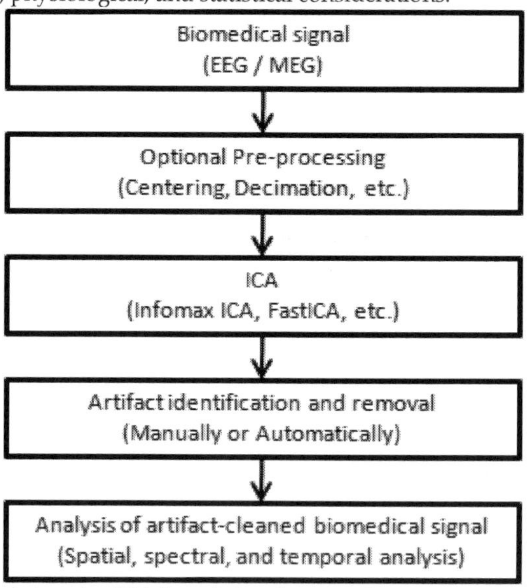

Fig. 1. Computational steps for ICA-based signal processing.

In general, the independent components related to the suspected artifacts must be manually assigned to an artifact type based on the attributes of the independent components (e.g., amplitude peak, frequency patterns). However, since the criteria to decide to remove such a component can depend of subjective judgments, this approach is sensitive to biases.

Recently, several automatic artifact detection and removal methods have been introduced (Delorme et al., 2001; Rong & Contreras-Vidal, 2006). For example, the functionally similar independent components could be automatically categorized using neural network with respect to a set of features such as spatial maps, spectral properties, and higher-order statistics (Rong & Contreras-Vidal, 2006).

2.1.1.5 Limitation of ICA

Although ICA facilitates the analysis of the brain dynamics, this method cannot isolate highly correlated sources due to the assumption of statistical independence. Furthermore, it cannot identify uniquely ordered, correctly phased and properly scaled source signals, in other words, when using ICA, the independent components that are isolated could be randomly ordered, reversely phased, or ill scaled. However, in the case where such specific characteristics are of interest, it must be noted that ICA is not able to identify the source of the signals. Moreover, for practical bioengineering applications, artifact identification and removal based on ICA is not appropriate for real-time processing since it requires significant computational resources and a large amount of data collected from a sufficiently large number of channels. The next paragraph introduces adaptive filtering, another method that can be potentially useful for real-time applications.

2.1.2 Artifact removal using adaptive filtering

Despite the advantages of ICA as an artifact removal method, this technique is computationally very expensive and, thus, not well suited under some conditions such as real-time applications. However, other linear and nonlinear filtering based-techniques to remove specific artifacts in real-time are available. Among these methods, adaptive filtering has been introduced for removing ocular artifacts in real-time (He et al., 2004).

2.1.2.1 Principle of adaptive filtering

Adaptive filters are based on the principle that the desired (clean) signal can be extracted from the input signal through the adaptation of the filter parameters. The filter parameters are adapted based on minimizing an error function between the filter output signal and a desired signal. The most commonly used adaptive filtering algorithms are the Kalman filter, the least mean square (LMS) filter, and the recursive least square (RLS) filter (for more details on the implementations of these methods see Zaknich, 2005).

2.1.2.2 Removing ocular artifacts by adaptive filtering

Specifically, adaptive filtering has been used to remove ocular artifacts that could contaminate EEG/MEG (Georgiadis et al., 2005; Sanei & Chambers, 2007). For instance, He et al., (2004) suggested an adaptive filter that uses three inputs to the system. First, the actual EEG/MEG signal $x(k)$ with the ocular artifacts $z(k)$ as the primary input ($s(k)=x(k)+z(k)$). The second and third inputs are the vertical and horizontal eye movement (VEOG and HEOG) as two reference inputs ($r_v(k)$ and $r_h(k)$), respectively. Each reference input is first processed by a finite impulse response (FIR) filter using the RLS algorithm ($\hat{r}_v(k)$ and $\hat{r}_h(k)$, respectively) and then subtracted from the EEG signal under the assumption that the desired ocular artifacts cleaned EEG signal is a zero-mean stationary random signal that is uncorrelated with the ocular artifacts and the two reference signals. Thus, the desired output produced by the whole system is the EEG signal without ocular artifacts. Hence the whole system can be described using the following sets of equations and the corresponding scheme illustrated in Fig. 2:

$$e(k) = s(k) - \hat{r}_v(k) - \hat{r}_h(k) = x(k) + [z(k) - \hat{r}_v(k) - \hat{r}_h(k)] \tag{4}$$

where $\hat{r}_v(k) = \sum_{m=1}^{M} h_v(m) r_v(k+1-m)$ and $\hat{r}_h(k) = \sum_{m=1}^{M} h_h(m) r_h(k+1-m)$ for the filter parameters $h_v(m)$ and $h_h(m)$, respectively. $e(k)$ is the error between the observed signal and reference inputs.

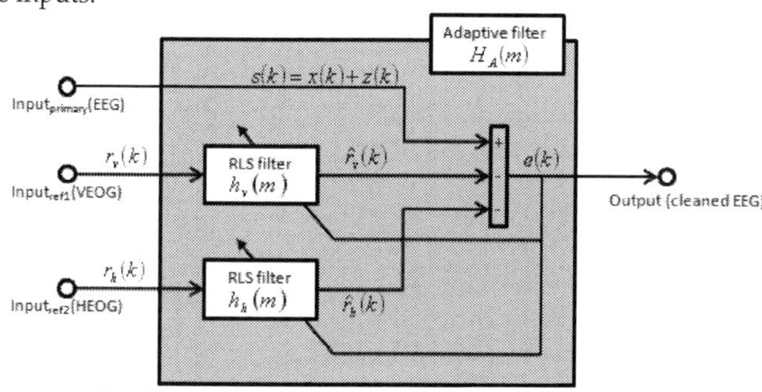

Fig. 2. Computational scheme of the adaptive filter configuration for eye artifact removal (EOG: Electrooculography). (The different symbols used in this figure are described in the text above).

2.1.2.3 Limitation of adaptive filtering

The LMS and RLS filters, popular alternative algorithms to the Kalman filter, also present some advantages and drawbacks. The LMS filter is one of the relatively simple adaptive filtering algorithms, so it is computationally very efficient, but it is not suitable for signals with high rate of sudden changes due to its slow rate of convergence (Vaseghi, 2007). In this case, the RLS filter offers relatively faster convergence and smaller error rate with more computations. More generally, a single type of artifact can be removed with a single filter, so multiple filtering must be performed when multiple forms of artifacts are present, increasing the chances of distorting the signals of interest.

2.1.3 Summary

To summarize, many novel artifact-removal techniques have been introduced along with some of their variants (He et al., 2004; Lee et al., 1999; Vaseghi 2007; Vigário et al., 2000). A common requirement for the artifact removal method is to remove the artifacts but keep the neurophysiological activities of interest intact. For this reason, the employment of algorithms for modeling and filtering must be carefully considered along with their underlying assumptions, since it may undesirably alter the estimated artifact-cleaned EEG/MEG signal (Hyvärinen & Oja, 2000; Oja, 2004; Vaseghi, 2007; Vigário et al., 2000). ICA is generally the most suitable artifacts removal algorithm with minimal affects on the interesting EEG/MEG signals, but it is very expensive in terms of both computation and memory usage. Adaptive filtering, on the other hand, can effectively remove artifacts from EEG/MEG signals in real-time fashion.

Once EEG/MEG signals are free of artifacts, the next step is to compute the brain biomarkers derived from these clean EEG/MEG signals in order to assess sensorimotor performance and learning. In this regard, the two main biomarkers that are available are derived from the spectral power and phase synchronisation between two signals located at different positions on the scalp. These two brain biomarkers are presented in the next two sections.

2.2 Spectral Power

A first type of brain biomarker that can be used to assess the level of mastery in sensorimotor performance and learning can be derived from the spectral power computed for specific frequency bands. Many different methods (e.g., parametric, non-parametric, and subspace methods) are available to compute the EEG/MEG spectral power (Kay, 1988; Sanei & Chambers, 2007; Shumway & Stoffer, 2000). For instance, some of these methods that have been applied are the classical fast Fourier transform (e.g., Hatfield et al., 1984; Haufler et al., 2000) and more sophisticated procedures such as the multitaper (e.g., Conteras-Vidal & Kerick, 2004) or wavelet (e.g., Mu et al., 2008) techniques. While some of these approaches have been applied with success in EEG/MEG studies that focus on sensorimotor performance and/or Brain Computer Interface (BCI) systems (McFarland et al., 2006; Pfurtscheller & Lopes da Silva, 1999), two methods are particularly popular to compute the EEG/MEG spectral power. The first approach uses autoregressive (AR) methods (e.g., McFarland et al., 2006, 2008) while the second one uses the band power method (Pfurtscheller & Lopes da Silva, 1999, 2005; Pfurtscheller & Neuper, 2006) providing changes in power amplitude that are often referred to as "event related desynchronization (ERD)" and "event related synchronization (ERS)."

2.2.1 Autoregressive filtering

The first technique that consists of using AR models is a classical parametric method (Marple, 1987; Sanei & Chambers, 2007; Shumway & Stoffer, 2000). Contrary to the fast Fourier transform, parametric spectral estimation by means of AR models offers various advantages by presenting a more general and flexible framework for parsimonious dynamical modeling of time series data useful for different applications such as prediction, classification or causality analysis of time series (Shumway & Stoffer, 2000; Wong et al., 2006). Specifically, an AR filter can be used for linear prediction in order to model the signal of interest; here an EEG or MEG signal. Namely, the real EEG/MEG signal can be considered as the sum of the signal modeled by the AR filter and an error term. Thus, by subtracting the real EEG/MEG signal to the one filtered by the AR model, the prediction error can be determined (Fig.3).

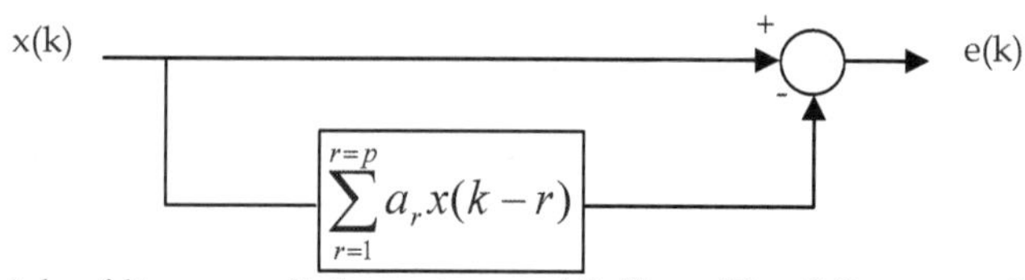

Fig. 3. Principle of linear prediction using an AR filter. (The different symbols used in this figure are described in the text below).

The prediction error for an AR model is defined as:

$$e(k) = x(k) - \sum_{r=1}^{r=p} a_r x(k-r) \tag{5}$$

where a_r (r = 1,2,3,…,p) are the coefficients, the constant p is the order of the filter, and k denotes the discrete time sample. $x(k)$ and $e(k)$ are respectively the input signal to approximate and the prediction error. For a given p, the coefficients are identified by minimization (e.g., LMS, Durbin method) of the error or driving signal that is considered to be zero mean white noise.

By applying the z-transform to equation (5) and considering Z= $e^{j\omega}$ we obtain:

$$\frac{X(\omega)}{E(\omega)} = \frac{1}{1 - \sum_{r=1}^{r=p} a_r e^{-jr\omega}} \tag{6}$$

Where $E(\omega)$ represents the power spectrum of the white noise that is constant (i.e., $E(\omega) = K_\omega$), and $X(\omega)$ represents the power spectrum of the signal. From this model, the spectral power can be estimated for any specific frequency band.

AR models may suffer from poor estimation of the model parameters mainly due to the limited length of the measured signal (Sanei & Chambers, 2007) while the order of the AR filter may influence the precision of the computation of power spectrum. For instance, McFarland et al., (2008) recently showed that the resolution of lower frequency signals requires higher AR model orders and also that increasing AR model order provided an enhanced spectral resolution. It must be noted that an increase of the AR model order results in a higher computational cost even if the tremendous advances in digital signal processor and field-programmable gate-array technology tend to weaken this drawback (Wang et al., 2006). Also, in the case of non-stationarity, parametric spectral estimation may also be applied with a moving window (Ozaki & Tong, 1975) or using some alternative approaches avoiding, thus, the introduction of such a moving window (Wong et al., 2006).

2.2.2 ERD/ERS method

The second method is well-established and has been successfully applied to many different EEG/MEG investigations (Gentili et al., 2008 ,2009a, 2009a; Kerick et al., 2004; Pfurtscheller & Lopes da Silva, 1999, 2005; Pfurtcheller & Neuper 2006; Tombini et al., 2009). Specifically, this method computes the spectral power by squaring and averaging across trials the output of a band pass filter in order to detect the changes in power amplitude. ERD and ERS correspond respectively to a decrease and an increase of the spectral power for specific frequency bands (e.g., alpha band) and brain regions (e.g., frontal region). These measures are often expressed as a percentage of a decrease or increase with respect to a baseline condition preceding task performance and are computed according to the following equation (for more details see Pfurtscheller & Lopes da Silva, 1999):

$$ERS/ERD = \frac{P_E - P_R}{P_R} \times 100\,(\%) \qquad (7)$$

where P_E and P_R correspond to the power computed within the frequency band of interest in the period after the event begins and during the preceding baseline or reference period, respectively.

It must be noted that although these ERD/ERS quantifications can be computed using different methods including AR filters, (e.g., see Table 1 in Pfurtscheller & Lopes da Silva, 1999) the term ERD/ERS is generally associated with the band pass method (see Pfurtscheller & Lopes da Silva, 1999, 2005 for a comprehensive review). From a physiological point of view, ERD/ERS mirror variations of the activity of local interactions between main neurons and interneurons that control the frequency components of the ongoing EEG (Pfurtscheller & Lopes da Silva 1999, 2005). As previously mentioned, although several methods can be used to isolate some specific frequency bands; one of the main problems of the EEG/MEG spectral analysis is the definition of the upper and lower bounds of the bands (Pfurtscheller & Lopes da Silva, 1999). Although the definition of the frequency band limits can slightly differ from one study to another, a possible approach for partitioning the frequency bands related to human motor performance for healthy adults is to consider the theta ([4-7 Hz]), alpha ([8-13 Hz]), beta ([14-35 Hz]) and gamma ([36-44 Hz]) frequency bands (e.g., Hatfield et al., 2004; Haufler et al., 2000; Tombini et al., 2009). Sometimes, the frequency range spread from 8 to 15 Hz (Blankertz & Vidaurre, 2009) or from 9 to 13Hz (Blankertz et al., 2009; Pfurtscheller & Neuper, 1997) are also named alpha frequency (or mu rhythm under certain conditions). Moreover, since it has been shown that certain frequency sub-bands are related to specific brain states during a sensorimotor task (e.g., Contreras-Vidal et al., 2004; Gentili et al., 2008; Hatfield et al., 2004; Tombini et al., 2009), most of the EEG/MEG studies refined their analysis by considering sub-frequency bands, typically, the low and high component of the original entire band. Therefore, for the bands previously defined, the low theta ([4-5 Hz]), high theta ([6-7 Hz]), low alpha ([8-10 Hz]), high alpha ([11-13 Hz]), low beta ([14-23 Hz]) and high beta ([24-35 Hz]) frequency bands can also be considered. In addition to the classical gamma band ([36-44 Hz]) it is also possible to consider the extended gamma band spread from 45 to 100 Hz or higher. This gamma band extension can be divided into several sub-bands with a method using a 10-Hz-wide band with an overlap of 5 Hz frequency bins ranging from 45 to 100 Hz (Crone et al.,

1998). Although, as previously mentioned, the limits of these bands can slightly change from one study to another; many EEG/MEG investigations consider frequency bands where upper and lower limits of the bandpass filter is the same for all the subjects tested. It must be noted that another approach (Pfurtscheller & Lopes da Silva, 1999, 2005) defines these frequency band limits for each individual subject in order to take into account some inter-individual differences. For instance, three possible methods can be used to determine the upper and lower limits of the bandpass filter; i) detection of the most reactive frequency band by comparing the two short-term power spectra; ii) use of a continuous wavelet transform; iii) definition of frequency bands relative to the spectral peak frequency (for more details see Pfurtscheller & Lopes da Silva, 1999, 2005).

2.3 Phase synchronization: Coherence and Phase Locking Value

Another important brain biomarker of sensorimotor performance can also be provided by analyzing the phase synchronization between different cortical sites. Such phase synchronization measures the level of interaction and cross talk among EEG/MEG channels allowing the identification of how signals propagate within the neural network of the brain. These spatial EEG/MEG coherence measures, generally presented for individual frequency bands, result from correlations among different cortical sources. Therefore, spectral coherence is a common method for determining synchrony in EEG/MEG activity.

Regarding the literature aiming to find brain biomarkers for human sensorimotor performance and learning, spectral power analysis has been widely used for a long time, however, the use of spectral coherence is relatively more recent, while the phase locking value (PLV), despite its advantages, still remains rarely used in this field. Generally, the literature focusing on EEG/MEG signal analysis computes the synchronization between two time signals recorded from two electrodes x and y by using classical coherence (Nunez & Srinivasan, 2006). First the cross-spectrum (CS) has to be computed using the following equation:

$$CS_{xy}(f) = \left\langle S_x(f)\bar{S}_y(f) \right\rangle \tag{8}$$

where $S_x(f)$ is the Fourier transform of the signal $s_x(t)$, $\bar{S}_x(f)$ is the complex conjugate of the Fourier transform of the signal $s_x(t)$ and $\langle\ \rangle$ is the expectation operator. Then, the complex coherence (CC) is computed by using the cross-spectrum normalized with respect to the two corresponding spectra of the two signals. Thus we have:

$$CC_{xy}(f) = \frac{CS_{xy}(f)}{\sqrt{CS_{xx}(f)CS_{yy}(f)}} \tag{9}$$

Where $CS_{xy}(f)$ is the cross-spectrum of the two time signals $s_x(t)$ and $s_y(t)$ and $CC_{xy}(f)$ the complex coherence.

Finally, the coherence (C) can be calculated by considering the absolute value of the complex coherence:

$$C_{xy}(f) = \left| CC_{xy}(f) \right| \tag{10}$$

Another way to interpret these equations is to consider the following equation:

$$S_x(f) = \rho_x e^{j\varphi_x} \tag{11}$$

where the Fourier transform $S_x(f)$ of the signal $s_x(t)$ is expressed in order to explicitly illustrate its amplitude ρ_x and its phase φ_x (here j denotes the imaginary unit and $j^2=-1$) .

Now the cross-spectrum expressed in equation (8) can be rewritten as:

$$CS_{xy}(f) = \left\langle \rho_x \rho_y e^{j\Delta\varphi} \right\rangle \tag{12}$$

where $\Delta\varphi$ denotes the phase difference between the two signals (i.e., $\Delta\varphi = \varphi_x - \varphi_y$). Thus, the complex coherence expressed in equation (9) can be rewritten as:

$$CC_{xy}(f) = \frac{\left\langle \rho_x \rho_y e^{j\Delta\varphi} \right\rangle}{\sqrt{\left\langle \rho_x^2 \right\rangle \left\langle \rho_y^2 \right\rangle}} \tag{13}$$

Leading to the classical coherence provided by the following equation:

$$C_{xy}(f) = \left| \frac{\left\langle \rho_x \rho_y e^{j\Delta\varphi} \right\rangle}{\sqrt{\left\langle \rho_x^2 \right\rangle \left\langle \rho_y^2 \right\rangle}} \right| \tag{14}$$

Although this measure of classical coherence is usually used in EEG/MEG studies, two main drawbacks have to be considered (Lachaux et al., 1999). First, the coherence can be applied only to stationary signals. Most of the time this assumption of stationarity (in time or across trials) is not strictly valid, however, the measure of phase-locking does not require this assumption on the signal. Second, coherence does not specifically quantify phase relationships. In fact, coherence increases with amplitude covariance (see the presence of the signal amplitudes ρ_x and ρ_y in the numerator and denominator of the formula in equation (14)) implying an uncertainty concerning the relative importance of amplitude and phase covariance in the coherence. In other words, the coherence does not separate the effects of amplitude and phase in the interrelations between two signals. Thus, based on these

premises and since phase-locking provides a measure that is sufficient to conclude if two brain regions interact, another measure of phase synchronization, the PLV, has been introduced, offering, thus, an alternative measure only based on the detection of phase covariance (Lachaux et al., 1999; Le Van Quyen et al., 2001; Tass et al., 1998).
Before computing the PLV, the frequency bands and sub-bands of interest mentioned in Section 2.2.2 are extracted for each subject and each single-trial by means of a filter bank using band-pass FIR (Lachaux et al., 1999) or IIR filters (Brunner et al., 2006).

Then, the PLV can be computed for each frequency band. Contrary to the classical coherence, it is defined by only considering the phases of the two signals.

$$PLV = \left|\left\langle e^{j\Delta\varphi} \right\rangle\right| \tag{15}$$

where $\Delta\varphi$ denotes the phase difference between the two signals $s_x(t)$ and $s_y(t)$ (i.e., $\Delta\varphi = \varphi_x - \varphi_y$).

It must be noted that equations (14) and (15) are comparable; however, the equation expressing the PLV does not include the amplitudes of the two signals, allowing examination of synchronization phenomena in EEG/MEG signals by directly capturing the phase synchronization.
Two methods to compute the phases φ_x and φ_y are available. The first one (Lachaux et al., 1999) uses a complex Gabor wavelet as defined by equation (16):

$$G(t,f) = e^{-a} e^{j2\pi ft} \tag{16}$$

Where a= $-\dfrac{t^2}{2\sigma_t^2}$, t represents the time and σ is the standard deviation of the Gaussian envelope.
The second method (Tass et al., 1998) uses the Hilbert transform as defined by the following equation:

$$\tilde{s}_x(t) = \frac{1}{\pi} PV \int_{-\infty}^{+\infty} \frac{s_x(t)}{t-\tau} d\tau \tag{17}$$

In this definition, $\tilde{s}_x(t)$ is the Hilbert transform of the time series $s_x(t)$ (in our case an EEG/MEG signal), and PV indicates that the integral is taken in the sense of Cauchy principal value. The instantaneous phase can then be calculated as:

$$\varphi_x(t) = \arctan \frac{\tilde{s}_x(t)}{s_x(t)} \tag{18}$$

It must be noted that these two methods provide very similar results when applied to EEG data (Le Van Quyen et al., 2001).
The averaging process can be performed either over time (i.e., in equation (19), n ∈ [1…N], where *n* is the sample number of the time series) for single-trial applications such as BCI approaches (Brunner et al., 2006; Lachaux et al., 2000) or over trials (Lachaux et al., 1999) (i.e., in equation (19), n ∈ [1…N], where *n* is the trial number). Thus, equation (19) is obtained:

$$PLV = \frac{1}{N}\left|\sum_{i=1}^{N} e^{j\Delta\varphi(t,n)}\right| \qquad (19)$$

where $\Delta\varphi(t,n)$ is the phase difference and $\Delta\varphi(t,n) = \varphi_x(t,n) - \varphi_y(t,n)$.

As for the coherence, the PLV is ranged from 0 to 1 indicating that during this time window the two channels considered are ranged from unsynchronized to perfectly synchronized, respectively. It must be noted that, despite the previously mentioned advantages of the PLV, it has been also suggested that one reason to use coherence rather than the PLV directly is that coherence measures are weighted in favor of epochs with large amplitudes. In particular, more consistent phase estimates will be probably obtained when amplitudes are large (if large amplitudes show a large signal-to-noise ratio as is generally the case in EEG/MEG) (Nunez & Srinivasan, 2006). Therefore, both coherence and PLV measures can be used. Interestingly, due to their unique advantages and pitfalls, some studies apply and compare both techniques that, in the case of convergence, lead to robust results, although in the case of EEG both approaches are subject to the electrode reference problem that can distort such measurements (Nunez & Srinivasan, 2006). Recently, Darvas et al., (2009) have proposed an extension of the PLV, called bi-PLV that is specifically sensitive to non-linear interactions providing, thus, robustness behavior to spurious synchronization arising from linear crosstalk. This property is particularly useful when analyzing data recorded by EEG or MEG. From a physiological point of view, both coherence and PLV methods quantify the magnitude of correlation, for a given frequency (or band), between different areas of the cerebral cortex. Thus, high coherence and/or PLV implies substantial communication between different cortical areas while low coherence and/or PLV reflects regional autonomy or independence (Nunez & Srinivasan, 2006).

3 Non-Invasive Functional Brain Biomarkers of Human Sensorimotor Performance:

Although the signal processing approaches described above are applicable to both EEG and MEG signals, we will focus mainly on brain biomarkers derived from EEG since, as mentioned in the introduction, this technique is portable and therefore is particularly well suited for ecological motor tasks such as aiming (e.g., marksmanship, archery), drawing, arm reaching and grasping task. Therefore, most of the examples below will present the results of brain biomarkers derived from EEG signals.

3.1 Spectral power

A series of studies that began in the early 80's provided a growing body of evidence that it is possible to assess the cortical dynamics of motor skills in novice and expert performers during visuomotor challenge such as marksmanship and archery tasks. These studies revealed changes in EEG activity with skill learning as well as differences in EEG power between novice and expert sport performers (Del Percio et al., 2008; Hatfield et al., 1984, 2004; Haufler et al., 2000; Kerick et al., 2004; Landers et al., 1994; Slobounov et al., 2007). Specifically, the power computed for the alpha and theta frequency bands were positively related to the level of motor performance (Del Percio et al., 2008; Hatfield et al., 2004; Haufler et al., 2000; Kerick et al., 2004).

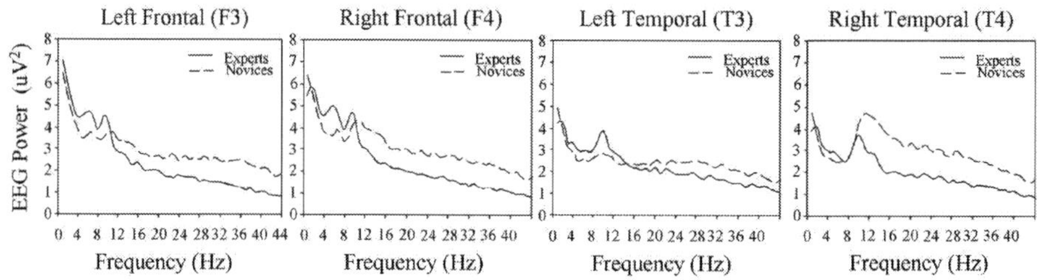

Fig. 4. Mean EEG power (mV^2) spectra (1–44 Hz) at left and right homologous sites in the frontal and temporal regions during the aiming period of the shooting task for expert marksmen versus novice shooters (Adapted from Haufler et al., (2000) with permission from Elsevier Science).

For instance, Haufler et al., (2000) showed that, compared to novices, experts revealed an overall increase in EEG alpha power in the left temporal lobe (i.e., T3) while the same comparison between novices and experts performing cognitive tasks that were equally familiar to them did not provide any differences. The authors concluded, therefore, that the EEG alpha power differences observed were likely due to the difference of level in mastery of the motor task (see Fig. 4). Obviously, the differences in cortical dynamic between novices and experts revealed by these studies were accompanied with important differences between performances (i.e., the novices scored lower and exhibited more variability in their performance than the experts). Thus, these studies provided brain biomarkers (e.g., alpha power) able to identify a high level of motor performance resulting from an extensive practice period, without, however, considering the changes of such brain biomarker throughout the training period itself.

Interestingly, in a more recent study Kerick et al., (2004) extended these investigations by assessing the dynamic changes throughout a marksmanship intensive training for novices during three months. The results revealed that, throughout the training, the performance for the shooting task was enhanced (Fig. 5A) concomitantly with an increased EEG alpha power (Fig. 5B) at the temporal level located on the contralateral side (i.e., T3, left temporal lobe) while such observation was not observed when the subjects were at rest. Such EEG changes are generally interpreted as indicative of high levels of skill and associated with a cortical refinement leading to reductions of nonessential cortical resources (Hatfield & Hillman, 2001). This kind of neural adaptation process may result in simplification of neurocognitive activity and less possibility of interference with essential visuomotor processes. Within an

activation context, a decrease in alpha power frequency band (i.e., desynchronization) represents an activated cortical site. Conversely, an increase in alpha power (i.e., synchronization) corresponds to a reduction of activation of a given cortical region (Pfurtscheller et al., 1996) indicating a decrease of the recruitment of neural resources.
In addition to the alpha frequency band, several studies suggested that theta oscillations are also related to performance enhancement (Caplan et al., 2003; Tombini et al., 2009). For instance, during a virtual maze navigation task, Caplan et al., (2003) observed that theta oscillations reflected an updating of motor plans in response to incoming sensory information that facilitates the information encoding of participant's cognitive map.

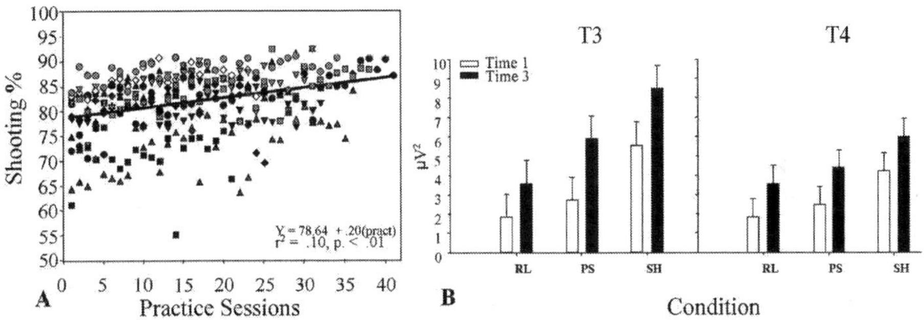

Fig. 5. A. Shooting percentages by practice session. The slope of the linear regression revealed a significant increase in performance over all practice sessions from time 1 to 3 (equation lower right corner). The different symbols represent the performance scores of individual participants on separate days of practice. B. Changes in mean power from time 1 to 3 during shooting (SH), postural (PS), and Baseline (BL) condition (T3, left panel; T4, right panel). (Adapted from Kerick et al., (2004) with permission from Wolters Kluwer/Lippincott Williams).

Although other interpretations of theta power increases are plausible (e.g., frontal theta EEG synchronization could also reflect an increased short term memory load; for a review see Klimesch et al., 2008), a growing body of work suggest that theta oscillations are functionally associated with error monitoring (Cavanagh et al., 2009; Larson & Lynch, 1989; Smith et al., 1999; Yordanova et al., 2004).
Thus, taken together these studies suggested that changes in alpha and theta power can be used as non-invasive functional brain biomarkers capable either to assess the level of mastery of a given sensori-motor task (e.g., marksmanship task) and/or to track the brain status during motor practice. However, these studies used visuomotor task where upper limb movements were extremely specific (e.g., archery, marksmanship task) without considering more familiar movements used in daily activities such as arm reaching, grasping and tool or object manipulations. Moreover, these investigations addressed the improvement of an established motor ability (e.g., Haulfer et al., 2000), or a long learning period of a skill involving no interference with previous motor experience (e.g., Caplan et al., 2003; Kerick et al., 2004). Interestingly, Kranczioch et al., (2008) showed that the learning of a visuomotor power grip tool led to EEG changes in spectral power and cortico-cortical coupling (i.e., coherence). However, this study did not involve a tool that required

suppression of a familiar response. Nevertheless, in daily activities, we frequently need to adapt our motor commands related to our upper limb to learn new input-output mappings characterizing novel tools by inhibiting familiar behavior or responses that are no longer valid to manipulate them. Such tool learning requires the selection and guidance of movements based on visual and proprioceptive inputs while frontal executive function would inhibit the pre-potent input-output relationships during acquisition of the internal model (also called internal representation) of the new tool. This would be typically the case if a person has to learn to manipulate a new tool such as a neuroprosthetic. It should be noted that Anguera et al., (2009) used a visuomotor adaptation task requiring suppression of preexisting motor responses in order to quantify the changes in error-related negativity associated with the magnitude of the error. However, this study did not focus on tracking the learning process by using brain biomarkers derived from spectral power and/or phase synchronization.

Based on this rational, a recent study (Gentili et al., 2008) intended to address this problem by analyzing the cortical dynamics during the learning of a new tool having unknown kinematics features. In this experiment, fifteen right-handed healthy adults subjects sat at a table facing a computer screen and, with their right hand, had to perform "centre-out" drawing movements (on a digitizing tablet) linking a central target and one of four peripheral targets. Movement paths were displayed on the screen, but a horizontal board prevented any vision of the moving limb on the tablet. EEG signals were acquired using an electro-cap with 64 tin electrodes, which was fitted to the participant's head in accordance with the standards of the extended International 10-20 system (Fig.6). First, the subjects performed 20 practice trials at the beginning of the experiment in order to be familiarized with the experimental setup. After this familiarization period, the experiment was divided into three sessions: i) pre-exposure, ii) exposure and iii) post-exposure. During the pre- and post-exposure phases the subjects performed, under normal visual conditions, 20 trials (i.e., 1 block). During the exposure phase, (180 trials, i.e., 20 trials x 9 blocks) ten subjects (i.e., learning croup) had to adapt to a 60° counter clock-wise screen cursor rotation. In addition, five healthy (i.e., control group) subjects were examined using the same protocol but in the absence of any visual distortion. Movements were self-initiated and targets were self-selected one at a time. All the targets were displayed throughout each trial. The instructions were to draw a line as straight and as fast as possible linking the home target and the peripheral target. Unknown to the participants, a trial was aborted and restarted if the time between entering the home target and movement onset was less than 2s. Therefore, participants had enough time to both select the target and plan their movement providing, thus, an extended time-window to analyze cortical activations related to preparation processes (i.e., planning) of the movement.

In order to quantify the motor performance during both movement planning and movement execution periods, the Movement Time (MT), Movement Length (ML) and Root Mean Square of the Error (RMSE) were computed from the 2D horizontal displacements. The MT was defined as the elapsed time between leaving the home circle and entering the target. The ML was defined as the distance traveled in each trial.

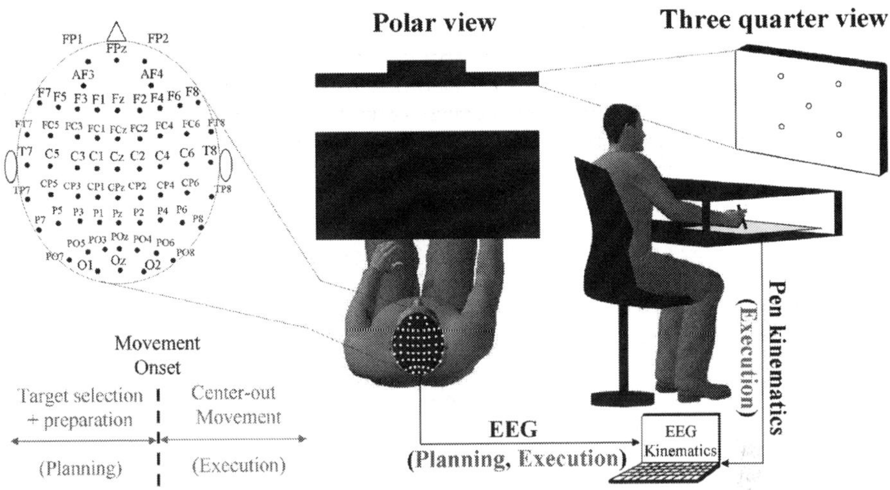

Fig. 6. Experimental device to record kinematics and EEG signals during the visuomotor adaptation task. Subjects sat at a table facing a computer screen located in front of them at a distance of ~60 cm and had to execute the motor task which consisted of drawing a line on a digitizing tablet (represented in light blue on the figure) that was displayed in real-time on the computer screen. The home target circle was the origin of a direct polar frame of reference, and the target circles were positioned 10 cm from the origin disposed at 45°, 135°, 225°, and 315°. Once a successful trial was performed, to prevent any feedback, all visual stimuli were erased from the screen in preparation for the next trial.

The RMSE was computed to assess the average deviation between the movement trajectory from the 'ideal' straight line connecting the home and the pointing target. For the nine learning blocks, the mean and standard deviation of the ML and MT were computed. In order to take into account any differences in subject's performance during the pre-exposure phase (i.e., baseline condition) and to focus on changes due solely to adaptation, the MT, ML and RMSE values were standardized with respect to the pre-exposure stage.

Continuous EEG data were epoched in 2-s windows centered at movement onset. Both pre- (i.e., planning) and post- (i.e., execution) movement time-windows were considered. Single-trial data were detrended to remove DC amplifier drift, low-pass filtered to suppress line noise, and baseline-corrected by averaging the mean potential from -1 to 1 s. The EEG signals were cleaned by means of the ICA Infomax method applied on a single-trial basis described in section 2.1.1. For each subject and each single-trial, the EEG power (ERS/ERD) were computed by squaring and integrating the output of a dual band-pass Butterworth fourth order filter, and standardized with respect to the pre-exposure stage. The EEG power was computed for the alpha (low: 8-10 Hz, high: 11-13 Hz), beta (low: 13-20 Hz, high: 21-35 Hz); theta (Low: 4-5 Hz, High: 6-7 Hz) and γ (36-44 Hz) bands. The entire alpha, beta and theta frequency bands were also analyzed. For the alpha band, two similar frequency ranges have been considered. i) alpha1: spread form 8 to 13Hz, and ii) alpha2: spreads from 9 to 13 Hz. For each sensor and each block, the average power changes (across subjects) were fitted using a linear model from which the coefficient of determination (R^2) and its slope were obtained. The sensors that showed a fit indicating a coefficient of determination capable to explain at least 50% of the variability of the data (i.e., $R^2 \geq 0.50$) allowed us to determine the sensor clusters and the frequency bands of interest. The results of this procedure led us to consider the two alpha frequency bands and the high component of the theta frequency band for the right (FT8, T8, TP8) and left (FT7, T7, TP7) temporal and right (FP2, AF4, F4, F6, F8) and left (FP1, AF3, F3, F5, F7,) frontal lobes. This procedure led us also to consider the two alpha frequency bands for the left (P1, P3, P5, P7, PO3, PO5, PO7) and right (P2, P4, P6, P8, PO4, PO6, PO8) parietal and left (O1) and right (O2) occipital regions (For the electrodes sites see Fig. 6). It must be noted that the results for both alpha bands were similar. However, since the findings for the second alpha band (i.e., [9-13Hz]) were slightly better only this frequency band will be presented and discussed. For the alpha (i.e., [9-13Hz]) and high theta (i.e., [6-7Hz]) bands and the eight clusters of interest, the average power values were computed, and the same fitting process was applied. Furthermore, in order to investigate any correlation between the kinematics data and the EEG power, the average EEG power values obtained for the clusters of interest were plotted versus the MT, ML and RMSE values. Exponential (single and double), linear and quadratic models were used to fit these relationships. The best fit was selected by considering the coefficient of determination and its adjusted value, the mean square error of the fit, and the sum of squares due to the fitting error.

The results showed that, during the early learning phase, the subjects performed distorted movement trajectories with a slow progression towards the targets. However, as the subjects of the learning group learned the unknown physical (kinematics) properties of the novel tool, the analysis of the motor performance revealed that the MT, ML and RMSE decreased throughout adaptation (Fig. 7A-C). From the early to the late learning period, the trajectories were straighter and smoother while the control group did not show any performance improvement (Fig. 7A-C).

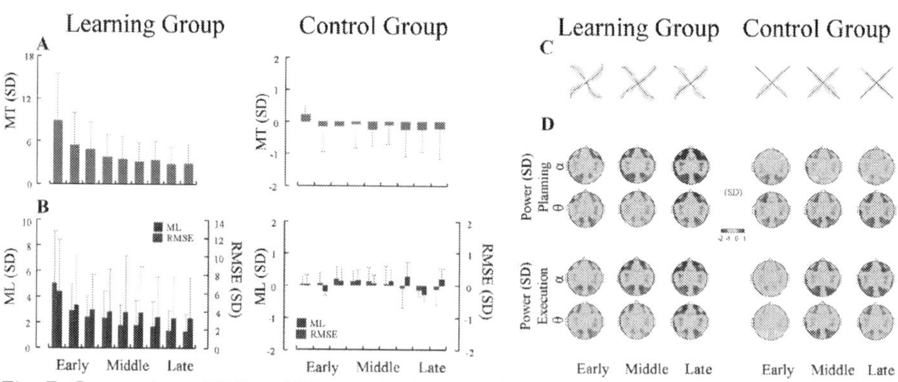

Fig. 7. Concomitant EEG and kinematic changes throughout learning for the learning and control groups. (A) Changes in MT (±SE) throughout the learning blocks. (B) Changes in ML (±SE) (purple) and RMSE (±SE) (blue) throughout the learning blocks. (C) Changes in average trajectory (thick black lines) throughout learning for early, middle and late exposure (the grey area represents the standard error across subjects). (D) Qualitative EEG changes in alpha (first and third row) and high theta (second and fourth row) frequency bands for the

frontal, temporal, parietal and occipital regions during planning (two first rows) and execution (two last rows). For the sake of clarity, sensors which did not belong to the clusters of interest were set to the minimal value of the scale for the scalp plot. The results of the learning group and control group are represented in the left and right column, respectively. (Adapted from Gentili et al., (2008) with permission from EURASIP).

Simultaneously to these behavioral changes, the results revealed that, as the subject adapt, the alpha and the high component of the theta power increased in the frontal and temporal lobes whereas an increased in alpha power also took place in the parietal lobes. Moreover, these spectral changes occurred during both movement planning (i.e., movement preparation) and movement execution. It must be noted that this alpha frequency band spread form 9 to 13Hz showed the largest reactivity during the adaptation to the novel tool and thus provides a better brain biomarker. Contrary to the learning group, the control group did not exhibit any changes in spectral power (Fig. 7D).

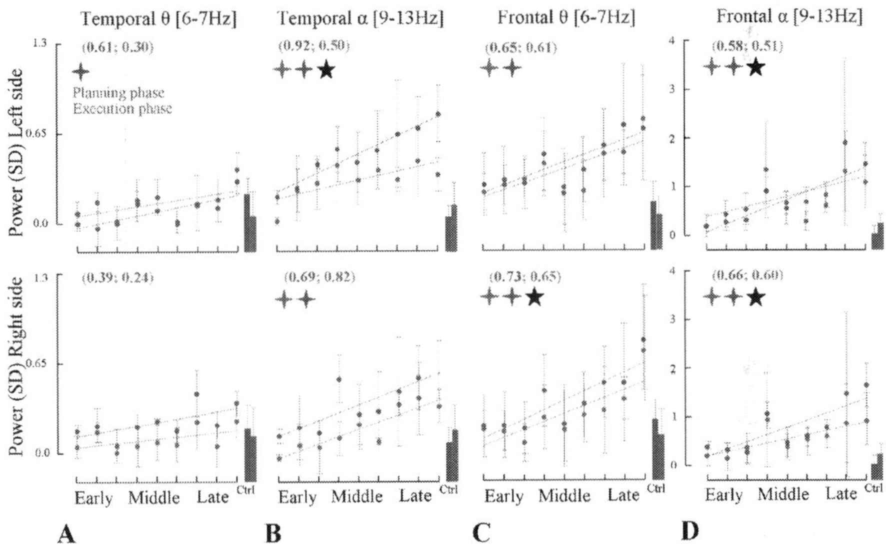

Fig. 8. Linear fits of EEG power changes for the frontal and temporal clusters for the participants of the learning group. Standardized values of the average EEG power computed across subjects (n=10) of the learning group and blocks (n=9) for the alpha and the high theta frequency bands recorded from the right (FT8, T8, TP8) and left (FT7, T7, TP7) temporal lobes and right (FP2, AF4, F4, F6, F8) and left (FP1, AF3, F3, F5, F7) frontal lobes. The blue and red stars indicate that the slopes were significantly different from zero for planning and execution, respectively. The black star indicates that the slopes between planning and execution were significantly different. The two bars on the right side of each panel represent the average value of the EEG power for the same cortical sites and the same frequency band for planning (blue) and execution (red) of the control group. (Adapted from Gentili et al., (2008) with permission from EURASIP).

Among the various models tested to fit these spectral changes, the best model that was able to capture these changes was linear. Only the left temporal lobe presented a significantly linear increase for the high component of theta power during movement planning (Fig. 8A). However, for the frontal lobes, the same linear theta power increase occurred during both movement planning and execution with similar slopes (Fig. 8C). For both the temporal and frontal lobes, the alpha power significantly increased linearly during both movement planning and execution. The slopes were also different between movement planning and execution (Fig. 8B, D). Finally, the alpha power showed a significant linear increase in the left and right parietal lobes for the planning while only a tendency was observed for the execution and both movement stages for the two occipital lobes (Fig. 9A, C).

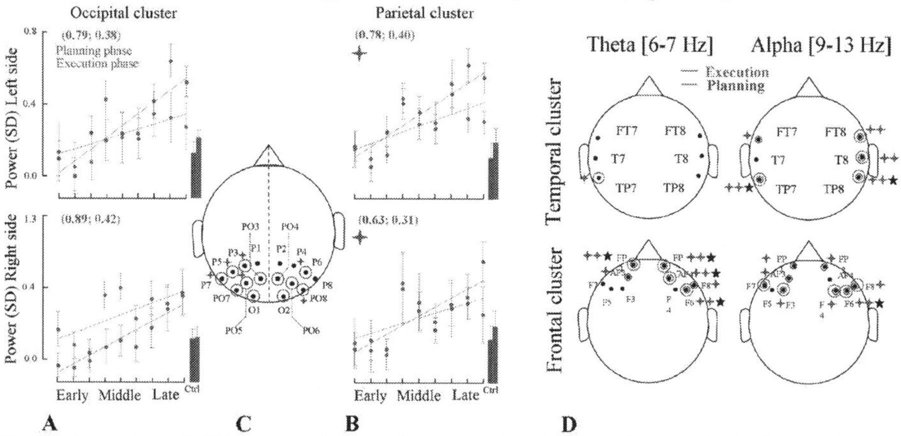

Fig. 9. Linear fits of EEG power changes for the occipital (A) and parietal (B) clusters for the learning group. Standardized values of the average EEG power computed across subjects (n=10) and blocks (n=9) for the alpha frequency bands recorded from the right (O2) and left (O1) occipital lobes and right (P2, P4, P6, P8, PO4, PO6, PO8) and left (P1, P3, P5, P7, PO3, PO5, PO7) parietal lobes. The blue stars indicate that the slopes were significantly different from zero for planning. The two bars on the right side of each panel represent the average value of the EEG power for the same cortical sites and the same frequency band for planning (blue) and execution (red) for the control group. The scalp plot depicts the clusters of electrodes in the occipital and parietal sites (C) and also for the frontal and temporal sites (D). For both panels, the blue and red circles indicate that the linear models for the alpha and theta power showed a coefficient of determination (R^2) greater than 0.5 for the planning and execution of movement, respectively. The blue and red stars indicate that the linear models had a slope significantly different from zero for planning and execution phases, respectively. The black star indicates that the slopes for planning and execution are significantly different from each other.

The previous results were obtained at a cluster level; however, a refined analysis conducted at the sensor level also showed that these linear changes where located on specific sensors (Fig. 9C, D) for these two frequency bands and both movement planning and execution. Finally, in order to find a correlation model between these spectral changes and those observed in kinematics during performance several models have been tested.

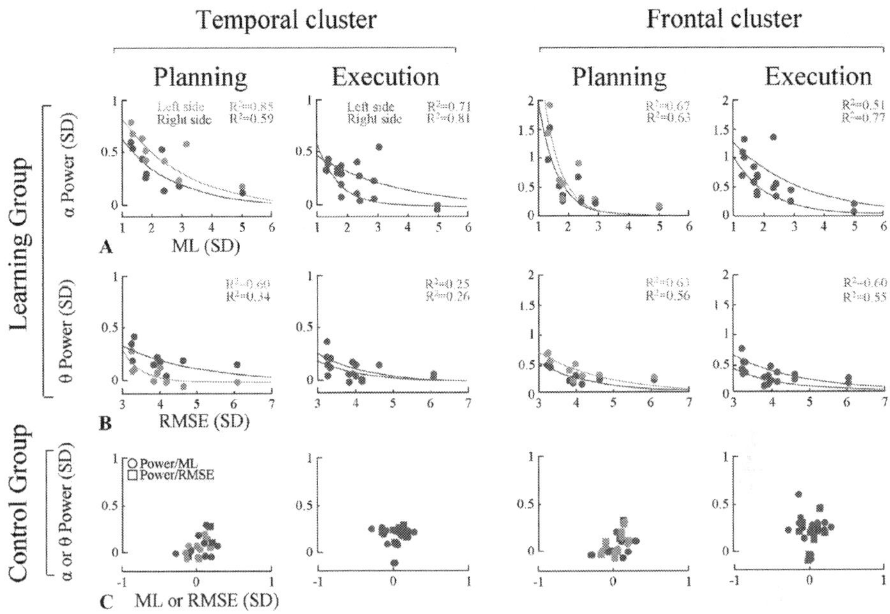

Fig. 10. Changes in EEG power in the alpha and high theta bands versus kinematics. The first two rows represent the average values of the standardized power of the alpha bands computed for the right and left temporal and frontal regions during planning and execution versus the concomitant changes in ML (first row) and RMSE (second row) for the learning group. The third row represents the same relationship for both alpha versus ML and high theta versus RMSE for the control group. (Adapted from Gentili et al., (2008) with permission from EURASIP).

The findings showed that, among the models tested, the single exponential was able to capture with the best accuracy these co-variations between EEG power changes and the corresponding motor production (Fig. 10A, B). The control group did not show any changes (Fig. 10C).

Thus, it appears that these changes in theta and alpha power provide informative brain biomarkers to track the cortical dynamics in order to assess the level of performance and also to track during both planning and execution the level of mastery of a novel tool throughout learning. Although useful, this first type of brain biomarker has the drawback to be univariate, that is, the power computed at a particular scalp site is able to characterize activation patterns for a particular channel (or brain region) without accounting for functional network connectivity or communications between different regions of the cortex during performance. It must be noted that these spectral power changes have been robustly observed in EEG/MEG studies and represent today a classical brain biomarker of human performance. Beside the spectral power, another type of brain biomarker, derived from EEG/MEG, is the computation of the phase synchronization between two scalp sites. Although initially less popular, this second technique (see section 2.3) is increasingly used to track the level of sensorimotor performance/learning. Recently this approach led to interesting results that will be presented in the next section.

3.2 Phase synchronisation

Contrary to the previously mentioned investigations focusing on the spectral power analysis, there are only a few studies that analyzed the cortical networking by means of coherence and/or PLV to assess the level of motor performance and/or to track the learning dynamic. For instance, Bell and Fox (1996) reported a decreased EEG coherence in experienced infant crawlers relative to novice crawlers and attributed their findings to a pruning of synaptic connections as crawling became more routine. Another experiment, further directly related to our purpose and conducted by Deeny et al., (2003), compared EEG coherence between a frontal site (i.e., sensor Fz) and several other cortical regions in two groups of highly skilled marksmen who were similar in expertise, but who differed in competitive performance history. One of the two groups performed consistently better in competition and exhibited significantly lower coherence between the left temporal region (i.e., T3) and the premotor area (i.e., Fz) in the low-alpha (8–10 Hz) and low-beta (13–22 Hz) bandwidths during the aiming period (Fig. 11).

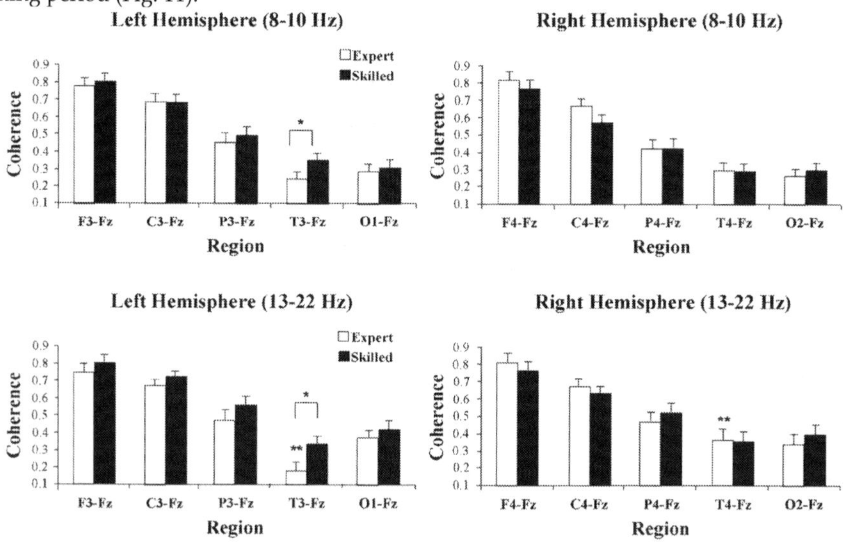

Fig. 11. Upper row. Expert and skilled group means for low-alpha (8–10 Hz) coherence estimates between Fz (premotor area) and frontal, central, temporal, parietal, and occipital sites in each cerebral hemisphere. Lower row. Expert and skilled group means for low-beta (13–22 Hz) coherence estimates between Fz (premotor area) and frontal, central, temporal, parietal, and occipital sites in each cerebral hemisphere. *Significant difference, $p < 0.05$; **T3–Fz coherence was significantly lower than T4–Fz coherence in the expert group only. (Adapted from Deeny et al., (2003) with permission from Human Kinetics Publishers).

More recently, Deeny et al., (2009) confirmed that the coherence could also be useful to assess the brain dynamic in relation to the level of mastery of a motor task. Specifically, they showed that experts generally exhibited lower coherence over the whole scalp compared with novices, with the effect most prominent in the right hemisphere. Coherence was positively related to aiming movement variability in experts (Fig. 12).

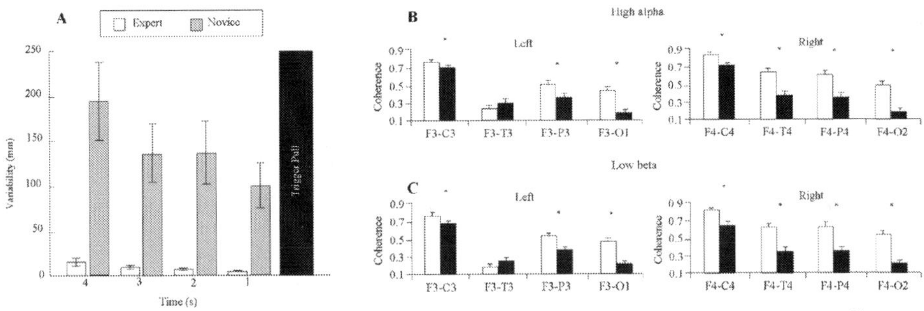

Fig. 12. A. Average variability of rifle aiming path during the 4 s prior to trigger pull in 1-s time bins for experts and novices. Error bars represent standard error. B. Coherence values for high alpha. C. Coherence values for low beta. *Indicate significantly higher coherence in novice shooters relative to experts (p <0.05). C = central; F = frontal; O = occipital; P = parietal; T = temporal. (Adapted from Deeny et al., (2009) with permission from Heldref Publications).

Taken together, the authors of these two studies suggested that these coherence results reflect a refinement of cortical networks in experts that was interpreted as a reduction of nonessential functional communications among the cortical regions of interest inducing in turn an improvement in motor performance. In other words, such coherence patterns provide brain biomarkers of specific motor planning as skill level increases allowing assessing the mastery level of a given task. As previously explained in the section related to the spectral power analysis, these studies assessed cortical dynamics for a well-established motor ability without addressing any learning manipulations of object or tool having unknown properties. As far as we know, only two investigations (Busk & Galbraith, 1975; Kranczioch et al., 2008) used coherence measurement to study learning during a visuomotor task. Specifically, Busk & Galbraith, (1975) reported decreased coherence between premotor (Fz) and motor (C3, C4) areas of the cortex and between the premotor and occipital regions, following practice on an eye-hand tracking task. More recently, Kranczioch et al., (2008) found changes in cortico-cortical coupling during learning of a visuomotor power grip tool. Specifically, they revealed that learning was variably associated with increased coherence between contralateral and/or ipsilateral frontal and parietal, fronto-central, and occipital brain regions. However, the learning period was relatively short (e.g., only the early learning stage was considered in Busk & Galbraith, (1975)) and these studies did not involve the suppression of familiar behavior used in the daily life.

By using the same tool learning protocol with unknown kinematics features (see section 3.1, Fig.6), a recent analysis (Gentili et al., 2009b) aimed to identify any changes in phase synchronization between two electrode pairs using both spectral coherence and PLV. The aim was to extract information from these measures to provide additional non-invasive functional brain biomarkers able to track the sensorimotor performance while subjects learned to manipulate a novel tool. The pre-processing of the EEG, the choice of the frequency bands of interest and the kinematics processing were similar to that previously described in section 3.1 for the same tool learning task. Both the spectral coherence and the PLV have been computed as mentioned in section 2.3. A visual inspection of the data led us to consider a linear and a logarithmic model to fit the relationship between the spectral coherence/PLV changes and the kinematics parameters (MT, ML, RMSE) throughout learning. However, based on the criteria previously mentioned (see section 3.1), the logarithmic model allowed a better fitting of these relationships. It must be noted that, since for this experiment both spectral coherence and PLV provided similar results, thus, only the PLV results are presented in the following. The kinematics results are the same that those presented in section 3.1 (see Fig. 7A-C) indicating that the subjects learned to manipulate correctly the novel tool.

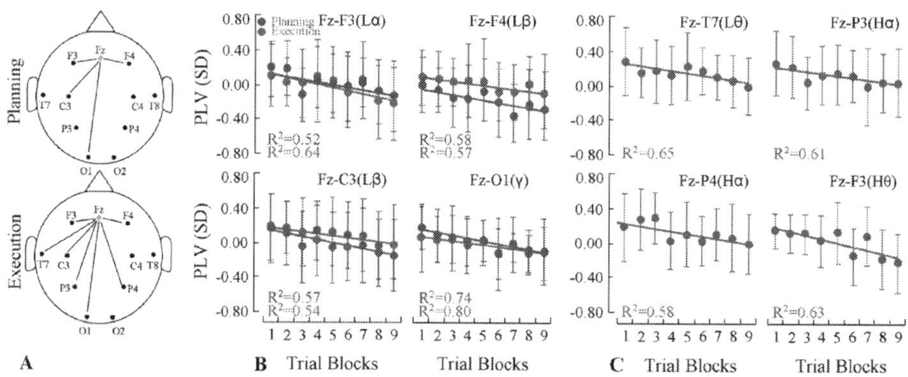

Fig. 13. Changes in PLV throughout the learning. A. Pair of electrodes showing a decrease of their synchronization throughout the learning during planning (top scalp plot) and execution (bottom scalp plot). B. Linear model capturing the changes in PLV during planning and execution for the pair of electrodes Fz-F3 (low alpha band), Fz-F4 (low beta band), Fz-C3 (low beta band) and Fz-O1 (gamma band). C. Linear model capturing the changes in PLV during execution for the pair of electrodes Fz-T7 (low theta band), Fz-P3 (high alpha band), Fz-P4 (high alpha band), and Fz-F3 (high theta band). (Panels A and B reproduced from Gentili et al., (2009b) with permission from IEEE).

While throughout learning the kinematics was enhanced (see Fig. 7A-C); electrophysiological changes in phase synchronization were simultaneously observed (Fig. 13A). Namely, as the subjects adapt, the electrodes pair Fz-F3 (low alpha band), Fz-F3 (low beta band), Fz-F4 (low beta band), Fz-C3 (low beta band) and Fz-O1 (gamma band) revealed a decrease captured by a linear model (i.e., $R^2 \geq 0.50$) for both movement planning and execution (Fig. 13B). For planning, the slopes of these linear models were significantly different from zero (t-test, $p<0.05$) for Fz-F3 (low components of the alpha and beta bands), Fz-C3 (low beta band), Fz-O1 (gamma band) and during execution for Fz-F3 (low alpha band) and Fz-C3 (low beta band) while a trend was observed for Fz-F3 (low beta band, $p=0.06$) and Fz-F4 (low beta band, $p=0.07$). Also, for execution, the same analysis revealed that the electrode pairs Fz-T7 (low theta band), Fz-P3 (high alpha band), Fz-P4 (high alpha band) and Fz-F3 (high theta band) showed a significant linear decrease of the PVL (t-test, $p<0.05$) throughout adaptation (Fig.13C).

Such linear decrease was correlated with an enhancement of the performance and particularly good logarithmic correlations were found between the changes in phase synchronization and the MT and ML parameters. The results for the correlation analyses showed that the relationships between the changes in PLV for the pairs Fz-F3, Fz-F4, Fz-C3, Fz-O1 and the MT and ML values were best fitted by using a logarithm ($R^2 \geq 0.40$) for both planning and execution. The same correlation analysis performed for the pairs Fz-T7, Fz-P3, Fz-P4, Fz-F3 and the MT and ML values revealed that the same results were obtained ($R^2 \geq 0.50$) only for movement execution.

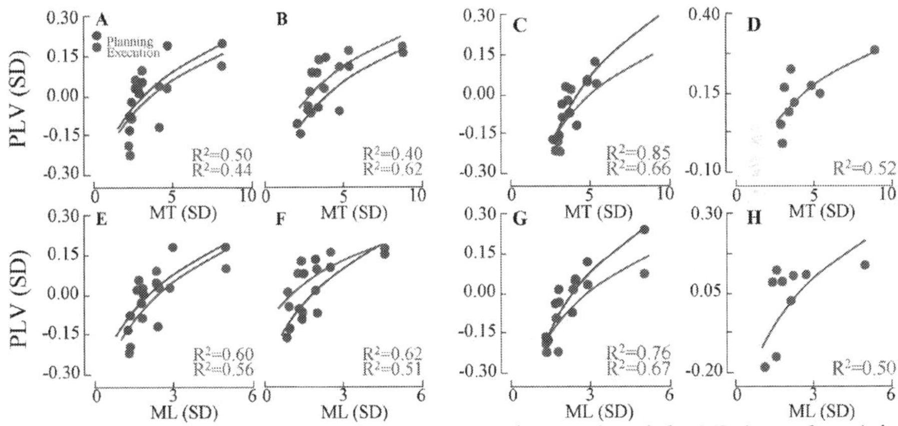

Fig. 14. Representation of the PLV versus the MT (first row) and the ML (second row) for both movement planning (blue color) and execution (red color). A. Pair Fz-F3 (low alpha band); B. Pair Fz-C3 (low beta band); C. Pair Fz-O1 (gamma band); D. Pair Fz-T7 (low theta band); E. Pair Fz-F3 (low alpha band); F. Pair Fz-C3 (low beta band); G. Pair Fz-O1 (gamma band); H. Pair Fz-F3 (high theta band). Since the Pair Fz-T7 (low theta band) and Fz-F3 (high theta band) revealed a non significant linear decrease during planning, the fits for PLV values versus MT and ML are only presented for execution (see panel D and H). (Panels A,B,E,F reproduced from Gentili et al., (2009b) with permission from IEEE).

As for the spectral power changes for the alpha and theta frequency bands, these changes in coherence/PLV presented above, allow assessing the level of performance but also its development throughout a learning period. Therefore, the spectral power and coherence/PLV provide brain biomarkers of the performance and learning in Human that may be useful in bioengineering/biomedical applications, particularly for brain monitoring applications and/or when the access to the actual performance is impossible. This will be presented in section 4, beforehand; the section 3.3 will present and discuss the advantages of these brain biomarkers but also their current limitations and the potential solutions to overcome them.

3.3 Strengths, weaknesses, and perspectives for brain biomarkers of the sensorimotor performance

3.3.1 Strengths and weaknesses

By revealing correlations between the spectral power, coherence/PLV and motor performance, the research lines presented in this chapter provide potential non-invasive functional brain biomarkers to assess and track the level of performance and learning. It is important to note that these biomarkers are able to detect important differences in skills level such as those existing between novices and experts (e.g., Hatfield et al., 1984, 2004; Haufler et al., 2000) as well as to identify the learning dynamic related to different types of tasks inducing different neural resources (e.g., Gentili et al., 2008, 2009a,b; Kerick et al., 2004). Moreover, although their scalp locations and frequency band of interest present slight variations from one task to another, it appears that these biomarkers share also some frequency (e.g., alpha band) and spatial (e.g., temporal region) features while being located on specific electrodes for the various tasks tested. Therefore, beyond certain specificities that are task-dependent, these biomarkers of human performance share a common consistent topology in term of frequency and spatial scalp locations across different tasks. Moreover, it must be noted that changes in phase synchronization for a specific frequency range do not necessarily imply similar power changes for the same electrodes (Kiroi & Aslanyan, 2006). Therefore, the availability of processing techniques for extracting and combining both univariate (i.e., spectral power) and multivariate (i.e., spectral coherence/PLV) cortical measures might provide "multidimensional" brain biomarkers in the future. Such multidimensionality resulting from the combination previously described is expected to provide enhanced, robust biomarkers capable of tracking performance and learning dynamics, thus providing a potential solution to overcome limitations in current practical applications. This will be explained in the section 3.3.2.

Another important point is directly linked to the fact that these biomarkers were derived from EEG during movement execution, but, more importantly, during movement preparation (i.e., planning; Deeny et al., 2003, 2009; Gentili et al., 2008, 2009a,b; Hatfield et al., 2004; Haufler et al., 2000). The availability of these biomarkers during movement execution and particularly during movement preparation (i.e., planning) involves two specific advantages.

First, a biomarker of the performance during execution can be considered as a good complement of the behavioral measures available during and/or after movement execution. More importanty, the presence of these brain biomarkers during planning also allow estimating/predicting the on-coming performance level that is not available with usual peripheral and behavioral measurements. This important feature is common to many biomarkers such as the bispectral index derived from EEG used for the identification of anesthetic depth during pediatric cardiac surgery while the usual clinical signs are not accessible (Williams & Ramamoorthy, 2009).

Second, the availability of brain biomarkers of the performance during movement preparation is a feature that becomes particularly important when considering overt but, more importantly, covert movement executions in the context of bioengineering and biomedical applications for rehabilitation. The expression "overt movement execution" corresponds to a movement actually performed such as those executed in daily activities. In this case, the person can see and feel his/her own limb moving. Conversely, the term "covert movement execution", also commonly named mental or motor imagery, refers to a dynamic mental process during which a subject internally simulates a motor action without activating the muscles and, therefore, without any apparent motion of the limbs involved in that action (Gentili et al., 2004, 2006; Jeannerod, 2001). Such motor imagery or covert execution is commonly used for mental practice/rehearsal of specific performance skills, BCI approaches and more generally in rehabilitation (see section 4 of this chapter). Interestingly, many studies revealed that common neurocognitive mechanisms in terms of both similar neural structures and behaviour exist between overt and covert motor actions (Fadiga & Craighero, 2004; Gentili et al., 2006; Jeannerod et al., 2001). In particular, several investigations suggest that motor imagery involves the same neural mechanisms as those activated during preparation (i.e., planning) and execution of overt movements (e.g., Jeannerod, 1994, 2001). Therefore, although our task involved actual movements, since the present results suggest that these brain biomarkers are accessible during movement preparation, they may also be suitable for covert movement execution when a task is performed using motor imagery.

Despite this research provided some interesting results and is still currently making progresses, two main limitations have to be considered. First, the present brain biomarkers of performance are based on a population analysis without considering subject individually. Second, their computation was based on the average value across several trials (e.g., 20 trials). Definitely, considering the variability of the MEG/EEG signals from one trial to another and also the sensitivity of the EEG signal to environmental noise and artefacts, the approach consisting in defining brain biomarkers of the performance needs to investigate, to what extent these results can be extended when single subject and single trials are considered. This is important for future applications since they will be designed for single subjects and ideally based on single or eventually few trials. Recently, by using MEG applied to a similar tool learning task (described in Fig. 6), we started to address these two problems by analyzing the alpha power band ([9-13Hz]) in individual subjects using the same ERD/ERS techniques and testing different sliding window (e.g., length, overlap) across trials. The preliminary results suggest that, at the individual level, the spectral power for the alpha band ([9-13Hz]) computed at the frontal, temporal and parietal regions during movement preparation were able to predict the motor performance (Gentili et al. 2009a).

3.3.2 Overcoming the current limitations by means of multiple constrains

As suggested in section 3.3.1, a possible way to overcome the two main limitations previously mentioned (i.e., single subject and computation based on single or few trials) is to obtain robust multidimensional EEG/MEG biomarkers able to assess the level of performance and learning by combining several individual biomarkers. In other words, the combination of several biomarkers would result in an increased number of conditions that have to be satisfied for estimating reliably any enhancement of the performance. The prediction problem is therefore constrained since a reliable estimation of performance needs to satisfy several constraints represented by the right combinations of biomarkers. For instance, if both a power increase and a coherence/PLV decrease are simultaneously observed for specific frequency bands and brain regions, it seems reasonable to predict with a certain confidence that the subjects are successfully learning the task. Conversely, if we would have only one biomarker, this prediction would be less reliable. Therefore, the combination of several brain biomarkers such as phase synchronization and spectral power would provide cross-information resulting in the generation of robust and accurate non-

invasive brain biomarkers of the motor performance. This approach could also give insight into possible reasons for the failure of sensorimotor learning and adaptations. Thus, such multidimensional brain biomarkers might be better suited for applications based on individual subjects and single or few trials.
It must be noted that, this first type of constraint was related to a combination of various biomarkers using the same brain imaging modality, i.e., EEG/MEG signals. However, another type of combination could also be considered by using the fusion across multiple recoding modalities in order to complement information provided from each imaging technique. For instance, in order to complement EEG/MEG signals analysis, fNIRS signals processing could provide additional brain biomarker by measuring the hemodynamic of brain activity. The choice to use fNIRS is guided by three reasons: First, although the hemodynamic activity has a lower temporal resolution than EEG, the fNIRS potentially provides more direct spatial resolution or localization abilities over EEG (Soraghan et al., 2008). Thus, with the superior temporal resolution of EEG, merging these two techniques would allow for "the best of both worlds" (Coyle et al., 2007). Second, contrary to EEG, the hemodynamic response is influenced by head/body orientation with respect to the gravitational axis whereas fNRIS signal is relatively less sensitive to artefact and environmental noise than EEG. Once again, since both do not have these two common weaknesses their combination appears to be advantageous. Third, although fNIRS only penetrate the cortex relatively superficially (~2.0 cm; Rolfe, 2003) contrary to classical fMRI, these signals can be recorded by portable devices as it is also the case for EEG, making them, particularly well suited for applications in practical/ecological situations with various populations (e.g., healthy persons, patients, children, elderly, military personnel, etc.). It must be noted that the idea to combine several biomarkers within (power, coherence/PLV) and between (fNIRS) imaging modalities has already been proposed for clinical applications (Guarracino et al., 2008) such as for brain injury prediction (Ramaswamy et al., 2009) and amyotrophic lateral sclerosis (Turner et al., 2009). From a practical point of view, this signal fusion across multiple imaging modalities could ideally be performed by using a recoding system that embed both EEG and fNIRS sensors.

3.3.3 Emotional states on brain biomarkers of the performance

A question that is naturally raised is the influence that some psychological and mental states such as emotion, stress or fatigue could exert over the quality of sensorimotor performance. If such adverse psychological and mental states disrupt the motor performance, it is legitimate to wonder to which extent the biomarkers tracking this same performance would also be affected. However, the majority of the performance stress-related studies focus on behavioural aspects without analyzing the cortical dynamics (Staal et al., 2004). Ongoing research by Hatfield and colleagues is beginning to provide some insight into such questions by placing performers under stressful conditions. For instance, Rietschel et al., (2008) asked participants to perform a marksmanship task under both regular performance-alone and competitive conditions. Changes in the Spielberger State Anxiety Inventory (STAI), heart rate, cortisol and skin conductance evidenced an increased state anxiety during the competitive condition. Furthermore, the performance was affected during the competition along with a significant decrease in alpha power. Similarly, when subjects performed a drawing movement task under high level arousal conditions they exhibited higher levels of coherence associated with decreases in performance (Rietschel et al., 2006).

Therefore, these results provide evidence that the brain biomarkers of sensorimotor performance can be disrupted by psychological and mental states such as emotion, stress. Thus, from a physiological point of view, it is possible to consider that an increased degree of stress would induce the recruitment of nonessential neural resources during task execution, leading to a reduction of cortical refinement (i.e., a reduction of alpha power and an increase in cortico-cortical communication) that reflects sub-optimal performance. In other words, we could consider that, to some degree, the brain biomarkers are contaminated with a sort of noise. However, even in this case, they may still be informative since in some instances they could also unravel the possible causes (e.g., stress, fatigue) of alterations in behavioral performance which cannot be revealed by peripheral motion parameters (e.g., kinematics) alone. For instance, in the study where subjects learn a novel tool, the absence of learning/adaptation could also be due to fatigue. Nevertheless, when considering the spectral power, the frontal biomarkers evidenced here are neither in the same spatial location (frontal midline) nor in the same frequency band (low theta band) than the fatigue-related EEG power (Makeig et al., 2000; Oken et al., 2006). Similarly, when considering the coherence/PLV, factors such as stress or fatigue imply an increase and not a decrease in phase synchronization and is generally identified for different electrodes pairs and/or frequency bands (Andersen et al., 2009; Lorist et al., 2009) than those found in the tool learning study (see section 3.2). Therefore, this clearly illustrates: i) the advantage to combine different biomarkers of the performance to obtain more robust predictions, ii) the benefit to combine them with other biomarkers identifying some adverse mental states (e.g., fatigue, stress) to be able to better decipher or indicate potential causes of a poor learning performance. Futures research should provide insights about these various possibilities, their benefit and limits.

3.3.4 Fusion of structural and functional brain biomarkers

Although the two previous sections (3.3.2 and 3.3.3) focused on different problems, both of them emphasized the importance for cross-information by combining several biomarkers. Indeed, it can be reasonably expected that such combination of biomarkers would lead to a robust tracking of motor performance and learning. It must be noted that such a combination can be performed not only between functional biomarkers but also between both structural and functional biomarkers. For instance, biomarkers can predict the performance based on information at the genetic/molecular level (e.g., naloxone, cortisol) or from behaviour such as heart rate or skin conductance (Armstrong & Hatfield, 2006). Thus, such convergence between these biomarkers, different in nature, would allow performing an even more robust prediction to assess accurately the level of performance and to track/predict precisely the learning dynamic. Although this chapter introduced mainly the concept of functional brain biomarkers for performance assessment, it appears clearly that both structural and functional brain biomarkers must be seen as a complementary source of information. Interestingly, while structural brain biomarkers using methods form genetic may be more appropriate on a long timescale prediction such as very early diagnostic, functional biomarkers may be better suited for short timescale prediction such as a real-time tracking of the neural events. Such combination of structural and functional brain biomarkers is an emerging research line. For instance, recently Deeny et al., (2008) investigated MEG measurements in relation to genetic markers such as the epsilon4 allele of the apolipoprotein, providing a method to detect risk factors for Alzheimer's disease (Corder et al., 1993).

4. Current Brain Biomarkers for Sensorimotor Performance and Bioengineering Applications

Beyond the considerations presented in section 3, the techniques presented to record and process brain biomarkers non-invasively using portable systems make them particularly well suited for real-time (or close to real-time) prediction in practical/ecological applications. Although multiple potential applications can be considered for the future, this section will illustrate two possible applications. The first one will be the design of future smart neuroprosthetics by proposing solutions to overcome some well-known BCI-related problems. The second application (that is actually to some extent a generalization of the first one) will be related to brain monitoring in the context of overt and covert movement execution to accelerate learning or re-learning when a task is performed/learned using actual movements and/or motor imagery.

4.1 Neuroprosthetic applications: towards a smart Brain Computer Interface

The changes previously described in EEG power and coherence/PLV that mirror human motor performance may potentially provide powerful biomarkers for tracking human learning/adaptation status when one has to learn/adapt to a new tool. A first potential interesting role of these brain biomarkers would be to overcome the well-known difficulties related to BCI systems such as adaptive decoding, constant recalibration and the maintenance of stable performance while a user tries to control a neuroprosthesis (Vaughan et al., 2003). Traditionally, motor-imagery-based BCI approaches are divided into two phases. The first one consists of a calibration phase to determine the parameters of a decoding algorithm, which has to map neural signals to a class of imagined movement. The second phase aims to train the subject by providing him/her sufficient feedback to change his/her cortical dynamics in order to control an external device via the BCI system. It is important to note that during this second stage, since the adaptation depends on the capacity of the user's brain to change its cortical dynamics, frequent recalibrations of the decoding algorithms are required when the user's performance degrades (Blankertz et al., 2009). In order to address these problems, some solutions have been proposed and notably by means of adaptive algorithms (Blankertz et al., 2006; Sykacek et al., 2004). However, these approaches use supervised adaptation based on *a priori* knowledge of an external target. Although helpful, the requirement of such *a priori* information actually represents a major pitfall for practical BCI applications since the user should decide when and where to direct his/her intentions. In other words, no information of external targets is available to the decoding algorithm (Blankertz et al., 2006; Vidaurre et al., 2007). The complexity of using two adaptive controllers (the user's brain and the decoding algorithm) is not new and has been already raised (McFarland et al., 2006; Vaughan et al., 1996); however, it continues to be an issue, and no satisfying solutions of this problem have been provided (McFarland et al., 2006). The brain biomarkers of performance presented in this chapter may help to overcome such important drawbacks of BCI. Indeed, such biomarkers could be used to continuously adapt the decoding algorithm to the subject's mental states, thereby allowing a stable co-adaptation/cooperation between the user and the BCI system. This is especially relevant when the user has to learn the physical properties of a new tool and/or a novel environment as is the case when a user intends to control a neuroprosthetic device. For example, the alpha power at the frontal, temporal and parietal sites combined with coherence/PLV for the low beta frequency bands between the pair of electrodes Fz-F3 and Fz-C3 could be computed using a sliding window (e.g., 15-20 trials). If the user's brain considerably adapts as indicated by an increased alpha power combined with a reduced coherence/PLV at the brain sites mentioned above, then the BCI decoding algorithm should not update its parameters. Conversely, it should adjust the parameters, by using, for instance, a reinforcement learning signal, to compensate for a user's poor performance (in that case reflected by a decreased alpha power and an increased coherence/PLV at the brain sites mentioned above).

As previously mentioned in section 3.3.3, the use of such biomarkers could also reveal the sources of alteration in behavioral performance which cannot be revealed by kinematics parameters alone. For instance, poor learning/adaptation performance could be due to other factors such as stress or fatigue. These biomarkers, thanks to their specificities in term of scalp sites and frequency bands (and also with eventual additional information such as hemodynamic response provided by fNIRS), could reasonably unravel the possible origin of poor motor learning, providing, therefore, relevant covert supervision of the user during BCI training. For example, in practical use, it is important to decipher if a user's poor BCI performance is related to fatigue or to bottlenecks related to information processing guiding the algorithm to adapt to the user's cognitive state, which is usually impossible to access from behavior.

4.2 Brain monitoring applications

Another possible application of functional brain biomarkers would be related to brain monitoring for overt and more importantly for covert execution. It is well known that motor imagery, or covert execution, share a lot of functional commonalities and that many neural structures are commonly activated during both overt and covert movement. On the other hand, there is also a growing body of evidence that suggests that it is possible to learn, or at least improve, performance with practice using motor imagery also called mental training. Most of the studies focusing on mental practice either considered performance enhancement in a healthy population (e.g., Gentili et al., 2006; Yaguez et al., 1998) or a rehabilitation (e.g., Jackson et al., 2004; Page et al., 2001) context where a positive effect on subsequent actual motor performance was evidenced. While it is possible to assess the effects of such covert practice on subsequent actual movements, it is impossible to continuously monitor mental training (unless a trial is actually executed) since no overt execution is available. However, the brain biomarkers presented here would allow for assessing the level of performance during mental training and tracking of learning dynamics. Such brain biomarkers could be coupled to a neurofeedback system providing, thus, an enhanced feedback of performance during overt execution (in addition to classical feedback) or covert execution where usually no feedback is available. Such brain monitoring systems for covert/overt movement execution would allow efficient supervision of performance, resulting in an accelerated learning or re-learning. Such bioengineering systems could be applied in various populations ranging from military personnel desiring to rapidly acquire skills to any persons subjected to a motor impairment undergoing rehabilitation where enhanced guidance for both patient and therapist would be beneficial. It must be noted that these biomarkers would allow monitoring and fitting of the training time-scale for each individual since it is reasonable to expect that two individuals will not mentally learn at the same speed. For instance, for the same task some individuals using mental practice may need 40 trials to reach acceptable performance while others would need 60 trials to reach the same level of performance. However, it is not possible to detect any progression in performance when using motor imagery (except by occasionally using actual execution) unless we use these brain biomarkers to create a customized training timescale for each individual. Moreover, as for BCI application, it would also be possible to know if a poor performance is related to sensorimotor learning processes or induced by some adverse mental states such as fatigue. Thus, the therapist could adapt the current rehabilitation session to the patient's cognitive state in order to improve training efficiency without having to access behavioral measures.

At present, the current research focuses mainly on brain biomarkers for healthy people since a well-established model of these brain biomarkers needs to be defined before moving towards practical applications for pathology in a rehabilitation context. It is of interest to consider if such brain biomarkers would be applicable for patients subjected to neural pathologies. Although these biomarkers should be affected by a given pathological state, it is still possible to find their modified version adapted to this pathology as a BCI decoding algorithm is able to map a pathological neural activity to the desired output (Neuper et al., 2003). This would necessitate applying the same techniques and approaches, albeit with some modifications, to provide biomarkers engineered for specific neural pathologies. For instance, it has been suggested that mental imagery practice would have positive effects on persons subjected to cerebral palsy (Trusceli et al., 2008; Zabalia, 2002). Therefore, under such conditions, the cerebral palsy-specific performance biomarkers would allow monitoring of the brain to provide feedback for a therapist in order to accelerate and improve performance and, thus, the physical therapy process. It must be noted that, beyond application, such brain biomarkers could also provide useful information about the cortical neural networks of patients suffering from neural diseases. Still taking the example of patients with cerebral palsy, specifically, these brain biomarkers could provide insights into the effects of physical therapy by, for instance, estimating the benefit of motor imagery on reorganization of cortical dynamics and the degree of automatization of the movement. Namely, the coherence/PLV biomarker (Busk & Galbraith, 1975; Deeny et al., 2003, 2009; Gentili et al., 2009b) may be of particular interest to analyze any possible changes in cortical network recruitments throughout the rehabilitation procedure associated with any potential motor performance improvement. Moreover, several investigations have suggested that an increase in alpha power in the temporal, frontal regions would reflect that movement become more automatized as a function of practice, requiring less attentional and processing resources, since as strategies and skills are developed, there is a less extensive cortical contribution to task performance, resulting in increased alpha power (Gentili et al., 2008, 2009a; Hatfield et al., 2004; Smith et al., 1999). Therefore, when using mental imagery the computation of such spectral power could provide a biomarker able to assess the degree of automatization of the repeated actions throughout a rehabilitation session. Finally, as previously mentioned, a multidimensional brain biomarker could be even more effective by combining information such as the spectral power, coherence/PLV and hemodynamic responses using fNIRS.

5. Conclusions and Perspectives

Nowadays, some non-invasive functional brain biomarkers able to assess cognitive-motor/sensorimotor performance and learning level are available. However, they were mainly analyzed by means of investigations based on populations of subjects. The next challenge is to generalize these biomarkers to single subjects using single or few trials in tasks using actual movements or motor imagery. In order to reach these new aims, further research is needed to provide multidimensional biomarkers by considering the fusion of both processing techniques (e.g., EEG/MEG spectral power and coherence) and the nature of neural signals (e.g., hemodynamic response with fNIRS). Such approaches are expected to provide robust models for these biomarkers. Today, these brain biomarkers are engineered based on healthy people; however, in the future these methods could be transferred to alleviate neural disorders, provide new types of smart neural prostheses, and create brain monitoring tools to allow the emergence of a new generation of assistive technology for both healthy (e.g., accelerated learning) and pathological (e.g., rehabilitation) human populations.

6. Acknowledgements

Rodolphe J. Gentili would like to sincerely thank La Fondation Motrice, Paris, France, for supporting continuously his research from several years.

7. References

Andersen, S.B.; Moore, R.A.; Venables, L. & Corr, P.J. (2009). Electrophysiological correlates of anxious rumination. *Int JPsychophysiol.*, Vol.71(2), pp.156-169.

Anguera, J.A.; Seidler, R.D.; Gehring, W.J. (2009). Changes in performance monitoring during sensorimotor adaptation. *J. Neurophysiol.*, Vol.102(3), pp.1868-1879.

Armstrong, D.W. & Hatfield, B.D. (2006). Hormonal responses to opioid receptor blockade: during rest and exercise in cold and hot environments. *Eur J Appl Physiol.*, Vol.97(1), pp.43-51.

Bell, M.A. & Fox, N.A. (1996). Crawling experience is related to changes in cortical organization during infancy: evidence from EEG coherence. *Dev Psychobiol.*, Vol.29(7), pp.551-61.

Bell, A.J. & Sejnowski, T.J. (1995). An Information-Maximization Approach to Blind Separation and Blind Deconvolution, *Neural Computation*, Vol.7(6), pp.1129-1159.

Berg, D. (2008). Biomarkers for the early detection of Parkinson's and Alzheimer's disease. *Neurodegener Dis.*, Vol.5(34), pp.133-136.

Blankertz, B. & Vidaurre, C. (2009). Towards a cure for BCI illiteracy: Machine-learning based co-adaptive learning.*BMC Neuroscience*, Vol.10(1), pp.85.

Blankertz, B.; Muller, K.R.; Krusienski, D. J.; Schalk, G.; Wolpaw, A. et al. (2006). The BCI competetion. III: Validating alternative approaches to actual BCI problems, *IEEE Trans Neural Syst Rehabil Eng.*, Vol.14(2), pp.153-159.

Blankertz, B.; Müller K.R. & Curio, G. (2009). Neuronal correlates of emotions in human-machine interaction. *BMC Neuroscience*, Vol.10(1), pp.80.

Brunner, C.; Scherer, R.; Graimann, B.; Supp, G. & Pfurtscheller, G. (2006). Online control of a brain-computer interface using phase synchronization. *IEEE Trans Biomed Eng.*, Vol.53(12 Pt 1), pp.2501-2506.

Busk, J. & Galbraith, G.C. (1975). EEG correlates of visual-motor practice in man. *Electroencephalogr Clin Neurophysiol,.* Vol.38(4), pp.415-22.

Caplan, J.B.; Madsen, J.R.; Schulze-Bonhage, A.; Aschenbrenner-Scheibe, R.; Newman E.L. et al. (2003). Human theta oscillations related to sensorimotor integration and spatial learning. *J Neurosci.,* Vol.23(11), pp.4726-736.

Carignan, C.R.; Naylor, M.P. & Roderick, S.N. (2008). Controlling shoulder impedance in a rehabilitation arm exoskeleton. *IEEE International Conference on Robotics and Automation,* Vol.19(23), pp.2453-2458.

Cavanagh, J.F.; Cohen, M.X. & Allen, J.J.B. (2009). Prelude to and Resolution of an Error: EEG Phase Synchrony Reveals Cognitive Control Dynamics during Action Monitoring. *J. Neurosc.,* Vol.29(1), pp.98-105.

Cipriani, C.; Zaccone, F.; Micera, S. & Carrozza, M.C. (2008). On the Shared Control of an EMG-Controlled Prosthetic Hand: Analysis of User–Prosthesis Interaction. *IEEE Trans on Robotics,* Vol.24(1), pp.170-184.

Contreras-Vidal, J.L. & Kerick, S.E. (2004). Independent component analysis of dynamic brain responses during visuomotor adaptation. *Neuroimage,* Vol.21(3), pp.936-945.

Corder, E.H.; Saunders, A.M.; Strittmatter, W.J.; Schmechel, D.E.; Gaskell, P.C. et al. (1993). Gene dose of apolipoproteine type 4 allele and the risk of Alzheimer's disease in late onset families, *Science,*Vol.261, pp.921–3.

Coyle, S.M.; Ward, T.E. & Markham, C.M. (2007). Brain-computer interface using a simplified functional near-infrared spectroscopy system. *J Neural Eng.,* Vol.4(3), pp.219-226.

Crone, N.E.; Miglioretti, D.L.; Gordon, B. & Lesser R.P. (1998). Functional mapping of human sensorimotor cortex with electrocorticographic spectral analysis. II. Event-related synchronization in the gamma band. *Brain,* Vol.121 (12), pp.2301-2315.

Dammann, O. & Leviton, A. (2004). Biomarker epidemiology of cerebral palsy. *Ann Neurol.,* Vol.55(2), pp.158-161.

Dammann, O. & Leviton, A. (2006). Neuroimaging and the prediction of outcomes in preterm infants. *N Engl J Med.,* Vol.355(7), pp.727-729.

Darvas, F.; Ojemann, J.G.; & Sorensen, L.B. (2009). Bi-phase locking - a tool for probing non-linear interaction in the human brain. *NeuroImage,* Vol.46(1), pp.123–132.

Deeny, S.P.; Poeppel, D.; Zimmerman, J.B.; Roth, S.M.; Brandauer, J. et al. (2008). Exercise, APOE, and working memory: MEG and behavioral evidence for benefit of exercise in epsilon4 carriers. *Biol Psychol.,* Vol.78(2), pp.179-187.

Deeny, S.P.; Hillman, C.H.; Janelle, C.M. & Hatfield, B.D. (2003). Cortico–cortical communication and superior performance in skilled marksmen:An EEG coherence analysis. *J Sport and Exercise Psychology,*Vol.25, pp.188–204.

Deeny, S.P.; Haufler, A.J.; Saffer, M. & Hatfield, B.D. (2009). Electroencephalographic coherence during visuomotor performance:a comparison of cortico-cortical communication in experts and novices.*J MotBehav.* Vol.41, p106-16.

Delorme, A.; Makeig, S. & Sejnowski, T.J. (2001). Automatic artifact rejection for EEG data using high-order statistics and independent component analysis. *Third International Workshop on Independent Component Analysis and Signal Separation,* pp.457-462.

Del Percio, C.; Rossini, P.M.; Marzano, N.; Iacoboni, M.; Infarinato, F. et al. (2008). Is there a "neural efficiency" in athletes? A high-resolution EEG study. *Neuroimage,* Vol. 42(4), pp.1544-1553.

Dengler, T.J.; Gleissner, C.A.; Klingenberg, R.; Sack, F.U.; Schnabel, P.A. et al. (2007). Biomarkers after heart transplantation: nongenomic. *Heart Fail Clin.*, Vol. 3(1), pp.69-81.

Eleuteri, E.; Magno, F.; Gnemmi, I.; Carbone, M.; Colombo, M. et al. (2009). Role of oxidative and nitrosative stress biomarkers in chronic heart failure. *Front Biosci.*, Vol.1(14), pp.2230-2237.

Fadiga, L. & Craighero, L. (2004). Electrophysiology of action representation. *J Clin Neurophysiol.*, Vol. 21(3), pp.157-169.

Gasser, T. (2009). Genomic and proteomic biomarkers for Parkinson disease. *Neurology,* Vol.72(7), pp.27-31.

Gentili, R.J.; Cahouet, V.; Ballay, Y. & Papaxanthis, C. (2004). Inertial properties of the arm are accurately predicted during motor imagery. *Behav Brain Res.*, Vol.155(2), pp.231-239.

Gentili, R.J.; Papaxanthis, C. & Pozzo, T. (2006). Improvement and generalization of arm motor performance through motor imagery practice. *Neuroscience,* Vol.137(3), pp.761-772.

Gentili, R.J.; Bradberry, T.J.; Hatfield, B.D. & Contreras-Vidal, J.L. (2008). A new generation of non-invasive biomarkers of cognitive-motor states with application to smart Brain Computer Interfaces. *Proceedings of the 16th European Signal Processing Conference - 2008,* Lausanne, Switzerland. http://www.eurasip.org/Proceedings/Eusipco/Eusipco2008/index.html/papers/1569105504.pdf.

Gentili, R.J.; Bradberry, T.J.; Rong, F.; Hatfield, B.D. & Contreras-Vidal, J.L. (2009a). Decoding of Non-Invasive Functional Brain Biomarkers for Sensorimotor Adaptation Assessed by MEG. *University of Maryland Graduate Research Interaction Day,* p.14.

Gentili, R.J.; Bradberry T.J.; Hatfield, B.D.; & Contreras-Vidal, J.L. (2009b). Brain Biomarkers of Motor Adaptation Using Phase Synchronization. *Proceedings of the IEEE International Conference of the Engineering in Medicine and Biology Society, September, 2-6, 2009, Minneapolis, Minnesota, USA.* Vol.1, pp.5930-3.

Georgiadis, S.D.; Ranta-aho, P.O.; Tarvainen, M.P. & Karjalainen, P.A. (2005). Single-trial dynamical estimation of event-related potentials: a Kalman filter-based approach. *IEEE Trans Biomed Eng.*, Vol.52(8), pp.1397-1406.

Georgopoulos, A.P.; Karageorgiou, E.; Leuthold, A.C.; Lewis, S.M.; Lynch, J et al.(2007).Synchronous neural interactions assessed by magnetoencephalography:a functional biomarker for brain disorders. *JNeuralEng.* Vol.4, pp.349-55.

Glass, K.A.; Frishkoff, G.A.; Frank, R.M.; Davey, C.; Dien, J. et al. (2004). A Framework for Evaluating ICA Methods of Artifact Removal from Multichannel EEG. In. Lecture Notes in Computer Science. *Independent Component Analysis and Blind Signal Separation,* Springer, Vol.3195, pp.1033-40, ISBN 978-3-540-23056-4, Berlin.

Guarracino, F. (2008). Cerebral monitoring during cardiovascular surgery. *Curr Opin Anaesthesiol.*, Vol. 21(1), pp.50-54.

Hatfield, B.D.; Landers, D.M. & Ray, W.J. (1984). Cognitive processes during self-paced motor performance: an electroencephalographic profile of skilled marksmen. *J Sport Psychol.*, Vol.6, pp.42–59.

Hatfield, B.D. & Hillman, C.H. (2001). The psychophysiology of sport: a mechanistic understanding of the psychology of superior performance. In: Singer RN, Hausenblas CH, Janelle CM, eds. Handbook of sport psychology. 2nd ed. New York: John Wiley & Sons, pp.362–386.

Hatfield, B.D.; Haufler, A.J.; Hung, T.M. & Spalding, T.W. (2004). Electroencephalographic studies of skilled psychomotor performance. *J Clin Neurophysiol.*, Vol.21(3), pp.144-156.

Haufler, A.J.; Spalding, T.W.; Santa Maria, D.L. & Hatfield, B.D. (2000). Neurocognitive activity during a self-paced visuospatial task: comparative EEG profiles in marksmen and novice shooters. *Biol Psychol.*Vol.53(3), pp.131–60

He, P.; Wilson, G. & Russell, C. (2004). Removal of ocular artifacts from electro-encephalogram by adaptive filtering, *Med. Biol. Eng. Comput.*, Vol.42(3), pp.407-412.

Hejjel, L. & Gál, I. (2001). Heart rate variability analysis. *Acta Physiol Hung.*, Vol.88(3), pp.219-230.

Hofstra, W.A. & de Weerd, A.W. (2008). How to assess circadian rhythm in humans: A review of literature. *Epilepsy & Behavior*, Vol.13(3), pp.438-444.

Hyvärinen, A. (1999). Fast and Robust Fixed-Point Algorithms for Independent Component Analysis, *IEEE Trans. On Neural Networks*, Vol.10(3), pp.626-634.

Hyvärinen, A.; & Oja, E. (2000). Independent Component Analysis: Algorithms and Applications, *Neural Networks*, Vol.13(4-5), pp.411-430.

Hyvärinen, A.; Karhunen, J. & Oja, E. (2001). *Independent component analysis.* ISBN:9780471405405, J.Wiley & Sons, NY.

Irani, F.; Platek, S.M.; Bunce, S.; Ruocco, A.C. & Chute, D. (2007). Functional near infrared spectroscopy (fNIRS): an emerging neuroimaging technology with important applications for the study of brain disorders. *ClinNeuropsychol.*, Vol.21(1), pp.9-37.

Isaac, D.L. (2008). Biomarkers in heart failure management. *Curr Opin Cardiol.*, Vol.23(2), pp.127-133.

Jackson, P.L.; Doyon, J.; Richards, C.L. & Malouin, F. (2004). The efficacy of combined physical and mental practice in the learning of a foot-sequence task after stroke: a case report. *Neurorehabil Neural Repair.*, Vol.18(2), pp.106-111.

Jeannerod, M. (2001).Neural simulation of action: a unifying mechanism for motor cognition.*Neuroimage*,Vol.14,pp.103-9.

Jeannerod, M. (1994). The representing brain: neural correlates of motor intention and imagery. *Behavioral and Brain Sciences*, Vol.17(2), pp.187–202 and pp.229–238.

Kaukola, T.; Satyaraj, E.; Patel, D.D.; Tchernev, V.T.; Grimwade, B.G. et al. (2004). Cerebral palsy is characterized by protein mediators in cord serum. *Ann Neurol.*, Vol.55(2), pp.136-194.

Kay, S.M. (1988). *Modern Spectral Estimation: Theory and Application.* ISBN:013598582X, Prentice-Hall, Englwood Cliffs, NJ.

Kerick, S.E.; Douglass, L.W. & Hatfield, B.D. (2004). Cerebral cortical adaptations associated with visuomotor practice. *Med Sci Sports Exerc.*, Vol.36(1), pp.118-129.

Kiroi, V.N.; & Aslanyan, E.V. (2006). General laws for the formation of the state of monotony. *Neurosci. Behav. Physiol*, Vol.36(9), pp.921-928.

Klimesch, W.; Freunberger, R.; Sauseng, P. & Gruber, W. (2008). A short review of slow phase synchronization and memory: evidence for control processes in different memory systems? *Brain Res.*, Vol.1235, pp.31-44.

Kranczioch, C.; Athanassiou, S.; Shen, S.; Gao, G. & Sterr, A. (2008). Short-term learning of a visually guided power-grip task is associated with dynamic changes in EEG oscillatory activity. *Clin Neurophysiol.*, Vol.119(6), pp.1419-1430.

Lachaux, J.P.; Rodriguez, E.; Martinerie, J. & Varela, F.J. (1999). Measuring phasesynchrony in brain signal. *Human Brain Mapping*, Vol.8(4), pp.194–208.

Lachaux, J.P.; Rodriguez, E.; Le Van Quyen, M.; Lutz, A.; Martinerie, J. et al. (2000). Studying single-trials of phase-synchronous activity in the brain. *Int J Bifurc Chaos.*, Vol.10(10), pp.2429-2439.

Landers, D.M.; Han, M.W.; Salazar, W.; Petruzzello, S.J.; Kubitz, K.A. et al. (1994). Effects of learning on electroencephalographic and electrocardiographic patterns in novice archers. *Int J Sport Psychol.*, Vol.25, pp.313-330.

Larson, J. & Lynch, G. (1989). Theta pattern stimulation and the induction of LTP: the sequence in which synapses are stimulated determines the degree to which they potentiate. *Brain Res.*, Vol.489(1), pp.49-45.

Le Van Quyen, M.; Foucher, J.; Lachaux, J.P.; Rodriguez, E.; Lutz, A. et al. (2001). Comparison of Hilbert transform and wavelet methods for the analysis of neuronal synchrony.*J.Neurosci.Meth.*,Vol.111(2), pp.83-98.

Lee, T.W.; Girolami, M. & Sejnowski, T.J. (1999). Independent Component Analysis Using an Extended Infomax Algorithm for Mixed Subgaussian and Supergaussian Sources, *Neural Computation*, Vol.11(2), pp.417-441.

Lorist, M.M.; Bezdan, E.; Ten Caat, M.; Span M.M.; Roerdink, J.B. et al. (2009). The influence of mental fatigue and motivation on neural network dynamics; an EEG coherence study, *Brain Res.*, Vol.1270, pp.95-106.

Makeig, S.; Jung, T.P. & Sejnowski, T. (2000). Awareness during drowsiness: dynamics and electrophysiological correlates, *Can J Exp Psychol.*, Vol.54(4), pp.266–273.

Marple S.L. (1987). *Digital spectral analysis with applications.* ISBN : 0132141493. Prentice-Hall, Englewood Cliffs, NJ.

McFarland, D.J.; Anderson, C.W.; Muller, K.R.; Schlogl, A.; & Krusienski, D.J. (2006). BCI Meeting 2005–workshop on BCI signal processing: feature extraction and translation, *IEEE Trans Neural Syst Rehabil Eng.*,Vol.14(2),pp.135-8.

McFarland, D.J.; & Wolpaw, J.R. (2008). Sensorimotor rhythm-based brain-computer interface (BCI): model order selection for autoregressive spectral analysis. *J Neural Eng.*, Vol.5(2), pp.155-162.

Moura, L.M.; Rocha-Gonçalves, F.; Zamorano, J.L.; Barros, I.; Bettencourt, P. et al.(2008).New cardiovascular biomarkers: clinical implications in patients with valvular heart disease. *Expert Rev Cardiovasc Ther.*, Vol.6(7), pp.945-954.

Mu, Y.; Fan, Y.; Mao, L.; & Han, S. (2008). Event-related theta and alpha oscillations mediate empathy for pain.*Brain Res.*, Vol.1234, pp.128-136.

Neuper, C.; Müller, G.R.; Kübler, A.; Birbaumer, N. & Pfurtscheller, G. (2003). Clinical application of an EEG-based brain-computer interface: a case study in a patient with severe motor impairment. *Clin Neurophysiol.*, Vol. 114(3), pp.399-409.

Newton, J.L.; Sheth, A.; Shin, J.; Pairman, J.; Wilton,. et al. (2009). Lower ambulatory blood pressure in chronic fatigue syndrome. *Psychosom Med.*, Vol.71(3), pp.361-365.

Nunez, P.L. & Srinivasan, R. (2006). *Electric fields of the brain:the neurophysics of EEG.* Oxford Univ. Press., New York.

Oja, E. (2004). Blind source separation: neural net principles and applications, Independent Component Analyses, Wavelets, Unsupervised Smart Sensors, and Neural Networks II, *Proceedings of SPIE*, Vol. 5439, pp.1-14.

Oken, B.S.; Salinsky, M.C. & Elsas, S.M. (2006). Vigilance, alertness, or sustained attention: physiological basis and measurement. *Clin Neurophys.*, Vol.117(9), pp.1885-1901.

Ozaki T. & Tong H. (1975). On the fitting of non-stationary autoregressive models in time series analysis, in: *Proceedings of the 8th Hawaii International Conference on System Sciences*, Western Periodical Co., Hawaii, pp.224-226.

Page, S.J.; Levine, P.; Sisto, S.A. & Johnston, M.V. (2001). Mental practice combined with physical practice for upper-limb motor deficit in subacute stroke. *Phys Ther.*, Vol.81(8), pp.1455-62.

Parasuraman, R. & Rizzo, M. (2007). *Neuroergonomics:The Brain at Work.* ISBN0195368657.Oxford Univ. Press Inc, USA

Pfurtscheller, G.; Stancák, A. & Neuper, C. (1996). Event-related synchronization (ERS) in the alpha band--an electrophysiological correlate of cortical idling: a review. *Int J Psychophysiol.*, Vol. 24(1-2), pp.39-46.

Pfurtscheller, G. & Lopes da Silva, F.H. (1999). Event-related EEG/MEG synchronization and desynchronization: basic principles. *Clin Neurophysiol.*, Vol. 110(11), pp.1842-1857.

Pfurtscheller, G. & Lopes da Silva, F.H. (2005). Event-related desynchronization (ERD) and event-related synchronization (ERS). In: E. Niedermeyer and F.H. Lopes da Silva, Editors, *Electroencephalography: basic principles, clinical applications and related fields (5th ed.)*, Lippincott, Williams & Wilkins, Philadelphia, PA, pp. 103-1016.

Pfurtscheller, G. & Neuper, C. (2006). Future prospects of ERD/ERS in the context of brain-computer interface (BCI) developments. *Prog Brain Res.*, Vol.159, pp.433-437.

Pfurtscheller, G. & Neuper, C. (1997). Motor imagery activates primary sensorimotor area in humans. *Neurosci Lett.*, Vol.239(2-3), pp.65-68.

Ramaswamy, V.; Horton, J.; Vandermeer, B.; Buscemi, N.; Miller, S. et al. (2009). Systematic review of biomarkers of brain injury in term neonatal encephalopathy. *Pediatr Neurol.*, Vol.40(3), pp.215-226.

Rietschel, J.C.; Goodman, R.N.; Lo, L.; Woo, M.; Haufler, A.J. et al. (2006). Explaining motor performance decrement associated with stress through electroencephalography (EEG) coherence. *North American Society for Psychology of Sport and Physical Activity Annual Conference*, Denver, CO, USA.

Rietschel, J.C.; Costanzo, M.E.; Goodman, R.N.; Haufler, A.J.; Lo, L.C. et al. (2008) Electrocortical dynamics during competitive psychomotor performance. *38th Annual Meeting of the Society for Neuroscience*, Washington DC, USA.

Rolfe, P. (2003). In Vivo Near-infrared spectroscopy. *Annu. Rev. Biomed. Eng.*, Vol.2, pp.715-754

Rong, F. & Contreras-Vidal, J.L. (2006). Magnetoencephalographic artifact identification and automatic removal based on independent component analysis and categorization approaches, *Journal of Neuroscience Methods*, Vol.157(2), pp.337-354.

Sanei, S.; & Chambers, J.A. (2007). *EEG signal processing.* ISBN:9780470025819.Wiley Ed., West Sussex, USA.

Schalk, G.; Miller, K.J.; Anderson, N.R.; Wilson, J.A.; Smyth, M.D. et al. (2008). Two-dimensional movement control using electrocorticographic signals in humans. *J Neural Eng.*, Vol 5(1), pp.75-84.

Shumway, R.H. & Stoffer D.S. (2006). *Time Series Analysis and its Applications.* ISBN:0387293175. Springer, NewYork.

Slobounov, S.; Ray, W.; Cao, C. & Chiang, H. (2007). Modulation of cortical activity as a result of task-specific practice. *Neurosci Lett.*, Vol.421(2), pp.126-31.

Smith, M.E.; McEvoy, L.K. & Gevins, A. (1999). Neurophysiological indices of strategy development and skill acquisition. *Cogn Brain Res.*, Vol.7(3), pp.389-404.

Soraghan, C.; Matthews, F.; Markham, C.; Pearlmutter, B.A.; O'Neill, R. et al. (2008). A 12-Channel, real-time near-infrared spectroscopy instrument for brain-computer interface applications. *Proceedings of the IEEE International Conference of the Engineering in Medicine and Biology Society, August, 20-24, British Columbia, Canada,* pp.5648-51.

Staal, M.A. (2004). Stress, Cognition, and Human Performance: A Literature Review and Conceptual Framework. Ames Research Center, Moffett Field, California. http://hsi.arc.nasa.gov/publications/20051028105746_IH-054%20Staal.pdf.

Storm, H. (2008). Changes in skin conductance as a tool to monitor nociceptive stimulation and pain. *Curr Opin Anaesthesiol.*, Vol. 21(6), pp.796-804.

Sykacek, P.; Roberts, S.J. & Stokes, M. (2004). Adaptive BCI based on variational Bayesian Kalman filtering: an empirical evaluation, *IEEE Trans Biomed Eng.*, Vol.51(5), pp.719-727.

Tass, P.; Rosenblum, M.G.; Weule, J.; Kurths, J.; Pikovsky, A. et al. (1998). Detection of n:m phase locking from noisy data: application to magnetoencephalography. *Phys Rev Lett.*, Vol. 81(15), pp.3291–3294.

Tombini, M.; Zappasodi, F.; Zollo, L.; Pellegrino, G.; Cavallo, G. et al. (2009). Brain activity preceding a 2D manual catching task. *Neuroimage.*, Vol.47(4), pp.1735-1746.

Trusceli, D.; Auferil, H.; de Barbot F.; Le Metayer, M.; Leroy-Malerbe, V. et al. (2008). *Les infirmités motrices cérébrales-Réflexions et perspectives sur la prise en charge.* ISBN:2294611934. Massion, Paris.

Turner, M.R.; Kiernan, M.C.; Leigh, P.N. & Talbot, K. (2009). Biomarkers in amyotrophic lateral sclerosis. *Lancet Neurol.*, Vol.8(1), pp.94-109.

van Putten, M.J.; Kind, T.; Visser, F. & Lagerburg, V. (2005). Detecting temporal lobe seizures from scalp EEG recordings: a comparison of various features. *Clin Neurophysiol.*, Vol.116(10), pp.2480-2489.

Vaseghi, S.V. (2007). *Multimedia Signal Processing: Theory and Applications in Speech, Music and Communications*, ISBN: 0470062010, John Wiley & Sons, New York.

Vaughan, T.M.; Wolpaw, J.R. & Donchin E. (1996). EEG-based communication: prospects and problems. *IEEE Trans Rehabil Eng.*, Vol.4(4), pp.425-30.

Vaughan, T.M.; Heetderks, W.J.; Trejo, L.J.; Rymer, W.Z.; Weinrich, M. et al. (2003). Brain-computer interface technology: a review of the Second International Meeting,*IEEE Trans Neural Syst Rehabil Eng*,Vol11(2),pp94-109.

Vidaurre, C.; Schlogl, A.; Cabeza, R.; Scherer, R. & Pfurtscheller, G. (2007). Study of on-line adaptive discriminant analysis for EEG-based brain computer interfaces. *IEEE Trans Biomed Eng.*, Vol.54(3), pp.550-556.

Vigário, R.; Särelä, J. & Oja, E. (2000). *Searching for Independence in Electromagnetic Brain Waves. In. Girolami, M. Advances in Independent Component Analysis.* ISBN:1852332638. Springer, pp.183-199.

Wang, X.; He, Y.; Peng, Y. & Xiong, J. (2006). A Neural Networks Approach for Designing FIR Notch Filters. Signal Processing, *8th International Conference on Signal processing.* Vol.1, pp.16-20.

Wei, X. & Li, L. (2009). Mass spectrometry-based proteomics and peptidomics for biomarker discovery in neurodegenerative diseases. *Int J Clin Exp Pathol.*, Vol.2(2), pp.132-148.

Williams, G.D. & Ramamoorthy, C. (2007). Brain monitoring and protection during pediatric cardiac surgery. *Semin Cardiothorac Vasc Anesth.*, Vol.11(1), pp.23-33.

Wolpaw, JR. (2007). Brain-computer interfaces as new brain output pathways. *J Physiol.*, Vol.15 (3), pp.613-619.

Wong, K.F.K.; Galka, A.; Yamashitad, O. & Ozaki, T. (2006). Modelling non-stationary variance in EEG time series by state space GARCH model. *Computers in Biology and Medicine*, Vol.36(12), pp.1327–1335

Yágüez, L.; Nagel, D.; Hoffman, H.; Canavan, A.G.; Wist, E. et al. (1998). A mental route to motor learning: improving trajectorial kinematics through imagery training. *Behav Brain Res.*, Vol.90(1), pp.95-106.

Yordanova, J.; Falkenstein, M.; Hohnsbein, J. & Kolev, V. (2004). Parallel systems of error processing in the brain. *Neuroimage*, Vol.22(2), pp.590-602.

Zabala, M. (2002). Apport d'exercice d'imagerie mentale dans la réalisation d'une tâche spatial chez l'enfant IMC. *Motricité Cérébral*, Vol.23, pp.21-29.

Zaknich, A. (2005). *Principles of adaptive filtering and self-learning systems.* ISBN: 1852339845. Springer, London.

25

The use of low-frequency ultrasonics in speech processing

Farzaneh Ahmadi and Ian McLoughlin
Nanyang Technological University
Singapore

1. Introduction

Audible sound analysis is assumed to be an integral part of any speech processing system, since the audible frequency ranges are naturally used for vocal communications. Inaudible sound, either ultrasonic or subsonic, is less widely researched - although sub-sonics (also called infrasound) have found a niche application in sound strengthening for spatial effects (Begault, 1994) and more immersive audio experiences (Kyriakakis, 1998) since there is evidence that these lower frequencies can be felt even if not heard. Higher frequency ultrasound is commonly used for diagnostic imaging in both medical and engineering fields (Szabo, 2004), and even sometimes for medical treatment (Haar, 1999). Due to the required resolution of these applications, they tend to operate at frequencies above the MHz range. In the animal kingdom, the majority of communication signals share a similar frequency range with humankind, although extending downward to infrasound in sea creatures such as whales (Clark, 2004), and upward to ultrasound in bats, moths, dolphins and so on (McLoughlin, 2009).

One phonetically significant and growing application of ultrasound is ultrasonic speech, as a contribution of ultrasound to speech analysis and processing. The technology acts to augment the human natural speech production system, using data extracted from ultrasonic analysis to synthesize elements of audible speech. In this application, an ultrasonic signal in the kHz range is injected into the vocal tract (VT), which propagates and resonates through the vocal cavities and is emitted from the mouth as ultrasonic speech. This signal could potentially be converted to audible speech by appropriate down-conversion.

This chapter introduces ultrasonics, particularly low frequency (LF) ultrasonic waves, and analyses their interaction with the human vocal tract. Ultrasonic frequencies used in this application are relatively low (near-audible), extending upwards from the upper threshold of human hearing to around 100 kHz in frequency. These frequencies are easily generated, captured and recorded by much existing audio equipment - and can be readily processed in real-time with available hardware.

In this chapter, the basic principles of ultrasonic speech technology and the most important issues concerning its implementation and signal processing are addressed. Most importantly, a modelling scheme describing ultrasonic behaviour within the VT is proposed and proven as the theoretical basis and the main framework of implementation of ultrasonic speech. This chapter concludes with open areas of research concerning the technology.

The scope of this chapter is as follows: In order to have a precise understanding of the problem, first the attributes of ultrasonic propagation are analyzed physically and mathematically in section 2. This section investigates these attributes, and describes linearity preconditions of any gas medium, the compliance with which, would allow ultrasonic propagation in that medium to be considered linear and lossless.
Section 3 analyses the plausibility of the linearity assumption for the propagation of the low frequency portion of the ultrasound bandwidth in the VT by a numerical analysis of the impact of dispersion and attenuation of LF ultrasound and addresses issues such as exhaled CO_2 as a dispersive wave medium for ultrasound, losses and cross modes of resonance of the VT in such frequencies.
Given this basic perspective, section 4 introduces ultrasonic speech as the usage of LF ultrasound for speech processing, surveys previous implementations of the technology and describes the necessary requirements of the implementation. As in this method, the human VT is used to produce the ultrasonic output signal, there is a need to study the anatomy and physiology of human speech production system in general in section 5. The necessary pre-conditions for linear modelling in section 2 along with the numerical analysis of section 3, lead to the derivation of a linear source-filter model for the ultrasonic speech process in section 6. Many applications in the theory of speech processing rely on the classical source-filter model of speech production. Section 6 considers how this model can be adapted to ultrasonic wave propagation in the vocal tract by manipulating the sonic wave equations and deriving the vocal tract transfer function for ultrasonic propagation.
At audible frequencies, linear predictive analysis (LPA) applies a linear source-filter model to speech production, to yield accurate estimates of speech parameters. Section 7 investigates the possibility of extension of LPA to cover ultrasonic speech. Discussing some simplifying assumptions, the section leads to the application of LPA for the analysis of ultrasonic speech. By the extension of LPA to ultrasonic speech, we introduce the main set of features needed to be extracted from the ultrasonic output of the VT to be utilized in speech augmentation. The chapter then presents a concise outline of current research questions related to this topic in section 8. Section 9 finally concludes the discussion.

2. Attributes of ultrasonic propagation

Ultrasound can be defined as "Sound waves or vibrations with frequencies greater than those audible to the human ear, or greater than 20,000 Hz" (Simpson & Weiner, 1989). The starting point of the ultrasonic bandwidth resides implicitly somewhere between 16-20 kHz due to variations in the hearing thresholds of different people. The bandwidth continues up to higher levels[1] where it goes over to what is conventionally called the hypersonic regime (David & Cheeke, 2002). The upper limit of ultrasound bandwidth in a gas is around 1 GHz and in a solid is around 10^{13} Hz (Ingard, 2008). At such mechanical vibrations exceeding the GHz range, electromagnetic waves may be emitted so that the upper limit of ultrasound may induce RF (radio frequency) electromagnetic waves (Lempriere, 2002).
The general definition of sound indicates that "sound is a pressure-wave which transports mechanical energy in a material medium" (Webster, 1986). This definition can extend the

1 which in a gas is of the order of the intermolecular collision frequency and in a solid is the upper vibration frequency (Ingard, 2008).

margins of understanding of sound beyond the hearing limitations of humans to cover any pressure wave including ultrasound. It has to be noted that similar to the sense of sight, which subjects the visible light region of the EM spectrum to special attention, the human sense of hearing has differentiated the "audio" segment of sound to be classically termed as "sound" in common language and other portions of the bandwidth have thus been classified in relation to the audible part as ultra or infrasound (similarly to visible light and infrared, ultraviolet terminology).
The fact which should not be concealed is that the audible sub-band is only a tiny slice of the total available bandwidth of sound waves, and the full bandwidth, except at its extreme limits can be described by a complete and unique theory of sound wave propagation in acoustics (David & Cheeke, 2002). Accordingly all of the phenomena occurring in the ultrasonic range occur throughout the full acoustic spectrum and there is no propagation theory that works only for ultrasound.
The theory of sound wave propagation in certain cases simplifies to the theory of linear acoustics which eases linear modelling of acoustic systems. It is generally preferential to approximate a system with a linear model where the assumptions of such modelling are plausible. Ultrasound inherits some of its behaviours from its nature of being a sound wave. There are also characteristics of the medium which impose some medium specific constraints on ultrasonic waves. Based on these facts we will review the general characteristics of ultrasound propagation as a sound wave and the effects of the medium, paying special attention to the required pre-conditions of linearity.

2.1 Wave based attributes of sound

Ultrasound as a sound wave, obeys the general principles of wave phenomena. The theory of wave propagation stems from a rich mathematical foundation of partial differential equations which are valid for all types of waves (Ikawa, 2000). In other words every wave, regardless of its production and physical detail of propagation can be described by a set of partial differential equations. All common behaviours observed in waves are mathematically proven by these equations (Rauch, 2008).
To rest under the scope of generalization of the theory of waves, a physical phenomenon solely needs to fulfil the preconditions of being a wave by complying with the restrictions imposed by the wave equations. Afterwards the common behaviour of waves, proven mathematically for the solutions of these equations, would be valid for that specific physical phenomenon too. It has to be noted that although in today's understanding of waves we are quite confident that for example, sound "is" a wave, however compliance of each wave type with the wave equations as the necessary pre-condition, has long ago been proven by scientists of the corresponding discipline (Pujol, 2003).
When the dimensions of the material are large in comparison to the wavelength, the wave equations become further simplified and can approximate the wave propagation as rays[2]. These simplified sets of wave equations are the basis of geometric wave theory (aka ray theory) of wave propagation (Bühler, 2006). The geometric wave theory permits freedom of microscopic details of wave propagation and describes the wave movement, reflection and refraction in terms of rays. The theory has been initially observed in optics and owes its

2 A ray is a straight or curved line which follows the normal to the wave-front and represents the two or three dimensional path of the wave (Lempriere, 2002).

application to acoustic waves to (Karal & Keller, 1959; 1964) and has yielded geometric acoustics (Crocker, 1998) as the dual to wave acoustics (Watkinson, 1998).

As a high frequency approximation solution to the wave equations, ray theory fails to describe the wave phenomenon in low frequencies when the wavelength is large compared to the dimensions of the medium. Consequently, in low frequencies we have to refer to general wave equations as the wave theory to describe the wave phenomenon. It has to be noted that wave theory is always valid but only in smaller wavelengths in comparison to the dimensions of the medium can the analysis be simplified by the geometric theory.

In any case, because all the waves obey the same sets of partial differential equations, they have common attributes which are guaranteed by several principles extracted out of the wave equations. These principles manifest geometric and wave behaviour and are the general laws which impose similar conditions upon the propagation of waves in microscopic and macroscopic scales. The Doppler effect (Harris & Benenson et al., 2002), principle of superposition of waves in linear media (Avallone & Baumeister et al., 2006), Fermat's (Blitz, 1967) and Huygens principles (Harris & Benenson et al., 2002) are the fundamental laws of propagation for all the waves including ultrasound in wave and geometric theory. For interested readers, the mathematical derivation of some of these principles using wave equations is covered in (Rauch, 2008).

For universal wave events such as diffraction, reflection and refraction which obey the general principles of wave propagation, there would be no exception to the general theory of sound propagation for ultrasound (David & Cheeke, 2002) except only the change of length scale which means that we have moved to different scales of the wavelength so the scale of material in interaction with waves and the technologies used for generation and reception of these waves will be different (David & Cheeke, 2002).

2.2 Medium based attributes of sound

The exclusive wavelength-dependant behaviours of ultrasound will present itself in the influence of the medium on wave propagation and we expect to observe some differences with audible sound where the wave propagation is apt to be influenced by characteristics of the medium through which it travels. In this section we consider the general attributes of a medium which impose special behaviours on a sound wave. Next in section 2.3 we will consider the effect of such attributes on ultrasound waves. When the medium of sound wave propagation is considered, the first important attribute under question is the linearity of the medium. Also important is a consideration of the attenuation mechanisms by which the energy of a sound wave is dissipated in the medium.

2.2.1 Linearity

Propagation of sound involves variations of components of stress (pressure) and strain in a medium. For an isolated segment of the medium we may consider the incoming wave stress as the input and the resulting medium strain as the response of the system to that input. To consider a medium of sound propagation as a linear system the stress-strain relation should be a linear function around the equilibrium state (Sadd, 2005). Gas mediums such as the air, match closely to the ideal gas law in their equilibrium state (Fahy, 2001) which states that:

$$\tilde{p}\tilde{v} = nR\tilde{T} \tag{1}$$

Where $\tilde{p}$ is the gas pressure, $\tilde{v}$ is the volume, $\tilde{T}$ is temperature and n, R are constant coefficients depending on the gas. If one of the three variables of $\tilde{p}$, $\tilde{v}$ or $\tilde{T}$ remains constant, the relation of the other two, can easily be understood from (1) but sound wave propagation generally alters all of these three components in different regions of the gas medium. A general trend is to consider sound wave propagation in an ideal gas as an adiabatic process meaning no energy is transferred by heat between the medium and its surroundings when the wave propagates in the medium (Serway & Jewett, 2006). If the ideal gas is in an adiabatic condition we would have (2) as the relation of pressure ($\tilde{p}$) and density ($\tilde{\rho}$) where α is a constant and the exponent γ is the ratio of specific heats at constant pressure and constant volume for the gas (which has the value 1.4 for air) (Fahy, 2001):

$$\tilde{p} = \alpha\tilde{\rho}^{\gamma} \quad \rightarrow \quad \partial\tilde{p}/\partial\tilde{\rho} = \gamma(\tilde{p}/\tilde{\rho}) \tag{2}$$

Equation (2) does not generally demonstrate a linear relation between pressure and density in an ideal gas but in small variations of pressure and density around the equilibrium state, $\tilde{p}/\tilde{\rho}$ can be considered to be constant and we will have:

$$[\partial\tilde{p}/\partial\tilde{\rho}]_0 = \gamma\left(\frac{p_0}{\rho_0}\right) \rightarrow [\partial\tilde{p}/\partial\tilde{\rho}]_0 = K/\rho_0 \tag{3}$$

where $[\partial\tilde{p}/\partial\tilde{\rho}]_0$ denotes small variations around the equilibrium, p_0 and ρ_0 are the pressure and density of the gas at equilibrium and constant $K = \gamma p_0$ is called the adiabatic bulk modulus of the gas (Fahy, 2001). Based on the above discussion the linear stress-strain relation in an ideal gas medium can be considered to exist between variations of pressure ($\partial\tilde{p}$) and variations of density ($\partial\tilde{\rho}$), having an adiabatic process (no loss) and small variations of pressure and density around the equilibrium.

2.2.2 Dissipation mechanisms

In section 2.2.1 we observed that under three conditions of having an ideal gas with an adiabatic process (no loss) and small variations of pressure and density around the equilibrium as a result of sound wave, air can be considered a linear lossless medium of sound wave propagation. These assumptions are known to be reasonable for audible sound but we need to consider their validation for the ultrasound case. Although we can preserve the small pressure variations precondition of linearity for ultrasonic speech application, as we will observe shortly, the physics of the problem make the assumptions of an adiabatic process and ideal gas behaviour of the air for ultrasonic frequencies, to be more of an approximation.

We need to consider the effects of this approximation i.e. attenuation (heat loss) and also deviation of the air from linear state equation (3) of an ideal gas in the frequency range of LF ultrasound. These derivations could cause dissipative behaviours in the air medium of sound propagation as a result of several phenomena including viscosity, heat conduction and relaxation. We will describe each briefly.

2.2.2.1 Viscosity and heat conduction

Viscosity is a material property that measures a fluids resistance to deformation. Heat conduction on the other hand is the flow of thermal energy through a substance from a higher to a lower-temperature region (Licker, 2002). For air, viscosity and heat conduction are known to have negligible dispersive effects (section 2.3.4) for sound frequencies below

50 MHz (Blackstock, 2000) but these mechanisms cause absorption of sound energy. Their effect in an unbounded medium can be considered by introducing a visco-thermal absorption coefficient α_{tv} to the time harmonic solution of the wave equation, the amount of which demonstrates the necessity of switching to wave equations in thermo-viscous fluids for the analysis of waves in frequency range of interest.

2.2.2.2 Relaxation

Gases demonstrate a behaviour called relaxation in sound wave propagation. Relaxation denotes that there is a time-lag (relaxation delay time) between the initiation of the disturbance by the wave and application of this disturbance to the gas which is compared to the time a capacitor needs to reach its final voltage value in an RC circuit (Ensminger, 1988). This delay could result from several physical phenomena. First the viscosity, second heat conduction in the gas from the places which the wave has compressed to the places where the wave has rarefacted which will cause the energy of the wave to be distributed in an unwanted pattern delaying the energy from returning to the equilibrium. The third and the most important case of relaxation in LF ultrasound applications is the molecular relaxation resulting from the delays of multi-atomic gas molecules having several modes of movement, vibration and rotation and the delay for molecules to be excited in their special vibration mode (Crocker, 1998).

When a new cycle of the wave is applied to the relaxing medium, the delay between the previous cycle of the wave disturbance and the resulting response of the medium will consume some of the energy of the new cycle, to return the medium to its equilibrium. This will cause absorption of the wave energy which depends on the frequency of the wave and the amount of the delay. In addition, due to the relative variations of frequency and relaxation delay, waves of some frequency can propagate faster than other frequencies. Consequently, relaxation in the gases is the physical cause of frequency dependant energy absorption and dispersion of the wave. As for this being a reason for dispersion, readers may refer to a mathematical discussion in (Bauer, 1965), while for the absorption as a result of relaxation, the interesting discussions in (Ingard, 2008) and (Blitz, 1967) should be consulted.

2.3 Effects of the medium on ultrasound propagation

Having considered the dispersive mechanisms of a gas for ultrasound frequencies, now we can consider the effects of these mechanisms in attenuation and dispersion of ultrasound. We will also discuss the case of resonance in the medium of ultrasonic propagation because these analyses will finally be applied to the propagation of ultrasound in the vocal tract which is a resonant cavity.

2.3.1 Speed

The sound speed in a medium (not necessary linear) has been formulated by (Fahy, 2001) as:

$$c^2 = \partial\tilde{p}/\partial\tilde{\rho} \tag{4}$$

While a gas medium maintains a linear behaviour as an ideal gas, based on the discussion of section 2.2.1, this speed is not a function of frequency and is evaluated according to the formula (Blackstock, 2000):

$$c = \sqrt{K/\rho_0} \tag{5}$$

If the phase speed of sound propagation in a medium is independent of the frequency as per (5), the medium is non-dispersive (Harris & Benenson et al., 2002), and all the events which rely on the speed of propagation (such as refraction) will be similar for sound waves across the whole frequency range (including ultrasound and audio) in that medium.

2.3.2 Acoustic impedance

The concept of acoustic impedance[3] is analogous to electrical impedance and is defined as the ratio of acoustic pressure $\tilde{p}$ and the resultant particle velocity $\tilde{u}$ (Harris & Benenson et al., 2002). Impedances determine the reflection and refraction of waves over medium boundaries. In a homogenous material the acoustic impedance is a material characteristic, so it is called characteristic acoustic impedance and is formulated as:

$$Z = \frac{\tilde{p}}{\tilde{u}} = \rho_0 . c \tag{6}$$

Where ρ_0 is the density of undisturbed medium and c is the speed of sound (The formula is same for both solids and fluids when they are homogenous). From (6) it is observed that in a non-dispersive material the acoustic impedance is independent of the frequency, so the impedance based characteristics (such as reflection coefficients) will be general to the case of all sounds in a non-dispersive medium (Harris & Benenson et al., 2002).

2.3.3 Attenuation

Attenuation is the loss of the energy of sound beam passing through a material. Attenuation can be the result of scattering, diffraction or absorption (Subramanian, 2006). Scattering and diffraction losses are not of much concern in the current application of LF ultrasounds in the vocal tract so we are going to discuss absorption in more detail.

The main causes of absorption of energy in gases in ultrasound frequencies are the molecular relaxation and visco-thermal effects. Visco-thermal effects introduce a visco-thermal absorption coefficient α_{tv} while molecular relaxation introduces several molecular coefficients α_{M_i} for each of the M_i gases in an N gas mixture (like air). The total absorption coefficient α is the sum of these values (Blackstock, 2000).

$$\alpha = \alpha_{tv+} \sum_{i=1}^{N} \alpha_{M_i} \tag{7}$$

α_{tv} is a scalar multiplicand of f^2 , (f being the frequency of the sound wave) while α_{M_i} is a scalar multiplicand of $\frac{f^2}{f^2+f_r^2}$ (f_r is the relaxation frequency of the gas[4]) (Blackstock, 2000).

The impact of absorption is usually regarded by the value of absorption coefficient. In an unbounded medium for the time harmonic analysis of the wave, the role of absorption coefficient α would be an exponential multiplicand $e^{-\alpha r}$ to be multiplied by the lossless wave solution where r is the distance of the inspection point from the source. In bounded

---

3 The unit for acoustic impedance is $\mathrm{Kg/m^2}/s$ and is called Rayl, named after Lord Rayleigh.

4 $f_r = \dfrac{1}{2\pi\tau}$ where τ is the relaxation time delay of the gas.

media we need to switch to damped wave equations to consider the effect of absorption. Absorption is usually accompanied by dispersion (Blackstock, 2000).

2.3.4 Dispersion

There are several possible causes for dispersion in a gaseous medium among which viscosity, heat conduction and relaxation are the most applicable for propagation of ultrasound frequencies. It is known that the dispersive effects of viscosity and heat conduction in air at frequencies below 50 MHz are negligible (Blackstock, 2000), so the main cause of dispersion in lower frequency ultrasound will be molecular relaxation (Blackstock, 2000). Sound speed in a relaxing gas with standard temperature and pressure is computed by (Crocker, 1998):

$$\frac{c^2}{c_0^2} = 1 + \frac{\epsilon}{1+\epsilon} \cdot \frac{\omega^2\tau^2}{1+\omega^2\tau^2} \tag{8}$$

c is the speed at angular frequency $\omega = 2\pi f$, ϵ is the relaxation strength and τ is relaxation time which are constants for a specific gas. c_0 is the low frequency speed of sound in the gas. The value $\omega\tau = 1$ occurs at the relaxation frequency f_r and the effect of dispersion in frequencies around f_r is more intense. For example CO_2 introduces dispersion at ultrasonic frequencies around 28 kHz (Dean, 1979).

2.3.5 Resonance

An important attribute of some sound propagation media is resonance at certain frequencies. Resonance is tied closely with the presence of standing waves in a medium. A resonant medium for sound waves should first have the possibility of forming standing waves and second the capability of frequency selectivity. Standing waves are normally formed as a result of interference between two waves travelling in opposite directions. For an interesting description of how standing waves are formed in an open-closed end tube as a simplified model of vocal tract, readers may refer to (Johnson, 2003).

The major cause of resonance for sound waves of certain frequencies in a medium is the geometric structure of that medium. When the geometry is more suitable for sound waves of certain frequencies to be distributed as standing waves in the medium e.g. the medium dimensions are wider where the standing wave has a rarefaction and narrower where it has a compression point, resonance can happen at that frequency. The resonance frequencies of an open/open and closed/open tube are a clear example of this (Halliday & Resnick et al., 2004).

For the case of interest, namely ultrasonic propagation through the vocal tract, we need to emphasize that the resonant behaviour of the VT will have one major difference with the audible case. In audible frequencies, due to the relatively large wavelength of the sound, standing wave patterns establish mainly along the axial length of the tract. But as we move toward lower wavelengths, in addition to axial standing waves, cross-modes of resonance can be created across the width of the tract, resulting in more complex patterns of resonance. Analysis of these cross-modes urges us to consider three dimensional equations for ultrasonic wave propagation in the tract while in audible range we normally consider the one dimensional wave equation.

Now that we have understood the main characteristics of ultrasound and its deviations from the general sound category in terms of attenuation and dispersion, we will consider a numerical analysis of the impact of these characteristics in LF ultrasound.

3. Low-frequency ultrasound

A major application of ultrasound is scanning, both in medical and industrial applications, relying upon reflections of the wave by an object (such as a defect in non destructive testing or a human fetus in ultra-sonography). When the dimensions of the reflecting object are smaller than the wavelength, the wave does not reflect back but scatters as an unfavourable wave behaviour. So to detect a defect, one needs to use a wavelength equal or smaller than its dimensions e.g. for a defect size of millimetres we need to use a sound wave above MHz frequency (Subramanian, 2006). The demand for detecting smaller details moves us out of audible range to use higher ultrasound frequencies, limiting the application of LF ultrasound to special cases such as cavitation or industrial non destructive testing.

Low Frequency ultrasound in ultrasonic speech application is considered as a portion of the ultrasonic bandwidth, starting from human hearing threshold up to 100 kHz. We will discuss the reasons for selection of this portion of the bandwidth shortly. As we will see in this section, LF ultrasound has properties which make it a suitable substitute for audible excitation of the vocal tract to produce ultrasonic speech.

The discussion of this section is biased so that the numerical analysis will provide us with an insight about the impact of attenuation and dispersion effects of LF ultrasound propagation in the vocal tract which we should discuss before being capable of modelling ultrasonic speech process as a linear and lossless system.

We are going to consider attributes of LF ultrasonic propagation in the air, and through the air-tissue interface. Soft body tissues and the air in the vocal tract are the regions of interest for ultrasonic speech production and both can be considered as homogeneous fluids (Zangzebski, 1996). Sound waves in the volumes of fluids are longitudinal (Fahy, 2001) so the mode of ultrasound propagation in the vocal tract and soft tissues of our concern will be longitudinal. As we will see in this section, high reflection coefficients of the air-tissue interface will reflect back most of the ultrasound wave energy over vocal tract walls, so we do not need to consider LF propagation through human body tissue.

3.1 Propagation through air-tissue interface

As described in (Caruthers, 1977), if the wavelength of the wave is small enough in comparison to the dimensions of the boundary of two media, Fermat principle will govern and the wave will be reflected with an angle (to the normal) equal to the angle of incidence. The reflection coefficient (Crocker, 1998) determines the proportion of energy to be reflected. Referring to (Zangzebski, 1996), we observe that the acoustic impedance of the air is too small in comparison to other materials of our problem. The reflection coefficient for an air-tissue interface (acoustic impedance Z_1=0.0004$*$ 10^6 Rayls for air and Z_2=1.71$*$ 10^6 for muscle)[5], is computed to be -0.99 (same value with positive sign for the tissue-air interface)[6].

---

5 Speed of sound is approximated 1600 m/s in muscle and 330 m/s in the air.

6 The minus value merely indicates the phase difference between the incident and reflected signal to be 180 degrees.

The value illustrates that ultrasound will almost completely reflect back from an air/tissue or tissue/air interface. This is expected also by the impedance mismatch effect (Zangzebski, 1996).

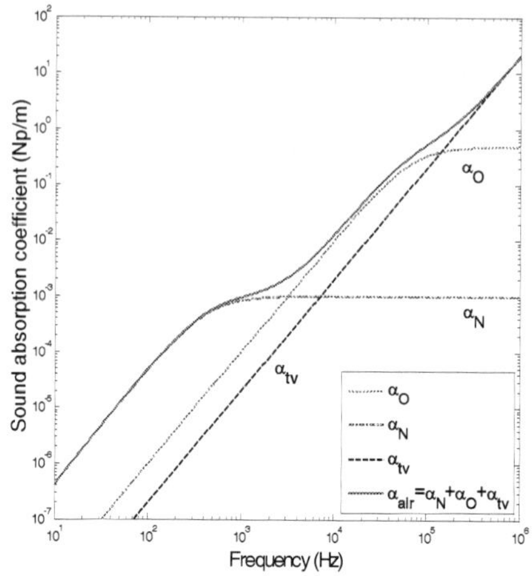

Fig. 1. Variation of the absorption coefficient of the air with frequency

3.2 Propagation through the air

In ultrasonic speech applications, the ultrasonic signal entering the vocal tract from the transducer has to travel through the air bounded by VT walls. As the exclusive effects of the medium on ultrasound, attenuation and dispersion are frequency-dependant, we need to have a numerical overview of the significance of these effects on ultrasound propagation in the air.

3.2.1 Attenuation

The absorption coefficient α was introduced in section 2.3.3 to be a sum of visco-thermal α_{tv} and molecular relaxation coefficients. For the air the two major components of oxygen and nitrogen have the molecular relaxation coefficients of α_N and α_O . Figure 1 demonstrates the variation of value of α (being equal to $\alpha_{tv} + \alpha_N + \alpha_O$) with frequency. As the figure demonstrates, this value reaches around 0.1 N_p/m in sound frequency of 100 KHz which is less than 1 dB/m.

3.2.2 Dispersion

As stated in 2.2.1 and 2.3.1, one precondition of linearity for ultrasound propagation in air is that the air medium should be an ideal gas in which the speed of sound is independent of sound frequency. For frequencies in the ultrasonic range, air deviates from this attribute as a result of being composed of dispersive carbon dioxide (CO_2) which should be considered in the VT due to the higher proportion of CO_2 in the exhaled air flow (The percentage of CO_2 in exhaled air is 4% which is 100 times that in normal air (Zemlin, 1997). This deviation initiates at frequencies above 28 kHz (Dean, 1979) and needs to be addressed here in detail.

The visco-thermal dispersion of sound in air for frequencies below several hundred MHz, depends on the square of the frequency but is negligible for frequencies between 1 Hz and 50 MHz at STP[7] (Blackstock, 2000; Dean, 1979). Thus there remains only molecular relaxation dispersion. Among the main components of air (nitrogen, oxygen, carbon dioxide and water), nitrogen and oxygen can be considered non-dispersive as the maximum variation of sound speed in these two gases with the increase of frequency from zero to infinity is only a few centimetres per second (Blackstock, 2000). Water and carbon dioxide have effects on variation of sound speed with frequency in the air. Specifically, pure carbon dioxide in which the speed of sound may vary about 8m/s between frequencies of 1kHz and 100 kHz (Crocker, 1998).

Equation (8) demonstrated the dispersion characteristics of the gas, and is shown in figure 2. The same figure is reported for air, which illustrates that the dispersive effect of humid air is negligible for frequencies up to 5 MHz (Crocker, 1998).

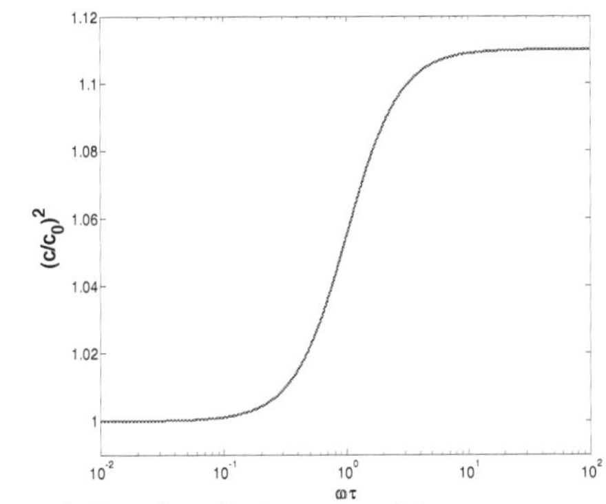

Fig. 2. Dispersion characteristics of a relaxing gas mixture

Based on studies of sound propagation in the atmosphere (Dean, 1979), the resulting variation of sound speed in air as a mixture of these gases (which obeys figure 2) over frequencies up to 5 MHz is in the order of few cm/s (for sound speed of approximately 343 m/s at STP). Referring to the monotonic pattern of increase of sound speed in (8) and figure 2, where the maximum speed variation for air at frequencies up to 5 MHz is negligible, and considering the percentage of gases other than carbon dioxide in the air, the dispersive effects of air can confidently be considered negligible for the dimensions of the vocal tract and the frequency range of interest (namely, less than 100 kHz).

As a conclusion of the preceding discussion, for ultrasonic frequencies of less than 100 kHz, and for the dimensions of our problem the air only has the effect of frequency dependant attenuation with an absorption coefficient of less than 1 dB/m and can be considered as a lossless non-dispersive linear medium in modelling ultrasonic propagation in the vocal tract. Linear systems are considered preferential for speech analysis and processing, and so we would prefer to limit our application to frequency ranges which can assure a linear relationship, if possible.

7 Standard temperature and pressure.

4. Application of LF ultrasound in speech augmentation

Having described the preliminary basics, we now turn our attention to the application of ultrasound in speech augmentation. We will divide these applications into two sets. The first set corresponds to applications in which ultrasonic excitation can act as a substitute to replace the natural excitation of the human voice production system. In this case, a person can speak without any voicing and an ultrasound to audible conversion system can produce a final audible sound. In the second set, ultrasonic excitation can be considered to act as a supplement to the natural excitation to provide additional data from the vocal tract for computational analysis.

Examples of the former set apply to people who suffer from impairments to their voice box and are incapable of producing natural excitations in their VT including laryngectomised patients and the voice-rest cases (Pozo, 2004). Another example is where audible speech is highly affected by surrounding or background noise and common levels of conversation or even high amplitude speech cannot be heard, such as at airports, on the battlefield, or in industrial environments (MacLeod, 1987). The other application in this set is when one does not wish to be heard in cases of talking in private places or when being heard will disturb other applications of a system like dictation in human-computer interfaces of crowded offices.

For the examples of the second set we may primarily consider ultrasound for providing additional data in speech recognition systems aiming to achieve higher levels of robustness. As another application in this set, we can mention cases where ultrasound can be augmented as an auxiliary excitation to the VT to provide voicing information when converting whispered speech to normally phonated speech. In this application, while a person whispers, the unvoiced segments of speech are extracted from the whispered signal but the voiced segments are reconstructed using the VT resonance data extracted from the ultrasonic output of the VT. This special augmentation can be used in whispered speech communications over telephone, and speech aids for people who have to speak in whisper mode for medical reasons.

4.1 Ultrasonic speech

In this chapter the application of LF ultrasonic waves in speech augmentation is termed ultrasonic speech. By ultrasonic speech we mean a system which augments an ultrasonic excitation to the human voice production mechanism as a substitute or supplement to the natural excitation and extracts feature sets from the resulting ultrasonic output to be used in several tasks including conversion to the audible speech, speech regeneration, recognition, enhancement and communication. The signal which is injected from an ultrasonic transducer to the VT via several possible injection points propagates through the tract and emits out of the mouth, where it is picked by another transducer and is delivered to the processing algorithms in charge of feature extractions in the ultrasonic domain or the equivalent audible domain. The set of these extracted features are then delivered as the output of the ultrasonic speech system to other modules which may pursue classic tasks of speech generation, recognition, and so on.

The ultrasonic frequency range of this application starts from the higher threshold of human hearing up to around 100 kHz. As stated before, this frequency range has some characteristics which suit the propagation of ultrasonic waves in the vocal tract to be modelled in linear and lossless acoustic domains. In this domain we can be equipped with facilities of linear modelling of the VT behaviour in response to ultrasonic excitation.

4.2 Previous implementations

Speech processing science relies heavily on data provided by ultrasonic scanning of the position of VT articulators as an indirect contribution of ultrasound to speech processing (Kelsey & Minifie et al., 1969). As an example we can mention the data provided by real-time ultrasonic monitoring of the tongue (Shawker & Sonies, 2005) to speech processing. In direct applications, ultrasonic waves are used directly to produce an ultrasonic speech signal which is sought for speech processing features (MacLeod, 1987). Similarly, an audible signal modulated by an ultrasonic career in ultrasonic communication (Akerman & Ayers et al., 1994), or converted to audible speech as a consequence of the non-linearities of the system in ultrasonic hearing (Lenhardt & Skellett et al., 1991).

These are niche examples of several contributions of ultrasonics to speech processing, yet there are few examples of the implementation of low frequency ultrasound in speech augmentation (ultrasonic speech). To consider further, let us first review the implementations of these methods.

The history of ultrasonic speech goes as far back as 1987 when MacLeod filed a patent for a non audible speech generator system (MacLeod, 1987). The system augmented a series of pulses similar to the glottal pulse shape in ultrasonic frequency range of 15 to 105 kHz to the vocal tract. MacLeod considered the output at the mouth as being an amplitude modulation of the ultrasonic input. He then proposed the idea of passing the output to an ultrasonic detector where it was down converted to audible range to pursue a further goal of synthesis of artificial speech. He considered the injection transducer to be directly placed on the throat or in front of the mouth which was equipped with separate noise and pulse generation mechanisms to produce voiced and unvoiced phonemes.

Based on the classification in the preamble of this section, MacLeod's proposed system was a substitutive approach which converted a speaker's silently mouthed words into synthesized audible speech. Other later authors mainly considered supplementary ultrasonic excitation, mostly for speech recognition. (Tosaya & Sliwa, 2002; 1999) patented a system which applied ultrasonic signal injection to the vocal tract to make the task of audible voice recognition more robust. Their system was proposed to enhance or replace the natural excitation with an artificial excitation for which ultrasound was considered an option. The injection points for the artificial excitation were proposed to include: outside and within the mouth, nasal passage and on the neck.

Another instance of ultrasonic speech implementation was proposed by (Lahr, 2002). He considered the ultrasonic output of the VT as the third mode of a trimodal voice recognition system whose other two modes where audible voice and images of the lips, tongue and the teeth. In addition to greater transcription accuracy in the recognition task, the system was claimed to be capable of audible speech production when the speaker did not use vocal fold vibration and just shaped the VT in positions associated to several different voices. He elected to use the neck and mouth as possible injection points of 28 to 100 kHz excitations. He also stated that wearing a neck device was usually uncomfortable so he focused on signal injection over the lips where the mouth and teeth opening permitted the signal to penetrate in the VT. The ultrasonic output of his system was finally demodulated to the audible range and used directly as an input channel to a recognition system.

Another implementation was reported by (Douglass, 2006), who used ultrasonic excitation to add value in improving the reliability of speech recognition. His excitation points were below the chin, on the neck, in front, and inside of the mouth. He proposed employing the same means of demodulating commonly used in radio broadcasting for the output ultrasonic signal.

4.3 Necessary considerations for implementation

There are several considerations which are necessary for implementation of an ultrasonic speech system. These considerations include, signal injection points, excitation waveforms, feature extraction method and hardware setup.

As stated in section 4.2, in spite of its various applications, ultrasonic speech has been a little researched area and there have been few cases of attempts of implementation. One of the reasons for unpopularity might be problems associated with signal injection to the vocal tract. The choice of injection position has a great impact on system design. Ultrasound, as we have observed in section 3.1, reflects back almost totally from the air-tissue interface. Another strong reflecting boundary is the bone/soft tissue interface. The bone is normally avoided in ultrasound propagation, because it distorts the ultrasonic beam (Zangzebski, 1996) (so we will not consider placing the transducer on the jaw or skull bones in this chapter). Consequently, injecting the signal through the bone or when the signal is going to face an air-tissue interface before entering the VT are not promising options.

Nevertheless, the task of signal injection is possible via some considerations to prevent or compensate for injection problems. Possible injection points introduced by previous implementations include the throat, on the neck, against the cheek, in the nasal cavity, inside and in front of the mouth. Each of these injection points imposes special considerations to fulfil the task of augmentation of an ultrasonic excitation to the VT.

As an example, for signal injection over the neck skin which has been used by (Lahr, 2002; MacLeod, 1987; Tosaya & Sliwa, 2002), the ultrasound wave propagates from the transducer to the air gap between the transducer and skin. As we have previously observed, this air/tissue boundary totally reflects the signal back. We can compensate for the effect of the reflection by using a coupling gel on the skin to eliminate the air from the transducer/skin interface. The signal entering the skin passes the tissue and encounters another tissue/air boundary before being able to enter the vocal tract where it will almost totally reflect back. So to consider signal injection over the neck skin we may need to apply the injection where the tissues are relatively thin to minimize reflection effects over the thin boundary. Another convenient option is signal injection in front of the mouth.

Excitation signal waveform design is another task which could simplify and optimize the operation of the system. Another brain-storming task is the down conversion of ultrasonic output and extraction of features which will be used for the reconstruction or recognition of audible speech. Although some of the previously mentioned implementations have considered the demodulation of ultrasonic speech to gain the audible equivalent, when the resulting converted signal is going to provide features to produce audible speech, the design of ultrasonic speech systems will require greater attention. This chapter addresses a solution to this issue by mathematically proving the possibility of linear predictive analysis (LPA) of ultrasonic speech. LPA is one of the strong feature extraction facilities based on a linear source-filter model of speech production. Extension of LPA to the ultrasonic domain will significantly simplify processing and analysis requirements in the audible domain.

The choice of hardware components in any ultrasonic system is another implementation consideration. Transducers are the core of a typical ultrasonic set up, fulfilling the task of transmit and receive, but ultrasonic system set up comprises several other hardware components including a signal generator to supply input energy to the transmitting transducer, and a data acquisition system to capture the signals for analysis.

5. Human speech production anatomy and physiology

The human speech production apparatus is well designed for the task of generating, modulating, and projecting intelligible sound. Controlled, in part by the Broca nucleus in the frontal cortex and Wernicke nucleus in the temporal cortex of the brain, the muscles controlling lung exhalation, glottal tension, epiglottis, tongue, throat and lip position, must work in concert to create and modulate the sounds that make up language.
Although speech can be considered as simply as a set of complex waveforms, and indeed sinewave speech can be created from simple waveforms (McLoughlin, 2009), it is in reality a complex and rich set of auditory symbols differentiated through several production mechanisms. These are illustrated in figure 3, and include the following:

- airflow from the lungs, either restricted, diverted through the nasal passages, around the tongue, through the lips or teeth, modulated in speed and intensity, or blocked momentarily, as in a plosive sound like /p/. It is the job of the lungs to provide the airflow, and to modulate its intensity (although the glottis and lips can both be used to block airflow for a time).
- pitch comes from the vibration of the flap-like vocal cords in the glottis, induced by airflow from the lungs. As some muscles in the glottis tauten, the glottal opening narrows and the vibration consequently increases in frequency. Pitch not only provides the characteristic frequency of our speech, but contributes a lexical meaning in several languages, particularly Chinese. Perhaps the most important role of pitch, which is similar in many ways to a periodic pulse train, is to resonate through the vocal tract.
- vocal tract geometry dictates the resonance patterns produced by the excitation. A pitch train flowing through the VT causes these resonances which affect the frequency of the sound exiting the tract in much the same way as most wind instruments operate.

Consider further this analogy with a wind instrument: a trumpet player relies upon a mouthpiece which, when blown, acts with the lips to produce a buzzing sound. This takes the place of the glottis in the speech production mechanism (and both examples require lungs to make the air move in the first place). The annoying buzzing sound from a trumpet mouthpiece, when fed through the smooth tubes of a trumpet, results in a beautiful resonant horn sound. Pressing or releasing the trumpet valves (keys) selects the tubes that the air passes through, resulting in different notes being played. Similarly, the glottal vibration is modified by the vocal tract to produce speech sounds. Changing the geometry of the vocal tract under muscular control changes the sounds produced in speech (McLoughlin, 2009).

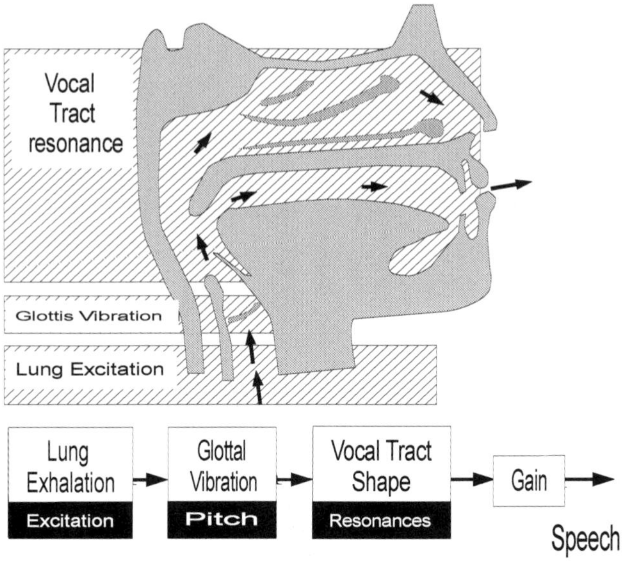

Fig. 3. A cut-away diagram of the human speech production mechanism, namely the human head (top), along with a block diagram representation below, showing lung excitation causing pitch to be produced by the glottis, acted upon by the vocal tract, and emitted from the mouth and nose

In speech, pitch is not present in all sounds: the vowel /a/ is voiced, meaning that it contains pitch, whereas the letter /f/ is unvoiced - meaning there is no pitch, so the sound is all lung excitation plus vocal tract shape. However all vowels are voiced, as are many consonants.

In ultrasonic speech production, an ultrasonic pulse-train usually replaces the pitch component generated by the glottis. All other articulators remain: the lungs still exhale, and provide airflow for the quiet unvoiced sounds (which are around 16dB quieter than voiced sounds). The tongue, lips and throat muscles still act together and the human brain can still direct the voice production apparatus to form words, as if whispering (which is naturally unvoiced). The main difference being that the pulse-producing glottis does not resonate.

Finally, understanding the speech production mechanism led many researchers to adopt a source-filter model for speech. This model separates the sound source (lung and glottis), from the filter (vocal tract), and assumes that these two parts are independent, but when directed by the brain to act in concert, produce the required sounds. Almost all modern speech analysis and processing systems rely heavily upon the source-filter model, and in particular assume that the filter part of the model can be represented by a linear polynomial function. It is this important relationship that we aim to establish for the case of LF ultrasonic speech.

6. Modelling ultrasonic speech process

Linear partial differential equations (PDEs) are the basic descriptors of linear systems, as a consequence of allowance to the principle of superposition (Coleman, 2005). Well known for benign impulse response and convolutional characteristics, linear time invariant (LTI) systems theory has underpinned the source-filter model of speech production for decades. The aim of this section is to derive a linear model for the propagation of ultrasonic signals through the vocal tract. We have seen in the previous sections that the assumptions of lossless propagation and ideal gas behaviour are plausible for small amplitude LF ultrasound propagation within the vocal tract. We commence our modelling from basic acoustic equations and apply these.

6.1 Mathematical description of ultrasonic propagation in the VT

The theory of acoustics stems from four main PDEs based on the conservation of mass, momentum and energy and also equations of the state of the medium (Blackstock, 2000), valid in three dimensional space over the frequency range of sound waves (including infrasound, audio and ultrasound). These equations are generally not linear but they are linearized in acoustics under several simplifying assumptions (Reynolds, 1981) and lead to the facilities of the theory of linear acoustics. We have theoretically described these assumptions earlier but will now review them mathematically before building on them further.

The first assumption is to consider ultrasonic wave propagation to be an adiabatic (lossless) phenomenon. We observed that the main causes of attenuation in ultrasound frequencies in a fluid medium are heat conduction, relaxation and viscosity. We then observed in section 3.2.1 that the effect of this attenuation in the frequency range of our application is negligible. So the process could be considered lossless (adiabatic) in which case, the equation of energy conservation will not be necessary (Blackstock, 2000).

The remaining equations are conservation of momentum (9) and mass (10) and equations of state of the gas. These equations describe the evolution of pressure $\tilde{p}$ and particle velocity vector $\tilde{\boldsymbol{u}}$ as functions of time t and three dimensional coordinates, $\boldsymbol{r} = [x\ y\ z]$. The general form of these equations is as stated below (Reynolds, 1981) where $\tilde{\rho}$ is the density, μ and λ are viscosity coefficients of the medium and F is the external excitation force.

$$\tilde{\rho}\left({\partial\tilde{\boldsymbol{u}}}/{\partial t} + \nabla.(\tilde{\boldsymbol{u}} \otimes \tilde{\boldsymbol{u}})\right) = -\nabla\tilde{p} + (2\mu + \lambda)\nabla(\nabla.\tilde{\boldsymbol{u}}) - \mu\nabla \times \nabla \times \tilde{\boldsymbol{u}} + F \tag{9}$$

$$ {\partial\tilde{\rho}}/{\partial t} + \nabla.(\tilde{\rho}\tilde{\boldsymbol{u}}) = 0 \tag{10}$$

Equation (9) includes the divergence of a dyadic product which is defined as:

$$\boldsymbol{v} \otimes \boldsymbol{u} = \begin{bmatrix} v_1 \\ v_2 \\ v_3 \end{bmatrix} [u_1 \quad u_2 \quad u_3] = \begin{bmatrix} v_1u_1 & v_1u_2 & v_1u_3 \\ v_2u_1 & v_2u_2 & v_2u_3 \\ v_3u_1 & v_3u_2 & v_3u_3 \end{bmatrix} \tag{11}$$

where u_i is the ith element of the vector $\boldsymbol{u}$.

The system (9-10) is completed by the equation of state that gives the pressure as a function of the density and temperature. When the flow is adiabatic in a gas, that is, no heat is transferred to or from the gas, and is reversible, that is, the flow conditions can return to their original values, the pressure is a function of the density only (Fahy, 2001), and the equation of state of the gas reduces to:

$$\tilde{p} = \tilde{p}(\tilde{\rho}) \tag{12}$$

Considering the equation of conservation of momentum (9), with adiabatic and reversible wave deformation in the medium, the next assumption is irrotational flow, $\nabla \times \tilde{\boldsymbol{u}} = 0$. This assumption has been somehow challenged by the existence of rotational flows in turbulent and jet flows in the classical linear modelling of audible sound propagation in the vocal tract during articulation of unvoiced utterances.

Due to the work of (Lighthill, 1952) and (Goldstein, 1984) the production of turbulent flow is governed by nonlinear equations of acoustics but once fully developed, we can describe its propagation as irrotational, governed by equations of linear acoustics (Crocker, 2007). We have conventionally used this assumption for the audible case, transferring the non-linearity of turbulent flow production to the source and dealing with the VT as a linear filter in the conventional source-filter modelling of the speech production system (Sinder, 1999). The same considerations apply to the ultrasonic range and make the assumption of $\nabla \times \tilde{\boldsymbol{u}} = 0$ a plausible statement.

The next step is to consider the effects of viscosity. Based on the discussions of section 3.2.2 about negligible dispersive effects of viscosity for frequencies below 50 MHz and referring to section 3.2.1 about values of visco-thermal absorption coefficient of the air in the frequency range of the current application, we can consider μ and λ to be very small, to neglect the effects of viscosity for LF ultrasound propagating in the air. We may now rewrite (9) in a clearer notation of (13) for each j from 1 to 3 as:

$$\tilde{\rho}\left(\frac{\partial \tilde{u}_j}{\partial t} + \sum_{i=1}^{3} \frac{\partial(\tilde{u}_i \tilde{u}_j)}{\partial x_i}\right) + \frac{\partial \tilde{p}}{\partial x_j} = F_i \tag{13}$$

Considering Small disturbances in pressure and density we will have (14, 15) where p_0, ρ_0, $\boldsymbol{u}_0$ are attributes of the medium at equilibrium state which are actually the time averages of $\tilde{p}$, $\tilde{\rho}$ and $\tilde{\boldsymbol{u}}$ respectively. "Acoustic pressure" p is introduced here then as the small variations of pressure around the equilibrium value p_0.

$$\tilde{p} = p_0 + p; \qquad \tilde{\rho} = \rho_0 + \rho\,; \qquad \tilde{\boldsymbol{u}} = \boldsymbol{u}_0 + \boldsymbol{u} \tag{14}$$

$$\frac{\partial p_0}{\partial t} = 0\,; \qquad \frac{\partial \rho_0}{\partial t} = 0; \qquad \frac{\partial \boldsymbol{u}_0}{\partial t} = 0 \tag{15}$$

Assuming the homogeneous (16) medium initially at rest (17):

$$\nabla p_0 = 0 \quad ; \quad \nabla \rho_0 = 0 \tag{16}$$

$$\boldsymbol{u}_0 = 0 \tag{17}$$

And manipulating conditions of (14-17) in (13), the linear equation of conservation of acoustic momentum for a lossless homogeneous medium initially at rest is derived for ultrasonic propagation inside the vocal tract by (18):

$$\rho_0 \frac{\partial \boldsymbol{u}}{\partial t} + \nabla p = F \tag{18}$$

For the equation of conservation of mass (10), using the above assumptions of homogeneous medium, small disturbances and medium at rest (14-17), we can determine the following:

$$\frac{\partial \rho}{\partial t} + \rho_0 \nabla . \boldsymbol{u} = 0 \tag{19}$$

The equation of state for an ideal gas states that:

$$\frac{p}{\rho} = \frac{\partial \tilde{p}}{\partial \tilde{\rho}} = c^2 \tag{20}$$

Where c is the speed of sound. The dispersive effects of air medium are discarded in (20) based on the discussions of section 3.2.2. Taking the derivative of (20) with respect to time, we will have:

$$\frac{\partial p}{\partial t} = c^2 \frac{\partial \rho}{\partial t} \tag{21}$$

Substituting (21) in (19) we would reach to the conservation of mass equation for ultrasonic propagation in the vocal tract:

$$\frac{1}{c^2}\frac{\partial p}{\partial t} + \rho_0 \nabla . \boldsymbol{u} = 0 \tag{22}$$

We would rewrite (18,22), i.e. lossless linear acoustic equations in (23,24) as the basic equations of ultrasound propagation in the vocal tract where p is the acoustic pressure and $\boldsymbol{u}$ is the acoustic velocity vector, ρ_0 is the static mass density of the medium and K is the adiabatic bulk modulus of the air:

$$\rho_0 \frac{\partial \boldsymbol{u}}{\partial t} + \nabla p = F \tag{23}$$

$$\frac{\partial p}{\partial t} + K \nabla . \boldsymbol{u} = 0 \tag{24}$$

As observed mathematically, the derivation of ultrasonic wave propagation in the vocal tract, with the simplifying assumptions which we have described in detail, has led to equations (23), (24) which are the general equations of linear acoustics, now applicable for ultrasonic propagation through the vocal tract.

6.2 Vocal tract transfer function for ultrasonic speech

In our approach to derive a linear model, in this section the VT transfer function is determined using the functional transformation method (FTM) which converts the linear PDEs to algebraic equations including boundary and initial conditions, similarly to Laplace transformation in ordinary PDEs (Rabenstein, 1999).

Combining (23) and (24) yields the wave equation for $p(t, \boldsymbol{r})$ and $\boldsymbol{u}(t, \boldsymbol{r})$:

$$\frac{1}{c^2}\frac{\partial^2 p}{\partial t^2} - \nabla^2 p = 0 \quad ; \quad \frac{1}{c^2}\frac{\partial^2 \boldsymbol{u}}{\partial t^2} - \nabla^2 \boldsymbol{u} = 0 \tag{25}$$

where $\boldsymbol{r} = [x\ y\ z]$ is the three dimensional coordinates vector and c is the speed of sound.

For audible sound production, since the cross section of the VT is small compared to the wavelength, the wave can propagate along the tract axis and we can model the VT simply as a single narrow tube. However the smaller wavelength of ultrasound means the wave can propagate across the width of the tract and the resulting cross modes require (25) solving in three dimensions. Thus the task of derivation of the three dimensional VT transfer function may not be as simple as the one dimensional wave equation for audible sound. We are considering the placement of the source in front of the mouth, however the general method is applicable to other injection positions.
Representing VT volume as Ω and its boundary as Γ being comprised of boundaries Γ_1 (the glottis), Γ_2 (VT walls) and Γ_3 (the mouth), having $f(r,t)$ to be the ultrasonic excitation source placed in front of the mouth, the general boundary and initial conditions of ultrasonic wave propagation in the VT can be found, with $Z(\boldsymbol{r})$ being the impedance of the VT and closed glottis walls, as:

$$\begin{cases} p(0,\boldsymbol{r}) = 0\,; \quad \boldsymbol{r}\epsilon\Omega; & \textit{medium initially at rest} \\ \frac{\partial p}{\partial t}(0,\boldsymbol{r}) = p_0(\boldsymbol{r}); & \boldsymbol{r}\epsilon\Omega \\ (n.\left(\frac{1}{\rho_0}\nabla\right) + \frac{1}{Z(r)}\frac{\partial}{\partial t})p(\boldsymbol{r},t) = 0 & \boldsymbol{r}\epsilon\Gamma_1,\Gamma_2 \\ n.\nabla p(\boldsymbol{r},t) = f(\boldsymbol{r},t) & \boldsymbol{r}\epsilon\Gamma_3 \end{cases} \tag{26}$$

Defining linear differential operators: $D_t = \frac{\partial^2}{\partial t^2}$, $D_r = \nabla^2 = \frac{\partial^2}{\partial x^2} + \frac{\partial^2}{\partial y^2} + \frac{\partial^2}{\partial z^2}$, we can rewrite (25) for pressure as:

$$\frac{1}{c^2}D_t(p(\boldsymbol{r},t)) - D_r(p(\boldsymbol{r},t)) = 0 \tag{27}$$

Taking the Laplace transform of (27) and considering the initial conditions of (26), we convert differential operator $D_t(p)$ to the algebraic form:

$$\begin{cases} \frac{1}{c^2}s^2P(\boldsymbol{r},s) - \frac{1}{c^2}p_0(\boldsymbol{r}) - D_r(P(\boldsymbol{r},s)) = 0 & & \text{(28.a)} \\ (n.\left(\frac{1}{\rho_0}\nabla\right) + \frac{1}{Z(r)}s)P(\boldsymbol{r},s) = 0 & \boldsymbol{r}\epsilon\Gamma_1,\Gamma_2 & \text{(28.b)} \\ n.\nabla P(\boldsymbol{r},s) = F(\boldsymbol{r},s) & \boldsymbol{r}\epsilon\Gamma_3 & \text{(28.c)} \end{cases}$$

$P(\mathbf{r},s)$ is the Laplace transform of $p(\mathbf{r},t)$. Next we seek another transform T which can convert the spatial differential operator D_r to algebraic equations. Lacking a general transform similar to the Laplace transform in the spatial domain, the spatial Sturm-Liouville transform (SLT) (Rabenstein, 1999) is applied:

$$T(P(\boldsymbol{r})) = P_T(\beta_k) = \iiint_\Omega P(\boldsymbol{r}).K(\boldsymbol{r},\beta_k)dV \tag{29}$$

The dependence upon Laplace transform parameter (s) is omitted for convenience from this point on (so $P(\mathbf{r},s)$ is written as $P(\mathbf{r})$ for instance). The aim is to evaluate the kernel function $K(\boldsymbol{r},\beta_k)$ so that:

$$T(D_r\{P(\boldsymbol{r})\}) = {\beta_k}^2T(P(\boldsymbol{r})) + \Phi_b(\Gamma) \tag{30}$$

Where β_k is a scalar coefficient and $\Phi_b(\Omega)$ is a function which depends on the boundary conditions of the problem. To reach this goal, we first multiply (28.a) by $K(\boldsymbol{r},\beta_k)$.

$$K(\boldsymbol{r},\beta_k)\left\{\frac{1}{c^2}s^2P(\boldsymbol{r})-\frac{1}{c^2}p_0(\boldsymbol{r})-D_r\{P(\boldsymbol{r})\}=0\right\} \tag{31}$$

Next we take the integral $\iiint_\Omega dV$, dV is the volume element.

$$\frac{1}{c^2}s^2\iiint_\Omega P(\boldsymbol{r})K(\boldsymbol{r},\beta_k)\,dV-\frac{1}{c^2}\iiint_\Omega p_0(\boldsymbol{r})K(\boldsymbol{r},\beta_k)dV-\iiint_\Omega K(\boldsymbol{r},\beta_k)D_r\{P(\boldsymbol{r})\}\,dV \;=0 \tag{32}$$

Referring to the definition of the SL transform (29), (32) yields:

$$\frac{1}{c^2}s^2P_T(\beta_k)-\frac{1}{c^2}p_{0_T}(\beta_k)-\iiint_\Omega K(\boldsymbol{r},\beta_k)D_r\{P(\boldsymbol{r})\}\,dV \;=0 \tag{33}$$

Considering $D_r=\nabla^2$ and by Green's theorem (Rabenstein, 1999), the integral in (33) is:

$$\begin{aligned}T\{D_r\{P(\boldsymbol{r})\}\}&=\iiint_\Omega K(\boldsymbol{r},\beta_k)D_r\{P(\boldsymbol{r})\}dV=\iiint_\Omega K(\boldsymbol{r},\beta_k)\nabla^2P(\boldsymbol{r})dV\\&=\iiint_\Omega [P(\boldsymbol{r})\nabla^2K(\boldsymbol{r},\beta_k)]dV\\&\quad+\iint_\Gamma K(\boldsymbol{r},\beta_k)\nabla P(\boldsymbol{r}).\boldsymbol{n}d\sigma-\iint_\Gamma P(\boldsymbol{r})\nabla K(\boldsymbol{r},\beta_k).\boldsymbol{n}d\sigma\end{aligned} \tag{34}$$

$\boldsymbol{n}d\sigma$ is the surface element. Comparing (34), and (30), the first integral in the right hand side of (34) should be converted to a multiplicand of $T\{P(\boldsymbol{r})\}$ (29). The second integral uses the values of $\nabla P(\boldsymbol{r})$ on the boundary Γ, which we have by the boundary conditions of (26). The last term is unwanted because we do not have the value of $\{P(\boldsymbol{r})\}$ over the boundary so we define kernel $K(\boldsymbol{r},\beta_k)$ to fulfil the following requirements as:

$$\begin{cases}\nabla^2K(\boldsymbol{r},\beta_k)={\beta_k}^2K(\boldsymbol{r},\beta_k)\\ \nabla K(\boldsymbol{r},\beta_k)=0 \qquad \boldsymbol{r}\epsilon\Gamma\end{cases} \tag{35}$$

Equation (35) is the well known Helmholtz equation (Blackstock, 2000) and its general solution relies strongly to the geometry Ω. Values of $K(\boldsymbol{r},\beta_k)$, β_k are Eigen functions and Eigen values of the operator $D_r=\nabla^2$ (Rabenstein, 1999). We then substitute the results in (33):

$$\frac{1}{c^2}s^2P_T(\beta_k)-\frac{1}{c^2}p_{0_T}(\beta_k)-\iiint_\Omega {\beta_k}^2K(\boldsymbol{r},\beta_k)P(\boldsymbol{r})\,dV \;=\iint_\Gamma \{K(\boldsymbol{r},\beta_k)\}\nabla P(\boldsymbol{r}).\boldsymbol{n}d\sigma \tag{36}$$

Referring to the definition of SLT (29) and substituting the values of $\nabla P(\boldsymbol{r})$ from boundary conditions (28.a,b), we may rewrite (36) as:

$$\begin{aligned}(\frac{1}{c^2}s^2-{\beta_k}^2)P_T(\beta_k)&=\frac{1}{c^2}p_{0_T}(\beta_k)-s\rho_0\iint_{\Gamma_{1,2}}\frac{P(r)}{Z(r)}K(\boldsymbol{r},\beta_k)d\sigma+\iint_{\Gamma_3}K(\boldsymbol{r},\beta_k)F(\boldsymbol{r})d\sigma=\\&\frac{1}{c^2}p_{0_T}(\beta_k)-s\rho_0G\left(\frac{P(r)}{Z(r)},\Gamma_{1,2},\beta_k\right)+G(F(\boldsymbol{r}),\Gamma_3,\beta_k)\end{aligned} \tag{37}$$

Equation (37), where $G(F(\boldsymbol{r}),\Gamma_j,\beta_k)\triangleq\iint_{\Gamma_j}K(\boldsymbol{r},\beta_k)F(\boldsymbol{r})d\sigma$, is the general equation relating the output $P_T(\beta_k)$ of the VT to the input $F(\boldsymbol{r})$ and initial and boundary conditions.
Considering hard walls for both the vocal tract and closed glottis, $Z(\boldsymbol{r})\rightarrow\infty$ (based on the impedance values of the soft tissue in section 3.1) and $p_{0_T}(\beta_k)=0$, i.e. zero initial conditions,

and $F(r,s) = F(s)$ meaning that the ultrasound source has uniform spatial distribution pattern, which is a plausible simplification we have:

$$G(F(\boldsymbol{r}),\Gamma_3,\beta_k) = F \iint_{\Gamma_3} K(\boldsymbol{r},\beta_k)d\sigma \tag{38}$$

And consequently:

$$P_T(\beta_k) = \frac{(c^2F).\iint_{\Gamma_3} K(\boldsymbol{r},\beta_k)d\sigma}{s^2 - c^2{\beta_k}^2} \tag{39}$$

Since $P_T(\beta_k) = T\{P(\boldsymbol{r})\}$, we need to take the inverse SL transform (Rabenstein, 1999) to reach $P(\boldsymbol{r})$.

$$T^{-1}(P_T(\beta_k)) = P(\boldsymbol{r}) = \sum_{k=1}^{\infty} \frac{1}{N_k} P_T(\beta_k)K(\boldsymbol{r},\beta_k)$$

$$N_k = \iiint_{\Omega} K^2(\boldsymbol{r},\beta_k)dV \tag{40}$$

$P(\boldsymbol{r}) = P(\boldsymbol{r},s)$ is the Laplace transform of $p(\boldsymbol{r},t)$. Using simplifications of (39), (40) becomes:

$$P(\boldsymbol{r}) = Fc^2\left[\sum_{k=1}^{\infty} \frac{1}{N_k}\{\iint_{\Gamma_3} K(\boldsymbol{r},\beta_k)d\sigma\}K(\boldsymbol{r},\beta_k)\right] \tag{41}$$

And consequently we will reach the transfer function of vocal tract for ultrasonic speech:

$$H(\boldsymbol{r}) = \frac{P(\boldsymbol{r})}{F} = c^2\left[\sum_{k=1}^{\infty} \frac{1}{N_k}\{\iint_{\Gamma_3} K(\boldsymbol{r},\beta_k)d\sigma\}K(\boldsymbol{r},\beta_k)\right] \tag{42}$$

$H(\boldsymbol{r})$is the three dimensional transfer function of the vocal tract when excited in front of the mouth which explicitly is a function of $\boldsymbol{r}$ but in its formation, the integrals were on the geometry of volume Ω and its boundaries Γ, so $H(\boldsymbol{r})$ is strongly relied on the definition of the geometry. Thus the three-dimensional wave equation applied to the near-audio ultrasonic speech, with several realistic assumptions as described, yields the linear transfer function (42).

6.3 Linear source filter model for ultrasonic speech

Showing the Laplace transform parameter (s) again - which we had omitted in our equations up to the point for simplicity - we recall that $H(\boldsymbol{r})$ was actually $H(r,s)$, the Laplace transform of $h(\boldsymbol{r},t)$. If sampling time intervals are small enough to consider the VT shape pseudo-static, a system with transfer function $h(\boldsymbol{r},t)$ will be an LTI system, leading to a convolutional relation between its output and input as (43). So $h(\boldsymbol{r},t)$ can be considered as a linear time-invariant (LTI) filter for small time intervals and by the benefit of LTI systems, the conventional source-filter model of audible speech can be extended to cover ultrasonic speech production.

$$p(\boldsymbol{r},t) = h(\boldsymbol{r},t) * f(t) \tag{43}$$

The classical source-filter modelling of VT enjoys independence between source and filter. In the case of ultrasonic speech, the source and the filter are intrinsically independent.

7. Extension of LPA to the analysis of ultrasonic speech

In the previous section, linear source filter model of speech production was mathematically proven to be valid for ultrasonic speech. Linear source filter modelling of ultrasonic speech is the basis of linear predictive analysis as a powerful feature extraction method as will be observed in this section.

The Z transform of $h(\boldsymbol{r}, t)$, can be described as an IIR filter as in (44).

$$H(\boldsymbol{r}, z) = \frac{\sum_{i=1}^{N} b_i(\boldsymbol{r}) z^{-i}}{1 + \sum_{i=1}^{M} a_i(\boldsymbol{r}) z^{-i}} \tag{44}$$

There is a need to inspect the dependence of $H(\boldsymbol{r}, z)$ on coordinates vector $\boldsymbol{r}$ more carefully. The VT is a resonant cavity and at ultrasonic frequencies will have cross modes of resonance. If the excitation signal is a sine function of the same frequency of one of the modes of the resonance, a standing wave of that frequency will form and as a consequence of linearity, the output wave at any point, except nodes, will have the same frequency as the input. The impulse function is the integral sum of an infinite number of sine waves in the time domain. As another consequence of LTI systems, the response of the VT to the impulse will be the summation of its output to sine waves of all frequencies including all its resonances with different amplitudes. Accordingly although the transfer function would have different values in different $\boldsymbol{r}$, it will have the same set of common poles as the resonances of the tract. These common resonances can be calculated with several methods as per (Haneda & Makino et al., 1994).

Linear predictive analysis utilizes the autoregressive (all pole) representation of the transfer function of VT and provides the procedures to evaluate the coefficients of the denominator. The same procedure can be applied to the Z transform of the VT transfer function in (44) which as the transfer function of a minimum phase system, has both poles and zeros inside the unit circle and can be represented as an all pole transfer function, with any zeros being approximated by additional poles (Rabiner & Schafer, 1978).

8. Open research questions

This chapter has presented a mathematical model for ultrasound propagation in the vocal tract and has proven the possibility of application of linear predictive analysis to the ultrasonic speech. The source-filter model of speech production and LPA are the basic building blocks of audible speech processing. Expanding their implementation to ultrasonic speech is the major basis of implementation of this technology. Having the findings of this chapter in hand, ultrasonic speech can begin to enjoy further research effort to reach a state of maturity.

For ultrasonic speech, an ultrasound excitation is injected into the vocal tract. The choice of optimum excitation point and excitation signal wave-form is a topic for further research. Based on the achievements of this chapter, the ultrasonic speech at the output of the mouth can be treated as the output of a LTI source-filter model and can be subjected to LPA analysis to retrieve a set of common poles of the transfer function. The extracted features, converted to a set of parameters, are suitable for production of audible speech. Efficient and accurate down-conversion is also a topic of further research which involves the choice of suitable deterministic or statistic conversion methods.

Finally, as ultrasonic speech involves long term exposure to ultrasound frequencies below 100 kHz, medical standards in place relating to the health effects of the technology need to be assessed and possibly revised as a pre-condition to widespread adoption.

9. Conclusion

This chapter has presented ultrasonic speech as a novel application of ultrasound in speech augmentation. Ultrasonic speech, operating by replacing the natural excitation in audible speech with an LF ultrasonic signal, has applications in speech augmentation for the speech rehabilitation and secure communications communities. This chapter has studied the requirements in modelling ultrasonic speech as a linear system of sound propagation and has proven that LPA, a major tool in the analysis of normal speech, is also extendible to ultrasonic speech.

In pursuing this aim, we first introduced the attributes of ultrasonic propagation in a linear lossless gas medium. We observed that if the sound propagation is an adiabatic procedure and the gas obeys the ideal gas law and with small disturbances in the medium as a result of wave propagation, the gas medium can be considered a linear lossless medium for ultrasound propagation. We then discussed deviations of these conditions for ultrasound propagation in the air medium.

Subsequently, LF ultrasound was introduced, and the impacts of the deviations of linear acoustic behaviour were numerically analyzed for propagation of low frequency ultrasound in the vocal tract. Then we considered the application of LF ultrasound in speech augmentation and discussed the aspects of system design which seek more attention. By a review of previous implementations, we investigated how they had addressed these aspects including the injection points and methods of down-conversion to audible domain.

Afterwards we considered the physiology and anatomy of the human speech production mechanism and how we can substitute the natural excitation with an ultrasonic waveform in speech augmentation. We also stated that the ultrasonic excitation could be applied as a supplement to natural excitation to provide additional data for speech processing applications. The chapter then demonstrated a linear modelling scheme in addition to the fact that speech LPA tools can be extended to sound propagation at lower ultrasonic frequencies. Starting with basic wave equations, and making several simplifying assumptions such as rigid walls for closed glottis and VT, relatively small signal disturbance, and a spatially flat (uniform) excitation source , the VT has been shown to be LTI with the transfer function in the form of a pole-zero IIR filter. By means of this derivation, the conventional source-filter model was proven to be extendable for an ultrasonic speech production system, and thus the powerful tools of LPA can be used.

In this chapter we have tried to bridge from audible speech processing methods to ultrasonics by mathematically and physically demonstrating that the extension of principles of audible speech processing to the analysis of ultrasonic speech is plausible. This significantly simplifies ultrasonic speech processing. The currently neglected area of LF ultrasonics research in speech analysis and processing can now be explored with relative ease. Further research effort is necessary, and welcomed in this area, as it moves toward further maturity and future real-life applications.

10. References

Akerman, M. A.; C. W. Ayers & H. D. Haynes (1994). Ultrasonic speech translator and communications system, United States Patent and Trademark Office, No. 5539705, 1996, United States.

Avallone, E. A.; T. Baumeister; A. Sadegh & L. S. Marks (2006). *Marks Standard handbook for mechanical engineers,* McGraw-Hill Professional.

Bauer, H. J. (1965). Theory of relaxation phenomena in gases, *Physical acoustics,* Vol. IIA.

Begault, D. R. (1994). *3-D sound for virtual reality and multimedia,* Academic Press.

Blackstock, D. T. (2000). *Fundamentals of physical acoustics,* Wiley Interscience.

Blitz, J. (1967). *Fundamentals of ultrasonics,* Butterworth and Co.

Bühler, O. (2006). *A Brief Introduction to classical, statistical, and quantum mechanics,* American Mathematical Society.

Caruthers, J. W. (1977). *fundamentals of marine Acoustics,* Elsevier.

Clark, C. W. (2004). Baleen whale infrasonic sounds: Natural variability and function, *Journal of Acoustical Society of America,* Vol. 115, No. 5, pp. 2554-2554.

Coleman, M. P. (2005). *An introduction to partial differential equations with MATLAB,* CRC Press.

Crocker, M. J. (1998). *Handbook of acoustics,* Wiley Interscience.

Crocker, M. J. (2007). *Handbook of noise and vibration control,* John Wiley and Sons.

David, J. & N. Cheeke (2002). *Fundamentals and applications of ultrasonic waves,* CRC press LLC.

Dean, E. A. (1979). Atmospheric effects on the speed of sound. Technical report of Defense Technical Information Center.

Douglass, B. G. (2006). Apparatus and method for detecting speech using acoustic signals outside the audible frequency range, United States Patent and Trademark Office, No. US 200710276658, United States.

Ensminger, D. (1988). *Ultrasonics, fundamentals, technology, applications,* Marecel Dekker.

Fahy, F. (2001). *Foundations of Engineering Acoustics,* Elsevier.

Goldstein, M. (1984). *Aeroacoustics,* McGraw Hill.

Haar, G. (1999). Theraputic ultrasound, *European Journal of Ultrasound,* Vol. 9, No. 1, pp. 3-9.

Halliday, D.; R. Resnick & J. Walker (2004). *Fundamentals of Physics,* John Wiley & Sons.

Haneda, Y.; S. Makino & Y. Kaneda (1994). Common acoustical pole and zero modeling of room transfer functions. *IEEE trans. speech and audio proc.,* Vol. 2, No. 2.

Harris, J. W.; W. Benenson; H. Stoecker & H. Lutz (2002). *Handbook of physics: with 797 illustrations,* Springer.

Ikawa, M. (2000). *Partial differential equations,* American Mathematical Society.

Ingard, U. (2008). *Notes on acoustics,* Infinity Science Press, LLC.

Johnson, K. (2003). *Acoustic and auditory phonetics,* Blackwell Publishing.

Karal, F. C. & J. B. Keller (1959). Elastic wave propagation in homogeneous and inhomogeneous media, *The journal of the acoustical society of America,* Vol. 31, No. 6, pp. 694-705.

Karal, F. C. & J. B. Keller (1964). Geometrical theory of elastic surface-wave excitation and propagation, *The journal of the acoustical society of America,* Vol. 36, No. 1, pp. 32-40.

Kelsey, C. A.; F. D. Minifie & T. J. Hixon (1969), Applications of ultrasound in speech research. *Journal of Speech and Hearing Research,* Vol. 12, pp. 564-575.

Kyriakakis, C. (1998). Fundamental and technological limitations of immersive audio systems, *Proceedings of IEEE,* Vol. 86, No. 5.

Lahr, R. J. (2002). Head-worn, trimodal device to increase transcription accuracy in a voice recognition system and to process unvocalized speech, United States Patent and Trademark Office, No. US 2002/0194005, 2002.

Lempriere, B. M. (2002). *Ultrasound and elastic waves, Frequently asked questions,* Elsevier Science.

Lenhardt, M. L.; R. Skellett; P. Wang & A. M. Clarke (1991). Human ultrasonic speech perception. *Science, New Series,*Vol. 253, No. 5015, pp. 82 - 85.

Licker, M. (2002). *McGraw-Hill Dictionary of Scientific and Technical Terms,* McGraw-Hill Companies.

Lighthill, M. J. (1952). On sound generated aerodynamically. i. general theory, *Proceedings of the Royal Society of London. Series A, Mathematical and Physical Sciences,* Vol. 211, No. 1107, pp. 564-587.

MacLeod, N. (1987). Non-audible speech generation method and apparatus, U. S. Patent, No. 4821326, 1989.

McLoughlin, I. V. (2009). *Applied speech and audio processing: with Matlab examples,* Cambridge University Press.

Pozo, A. D. (2004). Laryngectomee speech enhancement using voice conversion techniques, Christ's College, University of Cambridge, M.Sc Thesis.

Pujol, J. (2003). *Elastic wave propagation and generation in seismology,* Cambridge University Press.

Rabenstein, R. (1999). Transfer function models for multidimensional systems with bounded spatial domains, *Mathematical and Computer Modelling of Dynamical Systems,* Vol. 5, pp. 259—278.

Rabiner, L. R. & R. W. Schafer (1978). *Digital processing of speech signals,* Prentice-Hall.

Rauch, J. (2008). *Hyperbolic partial differential equations and geometric optics.*

Reynolds, D. D. (1981). *Engineering principles in acoustics,* Allyn and Bacon Inc.

Sadd, M. H. (2005). *Elasticity: Theory, applications and numerics,* Academic Press.

Serway, R. A. & J. W. Jewett (2006). *Principles of physics: a calculus-based text,* Thomson Brooks/Cole.

Shawker, T. H. & B. C. Sonies (2005). Tongue movement during speech: a real-time ultrasound evaluation, *Journal of Clinical Ultrasound,* Vol. 12, No. 3, pp. 125 - 133.

Simpson, J. A. & E. S. C. Weiner (1989). *The Oxford English Dictionary,* Clarendon Press.

Sinder, D. J. (1999). Speech synthesis using an aeroacoustic fricative model, Graduate school-New Brunswick Rutgers, The State University of New Jersey, PhD thesis.

Subramanian, C. V. (2006). *Practical ultrasonics,* Alpha Science.

Szabo, T. L. (2004). *Diagnostic ultrasound imaging: inside out,* Academic Press.

Tosaya, C. A. & J. W. Sliwa (2002, 1999). Signal Injection coupling into the human vocal tract for robust audible and inaudible voice recognition, United States Patent and Trademark Office, No. 7082395 & No. 6487531, United States.

Watkinson, J. (1998). *The art of sound reproduction,* Focal Press.

Webster, M. (1986). *Webster's ninth collegiate dictionary,* Springfield.

Zangzebski, J. A. (1996). *Essentials of ultrasound physics,* Mosby, Elsevier.

Zemlin, W. R. (1997). *Speech and hearing science anatomy and physiology,* Allyn and Bacon.